C000297128

# BRITISH RAILWAYS
# LOCOMOTIVES & COACHING STOCK
# 2010

The Complete Guide to all
Locomotives & Coaching Stock which
operate on the National Rail network and
Eurotunnel

Robert Pritchard, Peter Fox & Peter Hall

ISBN 978 1 902336 78 7

© 2010. Platform 5 Publishing Ltd., 3 Wyvern House, Sark Road, Sheffield,
S2 4HG, England.

# CONTENTS

## SECTION 1 – LOCOMOTIVES

## SECTION 2 – LOCO-HAULED COACHING STOCK

## SECTION 3 – DIESEL MULTIPLE UNITS

# CONTENTS

## SECTION 4 – ELECTRIC MULTIPLE UNITS

## SECTION 5 – UK Light Rail & Metro Systems

## SECTION 6 – CODES

## COVER PHOTOGRAPHS

**Front Cover:** The first of Freightliner's Class 70 fleet arrived in November 2009. On 17 December 2009 70003 passes Croome Perry wood, Worcestershire with 4Z70 08.53 Rugeley–Stoke Gifford (Bristol Parkway) empty coal. **Matt Clarke**

**Rear Cover:** Nottingham tram 205 "Lord Byron" is seen at Wilkinson Street with a Phoenix Park–Station Street service on 20 December 2009. **Jason Cross**

**Keep this book up to date with official stock changes published every month in Today's Railways UK magazine.**

**Today's Railways UK** is the only magazine to publish official Platform 5 stock changes for Locomotives, Coaching Stock, Diesel Multiple Units and Electric Multiple Units, presented in the same clear format used in this book. Keeping your book up to date couldn't be easier!

And of course every issue of **Today's Railways UK** also contains the very latest news, interesting articles and regular features. Please see pages 364 & 365 for further details.

**Today's Railways UK – The UK railway magazine from Platform 5 Publishing On sale 2nd Monday of every month.**

# PROVISION OF INFORMATION

This book has been compiled with care to be as accurate as possible, but in some cases information is not officially available and the publisher cannot be held responsible for any errors or omissions. We would like to thank the companies and individuals which have been co-operative in supplying information to us. The authors of this book will be pleased to receive notification of any inaccuracies readers may find in the series, and also any additional information to supplement our records and thus enhance future editions. Please send comments to:

Robert Pritchard, Platform 5 Publishing Ltd., 3 Wyvern House, Sark Road, Sheffield, S2 4HG, England.

**Tel:** 0114 255 2625 **Fax:** 0114 255 2471
**e-mail:** <u>robert@platform5.com</u>

This book is updated to January 2010.

# ACKNOWLEDGEMENTS

The author would like to thank all Train Operating Companies, Freight Companies, Rolling Stock Leasing Companies and spot-hire companies that have helped with the compilation of this book.

Thanks are also due to those who sent reports of changes observed during 2009 for the **Today's Railways UK** magazine "Stock Changes" column and for corrections given to the 2010 "pocket book" series.

# BRITAIN'S RAILWAY SYSTEM

## INFRASTRUCTURE & OPERATION

Britain's national railway infrastructure is owned by a "not for dividend" company, Network Rail. Many stations and maintenance depots are leased to and operated by Train Operating Companies (TOCs), but some larger stations remain under Network Rail control. The only exception is the infrastructure on the Isle of Wight, which is nationally owned and is leased to South West Trains.

Trains are operated by TOCs over Network Rail, regulated by access agreements between the parties involved. In general, TOCs are responsible for the provision and maintenance of the locos, rolling stock and staff necessary for the direct operation of services, whilst NR is responsible for the provision and maintenance of the infrastructure and also for staff to regulate the operation of services.

## DOMESTIC PASSENGER TRAIN OPERATORS

The large majority of passenger trains are operated by the TOCs on fixed term franchises. Franchise expiry dates are shown in the list of franchisees below:

| Franchise | Franchisee | Trading Name |
|---|---|---|
| Chiltern Railways | Deutsche Bahn (until 31 December 2021) | Chiltern Railways |
| Cross-Country[1] | Arriva Trains Ltd. (until 1 November 2013) | CrossCountry |
| East Midlands[2] | Stagecoach Holdings plc (until 11 November 2013) | East Midlands Trains |
| Greater Western[3] | First Group plc (until 1 April 2013) | First Great Western |
| Greater Anglia | National Express Group plc (until 1 April 2011) | National Express East Anglia |
| Integrated Kent[4] | GoVia Ltd. (Go-Ahead/Keolis) (until 3 March 2012) | Southeastern |
| InterCity East Coast[5] | | East Coast |
| InterCity West Coast | Virgin Rail Group Ltd. (until 31 March 2012) | Virgin Trains |
| London Rail[6] | MTR/Laing Rail (until 14 March 2014) | London Overground |
| LTS Rail | National Express Group plc (until 25 May 2011) | c2c |
| Merseyrail Electrics[7] | Serco/NedRail (until 20 July 2028) | Merseyrail |
| Northern Rail[8] | Serco/NedRail (until 13 September 2011) | Northern |
| ScotRail | First Group plc (until 8 November 2014) | ScotRail |
| South Central[9] | GoVia Ltd. (Go-Ahead/Keolis) (until 25 July 2015) | Southern |

| South Western[10] | Stagecoach Holdings plc (until 4 February 2014) | South West Trains |
| Thameslink/Great Northern[11] | First Group plc (until 1 April 2012) | First Capital Connect |
| Trans-Pennine Express[12] | First Group/Keolis (until 1 February 2012) | TransPennine Express |
| Wales & Borders | Arriva Trains Ltd. (until 6 December 2018) | Arriva Trains Wales |
| West Midlands[13] | GoVia Ltd. (Go-Ahead/Keolis) (until 19 September 2013) | London Midland |

**Notes:**

[1] Awarded for six years to 2013 with an extension for a further two years and five months to 1 April 2016 if performance targets are met.

[2] Awarded for six years to 2013 with an extension for a further one year and five months to 1 April 2015 if performance targets are met.

[3] Awarded for seven years to 2013 with an extension for a further three years to 1 April 2016 if performance targets are met.

[4] The Integrated Kent franchise started on 1 April 2006 for an initial period of six years to 2012, with an extension for a further two years to 1 April 2014 if performance targets are met.

[5] Currently run on an interim basis by DfT management company Directly Operated Railways (trading as East Coast) following financial difficulties experienced by National Express Group. The franchise is due to be relet to the private sector by late 2011.

[6] The London Rail Concession is different from all other rail franchises, as fares and service levels are set by Transport for London instead of the DfT. Incorporates the North and West London lines, the Gospel Oak–Barking line and Euston–Watford local services.

[7] Now under control of Merseytravel PTE instead of the DfT. Franchise due to be reviewed after seven years (in July 2010) and then every five years to fit in with the Merseyside Local Transport Plan.

[8] Awarded for six years and nine months to 2011 with an extension for a further two years to 13 September 2013 if performance targets are met.

[9] Awarded for five years and ten months to 2015 with a possible extension for a further two years to 25 July 2017.

[10] Awarded for seven years to 2014 with an extension for a further three years to 4 February 2017 if performance targets are met.

[11] Awarded for six years to 2012 with an extension for up to a further three years to 1 April 2015 if performance targets are met.

[12] Awarded for eight years to 2012 with an extension a further five years to 1 February 2017 if performance targets are met.

[13] Awarded for six years to 2013 with an extension for a further two years to 19 September 2015 if performance targets are met.

All new franchises officially start at 02.00 on the first day. Because of this the finishing date of an old franchise and the start date of its successor are the same.

Where termination dates are dependent on performance targets being met, the earliest possible termination date is given. However, with Merseyrail the termination date is based on the maximum franchise length.

The following operators run non-franchised services only:

| Operator | Trading Name | Route |
|---|---|---|
| BAA | Heathrow Express | London Paddington–Heathrow Airport |
| First Hull Trains | First Hull Trains | London King's Cross–Hull |
| Grand Central | Grand Central | London King's Cross–Sunderland† |
| North Yorkshire Moors Railway | North Yorkshire Moors Railway | Pickering–Grosmont–Whitby/ Battersby |
| West Coast Railway Company | West Coast Railway Company | Birmingham–Stratford-upon-Avon Fort William–Mallaig* York–Harrogate–Leeds–York–Scarborough* Machynlleth–Porthmadog/Pwllheli* |
| Wrexham, Shropshire & Marylebone Railway | Wrexham & Shropshire | London Marylebone–Wrexham General |

* Special summer-dated services only.
† Services from London King's Cross to Bradford Interchange due to start in summer 2010.

# INTERNATIONAL PASSENGER OPERATIONS

Eurostar (UK) operates passenger services between the UK and mainland Europe, jointly with the national operators of France (SNCF) and Belgium (SNCB/NMBS). Eurostar (UK) is a subsidiary of London & Continental Railways, which is jointly owned by National Express Group and British Airways.

In addition, a service for the conveyance of accompanied road vehicles through the Channel Tunnel is provided by the tunnel operating company, Eurotunnel.

# FREIGHT TRAIN OPERATIONS

The following operators operate freight train services under "Open Access" arrangements:

DB Schenker (formerly EWS)
Freightliner
First GBRf
Direct Rail Services (DRS)

Fastline (Jarvis)
Colas Rail
West Coast Railway Company

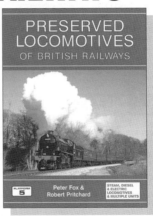

# 1. LOCOMOTIVES

# INTRODUCTION

## SCOPE

This section contains details of all locomotives which can run on Britain's national railway network, plus those of Eurotunnel. Locomotives which are owned by, for example, DB Schenker and Freightliner which have been withdrawn from service and awaiting disposal are listed in the main part of the book. Locos which are awaiting disposal at scrapyards are listed in the "Locomotives Awaiting Disposal" section.

Only preserved locomotives which are currently used on the National Rail network are included. Others, which may still be Network Rail registered but not at present certified for use, are not included, but will be found in the new thirteenth edition of the Platform 5 book, "Preserved Locomotives and Multiple Units" (published December 2009).

## LOCO CLASSES

Loco classes are listed in numerical order of class. Principal details and dimensions are quoted for each class in metric and/or imperial units as considered appropriate bearing in mind common UK usage.

**Builders:** These are shown in class headings. Abbreviations used are found in section 6.6.

All dimensions and weights are quoted for locomotives in an "as new" condition with all necessary supplies (e.g. oil, water and sand) on board. Dimensions are quoted in the order length x width. Lengths quoted are over buffers or couplers as appropriate. All widths quoted are maxima. Where two different wheel diameter dimensions are shown, the first refers to powered wheels and the second refers to non-powered wheels.

## NUMERICAL LISTINGS

Locomotives are listed in numerical order. Where numbers actually carried are different from those officially allocated, these are noted in class headings where appropriate. Where locomotives have been recently renumbered, the most immediate previous number is shown in parentheses. Each locomotive entry is laid out as in the following example:

| RSL No. | Detail | Livery | Owner | Pool | Allocn. | Name |
|---------|--------|--------|-------|------|---------|------|
| 57302 | d | **VT** | P | IWCA | MA | VIRGIL TRACY |

**Detail Differences**. Only detail differences which currently affect the areas and types of train which locomotives may work are shown. All other detail differences are specifically excluded. Where such differences occur within a class or part class, they are shown in the "Detail" column alongside the individual locomotive number.

Standard abbreviations used for the locomotives section are:

| | |
|---|---|
| a | Train air brake equipment only. |
| b | Drophead buckeye couplers. |
| c | Scharfenberg couplers. |
| d | Fitted with retractable Dellner couplers. |
| e | European Railway Traffic Management System (ERTMS) signalling equipment fitted. |
| k | Fitted with Swinghead Automatic "buckeye" combination couplers. |
| p | Train air, vacuum and electro-pneumatic brakes. |
| r | Radio Electric Token Block signalling equipment fitted. |
| s | Slow Speed Control equipment. |
| v | Train vacuum brake only. |
| x | Train air and vacuum brakes ("Dual brakes"). |
| + | Additional fuel tank capacity. |
| § | Sandite laying equipment. |

In all cases use of the above abbreviations indicates the equipment indicated is normally operable. Meaning of non-standard abbreviations and symbols is detailed in individual class headings.

**Codes**. Codes are used to denote the livery, owner, pool and depot of each locomotive. Details of these will be found in section 6 of this book.

**Names**. Only names carried with official sanction are listed. Names are shown in UPPER/lower case characters as actually shown on the name carried on the locomotive.

# GENERAL INFORMATION

## CLASSIFICATION AND NUMBERING

All locomotives are classified and allocated numbers by the Rolling Stock Library under the TOPS numbering system, introduced in 1972. This comprises a two-digit class number followed by a three-digit serial number. Where the actual number carried by a locomotive differs from the allocated number, or where an additional number is carried to the allocated number, this is shown by a note in the class heading.

For diesel locomotives, class numbers offer an indication of engine horsepower as shown in the table below.

| Class No. Range | Engine h.p. |
|---|---|
| 01–14 | 0–799 |
| 15–20 | 800–1000 |
| 21–31 | 1001–1499 |
| 32–39 | 1500–1999 |
| 40–54, 57 | 2000–2999 |
| 55–56, 58–69 | 3000+ |

For electric locomotives class numbers are allocated in ascending numerical order under the following scheme:

Class 70–80          direct current and DC/diesel dual system locomotives.
Class 81 onwards     alternating current and AC/DC dual system locos.

Numbers in the 89xxx series are allocated by the Rolling Stock Library to locomotives which have been de-registered but subsequently re-registered for use on the Network Rail network and whose original number has already been re-used. 89xxx numbers are normally only carried inside locomotive cabs and are not carried externally in normal circumstances.

# WHEEL ARRANGEMENT

For main line locomotives the number of driven axles on a bogie or frame is denoted by a letter (A = 1, B = 2, C = 3 etc.) and the number of non-powered axles is denoted by a number. The use of the letter "o" after a letter indicates each axle is individually powered, whilst the "+" symbol indicates bogies are inter-coupled.

For shunting locomotives, the Whyte notation is used. In this notation the number of leading wheels are given, followed by the number of driving wheels and then the trailing wheels.

# HAULAGE CAPABILITY OF DIESEL LOCOMOTIVES

The haulage capability of a diesel locomotive depends upon three basic factors:

1. Adhesive weight. The greater the weight on the driving wheels, the greater the adhesion and more tractive power can be applied before wheelslip occurs.

2. The characteristics of its transmission. To start a train the locomotive has to exert a pull at standstill. A direct drive diesel engine cannot do this, hence the need for transmission. This may be mechanical, hydraulic or electric. The present British Standard for locomotives is electric transmission. Here the diesel engine drives a generator or alternator and the current produced is fed to the traction motors. The force produced by each driven wheel depends on the current in its traction motor. In other words, the larger the current, the harder it pulls. As the locomotive speed increases, the current in the traction motor falls, hence the *Maximum Tractive Effort* is the maximum force at its wheels the locomotive can exert at a standstill. The electrical equipment cannot take such high currents for long without overheating. Hence the *Continuous Tractive Effort* is quoted which represents the current which the equipment can take continuously.

3. The power of its engine. Not all power reaches the rail, as electrical machines are approximately 90% efficient. As the electrical energy passes through two such machines (the generator or alternator and the traction motors), the *Power at Rail* is approximately 81% (90% of 90%) of the engine power, less a further amount used for auxiliary equipment such as radiator fans, traction motor blowers, air compressors, battery charging, cab heating, Electric Train Supply (ETS) etc. The power of the locomotive is proportional to the tractive effort times the speed. Hence when on full power there is a speed corresponding to the continuous tractive effort.

# HAULAGE CAPABILITY OF ELECTRIC LOCOMOTIVES

Unlike a diesel locomotive, an electric locomotive does not develop its power on board and its performance is determined only by two factors, namely its weight and the characteristics of its electrical equipment. Whereas a diesel locomotive tends to be a constant power machine, the power of an electric locomotive varies considerably. Up to a certain speed it can produce virtually a constant tractive effort. Hence power rises with speed according to the formula given in section three above, until a maximum speed is reached at which tractive effort falls, such that the power also falls. Hence the power at the speed corresponding to the maximum tractive effort is lower than the maximum speed.

# BRAKE FORCE

The brake force is a measure of the braking power of a locomotive. This is shown on the locomotive data panels so operating staff can ensure sufficient brake power is available on freight trains.

# ELECTRIC TRAIN SUPPLY (ETS)

A number of locomotives are equipped to provide a supply of electricity to the train being hauled to power auxiliaries such as heating, cooling fans, air conditioning and kitchen equipment. ETS is provided from the locomotive by means of a separate alternator (except Class 33 locos, which have a DC generator). The ETS index of a locomotive is a measure of the electrical power available for train supply.

Similarly, most loco-hauled coaches also have an ETS index, which in this case is a measure of the power required to operate equipment mounted in the coach. The sum of the ETS indices of all the hauled vehicles in a train must not exceed the ETS index of the locomotive.

ETS is commonly (but incorrectly) known as ETH (Electric Train Heating), which is a throwback to the days before loco-hauled coaches were equipped with electrically powered auxiliary equipment other than for train heating.

# ROUTE AVAILABILITY (RA)

This is a measure of a railway vehicle's axle load. The higher the axle load of a vehicle, the higher the RA number on a scale from 1 to 10. Each Network Rail route has a RA number and in general no vehicle with a higher RA number may travel on that route without special clearance.

# MULTIPLE & PUSH-PULL WORKING

Multiple working between vehicles (i.e. two or more powered vehicles being driven from one cab) is facilitated by jumper cables connecting the vehicles. However, not all types are compatible with each other, and a number of different systems are in use, each system being incompatible with any other.

**Association of American Railroads (AAR) System**: Classes 59, 66, and 67.
**Blue Star Coupling Code:** Classes 20, 25, 31, 33, 37 40 and 73.
**DRS System:** Classes 20/3, 37 and 47.
**Green Circle Coupling Code:** Class 47 (not all equipped).
**Orange Square Coupling Code:** Class 50.
**Red Diamond Coupling Code:** Classes 56 and 58.
**SR System:** Classes 33/1, 73 and various electric multiple units.
**Within Own Class only:** Classes 43 and 60.

Many locomotives use a time-division multiplex (TDM) system for push-pull and multiple working which utilises the existing RCH jumper cables fitted to coaching stock vehicles. Previously these cables had only been used to control train lighting and public address systems.

Class 47 locos 47701–47717 were equipped with an older non-standard TDM system.

# 1.1. DIESEL LOCOMOTIVES

## CLASS 08          BR/ENGLISH ELECTRIC          0-6-0

**Built:** 1955–1962 by BR at Crewe, Darlington, Derby Locomotive, Doncaster or Horwich Works.
**Engine:** English Electric 6KT of 298 kW (400 h.p.) at 680 r.p.m.
**Main Generator:** English Electric 801.
**Traction Motors:** Two English Electric 506.
**Maximum Tractive Effort:** 156 kN (35000 lbf).
**Continuous Tractive Effort:** 49 kN (11100 lbf) at 8.8 m.p.h.

| | |
|---|---|
| **Power At Rail:** 194 kW (260 h.p.). | **Train Brakes:** Air & vacuum. |
| **Brake Force:** 19 t. | **Dimensions:** 8.92 x 2.59 m. |
| **Weight:** 49.6–50.4 t. | **Wheel Diameter:** 1372 mm. |
| **Design Speed:** 20 m.p.h. | **Maximum Speed:** 15 m.p.h. |
| **Fuel Capacity:** 3037 litres. | **RA:** 5. |
| **Train Supply:** Not equipped. | |

**Multiple Working:** m Equipped for multiple working. All others not equipped.

**Notes:** † – Fitted with remote control equipment.

Actual locations for all operational shunters are given, apart from DB Schenker and Freightliner-operated locos which generally move about on a more regular basis.

Certain Class 08s that don't have Network Rail engineering acceptance are classed as "in industrial service" and can be found in section 1.4 of this book.

08850 is registered for use between Battersby and Whitby only, for rescue purposes.

**Non-standard liveries/numbering:**

08308 All over ScotRail "Caledonian Sleeper" purple.
08442 Dark grey lower bodyside with light grey upper bodyside. Carries no number.
08480 Yellow with a red bodyside band. Carries number "TOTON No 1".
08499 Pullman Rail blue & white.
08616 Carries number 3783.
08701 Carries number "Tyne 100".
08721 As **B**, but with a black roof & "Express parcels" branding with red & yellow stripe.
08810 and 08868 Two-tone light grey.
08824 Carries number "IEMD01".

Originally numbered in series D3000–D4192.

**Class 08/0. Standard Design.**

| | | | | |
|---|---|---|---|---|
| 08077 | **FL** | P | DFLS | LH (S) |
| 08308 | a **0** | RL | MRSO | IS |
| 08389 | a **E** | DB | WNTS | TO |
| 08393 | a **E** | DB | WNTS | BS |

| 08397 | a  | E  | DB | WZTS | TO |  |
|-------|----|----|----|------|----|--|
| 08401 | a  | DG | DB | WSXX | IM |  |
| 08405 | a  | E  | DB | WNTR | TO |  |
| 08410 | a  | GL | FG | EFSH | PZ |  |
| 08417 | a  | BS | SO | CDJD | ZA |  |
| 08418 | a  | E  | DB | WZTS | BS |  |
| 08428 | a  | E  | DB | WSSN | TO |  |
| 08442 | a  | O  | DB | WSXX | EH | RICHARD J. WENHAM EASTLEIGH DEPOT DECEMBER 1989–JULY 1999 |
| 08451 |    | GB | AM | ATZZ | MA |  |
| 08454 |    | K  | AM | ATLO | WB |  |
| 08466 | a† | E  | DB | WNTS | TO |  |
| 08472 | a  | WA | WA | RFSH | EC |  |
| 08480 | a  | O  | DB | WSXX | TO |  |
| 08482 | a  | E  | DB | WSSN | TO | DON GATES 1952–2000 |
| 08483 | a  | GL | FG | EFSH | OO | DUSTY Driver David Miller |
| 08485 | a  | B  | DB | WZTS | Carlisle Yard |  |
| 08495 | †  | E  | DB | WSSN | TO | NOEL KIRTON OBE |
| 08499 | a  | O  | PU |      | CF |  |
| 08500 |    | E  | DB | WNTS | DR |  |
| 08502 |    | NO | HN | HNRL | HT | Lybert Dickinson |
| 08507 | a  | HN | HN | HNRL | CZ |  |
| 08512 | a  | E  | DB | WNTS | DR |  |
| 08514 | a  | E  | DB | WNTS | DR |  |
| 08516 | a  | E  | DB | WSXX | BK |  |
| 08525 |    | MA | EM | EMSL | NL |  |
| 08527 |    | FA | HN | HNRL | RR |  |
| 08528 |    | DG | DB | WNTS | BS |  |
| 08530 |    | FL | P  | DFLS | FD |  |
| 08531 | a  | DG | P  | DFLS | FD |  |
| 08536 |    | B  | PO |      | DY (S) |  |
| 08538 |    | DG | DB | WNTS | BS |  |
| 08540 |    | E  | DB | WNTS | TO |  |
| 08543 |    | DG | DB | WNYX | BS |  |
| 08561 |    | B  | DB | WNXX | TO |  |
| 08567 |    | E  | DB | WSSN | TO |  |
| 08569 |    | E  | DB | WNYX | DR |  |
| 08571 | a  | WA | WA | HBSH | BN |  |
| 08575 |    | FL | P  | DFLS | FD |  |
| 08577 |    | E  | DB | WNTS | BS |  |
| 08578 |    | E  | DB | WSSN | TO |  |
| 08580 |    | E  | DB | WNYX | BS |  |
| 08585 |    | FL | P  | DFLS | FD | Vicky |
| 08593 |    | E  | DB | WNTS | TO |  |
| 08596 | a† | WA | WA | RFSH | BN |  |
| 08597 |    | E  | DB | WNTS | TE |  |
| 08605 |    | E  | DB | WSSN | TO |  |
| 08611 |    | V  | AM | ATLO | LL | DOWNHILL C.S. |
| 08615 |    | WA | WA | RFSH | EC |  |
| 08616 |    | LM | LM | EJLO | TS | TYSELEY 100 |
| 08617 |    | K  | AM | ATLO | WB |  |

| 08623 |    | E  | DB | WSSI | TO     |                 |
|-------|----|----|----|------|--------|-----------------|
| 08624 |    | FL | P  | DFLS | FD     |                 |
| 08630 |    | E  | DB | WSSI | TO     | BOB BROWN       |
| 08632 |    | E  | DB | WNTR | TO     |                 |
| 08633 |    | E  | DB | WNTR | TO     |                 |
| 08641 |    | FB | FG | EFSH | LA     |                 |
| 08644 |    | GL | FG | EFSH | LA     |                 |
| 08645 |    | FB | FG | EFSH | LA     | Mike Baggott    |
| 08646 |    | F  | DB | WNTS | MG     |                 |
| 08651 | a  | DG | DB | WNYX | BS     |                 |
| 08653 |    | E  | DB | WSSN | TO     |                 |
| 08662 |    | E  | DB | WNTS | SP     |                 |
| 08663 | a  | GL | FG | EFSH | PM     |                 |
| 08664 |    | E  | DB | WNTR | DR     |                 |
| 08669 | a  | WA | WA | RFSH | ZB     | Bob Machin      |
| 08676 |    | E  | DB | WSSN | TO     |                 |
| 08685 |    | E  | DB | WNTS | IM     |                 |
| 08689 | a  | E  | DB | WNTS | TO     |                 |
| 08690 |    | MA | EM | EMSL | NL     |                 |
| 08691 |    | FL | FL | DFLS | FD     | Terri           |
| 08696 | a  | G  | AM | ATLO | MA     | LONGSIGHT TMD   |
| 08697 |    | B  | EM | EMSL | DY (S) |                 |
| 08698 | a  | E  | DB | WNTS | TE     |                 |
| 08701 | a  | RX | DB | WNTR | TO     |                 |
| 08703 | a  | E  | DB | WSSK | TO     |                 |
| 08706 | †  | E  | DB | WNTR | TO     |                 |
| 08709 |    | E  | DB | WNTS | BS     |                 |
| 08711 | k  | RX | DB | WNTR | DR     |                 |
| 08714 |    | E  | DB | WSSI | TO     | Cambridge       |
| 08721 |    | O  | AM | ATLO | MA     | M.A. Smith      |
| 08724 |    | WA | WA | HBSH | NL     |                 |
| 08735 | †  | E  | DB | WSSN | TO     |                 |
| 08737 | a  | E  | DB | WNTR | TO     |                 |
| 08742 |    | RX | DB | WNTR | TO     |                 |
| 08745 |    | FE | P  | DHLT | SZ (S) |                 |
| 08750 | a  | K  | RL | MRSO | HE     |                 |
| 08752 | †  | E  | DB | WSSI | TO     |                 |
| 08757 |    | RG | DB | WSSN | TO     |                 |
| 08765 |    | E  | DB | WNTS | EH     |                 |
| 08770 | a  | DG | DB | WNTS | MG     |                 |
| 08776 | a  | DG | DB | WNTS | TE     |                 |
| 08782 | a† | CU | DB | WSSI | TO     | CASTLETON WORKS |
| 08783 |    | E  | DB | WNTS | TO     |                 |
| 08784 |    | E  | DB | WNTS | TO     |                 |
| 08785 | a  | FL | P  | DFLS | FD     |                 |
| 08786 | a  | DG | DB | WNTS | DR     |                 |
| 08788 |    | RT | RL | MRSO | IS     |                 |
| 08790 |    | B  | AM | ATLO | OY     | STARLET         |
| 08795 |    | GL | FG | EFSH | LE     |                 |
| 08798 |    | E  | DB | WNTS | TO     |                 |
| 08799 | a  | E  | DB | WSSN | TO     | ANDY BOWER      |

| | | | | | |
|---|---|---|---|---|---|
| 08802 † | **E** | DB | WNTR | TO | |
| 08804 | **E** | DB | WNTR | TO | |
| 08805 | **B** | LM | EJLO | SO | CONCORDE |
| 08810 a | **O** | LW | MBDL | CP | |
| 08822 | **GL** | FG | EFSH | PM | |
| 08824 ak | **K** | DB | WSXX | CE | |
| 08828 a | **E** | DB | WNYX | BS | |
| 08834 | **DR** | HN | HNRL | OD | |
| 08836 | **GL** | FG | EFSH | OO | |
| 08842 | **E** | DB | WNTS | BS | |
| 08844 | **E** | DB | WNTS | BS | CHRIS WREN 1955–2002 |
| 08847 | **CD** | RL | MRSO | NC | |
| 08850 | **B** | NY | MBDL | NY | |
| 08853 a | **WA** | WA | RFSH | ZB | |
| 08854 † | **E** | DB | WNTS | MG | |
| 08856 | **B** | DB | WNXX | DC | |
| 08865 | **E** | DB | WSSK | TO | |
| 08866 | **E** | DB | WNTS | DR | |
| 08868 | **O** | HN | HNRL | CP | |
| 08872 | **E** | DB | WZTS | IM | TONY LONG STRATFORD DEPOT 1971–2002 |
| 08874 | **SL** | RL | MRSO | NC | |
| 08877 | **DG** | DB | WSXX | SP | |
| 08879 | **E** | DB | WNTR | TO | |
| 08884 | **B** | DB | WZTS | BS | |
| 08886 † | **E** | DB | WSSN | TO | |
| 08887 a | **VP** | AM | ATZZ | MA | |
| 08888 | **E** | DB | WSSN | TO | |
| 08891 | **FL** | P | DFLS | FD | J.R 1951–2005 |
| 08897 | **E** | DB | WNTS | DR | |
| 08899 | **MA** | EM | EMSL | DY | |
| 08904 | **E** | DB | WSSN | TO | |
| 08905 | **E** | DB | WNTS | BS | |
| 08907 | **E** | DB | WSSN | TO | MOLLY'S DAY |
| 08908 | **MM** | EM | EMSL | NL | |
| 08909 | **E** | DB | WSSN | TO | |
| 08918 | **DG** | DB | WNTS | TO | |
| 08920 | **F** | DB | WNXX | BS | |
| 08921 † | **E** | DB | WNTR | SP | |
| 08922 | **DG** | DB | WNTR | Carlisle Yard | |
| 08924 | **E** | DB | WNTS | TY | |
| 08925 | **B** | DB | WNXX | DR | |
| 08934 a | **VP** | AM | ATLO | WB | |
| 08941 | **E** | DB | WNTS | DR | |
| 08948 c | **EP** | EU | GPSS | TI | |
| 08950 | **MA** | EM | EMSL | NL (S) | |
| 08951 † | **E** | DB | WNTS | TO | FRED |
| 08953 a | **DG** | DB | WNXX | DR | |
| 08954 | **F** | DB | WNXX | TO | |
| 08956 | **BS** | SO | CDJD | OD | |

**Class 08/9. Reduced height cab.** Converted 1985–1987 by BR at Landore.

| | | | | | |
|---|---|---|---|---|---|
| 08993 | E | DB | WSSN | TO | |
| 08994 a | E | DB | WNTR | DR | SPIRIT OF INNOVATION |
| 08995 a | E | DB | WSSN | TO | |

# CLASS 09        BR/ENGLISH ELECTRIC        0-6-0

**Built:** 1959–1962 by BR at Darlington or Horwich Works.
**Engine:** English Electric 6KT of 298 kW (400 h.p.) at 680 r.p.m.
**Main Generator:** English Electric 801.
**Traction Motors:** English Electric 506.
**Maximum Tractive Effort:** 111 kN (25000 lbf).
**Continuous Tractive Effort:** 39 kN (8800 lbf) at 11.6 m.p.h.
**Power At Rail:** 201 kW (269 h.p.).          **Train Brakes:** Air & vacuum.
**Brake Force:** 19 t.                         **Dimensions:** 8.92 x 2.59 m.
**Weight:** 49 t.                              **Wheel Diameter:** 1372 mm.
**Design Speed:** 27 m.p.h.                    **Maximum Speed:** 27 m.p.h.
**Fuel Capacity:** 3037 litres.                **RA:** 5.
**Train Supply:** Not equipped.                **Multiple Working:** Not equipped.

Class 09/0 were originally numbered D3665–D3671, D3719–D3721, D4099–D4114.

**Class 09/0. Built as Class 09.**

| | | | | | |
|---|---|---|---|---|---|
| 09001 | E | DB | WNTS | DR | |
| 09003 | E | DB | WNTS | MG | |
| 09005 k | E | DB | WNTS | Hoo Jn. | |
| 09006 | E | DB | WNTS | DR | |
| 09007 | ML | DB | WNTR | TO | |
| 09008 | E | DB | WNTS | BS | |
| 09009 | E | DB | WNXX | TO | Three Bridges C.E.D. |
| 09010 | DG | DB | WNTS | HG | |
| 09011 | DG | DB | WNTS | MG | |
| 09012 | DG | DB | WNXX | HG | |
| 09013 | DG | DB | WNTS | TO | |
| 09014 | DG | DB | WNTS | DR | |
| 09015 | E | DB | WNTS | MG | |
| 09016 | E | DB | WNXX | BZ | |
| 09017 | E | DB | WSSI | TO | |
| 09018 | E | DB | WNXX | HG | |
| 09019 | ML | DB | WSSI | TO | |
| 09020 | E | DB | WNTS | MG | |
| 09022 a | E | DB | WSSN | TO | |
| 09023 a | E | DB | WNTR | IM | |
| 09024 | ML | DB | WNTS | EH | |
| 09026 a | G | SN | HWSU | BI | Cedric Wares |

**Class 09/1. Converted from Class 08. 110 V electrical equipment.**
**Converted:** 1992–1993 by RFS Industries, Kilnhurst.

| | | | | | | |
|---|---|---|---|---|---|---|
| 09101 | (08833) | **DG** | DB | WNTR | DR |
| 09102 | (08832) | **DG** | DB | WNTS | MG |
| 09103 | (08766) | **DG** | DB | WNTS | AY |
| 09104 | (08749) | **DG** | DB | WNXX | TE |
| 09105 | (08835) | **DG** | DB | WNTS | DR |
| 09106 | (08759) | **E** | DB | WSSN | TO |
| 09107 | (08845) | **E** | DB | WNTR | DR |

**Class 09/2. Converted from Class 08. 90 V electrical equipment.**
**Converted:** 1992 by RFS Industries, Kilnhurst.

| | | | | | | |
|---|---|---|---|---|---|---|
| 09201 | (08421) | ak | **DG** | DB | WSSM | TO |
| 09202 | (08732) | | **DG** | DB | WNYX | DR |
| 09203 | (08781) | | **DG** | DB | WNYX | CE |
| 09204 | (08717) | | **DG** | DB | WNXX | TY |
| 09205 | (08620) | | **DG** | DB | WNTS | TE |

# CLASS 20        ENGLISH ELECTRIC        Bo-Bo

**Built:** 1957–1968 by English Electric at Vulcan Foundry, Newton-le-Willows or by Robert Stephenson & Hawthorns at Darlington.
**Engine:** English Electric 8SVT Mk. II of 746 kW (1000 h.p.) at 850 r.p.m.
**Main Generator:** English Electric 819/3C.
**Traction Motors:** English Electric 526/5D or 526/8D.
**Maximum Tractive Effort:** 187 kN (42000 lbf).
**Continuous Tractive Effort:** 111 kN (25000 lbf) at 11 m.p.h.

| | |
|---|---|
| **Power At Rail:** 574 kW (770 h.p.). | **Train Brakes:** Air & vacuum. |
| **Brake Force:** 35 t. | **Dimensions:** 14.25 x 2.67 m. |
| **Weight:** 73.4–73.5 t. | **Wheel Diameter:** 1092 mm. |
| **Design Speed:** 75 m.p.h. | **Maximum Speed:** 75 m.p.h. |
| **Fuel Capacity:** 1727 litres. | **RA:** 5. |
| **Train Supply:** Not equipped. | **Multiple Working:** Blue Star. |

Originally numbered in series D8007–D8190, D8315–D8325.

**Non-standard liveries/numbering:**

20088 & 20105 RFS grey (20105 carries numbers 2016 and 36).
20132 Carries number D8132.
20138 As **F0** but with a red solebar stripe.
20906 Carries no number.

**Class 20/0. Standard Design.**

| | | | | |
|---|---|---|---|---|
| 20016 | **B** | HN | HNRS | LM |
| 20032 | **B** | HN | HNRS | LM |
| 20057 | **B** | HN | HNRS | LM |
| 20072 | **B** | HN | HNRS | LM |
| 20081 | **B** | HN | HNRS | LM |
| 20088 | **0** | HN | HNRS | LM |

| 20092 | U  | HN | HNRS | BH |                    |
|-------|----|----|------|----|--------------------|
| 20096 | B  | HN | HNRL | BH |                    |
| 20105 | O  | HN | HNRS | BH |                    |
| 20107 | B  | HN | HNRS | BH |                    |
| 20121 | B  | HN | HNRS | BH |                    |
| 20132 | G  | HN | HNRS | BH | Barrow Hill Depot  |
| 20138 | O  | HN | HNRS | LM |                    |
| 20189 | G  | 20 | MOLO | SK |                    |
| 20197 | B  | HN | HNRS | LM |                    |
| 20227 | FO | 2L | MOLO | SK |                    |

**Class 20/3. Direct Rail Services refurbished locos.** Details as Class 20/0 except:

**Refurbished:** 1995–1996 by Brush Traction at Loughborough (20301–20305) or 1997–1998 by RFS(E) at Doncaster (20306–20315). Disc indicators or headcode panels removed.

| | |
|---|---|
| **Train Brakes:** Air. | **Maximum Speed:** 75 m.p.h. |
| **Weight:** 76 t. | **Fuel Capacity:** 2900 (+ 4909) litres. |
| **Brake Force:** 35 t. | **RA:** 5 (+ 6). |
| **Multiple Working:** DRS system. | |

| 20301 | (20047) | + | DS | DR XHNC | KM        | Max Joule 1958–1999 |
|-------|---------|---|----|---------|-----------|---------------------|
| 20302 | (20084) |   | DS | DR XHSS | ZG        |                     |
| 20303 | (20127) | + | DS | DR XHSS | ZG        |                     |
| 20304 | (20120) |   | DS | DR XHNC | KM        |                     |
| 20305 | (20095) |   | DS | DR XHSS | Stowmarket | Gresty Bridge      |
| 20306 | (20131) | + | DR | DR XHSS | CR        |                     |
| 20307 | (20128) | + | DR | DR XHSS | ZG        |                     |
| 20308 | (20187) | + | DS | DR XHSS | ZG        |                     |
| 20309 | (20075) | + | DS | DR XHSS | ZG        |                     |
| 20310 | (20190) | + | DR | DR XHSS | ZG        |                     |
| 20311 | (20012) | + | DR | DR XHSS | ZG        | Class 20 'Fifty'    |
| 20312 | (20042) | + | DS | DR XHSS | ZG        |                     |
| 20313 | (20194) | + | DR | DR XHSS | ZG        |                     |
| 20314 | (20117) | + | DS | DR XHSS | ZG        |                     |
| 20315 | (20104) | + | DR | DR XHSS | ZG        |                     |

**Class 20/9. Harry Needle Railroad Company (former Hunslet-Barclay/DRS) locos.** Details as Class 20/0 except:

**Refurbished:** 1989 by Hunslet-Barclay at Kilmarnock.

| | |
|---|---|
| **Train Brakes:** Air. | **Fuel Capacity:** 1727 (+ 4727) litres. |
| **RA:** 5 (+ 6). | |

| 20901 | (20101) |   | F  | HN MOLO | BH |
|-------|---------|---|----|---------|----|
| 20902 | (20060) | + | DR | HN HNRS | LM |
| 20903 | (20083) | + | DR | HN HNRS | LM |
| 20904 | (20041) |   | DR | HN HNRS | BH |
| 20905 | (20225) | + | F  | HN MOLO | BH |
| 20906 | (20219) |   | DR | HN HNRS | CP |

# CLASS 25 BR/BEYER PEACOCK/SULZER Bo-Bo

**Built:** 1965 by Beyer Peacock at Gorton.
**Engine:** Sulzer 6LDA28-B of 930 kW (1250 h.p.) at 750 r.p.m.
**Main Generator:** AEI RTB15656.       **Traction Motors:** AEI 253AY.
**Maximum Tractive Effort:** 200 kN (45000 lbf).
**Continuous Tractive Effort:** 93 kN (20800 lbf) at 17.1 m.p.h.
**Power At Rail:** 708 kW (949 h.p.).      **Train Brakes:** Air & vacuum.
**Brake Force:** 38 t.                      **Dimensions:** 15.39 x 2.73 m.
**Weight:** 71.5 t.                         **Wheel Diameter:** 1143 mm.
**Design Speed:** 90 m.p.h.                 **Maximum Speed:** 60 m.p.h.
**Fuel Capacity:** 2270 litres.             **RA:** 5.
**Train Supply:** Not equipped.             **Multiple Working:** Blue Star.

Original number is D7628, which the loco currently carries.

**Note:** Only certified for use on Network Rail metals between Whitby and
Battersby, as an extension of North Yorkshire Moors Railway services.

| 25278 | **GG** | NY | MBDL | NY | SYBILLA |

# CLASS 31 BRUSH/ENGLISH ELECTRIC A1A-A1A

**Built:** 1958–1962 by Brush Traction at Loughborough.
**Engine:** English Electric 12SVT of 1100 kW (1470 h.p.) at 850 r.p.m.
**Main Generator:** Brush TG160-48.       **Traction Motors:** Brush TM73-68.
**Maximum Tractive Effort:** 160 kN (35900 lbf).
**Continuous Tractive Effort:** 83 kN (18700 lbf) at 23.5 m.p.h.
**Power At Rail:** 872 kW (1170 h.p.).     **Train Brakes:** Air & vacuum.
**Brake Force:** 49 t.                      **Dimensions:** 17.30 x 2.67 m.
**Weight:** 106.7–111 t.                    **Wheel Diameter:** 1092/1003 mm.
**Design Speed:** 90 m.p.h.                 **Maximum Speed:** 90 m.p.h.
**Fuel Capacity:** 2409 litres.             **RA:** 5 or 6.
**Train Supply:** Not equipped.             **Multiple Working:** Blue Star.

Originally numbered D5520–D5699, D5800–D5862 (not in order).

**Non-standard numbering:**

31190 Also carries number D5613.

**Class 31/1. Standard Design.** RA: 5.

| 31105 | **Y**   | NR | QADD | DF |           |
| 31106 a | **B** | HJ | RVLO | DF |           |
| 31128 | **B**   | NS | NRLO | BH | CHARYBDIS |
| 31190 | **G**   | HS | HTLX | DF |           |
| 31233 a | **Y** | NR | QADD | DF |           |
| 31285 | **Y**   | NR | QADD | DF |           |

**Class 31/4. Electric Train Supply equipment.** RA: 6.
**Train Supply:** Electric, index 66.

| 31422 | **IC** | BA | RVLO | DF (S) |
| 31452 | **BA** | BA | RVLO | DF |

| 31454 | **IC** | BA | RVLO | DF | |
|--------|--------|-----|------|-------|-----------|
| 31459 | **K** | RE | RVLO | DF | CERBERUS |
| 31465 | **Y** | NR | QADD | DF | |
| 31468 | **FR** | BA | RVLO | DF (S) | HYDRA |

**Class 31/6. ETS through wiring and controls. RA: 5.**

| 31601 (31186) | **BA** | BA | RVLO | DF | |
|---------------|--------|-----|------|-------|--------------------|
| 31602 (31191) | **Y** | RE | RVLO | DF | DRIVER DAVE GREEN |

# CLASS 33          BRCW/SULZER          Bo-Bo

**Built:** 1960–1962 by the Birmingham Railway Carriage & Wagon Company at Smethwick.
**Engine:** Sulzer 8LDA28 of 1160 kW (1550 h.p.) at 750 r.p.m.
**Main Generator:** Crompton Parkinson CG391B1.
**Traction Motors:** Crompton Parkinson C171C2.
**Maximum Tractive Effort:** 200 kN (45000 lbf).
**Continuous Tractive Effort:** 116 kN (26000 lbf) at 17.5 m.p.h.
**Power At Rail:** 906 kW (1215 h.p.).      **Train Brakes:** Air & vacuum.
**Brake Force:** 35 t.                      **Dimensions:** 15.47 x 2.82 (2.64 m. 33/2).
**Weight:** 76-78 t.                        **Wheel Diameter:** 1092 mm.
**Design Speed:** 85 m.p.h.                 **Maximum Speed:** 85 m.p.h.
**Fuel Capacity:** 3410 litres.             **RA:** 6.
**Train Supply:** Electric, index 48 (750 V DC only).
**Multiple Working:** Blue Star.

Originally numbered in series D6500–D6597 but not in order.

**Class 33/0. Standard Design.**

| 33025 | **WC** | WC | MBDL | CS | Glen Falloch |
|-------|--------|-----|------|-------|--------------|
| 33029 | **WC** | WC | MBDL | CS (S) | Glen Loy |
| 33030 | **DR** | WC | MBDL | CS (S) | |

**Class 33/2. Built to former Loading Gauge of Tonbridge–Battle Line.**
Equipped with slow speed control.

| 33207 | **WC** | WC | MBDL | CS | Jim Martin |
|-------|--------|-----|------|-------|------------|

# CLASS 37          ENGLISH ELECTRIC          Co-Co

**Built:** 1960–1965 by English Electric at Vulcan Foundry, Newton-le-Willows or by Robert Stephenson & Hawthorns at Darlington.
**Engine:** English Electric 12CSVT of 1300 kW (1750 h.p.) at 850 r.p.m.
**Main Generator:** English Electric 822/10G.
**Traction Motors:** English Electric 538/A.
**Maximum Tractive Effort:** 245 kN (55500 lbf).
**Continuous Tractive Effort:** 156 kN (35000 lbf) at 13.6 m.p.h.
**Power At Rail:** 932 kW (1250 h.p.).      **Train Brakes:** Air & vacuum.
**Brake Force:** 50 t.                      **Dimensions:** 18.75 x 2.74 m.
**Weight:** 102.8–108.4 t.                  **Wheel Diameter:** 1092 mm.
**Design Speed:** 90 m.p.h.                 **Maximum Speed:** 80 m.p.h.
**Fuel Capacity:** 4046 (+ 7678) litres.    **RA:** 5 (§ 6).

**Train Supply:** Not equipped.
**Multiple Working:** Blue Star († DRS system).

Originally numbered D6600–D6608, D6700–D6999 (not in order).

**Note:** Class 37s in use abroad are listed in a new section of this book (section 1.6).

**Non-standard liveries/numbering:**

37402 Light grey lower bodyside & dark grey upper bodyside.
37411 Also carries number D6990.

**Class 37/0. Standard Design.** Details as above.

| | | | | | |
|---|---|---|---|---|---|
| 37029 | § | **DR** | HN | HNRS | LM |
| 37038 | † | **DR** | DR | XHNC | KM |
| 37042 | + | **E** | DB | WNXX | DR |
| 37057 | + | **E** | HN | HNRS | BH |
| 37059 | a+†**DS** | | DR | XHNC | KM |
| 37069 | a+†**DS** | | DR | XHNC | KM |
| 37087 | a† | **DR** | DR | XHNC | KM | Keighley & Worth Valley Railway 40th Anniversary 1968–2008 |
| 37108 | + | **WC** | TT | TTTC | CS (S) |
| 37165 | a+ | **CE** | HN | HNRS | CS |
| 37194 | † | **DS** | DR | XHNC | KM |
| 37197 | | **DS** | DR | XHHP | BH |
| 37198 | + | **Y** | NR | MBDL | GCR |
| 37214 | | **WC** | WC | MBDL | CS (S) | Loch Laidon |
| 37218 | † | **DS** | DR | XHNC | KM |
| 37229 | † | **DS** | DR | XHNC | KM | Jonty Jarvis 8-12-1998 to 18-3-2005 |
| 37259 | † | **DS** | DR | XHNC | KM |
| 37261 | a+†**DR** | | DR | XHSS | ZG |

**Class 37/4. Refurbished with electric train supply equipment.** Main generator replaced by alternator. Re-geared (CP7) bogies. Details as Class 37/0 except:
**Main Alternator:** Brush BA1005A.        **Power At Rail:** 935 kW (1254 h.p.).
**Traction Motors:** English Electric 538/5A.
**Maximum Tractive Effort:** 256 kN (57440 lbf).
**Continuous Tractive Effort:** 184 kN (41250 lbf) at 11.4 m.p.h.
**Weight:** 107 t.
**Design Speed:** 80 m.p.h.
**Fuel Capacity:** 7678 litres.
**Train Supply:** Electric, index 30.

| | | | | | |
|---|---|---|---|---|---|
| 37401 | r | **E** | DB | WKBN | TO |
| 37402 | | **O** | DB | WNXX | TO | Bont Y Bermo |
| 37405 | r | **E** | DB | WNTS | TO |
| 37406 | r | **E** | DB | WNXX | CD | The Saltire Society |
| 37409 | | **DS** | DR | XHSS | BH |
| 37410 | r | **E** | DB | WNTS | ZJ |
| 37411 | | **G** | DB | WNTS | EH | CAERPHILLY CASTLE/CASTELL CAERFFILI |
| 37412 | | **F** | DR | XHSS | LM |
| 37416 | | **GS** | DB | WNXX | EH |
| 37417 | ra | **E** | DB | WNXX | EH |
| 37419 | | **DB** | DB | WNTS | CE |

| 37422 r | **E** | DB | WNTS | TO | Cardiff Canton |
|---|---|---|---|---|---|
| 37423 † | **DS** | DR | XHNC | KM | Spirit of the Lakes |
| 37425 | **BL** | DB | WKBN | TO | Pride of the Valleys/ |
| | | | | | Balchder y Cymoedd |
| 37426 | **E** | DB | WNXX | CD | |
| 37427 r | **E** | DB | WNXX | TY | |

**Class 37/5. Refurbished without train supply equipment. Main generator replaced by alternator. Re-geared (CP7) bogies.** Details as Class 37/4 except:
**Maximum Tractive Effort:** 248 kN (55590 lbf).
**Weight:** 106.1–110.0 t.

| 37503 r§ | **E** | DB | WNXX | DR | |
|---|---|---|---|---|---|
| 37510 a† | **DS** | DR | XHNC | KM | |
| 37515 a† | **DR** | DR | XHHP | BH | |
| 37516 s | **WC** | WC | MBDL | CS | |
| 37517 as | **LH** | WC | MBDL | CS (S) | |
| 37521 r§ | **E** | DB | WNXX | DR | |

**Class 37/6. Originally refurbished for Nightstar services.** Main generator replaced by alternator. UIC jumpers. Details as Class 37/5 except:
**Maximum Speed:** 90 m.p.h.            **Train Brake:** Air.
**Train Supply:** Not equipped, but electric through wired.
**Multiple Working:** DRS system.

| 37601 | **DS** | DR | XHNC | KM | |
|---|---|---|---|---|---|
| 37602 | **DS** | DR | XHSS | KM | |
| 37603 | **DS** | DR | XHNC | KM | |
| 37604 | **DS** | DR | XHNC | KM | |
| 37605 | **DR** | DR | XHSS | ZG | |
| 37606 | **DR** | DR | XHSS | CR | |
| 37607 | **DR** | DR | XHNC | KM | |
| 37608 | **DS** | DR | XHNC | KM | |
| 37609 | **DR** | DR | XHNC | KM | |
| 37610 | **DS** | DR | XHNC | KM | T.S.(Ted) Cassady 14.5.61–6.4.08 |
| 37611 | **DS** | DR | XHNC | KM | |
| 37612 | **DR** | DR | XHSS | ZG | |

**Class 37/5 continued.**

| 37667 s† | **DS** | DR | XHNC | KM | |
|---|---|---|---|---|---|
| 37668 s | **E** | WC | MBDL | CS (S) | |
| 37669 r | **E** | DB | WNTS | TO | |
| 37670 r | **DB** | DB | WFMU | CD | St. Blazey T&RS Depot |
| 37671 a | **F** | DB | WNXX | TY | |
| 37672 as | **F** | HN | HNRS | LM | |
| 37675 as§ | **F** | DB | WNXX | MG | Margam TMD |
| 37676 a | **WC** | WC | MBDL | CS | Loch Rannoch |
| 37680 a§ | **F** | HN | HNRS | HP | |
| 37682 r† | **DS** | DR | XHHP | KM | |
| 37683 a | **DS** | DR | XHHP | BH | |
| 37685 a | **IC** | WC | MBDL | CS (S) | |
| 37688 † | **DS** | DR | XHNC | KM | Kingmoor TMD |
| 37689 a§ | **F** | DB | WNXX | DR | |

| 37693 as | **F** | DB | WNXX | TY |
| 37696 as | **F** | HN | HNRS | LM |

**Class 37/7. Refurbished locos. Main generator replaced by alternator. Re-geared (CP7) bogies. Ballast weights added. Details as Class 37/5 except:**
**Main Alternator:** GEC G564AZ (37796–803) Brush BA1005A (others).
**Maximum Tractive Effort:** 276 kN (62000 lbf).
**Weight:** 120 t.                                    **RA:** 7.

| 37706 |   | **WC** | WC | MBDL | CS |   |
| 37707 |   | **E** | DB | WNXX | BS |   |
| 37709 |   | **F** | DB | WNXX | MH |   |
| 37710 |   | **LH** | WC | MBDL | CS (S) |   |
| 37712 | a | **WC** | WC | MBDL | CS (S) |   |
| 37886 |   | **E** | DB | WNXX | MH | Sir Dyfed/County of Dyfed |
| 37891 | a | **F** | DB | WNXX | TY |   |
| 37895 | s | **E** | DB | WNXX | BS |   |
| 37898 | s | **F** | HN | HNRS | LM |   |

**Class 97/3. Class 37s refurbished for Network Rail for use on the Cambrian Lines pilot ERTMS signalling project.** Details as Class 37/0.

| 97301 | (37100) | e | **Y** | NR | QETS | BH |   |
| 97302 | (37170) | e | **Y** | NR | QETS | BH |   |
| 97303 | (37178) | e | **Y** | NR | QETS | BH |   |
| 97304 | (37217) | e | **Y** | NR | QETS | BH | John Tiley |

# CLASS 40     ENGLISH ELECTRIC     1Co-Co1

**Built:** 1958–1962 by English Electric at Vulcan Foundry, Newton-le-Willows.
**Engine:** English Electric 16SVT Mk2 of 1490 kW (2000 h.p.) at 850 r.p.m.
**Main Generator:** English Electric 822/4C.
**Traction Motors:** English Electric 526/5D or EE526/7D.
**Maximum Tractive Effort:** 231 kN (52000 lbf).
**Continuous Tractive Effort:** 137 kN (30900 lbf) at 18.8 m.p.h.
**Power At Rail:** 1160 kW (1550 h.p.).      **Train Brakes:** Air & vacuum.
**Brake Force:** 51 t.                        **Dimensions:** 21.18 x 2.78 m.
**Weight:** 132 t.                            **Wheel Diameter:** 914/1143 mm.
**Design Speed:** 90 m.p.h.                   **Maximum Speed:** 90 m.p.h.
**Fuel Capacity:** 3250 litres.               **RA:** 6.
**Train Supply:** Steam.                      **Multiple Working:** Blue Star.

Originally numbered D345.

| 40145 | **BL** | 40 | ELRD | BQ | East Lancashire Railway |

# CLASS 43          BREL/PAXMAN          Bo-Bo

**Built:** 1975–1982 by BREL at Crewe Works.
**Engine:** Paxman Valenta 12RP200L of 1680 kW (2250 h.p.) at 1500 r.p.m.
(* Paxman 12VP185 of 1565 kW (2100 h.p.) at 1500 r.p.m.).
(m MTU 16V4000 R41R of 1680kW (2250 h.p.) at 1500 r.p.m.). Fitted to all FGW,
East Coast, CrossCountry and Network Rail power cars.
**Main Alternator:** Brush BA1001B.
**Traction Motors:** Brush TMH68–46 or GEC G417AZ, frame mounted.
**Maximum Tractive Effort:** 80 kN (17980 lbf).
**Continuous Tractive Effort:** 46 kN (10340 lbf) at 64.5 m.p.h.
**Power At Rail:** 1320 kW (1770 h.p.).     **Train Brakes:** Air.
**Brake Force:** 35 t.                      **Dimensions:** 17.79 x 2.74 m.
**Weight:** 70.25 t.                        **Wheel Diameter:** 1020 mm.
**Design Speed:** 125 m.p.h.                **Maximum Speed:** 125 m.p.h.
**Fuel Capacity:** 4500 litres.             **RA:** 5.
**Train Supply:** Three-phase electric.
**Multiple Working:** Within class, jumpers at non-driving end only.

**Notes:** † Buffer fitted.

43013, 43014 & 43062 are fitted with measuring apparatus & front-end cameras.

| | | | | | |
|---|---|---|---|---|---|
| 43002 | m | **FB** | A | EFPC | LA |
| 43003 | m | **FB** | A | EFPC | LA | ISAMBARD KINGDOM BRUNEL |
| 43004 | m | **FB** | A | EFPC | LA | First for the future/ |
| | | | | | | First ar gyfer y dyfodol |
| 43005 | m | **FB** | A | EFPC | LA | |
| 43009 | m | **FB** | A | EFPC | LA | First transforming travel |
| 43010 | m | **FB** | A | EFPC | LA | |
| 43012 | m | **FB** | A | EFPC | LA | |
| 43013 | m† | **Y** | P | QCAR | EC | |
| 43014 | m† | **Y** | P | QCAR | EC | |
| 43015 | m | **FB** | A | EFPC | LA | |
| 43016 | m | **FB** | A | EFPC | LA | |
| 43017 | m | **FB** | A | EFPC | LA | |
| 43018 | m | **FB** | A | EFPC | LA | |
| 43020 | m | **FB** | A | EFPC | LA | |
| 43021 | m | **FB** | A | EFPC | LA | David Austin – Cartoonist |
| 43022 | m | **FB** | A | EFPC | LA | |
| 43023 | m | **FB** | A | EFPC | LA | |
| 43024 | m | **FB** | A | EFPC | LA | |
| 43025 | m | **FB** | A | EFPC | LA | |
| 43026 | m | **FB** | A | EFPC | LA | |
| 43027 | m | **FB** | A | EFPC | LA | Glorious Devon |
| 43028 | m | **FB** | A | EFPC | LA | |
| 43029 | m | **FB** | A | EFPC | LA | |
| 43030 | m | **FB** | A | EFPC | LA | Christian Lewis Trust |
| 43031 | m | **FB** | A | EFPC | LA | |
| 43032 | m | **FB** | A | EFPC | LA | |
| 43033 | m | **FB** | A | EFPC | LA | Driver Brian Cooper |
| | | | | | | 15 June 1947–5 October 1999 |

| | | | | | |
|---|---|---|---|---|---|
| 43034 | m | **FB** | A | EFPC | LA | TravelWatch SouthWest |
| 43035 | m | **FB** | A | EFPC | LA | |
| 43036 | m | **FB** | A | EFPC | LA | |
| 43037 | m | **FB** | A | EFPC | LA | PENYDARREN |
| 43040 | m | **FB** | A | EFPC | LA | Bristol St. Philip's Marsh |
| 43041 | m | **FB** | A | EFPC | OO | |
| 43042 | m | **FB** | A | EFPC | OO | |
| 43043 | * | **MN** | P | EMPC | NL | |
| 43044 | * | **MN** | P | EMPC | NL | |
| 43045 | * | **MN** | P | EMPC | NL | |
| 43046 | * | **ST** | P | EMPC | NL | |
| 43047 | * | **MN** | P | EMPC | NL | |
| 43048 | * | **ST** | P | EMPC | NL | T.C.B. Miller MBE |
| 43049 | * | **ST** | P | EMPC | NL | Neville Hill |
| 43050 | * | **ST** | P | EMPC | NL | |
| 43052 | * | **ST** | P | EMPC | NL | |
| 43053 | m | **FB** | P | EFPC | LE | |
| 43054 | * | **MN** | P | EMPC | NL | |
| 43055 | * | **ST** | P | EMPC | NL | |
| 43056 | m | **FB** | P | EFPC | LE | |
| 43058 | * | **ST** | P | EMPC | NL | |
| 43059 | * | **MN** | P | EMPC | NL | |
| 43060 | * | **MN** | P | EMPC | NL | |
| 43061 | * | **ST** | P | EMPC | NL | |
| 43062 | m | **Y** | P | QCAR | EC | John Armitt |
| 43063 | m | **FB** | P | EFPC | OO | |
| 43064 | * | **ST** | P | EMPC | NL | |
| 43065 | † | **GC** | ST | GCHP | HT | |
| 43066 | * | **MN** | P | EMPC | NL | |
| 43067 | † | **GC** | ST | GCHP | HT | |
| 43068 | † | **GC** | ST | GCHP | HT | |
| 43069 | m | **FB** | P | EFPC | OO | |
| 43070 | m | **FB** | P | EFPC | OO | The Corps of Royal Electrical and Mechanical Engineers |
| 43071 | m | **FB** | P | EFPC | OO | |
| 43072 | * | **ST** | P | EMPC | NL | |
| 43073 | * | **MN** | P | EMPC | NL | |
| 43074 | * | **MN** | P | EMPC | NL | |
| 43075 | * | **MN** | P | EMPC | NL | |
| 43076 | * | **MN** | P | EMPC | NL | |
| 43078 | m | **FB** | P | EFPC | OO | |
| 43079 | m | **FB** | P | EFPC | OO | |
| 43080 | † | **GC** | ST | GCHP | HT | |
| 43081 | * | **MN** | P | EMPC | NL | |
| 43082 | * | **ST** | P | EMPC | NL | RAILWAY children – THE VOICE FOR STREET CHILDREN WORLDWIDE |
| 43083 | * | **ST** | P | EMPC | NL | |
| 43084 | † | **GC** | ST | GCHP | HT | |
| 43086 | m | **FB** | P | EFPC | OO | |
| 43087 | m | **FB** | P | EFPC | OO | |
| 43088 | m | **FB** | P | EFPC | OO | |

| 43089 | * | **ST** | P | EMPC | NL | |
|-------|---|--------|---|------|----|-|
| 43091 | m | **FB** | P | EFPC | OO | |
| 43092 | m | **FB** | FG | EFPC | OO | |
| 43093 | m | **FB** | FG | EFPC | OO | |
| 43094 | m | **FB** | FG | EFPC | OO | |
| 43097 | m | **FB** | FG | EFPC | OO | Environment Agency |
| 43098 | m | **FB** | FG | EFPC | OO | |
| 43122 | m | **FB** | FG | EFPC | OO | |
| 43123 | † | **GC** | ST | GCHP | HT | |
| 43124 | m | **FB** | A | EFPC | LE | |
| 43125 | m | **FB** | A | EFPC | LE | |
| 43126 | m | **FB** | A | EFPC | LE | |
| 43127 | m | **FB** | A | EFPC | LE | Sir Peter Parker 1924–2002 Cotswold Line 150 |
| 43128 | m | **FB** | A | EFPC | LE | |
| 43129 | m | **FB** | A | EFPC | LE | |
| 43130 | m | **FB** | A | EFPC | LE | |
| 43131 | m | **FB** | A | EFPC | LE | |
| 43132 | m | **FB** | A | EFPC | LE | We Save the Children – Will You? |
| 43133 | m | **FB** | A | EFPC | LE | |
| 43134 | m | **FB** | A | EFPC | LE | |
| 43135 | m | **FB** | A | EFPC | LE | |
| 43136 | m | **FB** | A | EFPC | LE | |
| 43137 | m | **FB** | A | EFPC | LE | |
| 43138 | m | **FB** | A | EFPC | LE | |
| 43139 | m | **FB** | A | EFPC | LE | Driver Stan Martin 25 June 1950 – 6 November 2004 |
| 43140 | m | **FB** | A | EFPC | LE | |
| 43141 | m | **FB** | A | EFPC | LE | |
| 43142 | m | **FB** | A | EFPC | LE | |
| 43143 | m | **FB** | A | EFPC | LE | Stroud 700 |
| 43144 | m | **FB** | A | EFPC | LE | |
| 43145 | m | **FB** | A | EFPC | LE | |
| 43146 | m | **FB** | A | EFPC | LE | |
| 43147 | m | **FB** | A | EFPC | LE | |
| 43148 | m | **FB** | A | EFPC | LE | |
| 43149 | m | **FB** | A | EFPC | LE | |
| 43150 | m | **FB** | A | EFPC | LE | |
| 43151 | m | **FB** | A | EFPC | LE | |
| 43152 | m | **FB** | A | EFPC | LE | |
| 43153 | m | **FB** | FG | EFPC | OO | |
| 43154 | m | **FB** | FG | EFPC | OO | |
| 43155 | m | **FB** | FG | EFPC | OO | |
| 43156 | m | **FB** | P | EFPC | OO | Dartington International Summer School |
| 43158 | m | **FB** | FG | EFPC | OO | |
| 43159 | m | **FB** | P | EFPC | OO | |
| 43160 | m | **FB** | P | EFPC | OO | |
| 43161 | m | **FB** | P | EFPC | OO | |
| 43162 | m | **FB** | P | EFPC | OO | |
| 43163 | m | **FB** | A | EFPC | OO | Exeter Panel Signal Box 21st Anniversary 2009 |

| | | | | | | |
|---|---|---|---|---|---|---|
| 43164 | m | **FB** | A | EFPC | OO | |
| 43165 | m | **FB** | A | EFPC | OO | Prince Michael of Kent |
| 43168 | m | **FB** | A | EFPC | OO | |
| 43169 | m | **FB** | A | EFPC | OO | THE NATIONAL TRUST |
| 43170 | m | **FB** | A | EFPC | OO | |
| 43171 | m | **FB** | A | EFPC | OO | |
| 43172 | m | **FB** | A | EFPC | OO | |
| 43174 | m | **FB** | A | EFPC | OO | |
| 43175 | m | **FB** | A | EFPC | OO | |
| 43176 | m | **FB** | A | EFPC | OO | |
| 43177 | m | **FB** | A | EFPC | OO | |
| 43179 | m | **FB** | A | EFPC | OO | Pride of Laira |
| 43180 | m | **FB** | P | EFPC | OO | |
| 43181 | m | **FB** | A | EFPC | OO | |
| 43182 | m | **FB** | A | EFPC | OO | |
| 43183 | m | **FB** | A | EFPC | OO | |
| 43185 | m | **FB** | A | EFPC | OO | Great Western |
| 43186 | m | **FB** | A | EFPC | OO | |
| 43187 | m | **FB** | A | EFPC | OO | |
| 43188 | m | **FB** | A | EFPC | OO | |
| 43189 | m | **FB** | A | EFPC | OO | |
| 43190 | m | **FB** | A | EFPC | OO | |
| 43191 | m | **FB** | A | EFPC | OO | |
| 43192 | m | **FB** | A | EFPC | OO | |
| 43193 | m | **FB** | P | EFPC | OO | |
| 43194 | m | **FB** | FG | EFPC | OO | |
| 43195 | m | **FB** | P | EFPC | OO | |
| 43196 | m | **FB** | P | EFPC | OO | |
| 43197 | m | **FB** | P | EFPC | OO | |
| 43198 | m | **FB** | FG | EFPC | OO | Oxfordshire 2007 |

**Class 43/2. Rebuilt East Coast and CrossCountry power cars.** Power cars have been renumbered by adding 200 to their original number.

| | | | | | | |
|---|---|---|---|---|---|---|
| 43206 | (43006) | m | **NX** | A | IECP | EC | |
| 43207 | (43007) | m | **XC** | A | EHPC | EC | |
| 43208 | (43008) | m | **NX** | A | IECP | EC | |
| 43238 | (43038) | m | **NX** | A | IECP | EC | |
| 43239 | (43039) | m | **NX** | A | IECP | EC | |
| 43251 | (43051) | m | **NX** | P | IECP | EC | |
| 43257 | (43057) | m | **NX** | P | IECP | EC | |
| 43277 | (43077) | m | **NX** | P | IECP | EC | |
| 43285 | (43085) | m | **XC** | P | EHPC | EC | |
| 43290 | (43090) | m | **NX** | P | IECP | EC | mtu fascination of power |
| 43295 | (43095) | m | **NX** | A | IECP | EC | |
| 43296 | (43096) | m | **NX** | A | IECP | EC | |
| 43299 | (43099) | m | **NX** | P | IECP | EC | |
| 43300 | (43100) | m | **NX** | P | IECP | EC | Craigentinny |
| 43301 | (43101) | m | **XC** | P | EHPC | EC | |
| 43302 | (43102) | m | **NX** | P | IECP | EC | |
| 43303 | (43103) | m | **XC** | P | EHPC | EC | |
| 43304 | (43104) | m | **XC** | A | EHPC | EC | |

| | | | | | | |
|---|---|---|---|---|---|---|
| 43305 | (43105) | m | **NX** | A | IECP | EC |
| 43306 | (43106) | m | **NX** | A | IECP | EC |
| 43307 | (43107) | m | **NX** | A | IECP | EC |
| 43308 | (43108) | m | **NX** | A | IECP | EC |
| 43309 | (43109) | m | **NX** | A | IECP | EC |
| 43310 | (43110) | m | **NX** | A | IECP | EC |
| 43311 | (43111) | m | **NX** | A | IECP | EC |
| 43312 | (43112) | m | **NX** | A | IECP | EC |
| 43313 | (43113) | m | **GN** | A | IECP | EC |
| 43314 | (43114) | m | **NX** | A | IECP | EC |
| 43315 | (43115) | m | **NX** | A | IECP | EC |
| 43316 | (43116) | m | **NX** | A | IECP | EC |
| 43317 | (43117) | m | **NX** | A | IECP | EC |
| 43318 | (43118) | m | **NX** | A | IECP | EC |
| 43319 | (43119) | m | **NX** | A | IECP | EC |
| 43320 | (43120) | m | **NX** | A | IECP | EC |
| 43321 | (43121) | m | **XC** | P | EHPC | EC |
| 43357 | (43157) | m | **XC** | P | EHPC | EC |
| 43366 | (43166) | m | **XC** | A | EHPC | EC |
| 43367 | (43167) | m | **NX** | A | IECP | EC | DELTIC 50 1955–2005 |
| 43378 | (43178) | m | **XC** | A | EHPC | EC |
| 43384 | (43184) | m | **XC** | A | EHPC | EC |

# CLASS 47          BR/BRUSH/SULZER          Co-Co

**Built:** 1963–1967 by Brush Traction, at Loughborough or by BR at Crewe Works.
**Engine:** Sulzer 12LDA28C of 1920 kW (2580 h.p.) at 750 r.p.m.
**Main Generator:** Brush TG160-60 Mk4 or TM172-50 Mk1.
**Traction Motors:** Brush TM64-68 Mk1 or Mk1A.
**Maximum Tractive Effort:** 267 kN (60000 lbf).
**Continuous Tractive Effort:** 133 kN (30000 lbf) at 26 m.p.h.
**Power At Rail:** 1550 kW (2080 h.p.)    **Train Brakes:** Air.
**Brake Force:** 61 t.                    **Dimensions:** 19.38 x 2.79 m.
**Weight:** 111.5–120.6 t.                **Wheel Diameter:** 1143 mm.
**Design Speed:** 95 m.p.h.
**Maximum Speed:** 95 m.p.h. (* 75 m.p.h.).
**Fuel Capacity:** 3273 (+ 5550).        **RA:** 6 or 7.
**Train Supply:** Not equipped.
**Multiple Working:** † DRS system, m Green Circle (operational locos only).

Originally numbered in series D1100–D1111, D1500–D1999 but not in order.

**Non-standard liveries/numbering:**

47270 Also carries number D1971.
47773 Also carries number D1755.
47812 Also carries number D1916.
47815 Also carries number D1748.
47829 "Police" livery of white with a broad red band outlined in yellow.
47851 Also carries number D1648.
47853 "XP64 blue" with red cabside panels. Also carries number D1733.
47972 BR Central Services red & grey.

**Class 47/0 (Dual-braked locos) or Class 47/2 (Air-braked locos). Standard Design.** Details as above.

| 47150 *+ | **FL** | HN | HNRS | BA | |
| 47194 | **F** | WC | MBDL | CS (S) | |
| 47236 + | **FE** | WC | MBDL | CS (S) | |
| 47237 + | **AZ** | CD | ADFL | GL (S) | |
| 47245 x+m | **WC** | WC | MBDL | CS | |
| 47270 | **B** | BD | BREL | WH | SWIFT |
| 47289 *+ | **FF** | HN | HNRS | BA | |
| 47295 a | **FF** | HN | HNRS | LM | |

**Class 47/3 (Dual-braked locos) or Class 47/2 (Air-braked locos).**
Details as Class 47/0 except: **Weight:** 113.7 t.

| 47355 m | **K** | X | MBDL | CS (S) | |
| 47363 | **F** | WC | MBDL | CS (S) | |
| 47368 x | **F** | WC | MBDL | CS (S) | |
| 47375 + | **AZ** | NS | NRLO | BH (S) | |

**Class 47/4. Electric Train Supply equipment.**
Details as Class 47/0 except:

**Weight:** 120.4–125.1 t.                 **Fuel Capacity:** 3273 (+ 5887) litres.
**Train Supply:** Electric. ETH 66.       **RA:** 7.

| 47489 x | **RG** | WC | MBDL | CS (S) | |
| 47492 x | **RX** | WC | MBDL | CS (S) | |
| 47501 x†+ | **DS** | DR | XHAC | KM | Craftsman |
| 47525 x | **FE** | WC | MBDL | CS (S) | |
| 47526 x | **BL** | WC | MBDL | CS (S) | |
| 47575 x | **RG** | RV | RTLS | CQ | |
| 47580 x | **BL** | 47 | MBDL | TM | County of Essex |

**Class 47/7. Previously fitted with an older form of TDM.**

Details as Class 47/4 except:
**Weight:** 118.7 t.                       **Fuel Capacity:** 5887 litres.
**Maximum Speed:** 100 m.p.h.

| 47709 x† | **DS** | DR | XHHP | ZG | |
| 47712 x† | **DS** | DR | XHAC | KM | Pride of Carlisle |
| 47714 xm | **AR** | HN | HNRL | OD | |

**Class 47/7. Former Railnet dedicated locos.** All have twin fuel tanks.

| 47727 m | **CS** | CS | COLO | WH | Rebecca |
| 47739 m | **CS** | CS | COLO | WH | Robin of Templecombe |
| 47747 | **E** | RV | RTLO | CP (S) | |
| 47749 m | **CS** | CS | COLO | WH | Demelza |
| 47760 | **WC** | WC | MBDL | CS | |
| 47769 | **V** | RV | RTLO | CP | Resolve |
| 47770 | **RX** | WC | MBDL | CS (S) | |
| 47772 x | **RX** | WC | MBDL | CS (S) | |
| 47773 x | **GG** | 70 | MBDL | TM | |
| 47776 x | **RX** | WC | MBDL | CS (S) | |
| 47786 | **WC** | WC | MBDL | CS | Roy Castle OBE |

| 47787 | **WC** | WC | MBDL | CS | Windsor Castle |
| 47790 † | **DS** | DR | XHAC | KM | Galloway Princess |
| 47791 | **DS** | DR | XHHP | BH | |

**Class 47/4 continued**. RA6. Most fitted with extended-range fuel tanks (+).

| 47798 | **RP** | NM | MBDL | YK | Prince William |
| 47799 | **RP** | DB | WNXX | EH | |
| 47802 +† | **DS** | DR | XHAC | KM | Pride of Cumbria |
| 47804 | **WC** | WC | MBDL | CS | |
| 47805 +m | **RV** | RV | RTLO | CP | TALISMAN |
| 47810 + | **DS** | DR | XHSS | BH | |
| 47811 + | **GL** | FL | DFLH | Dagenham (S) | |
| 47812 +m | **GG** | RV | RTLO | CP | |
| 47813 +m | **CD** | HN | HNRL | DW (S) | |
| 47815 +m | **GG** | RV | RTLO | CP | GREAT WESTERN |
| 47816 + | **GL** | FL | DFLH | BA (S) | |
| 47818 + | **1** | HN | HNRL | BH (S) | |
| 47826 + | **WC** | WC | MBDL | CS | |
| 47828 +m | **CD** | CD | ADFL | DW (S)Joe Strummer | |
| 47829 + | **0** | HN | HNRS | LM | |
| 47830 + | **GL** | FL | DFLH | BA (S) | |
| 47832 +† | **DS** | DR | XHAC | KM | Solway Princess |
| 47839 +m | **RV** | RV | RTLO | CP | PEGASUS |
| 47841 + | **DS** | DR | XHHP | ZG | |
| 47843 +m | **RV** | RV | RTLO | CP | VULCAN |
| 47847 +m | **BL** | RV | RTLO | EH (S) | |
| 47848 +m | **RV** | RV | RTLO | CP | TITAN STAR |
| 47851 + | **GG** | WC | MBDL | CS | Traction Magazine |
| 47853 +m | **0** | RV | RTLO | CP | RAIL EXPRESS |
| 47854 + | **WC** | WC | MBDL | CS | |
| 47972 | **0** | WC | MBDL | CS (S) | |

# CLASS 50     ENGLISH ELECTRIC     Co-Co

**Built:** 1967–1968 by English Electric at Vulcan Foundry, Newton-le-Willows.
**Engine:** English Electric 16CVST of 2010 kW (2700 h.p.) at 850 r.p.m.
**Main Generator:** English Electric 840/4B.
**Traction Motors:** English Electric 538/5A.
**Maximum Tractive Effort:** 216 kN (48500 lbf).
**Continuous Tractive Effort:** 147 kN (33000 lbf) at 23.5 m.p.h.

| | |
|---|---|
| **Power At Rail:** 1540 kW (2070 h.p.). | **Train Brakes:** Air & vacuum. |
| **Brake Force:** 59 t. | **Dimensions:** 20.88 x 2.78 m. |
| **Weight:** 116.9 t. | **Wheel Diameter:** 1092 mm. |
| **Design Speed:** 105 m.p.h. | **Maximum Speed:** 90 m.p.h. |
| **Fuel Capacity:** 4796 litres. | **RA:** 6. |
| **Train Supply:** Electric, index 61. | **Multiple Working:** Orange Square. |

Originally numbered D444 & D449.

| 50044 | **GG** | 50 | CFOL | KR | EXETER |
| 50049 | **BL** | 50 | CFOL | CF | Defiance |

## CLASS 52      BR/MAYBACH      C-C

**Built:** 1961–1964 by BR at Swindon Works.
**Engine:** Two Maybach MD655 of 1007 kW (1350 h.p.) at 1500 r.p.m.
**Transmission:** Hydraulic. Voith L630rV.
**Maximum Tractive Effort:** 297 kN (66700 lbf).
**Continuous Tractive Effort:** 201 kN (45200 lbf) at 14.5 m.p.h.

| | |
|---|---|
| **Power At Rail:** 1490 kW (2000 h.p.). | **Train Brakes:** Air & vacuum. |
| **Brake Force:** 83 t. | **Dimensions:** 20.7 m x 2.78 m. |
| **Weight:** 110 t. | **Wheel Diameter:** 1092 mm. |
| **Design Speed:** 90 m.p.h. | **Maximum Speed:** 90 m.p.h. |
| **Fuel Capacity:** 3900 litres. | **RA:** 6. |
| **Train Supply:** Steam. | **Multiple Working:** Not equipped. |

Never allocated a number in the 1972 number series.

Registered on TOPS as No. 89416.

D1015    **M**    DT    MBDL      EH      WESTERN CHAMPION

## CLASS 55      ENGLISH ELECTRIC      Co-Co

**Built:** 1961 by English Electric at Vulcan Foundry, Newton-le-Willows.
**Engine:** Two Napier-Deltic D18-25 of 1230 kW (1650 h.p.) each at 1500 r.p.m.
**Main Generators:** Two English Electric 829/1A.
**Traction Motors:** English Electric 538/A.
**Maximum Tractive Effort:** 222 kN (50000 lbf).
**Continuous Tractive Effort:** 136 kN (30500 lbf) at 32.5 m.p.h.

| | |
|---|---|
| **Power At Rail:** 1969 kW (2640 h.p.). | **Train Brakes:** Air & vacuum. |
| **Brake Force:** 51 t. | **Dimensions:** 21.18 x 2.68 m. |
| **Weight:** 100 t. | **Wheel Diameter:** 1092 mm. |
| **Design Speed:** 105 m.p.h. | **Maximum Speed:** 100 m.p.h. |
| **Fuel Capacity:** 3755 litres. | **RA:** 5. |
| **Train Supply:** Electric, index 66. | **Multiple Working:** Not equipped. |

Originally numbered D9000.

Registered on TOPS as No. 89500.

55022    **B**    MW    ELRD      BQ      ROYAL SCOTS GREY

## CLASS 56      BRUSH/BR/RUSTON      Co-Co

**Built:** 1976–1984 by Electroputere at Craiova, Romania (as sub contractors for Brush) or BREL at Doncaster or Crewe Works.
**Engine:** Ruston Paxman 16RK3CT of 2460 kW (3250 h.p.) at 900 r.p.m.
**Main Alternator:** Brush BA1101A.
**Traction Motors:** Brush TM73-62.
**Maximum Tractive Effort:** 275 kN (61800 lbf).
**Continuous Tractive Effort:** 240 kN (53950 lbf) at 16.8 m.p.h.

| | |
|---|---|
| **Power At Rail:** 1790 kW (2400 h.p.). | **Train Brakes:** Air. |
| **Brake Force:** 60 t. | **Dimensions:** 19.36 x 2.79 m. |
| **Weight:** 126 t. | **Wheel Diameter:** 1143 mm. |

**Design Speed:** 80 m.p.h.  
**Fuel Capacity:** 5228 litres.  
**Train Supply:** Not equipped.  
**Maximum Speed:** 80 m.p.h.  
**RA:** 7.  
**Multiple Working:** Red Diamond.

**Note:** All equipped with Slow Speed Control.

**Non-standard liveries:**

56303 All over dark green.  
56311 Light grey with yellow cabsides.  
56312 Purple with yellow cabsides & green lining.

| | | | | |
|---|---|---|---|---|
| 56006 | **B** | DB | WNXX | BH |
| 56007 | **FER** | DB | WZGF | CE |
| 56018 | **FER** | DB | WZGF | WA |
| 56031 | **FER** | DB | WZGF | CD |
| 56032 | **FER** | DB | WZGF | CD |
| 56037 | **E** | DB | WZTS | CD |
| 56038 | **FER** | DB | WZGF | CD |
| 56041 | **E** | DB | WNXX | HM |
| 56046 | **CE** | DB | WNXX | TO |
| 56049 | **FER** | DB | WZGF | CD |
| 56051 | **FER** | DB | WZGF | CD |
| 56053 | **F** | DB | WNXX | HM |
| 56054 | **F** | DB | WNXX | CD |
| 56055 | **LH** | DB | WNXX | HM |
| 56058 | **FER** | DB | WZGF | CD |
| 56059 | **FER** | DB | WZGF | EH |
| 56060 | **FER** | DB | WZGF | CD |
| 56062 | **E** | DB | WNXX | MG |
| 56065 | **FER** | DB | WZGF | CD |
| 56067 | **E** | DB | WNXX | CD |
| 56069 | **FER** | DB | WZGF | CD |
| 56070 | **F** | DB | WNXX | CE |
| 56071 | **FER** | DB | WZGF | CD |
| 56072 | **F** | DB | WNXX | HM |
| 56073 | **F** | DB | WNXX | TO |
| 56074 | **FER** | DB | WZGF | CD |
| 56077 | **LH** | DB | WNXX | CD |
| 56078 | **FER** | DB | WZGF | CD |
| 56081 | **FER** | DB | WZGF | CD |
| 56083 | **LH** | DB | WNXX | CD |
| 56085 | **LH** | DB | WNXX | TE |
| 56087 | **FER** | DB | WZGF | CD |
| 56088 | **E** | DB | WNXX | TE |
| 56090 | **FER** | DB | WZGF | CD |
| 56091 | **FER** | DB | WZGF | EH |
| 56093 | **F** | DB | WNXX | HM |
| 56094 | **FER** | DB | WZGF | CD |
| 56095 | **FER** | DB | WZGF | EH |
| 56096 | **FER** | DB | WZGF | CD |
| 56099 | **F** | DB | WNXX | HM |
| 56100 | **LH** | DB | WNXX | MG |

| 56102 | **LH** | DB | WNXX | TE | |
|-------|--------|----|------|-----|---|
| 56103 | **FER** | DB | WZGF | CD | |
| 56104 | **FER** | DB | WZGF | CD | |
| 56105 | **FER** | DB | WZGF | CD | |
| 56106 | **FER** | DB | WZGF | CD | |
| 56107 | **LH** | DB | WNXX | CD | |
| 56108 | **F** | DB | WNXX | TE | |
| 56109 | **LH** | DB | WNXX | CD | |
| 56110 | **LH** | DB | WNXX | HM | |
| 56111 | **LH** | DB | WNXX | TE | |
| 56112 | **LH** | DB | WNXX | CE | |
| 56113 | **FER** | DB | WZGF | CD | |
| 56115 | **FER** | DB | WZGF | EH | |
| 56117 | **FER** | DB | WZGF | EH | |
| 56119 | **E** | DB | WNXX | HM | |
| 56120 | **E** | DB | WNXX | CD | |
| 56127 | **F** | DB | WNXX | TE | |
| 56129 | **F** | DB | WNXX | TE | |
| 56133 | **F** | DB | WZTS | CE | |
| | | | | | |
| 56301 (56045) | **FA** | FA | RCJZ | RR | |
| 56302 (56124) | **FA** | FA | RCJZ | RR | Wilson Walshe |
| 56303 (56125) | **0** | RE | RVLO | DF | |
| | | | | | |
| 56311 (56057) | **0** | HS | HTLX | WF | |
| 56312 (56003) | **0** | HS | HTLX | WF | ARTEMIS |
| 56313 (56128) | | HS | HTLX | WF (S) | |
| 56314 (56114) | | HS | HTLX | WH (S) | |

# CLASS 57            BRUSH/GM            Co-Co

**Built:** 1964–1965 by Brush Traction at Loughborough or BR at Crewe Works as Class 47. Rebuilt 1997–2004 by Brush Traction at Loughborough.
**Engine:** General Motors 12 645 E3 of 1860 kW (2500 h.p.) at 904 r.p.m.
**Main Alternator:** Brush BA1101D.
**Traction Motors:** Brush TM64-68 Mark 1 or Mark 1a.
**Maximum Tractive Effort:** 244.5 kN (55000 lbf).
**Continuous Tractive Effort:** 140 kN (31500 lbf) at ?? m.p.h.

| **Power at Rail:** 1507 kW (2025 h.p.). | **Train Brakes:** Air. |
|---|---|
| **Brake Force:** 80 t. | **Dimensions:** 19.38 x 2.79 m. |
| **Weight:** 120.6 t. | **Wheel Diameter:** 1143 mm. |
| **Design Speed:** 75 m.p.h. | **Maximum Speed:** 75 m.p.h. |
| **Fuel Capacity:** 5550 litres. | **RA:** 6 |
| **Train Supply:** Not equipped. | **Multiple Working:** † DRS system. |

**Class 57/0. No Train Supply Equipment. Rebuilt 1998–2000.**

| 57001 (47356) | | **FL** | P | SBXL | LB | |
|---------------|---|--------|----|------|-----|---|
| 57002 (47322) | † | **DS** | P | XHCK | KM | |
| 57003 (47317) | † | **DS** | P | XHCK | KM | |
| 57004 (47347) | † | **DS** | DR | XHCK | KM | |
| 57005 (47350) | | **AZ** | CD | ADFL | Cardiff Central (S) | |
| 57006 (47187) | | **AZ** | CD | ADFL | HT (S) | |

| | | | | | | |
|---|---|---|---|---|---|---|
| 57007 | (47332) | † **DS** | P | XHCK | KM | |
| 57008 | (47060) | † **DS** | P | XHCK | KM | Telford International |
| | | | | | | Railfreight Park June 2009 |
| 57009 | (47079) | † **DS** | P | XHCK | KM | |
| 57010 | (47231) | † **DS** | P | XHSS | KM | |
| 57011 | (47329) | † **DS** | P | XHSS | KM | |
| 57012 | (47204) | † **DS** | P | XHCK | KM | |

**Class 57/3. Electric Train Supply Equipment. Virgin Trains locos. Rebuilt 2002–2004.** Details as Class 57/0 except:

**Engine:** General Motors 12645F3B of 2050 kW (2750 h.p.) at 954 r.p.m.
**Main Alternator:** Brush BA1101F (recovered from a Class 56) or Brush BA1101G.
**Fuel Capacity:** 5887 litres.	**Train Supply:** Electric, index 100.
**Design Speed:** 95 m.p.h.	**Maximum Speed:** 95 m.p.h.
**Brake Force:** 60 t.	**Weight:** 117 t.

**Note:** 57313–316 are on sub-lease to Arriva Trains Wales and are used on the Holyhead–Cardiff loco-hauled service.

**Non-standard livery:** 57313 & 57316 All over blue.

| | | | | | | |
|---|---|---|---|---|---|---|
| 57301 | (47845) | d **VT** | P | IWCA | MA | SCOTT TRACY |
| 57302 | (47827) | d **VT** | P | IWCA | MA | VIRGIL TRACY |
| 57303 | (47705) | d **VT** | P | IWCA | MA | ALAN TRACY |
| 57304 | (47807) | d **VT** | P | IWCA | MA | GORDON TRACY |
| 57305 | (47822) | d **VT** | P | IWCA | MA | JOHN TRACY |
| 57306 | (47814) | d **VT** | P | IWCA | MA | JEFF TRACY |
| 57307 | (47225) | d **VT** | P | IWCA | MA | LADY PENELOPE |
| 57308 | (47846) | d **VT** | P | IWCA | MA | TIN TIN |
| 57309 | (47806) | d **VT** | P | IWCA | MA | BRAINS |
| 57310 | (47831) | d **VT** | P | IWCA | MA | KYRANO |
| 57311 | (47817) | d **VT** | P | IWCA | MA | PARKER |
| 57312 | (47330) | d **VT** | P | IWCA | MA | THE HOOD |
| 57313 | (47371) | d **0** | P | IWCA | MA | |
| 57314 | (47372) | d **AB** | P | IWCA | MA | |
| 57315 | (47234) | d **AB** | P | IWCA | MA | |
| 57316 | (47290) | d **0** | P | IWCA | MA | |

**Class 57/6. Electric Train Supply Equipment. Prototype ETS loco. Rebuilt 2001.** Details as Class 57/0 except:

**Main Alternator:** Brush BA1101E.	**Fuel Capacity:** 3273 litres.
**Train Supply:** Electric, index 100.	**Weight:** 113 t.
**Design Speed:** 95 m.p.h.	**Maximum Speed:** 95 m.p.h.
**Brake Force:** 60 t.

| | | | | | |
|---|---|---|---|---|---|
| 57601 | (47825) | **WC** | WC MBDL | CS | |

**Class 57/6. Electric Train Supply Equipment. First Great Western locos. Rebuilt 2004.** Details as Class 57/3.

| | | | | | | |
|---|---|---|---|---|---|---|
| 57602 | (47337) | **FB** | P | EFOO | OO | Restormel Castle |
| 57603 | (47349) | **GL** | P | EFOO | OO | Tintagel Castle |
| 57604 | (47209) | **GL** | P | EFOO | OO | Pendennis Castle |
| 57605 | (47206) | **FB** | P | EFOO | OO | Totnes Castle |

# CLASS 58          BREL/RUSTON          Co-Co

**Built:** 1983–1987 by BREL at Doncaster Works.
**Engine:** Ruston Paxman 12RK3ACT of 2460 kW (3300 h.p.) at 1000 r.p.m.
**Main Alternator:** Brush BA1101B.     **Traction Motors:** Brush TM73-62.
**Maximum Tractive Effort:** 275 kN (61800 lbf).
**Continuous Tractive Effort:** 240 kN (53950 lbf) at 17.4 m.p.h.
**Power At Rail:** 1780 kW (2387 h.p.).     **Train Brakes:** Air.
**Brake Force:** 60 t.                      **Dimensions:** 19.13 x 2.72 m.
**Weight:** 130 t.                          **Wheel Diameter:** 1120 mm.
**Design Speed:** 80 m.p.h.                 **Maximum Speed:** 80 m.p.h.
**Fuel Capacity:** 4214 litres.             **RA:** 7.
**Train Supply:** Not equipped.             **Multiple Working:** Red Diamond.

**Notes:** All equipped with Slow Speed Control.

Class 58s in use abroad are listed in a new section of this book (section 1.6).

| 58002 | **ML**  | DB | WZTS | EH |
|-------|---------|----|------|----|
| 58003 | **F**   | DB | WZTS | TO |
| 58008 | **ML**  | DB | WZTS | EH |
| 58012 | **F**   | DB | WZTS | TO |
| 58014 | **ML**  | DB | WZTS | TO |
| 58016 | **FER** | DB | WZTS | CE |
| 58017 | **F**   | DB | WZTS | EH |
| 58019 | **F**   | DB | WZTS | TO |
| 58022 | **F**   | DB | WZTS | CD |
| 58023 | **ML**  | DB | WZTS | TO |
| 58028 | **F**   | DB | WZTS | TO |
| 58037 | **E**   | DB | WZTS | EH |
| 58045 | **F**   | DB | WZTS | CE |
| 58048 | **E**   | DB | WZTS | CE |

# CLASS 59          GENERAL MOTORS          Co-Co

**Built:** 1985 (59001/59002/59004) or 1989 (59005) by General Motors, La Grange, Illinois, USA or 1990 (59101–59104), 1994 (59201) and 1995 (59202–59206) by General Motors, London, Ontario, Canada.
**Engine:** General Motors 16-645E3C two stroke of 2460 kW (3300 h.p.) at 904 r.p.m.
**Main Alternator:** General Motors AR11 MLD-D14A.
**Traction Motors:** General Motors D77B.
**Maximum Tractive Effort:** 506 kN (113 550 lbf).
**Continuous Tractive Effort:** 291 kN (65 300 lbf) at 14.3 m.p.h.
**Power At Rail:** 1889 kW (2533 h.p.).     **Train Brakes:** Air.
**Brake Force:** 69 t.                       **Dimensions:** 21.35 x 2.65 m.
**Weight:** 121 t.                           **Wheel Diameter:** 1067 mm.
**Design Speed:** 60 (* 75) m.p.h.           **Maximum Speed:** 60 (* 75) m.p.h.
**Fuel Capacity:** 4546 litres.              **RA:** 7.
**Train Supply:** Not equipped.              **Multiple Working:** AAR System.

**Class 59/0. Owned by Aggregate Industries.**

| | | | | | |
|---|---|---|---|---|---|
| 59001 | **AI** | AI | XYPO | MD | YEOMAN ENDEAVOUR |
| 59002 | **FY** | AI | XYPO | MD | ALAN J DAY |
| 59004 | **FY** | AI | XYPO | MD | PAUL A HAMMOND |
| 59005 | **AI** | AI | XYPO | MD | KENNETH J PAINTER |

**Class 59/1. Owned by Hanson Quarry Products.**

| | | | | | |
|---|---|---|---|---|---|
| 59101 | **HA** | HA | XYPA | MD | Village of Whatley |
| 59102 | **HA** | HA | XYPA | MD | Village of Chantry |
| 59103 | **HA** | HA | XYPA | MD | Village of Mells |
| 59104 | **HA** | HA | XYPA | MD | Village of Great Elm |

**Class 59/2. Owned by DB Schenker.**

| | | | | | | |
|---|---|---|---|---|---|---|
| 59201 | * | **E** | DB | WDAK | TO | Vale of York |
| 59202 | * | **E** | DB | WDAK | TO | Vale of White Horse |
| 59203 | * | **E** | DB | WDAK | TO | Vale of Pickering |
| 59204 | * | **E** | DB | WDAK | TO | Vale of Glamorgan |
| 59205 | *b | **E** | DB | WDAK | TO | L Keith McNair |
| 59206 | *b | **DB** | DB | WDAK | TO | John F. Yeoman Rail Pioneer |

---

# CLASS 60     BRUSH/MIRRLEES     Co-Co

**Built:** 1989–1993 by Brush Traction at Loughborough.
**Engine:** Mirrlees 8MB275T of 2310 kW (3100 h.p.) at 1000 r.p.m.
**Main Alternator:** Brush BA1006A.
**Traction Motors:** Brush TM2161A.
**Maximum Tractive Effort:** 500 kN (106500 lbf).
**Continuous Tractive Effort:** 336 kN (71570 lbf) at 17.4 m.p.h.

| | |
|---|---|
| **Power At Rail:** 1800 kW (2415 h.p.). | **Train Brakes:** Air. |
| **Brake Force:** 74 (+ 62) t. | **Dimensions:** 21.34 x 2.64 m. |
| **Weight:** 129 (+ 131) t. | **Wheel Diameter:** 1118 mm. |
| **Design Speed:** 62 m.p.h. | **Maximum Speed:** 60 m.p.h. |
| **Fuel Capacity:** 4546 (+ 5225) litres. | **RA:** 8. |
| **Train Supply:** Not equipped. | |

**Multiple Working:** Within class.

**IMPORTANT NOTE: DB Schenker Fleet Management Unit:** As all operational Class 60s are effectively now treated as "common user" by DB Schenker, and allocated to operational pools depending on which duties they are on at the time (sometimes changing between different business units several times per month), all operational locos are shown in the WFMU Fleet Management pool here. Details of the other individual pools can be found in the codes section of this book.

**Notes:** All equipped with Slow Speed Control.

60034, 60061, 60063, 60064, 60066, 60072, 60073, 60077, 60079, 60082, 60084, 60088, 60090 and 60091 carry their names on one side only.

60500 used to carry the number 60016.

60007, 60044 and 60078 carry EWS logos on their **LH** or **ML** liveries.

**Advertising liveries:**

60040 Territorial Army Centenary (maroon).
60074 Teenage Cancer Trust (light blue).

| | | | | | |
|---|---|---|---|---|---|
| 60001 |   | E  | DB | WNTS | TO | The Railway Observer |
| 60002 | + | E  | DB | WNTS | CD | High Peak |
| 60003 | + | E  | DB | WNTS | TO | FREIGHT TRANSPORT ASSOCIATION |
| 60004 | + | E  | DB | WNTR | TO | |
| 60005 | + | E  | DB | WNTS | TO | |
| 60006 |   | CU | DB | WNTS | TO | |
| 60007 | + | LH | DB | WNTS | CD | |
| 60008 |   | E  | DB | WNTS | TO | Sir William McAlpine |
| 60009 | + | E  | DB | WFMU | TO | |
| 60010 | + | E  | DB | WNTS | TO | |
| 60011 |   | ML | DB | WNTR | TO | |
| 60012 | + | E  | DB | WNTS | TO | |
| 60013 |   | EG | DB | WNTR | TO | Robert Boyle |
| 60014 |   | EG | DB | WNTS | TO | |
| 60015 | + | EG | DB | WNTS | TO | Bow Fell |
| 60017 | + | E  | DB | WNTS | TO | Shotton Works Centenary Year 1996 |
| 60018 |   | E  | DB | WNTS | TO | |
| 60019 |   | E  | DB | WNTR | TO | PATHFINDER TOURS 30 YEARS OF RAILTOURING 1973–2003 |
| 60020 | + | E  | DB | WNTS | TO | |
| 60021 | + | E  | DB | WNTS | TO | Star of the East |
| 60022 | + | E  | DB | WNTS | EH | |
| 60023 | + | E  | DB | WNTS | TO | |
| 60024 |   | E  | DB | WNTS | TO | |
| 60025 | + | E  | DB | WNTS | TO | |
| 60026 | + | E  | DB | WNTS | MG | |
| 60027 | + | E  | DB | WNTR | TO | |
| 60028 | + | EG | DB | WNTS | CD | John Flamsteed |
| 60029 |   | E  | DB | WNTS | CD | Clitheroe Castle |
| 60030 | + | E  | DB | WNTS | TO | |
| 60031 |   | E  | DB | WNTS | TO | ABP Connect |
| 60032 |   | F  | DB | WNTS | TO | William Booth |
| 60033 | + | CU | DB | WNTS | TO | Tees Steel Express |
| 60034 |   | EG | DB | WNTS | TO | Carnedd Llewelyn |
| 60035 |   | E  | DB | WNTS | TO | |
| 60036 |   | E  | DB | WNTS | TO | GEFCO |
| 60037 | + | E  | DB | WNTS | TO | Aberddawan/Aberthaw |
| 60038 | + | E  | DB | WNTR | CD | AvestaPolarit |
| 60039 |   | E  | DB | WFMU | TO | |
| 60040 |   | AL | DB | WFMU | TO | The Territorial Army Centenary |
| 60041 | + | E  | DB | WNTR | TO | |
| 60042 |   | E  | DB | WNTS | TO | The Hundred of Hoo |
| 60043 |   | E  | DB | WNTR | CD | |
| 60044 |   | ML | DB | WNTS | TO | |
| 60045 |   | E  | DB | WNTR | TO | The Permanent Way Institution |
| 60046 | + | EG | DB | WNTR | CD | William Wilberforce |
| 60047 |   | E  | DB | WNTS | CD | |

| | | | | | |
|---|---|---|---|---|---|
| 60048 | **E** | DB | WNTR | TO | EASTERN |
| 60049 | **E** | DB | WNTR | TO | |
| 60050 | **E** | DB | WNTS | TO | |
| 60051 + | **E** | DB | WNTR | TO | |
| 60052 + | **E** | DB | WNTS | TO | Glofa Twr – The last deep mine in Wales – Tower Colliery |
| 60053 | **E** | DB | WNTS | TO | |
| 60054 + | **F** | DB | WNTR | TO | Charles Babbage |
| 60055 + | **EG** | DB | WNTS | CD | Thomas Barnardo |
| 60056 + | **EG** | DB | WNTR | CD | William Beveridge |
| 60057 | **EG** | DB | WNTS | TO | Adam Smith |
| 60058 + | **E** | DB | WNTS | TO | |
| 60059 + | **LH** | DB | WNTR | TO | Swinden Dalesman |
| 60060 | **EG** | DB | WNTS | TO | James Watt |
| 60061 | **F** | DB | WNTS | TO | Alexander Graham Bell |
| 60062 | **E** | DB | WNTS | MG | |
| 60063 | **EG** | DB | WNTR | DR | James Murray |
| 60064 + | **EG** | DB | WNTS | TO | Back Tor |
| 60065 | **E** | DB | WNTS | TO | Spirit of JAGUAR |
| 60066 | **EG** | DB | WNTS | TO | John Logie Baird |
| 60067 | **EG** | DB | WNTS | TO | James Clerk-Maxwell |
| 60068 | **EG** | DB | WNTS | TO | |
| 60069 | **E** | DB | WNTS | TO | Slioch |
| 60070 + | **F** | DB | WNTS | TO | John Loudon McAdam |
| 60071 + | **E** | DB | WNTR | TO | Ribblehead Viaduct |
| 60072 | **EG** | DB | WNTS | TO | Cairn Toul |
| 60073 | **EG** | DB | WNTR | TO | Cairn Gorm |
| 60074 | **AL** | DB | WFMU | TO | Teenage Spirit |
| 60075 | **E** | DB | WNTS | TO | |
| 60076 | **EG** | DB | WNTR | CD | |
| 60077 + | **EG** | DB | WNTR | TO | Canisp |
| 60078 | **ML** | DB | WNTS | TO | |
| 60079 | **EG** | DB | WNTS | CD | Foinaven |
| 60080 + | **E** | DB | WNTS | TO | |
| 60081 + | **GW** | DB | WNTS | TO | |
| 60082 | **EG** | DB | WNTS | CD | Mam Tor |
| 60083 | **E** | DB | WNTS | TO | |
| 60084 | **EG** | DB | WNTR | TO | Cross Fell |
| 60085 | **E** | DB | WNTR | TO | MINI Pride of Oxford |
| 60086 | **EG** | DB | WNTS | TO | Schiehallion |
| 60087 | **E** | DB | WNTS | TO | Barry Needham |
| 60088 | **F** | DB | WNTS | TO | Buachaille Etive Mor |
| 60089 + | **E** | DB | WNTS | TO | |
| 60090 + | **EG** | DB | WNTS | TO | Quinag |
| 60091 + | **EG** | DB | WNTS | TO | An Teallach |
| 60092 + | **EG** | DB | WNTR | CD | Reginald Munns |
| 60093 | **E** | DB | WNTS | TO | |
| 60094 | **E** | DB | WNTR | Scunthorpe | Rugby Flyer |
| 60095 | **EG** | DB | WNTR | CD | |
| 60096 + | **E** | DB | WFMU | TO | |
| 60097 + | **E** | DB | WNTS | TO | |

| 60098 | + | E  | DB | WNTS | TO | |
|-------|---|----|----|------|----|---------------|
| 60099 |   | EG | DB | WNTS | TO | Ben More Assynt |
| 60100 |   | E  | DB | WNTS | TO | Pride of Acton |
| 60500 |   | E  | DB | WNTS | TO | |

# CLASS 66    GENERAL MOTORS/EMD    Co-Co

**Built:** 1998–2008 by General Motors/EMD, London, Ontario, Canada (Model JT42CWR (low emission locos Model JT42CWRM)).
**Engine:** General Motors 12N-710G3B-EC two stroke of 2385 kW (3200 h.p.) at 904 r.p.m.
**Main Alternator:** General Motors AR8/CA6.
**Traction Motors:** General Motors D43TR.
**Maximum Tractive Effort:** 409 kN (92000 lbf).
**Continuous Tractive Effort:** 260 kN (58390 lbf) at 15.9 m.p.h.

| | |
|---|---|
| **Power At Rail:** 1850 kW (2480 h.p.). | **Train Brakes:** Air. |
| **Brake Force:** 68 t. | **Dimensions:** 21.35 x 2.64 m. |
| **Weight:** 127 t. | **Wheel Diameter:** 1120 mm. |
| **Design Speed:** 87.5 m.p.h. | **Maximum Speed:** 75 m.p.h. |
| **Fuel Capacity:** 6550 litres. | **RA:** 7. |
| **Train Supply:** Not equipped. | **Multiple Working:** AAR System. |

**IMPORTANT NOTE: DB Schenker Fleet Management Unit:** As all DB Schenker Class 66s are effectively now treated as "common user" by DB Schenker, and allocated to operational pools depending on which duties they are on at the time (sometimes changing between different business levels several times per month), all operational locos are shown in the WFMU Fleet Management pool here. Details of the other individual pools can be found in the codes section of this book.

**Notes:** All equipped with Slow Speed Control.

Class 66s in use abroad with Euro Cargo Rail and Freightliner Poland are listed in a new section of this book (section 1.6).

**Advertising livery:** 66048 Stobart Rail (two tone blue & white).

**Class 66 delivery dates.** The Class 66 design has evolved over more than a ten year period with over 400 of these locos now in use in the UK. For clarity the delivery dates (by year) for each batch of locos delivered to the UK is as follows:

| | |
|---|---|
| 66001–66250 | EWS (now DB Schenker). 1998–2000 |
| 66301–66305 | Fastline. 2008 |
| 66401–66410 | DRS. 2003. Now stored or in use with other operators. 66406–410 renumbered 66841–844. |
| 66411–66420 | DRS. 2006 |
| 66421–66430 | DRS. 2007 |
| 66431–66434 | DRS. 2008 |
| 66501–66505 | Freightliner. 1999 |
| 66506–66520 | Freightliner. 2000 |
| 66521–66525 | Freightliner. 2000 (66521 since scrapped). |
| 66526–66531 | Freightliner. 2001 |
| 66532–66537 | Freightliner. 2001 |
| 66538–66543 | Freightliner. 2001 |

| 66544–66553 | Freightliner. 2001 |
| 66554 | Freightliner. 2002* |
| 66555–66566 | Freightliner. 2002 |
| 66567–66574 | Freightliner. 2003 |
| 66575–66577 | Freightliner. 2004 |
| 66578–66581 | Freightliner. 2005 |
| 66582–66594 | Freightliner. 2007 (66582/583/584/586 exported to Poland). |
| 66595–66599 | Freightliner. 2008 |
| 66601–66606 | Freightliner. 2000 |
| 66607–66612 | Freightliner. 2002 |
| 66613–66618 | Freightliner. 2003 |
| 66619–66622 | Freightliner. 2005 |
| 66623–66625 | Freightliner. 2007 (66625 exported to Poland). |
| 66701–66707 | First GBRf. 2001 |
| 66708–66712 | First GBRf. 2002 |
| 66713–66717 | First GBRf. 2003 |
| 66718–66722 | First GBRf. 2006 |
| 66723–66727 | First GBRf. 2006 |
| 66728–66732 | First GBRf. 2008 |
| 66951–66952 | Freightliner. 2004 |
| 66953–66957 | Freightliner. 2008 |

* Replacement for 66521, written off in the Great Heck accident in 2001.

### Class 66/0. DB Schenker-operated locomotives.

All fitted with Swinghead Automatic "Buckeye" Combination Couplers except 66001 and 66002.

† Fitted with additional lights and drawgear for Lickey banking duties.

| 66001 | E | A | WFMU | TO | |
| 66002 | E | A | WFMU | TO | Lafarge Quorn |
| 66003 | E | A | WFMU | TO | |
| 66004 | E | A | WFMU | TO | |
| 66005 | E | A | WFMU | TO | |
| 66006 | E | A | WFMU | TO | |
| 66007 | E | A | WFMU | TO | |
| 66008 | E | A | WFMU | TO | |
| 66009 | E | A | WFMU | TO | |
| 66011 | E | A | WFMU | TO | |
| 66012 | E | A | WFMU | TO | |
| 66013 | E | A | WFMU | TO | |
| 66014 | E | A | WFMU | TO | |
| 66015 | E | A | WFMU | TO | |
| 66016 | E | A | WFMU | TO | |
| 66017 | E | A | WFMU | TO | |
| 66018 | E | A | WFMU | TO | |
| 66019 | E | A | WFMU | TO | |
| 66020 | E | A | WFMU | TO | |
| 66021 | E | A | WFMU | TO | |
| 66023 | E | A | WFMU | TO | |
| 66024 | E | A | WFMU | TO | |

| 66025   | E  | A | WFMU | TO |                      |
|---------|----|---|------|----|----------------------|
| 66027   | E  | A | WFMU | TO |                      |
| 66030   | E  | A | WFMU | TO |                      |
| 66031   | E  | A | WFMU | TO |                      |
| 66034   | E  | A | WFMU | TO |                      |
| 66035   | E  | A | WFMU | TO |                      |
| 66037   | E  | A | WFMU | TO |                      |
| 66039   | E  | A | WFMU | TO |                      |
| 66040   | E  | A | WFMU | TO |                      |
| 66041   | E  | A | WFMU | TO |                      |
| 66043   | E  | A | WFMU | TO |                      |
| 66044   | E  | A | WFMU | TO |                      |
| 66046   | E  | A | WFMU | TO |                      |
| 66047   | E  | A | WFMU | TO |                      |
| 66048   | AL | A | WFMU | TO | James the Engine     |
| 66050   | E  | A | WFMU | TO | EWS Energy           |
| 66051   | E  | A | WFMU | TO |                      |
| 66053   | E  | A | WFMU | TO |                      |
| 66054   | E  | A | WFMU | TO |                      |
| 66055 † | E  | A | WFMU | TO |                      |
| 66056 † | E  | A | WFMU | TO |                      |
| 66057 † | E  | A | WFMU | TO |                      |
| 66058 † | E  | A | WFMU | TO |                      |
| 66059 † | E  | A | WFMU | TO |                      |
| 66060   | E  | A | WFMU | TO |                      |
| 66061   | E  | A | WFMU | TO |                      |
| 66063   | E  | A | WFMU | TO |                      |
| 66065   | E  | A | WFMU | TO |                      |
| 66066   | E  | A | WFMU | TO |                      |
| 66067   | E  | A | WFMU | TO |                      |
| 66068   | E  | A | WFMU | TO |                      |
| 66069   | E  | A | WFMU | TO |                      |
| 66070   | E  | A | WFMU | TO |                      |
| 66074   | E  | A | WFMU | TO |                      |
| 66075   | E  | A | WFMU | TO |                      |
| 66076   | E  | A | WFMU | TO |                      |
| 66077   | E  | A | WFMU | TO | Benjamin Gimbert G.C.|
| 66078   | E  | A | WFMU | TO |                      |
| 66079   | E  | A | WFMU | TO | James Nightall G.C.  |
| 66080   | E  | A | WFMU | TO |                      |
| 66081   | E  | A | WFMU | TO |                      |
| 66082   | E  | A | WFMU | TO |                      |
| 66083   | E  | A | WFMU | TO |                      |
| 66084   | E  | A | WFMU | TO |                      |
| 66085   | E  | A | WFMU | TO |                      |
| 66086   | E  | A | WFMU | TO |                      |
| 66087   | E  | A | WFMU | TO |                      |
| 66088   | E  | A | WFMU | TO |                      |
| 66089   | E  | A | WFMU | TO |                      |
| 66090   | E  | A | WFMU | TO |                      |
| 66091   | E  | A | WFMU | TO |                      |

| | | | | |
|---|---|---|---|---|
| 66092 | E | A | WFMU | TO |
| 66093 | E | A | WFMU | TO |
| 66094 | E | A | WFMU | TO |
| 66095 | E | A | WFMU | TO |
| 66096 | E | A | WFMU | TO |
| 66097 | E | A | WFMU | TO |
| 66098 | E | A | WFMU | TO |
| 66099 r | E | A | WFMU | TO |
| 66100 r | E | A | WFMU | TO |
| 66101 r | E | A | WFMU | TO |
| 66102 r | E | A | WFMU | TO |
| 66103 r | E | A | WFMU | TO |
| 66104 r | E | A | WFMU | TO |
| 66105 r | E | A | WFMU | TO |
| 66106 r | E | A | WFMU | TO |
| 66107 r | E | A | WFMU | TO |
| 66108 r | E | A | WFMU | TO |
| 66109 | E | A | WFMU | TO |
| 66110 r | E | A | WFMU | TO |
| 66111 r | E | A | WFMU | TO |
| 66112 r | E | A | WFMU | TO |
| 66113 r | E | A | WFMU | TO |
| 66114 r | E | A | WFMU | TO |
| 66115 | E | A | WFMU | TO |
| 66116 | E | A | WFMU | TO |
| 66117 | E | A | WFMU | TO |
| 66118 | E | A | WFMU | TO |
| 66119 | E | A | WFMU | TO |
| 66120 | E | A | WFMU | TO |
| 66121 | E | A | WFMU | TO |
| 66122 | E | A | WFMU | TO |
| 66124 | E | A | WFMU | TO |
| 66125 | E | A | WFMU | TO |
| 66126 | E | A | WFMU | TO |
| 66127 | E | A | WFMU | TO |
| 66128 | E | A | WFMU | TO |
| 66129 | E | A | WFMU | TO |
| 66130 | E | A | WFMU | TO |
| 66131 | E | A | WFMU | TO |
| 66132 | E | A | WFMU | TO |
| 66133 | E | A | WFMU | TO |
| 66134 | E | A | WFMU | TO |
| 66135 | E | A | WFMU | TO |
| 66136 | E | A | WFMU | TO |
| 66137 | E | A | WFMU | TO |
| 66138 | E | A | WFMU | TO |
| 66139 | E | A | WFMU | TO |
| 66140 | E | A | WFMU | TO |
| 66141 | E | A | WFMU | TO |
| 66142 | E | A | WFMU | TO |
| 66143 | E | A | WFMU | TO |

| 66144 | E  | A | WFMU | TO |
|-------|----|---|------|----|
| 66145 | E  | A | WFMU | TO |
| 66146 | E  | A | WFMU | TO |
| 66147 | E  | A | WFMU | TO |
| 66148 | E  | A | WFMU | TO |
| 66149 | E  | A | WFMU | TO |
| 66150 | E  | A | WFMU | TO |
| 66151 | E  | A | WFMU | TO |
| 66152 | DB | A | WFMU | TO |
| 66153 | E  | A | WFMU | TO |
| 66154 | E  | A | WFMU | TO |
| 66155 | E  | A | WFMU | TO |
| 66156 | E  | A | WFMU | TO |
| 66157 | E  | A | WFMU | TO |
| 66158 | E  | A | WFMU | TO |
| 66159 | E  | A | WFMU | TO |
| 66160 | E  | A | WFMU | TO |
| 66161 | E  | A | WFMU | TO |
| 66162 | E  | A | WFMU | TO |
| 66163 | E  | A | WFMU | TO | skour 3/12 |
| 66164 | E  | A | WFMU | TO |
| 66165 | E  | A | WFMU | TO |
| 66166 | E  | A | WFMU | TO |
| 66167 | E  | A | WFMU | TO |
| 66168 | E  | A | WFMU | TO |
| 66169 | E  | A | WFMU | TO |
| 66170 | E  | A | WFMU | TO |
| 66171 | E  | A | WFMU | TO |
| 66172 | E  | A | WFMU | TO | PAUL MELLENEY |
| 66173 | E  | A | WFMU | TO |
| 66174 | E  | A | WFMU | TO |
| 66175 | E  | A | WFMU | TO |
| 66176 | E  | A | WFMU | TO |
| 66177 | E  | A | WFMU | TO |
| 66178 | E  | A | WFMU | TO |
| 66180 | E  | A | WFMU | TO |
| 66181 | E  | A | WFMU | TO |
| 66182 | E  | A | WFMU | TO |
| 66183 | E  | A | WFMU | TO |
| 66184 | E  | A | WFMU | TO |
| 66185 | E  | A | WFMU | TO |
| 66186 | E  | A | WFMU | TO |
| 66187 | E  | A | WFMU | TO |
| 66188 | E  | A | WFMU | TO |
| 66189 | E  | A | WFMU | TO |
| 66192 | E  | A | WFMU | TO |
| 66193 | E  | A | WFMU | TO |
| 66194 | E  | A | WFMU | TO |
| 66196 | E  | A | WFMU | TO |
| 66197 | E  | A | WFMU | TO |
| 66198 | E  | A | WFMU | TO |

| 66199 | **E** | A | WFMU | TO |
| 66200 | **E** | A | WFMU | TO |
| 66201 | **E** | A | WFMU | TO |
| 66204 | **E** | A | WFMU | TO |
| 66206 | **E** | A | WFMU | TO |
| 66207 | **E** | A | WFMU | TO |
| 66213 | **E** | A | WFMU | TO |
| 66221 | **E** | A | WFMU | TO |
| 66227 | **E** | A | WFMU | TO |
| 66230 | **E** | A | WFMU | TO |
| 66232 | **E** | A | WFMU | TO |
| 66237 | **E** | A | WFMU | TO |
| 66238 | **E** | A | WFMU | TO |
| 66248 | **E** | A | WFMU | TO |
| 66250 | **E** | A | WFMU | TO |

RAILWAY HERITAGE COMMITTEE

**Class 66/3. Fastline-operated locomotives. Low emission.** Details as Class 66/0 except:

**Engine:** EMD 12N-710G3B-U2 two stroke of 2420 kW (3245 h.p.) at 904 r.p.m.
**Traction Motors:** General Motors D43TRC.
**Fuel Capacity:** 5150 litres.

| 66301 | **FA** | BN | RCJB | KM |
| 66302 | **FA** | BN | RCJB | KM |
| 66303 | **FA** | BN | RCJB | KM |
| 66304 | **FA** | BN | RCJB | KM |
| 66305 | **FA** | BN | RCJB | KM |

**Class 66/4. Former Direct Rail Services-operated locomotives.**
**66401–66410. Porterbrook locos.** Details as Class 66/0. Most off-lease at the time of writing.

**Advertising livery:** 66405 WH Malcolm (DRS Blue with WH Malcolm logos).

| 66401 | **DS** | P | GBRT | WB |
| 66402 | **DS** | P | GBRT | WB |
| 66403 | **DS** | P | SBXL | WR |
| 66404 | **DS** | P | SBXL | WR |
| 66405 | **AL** | P | SBXL | WR |
| 66410 | **DS** | P | SBXL | WR |

**66411–66434. Low emission. HBOS-owned.** Details as Class 66/0 except:

**Engine:** EMD 12N-710G3B-U2 two stroke of 2420 kW (3245 h.p.) at 904 r.p.m.
**Traction Motors:** General Motors D43TRC.
**Fuel Capacity:** 5150 litres.

**Advertising liveries:** 66411 & 66414 Stobart Rail (two tone blue & white).
66412 Malcolm Rail (black with a red solebar stripe).

| 66411 | **AL** | HX | XHIM | KM | Eddie the Engine |
| 66412 | **AL** | HX | XHIM | KM | |
| 66413 | **DS** | HX | XHIM | KM | |
| 66414 | **AL** | HX | XHIM | KM | James the Engine |
| 66415 | **DS** | HX | XHIM | KM | |

| 66416 | **DS** | HX | XHIM | KM |
| 66417 | **DS** | HX | XHIM | KM |
| 66418 | **DS** | HX | XHIM | KM |
| 66419 | **DS** | HX | XHIM | KM |
| 66420 | **DS** | HX | XHIM | KM |
| 66421 | **DS** | HX | XHIM | KM |
| 66422 | **DS** | HX | XHIM | KM |
| 66423 | **DS** | HX | XHIM | KM |
| 66424 | **DS** | HX | XHIM | KM |
| 66425 | **DS** | HX | XHIM | KM |
| 66426 | **DS** | HX | XHIM | KM |
| 66427 | **DS** | HX | XHIM | KM |
| 66428 | **DS** | HX | XHIM | KM |
| 66429 | **DS** | HX | XHIM | KM |
| 66430 | **DS** | HX | XHIM | KM |
| 66431 | **DS** | HX | XHIM | KM |
| 66432 | **DS** | HX | XHIM | KM |
| 66433 | **DS** | HX | XHIM | KM |
| 66434 | **DS** | HX | XHIM | KM |

**Class 66/5. Freightliner-operated locomotives.** Details as Class 66/0.

**Advertising livery:** 66522 Shanks Waste (one half of loco Freightliner green and one half Shanks' Waste light green).

| 66501 | **FL** | P | DFGM | FD | Japan 2001 |
| 66502 | **FL** | P | DFGM | FD | Basford Hall Centenary 2001 |
| 66503 | **FL** | P | DFGM | FD | The RAILWAY MAGAZINE |
| 66504 | **FL** | P | DFGM | FD | |
| 66505 | **FL** | P | DFGM | FD | |
| 66506 | **FL** | H | DFHH | FD | Crewe Regeneration |
| 66507 | **FL** | H | DFRT | FD | |
| 66508 | **FL** | H | DFHH | FD | |
| 66509 | **FL** | H | DFHH | FD | |
| 66510 | **FL** | H | DFRT | FD | |
| 66511 | **FL** | H | DFRT | FD | |
| 66512 | **FL** | H | DFHH | FD | |
| 66513 | **FL** | H | DFHH | FD | |
| 66514 | **FL** | H | DFRT | FD | |
| 66515 | **FL** | H | DFRT | FD | |
| 66516 | **FL** | H | DFGM | FD | |
| 66517 | **FL** | H | DFGM | FD | |
| 66518 | **FL** | H | DFRT | FD | |
| 66519 | **FL** | H | DFHH | FD | |
| 66520 | **FL** | H | DFRT | FD | |
| 66522 | **AL** | H | DFRT | LD | |
| 66523 | **FL** | H | DFRT | FD | |
| 66524 | **FL** | H | DFHH | LD | |
| 66525 | **FL** | H | DFHH | FD | |
| 66526 | **FL** | P | DFRT | LD | Driver Steve Dunn (George) |
| 66527 | **FL** | P | DFRT | LD | Don Raider |
| 66528 | **FL** | P | DFHH | FD | |

| | | | | | |
|---|---|---|---|---|---|
| 66529 | **FL** | P | DFHH | FD | |
| 66530 | **FL** | P | DFGM | FD | |
| 66531 | **FL** | P | DFGM | FD | |
| 66532 | **FL** | P | DFGM | FD | P&O Nedlloyd Atlas |
| 66533 | **FL** | P | DFGM | FD | Hanjin Express/Senator Express |
| 66534 | **FL** | P | DFGM | FD | OOCL Express |
| 66535 | **FL** | P | DFGM | FD | |
| 66536 | **FL** | P | DFGM | FD | |
| 66537 | **FL** | P | DFGM | FD | |
| 66538 | **FL** | H | DFIM | FD | |
| 66539 | **FL** | H | DFIM | FD | |
| 66540 | **FL** | H | DFIM | FD | Ruby |
| 66541 | **FL** | H | DFIM | FD | |
| 66542 | **FL** | H | DFIM | FD | |
| 66543 | **FL** | H | DFIM | FD | |
| 66544 | **FL** | P | DFHG | LD | |
| 66545 | **FL** | P | DFHG | FD | |
| 66546 | **FL** | P | DFNR | FD | |
| 66547 | **FL** | P | DFNR | LD | |
| 66548 | **FL** | P | DFHG | LD | |
| 66549 | **FL** | P | DFHG | LD | |
| 66550 | **FL** | P | DFHG | LD | |
| 66551 | **FL** | P | DFHG | LD | |
| 66552 | **FL** | P | DFHG | LD | Maltby Raider |
| 66553 | **FL** | P | DFHG | LD | |
| 66554 | **FL** | H | DFHG | LD | |
| 66555 | **FL** | H | DFHG | LD | |
| 66556 | **FL** | H | DFHG | LD | |
| 66557 | **FL** | H | DFHG | FD | |
| 66558 | **FL** | H | DFIM | FD | |
| 66559 | **FL** | H | DFIM | FD | |
| 66560 | **FL** | H | DFHG | FD | |
| 66561 | **FL** | H | DFHG | FD | |
| 66562 | **FL** | H | DFIM | LD | |
| 66563 | **FL** | H | DFIM | FD | |
| 66564 | **FL** | H | DFIM | LD | |
| 66565 | **FL** | H | DFIM | LD | |
| 66566 | **FL** | H | DFIM | LD | |
| 66567 | **FL** | H | DFIM | FD | |
| 66568 | **FL** | H | DFIM | FD | |
| 66569 | **FL** | H | DFIM | FD | |
| 66570 | **FL** | H | DFIM | FD | |
| 66571 | **FL** | H | DFIM | FD | |
| 66572 | **FL** | H | DFIM | FD | |
| 66573 | **FL** | H | DFTZ | LD | |
| 66574 | **FL** | H | DFTZ | LD | |
| 66575 | **FL** | H | DFIM | FD | |
| 66576 | **FL** | H | DFIM | FD | Hamburg Sud Advantage |
| 66577 | **FL** | H | DFIM | FD | |
| 66578 | **FL** | H | DFTZ | LD | |
| 66579 | **FL** | H | DFTZ | LD | |

| 66580 | **FL** | H | DFTZ | LD | |
| 66581 | **FL** | H | DFTZ | LD | Sophie |

**Class 66/5. Freightliner-operated low emission locos.** Details as Class 66/0 except:

**Engine:** EMD 12N-710G3B-U2 two stroke of 2420 kW (3245 h.p.) at 904 r.p.m.
**Traction Motors:** General Motors D43TRC.
**Fuel Capacity:** 5150 litres.

| 66585 | **FL** | HX | DFHG | FD | The Drax Flyer |
| 66587 | **FL** | HX | DFIN | FD | |
| 66588 | **FL** | HX | DFIN | FD | |
| 66589 | **FL** | HX | DFIN | FD | |
| 66590 | **FL** | HX | DFIN | FD | |
| 66591 | **FL** | LY | DFIN | FD | |
| 66592 | **FL** | LY | DFIN | FD | Johnson Stevens Agencies |
| 66593 | **FL** | LY | DFIN | FD | 3MG MERSEY MULTIMODAL GATEWAY |
| 66594 | **FL** | LY | DFIN | FD | NYK Spirit of Kyoto |
| 66595 | **FL** | BN | DFHG | FD | |
| 66596 | **FL** | BN | DFHG | FD | |
| 66597 | **FL** | BN | DFHG | FD | |
| 66598 | **FL** | BN | DFHG | FD | |
| 66599 | **FL** | BN | DFHG | FD | |

**Class 66/6. Freightliner-operated locomotives with modified gear ratios.** Details as Class 66/0 except:

**Maximum Tractive Effort:** 467 kN (105080 lbf).
**Continuous Tractive Effort:** 296 kN (66630 lbf) at 14.0 m.p.h.
**Design Speed:** 65 m.p.h.          **Maximum Speed:** 65 m.p.h.

| 66601 | **FL** | P | DFHH | LD | The Hope Valley |
| 66602 | **FL** | P | DFRT | FD | |
| 66603 | **FL** | P | DFRT | FD | |
| 66604 | **FL** | P | DFRT | FD | |
| 66605 | **FL** | P | DFRT | FD | |
| 66606 | **FL** | P | DFRT | FD | |
| 66607 | **FL** | P | DFHG | FD | |
| 66608 | **FL** | P | DFHG | FD | |
| 66609 | **FL** | P | DFHG | LD (S) | |
| 66610 | **FL** | P | DFHG | FD | |
| 66611 | **FL** | P | DFHG | FD | |
| 66612 | **FL** | P | DFHG | FD | Forth Raider |
| 66613 | **FL** | H | DFHG | FD | |
| 66614 | **FL** | H | DFHG | FD | |
| 66615 | **FL** | H | DFHG | FD | |
| 66616 | **FL** | H | DFHG | FD | |
| 66617 | **FL** | H | DFHG | FD | |
| 66618 | **FL** | H | DFHG | FD | Railways Illustrated Annual Photographic Awards Alan Barnes Derek W. Johnson MBE |
| 66619 | **FL** | H | DFHG | FD | |
| 66620 | **FL** | H | DFHG | FD | |
| 66621 | **FL** | H | DFHG | FD | |

66622   **FL**   H    DFHG        FD

**Class 66/6. Freightliner-operated low emission locos with modified gear ratios.**
**Fuel Capacity:** 5150 litres.

**Advertising livery:** 66623 Bardon Aggregates (blue).

66623   **AL**   HX   DFHG        FD        Bill Bolsover
66624   **FL**   HX   DFHG        FD

**Class 66/7. First GBRf-operated locomotives.** Details as Class 66/0.

**Non-standard/Advertising liveries:**

66705 **GB** livery but with the addition of "Union Jack" bodyside vinyls.
66709 Black & orange with MEDITE branding.

66701   **GB**   H    GBRT        WB        Whitemoor
66702   **GB**   H    GBRT        WB        Blue Lightning
66703   **GB**   H    GBCM        WB        Doncaster PSB 1981–2002
66704   **GB**   H    GBCM        WB        Colchester Power Signalbox
66705   **GB**   H    GBCM        WB        Golden Jubilee
66706   **GB**   H    GBCM        WB        Nene Valley
66707   **GB**   H    GBRT        WB        Sir Sam Fay GREAT CENTRAL RAILWAY
66708   **GB**   H    GBRT        WB
66709   **AL**   H    GBRT        WB        Joseph Arnold Davies
66710   **GB**   H    GBCM        WB
66711   **GB**   H    GBCM        WB
66712   **GB**   H    GBCM        WB        Peterborough Power Signalbox
66713   **GB**   H    GBCM        WB        Forest City
66714   **GB**   H    GBCM        WB        Cromer Lifeboat
66715   **GB**   H    GBCM        WB        VALOUR – IN MEMORY OF ALL RAILWAY
                                            EMPLOYEES WHO GAVE THEIR LIVES FOR
                                            THEIR COUNTRY
66716   **GB**   H    GBCM        WB
66717   **GB**   H    GBCM        WB        Good Old Boy

**66718–66732. Low emission.** Details as Class 66/0 except:

**Engine:** EMD 12N-710G3B-U2 two stroke of 2420 kW (3245 h.p.) at 904 r.p.m.
**Traction Motors:** General Motors D43TRC.
**Fuel Capacity:** 5546 litres (66718–722) or 5150 litres (66723–732).

66718   **MT**   H    GBCM        WB        Gwyneth Dunwoody
66719   **MT**   H    GBCM        WB        METRO-LAND
66720   **MT**   H    GBCM        WB        Metronet Pathfinder N M 3/12
66721   **MT**   H    GBCM        WB        Harry Beck
66722   **MT**   H    GBCM        WB        Sir Edward Watkin
66723   **FS**   H    GBCM        WB        Chinook
66724   **FS**   H    GBCM        WB        Drax Power Station
66725   **FS**   H    GBCM        WB        SUNDERLAND
66726   **FS**   H    GBCM        WB        SHEFFIELD WEDNESDAY
66727   **FS**   H    GBCM        WB        Andrew Scott CBE
66728   **FS**   P    GBCM        WB        Institution of Railway Operators
66729   **FS**   P    GBCM        WB
66730   **FS**   P    GBCM        WB

| 66731 | **FS** | P | GBCM | WB | |
| 66732 | **FS** | P | GBCM | WB | GBRf The First Decade 1999–2009 |
| | | | | | John Smith – MD |

**Class 66/8. Former DRS Class 66/4s originally overhauled for Advenza Freight.**
Details as Class 66/4 (66401–410):

| 66841 | (66406) | **CS** | P | COLO | FD |
| 66842 | (66407) | **CS** | P | COLO | FD |
| 66843 | (66408) | **CS** | P | COLO | FD |
| 66844 | (66409) | **AZ** | P | GBRT | WB |

**Class 66/9. Freightliner locos. Low emission "demonstrator" locos.** Details as
Class 66/0 except:

**Engine:** EMD 12N-710G3B-U2 two stroke of 2420 kW (3245 h.p.) at 904 r.p.m.
**Traction Motors:** General Motors D43TRC.
**Fuel Capacity:** 5905/5150 litres.

| 66951 | **FL** | H | DFHG | FD |
| 66952 | **FL** | H | DFHG | FD |

**Class 66/9. Freightliner-operated low emission locos.** Due to the 665xx number
range being full further orders of 66/5s are to be numbered from 66953 onwards.
Details as Class 66/5 (low emission):

| 66953 | **FL** | BN | DFHG | FD | |
| 66954 | **FL** | BN | DFIN | FD | |
| 66955 | **FL** | BN | DFIN | FD | |
| 66956 | **FL** | BN | DFIN | FD | |
| 66957 | **FL** | BN | DFHG | FD | Stephenson Locomotive Society |
| | | | | | 1909–2009 |

# CLASS 67  ALSTOM/GENERAL MOTORS EMD  Bo-Bo

**Built:** 1999–2000 by Alstom at Valencia, Spain, as sub-contractors for General
Motors (General Motors model JT42 HW-HS).
**Engine:** GM 12N-710G3B-EC two stroke of 2385 kW (3200 h.p.) at 904 r.p.m.
**Main Alternator:** General Motors AR9A/HEP7/CA6C.
**Traction Motors:** General Motors D43FM.
**Maximum Tractive Effort:** 141 kN (31770 lbf).
**Continuous Tractive Effort:** 90 kN (20200 lbf) at 46.5 m.p.h.
**Power At Rail:** 1860 kW.                    **Train Brakes:** Air.
**Brake Force:** 78 t.                         **Dimensions:** 19.74 x 2.72 m.
**Weight:** 90 t.                              **Wheel Diameter:** 965 mm.
**Design Speed:** 125 m.p.h.
**Maximum Speed:** 125 m.p.h. (but only currently authorised for 110 m.p.h.).
**Fuel Capacity:** 4927 litres.               **RA:** 8.
**Train Supply:** Electric, index 66.         **Multiple Working:** AAR System.
**Notes:** All equipped with Slow Speed Control and Swinghead Automatic
"Buckeye" Combination Couplers.

67004, 67007, 67009, 67011 and 67030 are fitted with cast iron brake blocks for working the Fort William Sleeper. **Maximum Speed:** 80 m.p.h.

67004 and 67027 carry their names on one side only.

**Non-standard livery:** 67029 All over silver with EWS logos (EWS "Special Train").

| | | | | | |
|---|---|---|---|---|---|
| 67001 | E | A | WNTR | TO | |
| 67002 | E | A | WAAN | CE | Special Delivery |
| 67003 | E | A | WNTR | CE | |
| 67004 r | E | A | WABN | CE | Post Haste |
| 67005 | RZ | A | WAAN | CE | Queen's Messenger |
| 67006 | RZ | A | WAAN | CE | Royal Sovereign |
| 67007 r | E | A | WABN | CE | |
| 67008 | E | A | WAAN | CE | |
| 67009 r | E | A | WABN | CE | |
| 67010 | WS | A | WAWN | CE | |
| 67011 r | E | A | WABN | CE | |
| 67012 | WS | A | WAWN | CE | A Shropshire Lad |
| 67013 | WS | A | WAWN | CE | Dyfrbont Pontcysyllte |
| 67014 | WS | A | WNTR | CE | Thomas Telford |
| 67015 | WS | A | WFMU | CE | David J. Lloyd |
| 67016 | E | A | WAFN | CE | |
| 67017 | E | A | WAFN | CE | Arrow |
| 67018 | DB | A | WAAN | CE | Keith Heller |
| 67019 | E | A | WAAN | CE | |
| 67020 | E | A | WAAN | CE | |
| 67021 | E | A | WNTR | CE | |
| 67022 | E | A | WAAN | CE | |
| 67023 | E | A | WNTR | CE | |
| 67024 | E | A | WAAN | CE | |
| 67025 | E | A | WAAN | CE | Western Star |
| 67026 | E | A | WAAN | CE | |
| 67027 | E | A | WAAN | CE | Rising Star |
| 67028 | E | A | WNTR | CE | |
| 67029 | O | A | WAAN | CE | Royal Diamond |
| 67030 r | E | A | WFMU | CE | |

# CLASS 70        GENERAL ELECTRIC        Co-Co

30 new General Electric "PowerHaul" locos are currently being delivered to
Freightliner. The first six locos arrived in the UK in late 2009, but the remaining
24 locos are due to arrive over a protracted period, with the next six due in
September 2010.

**Built:** 2009–2011 by General Electric, Erie, Pennsylvania, USA.
**Engine:** General Electric PowerHaul P616 of 2750 kW (3700 h.p.) at 904 r.p.m.
**Main Alternator:** General Electric GTA series.
**Traction Motors:** AC-GE 5GEB30.
**Maximum Tractive Effort:** 544 kN (122 000 lbf).
**Continuous Tractive Effort:** 427 kN (96 000 lbf) at ?? m.p.h.

| | |
|---|---|
| **Power At Rail:** | **Train Brakes:** Air. |
| **Brake Force:** 97.6 t. | **Dimensions:** 21.71 x 2.64 m. |
| **Weight:** 129 t. | **Wheel Diameter:** 1007 mm. |
| **Design Speed:** 75 m.p.h. | **Maximum Speed:** 75 m.p.h. |
| **Fuel Capacity:** 6000 litres. | **RA:** 7. |
| **Train Supply:** Not equipped. | **Multiple Working:** |

| | | | | | |
|---|---|---|---|---|---|
| 70001 | FH | LY | DFGI | LD | PowerHaul |
| 70002 | FH | LY | DFGH | LD | |
| 70003 | FH | LY | DFGH | LD | |
| 70004 | FH | LY | DFGH | LD | |
| 70005 | FH | LY | DFGH | LD | |
| 70006 | FH | LY | DFGH | LD | |
| 70007 | | | | | |
| 70008 | | | | | |
| 70009 | | | | | |
| 70010 | | | | | |
| 70011 | | | | | |
| 70012 | | | | | |
| 70013 | | | | | |
| 70014 | | | | | |
| 70015 | | | | | |
| 70016 | | | | | |
| 70017 | | | | | |
| 70018 | | | | | |
| 70019 | | | | | |
| 70020 | | | | | |
| 70021 | | | | | |
| 70022 | | | | | |
| 70023 | | | | | |
| 70024 | | | | | |
| 70025 | | | | | |
| 70026 | | | | | |
| 70027 | | | | | |
| 70028 | | | | | |
| 70029 | | | | | |
| 70030 | | | | | |

# 1.2. ELECTRO-DIESEL & ELECTRIC LOCOMOTIVES

## CLASS 73          BR/ENGLISH ELECTRIC          Bo-Bo

Electro-diesel locomotives which can operate either from a DC supply or using power from a diesel engine.

**Built:** 1965–1967 by English Electric Co. at Vulcan Foundry, Newton-le-Willows.
**Engine:** English Electric 4SRKT of 447 kW (600 h.p.) at 850 r.p.m.
**Main Generator:** English Electric 824/5D.
**Electric Supply System:** 750 V DC from third rail.
**Traction Motors:** English Electric 546/1B.
**Maximum Tractive Effort (Electric):** 179 kN (40000 lbf).
**Maximum Tractive Effort (Diesel):** 160 kN (36000 lbf).
**Continuous Rating (Electric):** 1060 kW (1420 h.p.) giving a tractive effort of 35 kN (7800 lbf) at 68 m.p.h.
**Continuous Tractive Effort (Diesel):** 60 kN (13600 lbf) at 11.5 m.p.h.
**Maximum Rail Power (Electric):** 2350 kW (3150 h.p.) at 42 m.p.h.
**Train Brakes:** Air, vacuum & electro-pneumatic († Air & electro-pneumatic).
**Brake Force:** 31 t.                    **Dimensions:** 16.36 x 2.64 m.
**Weight:** 77 t.                          **Wheel Diameter:** 1016 mm.
**Design Speed:** 90 m.p.h.                **Maximum Speed:** 90 m.p.h.
**Fuel Capacity:** 1409 litres.            **RA:** 6.
**Train Supply:** Electric, index 66 (on electric power only).
**Multiple Working:** SR 27-way System & Blue Star.

Formerly numbered E6001–E6020/E6022–E6026/E6028–E6049 (not in order).

**Note:** Locomotives numbered in the 732xx series are classed as 73/2 and were originally dedicated to Gatwick Express services.

**Non-standard livery:** 73107 Two-tone grey.

| | | | | | |
|---|---|---|---|---|---|
| 73107 | **O** | 20 | MBED | SE | SPITFIRE |
| 73109 | **SD** | 73 | MBED | SL | Battle of Britain 50th Anniversary |
| 73141 | **FS** | GB | GBED | SE | Charlotte |
| 73201 † | **B** | P | MBED | SE | Broadlands |
| 73202 † | **GV** | P | IVGA | SL | Dave Berry |
| 73203 † | **GX** | GB | GBZZ | SE | |
| 73204 † | **GB** | GB | GBED | SE | Janice |
| 73205 † | **GB** | GB | GBED | SE | Jeanette |
| 73206 † | **GB** | GB | GBED | SE | Lisa |
| 73207 † | **BL** | GB | GBWM | SE | |
| 73208 † | **B** | GB | GBED | SE | Kirsten |
| 73209 † | **GB** | GB | GBZZ | SE | Alison |
| 73212 † | **Y** | GB | GBED | SE | |
| 73213 † | **FS** | GB | GBED | SE | |
| 73235 † | **SD** | P | HYWD | WD | |

# CLASS 86     BR/ENGLISH ELECTRIC     Bo-Bo

**Built:** 1965–1966 by English Electric Co. at Vulcan Foundry, Newton-le-Willows or by BR at Doncaster Works.
**Electric Supply System:** 25 kV AC 50 Hz overhead.
**Train Brakes:** Air.                          **Brake Force:** 40 t.
**Dimensions:** 17.83 x 2.65 m.               **Weight:** 83–86.8 t.
**RA:** 6.                                      **Multiple Working:** TDM system.
**Train Supply:** Electric, index 66.

Formerly numbered E3101–E3200 (not in order).

**Class 86/1. Class 87-type bogies & motors.**

Details as above except:
**Traction Motors:** GEC 412AZ frame mounted.
**Maximum Tractive Effort:** 258 kN (58000 lbf).
**Continuous Rating:** 3730 kW (5000 h.p.) giving a tractive effort of 95 kN (21300 lbf) at 87 m.p.h.
**Maximum Rail Power:** 5860 kW (7860 h.p.) at 50.8 m.p.h.
**Wheel Diameter:** 1150 mm.                   **Weight:** 86.8 t.
**Design Speed:** 110 m.p.h.                   **Maximum Speed:** 110 m.p.h.

| 86101 | **B** | EL | ACAC | CP | Sir William A Stanier FRS |

**Class 86/2. Standard design rebuilt with resilient wheels and Flexicoil suspension.**

**Traction Motors:** AEI 282BZ axle hung.
**Maximum Tractive Effort:** 207 kN (46500 lbf).
**Continuous Rating:** 3010 kW (4040 h.p.) giving a tractive effort of 85 kN (19200 lbf) at 77.5 m.p.h.
**Maximum Rail Power:** 4550 kW (6100 h.p.) at 49.5 m.p.h.
**Wheel Diameter:** 1156 mm.                   **Weight:** 85–86.2 t.
**Design Speed:** 125 m.p.h.                   **Maximum Speed:** 100 m.p.h.

**Non-standard livery/numbering:** 86233 & 86259 BR "Electric blue" livery. 86233 Also carries number E3172.

| 86212 | **V**  | H  | SAXL | LM |                   |
| 86213 | **IC** | EL | ACXX | WB | Lancashire Witch  |
| 86215 | **AR** | H  | SAXL | LM | The Round Tabler  |
| 86217 | **AR** | H  | SAXL | LM |                   |
| 86218 | **AR** | H  | SAXL | LM |                   |
| 86223 | **AR** | H  | SAXL | LM |                   |
| 86226 | **V**  | H  | SAXL | LM |                   |
| 86228 | **IC** | H  | SAXL | LM | Vulcan Heritage   |
| 86229 | **V**  | H  | SAXL | LM |                   |
| 86230 | **AR** | H  | SAXL | LM |                   |
| 86231 | **V**  | H  | SAXL | LM |                   |
| 86232 | **AR** | H  | SAXL | LM |                   |
| 86233 | **0**  | EP | EPXX | LM |                   |
| 86234 | **AR** | H  | SAXL | LM |                   |
| 86235 | **AR** | H  | SAXL | LM |                   |

| 86242 | **AR** | H   | SAXL | LM |          |
|-------|--------|-----|------|----|----------|
| 86245 | **V**  | H   | SAXL | LM |          |
| 86246 | **AR** | H   | SAXL | LM |          |
| 86247 | **EL** | EP  | EPXX | LM |          |
| 86251 | **V**  | H   | SAXL | LM |          |
| 86259 | **0**  | LR  | MBEL | TM | Les Ross |

**Class 86/4.**

**Traction Motors:** AEI 282AZ axle hung.
**Maximum Tractive Effort:** 258 kN (58000 lbf).
**Continuous Rating:** 2680 kW (3600 h.p.) giving a tractive effort of 89 kN (20000 lbf) at 67 m.p.h.
**Maximum Rail Power:** 4400 kW (5900 h.p.) at 38 m.p.h.
**Wheel Diameter:** 1156 mm.     **Weight:** 83–83.9 t.
**Design Speed:** 100 m.p.h.     **Maximum Speed:** 100 m.p.h.

| 86401 | **N** | EL | ACXX | WN | Northampton Town |
|-------|-------|----|------|----|------------------|
| 86424 | **Y** | NR | QSTR | CP |                  |

**Class 86/5. Regeared locomotive operated by Freightliner.**

Details as Class 86/4 except:

**Continuous Rating:** 2680 kW (3600 h.p.) giving a tractive effort of 117 kN (26300 lbf) at 67 m.p.h.
**Maximum Speed:** 75 m.p.h.     **Train Supply:** Electric, isolated.

86501 (86608)  **FL**  FL  DFGC     FE

**Class 86/6. Freightliner-operated locomotives.**

Details as Class 86/4 except:

**Maximum Speed:** 75 m.p.h.     **Train Supply:** Electric, isolated.

| 86604 | **FL** | FL | DFNC | FE |
|-------|--------|----|------|----|
| 86605 | **FL** | FL | DFNC | FE |
| 86607 | **FL** | FL | DFNC | FE |
| 86609 | **FL** | FL | DFNC | FE |
| 86610 | **FL** | FL | DFNC | FE |
| 86612 | **FL** | P  | DFNC | FE |
| 86613 | **FL** | P  | DFNC | FE |
| 86614 | **FL** | P  | DFNC | FE |
| 86621 | **FL** | P  | DFNC | FE |
| 86622 | **FF** | P  | DFNC | FE |
| 86627 | **FL** | P  | DFNC | FE |
| 86628 | **FL** | P  | DFNC | FE |
| 86632 | **FL** | P  | DFNC | FE |
| 86633 | **FF** | P  | DHLT | CP |
| 86635 | **FL** | P  | DHLT | CP |
| 86637 | **FF** | P  | DFNC | FE |
| 86638 | **FL** | P  | DFNC | FE |
| 86639 | **FL** | P  | DFNC | FE |

**Class 86/7. Europhoenix-owned locomotives.** Refurbished Class 86/2s for the UK spot-hire market. Details as Class 86/2 unless stated.

**Maximum Speed:** 110 m.p.h.        **Weight:** 85 t.
**Train Supply:** Electric, index 74.

| 86701 | (86205) | **EL** | EP | ETLO | CP | Orion |
| 86702 | (86260) | **EL** | EP | ETLO | CP | Cassiopeia |

**Class 86/9. Network Rail-owned locomotives.** Rebuilt from Class 86/2s for use as Mobile Load Bank test locos to test Overhead Line Equipment, initially on the WCML. No. 1 end Traction Motors isolated. Can still move under own power.

**Maximum Speed:** 60 m.p.h.        **Train Supply:** Electric, isolated.

| 86901 | (86253) | **Y** | NR | QACL | CP | CHIEF ENGINEER |
| 86902 | (86210) | **Y** | NR | QACL | CP | RAIL VEHICLE ENGINEERING |

# CLASS 87            BREL/GEC            Bo-Bo

**Built:** 1973–1975 by BREL at Crewe Works.
**Electric Supply System:** 25 kV AC 50 Hz overhead.
**Traction Motors:** GEC G412AZ frame mounted.
**Maximum Tractive Effort:** 258 kN (58000 lbf).
**Continuous Rating:** 3730 kW (5000 h.p.) giving a tractive effort of 95 kN (21300 lbf) at 87 m.p.h.
**Maximum Rail Power:** 5860 kW (7860 h.p.) at 50.8 m.p.h.
**Train Brakes:** Air.                          **Brake Force:** 40 t.
**Dimensions:** 17.83 x 2.65 m.                 **Weight:** 83.3 t.
**Wheel Diameter:** 1150 mm.                    **Design Speed:** 110 m.p.h.
**Maximum Speed:** 110 m.p.h.                   **Train Supply:** Electric, index 95.
**RA:** 6.                                      **Multiple Working:** TDM system.

**Note:** Apart from 87002, this class have now finished work in the UK and all locos listed below except 87002 and 87027 (the latter being used for spares only) are due to be exported to Bulgaria during 2010. Locos already moved to Bulgaria are listed in section 1.6 of this book.

| 87002 | **B** | EL | ACAC | CP | Royal Sovereign |
| 87009 | **V** | BU | SBXL | LM | |
| 87011 | **V** | BU | SBXL | LM | |
| 87017 | **V** | BU | SBXL | LM | |
| 87018 | **V** | BU | SBXL | LM | |
| 87021 | **V** | BU | SBXL | LM | |
| 87023 | **V** | BU | SBXL | LM | |
| 87025 | **V** | BU | SBXL | LM | |
| 87027 | **V** | P  | SBXL | LM | |
| 87030 | **V** | BU | SBXL | LM | |
| 87031 | **V** | P  | SBXL | LM | |
| 87032 | **V** | BU | SBXL | LM | |

## CLASS 90 GEC Bo-Bo

**Built:** 1987–1990 by BREL at Crewe Works (as sub contractors for GEC).
**Electric Supply System:** 25 kV AC 50 Hz overhead.
**Traction Motors:** GEC G412CY frame mounted.
**Maximum Tractive Effort:** 258 kN (58000 lbf).
**Continuous Rating:** 3730 kW (5000 h.p.) giving a tractive effort of 95 kN (21300 lbf) at 87 m.p.h.
**Maximum Rail Power:** 5860 kW (7860 h.p.) at 68.3 m.p.h.
**Train Brakes:** Air.
**Brake Force:** 40 t.
**Weight:** 84.5 t.
**Design Speed:** 110 m.p.h.
**Train Supply:** Electric, index 95.
**Multiple Working:** TDM system.

**Dimensions:** 18.80 x 2.74 m.
**Wheel Diameter:** 1150 mm.
**Maximum Speed:** 110 m.p.h.
**RA:** 7.

**Non-standard livery:** 90036 As **FE** but with a yellow roof. EWS stickers.

| | | | | | |
|---|---|---|---|---|---|
| 90001 | b | 1 | P | IANA | NC |
| 90002 | b | 1 | P | IANA | NC |
| 90003 | b | NX | P | IANA | NC | Raedwald of East Anglia |
| 90004 | b | 1 | P | IANA | NC |
| 90005 | b | 1 | P | IANA | NC | Vice-Admiral Lord Nelson |
| 90006 | b | 1 | P | IANA | NC | Modern Railways Magazine/ Roger Ford |
| 90007 | b | 1 | P | IANA | NC | Sir John Betjeman |
| 90008 | b | NX | P | IANA | NC |
| 90009 | b | 1 | P | IANA | NC |
| 90010 | b | 1 | P | IANA | NC |
| 90011 | b | 1 | P | IANA | NC | Let's Go East of England |
| 90012 | b | 1 | P | IANA | NC | Royal Anglian Regiment |
| 90013 | b | 1 | P | IANA | NC |
| 90014 | b | 1 | P | IANA | NC | Norfolk and Norwich Festival |
| 90015 | b | NX | P | IANA | NC | Colchester Castle |
| 90016 | | FL | P | DFLC | FE |
| 90017 | b | E | DB | WNTS | CE |
| 90018 | b | E | DB | WEFE | CE |
| 90019 | b | FS | DB | WEFE | CE |
| 90020 | b | E | DB | WEFE | CE | Collingwood |
| 90021 | | FS | DB | WEFE | CE |
| 90022 | | EG | DB | WNTS | CE | Freightconnection |
| 90023 | | E | DB | WNTS | CE |
| 90024 | | FS | DB | WEFE | CE |
| 90025 | | F | DB | WNTS | CE |
| 90026 | | E | DB | WEFE | CE |
| 90027 | | F | DB | WNTS | CE | Allerton T&RS Depot |
| 90028 | | E | DB | WNTS | CE |
| 90029 | | E | DB | WEFE | CE | The Institution of Civil Engineers |
| 90030 | | E | DB | WNTS | CE | Crewe Locomotive Works |
| 90031 | | E | DB | WNTS | CE | The Railway Children Partnership Working For Street Children Worldwide |

| 90032 | E  | DB | WNTS | CE |                        |
|-------|----|----|------|----|------------------------|
| 90033 | FE | DB | WNTS | CE |                        |
| 90034 | E  | DB | WNTS | CE |                        |
| 90035 | E  | DB | WEFE | CE |                        |
| 90036 | O  | DB | WEFE | CE |                        |
| 90037 | E  | DB | WNTS | CE | Spirit of Dagenham     |
| 90038 | FE | DB | WNTS | CE |                        |
| 90039 | E  | DB | WFMU | CE |                        |
| 90040 | E  | DB | WNTS | CE | The Railway Mission    |
| 90041 | FL | P  | DFLC | FE |                        |
| 90042 | FF | P  | DFLC | FE |                        |
| 90043 | FF | P  | DFLC | FE | Freightliner Coatbridge|
| 90044 | FF | P  | DFLC | FE |                        |
| 90045 | FF | P  | DFLC | FE |                        |
| 90046 | FL | P  | DFLC | FE |                        |
| 90047 | FF | P  | DFLC | FE |                        |
| 90048 | FF | P  | DFLC | FE |                        |
| 90049 | FF | P  | DFLC | FE |                        |
| 90050 | FF | DB | WNTS | CE |                        |

---

## CLASS 91                          GEC                          Bo-Bo

**Built:** 1988–1991 by BREL at Crewe Works (as sub contractors for GEC).
**Electric Supply System:** 25 kV AC 50 Hz overhead.
**Traction Motors:** GEC G426AZ.
**Maximum Tractive Effort:** 190 kN (43 000 lbf).
**Continuous Rating:** 4540 kW (6090 h.p.) giving a tractive effort of 170 kN at 96 m.p.h.
**Maximum Rail Power:** 4700 kW (6300 h.p.) at ?? m.p.h.
**Train Brakes:** Air.

| | |
|---|---|
| **Brake Force:** 45 t. | **Dimensions:** 19.41 x 2.74 m. |
| **Weight:** 84 t. | **Wheel Diameter:** 1000 mm. |
| **Design Speed:** 140 m.p.h. | **Maximum Speed:** 125 m.p.h. |
| **Train Supply:** Electric, index 95. | **RA:** 7. |
| **Multiple Working:** TDM system. | |

**Note:** Locos originally numbered in the 910xx series, but renumbered upon completion of overhauls at Bombardier, Doncaster by the addition of 100 to their original number. The exception to this rule was 91023 which was renumbered 91132.

| 91101 | GN | H | IECA | BN |
|-------|----|---|------|----|
| 91102 | GN | H | IECA | BN |
| 91103 | GN | H | IECA | BN |
| 91104 | GN | H | IECA | BN |
| 91105 | GN | H | IECA | BN |
| 91106 | GN | H | IECA | BN |
| 91107 | GN | H | IECA | BN |
| 91108 | GN | H | IECA | BN |
| 91109 | GN | H | IECA | BN |
| 91110 | GN | H | IECA | BN |

| 91111 | NX | H | IECA | BN |
| 91112 | GN | H | IECA | BN |
| 91113 | GN | H | IECA | BN |
| 91114 | GN | H | IECA | BN |
| 91115 | GN | H | IECA | BN |
| 91116 | GN | H | IECA | BN |
| 91117 | GN | H | IECA | BN |
| 91118 | GN | H | IECA | BN |
| 91119 | GN | H | IECA | BN |
| 91120 | GN | H | IECA | BN |
| 91121 | GN | H | IECA | BN |
| 91122 | GN | H | IECA | BN |
| 91123 | GN | H | IECA | BN |
| 91124 | GN | H | IECA | BN |
| 91125 | GN | H | IECA | BN |
| 91126 | GN | H | IECA | BN |
| 91127 | GN | H | IECA | BN |
| 91128 | GN | H | IECA | BN |
| 91129 | GN | H | IECA | BN |
| 91130 | GN | H | IECA | BN |
| 91131 | GN | H | IECA | BN |
| 91132 | GN | H | IECA | BN |

LDS 10/10

## CLASS 92     BRUSH     Co-Co

**Built:** 1993–1996 by Brush Traction at Loughborough.
**Electric Supply System:** 25 kV AC 50 Hz overhead or 750 V DC third rail.
**Traction Motors:** Asea Brown Boveri design. Model 6FRA 7059B (Asynchronous 3-phase induction motors).
**Maximum Tractive Effort:** 400 kN (90 000 lbf).
**Continuous Rating:** 5040 kW (6760 h.p.) on AC, 4000 kW (5360 h.p.) on DC.
**Maximum Rail Power:**     **Train Brakes:** Air.
**Brake Force:** 63 t.     **Dimensions:** 21.34 x 2.67 m.
**Weight:** 126 t.     **Wheel Diameter:** 1070 mm.
**Design Speed:** 140 km/h (87 m.p.h.).     **Maximum Speed:** 145 km/h (90 m.p.h.).
**Train Supply:** Electric, index 108 (AC), 70 (DC).
**RA:** 7.

**Advertising livery:** 92017 Stobart Rail (two tone blue & white).

| 92001 | E | HX | WTAE | CE | Victor Hugo |
| 92002 | EG | HX | WNTS | CE | H.G. Wells |
| 92003 | EG | HX | WFMU | CE | Beethoven |
| 92004 | EG | HX | WNTS | CE | Jane Austen |
| 92005 | EG | HX | WFMU | CE | Mozart |
| 92006 | EP | SF | WNWX | CE | Louis Armand |
| 92007 | EG | HX | WTAE | CE | Schubert |
| 92008 | EG | HX | WNTS | CE | Jules Verne |
| 92009 | EG | HX | WTAE | CE | Elgar |
| 92010 | EP | ET | PTXX | CO | Molière |
| 92011 | EG | HX | WNTS | CE | Handel |
| 92012 | EG | HX | WTAE | CE | Thomas Hardy |

| | | | | | |
|---|---|---|---|---|---|
| 92013 | EG | HX | WFMU | CE | Puccini |
| 92014 | EP | SF | WNWX | CE | Emile Zola |
| 92015 | EG | HX | WNTS | CE | D.H. Lawrence |
| 92016 | EG | HX | WNTS | CE | Brahms |
| 92017 | AL | HX | WTAE | CE | Bart the Engine |
| 92018 | EP | SF | WNWX | CE | Stendhal |
| 92019 | EG | HX | WTAE | CE | Wagner |
| 92020 | EP | ET | PTXX | LB (S) | Milton |
| 92021 | EP | ET | PTXX | LB (S) | Purcell |
| 92022 | EG | HX | WTAE | CE | Charles Dickens |
| 92023 | EP | SF | WNWX | CE | Ravel |
| 92024 | EG | HX | WNTS | CE | J.S. Bach |
| 92025 | EG | HX | WNTS | CE | Oscar Wilde |
| 92026 | EG | HX | WTAE | CE | Britten |
| 92027 | EG | HX | WNTS | CE | George Eliot |
| 92028 | EP | ET | PTXX | CO | Saint Saëns |
| 92029 | EG | HX | WNTS | CE | Dante |
| 92030 | EG | HX | WNTR | CE | Ashford |
| 92031 | E | HX | WTAE | CE | The Institute of Logistics and Transport |
| 92032 | EP | ET | PTXX | CO | César Franck |
| 92033 | EP | SF | WNWX | CE | Berlioz |
| 92034 | EG | HX | WTAE | CE | Kipling |
| 92035 | EP | HX | WNTS | CE | Mendelssohn |
| 92036 | EG | HX | WTAE | CE | Bertolt Brecht |
| 92037 | EG | HX | WTAE | CE | Sullivan |
| 92038 | EP | ET | PTXX | CO | Voltaire |
| 92039 | EG | HX | WNTS | CE | Johann Strauss |
| 92040 | EP | ET | PTXX | LB (S) | Goethe |
| 92041 | EG | HX | WTAE | CE | Vaughan Williams |
| 92042 | EG | HX | WTAE | CE | Honegger |
| 92043 | EP | ET | PTXX | CO | Debussy |
| 92044 | EP | ET | PTXX | CO | Couperin |
| 92045 | EP | ET | PTXX | LB (S) | Chaucer |
| 92046 | EP | ET | PTXX | LB (S) | Sweelinck |

▲ Classed as in industrial service, a shabby 08320 (numbered 402D) is seen waiting its next duty at Rock Works, Bugle (alongside the Newquay branch) on 30/08/09. **Andy Barclay**

▼ There are a few regular (and short) main line workings for DBS Class 08/09 shunters, including in South Wales and in the Doncaster and Knottingley areas. On 22/02/09 BR Departmental grey-liveried 09201 passes Burton Salmon with a Milford–Knottingley trip consisting of MEA wagons. **Gary Schofield**

▲ Recently overhauled and repainted by Arlington Fleet Services, 20304 displays the revised DRS livery at Eastleigh Works on 18/09/09. **Carl Watson**

▼ Network Rail yellow-liveried 31285 is seen shortly after departure from Drumgelloch with a test train to Hyndland loop on 11/02/09. **Ian Lothian**

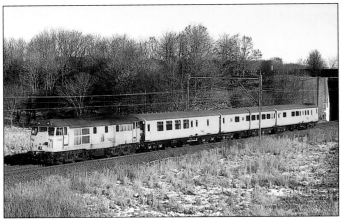

▲ West Coast Railway Company maroon-liveried 33207 leads 1Z37 06.45 Worksop–London Marylebone charter at Elford, between Burton and Tamworth, on 05/09/09 (37516 is on the rear). **Mick Tindall**

▼ One of the four Network Rail Class 37s refurbished and renumbered into the 973xx series for the ERTMS programme, 97301 passes Barton North Junction with 5Z97 08.21 Shrewsbury–Derby RTC on 12/06/09. **Phil Chilton**

WCRC's 37516 passes Atherstone with the Queen of Scots rake on 21/05/09, working as 5Z37 10.00 Carnforth–Eastleigh Works, en route for display at the open weekend. **Phil Chilton**

▲ A First Great Western HST led by 43027 passes Woolhampton, Midgham with the 05.46 Exeter St Davids–London Paddington on 27/06/08. **Neil Gibson**

▼ East Midlands Trains-liveried 43048 and 43055 (nearest camera) pass Dore & Totley with the 13.25 London St Pancras–Sheffield on 19/07/08. **Robert Pritchard**

▲ A CrossCountry HST powered by 43304 and 43378 passes Dobwalls, near Liskeard, with the 09.28 Penzance–Glasgow Central on 19/04/09. **Ron Westwater**

▼ West Coast Railway Company's 47760 and 47787 top-and-tail a 5Z55 12.20 Aberdeen–Bo'ness SRPS charter set e.c.s. on 17/08/09 at Powinwood, between Plean and Larbert. **Ian Lothian**

▲ DRS-liveried 47802 "Pride of Cumbria" passes Reedham with the 10.00 London Liverpool Street–Great Yarmouth on 04/07/09 (90013 is dead in train behind the Class 47). **Anthony Guppy**

▼ Hanson Traction's 56312 "ARTEMIS" works 6Z56 06.15 Washwood Heath–Boston Docks empty steel at Kelby Lane (Sleaford) on 19/08/09. **Aubrey Evans**

▲ Arriva "executive"-liveried 57315 leaves Hereford on 11/05/09 with the 16.17 Cardiff Central–Holyhead ATW loco-hauled service. **Dave Gommersall**

▼ Hanson Quarry Products-liveried 59104 "Village of Great Elm" passes Wyke Champflower (near Castle Cary) with 6W42 16.29 Westbury–Exeter engineers' train on 14/03/09. **Ron Westwater**

The first loco to receive DB Schenker red livery was 59206, which also also named "John F. Yeoman Rail Pioneer" at the same time. It is seen here on 26/05/09 at Hawkeridge Junction, Westbury with 6C83 11.40 Machen–Westbury stone train.

**Kevin Poole**

▲ In a promotional livery for the Teenage Cancer Trust charity, 60074 "Teenage Spirit" passes Newport on 02/06/09 with 6B13 05.10 Robeston–Westerleigh loaded oil tanks. **Darren Ford**

▼ Fastline-liveried 66302 heads north through Loughborough with 6D06 14.46 Daw Mill–Ratcliffe loaded coal on 01/04/09. **Paul Biggs**

By far the most common loco livery on the main line network is still EWS red & gold, although the company rebranded as DB Schenker at the start of 2009. On 02/06/09 66078 heads the weekly train of fuel tanks (TO 6V62 08.48 Fawley–Tavistock Junction) west over Dainton bank.

**Ron Westwater**

▲ Freightliner-liveried 66518 passes Tickhill on the former South Yorkshire Joint Line with a West Burton–Tyne Dock train of stone hoppers on 05/06/08.
**Peter Foster**

▼ Royal Train-liveried 67005 "Queen's Messenger" leads a private charter from Torquay to Cambridge at Dawlish on 20/04/09 (67029 is on the rear). **Colin Marsden**

▲ The first of the General Electric-built Class 70s for Freightliner were due to arrive at Newport docks in November 2009. Here 70006 is seen at GE's test track in Erie, Pennsylvania in September 2009. **Freightliner**

▼ Acting as a "super shunter" at March Whitemoor Yard on 20/07/09 is First GBRf's 73207 in BR Revised Blue livery, seen shunting the High Output Ballast Cleaning train. **John Pink**

▲ Freightliner-liveried 86607 and 86605 pass Weaver Junction with 4L92 14.03 Ditton–Felixstowe intermodal on 09/09/09. **Tom Mcatee**

▼ Two Electric Traction Limited Class 86/7s, 86701 "Orion" and 86702 "Cassiopeia" on display at Long Marston on 07/08/09. These locos are owned by Europhoenix. **Mark Beal**

▲ First Group-liveried 90019 passes Harringay working UK Railtours' 1Z20 07.07 London King's Cross–Durham charter on 24/06/09.   **Nigel Gibbs**

▼ National Express-liveried 91111 races past Bishopwood with the 15.00 London King's Cross–Glasgow Central on 25/07/09.   **Neil Gibson**

In two-tone grey livery with EWS logos, 92009 "Elgar" is seen near Polmadie with the morning Sleeper stock e.c.s. working from Glasgow Central to Polmadie depot on 09/06/09.

**Robert Pritchard**

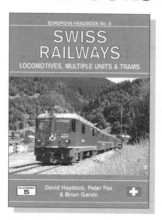

# 1.3. EUROTUNNEL LOCOMOTIVES

## DIESEL LOCOMOTIVES

### 0001–0005                   MaK                   Bo-Bo

**Built:** 1991–1992 by MaK at Kiel, Germany (Model DE1004).
**Engine:** MTU 12V 396 TC13 of 940 kW (1260 h.p.) at 1800 rpm.
**Main Alternator:** ABB.          **Traction Motors:** ABB.
**Maximum Tractive Effort:** 305 kN (68600 lbf).
**Continuous Tractive Effort:** 140 kN (31500 lbf) at 20 mph.
**Power At Rail:** 750 kW (1012 h.p.). **Dimensions:** 14.40 x ?? m.
**Brake Force:** 120 kN.            **Wheel Diameter:** 1000 mm.
**Weight:** 90 t.                  **Maximum Speed:** 100 km/h.
**Design Speed:** 120 km/h.        **Train Brakes:** Air.
**Fuel Capacity:** 3500 litres.    **Multiple Working:** Within class.
**Train Supply:** Not equipped.    **Signalling System:** TVM430 cab signalling.

**Note:** Registered on TOPS as 21901–905.

| | | | |
|---|---|---|---|
| 0001 | **GY** | ET | CO |
| 0002 | **GY** | ET | CO |
| 0003 | **GY** | ET | CO |
| 0004 | **GY** | ET | CO |
| 0005 | **GY** | ET | CO |

### 0031–0042         HUNSLET/SCHÖMA         0–4–0

**Built:** 1989–1990 by Hunslet Engine Company at Leeds as 900 mm gauge.
**Rebuilt:** 1993–1994 by Schöma in Germany to 1435 mm. gauge.
**Engine:** Deutz of 270 kW (200 h.p.) at ???? rpm.
**Transmission:** Mechanical.      **Maximum Tractive Effort:**
**Cont. Tractive Effort:**         **Power At Rail:**
**Brake Force:**                   **Dimensions:**
**Weight:**                        **Wheel Diameter:**
**Design Speed:** 50 km/h.         **Maximum Speed:** 50 km/h.
**Fuel Capacity:**                 **Train Brakes:** Air.
**Train Supply:** Not equipped.    **Multiple Working:** Not equipped.

| | | | | |
|---|---|---|---|---|
| 0031 | **GY** | ET | CO | FRANCES |
| 0032 | **GY** | ET | CO | ELISABETH |
| 0033 | **GY** | ET | CO | SILKE |
| 0034 | **GY** | ET | CO | AMANDA |
| 0035 | **GY** | ET | CO | MARY |
| 0036 | **GY** | ET | CO | LAWRENCE |
| 0037 | **GY** | ET | CO | LYDIE |
| 0038 | **GY** | ET | CO | JENNY |
| 0039 | **GY** | ET | CO | PACITA |
| 0040 | **GY** | ET | CO | JILL |

| 0041 | **GY** | ET | CO | KIM |
| 0042 | **GY** | ET | CO | NICOLE |

# ELECTRIC LOCOMOTIVES

## 9001–9838     BRUSH/ABB     Bo-Bo-Bo

**Built:** 1993–2002 by Brush Traction at Loughborough.
**Supply System:** 25 kV AC 50 Hz overhead.
**Traction Motors:** Asea Brown Boveri design. Asynchronous 3-phase motors. Model 6FHA 7059 (as built). Model 6FHA 7059C (7000 kW rated locos).
**Maximum Tractive Effort:** 400kN (90 000lbf).
**Continuous Rating:** Class 9/0 and 9/1: 5760 kW (7725 h.p.). Class 9/7 and 9/8: 7000 kW (9387 h.p.).

| | |
|---|---|
| **Maximum Rail Power:** | **Multiple Working:** TDM system. |
| **Brake Force:** 50 t. | **Dimensions:** 22.01 x 2.97 x 4.20 m. |
| **Weight:** 132 t. | **Wheel Diameter:** 1250 mm. |
| **Design Speed:** 100 m.p.h. | **Maximum Speed:** 87 m.p.h. |
| **Train Supply:** Electric. | **Train Brakes:** Air. |

**CLASS 9/0 Original build mixed traffic locos.**

| 9005 | **EB** | ET | CO | JESSYE NORMAN |
| 9006 | **EB** | ET | CO | REGINE CRESPIN |
| 9007 | **EB** | ET | CO | DAME JOAN SUTHERLAND |
| 9011 | **EB** | ET | CO | JOSÉ VAN DAM |
| 9013 | **EB** | ET | CO | MARIA CALLAS |
| 9015 | **EB** | ET | CO | LÖTSCHBERG 1913 |
| 9018 | **EB** | ET | CO | WILHELMENA FERNANDEZ |
| 9022 | **EB** | ET | CO | DAME JANET BAKER |
| 9023 | **EB** | ET | CO | DAME ELISABETH LEGGE-SCHWARZKOPF |
| 9024 | **EB** | ET | CO | GOTTHARD 1882 |
| 9026 | **EB** | ET | CO | FURKATUNNEL 1982 |
| 9027 | **EB** | ET | CO | BARBARA HENDRICKS |
| 9029 | **EB** | ET | CO | THOMAS ALLEN |
| 9031 | **EB** | ET | CO | |
| 9033 | **EB** | ET | CO | MONTSERRAT CABALLE |
| 9036 | **EB** | ET | CO | ALAIN FONDARY |
| 9037 | **EB** | ET | CO | GABRIEL BACQUIER |
| 9040 | **EB** | ET | CO | |

**CLASS 9/1. Freight Shuttle dedicated locos.**

| 9101 | **EB** | ET | CO |
| 9102 | **EB** | ET | CO |
| 9103 | **EB** | ET | CO |
| 9104 | **EB** | ET | CO |
| 9105 | **EB** | ET | CO |
| 9106 | **EB** | ET | CO |
| 9107 | **EB** | ET | CO |
| 9108 | **EB** | ET | CO |

| 9109 | **EB** | ET | CO |
|------|--------|----|----|
| 9110 | **EB** | ET | CO |
| 9111 | **EB** | ET | CO |
| 9112 | **EB** | ET | CO |
| 9113 | **EB** | ET | CO |

**CLASS 9/7. Later build (2001–2002) increased power freight shuttle locos.**

| 9701 | **EB** | ET | CO |
|------|--------|----|----|
| 9702 | **EB** | ET | CO |
| 9703 | **EB** | ET | CO |
| 9704 | **EB** | ET | CO |
| 9705 | **EB** | ET | CO |
| 9706 | **EB** | ET | CO |
| 9707 | **EB** | ET | CO |

**CLASS 9/8 Locos rebuilt from Class 9/0 by adding 800 to the loco number. Uprated to 7000 kW. Generally used on freight duties.**

| 9801 | **EB** | ET | CO |     | LESLEY GARRETT |
|------|--------|----|----|-----|----------------|
| 9802 | **EB** | ET | CO |     | STUART BURROWS |
| 9803 | **EB** | ET | CO |     | BENJAMIN LUXON |
| 9804 | **EB** | ET | CO |     | VICTORIA DE LOS ANGELES |
| 9808 | **EB** | ET | CO |     | ELISABETH SODERSTROM |
| 9809 | **EB** | ET | CO |     | FRANÇOIS POLLET |
| 9810 | **EB** | ET | CO |     | JEAN-PHILIPPE COURTIS |
| 9812 | **EB** | ET | CO |     | LUCIANO PAVAROTTI |
| 9814 | **EB** | ET | CO | (S) | LUCIA POPP |
| 9816 | **EB** | ET | CO |     | WILLARD WHITE |
| 9817 | **EB** | ET | CO | (S) | JOSÉ CARRERAS |
| 9819 | **EB** | ET | CO |     | MARIA EWING |
| 9820 | **EB** | ET | CO |     | NICOLAI GHIAUROV |
| 9821 | **EB** | ET | CO |     | TERESA BERGANZA |
| 9825 | **EB** | ET | CO |     | |
| 9828 | **EB** | ET | CO |     | DAME KIRI TE KANAWA |
| 9832 | **EB** | ET | CO |     | RENATA TEBALDI |
| 9834 | **EB** | ET | CO |     | MIRELLA FRENI |
| 9835 | **EB** | ET | CO |     | NICOLAI GEDDA |
| 9838 | **EB** | ET | CO |     | HILDEGARD BEHRENS |

# 1.4. FORMER BR MAIN LINE LOCOS IN INDUSTRIAL SERVICE

Former British Rail main line locomotives considered to be in "industrial use" are listed here. These locomotives do not currently have Network Rail engineering acceptance for operation on the national railway network.

*Number    Other no./name    Location*

## Class 11

| | | |
|---|---|---|
| 12082 | 01553 | Deanside Transit, Hillington, Glasgow |
| 12088 | | Johnson's (Chopwell), Widdrington Disposal Point |

## Class 03

| | | |
|---|---|---|
| 03112 | D2112 | Port of Boston, Boston Docks |
| 03179 | CLIVE | First Capital Connect, Hornsey Depot, London |
| 03196 | JOYCE/GLYNIS | West Coast Railway Company, Carnforth |
| D2381 | | West Coast Railway Company, Carnforth |

## Class 07

| | | |
|---|---|---|
| 07001 | | Barrow Hill Roundhouse, Chesterfield |
| D2991 | 07007 | Knights Rail Services, Eastleigh Works |

## Class 08

| | | |
|---|---|---|
| 08202 | | The Potter Group, Knowsley, Merseyside |
| 08320 | 400D | Imerys Clay Company, Rocks Works, Bugle |
| 08331 | | Midland Railway Butterley-Derbyshire |
| 08375 | | Corus, Trostre Works, Llanelli, Carmarthenshire |
| 08398 | 402D | Imerys Clay Company, Rocks Works, Bugle |
| 08411 | | Colne Valley Railway |
| 08423 | H011  14 | PD Ports, Teesport, Grangetown, Middlesbrough |
| 08441 | | Colne Valley Railway |
| 08445 | | Corus, Shotton Works, Flintshire |
| 08447 | | Deanside Transit, Hillington, Glasgow |
| 08460 | | Felixstowe Dock & Railway Company, Felixstowe |
| 08484 | CAPTAIN NATHANIEL DARELL | Felixstowe Dock & Railway Company, Felixstowe |
| 08492 | | Barrow Hill Roundhouse, Chesterfield |
| 08503 | | Rye Farm, Wishaw (Sutton Coldfield) |
| 08511 | | Felixstowe Dock & Railway Company, Felixstowe |
| 08517 | | St. Modwen Properties, Long Marston |
| 08523 | | Celtic Energy, Onllwyn Washery, West Glamorgan |
| 08568 | St. Rollox | Railcare, Springburn Works, Glasgow |
| 08573 | | Bombardier Transportation, Ilford Works, London |
| 08588 | 17 | PD Ports, Teesport, Grangetown, Middlesbrough |
| 08598 | H016 | The Potter Group, Knowsley, Merseyside |
| 08600 | | AV Dawson, Middlesbrough |
| 08602 | 004 | Bombardier Transportation, Derby Works |
| 08613 | H064 | Castle Cement, Ketton Cement Works, near Stamford |
| 08622 | H028 7 | PD Ports, Teesport, Grangetown, Middlesbrough |

| | | |
|---|---|---|
| 08629 | | Railcare, Wolverton Works |
| 08643 | | Hanson Aggregates, Whatley Quarry, near Frome |
| 08648 | OLD GEOFF | Wabtec Rail, Doncaster |
| 08649 | G.H. Stratton | Railcare, Wolverton Works |
| 08650 | ISLE OF GRAIN | Aggregate Industries UK, Isle of Grain |
| 08652 | | Hanson Aggregates, Whatley Quarry, near Frome |
| 08665 | | Barrow Hill Roundhouse, Chesterfield |
| 08668 | | St. Modwen Properties, Long Marston |
| 08670 | | Colne Valley Railway |
| 08678 | ARTILA | West Coast Railway Company, Carnforth |
| 08682 | Lionheart | Bombardier Transportation, Derby Works |
| 08683 | | Gloucestershire-Warwickshire Railway |
| 08699 | | Corus, Shotton Works, Flintshire |
| 08704 | D3871 | Port of Boston, Boston Docks |
| 08730 | The Caley | LH Group Services, Barton-under-Needwood |
| 08743 | Bryan Turner | SembCorp Utilities Teeside, Wilton, Middlesbrough |
| 08754 | | Wabtec Rail, Doncaster |
| 08756 | | Corus, Shotton Works, Flintshire |
| 08762 | | Wabtec Rail, Doncaster |
| 08764 | 003 FLORENCE | Transfesa, Tilbury Riverside Terminal, Tilbury |
| 08774 | ARTHUR VERNON DAWSON | AV Dawson, Middlesbrough |
| 08787 | 08296 | Hanson Aggregates, Machen Quarry, near Newport |
| 08807 | | AV Dawson, Middlesbrough |
| 08809 | | Corus, Shotton Works, Flintshire |
| 08813 | | St. Modwen Properties, Long Marston |
| 08818 | MOLLY | Faber Prest Ports, Flixborough Wharf, Scunthorpe |
| 08823 | D3991 | LH Group Services, Barton-under-Needwood |
| 08827 | | St. Modwen Properties, Long Marston |
| 08846 | 003 | Bombardier Transportation, Derby Works |
| 08869 | | St. Modwen Properties, Long Marston |
| 08870 | H024 | Castle Cement, Ketton Cement Works, near Stamford |
| 08871 | | Wabtec Rail, Doncaster |
| 08873 | | Round Oak Distribution Centre, Wednesbury, West Midlands |
| 08881 | | Gloucestershire-Warwickshire Railway |
| 08885 | H042 | PD Ports, Teesport, Grangetown, Middlesbrough |
| 08892 | | Lafarge, Blue Circle Cement Works, Hope, Derbyshire |
| 08903 | JOHN W. ANTILL | SembCorp Utilities Teeside, Wilton, Middlesbrough |
| 08912 | | AV Dawson, Middlesbrough |
| 08913 | | Daventry International Railfreight Terminal |
| 08915 | | Stephenson Railway Museum, West Chirton |
| 08928 | | St. Modwen Properties, Long Marston |
| 08933 | | Aggregate Industries UK, Merehead Stone Terminal |
| 08936 | | Corus, Shotton Works, Flintshire |
| 08937 | BLUEBELL MEL | Aggregate Industries UK, Meldon Quarry, Okehampton |
| 08943 | PET II | Bombardier Transportation, Crewe Works |
| 08947 | | Aggregate Industries UK, Merehead Stone Terminal |

**Class 14**

| D9504 | | Nene Valley Railway |
| D9529 | 14029 | Aggregate Industries UK, Bardon Hill Quarry, Coalville |

**Class 20**

| 20056 | 81 | Corus, Appleby-Frodingham Works, Scunthorpe |
| 20066 | 82 | Corus, Appleby-Frodingham Works, Scunthorpe |
| 20168 | SIR GEORGE EARLE | Lafarge, Blue Circle Cement Works, Hope, Derbyshire |

**Class 56**

| 56009 | 56201 | Brush Traction, Loughborough Works |

**Class 73**

| 73119 | Borough of Eastleigh | Knights Rail Services, Eastleigh Works |
| 73133 | | Amey Colas, Fairwater Yard, Taunton |

**NS Class 600**

This class is of a similar design to the BR Class 08 and this loco, now in industrial use in the UK, is included here for clarity (several other in this class are classed as preserved).

| 625 | 690 | H043 | 16 | PD Ports, Teesport, Grangetown, Middlesbrough |

# 1.5. LOCOMOTIVES AWAITING DISPOSAL

Locomotives that are still extant but at scrapyards or considered to be awaiting disposal are listed here. It should be noted that some of the locos listed here may see further use on the main line if they are resold by scrap merchants.

*Number   Livery    Location*

**Class 08**

| 08350 | G | Ron Hull Junior, Rotherham |
| 08402 | E | TJ Thomson, Stockton-on-Tees |

**Class 37**

| 37203 | ML | Ron Hull Junior, Rotherham |
| 37415 | E | CF Booth, Rotherham |
| 37428 | GS | CF Booth, Rotherham |
| 37684 | E | CF Booth, Rotherham |
| 37698 | LH | CF Booth, Rotherham |
| 37890 | F | Ron Hull Junior, Rotherham |
| 37893 | E | Allely's, Studley (Warwickshire) |
| 37896 | F | Ron Hull Junior, Rotherham |

**Class 47**

| 47550 | IM | Rye Farm, Wishaw (Sutton Coldfield) |

**Class 56**

| 56033 | F | Doncaster Carr Yard |
| 56048 | CE | Doncaster Carr Yard |
| 56056 | F | Doncaster Carr Yard |
| 56068 | E | Doncaster Carr Yard |
| 56079 | F | Doncaster Carr Yard |
| 56116 | LH | Doncaster Carr Yard |
| 56134 | F | Doncaster Carr Yard |

# 1.6. LOCOMOTIVES EXPORTED FOR USE ABROAD

This section details former BR (plus privatisation era) diesel and electric locomotives that have been exported from the UK for use in industrial locations or by a main line operator abroad. Not included are locos that are "preserved" abroad, which are included in our "Preserved Locomotives" publication. Generally locos are included here if they are expected to remain abroad for more than one year. The DB Schenker Class 66s in use with DBS subsidiary Euro Cargo Rail in France are now also listed here as these only now return to Toton for major maintenance.

*Number*  *Other no./name*  *Location*

## Class 04

| | | |
|---|---|---|
| D2289 | | Lonato SpA, Lonato Steelworks, Lonato, Brescia, Italy |

## Class 08

| | | |
|---|---|---|
| 08738 | | Euro Cargo Rail, Vallourec pipe works, Déville-les-Rouen, France |
| 08939 | | Euro Cargo Rail, Vallourec pipe works, Déville-les-Rouen, France |

## Class 37

| | | |
|---|---|---|
| 37702 | L30 | Continental Rail, Spain (withdrawn) |
| 37703 | L25 | Continental Rail, Spain |
| 37714 | L26 | Continental Rail, Spain |
| 37716 | L23 | Continental Rail, Spain |
| 37718 | L22 | Continental Rail, Spain |
| 37799 | L27 | Continental Rail, Spain (withdrawn) |
| 37800 | L33 | Continental Rail, Spain |
| 37801 | L29 | Continental Rail, Spain (withdrawn) |
| 37883 | L28 | Continental Rail, Spain (stored) |
| 37884 | L34 | Continental Rail, Spain |
| 37888 | L31 | Continental Rail, Spain (withdrawn) |

## Class 58

| | | |
|---|---|---|
| 58001 | | ETF, Villersexel, France |
| 58004 | | TSO, Villersexel, France |
| 58005 | | ETF, Villersexel, France |
| 58006 | | ETF, Villersexel, France |
| 58007 | | TSO, Villersexel, France |
| 58009 | | TSO, Villersexel, France |
| 58010 | | TSO, Villersexel, France |
| 58011 | | TSO, Villersexel, France |
| 58013 | | ETF, Villersexel, France |
| 58015 | L54 | Continental Rail, Spain |
| 58018 | | TSO, Villersexel, France |
| 58020 | L43 | Continental Rail, Spain |
| 58021 | | ETF, Villersexel, France |
| 58024 | L42 | Continental Rail, Spain |

| 58025 | L41 | Continental Rail, Spain |
| 58026 | | TSO, Villersexel, France |
| 58027 | L52 | Continental Rail, Spain |
| 58029 | L44 | Continental Rail, Spain |
| 58030 | L46 | Continental Rail, Spain |
| 58031 | L45 | Continental Rail, Spain |
| 58032 | | ETF, Villersexel, France |
| 58033 | | TSO, Villersexel, France |
| 58034 | | TSO, Villersexel, France |
| 58035 | | TSO, Villersexel, France |
| 58036 | | ETF, Villersexel, France |
| 58038 | | ETF, Villersexel, France |
| 58039 | | ETF, Villersexel, France |
| 58040 | | TSO, Villersexel, France |
| 58041 | L36 | Continental Rail, Spain |
| 58042 | | ETF, Villersexel, France |
| 58043 | L37 | Continental Rail, Spain |
| 58044 | | ETF, Villersexel, France |
| 58046 | | TSO, Villersexel, France |
| 58047 | L51 | Continental Rail, Spain |
| 58049 | | ETF, Villersexel, France |
| 58050 | L53 | Continental Rail, Spain |

## Class 59

| 59003 | YEOMAN HIGHLANDER | |
| | 259 003-2 | Heavy Haul Power International, Germany |

## Class 66

| 66010 | Euro Cargo Rail, France |
| 66022 | Euro Cargo Rail, France |
| 66026 | Euro Cargo Rail, France |
| 66028 | Euro Cargo Rail, France |
| 66029 | Euro Cargo Rail, France |
| 66032 | Euro Cargo Rail, France |
| 66033 | Euro Cargo Rail, France |
| 66036 | Euro Cargo Rail, France |
| 66038 | Euro Cargo Rail, France |
| 66042 | Euro Cargo Rail, France |
| 66045 | Euro Cargo Rail, France |
| 66049 | Euro Cargo Rail, France |
| 66052 | Euro Cargo Rail, France |
| 66062 | Euro Cargo Rail, France |
| 66064 | Euro Cargo Rail, France |
| 66071 | Euro Cargo Rail, France |
| 66072 | Euro Cargo Rail, France |
| 66073 | Euro Cargo Rail, France |
| 66123 | Euro Cargo Rail, France |
| 66179 | Euro Cargo Rail, France |
| 66190 | Euro Cargo Rail, France |
| 66191 | Euro Cargo Rail, France |
| 66195 | Euro Cargo Rail, France |

| | | |
|---|---|---|
| 66202 | | Euro Cargo Rail, France |
| 66203 | | Euro Cargo Rail, France |
| 66205 | | Euro Cargo Rail, France |
| 66208 | | Euro Cargo Rail, France |
| 66209 | | Euro Cargo Rail, France |
| 66210 | | Euro Cargo Rail, France |
| 66211 | | Euro Cargo Rail, France |
| 66212 | | Euro Cargo Rail, France |
| 66214 | | Euro Cargo Rail, France |
| 66215 | | Euro Cargo Rail, France |
| 66216 | | Euro Cargo Rail, France |
| 66217 | | Euro Cargo Rail, France |
| 66218 | | Euro Cargo Rail, France |
| 66219 | | Euro Cargo Rail, France |
| 66220 | | Euro Cargo Rail, France |
| 66222 | | Euro Cargo Rail, France |
| 66223 | | Euro Cargo Rail, France |
| 66224 | | Euro Cargo Rail, France |
| 66225 | | Euro Cargo Rail, France |
| 66226 | | Euro Cargo Rail, France |
| 66228 | | Euro Cargo Rail, France |
| 66229 | | Euro Cargo Rail, France |
| 66231 | | Euro Cargo Rail, France |
| 66233 | | Euro Cargo Rail, France |
| 66234 | | Euro Cargo Rail, France |
| 66235 | | Euro Cargo Rail, France |
| 66236 | | Euro Cargo Rail, France |
| 66239 | | Euro Cargo Rail, France |
| 66240 | | Euro Cargo Rail, France |
| 66241 | | Euro Cargo Rail, France |
| 66242 | | Euro Cargo Rail, France |
| 66243 | | Euro Cargo Rail, France |
| 66244 | | Euro Cargo Rail, France |
| 66245 | | Euro Cargo Rail, France |
| 66246 | | Euro Cargo Rail, France |
| 66247 | | Euro Cargo Rail, France |
| 66249 | | Euro Cargo Rail, France |
| 66582 | 66009 | Freightliner, Poland |
| 66583 | 66010 | Freightliner, Poland |
| 66584 | 66011 | Freightliner, Poland |
| 66586 | 66008 | Freightliner, Poland |
| 66625 | 66101 | Freightliner, Poland |

**Class 86**

| | | |
|---|---|---|
| 86248 | 0450 001-7 | FLOYD, Hungary |
| 86250 | 0450 002-5 | FLOYD, Hungary |

**Class 87**

| | | |
|---|---|---|
| 87003 | 87003-0 | BZK, Bulgaria |
| 87004 | 87004-8 Britannia | BZK, Bulgaria |
| 87006 | 87006-3 | BZK, Bulgaria |

| | | |
|---|---|---|
| 87007 | 87007-1 | BZK, Bulgaria |
| 87008 | 87008-9 | BZK, Bulgaria |
| 87010 | 87010-5 | BZK, Bulgaria |
| 87012 | 87012-1 | BZK, Bulgaria |
| 87013 | 87013-9 | BZK, Bulgaria |
| 87014 | 87014-7 | BZK, Bulgaria |
| 87019 | 87019-6 | BZK, Bulgaria |
| 87020 | 87020-4 | BZK, Bulgaria |
| 87022 | 87022-0 | BZK, Bulgaria |
| 87026 | 87026-1 | BZK, Bulgaria |
| 87028 | 87028-7 | BZK, Bulgaria |
| 87029 | 87029-5 | BZK, Bulgaria |
| 87033 | 87033-7 | BZK, Bulgaria |
| 87034 | 87034-5 | BZK, Bulgaria |

# 2. LOCO-HAULED COACHING STOCK

# INTRODUCTION

## NUMBERING SYSTEMS

Seven different numbering systems were in use on British Rail. These were the British Rail series, the four pre-nationalisation companies' series', the Pullman Car Company's series and the UIC (International Union of Railways) series. BR number series coaches and former Pullman Car Company series are listed separately. There is also a separate listing of "Saloon" type vehicles which are registered to run on the national railway system. Please note the Mark 2 Pullman vehicles were ordered after the Pullman Car Company had been nationalised and are therefore numbered in the British Rail series.

Also listed separately are the British Rail and Pullman Car Company number series coaches used on North Yorkshire Moors Railway services on the national railway system. This is due to their very restricted sphere of operation.

## LAYOUT OF INFORMATION

Coaches are listed in numerical order of painted number in batches according to type.

Each coach entry is laid out as in the following example (previous number(s) column may be omitted where not applicable):

| No. | Prev. No. | Notes | Livery | Owner | Operator | Depot/Location |
|-----|-----------|-------|--------|-------|----------|----------------|
| 42406 | (12112) | † | **GC** | ST | *GC* | HT |

**Notes:**

The owner is the responsible custodian of the coach and this may not always be the owner by law.

The operator is the organisation which facilitates the use of the coach and may not be the actual train operating company which runs the train.

The depot is the facility primarily responsible for the coaches maintenance. Light maintenance and heavy overhauls in particular may be carried out elsewhere.

The location is where coaches not in use are currently being kept/stored.

# DETAILED INFORMATION & CODES

Under each type heading, the following details are shown:

- "Mark" of coach (see below).
- Descriptive text.
- Number of first class seats, standard class seats, lavatory compartments and wheelchair spaces shown as F/S nT nW respectively.
- Bogie type (see below).
- Additional features.
- ETH Index.

# TOPS TYPE CODES

TOPS type codes are allocated to all coaching stock. For vehicles numbered in the passenger stock number series the code consists of:

(1) Two letters denoting the layout of the vehicle as follows:

AA   Gangwayed Corridor
AB   Gangwayed Corridor Brake
AC   Gangwayed Open (2+2 seating)
AD   Gangwayed Open (2+1 seating)
AE   Gangwayed Open Brake
AF   Gangwayed Driving Open Brake
AG   Micro-Buffet
AH   Brake Micro-Buffet
AI   As "AC" but with drop-head buckeye and gangway at one end only
AJ   Kitchen or Buffet Car with seating
AK   Kitchen Car
AL   As "AC" but with disabled person's toilet (Mark 4 only)
AN   Open Second with Miniature Buffet
AP   Pullman Kitchen with Servery
AQ   Pullman Parlour First
AR   Pullman Brake First
AS   Sleeping Car
AT   Royal Train Coach
AU   Sleeping Car with Pantry
AX   Generator Van
AZ   Special Saloon
NW   Desiro Barrier Vehicle
NZ   Driving Brake Van ("Driving Van Trailer")

(2) A digit denoting the class of passenger accommodation:

1   First
2   Standard (formerly second)
3   Composite (first & standard)
4   Unclassified
5   None

(3) A suffix relating to the build of coach.

| | |
|---|---|
| 1 | Mark 1 |
| Z | Mark 2 |
| A | Mark 2A |
| B | Mark 2B |
| C | Mark 2C |
| D | Mark 2D |
| E | Mark 2E |
| F | Mark 2F |
| G | Mark 3 or 3A |
| H | Mark 3B |
| J | Mark 4 |

# OPERATING CODES

Operating codes used by train company operating staff (and others) to denote vehicle types in general. These are shown in parentheses adjacent to TOPS type codes. Letters used are:

| | |
|---|---|
| B Brake | K Side corridor with lavatory |
| C Composite | O Open |
| F First Class | S Standard Class (formerly second) |

Various other letters are in use and the meaning of these can be ascertained by referring to the titles at the head of each type.

Readers should note the distinction between an SO (Open Standard) and a TSO (Tourist Open Standard) The former has 2+1 seating layout, whilst the latter has 2+2.

# BOGIE TYPES

**BR Mark 1 (BR1).** Double bolster leaf spring bogie. Generally 90 m.p.h., but Mark 1 bogies may be permitted to run at 100 m.p.h. with special maintenance. Weight: 6.1 t.

**BR Mark 2 (BR2).** Single bolster leaf-spring bogie used on certain types of non-passenger stock and suburban stock (all now withdrawn). Weight: 5.3 t.

**COMMONWEALTH (C).** Heavy, cast steel coil spring bogie. 100 m.p.h. Weight: 6.75 t.

**B4.** Coil spring fabricated bogie. Generally 100 m.p.h., but B4 bogies may be permitted to run at 110 m.p.h. with special maintenance. Weight: 5.2 t.

**B5.** Heavy duty version of B4. 100 m.p.h. Weight: 5.3 t.

**B5 (SR).** A bogie originally used on Southern Region EMUs, similar in design to B5. Now also used on locomotive hauled coaches. 100 m.p.h.

**BT10.** A fabricated bogie designed for 125 m.p.h. Air suspension.

**T4.** A 125 m.p.h. bogie designed by BREL (now Bombardier Transportation).

**BT41.** Fitted to Mark 4 vehicles, designed by SIG in Switzerland. At present limited to 125 m.p.h., but designed for 140 m.p.h.

# BRAKES

Air braking is now standard on British main line trains. Vehicles with other equipment are denoted:

v   Vacuum braked.
x   Dual braked (air and vacuum).

# HEATING & VENTILATION

Electric heating and ventilation is now standard on British main-line trains. Certain coaches for use on charter services may also have steam heating facilities, or be steam heated only.

# PUBLIC ADDRESS

It is assumed all coaches are now fitted with public address equipment, although certain stored vehicles may not have this feature. In addition, it is assumed all vehicles with a conductor's compartment have public address transmission facilities, as have catering vehicles.

# COOKING EQUIPMENT

It is assumed that Mark 1 catering vehicles have gas powered cooking equipment, whilst Mark 2, 3 and 4 catering vehicles have electric powered cooking equipment unless stated otherwise.

# ADDITIONAL FEATURE CODES

d    Secondary door locking.
dg   Driver–Guard communication equipment.
f    Facelifted or fluorescent lighting.
h    "High density" seating
k    Composition brake blocks (instead of cast iron).
n    Day/night lighting.
pg   Public address transmission and driver-guard communication.
pt   Public address transmission facility.
q    Catering staff to shore telephone.
W    Wheelchair space.
★    Blue star multiple working cables fitted.

# NOTES ON ETH INDICES

The sum of ETH indices in a train must not be more than the ETH index of the locomotive. The normal voltage on British trains is 1000 V. Suffix "X" denotes 600 amp wiring instead of 400 amp. Trains whose ETH index is higher than 66 must be formed completely of 600 amp wired stock. Class 33 and 73 locomotives cannot provide a suitable electric train supply for Mark 2D, Mark 2E, Mark 2F, Mark 3, Mark 3A, Mark 3B or Mark 4 coaches. Class 55 locomotives provide an e.t.s. directly from one of their traction generators into the train line. Consequently voltage fluctuations can result in motor-alternator flashover. Thus these locomotives are not suitable for use with Mark 2D, Mark 2E, Mark 2F, Mark 3, Mark 3A, Mark 3B or Mark 4 coaches unless modified motor-alternators are fitted. Such motor alternators were fitted to Mark 2D and 2F coaches used on the East Coast main line, but few remain fitted.

# BUILD DETAILS

### Lot Numbers
Vehicles ordered under the auspices of BR were allocated a lot (batch) number when ordered and these are quoted in class headings and sub-headings.

### Builders
These are shown for each lot. Abbreviations used are shown in Section 6.7.

Information on sub-contracting works which built parts of vehicles e.g. the underframes etc. is not shown.

In addition to the above, certain vintage Pullman cars were built or rebuilt at the following works:

Metropolitan Carriage & Wagon Company, Birmingham
Midland Carriage & Wagon Company, Birmingham
Pullman Car Company, Preston Park, Brighton
Conversions have also been carried out at the Railway Technical Centre, Derby, LNWR, Crewe and Blakes Fabrications, Edinburgh.

# VEHICLE NUMBERS

Where a coach has been renumbered, the former number is shown in parentheses. If a coach has been renumbered more than once, the original number is shown first in parentheses, followed by the most recent previous number.

# THE DEVELOPMENT OF BR STANDARD COACHES

### Mark 1

The standard BR coach built from 1951 to 1963 was the Mark 1. This type features a separate underframe and body. The underframe is normally 64 ft. 6 in. long, but certain vehicles were built on shorter (57 ft.) frames. Tungsten lighting was standard and until 1961, BR Mark 1 bogies were generally provided. In 1959 Lot No. 30525 (TSO) appeared with fluorescent lighting and melamine interior panels, and from 1961 onwards Commonwealth bogies were fitted in an attempt to improve the quality of ride which became very poor when the tyre profiles on the wheels of the BR1 bogies became worn. Later batches of TSO and BSO retained the features of Lot No. 30525, but compartment vehicles – whilst utilising melamine panelling in standard class – still retained tungsten lighting. Wooden interior finish was retained in first class vehicles where the only change was to fluorescent lighting in open vehicles (except Lot No. 30648, which had tungsten lighting). In later years many Mark 1 coaches had BR 1 bogies replaced by B4.

### XP64

In 1964, a new prototype train was introduced. Known as "XP64", it featured new seat designs, pressure heating & ventilation, aluminium compartment doors and corridor partitions, foot pedal operated toilets and B4 bogies. The vehicles were built on standard Mark 1 underframes. Folding exterior doors were fitted, but these proved troublesome and were later replaced with hinged doors. All XP64 coaches have been withdrawn, but some have been preserved.

### Mark 2

The prototype Mark 2 vehicle (W 13252) was produced in 1963. This was an FK of semi-integral construction and had pressure heating & ventilation, tungsten lighting, and was mounted on B4 bogies. This vehicle has now been preserved at the Mid Norfolk Railway. The production build was similar, but wider windows were used. The TSO and SO vehicles used a new seat design similar to that in the XP64 and fluorescent lighting was provided. Interior finish reverted to wood. Mark 2 vehicles were built from 1964–66.

### Mark 2A–2C

The Mark 2A design, built 1967–68, incorporated the remainder of the features first used in the XP64 coaches, i.e. foot pedal operated toilets (except BSO), new first class seat design, aluminium compartment doors and partitions together with fluorescent lighting in first class compartments. Folding gangway doors (lime green coloured) were used instead of the traditional one-piece variety.

Mark 2B coaches had wide wrap around doors at vehicle ends, no centre doors and a slightly longer body. In standard class there was one toilet at each end instead of two at one end as previously. The folding gangway doors were red.

Mark 2C coaches had a lowered ceiling with twin strips of fluorescent lighting and ducting for air conditioning, but air conditioning was never fitted.

### Mark 2D–2F

These vehicles were fitted with air conditioning. They had no opening top-lights in saloon windows, which were shallower than previous ones.

Mark 2E vehicles had smaller toilets with luggage racks opposite. The folding gangway doors were fawn coloured.

Mark 2F vehicles had a modified air conditioning system, plastic interior panels and Inter-City 70 type seats.

### Mark 3

The Mark 3 design has BT10 bogies, is 75 ft. (23 m.) long and is of fully integral construction with Inter-City 70 type seats. Gangway doors were yellow (red in RFB) when new, although these were changed on refurbishment. Loco-hauled coaches are classified Mark 3A, Mark 3 being reserved for HST trailers. A new batch of FO and BFO, classified Mark 3B, was built in 1985 with Advanced Passenger Train-style seating and revised lighting. These are now in use on First Great Western sleeping car trains. The last vehicles in the Mark 3 series were the driving brake vans ("Driving Van Trailers") built for West Coast Main Line services.

A number of Mark 3 vehicles have recently been converted for use as HST trailers with Grand Central, CrossCountry and First Great Western.

### Mark 4

The Mark 4 design was built by Metro-Cammell for use on the East Coast Main Line after electrification and featured a body profile suitable for tilting trains, although tilt is not fitted, and is not intended to be. This design is suitable for 140 m.p.h. running, although is restricted to 125 m.p.h. because the signalling system on the route is not suitable for the higher speed. The bogies for these coaches were built by SIG in Switzerland and are designated BT41. Power operated sliding plug exterior doors are standard. All Mark 4s were rebuilt with completely new interiors in 2003–05 for GNER and referred to as "Mallard" stock. These rakes generally run in fixed formations and are now operated by East Coast.

# 2.1. BR NUMBER SERIES COACHING STOCK

## AJ11 (RF)                                KITCHEN FIRST

Mark 1. Spent most of its life as a Royal Train vehicle and was numbered 2907 for a time. Built with Commonwealth bogies, but B5 bogies substituted. 24/–. ETH 2.

Lot No. 30633 Swindon 1961. 41 t.

| 325 | **VN** | VS | *VS* | CP | DUART |

## AP1Z (PFK) PULLMAN KITCHEN WITH SERVERY

Mark 2. Pressure Ventilated. Seating removed and replaced with servery. 2T. B5 bogies. ETH 6.

Lot No. 30755 Derby 1966. 40 t.

| 504 | **PC** | WC | *WC* | CS | ULLSWATER |
| 506 | **PC** | WC | *WC* | CS | WINDERMERE |

## AQ1Z (PFP)                     PULLMAN PARLOUR FIRST

Mark 2. Pressure Ventilated. 36/– 2T. B4 bogies. ETH 5.

**Non-standard livery:** 546 Maroon & beige.

Lot No. 30754 Derby 1966. 35 t.

| 546 | **0** | WC | | CS | CITY OF MANCHESTER |
| 548 | **PC** | WC | *WC* | CS | GRASMERE |
| 549 | **PC** | WC | *WC* | CS | BASSENTHWAITE |
| 550 | **PC** | WC | *WC* | CS | RYDAL WATER |
| 551 | **PC** | WC | *WC* | CS | BUTTERMERE |
| 552 | **PC** | WC | *WC* | CS | ENNERDALE WATER |
| 553 | **PC** | WC | *WC* | CS | CRUMMOCK WATER |

## AR1Z (PFB)                        PULLMAN BRAKE FIRST

Mark 2. Pressure Ventilated. 30/– 2T. B4 bogies. ETH 4.

Lot No. 30753 Derby 1966. 35 t.

| 586 | **PC** | WC | *WC* | CS | DERWENTWATER |

# AJ1F (RFB) BUFFET FIRST

Mark 2F. Air conditioned. Converted 1988–9/91 at BREL, Derby from Mark 2F FOs. 1200/1/3/11/14/20/21/50/2 have Stones equipment, others have Temperature Ltd. 25/– 1T 1W (except 1253 which is 26/– 1T). B4 bogies. d. ETH 6X.

**1200/3/11/14/20/52.** Lot No. 30845 Derby 1973. 33 t.
**1201/7/10/12/13/21/50/60.** Lot No. 30859 Derby 1973–74. 33 t.
**1253.** Lot No. 30873 Derby 1974–75. 33 t.

| | | | | |
|---|---|---|---|---|
| 1200 | (3287, 6459) | **RV** H | *RV* | EH |
| 1201 | (3361, 6445) | **CH** H | *VT* | TM |
| 1203 | (3291) | **IC** H | *RV* | EH |
| 1207 | (3328, 6422) | **V** H | | ZG |
| 1210 | (3405, 6462) | **FS** H | *SR* | IS |
| 1211 | (3305) | **IC** H | | LM |
| 1212 | (3427, 6453) | **V** H | *RV* | EH |
| 1213 | (3419) | **V** DM | | MQ |
| 1214 | (3317, 6433) | **AR** H | | KT |
| 1220 | (3315, 6432) | **FS** H | *SR* | IS |
| 1221 | (3371) | **IC** H | | ZG |
| 1250 | (3372) | **V** H | *RV* | EH |
| 1252 | (3280) | **V** H | | LM |
| 1253 | (3432) | **V** H | | KT |
| 1254 | (3391) | **BG** CG | *CG* | BH |
| 1258 | (3322) | **V** H | | KT |
| 1260 | (3378) | **V** H | | EH |

# AK51 (RKB) KITCHEN WITH BAR

Mark 1. Built with no seats but three Pullman-style seats now fitted in bar area. B5 bogies. ETH 1.

Lot No. 30624 Cravens 1960–61. 41 t.

| | | | | |
|---|---|---|---|---|
| 1566 | **VN** VS | *VS* | CP |

# AJ41 (RBR) UNCLASSIFIED KITCHEN BUFFET

Mark 1. Built with 23 loose chairs. All remaining vehicles refurbished with 23 fixed polypropylene chairs and fluorescent lighting. ETH 2 (* 2X). 1683/91/92/99 were further refurbished with 21 chairs, wheelchair space and carpets.

s Modified for use as servery vehicle with some or all seating removed.
t Modified with 11 chairs with a food preparation area replacing the former seating area.

**1651–1699.** Lot No. 30628 Pressed Steel 1960–61. Commonwealth bogies. 39 t.
**1730.** Lot No. 30512 BRCW 1960–61. B5 bogies. 37 t.

**Non-standard liveries:** 1683 and 1699 Oxford Blue.
1679, 1680 & 1698 British racing green & cream lined out in gold.

| 1651 | t   | **CC** | RV | | EH | | 1683 | | **0** | RV | | EH |
|---|---|---|---|---|---|---|---|---|---|---|---|---|
| 1657 | s   | **DR** | DR | | ZG | | 1691 | t | **CC** | RV | *RV* | EH |
| 1658 | t   | **BG** | DB | | FA | | 1692 | t | **CH** | RV | *RV* | EH |
| 1659 | s   | **PC** | RA | *RA* | EH | | 1696 | t | **G** | DB | | FA |
| 1671 | x*t | **M**  | RV | *RV* | EH | | 1698 | s | **0** | RV Long Marston Aerodrome |
| 1679 | t   | **0**  | DB | | EH | | 1699 | t | **0** | RV | *RV* | EH |
| 1680 | *t  | **0**  | DB | *DB* | CE | | 1730 | x | **M** | BK | *BK* | BT |

# AN2F (RSS)                                 SELF-SERVICE BUFFET

Mark 2F. Air conditioned. Temperature Ltd. equipment. Inter-City 70 seats. Converted 1974 from Mark 2F TSO 5970 as a prototype self-service buffet for APT-P. Sold to Northern Ireland Railways 1983, regauged to 5'3" and numbered 546. Since withdrawn, repatriated to Great Britain and converted back to standard gauge. –/24. B5 bogies. ETH 12X.

Lot No. 30860 Derby 1973–74. 33 t.

| 1800 | | **PC** | WT | | CS | | TINTAGEL |
|---|---|---|---|---|---|---|---|

# AN21 (RMB)
## OPEN STANDARD WITH MINIATURE BUFFET

Mark 1. –/44 2T. These vehicles are basically an open standard with two full window spaces removed to accommodate a buffet counter, and four seats removed to allow for a stock cupboard. All remaining vehicles now have fluorescent lighting. Commonwealth bogies. ETH 3.

**1813–1832.** Lot No. 30520 Wolverton 1960. 38 t.
**1840–1842.** Lot No. 30507 Wolverton 1960. 37 t.
**1859–1863.** Lot No. 30670 Wolverton 1961–62. 38 t.
**1882.** Lot No. 30702 Wolverton 1962. 38 t.

**Notes:**

1842 is refurbished and fitted with a microwave oven.
1861 has had its toilets replaced with store cupboards.

| 1813 | x | **M**  | RV | *RV* | EH | | 1860 | x | **M**  | WC | *WC* | CS |
|---|---|---|---|---|---|---|---|---|---|---|---|---|
| 1832 | x | **CC** | RV | | EH | | 1861 | x | **M**  | WC | *WC* | CS |
| 1840 | v | **G**  | WC | *WC* | CS | | 1863 | x | **CH** | RV | *RV* | EH |
| 1842 |   | **CH** | RV | *RV* | EH | | 1882 | x | **M**  | WC | *WC* | CS |
| 1859 | x | **M**  | BK | *BK* | BT | | | | | | | |

# AJ41 (RBR)     UNCLASSIFIED KITCHEN BUFFET

Mark 1. These vehicles were built as unclassified restaurant (RU). They were rebuilt with buffet counters and 23 fixed polypropylene chairs (RBS), then further refurbished by fitting fluorescent lighting and reclassified RBR. ETH 2X.

s Modified for use as servery vehicle with seating removed.

**1953.** Lot No. 30575 Swindon 1960. B4/B5 bogies. 36.5 t.
**1961.** Lot No. 30632 Swindon 1961. Commonwealth bogies. 39 t.

1953 s    **VN** VS *VS* CP    | 1961 x    **G** WC *WC* CS

## AU51      CHARTER TRAIN STAFF COACHES

Mark 1. Converted from BCKs in 1988. Commonwealth bogies. ETH 2.

Lot No. 30732 Derby 1964. 37 t.

| | | | | | |
|---|---|---|---|---|---|
| 2833 | (21270) | **M** | WC | *WC* | CS |
| 2834 | (21267) | **M** | RV | *RV* | EH |

## AT5G      HM THE QUEEN'S SALOON

Mark 3. Converted from a FO built 1972. Consists of a lounge, bedroom and bathroom for HM The Queen, and a combined bedroom and bathroom for the Queen's dresser. One entrance vestibule has double doors. Air conditioned. BT10 bogies. ETH 9X.

Lot No. 30886 Wolverton 1977. 36 t.

| | | | | | |
|---|---|---|---|---|---|
| 2903 | (11001) | **RP** | NR | *RP* | ZN |

## AT5G   HRH THE DUKE OF EDINBURGH'S SALOON

Mark 3. Converted from a TSO built 1972. Consists of a combined lounge/dining room, a bedroom and a shower room for the Duke, a kitchen and a valet's bedroom and bathroom. Air conditioned. BT10 bogies. ETH 15X.

Lot No. 30887 Wolverton 1977. 36 t.

| | | | | | |
|---|---|---|---|---|---|
| 2904 | (12001) | **RP** | NR | *RP* | ZN |

## AT5G      ROYAL HOUSEHOLD SLEEPING CAR

Mark 3A. Built to similar specification as SLE 10647–729. 12 sleeping compartments for use of Royal Household with a fixed lower berth and a hinged upper berth. 2T plus shower room. Air conditioned. BT10 bogies. ETH 11X.

Lot No. 31002 Derby/Wolverton 1985. 44 t.

| | | | | |
|---|---|---|---|---|
| 2915 | **RP** | NR | *RP* | ZN |

## AT5G   HRH THE PRINCE OF WALES'S DINING CAR

Mark 3. Converted from HST TRUK built 1976. Large kitchen retained, but dining area modified for Royal use seating up to 14 at central table(s). Air conditioned. BT10 bogies. ETH 13X.

Lot No. 31059 Wolverton 1988. 43 t.

| | | | | | |
|---|---|---|---|---|---|
| 2916 | (40512) | **RP** | NR | *RP* | ZN |

## AT5G ROYAL KITCHEN/HOUSEHOLD DINING CAR

Mark 3. Converted from HST TRUK built 1977. Large kitchen retained and dining area slightly modified with seating for 22 Royal Household members. Air conditioned. BT10 bogies. ETH 13X.
Lot No. 31084 Wolverton 1990. 43 t.

2917   (40514)      **RP**   NR   *RP*        ZN

## AT5G                                  ROYAL HOUSEHOLD CARS

Mark 3. Converted from HST TRUKs built 1976/7. Air conditioned. BT10 bogies. ETH 10X.

Lot Nos. 31083 (31085*) Wolverton 1989. 41.05 t.

2918   (40515)        **RP**   NR              ZN
2919   (40518)    *   **RP**   NR              ZN

## AT5B                            ROYAL HOUSEHOLD COUCHETTES

Mark 2B. Converted from BFK built 1969. Consists of luggage accommodation, guard's compartment, workshop area, 350 kW diesel generator and staff sleeping accommodation. B5 bogies. ETH2X.

Lot No. 31044 Wolverton 1986. 48 t.

2920   (14109, 17109)    **RP**   NR   *RP*   ZN

Mark 2B. Converted from BFK built 1969. Consists of luggage accommodation, kitchen, brake control equipment and staff accommodation. B5 bogies. ETH7X.

Lot No. 31086 Wolverton 1990. 41.5 t.

2921   (14107, 17107)    **RP**   NR   *RP*   ZN

## AT5H HRH THE PRINCE OF WALES'S SLEEPING CAR

Mark 3B. BT10 bogies. Air conditioned. ETH 7X.
Lot No. 31035 Derby/Wolverton 1987.

2922                  **RP**   NR   *RP*        ZN

## AT5H                                        ROYAL SALOON

Mark 3B. BT10 bogies. Air conditioned. ETH 6X.
Lot No. 31036 Derby/Wolverton 1987.

2923                  **RP**   NR   *RP*        ZN

# AD11 (FO) OPEN FIRST

Mark 1. 42/– 2T. ETH 3. Many now fitted with table lamps.

**Non-standard livery:** British racing green & cream lined out in gold.

**3066–3069.** Lot No. 30169 Doncaster 1955. B4 bogies. 33 t.
**3093.** Lot No. 30472 BRCW 1959. B4 bogies. 33 t.
**3096–3098.** Lot No. 30576 BRCW 1959. B4 bogies. 33 t.

3068 was numbered DB 975606 and 3093 was numbered DB 977594 for a time when in departmental service for British Railways.

| | | | | | | | | | | |
|---|---|---|---|---|---|---|---|---|---|---|
| 3066 | **CC** | RV | *RV* | EH | | 3096 | x **M** | BK | *BK* | BT |
| 3068 | **CC** | RV | *RV* | EH | | 3097 | **CC** | RV | *RV* | EH |
| 3069 | **CC** | RV | *RV* | EH | | 3098 | x **CH** | RV | *RV* | EH |
| 3093 | **M** | WC | *WC* | CS | | | | | | |

Later design with fluorescent lighting, aluminium window frames and Commonwealth bogies.

**3105–3128.** Lot No. 30697 Swindon 1962–63. 36 t.
**3130–3150.** Lot No. 30717 Swindon 1963. 36 t.

3128/36/41/3/4/6/7/8 were renumbered 1058/60/3/5/6/8/9/70 when reclassified RUO, then 3600/5/8/9/2/6/4/10 when declassified to SO, but have since regained their original numbers. 3136 was numbered DB977970 for a time when in use with Serco Railtest as a Brake Force Runner.

**Note:** 3105 has had its luggage racks removed and has tungsten lighting.

| | | | | | | | | | | |
|---|---|---|---|---|---|---|---|---|---|---|
| 3105 | x **M** | WC | *WC* | CS | | 3127 | **G** | RV | | EH |
| 3106 | x **M** | WC | *WC* | CS | | 3128 | x **M** | WC | *WC* | CS |
| 3107 | x **CH** | RV | *RV* | EH | | 3130 | v **M** | WC | *WC* | CS |
| 3110 | x **CH** | RV | *RV* | EH | | 3131 | x **M** | RV | | EH |
| 3112 | x **CH** | RV | *RV* | EH | | 3132 | x **M** | RV | | EH |
| 3113 | x **M** | WC | *WC* | CS | | 3133 | x **M** | RV | | EH |
| 3114 | **G** | RV | | EH | | 3136 | **M** | WC | *WC* | CS |
| 3115 | x **M** | BK | *BK* | BT | | 3140 | x **CH** | RV | *RV* | EH |
| 3117 | x **M** | WC | *WC* | CS | | 3141 | **M** | RV | *RV* | EH |
| 3119 | **CC** | RV | *RV* | EH | | 3143 | **M** | WC | *WC* | CS |
| 3120 | **CC** | RV | *RV* | EH | | 3144 | x **M** | RV | *RV* | EH |
| 3121 | **O** | RV | *RV* | EH | | 3146 | **M** | RV | *RV* | EH |
| 3122 | x **CH** | RV | *RV* | EH | | 3147 | **O** | RV | *RV* | EH |
| 3123 | **O** | RV | *RV* | EH | | 3148 | **M** | JH | *WC* | CS |
| 3124 | **G** | RV | | EH | | 3149 | **CC** | RV | *RV* | EH |
| 3125 | x **CH** | JH | *VT* | TM | | 3150 | **M** | BK | *BK* | BT |

**Names:**

| | | | | |
|---|---|---|---|---|
| 3105 | JULIA | | 3128 | VICTORIA |
| 3106 | ALEXANDRA | | 3136 | DIANA |
| 3113 | JESSICA | | 3143 | PATRICIA |

## AD1D (FO)                                                  OPEN FIRST

Mark 2D. Air conditioned. Stones equipment. 42/– 2T. B4 bogies. ETH 5.

† Interior modified to Pullman Car standards with new seating, new panelling, tungsten lighting and table lights for VSOE "Northern Belle".

Lot No. 30821 Derby 1971–72. 34 t.

| | | | | | | |
|---|---|---|---|---|---|---|
| 3174 | † | **VN** | VS | *VS* | CP | GLAMIS |
| 3182 | † | **VN** | VS | *VS* | CP | WARWICK |
| 3188 | | **PC** | RA | *RA* | EH | SOVEREIGN |

## AD1E (FO)                                                  OPEN FIRST

Mark 2E. Air conditioned. Stones equipment. 42/– 2T (w 41/– 2T 1W, p 36/– 2T). B4 bogies. ETH 5.

r Refurbished with new seats.
u Fitted with power supply for Mk. 1 RBR.
† Interior modified to Pullman Car standards with new seating, new panelling, tungsten lighting and table lights for VSOE "Northern Belle".

3255 was numbered 3525 for a time when fitted with a pantry.

Lot No. 30843 Derby 1972–73. 32.5 t. (35.8 t. †).

| | | | | | | |
|---|---|---|---|---|---|---|
| 3223 | | **RV** | RV | | CD | DIAMOND |
| 3228 | du | **RV** | RV | | CD | AMETHYST |
| 3231 | p | **PC** | RA | *RA* | EH | APOLLO |
| 3232 | dr | **BG** | VS | *CG* | BH | |
| 3240 | | **RV** | RV | | CD | SAPPHIRE |
| 3241 | dr | **FP** | H | | LM | |
| 3244 | d | **RV** | RV | | CD | EMERALD |
| 3247 | † | **VN** | VS | *VS* | CP | CHATSWORTH |
| 3255 | dr | **M** | DB | | FA | |
| 3261 | dw | **FP** | H | | EH | |
| 3267 | † | **VN** | VS | *VS* | CP | BELVOIR |
| 3269 | dr | **M** | DB | | EH | |
| 3273 | † | **VN** | VS | *VS* | CP | ALNWICK |
| 3275 | † | **VN** | VS | *VS* | CP | HARLECH |

## AD1F (FO)                                                  OPEN FIRST

Mark 2F. Air conditioned. 3277–3318/58–79 have Stones equipment, others have Temperature Ltd. 42/– 2T. All now refurbished with power-operated vestibule doors, new panels and new seat trim. B4 bogies. d. ETH 5X.

**3277–3318.** Lot No. 30845 Derby 1973. 33.5 t.
**3325–3426.** Lot No. 30859 Derby 1973–74. 33.5 t.
**3431–3438.** Lot No. 30873 Derby 1974–75. 33.5 t.

r Further refurbished with table lamps and modified seats with burgundy seat trim.
u Fitted with power supply for Mark 1 RBR.

| | | | | | | | | | | |
|---|---|---|---|---|---|---|---|---|---|---|
| 3277 | | **AR** | H | *RV* | EH | 3359 | r | **M** | WC | *WC* | CS |
| 3278 | r | **BP** | DR | | KM | 3360 | r | **IC** | WC | *WC* | CS |
| 3279 | u | **M** | DB | *DB* | CE | 3362 | r | **IC** | WC | *WC* | CS |
| 3292 | | **M** | DB | *DB* | CE | 3364 | r | **RV** | RV | *RV* | EH |
| 3295 | | **AR** | H | *RV* | EH | 3366 | r | **BG** | CG | *CG* | BH |
| 3303 | | **AR** | H | | CE | 3368 | | **M** | DB | | FA |
| 3304 | r | **V** | H | *RV* | EH | 3374 | | **BG** | CG | *CG* | BH |
| 3309 | | **IC** | H | | TM | 3375 | | **M** | DB | | EH |
| 3312 | | **IC** | H | | LM | 3379 | u | **AR** | H | *RV* | EH |
| 3313 | r | **M** | WC | *WC* | CS | 3384 | r | **RV** | RV | *RV* | EH |
| 3314 | r | **V** | H | *RV* | EH | 3385 | r | **BP** | DR | | BA |
| 3318 | | **M** | DB | *DB* | CE | 3386 | r | **V** | RV | *RV* | EH |
| 3325 | r | **V** | H | *RV* | EH | 3387 | r | **V** | DM | | MQ |
| 3326 | r | **BP** | WC | | CS | 3388 | | **M** | DB | | EH |
| 3330 | r | **RV** | RV | *RV* | EH | 3390 | r | **RV** | RV | *RV* | EH |
| 3331 | | **M** | DB | *DB* | CE | 3392 | r | **M** | WC | *WC* | CS |
| 3333 | r | **V** | H | *RV* | EH | 3395 | r | **M** | WC | *WC* | CS |
| 3334 | | **AR** | H | *RV* | EH | 3397 | r | **RV** | RV | *RV* | EH |
| 3336 | u | **AR** | H | *RV* | EH | 3399 | u | **M** | DB | | EH |
| 3338 | u | **M** | DB | | EH | 3400 | | **M** | DB | *DB* | CE |
| 3340 | r | **V** | H | *RV* | EH | 3402 | r | **V** | DM | | YJ |
| 3344 | r | **V** | RV | *RV* | EH | 3408 | r | **M** | WC | *WC* | CS |
| 3345 | r | **V** | H | *RV* | EH | 3411 | r | **V** | DM | | MQ |
| 3348 | r | **RV** | RV | *RV* | EH | 3414 | | **M** | DB | | EH |
| 3350 | r | **M** | WC | *WC* | CS | 3416 | | **IC** | H | | TM |
| 3351 | | **CH** | H | *VT* | TM | 3417 | | **AR** | H | *RV* | EH |
| 3352 | r | **M** | WC | *WC* | CS | 3424 | | **M** | DB | *DB* | CE |
| 3353 | r | **G** | DM | | MQ | 3425 | r | **V** | DM | | YJ |
| 3354 | r | **V** | DM | | YJ | 3426 | r | **RV** | RV | *RV* | EH |
| 3356 | r | **RV** | RV | *RV* | EH | 3431 | r | **M** | WC | *WC* | CS |
| 3358 | | **M** | DB | *DB* | CE | 3438 | r | **V** | H | | LM |

**Names:**

| | | | | |
|---|---|---|---|---|
| 3330 | BRUNEL | | 3384 | DICKENS |
| 3348 | GAINSBOROUGH | | 3390 | CONSTABLE |
| 3356 | TENNYSON | | 3397 | WORDSWORTH |
| 3364 | SHAKESPEARE | | 3426 | ELGAR |

## AC21 (TSO)                                    OPEN STANDARD

Mark 1. This coach has narrower seats than later vehicles. Built with BR Mark 1 bogies. –/64 2T. ETH 4.

Lot No. 30079 York 1953. Commonwealth bogies. 36 t.

3766  x  **M**  WC  *WC*  CS          |

## AC21 (TSO)                                    OPEN STANDARD

Mark 1. These vehicles are a development of the above with fluorescent lighting and modified design of seat headrest. Built with BR Mark 1 bogies. –/64 2T. ETH 4.

**4831–4836.** Lot No. 30506 Wolverton 1959. Commonwealth bogies. 33 t.
**4856.** Lot No. 30525 Wolverton 1959–60. B4 bogies. 33 t.

| 4831 | x | **M** | BK | *BK* | BT | | 4836 | x | **M** | BK | *BK* | BT |
| 4832 | x | **CC** | BK | *BK* | BT | | 4856 | x | **M** | BK | *BK* | BT |

## AC21 (TSO)                                    OPEN STANDARD

Mark 1. Later vehicles built with Commonwealth bogies. –/64 2T. ETH 4.

**4902–4912.** Lot No. 30646 Wolverton 1961.BR Mark 1 bogies substituted by the SR. All now re-rebogied. 34 t B4, 36 t C.
**4927–5044.** Lot No. 30690 Wolverton 1961–62. Aluminium window frames. 37 t.

| 4902 | x B4 | **CH** | RV | *RV* | EH | | 4994 | x | **M** | WC | *WC* | CS |
| 4905 | x C | **M** | WC | *WC* | CS | | 4996 | x | **M** | RV | *RV* | EH |
| 4912 | x C | **M** | WC | *WC* | CS | | 4998 | | **M** | RV | *RV* | EH |
| 4927 | x | **CH** | RV | *RV* | EH | | 4999 | | **BG** | RV | | EH |
| 4931 | v | **M** | WC | *WC* | CS | | 5007 | | **G** | RV | | EH |
| 4940 | x | **M** | WC | *WC* | CS | | 5008 | x | **M** | RV | *RV* | EH |
| 4946 | x | **M** | RV | *RV* | EH | | 5009 | x | **CH** | RV | *RV* | EH |
| 4949 | x | **M** | RV | *RV* | EH | | 5023 | | **G** | RV | | EH |
| 4951 | x | **M** | WC | *WC* | CS | | 5027 | | **G** | RV | | EH |
| 4954 | v | **M** | WC | *WC* | CS | | 5028 | x | **CC** | BK | *BK* | BT |
| 4959 | | **BG** | RV | | EH | | 5032 | x | **M** | WC | *WC* | CS |
| 4960 | x | **M** | WC | *WC* | CS | | 5033 | x | **M** | WC | *WC* | CS |
| 4973 | x | **M** | WC | *WC* | CS | | 5035 | x | **M** | WC | *WC* | CS |
| 4984 | x | **M** | WC | *WC* | CS | | 5040 | x | **CH** | RV | *RV* | EH |
| 4986 | | **G** | RV | *RV* | EH | | 5044 | x | **M** | WC | *WC* | CS |
| 4991 | | **BG** | RV | | EH | | | | | | | |

## AC2Z (TSO)                                    OPEN STANDARD

Mark 2. Pressure ventilated. –/64 2T. B4 bogies. ETH 4.

Lot No. 30751 Derby 1965–67. 32 t.

| 5148 | v | **RR** | H | | TM | | 5193 | v | **LN** | H | | TM |
| 5157 | v | **CH** | H | *VT* | TM | | 5194 | v | **RR** | H | | TM |
| 5171 | v | **G** | WC | *WC* | CS | | 5198 | v | **CH** | H | *VT* | TM |
| 5177 | v | **CH** | H | *VT* | TM | | 5200 | v | **G** | WC | *WC* | CS |
| 5179 | v | **RR** | H | | TM | | 5212 | v | **LN** | H | | TM |
| 5183 | v | **RR** | H | | TM | | 5216 | v | **G** | WC | *WC* | CS |
| 5186 | v | **RR** | H | | TM | | 5221 | v | **RR** | H | | TM |
| 5191 | v | **CH** | H | *VT* | TM | | 5222 | v | **M** | WC | *WC* | CS |

**Names:**

| 5193 | CLAN MACLEOD | | 5212 | CAPERKAILZIE |

## AD2Z (SO)                                    OPEN STANDARD

Mark 2. Pressure ventilated. –/48 2T. B4 bogies. ETH 4.

Lot No. 30752 Derby 1966. 32 t.

**Non-standard livery:** 5229 Green & Cream with gold lettering lined out in gold.

| 5229 | | **0** | WT | *WC* | CS | THE GREEN KNIGHT |
| 5236 | v | **G** | WC | *WC* | CS | |
| 5237 | v | **G** | WC | *WC* | CS | |
| 5239 | | **PC** | WT | *WC* | CS | THE RED KNIGHT |
| 5249 | v | **G** | WC | *WC* | CS | |

## AC2A (TSO)                                   OPEN STANDARD

Mark 2A. Pressure ventilated. –/64 2T (–/62 2T w). B4 bogies. ETH 4.

**5276–5341.** Lot No. 30776 Derby 1967–68. 32 t.
**5350–5419.** Lot No. 30787 Derby 1968. 32 t.

f Facelifted vehicles.

| 5276 | f | **RV** | RV | *RV* | EH | | 5365 | | **RV** | RV | | EH |
| 5278 | | **PC** | WT | *WC* | CS | | 5366 | f | **RV** | RV | *RV* | EH |
| 5292 | f | **RV** | RV | *RV* | EH | | 5376 | | **RV** | RV | | EH |
| 5322 | f | **RV** | RV | *RV* | EH | | 5386 | w | **M** | DB | | FA |
| 5331 | | **M** | DB | | FA | | 5412 | w | **M** | BK | *BK* | BT |
| 5341 | f | **CC** | RV | *RV* | EH | | 5419 | w | **PC** | WT | *WC* | CS |
| 5350 | | **CH** | RV | *RV* | EH | | | | | | | |

**Names:**

| 5278 | MELISANDE | | 5376 | Michaela |
| 5365 | Deborah | | 5419 | SIR. LANCELOT |

## AC2B (TSO)                                   OPEN STANDARD

Mark 2B. Pressure ventilated. –/62 2T. B4 bogies. d. ETH 4.

Lot No. 30791 Derby 1969. 32 t.

| 5453 | **M** | WC | *WC* | CS | | 5487 | **M** | WC | *WC* | CS |
| 5463 | **M** | WC | *WC* | CS | | 5491 | **M** | WC | *WC* | CS |
| 5478 | **M** | WC | *WC* | CS | | | | | | |

## AC2C (TSO)                                   OPEN STANDARD

Mark 2C. Pressure ventilated. –/62 2T. B4 bogies. d. ETH 4.

Lot No. 30795 Derby 1969–70. 32 t.

| 5569 | **M** | WC | *WC* | CS | |

## AC2D (TSO)                                    OPEN STANDARD

Mark 2D. Air conditioned. Stones equipment. Refurbished with new seats and end luggage stacks. –/58 2T. B4 bogies. d. ETH 5.

Lot No. 30822 Derby 1971. 33 t.

| | | | | | | | | |
|---|---|---|---|---|---|---|---|---|
| 5631 | **M** | DB | EH | | 5700 | **FP** | H | HT |
| 5632 | **M** | DB | EH | | 5710 | **FP** | H | HT |
| 5657 | **M** | DB | EH | | 5737 | **FP** | H | KT |
| 5669 | **BP** | WC | CS | | 5740 | **FP** | H | KT |
| 5679 | **FP** | H | KT | | | | | |

## AC2E (TSO)                                    OPEN STANDARD

Mark 2E. Air conditioned. Stones equipment. –/64 2T (w –/62 2T 1W). B4 bogies. d. ETH 5.

**5745–5797**. Lot No. 30837 Derby 1972. 33.5 t.
**5810–5906**. Lot No. 30844 Derby 1972–73. 33.5 t.

r Refurbished with new interior panelling.
s Refurbished with new interior panelling, modified design of seat headrest and centre luggage stack. –/60 2T (w –/58 2T 1W).
t Refurbished with new interior panelling and new seats.

| | | | | | | | | | |
|---|---|---|---|---|---|---|---|---|---|
| 5745 | s | **V** | H | | KT | 5853 | t | **AV** | AW | CF |
| 5748 | r pt | **IC** | H | GW | CF | 5866 | r pt★ | **IC** | H | BH |
| 5750 | s | **V** | H | | KT | 5869 | t | **AV** | AW | LM |
| 5754 | ws | **V** | H | | KT | 5874 | t | **M** | WC | CS |
| 5769 | r | **IC** | H | GW | CF | 5876 | s pt | **V** | H | LM |
| 5787 | s | **V** | H | | LM | 5881 | ws | **V** | H | KT |
| 5788 | r | **IC** | H | | KT | 5886 | s | **V** | H | KT |
| 5789 | r pt | **IC** | H | | LM | 5888 | wr | **IC** | H | KT |
| 5792 | r | **IC** | H | GW | CF | 5899 | s | **V** | H | KT |
| 5793 | wspt | **V** | H | | KT | 5900 | wspt | **V** | H | KT |
| 5797 | r★ | **IC** | H | | LM | 5901 | s | **BG** | CG | CG | BH |
| 5810 | s | **BG** | CG | CG | BH | 5903 | s | **V** | H | KT |
| 5815 | ws | **V** | H | | LM | 5905 | s | **V** | H | KT |
| 5821 | r pt | **V** | H | | KT | 5906 | wspt★ | **IC** | H | BH |

## AC2F (TSO)                                    OPEN STANDARD

Mark 2F. Air conditioned. Temperature Ltd. equipment. Inter-City 70 seats. All were refurbished in the 1980s with power-operated vestibule doors, new panels and new seat trim. –/64 2T. (w –/62 2T 1W) B4 bogies. d. ETH 5X.

**5908–5958**. Lot No. 30846 Derby 1973. 33 t.
**5959–6170**. Lot No. 30860 Derby 1973–74. 33 t.
**6173–6183**. Lot No. 30874 Derby 1974–75. 33 t.

* Early Mark 2 style seats.

These vehicles have undergone a second refurbishment with carpets & new seat trim.

q   Fitted with two wheelchair spaces. –/60 2T 2W.
s   Fitted with centre luggage stack. –/60 2T.
t   Fitted with centre luggage stack and wheelchair space. –/58 2T 1W.

| | | | | | | | | | | |
|---|---|---|---|---|---|---|---|---|---|---|
| 5908 | | **V** | H | | ZG | 5983 | s | **V** | H | KT |
| 5910 | q | **V** | H | *RV* | EH | 5984 | | **V** | H | EH |
| 5911 | s | **V** | RV | | CD | 5985 | | **AR** | H | *RV* | EH |
| 5912 | s | **V** | H | | KT | 5986 | | **V** | H | EH |
| 5913 | | **AV** | AW | | LM | 5987 | | **V** | H | *RV* | EH |
| 5917 | s | **V** | WC | | CS | 5989 | t | **V** | DR | BA |
| 5919 | s pt | **BG** | CG | *CG* | BH | 5991 | s | **V** | H | KT |
| 5920 | | **V** | DM | | YJ | 5995 | s | **BG** | CG | *SR* | BH |
| 5921 | | **AR** | H | *RV* | EH | 5997 | | **V** | H | *RV* | EH |
| 5922 | | **M** | DB | *SR* | CE | 5998 | | **AR** | H | *GW* | CF |
| 5924 | | **M** | DB | *SR* | CE | 6000 | t | **M** | WC | *WC* | CS |
| 5925 | s pt★ | **IC** | H | | LM | 6001 | q | **BG** | CG | *CG* | BH |
| 5928 | | **CH** | H | | TM | 6002 | | **V** | DM | YJ |
| 5929 | | **AR** | H | *GW* | CF | 6006 | | **AR** | H | *RV* | EH |
| 5930 | t | **V** | H | | KT | 6008 | s | **BG** | CG | *GW* | BK |
| 5932 | | **V** | H | | EH | 6009 | | **V** | H | ZG |
| 5933 | | **V** | H | | ZG | 6012 | | **V** | H | ZG |
| 5934 | | **V** | RV | | EH | 6013 | s | **AV** | AW | LM |
| 5936 | | **AR** | H | | LM | 6016 | | **V** | H | ZG |
| 5937 | | **V** | RV | | EH | 6021 | | **V** | H | ZG |
| 5940 | q | **V** | H | | ZG | 6022 | s | **M** | WC | *WC* | CS |
| 5941 | | **BG** | CG | *CG* | BH | 6024 | s | **V** | RV | *RV* | EH |
| 5943 | w | **V** | H | | ZG | 6027 | q | **V** | RV | *RV* | EH |
| 5945 | | **V** | H | *RV* | EH | 6028 | | **AR** | H | ZG |
| 5946 | | **V** | H | *RV* | EH | 6029 | | **V** | H | ZG |
| 5948 | q | **V** | H | | KT | 6031 | | **V** | H | ZG |
| 5949 | q | **V** | H | | ZG | 6035 | t★ | **AV** | AW | LM |
| 5950 | | **AR** | H | | EH | 6036 | * | **M** | DB | *SR* | CE |
| 5952 | | **V** | RV | *RV* | EH | 6037 | | **AR** | H | ZG |
| 5954 | | **M** | DB | | EH | 6038 | s | **V** | RV | EH |
| 5955 | | **V** | RV | *RV* | EH | 6041 | s | **M** | WC | *WC* | CS |
| 5957 | | **V** | H | | ZG | 6042 | | **AR** | H | *RV* | EH |
| 5958 | s★ | **IC** | H | | BH | 6045 | w | **V** | CG | KT |
| 5959 | n | **M** | DB | *SR* | CE | 6046 | s | **BG** | CG | *GW* | BK |
| 5960 | s | **V** | H | | KT | 6049 | | **V** | H | KT |
| 5961 | s pt | **V** | RV | *RV* | EH | 6050 | s | **IC** | H | ZG |
| 5962 | s pt | **V** | H | | KT | 6051 | | **V** | RV | *RV* | EH |
| 5963 | | **V** | H | | EH | 6052 | tw | **IC** | H | KT |
| 5964 | | **AR** | H | *GW* | CF | 6053 | * | **AR** | H | KT |
| 5965 | t | **AB** | AW | *AW* | CF | 6054 | | **V** | H | *RV* | EH |
| 5969 | q | **V** | H | | ZG | 6056 | | **V** | RV | EH |
| 5971 | s | **BG** | CG | *SR* | BH | 6059 | s | **V** | H | KT |
| 5976 | t | **AB** | AW | *AW* | CF | 6064 | s | **BG** | CG | *GW* | BK |
| 5977 | | **V** | H | | ZG | 6065 | | **V** | DM | KT |
| 5978 | | **V** | H | | ZG | 6066 | s★ | **AV** | AW | CF |
| 5980 | | **V** | H | | ZG | 6067 | s pt | **V** | RV | *RV* | EH |

| 6073 | s | **V** | H | | KT |
| 6101 | | **V** | H | | ZG |
| 6103 | | **M** | WC | *WC* | CS |
| 6104 | | **V** | H | | EH |
| 6107 | | **V** | H | *RV* | EH |
| 6110 | | **M** | DB | *SR* | CE |
| 6115 | s | **M** | WC | *WC* | CS |
| 6117 | t★ | **BG** | CG | *GW* | BK |
| 6119 | s | **AV** | AW | | CF |
| 6120 | s | **V** | H | | KT |
| 6122 | s★ | **BG** | CG | *SR* | BH |
| 6124 | s pt★ | **AV** | CG | | LM |
| 6134 | | **V** | CG | | KT |
| 6136 | | **V** | H | | ZG |
| 6137 | s pt | **AV** | AW | | CF |
| 6138 | | **V** | RV | *RV* | EH |
| 6139 | n* | **M** | DB | *SR* | CE |
| 6141 | q | **V** | RV | *RV* | EH |
| 6148 | s | **IC** | WC | | CS |
| 6150 | s | **IC** | H | | ZG |
| 6151 | * | **V** | CG | | KT |
| 6152 | * | **M** | DB | *SR* | CE |
| 6153 | | **V** | H | | ZG |
| 6154 | pt | **IC** | H | | LM |
| 6158 | | **V** | H | *RV* | EH |
| 6162 | s pt | **AV** | AW | | LM |
| 6165 | | **V** | DM | | KT |
| 6168 | s★ | **IC** | H | | BH |
| 6170 | s★ | **AV** | AW | | LM |
| 6173 | s★ | **BG** | CG | *CG* | BH |
| 6175 | | **V** | H | | ZG |
| 6176 | t | **V** | RV | *RV* | EH |
| 6177 | s | **V** | RV | *RV* | EH |
| 6179 | | **V** | H | | ZG |
| 6181 | wn | **V** | DM | | YJ |
| 6183 | s | **AB** | AW | *AW* | CF |

## AX51                                                    BRAKE GENERATOR VAN

Mark 1. Renumbered 1989 from BR departmental series. Converted from NDA in 1973 to three-phase supply brake generator van for use with HST trailers. Modified 1999 for use with loco-hauled stock. B5 bogies.

Lot No. 30400 Pressed Steel 1958.

| 6310 | (81448, 975325) | **CH** | RV | *RV* | EH |

## AX51                                                             GENERATOR VAN

Mark 1. Converted from NDA in 1992 to generator vans for use on Anglo-Scottish sleeping car services. Now normally used on trains hauled by steam locomotives. B4 bogies. ETH75.

**6311.** Lot No. 30162 Pressed Steel 1958. 37.25 t.
**6312.** Lot No. 30224 Cravens 1956. 37.25 t.
**6313.** Lot No. 30484 Pressed Steel 1958. 37.25 t.

| 6311 | (80903, 92911) | **B** | DB | | TO |
| 6312 | (81023, 92925) | **PC** | WC | *WC* | CS |
| 6313 | (81553, 92167) | **PC** | VS | *VS* | SL |

## AG2C (TSOT)                            OPEN STANDARD (TROLLEY)

Mark 2C. Converted from TSO by removal of one seating bay and replacing this by a counter with a space for a trolley. Adjacent toilet removed and converted to steward's washing area/store. Pressure ventilated. –/55 1T. B4 bogies. ETH 4.

Lot No. 30795 Derby 1969–70. 32.5 t.

| 6528 | (5592) | **M** | WC | *WC* | CS |

## AN1F (RLO)  SLEEPER RECEPTION CAR

Mark 2F. Converted from FO, these vehicles consist of pantry, microwave cooking facilities, seating area for passengers (with loose chairs, staff toilet plus two bars). Now refurbished again with new "sofa" seating as well as the loose chairs. Converted at RTC, Derby (6700), Ilford (6701–5) and Derby (6706–8). Air conditioned. 6700/1/3/5–8 have Stones equipment and 6702/4 have Temperature Ltd. equipment. The number of seats per coach can vary but typically is 25/– 1T (12 seats as "sofa" seating and 13 loose chairs). B4 bogies. d. ETH 5X.

**6700–2/4/8.** Lot No. 30859 Derby 1973–74. 33.5 t.
**6703/5–7.** Lot No. 30845 Derby 1973. 33.5 t.

| | | | | | |
|---|---|---|---|---|---|
| 6700 | (3347) | **FB** | H | *SR* | IS |
| 6701 | (3346) | **FS** | H | *SR* | IS |
| 6702 | (3421) | **FS** | H | *SR* | IS |
| 6703 | (3308) | **FS** | H | *SR* | IS |
| 6704 | (3341) | **FS** | H | *SR* | IS |
| 6705 | (3310, 6430) | **FS** | H | *SR* | IS |
| 6706 | (3283, 6421) | **FS** | H | *SR* | IS |
| 6707 | (3276, 6418) | **FS** | H | *SR* | IS |
| 6708 | (3370) | **FS** | H | *SR* | IS |

## AN1D (RFB)  BUFFET FIRST

Mark 2D. Converted from TSOT by the removal of another seating bay and fitting a proper buffet counter with boiler and microwave oven. Now converted to First Class with new seating and end luggage stacks. Air conditioned. Stones equipment. 30/– 1T. B4 bogies. d. ETH 5.

Lot No. 30822 Derby 1971. 33 t.

| | | | | | |
|---|---|---|---|---|---|
| 6720 | (5622, 6652) | **M** | DB | *DB* | CE |
| 6722 | (5736, 6661) | **FP** | H | | LM |
| 6723 | (5641, 6662) | **FP** | WC | | CS |
| 6724 | (5721, 6665) | **FP** | WC | | CS |

## AH2Z (BSOT)  OPEN BRAKE STANDARD (TROLLEY)

Mark 2. These vehicles use the same body shell as the Mark 2 BFK. Converted from BSO by removal of one seating bay and replacing this with a counter with a space for a trolley. Adjacent toilet removed and converted to a steward's washing area/store. –/23 0T. B4 bogies. ETH 4.

Lot No. 30757 Derby 1966. 31 t.

| | | | | | | |
|---|---|---|---|---|---|---|
| 9101 | (9398) | v | **CH** | H | *VT* | TM |
| 9104 | (9401) | v | **G** | WC | *WC* | CS |

## AE2Z (BSO)                    OPEN BRAKE STANDARD

Mark 2. These vehicles use the same body shell as the Mark 2 BFK and have
First Class seat spacing and wider tables. Pressure ventilated. –/31 1T. B4 bogies.
ETH 4.

Lot No. 30757 Derby 1966. 31.5 t.

| | | | | | |
|---|---|---|---|---|---|
| 9391 | | **PC** | WT *WC* | CS | PENDRAGON |
| 9392 | v | **M** | WC *WC* | CS | |

## AE2C (BSO)                    OPEN BRAKE STANDARD

Mark 2C. Pressure ventilated. –/31 1T. B4 bogies. ETH 4.

Lot No. 30798 Derby 1970. 32 t.

| | | | | | |
|---|---|---|---|---|---|
| 9440 | d | **M** | WC *WC* | CS | &#124; |

## AE2D (BSO)                    OPEN BRAKE STANDARD

Mark 2D. Air conditioned (Stones). –/31 1T. B4 bogies. d. pg. ETH 5.

r Refurbished with new interior panelling.
s Refurbished with new seating –/22 1TD.
w Facelifted –/28 1W 1T.

Lot No. 30824 Derby 1971. 33 t.

| | | | | | | | | | | |
|---|---|---|---|---|---|---|---|---|---|---|
| 9479 | r | **IC** | DR | BA | | 9490 | s | **FP** | H | KT |
| 9480 | w | **FP** | H | KT | | 9492 | w | **FP** | DM | YJ |
| 9488 | s | **FP** | H | Darlington | | 9493 | s | **M** | WC *WC* | CS |
| 9489 | r | **V** | H | KT | | 9494 | s | **M** | DB *DB* | CE |

## AE2E (BSO)                    OPEN BRAKE STANDARD

Mark 2E. Air conditioned (Stones). –/32 1T. B4 bogies. d. pg. ETH 5.

Lot No. 30838 Derby 1972. 33 t.

**Non-standard livery:** 9502 Pullman umber & cream.

r Refurbished with new interior panelling.
s Refurbished with modified design of seat headrest and new interior panelling.
w Facelifted –/28 1W 1T.

| | | | | | | | | | | | |
|---|---|---|---|---|---|---|---|---|---|---|---|
| 9496 | r | **IC** | H | *DR* | KM | | 9504 | s | **V** | H | *RV* | EH |
| 9497 | r★ | **IC** | H | | BH | | 9505 | s★ | **IC** | H | | LM |
| 9498 | r | **V** | H | | KT | | 9506 | s★ | **BG** | CG | *SR* | BH |
| 9500 | r | **IC** | H | | LM | | 9507 | s | **V** | H | *RV* | EH |
| 9501 | w | **FP** | DM | | MQ | | 9508 | s | **BG** | CG | *GW* | BK |
| 9502 | s | **O** | H | *VS* | SL | | 9509 | s | **AV** | AW | | LM |
| 9503 | s | **AV** | AW | | CF | | | | | | | |

# AE2F (BSO)                        OPEN BRAKE STANDARD

Mark 2F. Air conditioned (Temperature Ltd.). All now refurbished with power-operated vestibule doors, new panels and seat trim. All now further refurbished with carpets. –/32 1T. B4 bogies. d. pg. ETH5X.

Lot No. 30861 Derby 1974. 34 t.

| | | | | | | | | | | |
|---|---|---|---|---|---|---|---|---|---|---|
| 9513 | | **BP** | DR | | BA | 9526 | n★ | **IC** | H | *GW* | CF |
| 9516 | n | **V** | H | | KT | 9527 | n | **V** | RV | | EH |
| 9520 | n | **AR** | RV | *GW* | CF | 9529 | n | **M** | DB | *SR* | CE |
| 9521 | ★ | **AB** | AW | *AW* | CF | 9531 | | **M** | DB | *SR* | CE |
| 9522 | | **V** | H | | KT | 9537 | n | **V** | H | *RV* | EH |
| 9523 | | **V** | H | | KT | 9538 | | **V** | H | | KT |
| 9524 | n★ | **AV** | AW | | LM | 9539 | | **AB** | AW | *AW* | CF |
| 9525 | | **BG** | H | *CG* | BH | | | | | | |

# AF2F (DBSO)  DRIVING OPEN BRAKE STANDARD

Mark 2F. Air conditioned (Temperature Ltd.). Push & pull (t.d.m. system). Converted from BSO, these vehicles originally had half cabs at the brake end. They have since been refurbished and have had their cabs widened and the cab-end gangways removed. Five vehicles (9701–03/08/14) have been converted for use in Network Rail test trains and can be found in the Service Stock section of this book. –/30 1W 1T. B4 bogies. d. pg. Cowcatchers. ETH 5X.

**9704–9710.** Lot No. 30861 Derby 1974. Converted Glasgow 1979. Disc brakes. 34 t.
**9711/9713.** Lot No. 30861 Derby 1974. Converted Glasgow 1985. 34 t.

| | | | | | | | | | | |
|---|---|---|---|---|---|---|---|---|---|---|
| 9704 | (9512) | **AR** | H | | ZG | 9710 | (9518) | **1** | H | | ZG |
| 9705 | (9519) | **AR** | H | | ZG | 9711 | (9532) | **AR** | H | | TS |
| 9707 | (9511) | **AR** | H | | ZG | 9713 | (9535) | **AR** | H | | EH |
| 9709 | (9515) | **AR** | H | | ZG | | | | | | |

# AE4E (BUO)      UNCLASSIFIED OPEN BRAKE

Mark 2E. Converted from TSO with new seating for use on Anglo-Scottish overnight services by Railcare, Wolverton. Air conditioned. Stones equipment. B4 bogies. d. –/31 2T. B4 bogies. ETH 4X.

**9801–9803.** Lot No. 30837 Derby 1972. 33.5 t.
**9804–9810.** Lot No. 30844 Derby 1972–73. 33.5 t.

| | | | | | | | | | | | |
|---|---|---|---|---|---|---|---|---|---|---|---|
| 9800 | (5751) | **FS** | H | *SR* | IS | 9806 | (5840) | **FS** | H | *SR* | IS |
| 9801 | (5760) | **FS** | H | *SR* | IS | 9807 | (5851) | **FS** | H | *SR* | IS |
| 9802 | (5772) | **FS** | H | *SR* | IS | 9808 | (5871) | **FS** | H | *SR* | IS |
| 9803 | (5799) | **FS** | H | *SR* | IS | 9809 | (5890) | **FS** | H | *SR* | IS |
| 9804 | (5826) | **FS** | H | *SR* | IS | 9810 | (5892) | **FS** | H | *SR* | IS |
| 9805 | (5833) | **FS** | H | *SR* | IS | | | | | | |

## AJ1G (RFB)                    KITCHEN BUFFET FIRST

Mark 3A. Air conditioned. Converted from HST TRFKs, RFBs and FOs. Refurbished with table lamps and burgundy seat trim (except *). 18/– plus two seats for staff use (* 24/–, † 24/–, § 24/–). BT10 bogies. d. ETH 14X.

**10200–10211.** Lot No. 30884 Derby 1977. 39.8 t.
**10212–10229.** Lot No. 30878 Derby 1975–76. 39.8 t.
**10230–10259.** Lot No. 30890 Derby 1979. 39.8 t.

§ First Great Western Sleeper "day coaches" that have been fitted with former HST First Class seats to a 2+1 layout.

Coaches in **WS** livery have been refurbished for Wrexham & Shropshire. Fitted with new Primarius seating, new kitchen area and universal-access toilet. 30/– 1TD 1W.

**Non-standard livery:** 10211 EWS dark maroon.

| | | | | | | | | | | | | |
|---|---|---|---|---|---|---|---|---|---|---|---|---|
| 10200 | (40519) | * | **1** | P | *EA* | NC | 10231 | (10016) | | **V** | P | LM |
| 10202 | (40504) | † | **BG** | CG | *AW* | CF | 10232 | (10027) | § | **FD** | P | *GW* | PZ |
| 10203 | (40506) | * | **1** | P | *EA* | NC | 10233 | (10013) | | **V** | DB | | LM |
| 10206 | (40507) | | **V** | P | | NC | 10235 | (10015) | † | **BG** | DB | *WS* | CE |
| 10208 | (40517) | | **WS** | DB | *WS* | AL | 10236 | (10018) | | **WS** | DB | *WS* | AL |
| 10211 | (40510) | | **0** | DB | *DB* | TO | 10237 | (10022) | | **DR** | DR | | BA |
| 10212 | (11049) | | **VT** | P | *VW* | WB | 10240 | (10003) | | **V** | P | | LM |
| 10213 | (11050) | | **V** | CG | | HT | 10241 | (10009) | * | **1** | P | *EA* | NC |
| 10214 | (11034) | * | **1** | P | *EA* | NC | 10242 | (10002) | | **BG** | CG | | WN |
| 10215 | (11032) | | **BG** | DB | *WS* | CE | 10245 | (10019) | | **V** | CG | | ZB |
| 10216 | (11041) | * | **1** | P | *EA* | NC | 10246 | (10014) | † | **BG** | CG | *CG* | BH |
| 10217 | (11051) | | **VT** | P | *VW* | WB | 10247 | (10011) | * | **NX** | P | *EA* | NC |
| 10219 | (11047) | § | **FD** | P | *GW* | PZ | 10249 | (10012) | | **AB** | CG | *AW* | CF |
| 10223 | (11043) | * | **1** | P | *EA* | NC | 10250 | (10020) | | **V** | DB | | LM |
| 10225 | (11014) | § | **FD** | P | *GW* | PZ | 10253 | (10026) | | **V** | P | | LM |
| 10226 | (11015) | | **V** | DB | | LM | 10255 | (10010) | | **WS** | DB | *WS* | AL |
| 10228 | (11035) | * | **1** | P | *EA* | NC | 10257 | (10007) | † | **BG** | DB | *WS* | CE |
| 10229 | (11059) | * | **1** | P | *EA* | NC | 10259 | (10025) | | **V** | P | | LM |
| 10230 | (10021) | | **WS** | DB | *WS* | AL | | | | | | | |

## AG2J (RSB)          KITCHEN BUFFET STANDARD

Mark 4. Air conditioned. BT41 bogies. ETH 6X. Rebuilt from First to Standard Class with bar adjacent to seating area instead of adjacent to end of coach. –/ 30 1T.

Lot No. 31045 Metro-Cammell 1989–1992. 43.2 t.

| | | | | | | | | | |
|---|---|---|---|---|---|---|---|---|---|
| 10300 | **GN** | H | *EC* | BN | 10306 | **GN** | H | *EC* | BN |
| 10301 | **GN** | H | *EC* | BN | 10307 | **GN** | H | *EC* | BN |
| 10302 | **GN** | H | *EC* | BN | 10308 | **GN** | H | *EC* | BN |
| 10303 | **GN** | H | *EC* | BN | 10309 | **GN** | H | *EC* | BN |
| 10304 | **GN** | H | *EC* | BN | 10310 | **GN** | H | *EC* | BN |
| 10305 | **GN** | H | *EC* | BN | 10311 | **GN** | H | *EC* | BN |

| | | | | | | | | |
|---|---|---|---|---|---|---|---|---|
| 10312 | **GN** | H *EC* | BN | | 10324 | **GN** | H *EC* | BN |
| 10313 | **GN** | H *EC* | BN | | 10325 | **GN** | H *EC* | BN |
| 10315 | **GN** | H *EC* | BN | | 10326 | **GN** | H *EC* | BN |
| 10317 | **GN** | H *EC* | BN | | 10328 | **GN** | H *EC* | BN |
| 10318 | **GN** | H *EC* | BN | | 10329 | **GN** | H *EC* | BN |
| 10319 | **GN** | H *EC* | BN | | 10330 | **GN** | H *EC* | BN |
| 10320 | **GN** | H *EC* | BN | | 10331 | **GN** | H *EC* | BN |
| 10321 | **GN** | H *EC* | BN | | 10332 | **GN** | H *EC* | BN |
| 10323 | **GN** | H *EC* | BN | | 10333 | **GN** | H *EC* | BN |

## AN2G (RMB)
## OPEN STANDARD WITH MINIATURE BUFFET

Mark 3A. Air conditioned. Converted from Mark 3 TSOs at Derby 2006. –/52 1T (including 6 Compin Pegasus seats for "priority" use).

Lot No. 30877 Derby 1975–77. 37.8 t.

| | | | | | | | | | | |
|---|---|---|---|---|---|---|---|---|---|---|
| 10401 | (12168) | **NX** | P | *EA* | NC | | 10404 | (12068) | **1** | P *EA* NC |
| 10402 | (12010) | **1** | P | *EA* | NC | | 10405 | (12157) | **1** | P *EA* NC |
| 10403 | (12135) | **1** | P | *EA* | NC | | 10406 | (12020) | **1** | P *EA* NC |

## AU4G (SLEP)　　　SLEEPING CAR WITH PANTRY

Mark 3A. Air conditioned. Retention toilets. 12 compartments with a fixed lower berth and a hinged upper berth, plus an attendants compartment. 2T. BT10 bogies. ETH 7X.

**Non-standard livery:** 10546 EWS dark maroon.

Lot No. 30960 Derby 1981–83. 41 t.

| | | | | | | | | | | | |
|---|---|---|---|---|---|---|---|---|---|---|---|
| 10501 | d | **FS** | P | *SR* | IS | | 10543 | d | **FS** | P | *SR* | IS |
| 10502 | d | **FS** | P | *SR* | IS | | 10544 | d | **FS** | P | *SR* | IS |
| 10504 | d | **FS** | P | *SR* | IS | | 10546 | d | **0** | DB | *DB* | TO |
| 10506 | d | **FS** | P | *SR* | IS | | 10548 | d | **FS** | P | *SR* | IS |
| 10507 | d | **FS** | P | *SR* | IS | | 10551 | d | **FS** | P | *SR* | IS |
| 10508 | d | **FS** | P | *SR* | IS | | 10553 | d | **FS** | P | *SR* | IS |
| 10513 | d | **FS** | P | *SR* | IS | | 10561 | d | **FS** | P | *SR* | IS |
| 10516 | d | **FS** | P | *SR* | IS | | 10562 | d | **FS** | P | *SR* | IS |
| 10519 | d | **FS** | P | *SR* | IS | | 10563 | d | **FD** | P | *GW* | PZ |
| 10520 | d | **FS** | P | *SR* | IS | | 10565 | d | **FS** | P | *SR* | IS |
| 10522 | d | **FS** | P | *SR* | IS | | 10580 | d | **FS** | P | *SR* | IS |
| 10523 | d | **FS** | P | *SR* | IS | | 10584 | d | **FD** | P | *GW* | PZ |
| 10526 | d | **FS** | P | *SR* | IS | | 10588 | d | **BG** | CG | *CG* | BH |
| 10527 | d | **FS** | P | *SR* | IS | | 10589 | d | **FD** | P | *GW* | PZ |
| 10529 | d | **FS** | P | *SR* | IS | | 10590 | d | **FD** | P | *GW* | PZ |
| 10531 | d | **FS** | P | *SR* | IS | | 10594 | d | **FD** | P | *GW* | PZ |
| 10532 | d | **FD** | P | *GW* | PZ | | 10596 | d | **IC** | P | | LM |
| 10534 | d | **FD** | P | *GW* | PZ | | 10597 | d | **FS** | P | *SR* | IS |
| 10542 | d | **FS** | P | *SR* | IS | | 10598 | d | **FS** | P | *SR* | IS |

| | | | | | | | | | |
|---|---|---|---|---|---|---|---|---|---|
| 10600 | d | **FS** | P | *SR* | IS | 10612 | d | **FD** | P | *GW* | PZ |
| 10601 | d | **FD** | P | *GW* | PZ | 10613 | d | **FS** | P | *SR* | IS |
| 10605 | d | **FS** | P | *SR* | IS | 10614 | d | **FS** | P | *SR* | IS |
| 10607 | d | **FS** | P | *SR* | IS | 10616 | d | **FD** | P | *GW* | PZ |
| 10610 | d | **FS** | P | *SR* | IS | 10617 | d | **FS** | P | *SR* | IS |

## AS4G/*AQ4G (SLE/*SLED)                    SLEEPING CAR

Mark 3A. Air conditioned. Retention toilets. 13 compartments with a fixed lower berth and a hinged upper berth (* 11 compartments with a fixed lower berth and a hinged upper berth + one compartment for a disabled person. 1TD). 2T. BT10 bogies. ETH 6X.

**Note:** 10734 was originally 2914 and used as a Royal Train staff sleeping car. It has 12 berths and a shower room and is ETH11X.

**10647–10729.** Lot No. 30961 Derby 1980–84. 43.5 t.
**10734.** Lot No. 31002 Derby/Wolverton 1985. 42.5 t.

| | | | | | | | | | | | |
|---|---|---|---|---|---|---|---|---|---|---|---|
| 10647 | d | **IC** | DB | | LM | 10699 | d | *FS | P | *SR* | IS |
| 10648 | d | *FS | P | *SR* | IS | 10701 | d | **IC** | DB | | LM |
| 10650 | d | *FS | P | *SR* | IS | 10703 | d | **FS** | P | *SR* | IS |
| 10666 | d | *FS | P | *SR* | IS | 10706 | d | *FS | P | *SR* | IS |
| 10675 | d | *FS | P | *SR* | IS | 10714 | d | *FS | P | *SR* | IS |
| 10680 | d | *FS | P | *SR* | IS | 10718 | d | *FS | P | *SR* | IS |
| 10683 | d | **FS** | P | *SR* | IS | 10719 | d | *FS | P | *SR* | IS |
| 10688 | d | *FS | P | *SR* | IS | 10722 | d | *FS | P | *SR* | IS |
| 10689 | d | *FS | P | *SR* | IS | 10723 | d | *FS | P | *SR* | IS |
| 10690 | d | **FS** | P | *SR* | IS | 10729 | | **VN** | VS | *VS* | CP |
| 10693 | d | **FS** | P | *SR* | IS | 10734 | | **VN** | VS | *VS* | CP |

**Names:**

| | | |
|---|---|---|
| 10729 | CREWE | 10734 | BALMORAL |

## AD1G (FO)                                      OPEN FIRST

Mark 3A. Air conditioned. All refurbished with table lamps and new seat cushions and trim. 48/– 2T (* 48/– 1T 1TD, † 47/– 2T 1W). BT10 bogies. d. ETH 6X.

§ 11029 and 11040 have been reseated with Standard Class seats. 11029 seats –/68 2T 2W and 11040 seats –/72 2T.

11005–7 were open composites 11905–7 for a time.

**Non-standard livery:** 11039 EWS dark maroon.

Lot No. 30878 Derby 1975–76. 34.3 t.

| | | | | | | | | | | | |
|---|---|---|---|---|---|---|---|---|---|---|---|
| 11005 | | **V** | DB | | LM | 11021 | | **V** | P | | NC |
| 11006 | | **V** | P | | LM | 11026 | | **V** | P | | LM |
| 11007 | | **VT** | P | *VW* | WB | 11027 | † | **V** | DB | | WN |
| 11011 | * | **V** | P | | LM | 11028 | | **V** | DR | | ZB |
| 11013 | | **DR** | DR | | ZN | 11029 | § | **BG** | DB | *WS* | CE |
| 11018 | | **VT** | P | *VW* | WB | 11030 | † | **DR** | DR | | BA |
| 11019 | † | **DR** | DR | *DR* | KM | 11031 | † | **BG** | DB | *WS* | CE |

| | | | |
|---|---|---|---|
| 11033 | **DR** DR | | ZN |
| 11039 | **0** DB *DB* | | TO |
| 11040 § | **BG** DB *WS* | | CE |
| 11042 | **V** DB | | ZB |
| 11044 † | **DR** DR | | BA |

| | | | |
|---|---|---|---|
| 11046 † | **DR** DR *DR* | | KM |
| 11048 | **VT** P *VW* | | WB |
| 11052 | **V** DB | | ZB |
| 11054 † | **DR** DR *DR* | | KM |
| 11058 | **V** DB | | ZB |

## AD1H (FO)            OPEN FIRST

Mark 3B. Air conditioned. Inter-City 80 seats. All refurbished with table lamps and new seat cushions and trim. 48/– 2T. BT10 bogies. d. ETH 6X.

† National Express East Anglia vehicles fitted with disabled toilet and reduced seating including three Compin "Pegasus" seats of the same type as used in Standard Class (but regarded as First Class!). 34/3 1T 1TD 2W.

Lot No. 30982 Derby 1985. 36.5 t.

| | | | | |
|---|---|---|---|---|
| 11064 | **BG** CG | | WN |
| 11065 | **BG** CG *CG* | BH |
| 11066 | **1** P | *EA* | NC |
| 11067 | **1** P | *EA* | NC |
| 11068 | **1** P | *EA* | NC |
| 11069 | **1** P | *EA* | NC |
| 11070 | **1** P | *EA* | NC |
| 11071 | **BG** CG *CG* | BH |
| 11072 | **1** P | *EA* | NC |
| 11073 | **1** P | *EA* | NC |
| 11074 | **V** P | | NC |
| 11075 | **1** P | *EA* | NC |
| 11076 | **1** P | *EA* | NC |
| 11077 | **1** P | *EA* | NC |
| 11078 † | **1** P | *EA* | NC |
| 11079 | **V** CG | | CE |
| 11080 | **1** P | *EA* | NC |
| 11081 | **1** P | *EA* | NC |
| 11082 | **1** P | *EA* | NC |

| | | | | |
|---|---|---|---|---|
| 11083 | **BG** CG *CG* | BH |
| 11084 | **BG** CG | | WN |
| 11085 † | **1** P | *EA* | NC |
| 11086 | **BG** CG | | WN |
| 11087 † | **NX** P | *EA* | NC |
| 11088 † | **1** P | *EA* | NC |
| 11089 | **BG** CG *CG* | BH |
| 11090 † | **1** P | *EA* | NC |
| 11091 | **NX** P | *EA* | NC |
| 11092 † | **1** P | *EA* | NC |
| 11093 † | **1** P | *EA* | NC |
| 11094 † | **1** P | *EA* | NC |
| 11095 † | **1** P | *EA* | NC |
| 11096 † | **1** P | *EA* | NC |
| 11097 | **V** CG | | LM |
| 11098 † | **1** P | *EA* | NC |
| 11099 † | **1** P | *EA* | NC |
| 11100 † | **1** P | *EA* | NC |
| 11101 † | **1** P | *EA* | NC |

## AD1J (FO)            OPEN FIRST

Mark 4. Air conditioned. Rebuilt with new interior by Bombardier Wakefield 2003–05 (some converted from Standard Class vehicles) 46/– 1T. BT41 bogies. ETH 6X.

**11201–11273**. Lot No. 31046 Metro-Cammell 1989–92. 41.3 t .
**11277–11299**. Lot No. 31049 Metro-Cammell 1989–92. 41.3 t .

| | | | | |
|---|---|---|---|---|
| 11201 (11201) | **GN** H *EC* | BN |
| 11219 (11219) | **GN** H *EC* | BN |
| 11229 (11229) | **GN** H *EC* | BN |
| 11237 (11237) | **GN** H *EC* | BN |
| 11241 (11241) | **GN** H *EC* | BN |
| 11244 (11244) | **GN** H *EC* | BN |
| 11273 (11273) | **GN** H *EC* | BN |

| | | | | |
|---|---|---|---|---|
| 11277 (12408) | **GN** H *EC* | BN |
| 11278 (12479) | **GN** H *EC* | BN |
| 11279 (12521) | **GN** H *EC* | BN |
| 11280 (12523) | **GN** H *EC* | BN |
| 11281 (12418) | **GN** H *EC* | BN |
| 11282 (12524) | **GN** H *EC* | BN |
| 11283 (12435) | **GN** H *EC* | BN |

| 11284 (12487) | **GN** H *EC* BN | 11291 (12535) | **GN** H *EC* BN |
| 11285 (12537) | **GN** H *EC* BN | 11292 (12451) | **GN** H *EC* BN |
| 11286 (12482) | **GN** H *EC* BN | 11293 (12536) | **GN** H *EC* BN |
| 11287 (12527) | **GN** H *EC* BN | 11294 (12529) | **GN** H *EC* BN |
| 11288 (12517) | **GN** H *EC* BN | 11295 (12475) | **GN** H *EC* BN |
| 11289 (12528) | **GN** H *EC* BN | 11298 (12416) | **GN** H *EC* BN |
| 11290 (12530) | **GN** H *EC* BN | 11299 (12532) | **GN** H *EC* BN |

## AD1J (FOD)                    OPEN FIRST (DISABLED)

Mark 4. Air conditioned. Rebuilt from FO by Bombardier Wakefield 2003–05.
42/– 1W 1TD. BT41 bogies. ETH 6X.

Lot No. 31046 Metro-Cammell 1989–92. 40.7 t.

| 11301 (11215) | **GN** H *EC* BN | 11316 (11227) | **GN** H *EC* BN |
| 11302 (11203) | **GN** H *EC* BN | 11317 (11223) | **GN** H *EC* BN |
| 11303 (11211) | **GN** H *EC* BN | 11318 (11251) | **GN** H *EC* BN |
| 11304 (11257) | **GN** H *EC* BN | 11319 (11247) | **GN** H *EC* BN |
| 11305 (11261) | **GN** H *EC* BN | 11320 (11255) | **GN** H *EC* BN |
| 11306 (11276) | **GN** H *EC* BN | 11321 (11245) | **GN** H *EC* BN |
| 11307 (11217) | **GN** H *EC* BN | 11322 (11228) | **GN** H *EC* BN |
| 11308 (11263) | **GN** H *EC* BN | 11323 (11235) | **GN** H *EC* BN |
| 11309 (11259) | **GN** H *EC* BN | 11324 (11253) | **GN** H *EC* BN |
| 11310 (11272) | **GN** H *EC* BN | 11325 (11231) | **GN** H *EC* BN |
| 11311 (11221) | **GN** H *EC* BN | 11326 (11206) | **GN** H *EC* BN |
| 11312 (11225) | **GN** H *EC* BN | 11327 (11236) | **GN** H *EC* BN |
| 11313 (11210) | **GN** H *EC* BN | 11328 (11274) | **GN** H *EC* BN |
| 11314 (11207) | **GN** H *EC* BN | 11329 (11243) | **GN** H *EC* BN |
| 11315 (11238) | **GN** H *EC* BN | 11330 (11249) | **GN** H *EC* BN |

## AD1J (FO)                                     OPEN FIRST

Mark 4. Air conditioned. Rebuilt from FO by Bombardier Wakefield 2003–05.
Separate area for 7 smokers, although smoking is no longer allowed. 46/– 1W
1TD. BT41 bogies. ETH 6X.

Lot No. 31046 Metro-Cammell 1989–92. 42.1 t.

| 11401 (11214) | **GN** H *EC* BN | 11415 (11208) | **GN** H *EC* BN |
| 11402 (11216) | **GN** H *EC* BN | 11416 (11254) | **GN** H *EC* BN |
| 11403 (11258) | **GN** H *EC* BN | 11417 (11226) | **GN** H *EC* BN |
| 11404 (11202) | **GN** H *EC* BN | 11418 (11222) | **GN** H *EC* BN |
| 11405 (11204) | **GN** H *EC* BN | 11419 (11250) | **GN** H *EC* BN |
| 11406 (11205) | **GN** H *EC* BN | 11420 (11242) | **GN** H *EC* BN |
| 11407 (11256) | **GN** H *EC* BN | 11421 (11220) | **GN** H *EC* BN |
| 11408 (11218) | **GN** H *EC* BN | 11422 (11232) | **GN** H *EC* BN |
| 11409 (11262) | **GN** H *EC* BN | 11423 (11230) | **GN** H *EC* BN |
| 11410 (11260) | **GN** H *EC* BN | 11424 (11239) | **GN** H *EC* BN |
| 11411 (11240) | **GN** H *EC* BN | 11425 (11234) | **GN** H *EC* BN |
| 11412 (11209) | **GN** H *EC* BN | 11426 (11252) | **GN** H *EC* BN |
| 11413 (11212) | **GN** H *EC* BN | 11427 (11200) | **GN** H *EC* BN |
| 11414 (11246) | **GN** H *EC* BN | 11428 (11233) | **GN** H *EC* BN |

| 11429 (11275) | **GN** H *EC* BN | | 11430 (11248) | **GN** H *EC* BN |

## AD1J (FO) — OPEN FIRST

Mark 4. Air conditioned. Converted from TFRB with new interior by Bombardier Wakefield 2005. 46/– 1T. BT41 bogies. ETH 6X.

Lot No. 31046 Metro-Cammell 1989–92. 41.3 t.

| 11998 (10314) | **GN** H *EC* BN | | 11999 (10316) | **GN** H *EC* BN |

## AC2G (TSO) — OPEN STANDARD

Mark 3A. Air conditioned. All refurbished with modified seat backs and new layout and further refurbished with new seat trim. –/76 2T (s –/70 2T 1W, t –/72 2T, z –/70 1TD 1T 2W, § –/45(2) 2T 1W). BT10 bogies. d. ETH 6X.

h National Express East Anglia modified coaches with eight Compin Pegasus seats at saloon ends for "priority" use and a high density layout with more unidirectional seating. –/80 2T.

§ First Great Western Sleeper "day coaches" that have been fitted with former HST First Class seats to a 2+1 layout and are effectively unclassified.

Coaches in **WS** livery have been refurbished for Wrexham & Shropshire. Original Inter-City 70 seats retained, but almost all arranged in a facing layout. –/72 2T.

**Note:** 12169–171 were converted from open composites 11908–10, formerly FOs 11008–10.

**12005–12167.** Lot No. 30877 Derby 1975–77. 34.3 t.
**12169–12171.** Lot No. 30878 Derby 1975–76. 34.3 t.

| 12005 | h | **1** | P | *EA* | NC |
| 12008 | | **V** | P | | LM |
| 12009 | h | **1** | P | *EA* | NC |
| 12011 | | **VT** | P | *VW* | WB |
| 12012 | h | **1** | P | *EA* | NC |
| 12013 | h | **1** | P | *EA* | NC |
| 12014 | t | **BG** | CG | *WS* | CE |
| 12015 | h | **1** | P | *EA* | NC |
| 12016 | | **1** | P | *EA* | NC |
| 12017 | | **V** | DB | | WN |
| 12019 | h | **1** | P | *EA* | NC |
| 12021 | | **NX** | P | *EA* | NC |
| 12022 | | **V** | P | | LM |
| 12024 | h | **1** | P | *EA* | NC |
| 12026 | h | **1** | P | *EA* | NC |
| 12027 | h | **1** | P | *EA* | NC |
| 12029 | | **V** | P | | LM |
| 12030 | h | **1** | P | *EA* | NC |
| 12031 | | **1** | P | *EA* | NC |
| 12032 | h | **1** | P | *EA* | NC |
| 12034 | h | **1** | P | *EA* | NC |
| 12035 | h | **NX** | P | *EA* | NC |
| 12036 | s | **V** | P | | LM |
| 12037 | h | **1** | P | *EA* | NC |
| 12038 | s | **BG** | CG | *WS* | CE |
| 12040 | h | **1** | P | *EA* | NC |
| 12041 | h | **1** | P | *EA* | NC |
| 12042 | h | **1** | P | *EA* | NC |
| 12043 | s | **BG** | CG | *WS* | CE |
| 12045 | | **V** | P | | LM |
| 12046 | h | **1** | P | *EA* | NC |
| 12047 | z | **V** | P | | LM |
| 12048 | | **WS** | DB | *WS* | AL |
| 12049 | | **1** | P | *EA* | NC |
| 12051 | h | **NX** | P | *EA* | NC |
| 12053 | t | **BG** | CG | *CG* | BH |
| 12054 | s | **V** | DB | | WN |
| 12056 | h | **1** | P | *EA* | NC |
| 12057 | h | **1** | P | *EA* | NC |
| 12058 | | **V** | ST | | LM |
| 12059 | | **WS** | DB | *WS* | AL |
| 12060 | h | **1** | P | *EA* | NC |
| 12061 | h | **1** | P | *EA* | NC |
| 12062 | h | **1** | P | *EA* | NC |

| | | | | | | | | | | |
|---|---|---|---|---|---|---|---|---|---|---|
| 12063 | | **V** | P | | NC | | 12120 | h | **1** | P |
| | | | | | | | | | | |

| No. | | Col1 | Col2 | Col3 | Col4 |
|---|---|---|---|---|---|
| 12063 | | **V** | P | | NC |
| 12064 | | **1** | P | *EA* | NC |
| 12065 | | **V** | P | | NC |
| 12066 | h | **1** | P | *EA* | NC |
| 12067 | | **1** | P | *EA* | NC |
| 12069 | | **WS** | DB | *WS* | AL |
| 12072 | | **WS** | DB | *WS* | AL |
| 12073 | h | **1** | P | *EA* | NC |
| 12078 | | **VT** | P | *VW* | WB |
| 12079 | | **1** | P | *EA* | NC |
| 12081 | | **1** | P | *EA* | NC |
| 12082 | h | **1** | P | *EA* | NC |
| 12083 | | **V** | P | | LM |
| 12084 | h | **1** | P | *EA* | NC |
| 12087 | s | **V** | P | | LM |
| 12089 | | **1** | P | *EA* | NC |
| 12090 | h | **1** | P | *EA* | NC |
| 12091 | h | **1** | P | *EA* | NC |
| 12092 | | **V** | P | | NC |
| 12093 | | **1** | P | *EA* | NC |
| 12094 | | **V** | DB | | WN |
| 12095 | | **V** | P | | LM |
| 12097 | h | **1** | P | *EA* | NC |
| 12098 | | **1** | P | *EA* | NC |
| 12099 | h | **1** | P | *EA* | NC |
| 12100 | § | **FD** | P | *GW* | PZ |
| 12101 | s | **V** | P | | LM |
| 12103 | | **1** | P | *EA* | NC |
| 12104 | | **V** | ST | | LM |
| 12105 | h | **1** | P | *EA* | NC |
| 12107 | h | **1** | P | *EA* | NC |
| 12108 | | **1** | P | *EA* | NC |
| 12109 | h | **1** | P | *EA* | NC |
| 12110 | h | **1** | P | *EA* | NC |
| 12111 | | **1** | P | *EA* | NC |
| 12114 | h | **1** | P | *EA* | NC |
| 12115 | h | **1** | P | *EA* | NC |
| 12116 | h | **1** | P | *EA* | NC |
| 12117 | | **WS** | DB | *WS* | AL |
| 12118 | | **1** | P | *EA* | NC |
| 12119 | s | **BG** | CG | *WS* | CE |
| 12120 | h | **1** | P | *EA* | NC |
| 12122 | z | **VT** | P | *VW* | WB |
| 12124 | | **V** | DB | | WN |
| 12125 | h | **1** | P | *EA* | NC |
| 12126 | h | **1** | P | *EA* | NC |
| 12127 | | **WS** | DB | *WS* | AL |
| 12129 | h | **NX** | P | *EA* | NC |
| 12130 | h | **1** | P | *EA* | NC |
| 12131 | | **WS** | DB | *WS* | AL |
| 12132 | | **NX** | P | *EA* | NC |
| 12133 | | **VT** | P | *VW* | WB |
| 12134 | | **V** | P | | LM |
| 12137 | h | **1** | P | *EA* | NC |
| 12138 | | **VT** | P | *VW* | WB |
| 12139 | | **V** | P | | NC |
| 12141 | | **1** | P | *EA* | NC |
| 12142 | z | **V** | P | | LM |
| 12143 | | **1** | P | *EA* | NC |
| 12144 | s | **V** | P | | LM |
| 12145 | | **WS** | DB | *WS* | AL |
| 12146 | | **1** | P | *EA* | NC |
| 12147 | | **1** | P | *EA* | NC |
| 12148 | | **1** | P | *EA* | NC |
| 12150 | h | **1** | P | *EA* | NC |
| 12151 | | **1** | P | *EA* | NC |
| 12153 | | **1** | P | *EA* | NC |
| 12154 | h | **1** | P | *EA* | NC |
| 12156 | | **V** | P | | LM |
| 12158 | | **V** | P | | LM |
| 12159 | | **1** | P | *EA* | NC |
| 12160 | s | **V** | P | | LM |
| 12161 | § | **FD** | P | *GW* | PZ |
| 12163 | | **V** | P | | LM |
| 12164 | | **1** | P | *EA* | NC |
| 12165 | | **V** | ST | | LM |
| 12166 | | **1** | P | *EA* | NC |
| 12167 | h | **1** | P | *EA* | NC |
| 12169 | | **WS** | DB | *WS* | AL |
| 12170 | | **1** | P | *EA* | NC |
| 12171 | | **1** | P | *EA* | NC |

## AI2J (TSOE)    OPEN STANDARD (END)

Mark 4. Air conditioned. Rebuilt with new interior by Bombardier Wakefield 2003–05. Separate area for 26 smokers, although smoking is no longer allowed. –/76 1T. BT41 bogies. ETH 6X.

**Note:** 12232 was converted from the original 12405.

**12200–12231.** Lot No. 31047 Metro-Cammell 1989–91. 39.5 t.
**12232.** Lot No. 31049 Metro-Cammell 1989–92. 39.5 t.

| | | | | | | | | |
|---|---|---|---|---|---|---|---|---|
| 12200 | **GN** | H *EC* | BN | | 12217 | **GN** | H *EC* | BN |
| 12201 | **GN** | H *EC* | BN | | 12218 | **GN** | H *EC* | BN |
| 12202 | **GN** | H *EC* | BN | | 12219 | **GN** | H *EC* | BN |
| 12203 | **GN** | H *EC* | BN | | 12220 | **GN** | H *EC* | BN |
| 12204 | **GN** | H *EC* | BN | | 12222 | **GN** | H *EC* | BN |
| 12205 | **GN** | H *EC* | BN | | 12223 | **GN** | H *EC* | BN |
| 12207 | **GN** | H *EC* | BN | | 12224 | **GN** | H *EC* | BN |
| 12208 | **GN** | H *EC* | BN | | 12225 | **GN** | H *EC* | BN |
| 12209 | **GN** | H *EC* | BN | | 12226 | **GN** | H *EC* | BN |
| 12210 | **GN** | H *EC* | BN | | 12227 | **GN** | H *EC* | BN |
| 12211 | **GN** | H *EC* | BN | | 12228 | **GN** | H *EC* | BN |
| 12212 | **GN** | H *EC* | BN | | 12229 | **GN** | H *EC* | BN |
| 12213 | **GN** | H *EC* | BN | | 12230 | **GN** | H *EC* | BN |
| 12214 | **GN** | H *EC* | BN | | 12231 | **GN** | H *EC* | BN |
| 12215 | **GN** | H *EC* | BN | | 12232 | **GN** | H *EC* | BN |
| 12216 | **GN** | H *EC* | BN | | | | | |

# AL2J (TSOD) OPEN STANDARD (DISABLED ACCESS)

Mark 4. Air conditioned. Rebuilt with new interior by Bombardier Wakefield 2003–05. –/68 2W 1TD. BT41 bogies. ETH 6X.

**Note:** 12331 has been converted from TSO 12531.

**12300–12330.** Lot No. 31048 Metro-Cammell 1989–91. 39.4 t.
**12331.** Lot No. 31049 Metro-Cammell 1989–92. 39.4 t.

| | | | | | | | | |
|---|---|---|---|---|---|---|---|---|
| 12300 | **GN** | H *EC* | BN | | 12317 | **GN** | H *EC* | BN |
| 12301 | **GN** | H *EC* | BN | | 12318 | **GN** | H *EC* | BN |
| 12302 | **GN** | H *EC* | BN | | 12319 | **GN** | H *EC* | BN |
| 12303 | **GN** | H *EC* | BN | | 12320 | **GN** | H *EC* | BN |
| 12304 | **GN** | H *EC* | BN | | 12321 | **GN** | H *EC* | BN |
| 12305 | **GN** | H *EC* | BN | | 12322 | **GN** | H *EC* | BN |
| 12307 | **GN** | H *EC* | BN | | 12323 | **GN** | H *EC* | BN |
| 12308 | **GN** | H *EC* | BN | | 12324 | **GN** | H *EC* | BN |
| 12309 | **GN** | H *EC* | BN | | 12325 | **GN** | H *EC* | BN |
| 12310 | **GN** | H *EC* | BN | | 12326 | **GN** | H *EC* | BN |
| 12311 | **GN** | H *EC* | BN | | 12327 | **GN** | H *EC* | BN |
| 12312 | **GN** | H *EC* | BN | | 12328 | **GN** | H *EC* | BN |
| 12313 | **GN** | H *EC* | BN | | 12329 | **GN** | H *EC* | BN |
| 12315 | **GN** | H *EC* | BN | | 12330 | **GN** | H *EC* | BN |
| 12316 | **GN** | H *EC* | BN | | 12331 | **GN** | H *EC* | BN |

# AC2J (TSO)                          OPEN STANDARD

Mark 4. Air conditioned. Rebuilt with new interior by Bombardier Wakefield 2003–05. –/76 1T. BT41 bogies. ETH 6X.
Lot No. 31049 Metro-Cammell 1989–92. 40.8 t.

**Note:** 12405 is the second coach to carry that number. It was built from the bodyshell originally intended for 12221. The original 12405 is now 12232.

| | | | | | | | | |
|---|---|---|---|---|---|---|---|---|
| 12400 | **GN** | H *EC* | BN | | 12452 | **GN** | H *EC* | BN |
| 12401 | **GN** | H *EC* | BN | | 12453 | **GN** | H *EC* | BN |
| 12402 | **GN** | H *EC* | BN | | 12454 | **GN** | H *EC* | BN |
| 12403 | **GN** | H *EC* | BN | | 12455 | **GN** | H *EC* | BN |
| 12404 | **GN** | H *EC* | BN | | 12456 | **GN** | H *EC* | BN |
| 12405 | **GN** | H *EC* | BN | | 12457 | **GN** | H *EC* | BN |
| 12406 | **GN** | H *EC* | BN | | 12458 | **GN** | H *EC* | BN |
| 12407 | **GN** | H *EC* | BN | | 12459 | **GN** | H *EC* | BN |
| 12409 | **GN** | H *EC* | BN | | 12460 | **GN** | H *EC* | BN |
| 12410 | **GN** | H *EC* | BN | | 12461 | **GN** | H *EC* | BN |
| 12411 | **GN** | H *EC* | BN | | 12462 | **GN** | H *EC* | BN |
| 12414 | **GN** | H *EC* | BN | | 12463 | **GN** | H *EC* | BN |
| 12415 | **GN** | H *EC* | BN | | 12464 | **GN** | H *EC* | BN |
| 12417 | **GN** | H *EC* | BN | | 12465 | **GN** | H *EC* | BN |
| 12419 | **GN** | H *EC* | BN | | 12466 | **GN** | H *EC* | BN |
| 12420 | **GN** | H *EC* | BN | | 12467 | **GN** | H *EC* | BN |
| 12421 | **GN** | H *EC* | BN | | 12468 | **GN** | H *EC* | BN |
| 12422 | **GN** | H *EC* | BN | | 12469 | **GN** | H *EC* | BN |
| 12423 | **GN** | H *EC* | BN | | 12470 | **GN** | H *EC* | BN |
| 12424 | **GN** | H *EC* | BN | | 12471 | **GN** | H *EC* | BN |
| 12425 | **GN** | H *EC* | BN | | 12472 | **GN** | H *EC* | BN |
| 12426 | **GN** | H *EC* | BN | | 12473 | **GN** | H *EC* | BN |
| 12427 | **GN** | H *EC* | BN | | 12474 | **GN** | H *EC* | BN |
| 12428 | **GN** | H *EC* | BN | | 12476 | **GN** | H *EC* | BN |
| 12429 | **GN** | H *EC* | BN | | 12477 | **GN** | H *EC* | BN |
| 12430 | **GN** | H *EC* | BN | | 12478 | **GN** | H *EC* | BN |
| 12431 | **GN** | H *EC* | BN | | 12480 | **GN** | H *EC* | BN |
| 12432 | **GN** | H *EC* | BN | | 12481 | **GN** | H *EC* | BN |
| 12433 | **GN** | H *EC* | BN | | 12483 | **GN** | H *EC* | BN |
| 12434 | **GN** | H *EC* | BN | | 12484 | **GN** | H *EC* | BN |
| 12436 | **GN** | H *EC* | BN | | 12485 | **GN** | H *EC* | BN |
| 12437 | **GN** | H *EC* | BN | | 12486 | **GN** | H *EC* | BN |
| 12438 | **GN** | H *EC* | BN | | 12488 | **GN** | H *EC* | BN |
| 12439 | **GN** | H *EC* | BN | | 12489 | **GN** | H *EC* | BN |
| 12440 | **GN** | H *EC* | BN | | 12513 | **GN** | H *EC* | BN |
| 12441 | **GN** | H *EC* | BN | | 12514 | **GN** | H *EC* | BN |
| 12442 | **GN** | H *EC* | BN | | 12515 | **GN** | H *EC* | BN |
| 12443 | **GN** | H *EC* | BN | | 12518 | **GN** | H *EC* | BN |
| 12444 | **GN** | H *EC* | BN | | 12519 | **GN** | H *EC* | BN |
| 12445 | **GN** | H *EC* | BN | | 12520 | **GN** | H *EC* | BN |
| 12446 | **GN** | H *EC* | BN | | 12522 | **GN** | H *EC* | BN |
| 12447 | **GN** | H *EC* | BN | | 12526 | **GN** | H *EC* | BN |
| 12448 | **GN** | H *EC* | BN | | 12533 | **GN** | H *EC* | BN |
| 12449 | **GN** | H *EC* | BN | | 12534 | **GN** | H *EC* | BN |
| 12450 | **GN** | H *EC* | BN | | 12538 | **GN** | H *EC* | BN |

## AA11 (FK) CORRIDOR FIRST

Mark 1. 42/– 2T. ETH 3.

Lot No. 30381 Swindon 1959. B4 bogies. 33 t.

| 13229 | xk | **M** | BK | *BK* | BT | | 13230 | xk | **M** | BK | *BK* | BT |

## AA11 (RK) KITCHEN CAR

Mark 1. ETH 3.

Lot No. 30667 Swindon 1961. Commonwealth bogies. This coach was converted in 2008 from an FK to a kitchen car with staff accommodation. 37 t.

| 13321 | x | **M** | WC | *WC* | CS | |

## AA1A (FK) CORRIDOR FIRST

Mark 2A. Pressure ventilated. 42/– 2T. B4 bogies. ETH 4.

Lot No. 30774 Derby 1968. 33 t.

| 13440 | v | **G** | WC | *WC* | CS | |

## AB11 (BFK) CORRIDOR BRAKE FIRST

Mark 1. 24/– 1T. Commonwealth bogies. ETH 2.

Lot No. 30668 Swindon 1961. 36 t.

Originally numbered in 14xxx series and then renumbered in 17xxx series.

| 17015 | x | **CC** | RV | *RV* | EH | | 17018 | v | **CH** | VT | | TM |

## AB1A (BFK) CORRIDOR BRAKE FIRST

Mark 2A. Pressure ventilated. 24/– 1T. B4 bogies. ETH 4.

**17056–17077.** Lot No. 30775 Derby 1967–8. 32 t.
**17080–17102.** Lot No. 30786 Derby 1968. 32 t.

Originally numbered 14056–102. 17080/090 were numbered 35516/503 for a time when declassified.

| 17056 | **M** | RV | *RV* | EH | | 17090 | v | **CH** | H | | TM |
| 17077 | **RV** | RV | *RV* | EH | | 17102 | | **M** | WC | *WC* | CS |
| 17080 | **PC** | RA | *RA* | EH | | | | | | | |

## AX5B COUCHETTE/GENERATOR COACH

Mark 2B. Formerly part of Royal Train. Converted from a BFK built 1969. Consists of luggage accommodation, guard's compartment, 350 kW diesel generator and staff sleeping accommodation. Pressure ventilated. B5 bogies. ETH 5X.

**Non-standard livery:** 17105 Oxford blue.

Lot No. 30888 Wolverton 1977. 46 t.

17105   (14105, 2905)          **0**    RV    *RV*        EH

# AB1D (BFK)                    CORRIDOR BRAKE FIRST

Mark 2D. Air conditioned (Stones equipment). 24/– 1T. B4 Bogies. ETH 5.

Lot No. 30823 Derby 1971–72. 33.5 t.

Originally numbered 14159–68.

| | | | | | |
|---|---|---|---|---|---|
| 17159 | (14159) | **DR** | DR | | ZG |
| 17167 | (14167) | **VN** | VS | *VS* | CP |
| 17168 | (14168) | d **M** | WC | | CS |

# AE1H (BUO)          UNCLASSIFIED OPEN BRAKE

Mark 3B. Air conditioned. Fitted with hydraulic handbrake. Used by First Great Western as Sleeper "day coaches" that have been fitted with former HST First Class seats to a 2+1 layout and are effectively unclassified. 36/– 1T. BT10 bogies. pg. d. ETH 5X.

Lot No. 30990 Derby 1986. 35.81 t.

| | | | | | | | | | |
|---|---|---|---|---|---|---|---|---|---|
| 17173 | **FD** P | *GW* PZ | | 17175 | **FD** P | *GW* PZ |
| 17174 | **FD** P | *GW* PZ | | | | |

# AA21 (SK)                       CORRIDOR STANDARD

Mark 1. Each vehicle has eight compartments. All remaining vehicles have metal window frames and melamine interior panelling. Commonwealth bogies. –/48 2T. ETH 4.

Lot No. 30685 Derby 1961–62. 36 t.

t Rebuilt internally as TSO using components from 4936. –/64 2T.

Originally numbered 25756–25862.

| | | | | | | | | | |
|---|---|---|---|---|---|---|---|---|---|
| 18756 | x **M** | WC | *WC* CS | | 18808 | x | **M** | WC | *WC* CS |
| 18767 | x **M** | WC | *WC* CS | | 18862 | x | **M** | WC | *WC* CS |
| 18806 | xt **M** | WC | *WC* CS | | | | | | |

# AB31 (BCK)          CORRIDOR BRAKE COMPOSITE

Mark 1. There are two variants depending upon whether the Standard Class compartments have armrests. Each vehicle has two First Class and three Standard Class compartments. 12/18 2T (* 12/24 2T). Commonwealth bogies. ETH 2.

**Non-standard livery:** 21269 British racing green & cream lined out in gold.

**21241–21245.** Lot No. 30669 Swindon 1961–62. Commonwealth bogies. 36 t.
**21256.** Lot No. 30731 Derby 1963. Commonwealth bogies. 37 t.
**21266–21272.** Lot No. 30732 Derby 1964. Commonwealth bogies. 37 t.

| | | | | | | | | | |
|---|---|---|---|---|---|---|---|---|---|
| 21241 | x **CC** | BK | *BK* | BT | | 21266 | x* **M** | WC | *WC* CS |
| 21245 | x **M** | RV | *RV* | EH | | 21269 | * **0** | RV | *RV* EH |
| 21256 | x **M** | WC | *WC* | CS | | 21272 | x* **CH** | RV | *RV* EH |

## AB21 (BSK)          CORRIDOR BRAKE STANDARD

Mark 1. Four compartments. Lot 30721 has metal window frames and melamine interior panelling. –/24 1T. ETH2.

g Fitted with an e.t.s. generator. Weight unknown.

**35185.** Lot No. 30427 Wolverton 1959. B4 bogies. 33 t.
**35459–35469.** Lot No. 30721 Wolverton 1963. Commonwealth bogies. 37 t.

| | | | | | | | | | |
|---|---|---|---|---|---|---|---|---|---|
| 35185 | x | **M** | BK | *BK* | BT | | | | |
| 35459 | x | **M** | WC | *WC* | CS | | 35469 | xg | **CC** | RV | *RV* | EH |

## AB5C                    BRAKE/POWER KITCHEN

Mark 2C. Pressure ventilated. Converted from BFK (declassified to BSK) built 1970. Converted at West Coast Railway Company 2000–01. Consists of 60 kVA generator, guard's compartment and electric kitchen. B5 bogies. ETH 4.

**Non-standard livery:** British Racing Green with gold lining.

Lot No. 30796 Derby 1969–70. 32.5 t.

| | | | | |
|---|---|---|---|---|
| 35511 | (14130, 17130) | **0** | RA | Railway Restorations North-East, Shildon |

## AK51 (RK)                       KITCHEN CAR

Mark 1. Converted 1989/2006 from RBR. Buffet and seating area replaced with additional kitchen and food preparation area. Fluorescent lighting. Commonwealth bogies. ETH 2X.

Lot No. 30628 Pressed Steel 1960–61. 39 t.

| | | | | | | |
|---|---|---|---|---|---|---|
| 80041 | (1690) | x | **M** | RV | *RV* | EH |
| 80042 | (1646) | | **DR** | DR | | ZG |

## NZ (DLV)        DRIVING BRAKE VAN (110 m.p.h.)

Mark 3B. Air conditioned. T4 bogies. dg. ETH 5X.

Lot No. 31042 Derby 1988. 45.18 t.

**Non-standard livery:** 82146 EWS silver.

| | | | | | | | | | |
|---|---|---|---|---|---|---|---|---|---|
| 82101 | **V** | P | *VW* | WB | | 82112 | **1** | P | *EA* | NC |
| 82102 | **1** | P | *EA* | NC | | 82113 | **V** | DB | | LM |
| 82103 | **1** | P | *EA* | NC | | 82114 | **1** | P | *EA* | NC |
| 82104 | **V** | P | | NC | | 82115 | **B** | P | | ZN |
| 82105 | **1** | P | *EA* | NC | | 82116 | **V** | DB | | LM |
| 82106 | **V** | CG | | LM | | 82118 | **1** | P | *EA* | NC |
| 82107 | **NX** | P | *EA* | NC | | 82120 | **V** | DB | | LM |
| 82108 | **V** | DB | | LM | | 82121 | **1** | P | *EA* | NC |
| 82110 | **V** | P | | LM | | 82122 | **V** | DB | | LM |
| 82111 | **V** | P | | LM | | 82123 | **V** | DB | | LM |

| | | | | | | | | |
|---|---|---|---|---|---|---|---|---|
| 82124 | **V** | P | | LM | 82138 | **V** | DB | | CE |
| 82125 | **V** | P | | LM | 82139 | **1** | P | *EA* | NC |
| 82126 | **VT** | P | *VW* | WB | 82140 | **V** | P | | LM |
| 82127 | **1** | P | *EA* | NC | 82141 | **V** | P | | LM |
| 82128 | **V** | P | | LM | 82143 | **1** | P | *EA* | NC |
| 82129 | **V** | P | | LM | 82144 | **V** | DB | | LM |
| 82131 | **V** | DB | | LM | 82145 | **V** | P | | LM |
| 82132 | **1** | P | *EA* | NC | 82146 | **0** | DB | *DB* | TO |
| 82133 | **1** | P | *EA* | NC | 82148 | **V** | DB | | LM |
| 82136 | **1** | P | *EA* | NC | 82150 | **V** | DB | | LM |
| 82137 | **V** | DB | | LM | 82152 | **1** | P | *EA* | NC |

## NZ (DLV)        DRIVING BRAKE VAN (140 m.p.h.)

Mark 4. Air conditioned. Swiss-built (SIG) bogies. dg. ETH 6X.

Fitted with transceiver "domes" for wi-fi.

Lot No. 31043 Metro-Cammell 1988. 43.5 t.

| | | | | | | | | | |
|---|---|---|---|---|---|---|---|---|---|
| 82200 | **GN** | H | *EC* | BN | 82216 | **GN** | H | *EC* | BN |
| 82201 | **GN** | H | *EC* | BN | 82217 | **GN** | H | *EC* | BN |
| 82202 | **GN** | H | *EC* | BN | 82218 | **GN** | H | *EC* | BN |
| 82203 | **GN** | H | *EC* | BN | 82219 | **GN** | H | *EC* | BN |
| 82204 | **GN** | H | *EC* | BN | 82220 | **GN** | H | *EC* | BN |
| 82205 | **GN** | H | *EC* | BN | 82222 | **GN** | H | *EC* | BN |
| 82206 | **GN** | H | *EC* | BN | 82223 | **GN** | H | *EC* | BN |
| 82207 | **GN** | H | *EC* | BN | 82224 | **GN** | H | *EC* | BN |
| 82208 | **GN** | H | *EC* | BN | 82225 | **GN** | H | *EC* | BN |
| 82209 | **GN** | H | *EC* | BN | 82226 | **GN** | H | *EC* | BN |
| 82210 | **GN** | H | *EC* | BN | 82227 | **GN** | H | *EC* | BN |
| 82211 | **GN** | H | *EC* | BN | 82228 | **GN** | H | *EC* | BN |
| 82212 | **GN** | H | *EC* | BN | 82229 | **GN** | H | *EC* | BN |
| 82213 | **GN** | H | *EC* | BN | 82230 | **GN** | H | *EC* | BN |
| 82214 | **GN** | H | *EC* | BN | 82231 | **GN** | H | *EC* | BN |
| 82215 | **GN** | H | *EC* | BN | | | | | |

## NZ (DLV)        DRIVING BRAKE VAN (110 m.p.h.)

Mark 3B. Air conditioned. T4 bogies. dg. ETH 6X.

Lot No. 31042 Derby 1988. 45.2 t.

These vehicles have been converted for use on Wrexham & Shropshire services.
Converted to operate in push-pull mode with 67010/012–015/029.

| | | | | | | |
|---|---|---|---|---|---|---|
| 82301 | (82117) | **WS** | DB | *WS* | AL |
| 82302 | (82151) | **CR** | DB | *WS* | AL |
| 82303 | (82135) | **WS** | DB | *WS* | AL |
| 82304 | (82130) | **WS** | DB | *WS* | AL |
| 82305 | (82134) | **WS** | DB | *WS* | AL |

# NE (BG) GANGWAYED BRAKE VAN (100 m.p.h.)

Mark 1. Short frame. Load 10 t. Adapted 199? for use as Brake Luggage Van. Guard's compartment retained and former baggage area adapted for secure stowage of passengers' luggage. B4 bogies. 100 m.p.h. ETH1X.

Lot No. 30162 Pressed Steel 1956–57. 30.5 t.

92904  (80867, 99554)  **VN**  VS  *VS*  CP

# NYMR COACHES FOR PASSENGER USE BETWEEN MIDDLESBROUGH & WHITBY ONLY

These coaches are permitted to operate on the National Rail system but may only be used to convey fare-paying passengers between Middlesbrough and Whitby on the Esk Valley branch line as an extension of North Yorkshire Moors Railway services between Pickering and Grosmont. Only those coaches currently registered for use on the National Rail system are listed here.

## AJ11 (RF)                          RESTAURANT FIRST

Mark 1. –/44 2T. Commonwealth bogies. 24/–. ETH 2.

Lot No. 30633 Swindon 1961. 42.5 t.

| 324 | x | **PC** | NY /NY | NY | | JOS de CRAU |
|-----|---|--------|--------|----|--|-------------|

## AN21 (RMB)
### OPEN STANDARD WITH MINIATURE BUFFET

Mark 1. –/44 2T. BR Mark 1 bogies. For details see page .

Lot No. 30520 Wolverton 1960. 38 t.

| 1823 | v | **M** | NY /NY | NY | | &#124; |
|------|---|-------|--------|----|--|---|

## AC21 (TSO)                              OPEN STANDARD

Mark 1. –/64 2T (* –/60 2W 2T, † –/60 3W 1T). BR Mark 1 bogies. ETH 4.

**3860/3872.** Lot No. 30080 York 1954. 33 t.
**3948.** Lot No. 30086 Eastleigh 1954–55. 33 t.
**4198/4252.** Lot No. 30172 York 1956. 33 t.
**4286/4290.** Lot No. 30207 BRCW 1956. 33 t.
**4455.** Lot No. 30226 BRCW 1957. 33 t.

| 3860 | v* | **M**  | NY /NY | NY | | 4252 | v* | **CC** | NY /NY | NY |
|------|----|--------|--------|----|--|------|----|--------|--------|----|
| 3872 | v† | **BG** | NY /NY | NY | | 4286 | v  | **CC** | NY /NY | NY |
| 3948 | v  | **CC** | NY /NY | NY | | 4290 | v  | **M**  | NY /NY | NY |
| 4198 | v  | **CC** | NY /NY | NY | | 4455 | v  | **CC** | NY /NY | NY |

## AD21 (TSO)                              OPEN STANDARD

Mark 1. –/48 2T. BR Mark 1 bogies. ETH 4.

**4786.** Lot No. 30376 York 1957. 33 t.
**4817.** Lot No. 30473 BRCW 1959. 33 t.

| 4786 | v | **M** | NY /NY | NY | | 4817 | v | **M** | NY /NY | NY |
|------|---|-------|--------|----|--|------|---|-------|--------|----|

## AC21 (TSO)     OPEN STANDARD

Mark 1. Later vehicles built with Commonwealth bogies. –/64 2T. ETH 4.
Lot No. 30690 Wolverton 1961–62. Aluminium window frames. 37 t.

5000 v   **M**   NY   *NY*   NY   | 5029 v   **CH**   NY   *NY*   NY

## AE21 (BSO)     OPEN BRAKE STANDARD

Mark 1. –/39 1T. BR Mark 1 bogies. ETH 4.
Lot No. 30170 Doncaster 1956. 34 t.

9267   v **BG** NY *NY*   NY   | 9274 v   **M**   NY *NY*    NY

## AA31 (CK)     CORRIDOR COMPOSITE

Mark 1. 24/18 1T. BR Mark 1 bogies. ETH 2.
Lot No. 30665 Derby 1961. 36 t.

16156   v **CC** NY *NY*   NY   |

## AB21 (BSK)     CORRIDOR BRAKE STANDARD

Mark 1. –/24 1T. BR Mark 1 bogies. ETH 2.
Lot No. 30233 Gloucester 1957. 35 t.

35089   v **CC** NY *NY*    NY   |

## PULLMAN BRAKE THIRD

Built 1928 by Metropolitan Carriage & Wagon Company. Gresley bogies. –/30. 37.5 t.

232    v **PC** NY *NY*    NY      CAR No.79

## PULLMAN KITCHEN FIRST

Built by Metro-Cammell 1960–61 for ECML services. Commonwealth bogies. 20/– 2T. ETH 4. 41.2 t.

318    x **PC** NY *NY*    NY      ROBIN

## PULLMAN PARLOUR FIRST

Built by Metro-Cammell 1960–61 for ECML services. Commonwealth bogies. 29/– 2T. 38.5 t.

328    x **PC** NY *NY*    NY      OPAL

# 2.2. HIGH SPEED TRAIN TRAILER CARS

HSTs consist of a number of trailer cars (usually seven to nine) with a power car at each end. All trailer cars are classified Mark 3 and have BT10 bogies with disc brakes and central door locking. Heating is by a 415 V three-phase supply and vehicles have air conditioning. Maximum speed is 125 m.p.h.

The trailer cars have one standard bodyshell for both First and Standard Class, thus facilitating easy conversion from one class to the other. As built all cars had facing seating around tables with Standard Class coaches having nine bays of seats per side which did not line up with the eight windows per side. This created a new unwelcome trend in British rolling stock of seats not lining up with windows.

All vehicles underwent a mid-life refurbishment in the 1980s with Standard Class seating layouts revised to incorporate unidirectional seating in addition to facing, in a somewhat higgeldy-piggeldy layout where seats did not line up either side of the aisle.

A further refurbishment programme was completed in November 2000, with each train operating company having a different scheme as follows:

**First Great Western.** Green seat covers and extra partitions between seat bays.

**Great North Eastern Railway.** New ceiling lighting panels and brown seat covers. First Class vehicles have table lamps and imitation walnut plastic end panels.

**Virgin Cross-Country.** Green seat covers. Standard Class vehicles had four seats in the centre of each carriage replaced with a luggage stack. All have now passed to other operators.

**Midland Mainline.** Grey seat covers, redesigned seat squabs, side carpeting and two seats in the centre of each standard class carriage and one in First Class carriages replaced with a luggage stack.

Since then the remaining three operators of HSTs have embarked on separate, and very different, refurbishment projects:

**Midland Mainline** was first to refurbish its vehicles a second time during 2003–04. This involved fitting new fluorescent and halogen ceiling lighting, although the original seats were retained in First and Standard Class, but with blue upholstery.

London St Pancras–Sheffield/Leeds and Nottingham services are now operated by **East Midlands Trains** and in late summer 2009 this operator embarked on another, less radical, refurbishment which included retention of the original seats but with red upholstery in Standard Class and blue in First Class. This programme was due for completion by late 2010.

**First Great Western** started a major rebuild of its HST sets in late 2006, with the programme completed in spring 2008. With an increased fleet of 54 sets the new interiors feature new lighting and seating throughout. First Class seats have leather upholstery, and are made by Primarius UK. Standard Class seats are of high-back design by Grammer. A small number of sets operate without a buffet car and 19 TS vehicles are currently being converted to TSRMB vehicles with a "mini buffet" area for use on shorter distance services.

**GNER** modernised its buffet cars with new corner bars in 2004 and at the same time each HST set was made up to 9-cars with an extra Standard Class vehicle added with a disabled person's toilet.

At the end of 2006 **GNER** embarked on a major rebuild of its sets, with the work being carried out at Wabtec, Doncaster. All vehicles will have similar interiors to the Mark 4 "Mallard" fleet, with new Primarius seats throughout. The refurbishment of 13 sets was completed in late 2009, now operated by **East Coast** (the DfT) following the demise of National Express East Coast.

Ten sets ex-Virgin Cross-Country, and some spare vehicles, were temporarily allocated to Midland Mainline for the interim service to Manchester during 2003–04 and had a facelift. Buffet cars were converted from TRSB to TRFB and renumbered in the 408xx series. These vehicles are now in use with First Great Western or East Coast.

Open access operator **Grand Central** started operation in December 2007 with a new service from Sunderland to London King's Cross. This operator has three sets mostly using stock converted from loco-hauled Mark 3s. The seats in Standard Class have First Class spacing and in some vehicles are all facing.

**CrossCountry** reintroduced HSTs to the Cross-Country network from summer 2008 using ex-Midland Mainline sets. Five sets have been refurbished at Wabtec, Doncaster for regular use on the Plymouth–Edinburgh corridor. Three of these sets use stock mostly converted from loco-hauled Mark 3s and two are sets ex-Midland Mainline. The interiors are similar to refurbished NXEC sets, although the seating layout is different and one toilet per coach has been removed for a luggage stack.

## TOPS Type Codes

TOPS type codes for HST trailer cars are made up as follows:

(1) Two letters denoting the layout of the vehicle as follows:

| | | | |
|---|---|---|---|
| GH | Open | GL | Kitchen |
| GJ | Open with Guard's compartment | GN | Buffet |

(2) A digit for the class of passenger accommodation

| | | | |
|---|---|---|---|
| 1 | First | 3 | Composite |
| 2 | Standard (formerly second) | | |

(3) A suffix relating to the build of coach.

G    Mark 3

## Operator Codes

The normal operator codes are given in brackets after the TOPS codes. These are as follows:

| | | | |
|---|---|---|---|
| TCC | Trailer Composite Catering | TRSB | Trailer Buffet Standard |
| TF | Trailer First | TS | Trailer Standard |
| TGS | Trailer Guard's Standard | TSRMB | Trailer Standard with |
| TRB | Trailer Buffet First | | Miniature Buffet |
| TRFB | Trailer Kitchen Buffet First | | |

## GN2G (TSRMB)
# TRAILER STANDARD WITH MINIATURE BUFFET

19 vehicles are being converted from HST TSs for First Great Western. Refurbished with Grammer seating.

**40101–40119.** For Lot No. details see TS. –/70 1T.   . t.

| | | | | |
|---|---|---|---|---|
| 40101 | (42170) | **FD** | P | |
| 40102 | (42223) | **FD** | P | |
| 40103 | (42316) | **FD** | P | |
| 40104 | (42254) | **FD** | P | |
| 40105 | (42084) | **FD** | P | |
| 40106 | (42162) | **FD** | P | *GW*  OO |
| 40107 | (42334) | **FD** | P | *GW*  OO |
| 40108 | (42314) | **FD** | P | *GW*  OO |
| 40109 | (42262) | **FD** | P | *GW*  OO |
| 40110 | (42187) | **FD** | P | *GW*  OO |
| 40111 | (42248) | **FD** | P | *GW*  OO |
| 40112 | (42336) | **FD** | P | *GW*  OO |
| 40113 | (42309) | **FD** | P | *GW*  OO |
| 40114 | (42086) | **FD** | P | *GW*  OO |
| 40115 | (42320) | **FD** | P | *GW*  OO |
| 40116 | (42147) | **FD** | P | *GW*  OO |
| 40117 | (42249) | **FD** | P | |
| 40118 | (42338) | **FD** | P | |
| 40119 | (42090) | **FD** | P | |

## GN1G (TRFB)                        TRAILER BUFFET FIRST

Converted from TRSB by fitting First Class seats. Renumbered from 404xx series by subtracting 200. 23/–.

**40204–40228.** Lot No. 30883 Derby 1976–77. 36.12 t.
**40231.** Lot No. 30899 Derby 1978–79. 36.12 t.

\* Refurbished First Great Western vehicles. Primarius leather seating.

| | | | | | | | | | | |
|---|---|---|---|---|---|---|---|---|---|---|
| 40204 | \* | **FD** | A | *GW* | LA | 40210 | \* | **FD** | A | *GW* | LA |
| 40205 | \* | **FD** | A | *GW* | LA | 40221 | \* | **FD** | A | *GW* | LA |
| 40207 | \* | **FD** | A | *GW* | LA | 40228 | | **FG** | A | | ZG |
| 40208 | | **FG** | A | | ZG | 40231 | \* | **FD** | A | *GW* | LA |
| 40209 | | **FG** | A | | ZG | | | | | | |

## GK2G (TRSB)           TRAILER BUFFET STANDARD

Renumbered from 400xx series by adding 400. –/33 1W.

**40402–40426.** Lot No. 30883 Derby 1976–77. 36.12 t.
**40433/40434.** Lot No. 30899 Derby 1978–79. 36.12 t.

**Note:** 40433/40434 were numbered 40233/40234 for a time when fitted with 23 First Class seats.

† Fitted with transceiver "dome" for wi-fi.

| | | | | | | | | | |
|---|---|---|---|---|---|---|---|---|---|
| 40402 | **V** | P | | LM | 40424 † | **GC** | ST | *GC* | HT |
| 40403 | **V** | P | | LM | 40426 † | **GC** | ST | *GC* | HT |
| 40416 | **V** | P | | LM | 40433 † | **GC** | ST | *GC* | HT |
| 40419 | **V** | P | | LM | 40434 | **V** | P | | LM |

## GK1G (TRFB)                 TRAILER BUFFET FIRST

These vehicles have larger kitchens than the 402xx and 404xx series vehicles, and are used in trains where full meal service is required. They were renumbered from the 403xx series (in which the seats were unclassified) by adding 400 to the previous number. 17/–.

**40700–40721**. Lot No. 30921 Derby 1978–79. 38.16 t.
**40722–40735**. Lot No. 30940 Derby 1979–80. 38.16 t.
**40736–40753**. Lot No. 30948 Derby 1980–81. 38.16 t.
**40754–40757**. Lot No. 30966 Derby 1982. 38.16 t.

\* Refurbished First Great Western vehicles. Primarius leather seating.
m Refurbished East Coast vehicles with Primarius seating.
† Fitted with transceiver "dome" for wi-fi.

| | | | | | | | | | |
|---|---|---|---|---|---|---|---|---|---|
| 40700 | | **MN** | P | *EM* | NL | 40730 | | **MN** | P | *EM* | NL |
| 40701 | m† | **NX** | P | *EC* | EC | 40731 | | **FD** | A | | ZG |
| 40702 | m† | **NX** | P | *EC* | EC | 40732 | | **MN** | A | | LM |
| 40703 | \* | **FD** | A | *GW* | LA | 40733 | \* | **FD** | A | *GW* | LA |
| 40704 | m† | **NX** | A | *EC* | EC | 40734 | \* | **FD** | A | *GW* | LA |
| 40705 | m† | **NX** | A | *EC* | EC | 40735 | m† | **NX** | A | *EC* | EC |
| 40706 | m† | **NX** | A | *EC* | EC | 40736 | | **FD** | A | | LA |
| 40707 | \* | **FD** | A | *GW* | LA | 40737 | m† | **NX** | A | *EC* | EC |
| 40708 | m† | **NX** | P | *EC* | EC | 40738 | | **FD** | A | *GW* | OO |
| 40709 | | **FG** | A | *GW* | OO | 40739 | \* | **FD** | A | *GW* | LA |
| 40710 | \* | **FD** | A | *GW* | LA | 40740 | m† | **NX** | A | *EC* | EC |
| 40711 | m† | **NX** | A | *EC* | EC | 40741 | | **MN** | P | *EM* | NL |
| 40712 | | **FD** | A | | LM | 40742 | m† | **NX** | A | *EC* | EC |
| 40713 | \* | **FD** | A | *GW* | LA | 40743 | \* | **FD** | A | *GW* | LA |
| 40714 | | **FD** | A | | LM | 40744 | | **FD** | A | *GW* | OO |
| 40715 | \* | **FD** | A | *GW* | LA | 40745 | | **FG** | A | | LA |
| 40716 | \* | **FD** | A | *GW* | LA | 40746 | | **ST** | P | *EM* | NL |
| 40717 | | **FD** | A | | ZG | 40747 | | **FD** | A | | ZG |
| 40718 | \* | **FD** | A | *GW* | OO | 40748 | m† | **NX** | A | *EC* | EC |
| 40720 | m† | **NX** | A | *EC* | EC | 40749 | | **ST** | P | *EM* | NL |
| 40721 | \* | **FD** | A | *GW* | LA | 40750 | m† | **NX** | A | *EC* | EC |
| 40722 | \* | **FD** | A | *GW* | LA | 40751 | | **MN** | P | *EM* | NL |
| 40723 | | **MN** | A | | LM | 40752 | \* | **FD** | A | *GW* | LA |
| 40724 | | **FD** | A | *GW* | OO | 40753 | | **MN** | P | *EM* | NL |
| 40725 | | **FD** | A | *GW* | OO | 40754 | | **ST** | P | *EM* | NL |
| 40726 | | **FD** | A | *GW* | OO | 40755 | \* | **FD** | A | *GW* | LA |
| 40727 | \* | **FD** | A | *GW* | LA | 40756 | | **MN** | P | *EM* | NL |
| 40728 | | **ST** | P | *EM* | NL | 40757 | \* | **FD** | A | *GW* | LA |
| 40729 | | **MN** | P | | NL | | | | | | |

## GL1G (TRFB)                          TRAILER BUFFET FIRST

These vehicles have been converted from TRSBs in the 404xx series to be similar to the 407xx series vehicles. 17/–.

**40801–40803/40805/40808/40809/40811.** Lot No. 30883 Derby 1976–77. 38.16 t.
**40804/40806/40807/40810.** Lot No. 30899 Derby 1978–79. 38.16 t.

**Note:** 40802/40804/40811 were numbered 40212/40232/40211 for a time when fitted with 23 First Class seats.

\* Refurbished First Great Western vehicles. Primarius leather seating.
m  Refurbished East Coast vehicle with Primarius seating.
†   Fitted with transceiver "dome" for wi-fi.

| 40801 | (40027, 40427) | \* | **FD** | P | *GW* | OO |
|-------|----------------|-----|--------|---|------|----|
| 40802 | (40012, 40412) | \* | **FD** | P | *GW* | OO |
| 40803 | (40018, 40418) | \* | **FD** | P | *GW* | OO |
| 40804 | (40032, 40432) | \* | **FD** | P | *GW* | OO |
| 40805 | (40020, 40420) | m† | **NX** | P | *EC* | EC |
| 40806 | (40029, 40429) | \* | **FD** | P | *GW* | OO |
| 40807 | (40035, 40435) | \* | **FD** | P | *GW* | LA |
| 40808 | (40015, 40415) | \* | **FD** | P | *GW* | OO |
| 40809 | (40014, 40414) | \* | **FD** | P | *GW* | LA |
| 40810 | (40030, 40430) | \* | **FD** | P | *GW* | LA |
| 40811 | (40011, 40411) | \* | **FD** | P | *GW* | LA |

## GN1G (TRB)                           TRAILER BUFFET FIRST

Vehicles owned by First Group. Converted from TRSB by First Great Western. Refurbished with Primarius leather seating. 23/–.

**40900/40902/40904.** Lot No. 30883 Derby 1976–77. 36.12 t.
**40901/40903.** Lot No. 30899 Derby 1978–79. 36.12 t.

| 40900 | (40022, 40422) | **FD** | FG | *GW* | LA |
|-------|----------------|--------|-----|------|----|
| 40901 | (40036, 40436) | **FD** | FG | *GW* | LA |
| 40902 | (40023, 40423) | **FD** | FG | *GW* | LA |
| 40903 | (40037, 40437) | **FD** | FG | *GW* | LA |
| 40904 | (40001, 40401) | **FD** | FG | *GW* | LA |

## GH1G (TF)                                    TRAILER FIRST

**41003–41056.** Lot No. 30881 Derby 1976–77. 33.66 t.
**41057–41120.** Lot No. 30896 Derby 1977–78. 33.66 t.
**41121–41148.** Lot No. 30938 Derby 1979–80. 33.66 t.
**41149–41166.** Lot No. 30947 Derby 1980. 33.66 t.
**41167–41169.** Lot No. 30963 Derby 1982. 33.66 t.
**41170.** Lot No. 30967 Derby 1982. Former prototype vehicle. 33.66 t.
**41176.** Lot No. 30897 Derby 1977. 33.66 t.
**41179/41180.** Lot No. 30884 Derby 1976–77. 33.66 t.
**41181–41184/41189.** Lot No. 30939 Derby 1979–80. 33.66 t.
**41185–41187/41191.** Lot No. 30969 Derby 1982. 33.66 t.

**41190.** Lot No. 30882 Derby 1976–77. 33.60 t.
**41192.** Lot No. 30897 Derby 1977–79. 33.60 t.
**41193–41195/41201–41206.** Lot No. 30878 Derby 1975–76. 34.3 t. Converted from Mark 3A FO.

As built and m 48/– 2T.
*   Refurbished First Great Western vehicles. Primarius leather seating.
c   Refurbished CrossCountry vehicles with Primarius seating and 2 tip-up seats. One toilet removed. 40/– 1TD 1W.
m   Refurbished East Coast vehicles with Primarius seating.
s   Fitted with centre luggage stack, disabled toilet and wheelchair space. 46/– 1T 1TD 1W.
w   Wheelchair space. 47/– 2T 1W.
x   Toilet removed for trolley space (FGW). 48/– 1T.

| No. | Code | Op | Own | Livery | Depot |
|---|---|---|---|---|---|
| 41003 | *x | FD | A | GW | LA |
| 41004 | *x | FD | A | GW | OO |
| 41005 | *x | FD | A | GW | OO |
| 41006 | *w | FD | A | GW | OO |
| 41007 | *x | FD | A | GW | OO |
| 41008 | *w | FD | A | GW | OO |
| 41009 | *x | FD | A | GW | LA |
| 41010 | *w | FD | A | GW | LA |
| 41011 | *x | FD | A | GW | LA |
| 41012 | *w | FD | A | GW | LA |
| 41015 | *x | FD | A | GW | LA |
| 41016 | *w | FD | A | GW | LA |
| 41017 | *x | FD | A | GW | OO |
| 41018 | *w | FD | A | GW | OO |
| 41019 | *x | FD | A | GW | LA |
| 41020 | *w | FD | A | GW | LA |
| 41021 | *x | FD | A | GW | LA |
| 41022 | *w | FD | A | GW | LA |
| 41023 | *x | FD | A | GW | LA |
| 41024 | *w | FD | A | GW | LA |
| 41026 | c | XC | A | XC | EC |
| 41027 | *x | FD | A | GW | OO |
| 41028 | *w | FD | A | GW | OO |
| 41029 | *x | FD | A | GW | OO |
| 41030 | *w | FD | A | GW | OO |
| 41031 | *x | FD | A | GW | LA |
| 41032 | *w | FD | A | GW | LA |
| 41033 | *x | FD | A | GW | OO |
| 41034 | *w | FD | A | GW | OO |
| 41035 | c | XC | A | XC | EC |
| 41037 | *x | FD | A | GW | LA |
| 41038 | *w | FD | A | GW | LA |
| 41039 | m | NX | A | EC | EC |
| 41040 | mw | NX | A | EC | EC |
| 41041 | s | ST | P | EM | NL |
| 41044 | mw | NX | A | EC | EC |
| 41045 | *x | FD | FG | GW | LA |
| 41046 | s | ST | P | EM | NL |
| 41051 | *x | FD | A | GW | LA |
| 41052 | *w | FD | A | GW | LA |
| 41055 | *x | FD | A | GW | OO |
| 41056 | *w | FD | A | GW | OO |
| 41057 | | MN | P | EM | NL |
| 41059 | *w | FD | FG | GW | LA |
| 41061 | | MN | P | EM | NL |
| 41062 | w | MN | P | EM | NL |
| 41063 | | MN | P | EM | NL |
| 41064 | s | ST | P | EM | NL |
| 41065 | *x | FD | A | GW | OO |
| 41066 | m | NX | A | EC | EC |
| 41067 | s | ST | P | EM | NL |
| 41068 | s | MN | P | EM | NL |
| 41069 | s | MN | P | EM | NL |
| 41070 | s | MN | P | EM | NL |
| 41071 | | MN | P | EM | NL |
| 41072 | s | MN | P | EM | NL |
| 41075 | | MN | P | EM | NL |
| 41076 | s | MN | P | EM | NL |
| 41077 | | ST | P | EM | NL |
| 41078 | | MN | P | EM | NL |
| 41079 | | MN | P | EM | NL |
| 41081 | *x | FD | P | GW | OO |
| 41083 | mw | NX | P | EC | EC |
| 41084 | s | MN | P | EM | NL |
| 41085 | *x | FD | FG | GW | LA |
| 41086 | *x | FD | FG | GW | LA |
| 41087 | m | NX | A | EC | EC |
| 41088 | mw | NX | A | EC | EC |
| 41089 | *w | FD | A | GW | OO |
| 41090 | m | NX | A | EC | EC |
| 41091 | m | NX | A | EC | EC |
| 41092 | mw | NX | A | EC | EC |
| 41093 | *x | FD | A | GW | LA |
| 41094 | *w | FD | A | GW | LA |

| 41095 | mw | **NX** | P | *EC* | EC |
|-------|----|--------|---|------|----|
| 41096 | *x | **FD** | P | *GW* | OO |
| 41097 | m  | **NX** | A | *EC* | EC |
| 41098 | mw | **NX** | A | *EC* | EC |
| 41099 | m  | **NX** | A | *EC* | EC |
| 41100 | mw | **NX** | A | *EC* | EC |
| 41101 | *x | **FD** | A | *GW* | OO |
| 41102 | *w | **FD** | A | *GW* | OO |
| 41103 | *x | **FD** | A | *GW* | LA |
| 41104 | *w | **FD** | A | *GW* | LA |
| 41105 | *x | **FD** | A | *GW* | OO |
| 41106 | *w | **FD** | A | *GW* | OO |
| 41108 | *w | **FD** | P | *GW* | OO |
| 41109 | *x | **FD** | P | *GW* | OO |
| 41110 | *w | **FD** | A | *GW* | OO |
| 41111 |    | **MN** | P | *EM* | NL |
| 41112 |    | **ST** | P | *EM* | NL |
| 41113 | s  | **MN** | P | *EM* | NL |
| 41114 | *x | **FD** | FG | *GW* | LA |
| 41115 | m  | **NX** | P | *EC* | EC |
| 41116 | *x | **FD** | A | *GW* | LA |
| 41117 |    | **ST** | P | *EM* | NL |
| 41118 | mw | **NX** | A | *EC* | EC |
| 41119 | *x | **FD** | P | *GW* | OO |
| 41120 | m  | **NX** | A | *EC* | EC |
| 41121 | *x | **FD** | A | *GW* | LA |
| 41122 | *w | **FD** | A | *GW* | LA |
| 41123 | *x | **FD** | A | *GW* | LA |
| 41124 | *w | **FD** | A | *GW* | LA |
| 41125 | *x | **FD** | A | *GW* | OO |
| 41126 | *w | **FD** | A | *GW* | OO |
| 41127 | *x | **FD** | A | *GW* | OO |
| 41128 | *w | **FD** | A | *GW* | OO |
| 41129 | *x | **FD** | A | *GW* | LA |
| 41130 | *w | **FD** | A | *GW* | LA |
| 41131 | *x | **FD** | A | *GW* | OO |
| 41132 | *w | **FD** | A | *GW* | OO |

| 41133 | *x | **FD** | A | *GW* | LA |
|-------|----|--------|---|------|----|
| 41134 | *w | **FD** | A | *GW* | LA |
| 41135 | *w | **FD** | A | *GW* | LA |
| 41136 | *w | **FD** | A | *GW* | LA |
| 41137 | *x | **FD** | A | *GW* | OO |
| 41138 | *w | **FD** | A | *GW* | OO |
| 41139 | *x | **FD** | A | *GW* | OO |
| 41140 | *w | **FD** | A | *GW* | OO |
| 41141 | *x | **FD** | A | *GW* | LA |
| 41142 | *w | **FD** | A | *GW* | LA |
| 41143 | *x | **FD** | A | *GW* | LA |
| 41144 | *w | **FD** | A | *GW* | LA |
| 41145 | *x | **FD** | A | *GW* | LA |
| 41146 | *w | **FD** | A | *GW* | LA |
| 41147 | *w | **FD** | P | *GW* | OO |
| 41148 | *x | **FD** | P | *GW* | OO |
| 41149 | *w | **FD** | P | *GW* | OO |
| 41150 | mw | **NX** | A | *EC* | EC |
| 41151 | m  | **NX** | A | *EC* | EC |
| 41152 | mw | **NX** | A | *EC* | EC |
| 41153 | *x | **FD** | P | *GW* | OO |
| 41154 | s  | **MN** | P | *EM* | NL |
| 41155 | *x | **FD** | P | *GW* | OO |
| 41156 |    | **ST** | P | *EM* | NL |
| 41157 | *x | **FD** | A | *GW* | LA |
| 41158 | *w | **FD** | A | *GW* | LA |
| 41159 | m  | **FD** | P | *EC* | EC |
| 41160 | *w | **FD** | FG | *GW* | LA |
| 41161 | *w | **FD** | P | *GW* | OO |
| 41162 | *w | **FD** | FG | *GW* | LA |
| 41163 | *x | **FD** | FG | *GW* | LA |
| 41164 | mw | **NX** | A | *EC* | EC |
| 41165 | mw | **NX** | P | *EC* | EC |
| 41166 | *w | **FD** | FG | *GW* | LA |
| 41167 | *w | **FD** | FG | *GW* | LA |
| 41168 | *x | **FD** | P | *GW* | OO |
| 41169 | *w | **FD** | P | *GW* | OO |

| 41170 | (41001)          | m  | **NX** | A | *EC* | EC |
|-------|------------------|----|--------|---|------|----|
| 41176 | (42142, 42352)   | *w | **FD** | P | *GW* | OO |
| 41179 | (40505)          | *x | **FD** | A | *GW* | OO |
| 41180 | (40511)          | *w | **FD** | A | *GW* | OO |
| 41181 | (42282)          | *x | **FD** | P | *GW* | OO |
| 41182 | (42278)          | *w | **FD** | P | *GW* | OO |
| 41183 | (42274)          | *w | **FD** | P | *GW* | OO |
| 41184 | (42270)          | *x | **FD** | P | *GW* | OO |
| 41185 | (42313)          | m  | **NX** | P | *EC* | EC |
| 41186 | (42312)          | *x | **FD** | P | *GW* | OO |
| 41187 | (42311)          | *w | **FD** | P | *GW* | OO |
| 41189 | (42298)          | *w | **FD** | P | *GW* | OO |
| 41190 | (42088)          | mw | **GN** | P | *EC* | EC |

| 41191 | (42318) | *x | **FD** | P | *GW* | OO |
| 41192 | (42246) | *w | **FD** | P | *GW* | OO |

The following coaches have been converted from loco-hauled Mark 3 vehicles for CrossCountry.

| 41193 | (11060) | c | **XC** | P | *XC* | EC |
| 41194 | (11016) | c | **XC** | P | *XC* | EC |
| 41195 | (11020) | c | **XC** | P | *XC* | EC |

The following coaches have been converted from loco-hauled Mark 3 vehicles for Grand Central. 48/– 2T.

| 41201 | (11045) | | **GC** | ST | *GC* | HT |
| 41202 | (11017) | | **GC** | ST | *GC* | HT |
| 41203 | (11038) | | **GC** | ST | | ZJ |
| 41204 | (11023) | | **GC** | ST | *GC* | HT |
| 41205 | (11036) | | **GC** | ST | *GC* | HT |
| 41206 | (11055) | | **GC** | ST | *GC* | HT |

# GH2G (TS)                               TRAILER STANDARD

**42003–42090/42362.** Lot No. 30882 Derby 1976–77. 33.60 t.
**42091–42250.** Lot No. 30897 Derby 1977–79. 33.60 t.
**42251–42305.** Lot No. 30939 Derby 1979–80. 33.60 t.
**42306–42322.** Lot No. 30969 Derby 1982. 33.60 t.
**42323–42341.** Lot No. 30983 Derby 1984–85. 33.60 t.
**42342/42360.** Lot No. 30949 Derby 1982. 33.47 t. Converted from TGS.
**42343/42345.** Lot No. 30970 Derby 1982. 33.47 t. Converted from TGS.
**42344/42361.** Lot No. 30964 Derby 1982. 33.47 t. Converted from TGS.
**42346/42347/42350/42351/42379/42380.** Lot No. 30881 Derby 1976–77. 33.66 t. Converted from TF.
**42348/42349/42363–42365/42381.** Lot No. 30896 Derby 1977–78. 33.66 t. Converted from TF.
**42354.** Lot No. 30897 Derby 1977. Was TF from 1983 to 1992. 33.66 t.
**42353/42355–42357.** Lot No. 30967 Derby 1982. Ex-prototype vehicles. 33.66 t.
**42366–42378/42382/42401–42409.** Lot No. 30877 Derby 1975–77. 34.3 t. Converted from Mark 3A TSO.

**Notes:** 42158 was numbered 41177 for a time when fitted with First Class seats.
42310 was numbered 41188 for a time when fitted with First Class seats.

Standard seating and m –/76 2T.
* Refurbished First Great Western vehicles. Grammer seating. –/80 2T (unless h – high density).
c Refurbished CrossCountry vehicles with Primarius seating. One toilet removed. –/82 1T.
§c Refurbished CrossCountry vehicles with Primarius seating and 2 tip-up seats. One toilet removed. –/66 1TD 2W. Note 42379/380 are –/71 1TD 1T 2W.
d FGW vehicles with disabled persons toilet and 5, 6 or 7 tip-up seats. –/68 1T 1TD 2W.
h "High density" FGW vehicles. –/84 2T.
k "High density" FGW refurbished vehicle with disabled persons toilet and 6 or 7 tip-up seats. –/72 1T 1TD 2W.

m  Refurbished East Coast vehicles with Primarius seating.
u  Centre luggage stack (EMT) –/74 2T.
w  Centre luggage stack and wheelchair space (EMT) –72 2T 1W.
†  Disabled persons toilet (East Coast) –/62 1T 1TD 1W.

| | | | | | | | | | | | |
|---|---|---|---|---|---|---|---|---|---|---|---|
| 42003 | *h | **FD** | A | *GW* | OO | | 42054 | * | **FD** | A | *GW* | LA |
| 42004 | *d | **FD** | A | *GW* | LA | | 42055 | * | **FD** | A | *GW* | LA |
| 42005 | *h | **FD** | A | *GW* | LA | | 42056 | * | **FD** | A | *GW* | LA |
| 42006 | *h | **FD** | A | *GW* | LA | | 42057 | m | **NX** | A | *EC* | EC |
| 42007 | *d | **FD** | A | *GW* | LA | | 42058 | m | **NX** | A | *EC* | EC |
| 42008 | *k | **FD** | A | *GW* | OO | | 42059 | m | **NX** | A | *EC* | EC |
| 42009 | *h | **FD** | A | *GW* | LA | | 42060 | *h | **FD** | A | *GW* | OO |
| 42010 | *h | **FD** | A | *GW* | LA | | 42061 | *h | **FD** | A | *GW* | OO |
| 42012 | *k | **FD** | A | *GW* | LA | | 42062 | *k | **FD** | A | *GW* | OO |
| 42013 | *h | **FD** | A | *GW* | LA | | 42063 | m | **NX** | A | *EC* | EC |
| 42014 | *h | **FD** | A | *GW* | LA | | 42064 | m | **NX** | A | *EC* | EC |
| 42015 | *k | **FD** | A | *GW* | LA | | 42065 | m | **NX** | A | *EC* | EC |
| 42016 | *h | **FD** | A | *GW* | LA | | 42066 | *k | **FD** | A | *GW* | OO |
| 42019 | * | **FD** | A | *GW* | LA | | 42067 | *h | **FD** | A | *GW* | OO |
| 42021 | *k | **FD** | A | *GW* | LA | | 42068 | *h | **FD** | A | *GW* | OO |
| 42023 | *h | **FD** | A | *GW* | LA | | 42069 | *k | **FD** | A | *GW* | OO |
| 42024 | *k | **FD** | A | *GW* | OO | | 42070 | *h | **FD** | A | *GW* | OO |
| 42025 | *h | **FD** | A | *GW* | OO | | 42071 | *h | **FD** | A | *GW* | OO |
| 42026 | *h | **FD** | A | *GW* | OO | | 42072 | * | **FD** | A | *GW* | LA |
| 42027 | *h | **FD** | A | *GW* | OO | | 42073 | *h | **FD** | A | *GW* | OO |
| 42028 | *h | **FD** | A | *GW* | LA | | 42074 | *h | **FD** | A | *GW* | OO |
| 42029 | *h | **FD** | A | *GW* | LA | | 42075 | * | **FD** | A | *GW* | LA |
| 42030 | *k | **FD** | A | *GW* | LA | | 42076 | * | **FD** | A | *GW* | LA |
| 42031 | *h | **FD** | A | *GW* | LA | | 42077 | * | **FD** | A | *GW* | LA |
| 42032 | *h | **FD** | A | *GW* | LA | | 42078 | * | **FD** | A | *GW* | LA |
| 42033 | * | **FD** | A | *GW* | LA | | 42079 | *h | **FD** | A | *GW* | OO |
| 42034 | * | **FD** | A | *GW* | LA | | 42080 | *h | **FD** | A | *GW* | OO |
| 42035 | * | **FD** | A | *GW* | LA | | 42081 | *k | **FD** | A | *GW* | OO |
| 42036 | c | **XC** | A | *XC* | EC | | 42083 | *h | **FD** | A | *GW* | OO |
| 42037 | c | **XC** | A | *XC* | EC | | 42084 | *h | **FD** | A | *GW* | OO |
| 42038 | c | **XC** | A | *XC* | EC | | 42085 | *h | **FD** | P | *GW* | OO |
| 42039 | *h | **FD** | A | *GW* | OO | | 42087 | *h | **FD** | P | *GW* | OO |
| 42040 | *h | **FD** | A | *GW* | OO | | 42089 | *h | **FD** | A | *GW* | OO |
| 42041 | *h | **FD** | A | *GW* | OO | | 42090 | *h | **FD** | P | *GW* | OO |
| 42042 | *h | **FD** | A | *GW* | OO | | 42091 | mt | **NX** | A | *EC* | EC |
| 42043 | *h | **FD** | A | *GW* | OO | | 42092 | *d | **FD** | FG | *GW* | LA |
| 42044 | *h | **FD** | A | *GW* | OO | | 42093 | *h | **FD** | FG | *GW* | LA |
| 42045 | * | **FD** | A | *GW* | LA | | 42094 | *h | **FD** | FG | *GW* | LA |
| 42046 | * | **FD** | A | *GW* | LA | | 42095 | * | **FD** | FG | *GW* | LA |
| 42047 | * | **FD** | A | *GW* | LA | | 42096 | *h | **FD** | A | *GW* | OO |
| 42048 | *h | **FD** | A | *GW* | OO | | 42097 | c | **XC** | A | *XC* | EC |
| 42049 | *h | **FD** | A | *GW* | OO | | 42098 | *h | **FD** | A | *GW* | OO |
| 42050 | *h | **FD** | A | *GW* | OO | | 42099 | *h | **FD** | A | *GW* | OO |
| 42051 | c | **XC** | A | *XC* | EC | | 42100 | u | **ST** | P | *EM* | NL |
| 42052 | c | **XC** | A | *XC* | EC | | 42101 | *h | **FD** | P | *GW* | OO |
| 42053 | c | **XC** | A | *XC* | EC | | 42102 | *h | **FD** | P | *GW* | OO |

| | | | | | | | | | | |
|---|---|---|---|---|---|---|---|---|---|---|
| 42103 | *k | **FD** | FG | *GW* | LA | 42157 | u | **MN** | P | *EM* | NL |
| 42104 | m | **NX** | A | *EC* | EC | 42158 | m | **NX** | A | *EC* | EC |
| 42105 | *d | **FD** | FG | *GW* | LA | 42159 | mt | **NX** | P | *EC* | EC |
| 42106 | m | **NX** | A | *EC* | EC | 42160 | m | **NX** | P | *EC* | EC |
| 42107 | * | **FD** | A | *GW* | LA | 42161 | mt | **NX** | A | *EC* | EC |
| 42108 | *h | **FD** | FG | *GW* | LA | 42163 | m | **NX** | P | *EC* | EC |
| 42109 | m | **NX** | P | *EC* | EC | 42164 | | **ST** | P | *EM* | NL |
| 42110 | m | **NX** | P | *EC* | EC | 42165 | | **ST** | P | *EM* | NL |
| 42111 | u | **MN** | P | *EM* | NL | 42166 | *h | **FD** | P | *GW* | OO |
| 42112 | u | **MN** | P | *EM* | NL | 42167 | *h | **FD** | FG | *GW* | LA |
| 42113 | u | **MN** | P | *EM* | NL | 42168 | *h | **FD** | FG | *GW* | LA |
| 42115 | *h | **FD** | P | *GW* | OO | 42169 | *h | **FD** | FG | *GW* | LA |
| 42116 | mt | **NX** | A | *EC* | EC | 42170 | *h | **FD** | P | *GW* | OO |
| 42117 | m | **NX** | P | *EC* | EC | 42171 | m | **NX** | A | *EC* | EC |
| 42118 | *h | **FD** | A | *GW* | OO | 42172 | m | **NX** | A | *EC* | EC |
| 42119 | u | **ST** | P | *EM* | NL | 42173 | *k | **FD** | P | *GW* | OO |
| 42120 | u | **MN** | P | *EM* | NL | 42174 | *k | **FD** | P | *GW* | OO |
| 42121 | u | **ST** | P | *EM* | NL | 42175 | *h | **FD** | FG | *GW* | LA |
| 42122 | m | **NX** | A | *EC* | EC | 42176 | *h | **FD** | FG | *GW* | LA |
| 42123 | u | **MN** | P | *EM* | NL | 42177 | *h | **FD** | FG | *GW* | LA |
| 42124 | u | **ST** | P | *EM* | NL | 42178 | *h | **FD** | P | *GW* | OO |
| 42125 | u | **MN** | P | *EM* | NL | 42179 | m | **NX** | A | *EC* | EC |
| 42126 | *h | **FD** | A | *GW* | OO | 42180 | m | **NX** | A | *EC* | EC |
| 42127 | mt | **NX** | A | *EC* | EC | 42181 | m | **NX** | A | *EC* | EC |
| 42128 | mt | **NX** | A | *EC* | EC | 42182 | m | **NX** | A | *EC* | EC |
| 42129 | * | **FD** | A | *GW* | LA | 42183 | *d | **FD** | A | *GW* | LA |
| 42130 | m | **NX** | P | *EC* | EC | 42184 | * | **FD** | A | *GW* | LA |
| 42131 | u | **ST** | P | *EM* | NL | 42185 | * | **FD** | A | *GW* | LA |
| 42132 | u | **ST** | P | *EM* | NL | 42186 | m | **NX** | A | *EC* | EC |
| 42133 | u | **ST** | P | *EM* | NL | 42188 | mt | **NX** | A | *EC* | EC |
| 42134 | m | **NX** | A | *EC* | EC | 42189 | mt | **NX** | A | *EC* | EC |
| 42135 | u | **MN** | P | *EM* | NL | 42190 | m | **NX** | A | *EC* | EC |
| 42136 | u | **MN** | P | *EM* | NL | 42191 | m | **NX** | A | *EC* | EC |
| 42137 | u | **MN** | P | *EM* | NL | 42192 | m | **NX** | A | *EC* | EC |
| 42138 | *k | **FD** | A | *GW* | OO | 42193 | m | **NX** | A | *EC* | EC |
| 42139 | u | **MN** | P | *EM* | NL | 42194 | w | **ST** | P | *EM* | NL |
| 42140 | u | **MN** | P | *EM* | NL | 42195 | *k | **FD** | P | *GW* | OO |
| 42141 | u | **MN** | P | *EM* | NL | 42196 | *h | **FD** | A | *GW* | OO |
| 42143 | * | **FD** | A | *GW* | LA | 42197 | *h | **FD** | A | *GW* | OO |
| 42144 | * | **FD** | A | *GW* | LA | 42198 | m | **NX** | A | *EC* | EC |
| 42145 | * | **FD** | A | *GW* | LA | 42199 | m | **NX** | A | *EC* | EC |
| 42146 | m | **NX** | A | *EC* | EC | 42200 | *d | **FD** | A | *GW* | LA |
| 42148 | u | **MN** | P | *EM* | NL | 42201 | *k | **FD** | A | *GW* | OO |
| 42149 | u | **MN** | P | *EM* | NL | 42202 | *k | **FD** | A | *GW* | OO |
| 42150 | m | **NX** | A | *EC* | EC | 42203 | *h | **FD** | A | *GW* | OO |
| 42151 | w | **ST** | P | *EM* | NL | 42204 | *h | **FD** | A | *GW* | OO |
| 42152 | u | **MN** | P | *EM* | NL | 42205 | u | **MN** | P | *EM* | NL |
| 42153 | u | **ST** | P | *EM* | NL | 42206 | *d | **FD** | A | *GW* | LA |
| 42154 | m | **NX** | A | *EC* | EC | 42207 | *d | **FD** | A | *GW* | LA |
| 42155 | w | **MN** | P | *EM* | NL | 42208 | * | **FD** | A | *GW* | LA |
| 42156 | u | **MN** | P | *EM* | NL | 42209 | * | **FD** | A | *GW* | LA |

| No. | | | | | |
|---|---|---|---|---|---|
| 42210 | u | MN | P | EM | NL |
| 42211 | *k | FD | A | GW | OO |
| 42212 | *h | FD | A | GW | OO |
| 42213 | *h | FD | A | GW | OO |
| 42214 | *h | FD | A | GW | OO |
| 42215 | m | NX | A | EC | EC |
| 42216 | *h | FD | A | GW | OO |
| 42217 | *k | FD | P | GW | OO |
| 42218 | *d | FD | P | GW | OO |
| 42219 | m | NX | A | EC | EC |
| 42220 | w | ST | P | EM | NL |
| 42221 | *h | FD | A | GW | OO |
| 42222 | *h | FD | P | GW | OO |
| 42223 | *h | FD | P | GW | OO |
| 42224 | *k | FD | P | GW | OO |
| 42225 | u | ST | P | EM | NL |
| 42226 | m | NX | A | EC | EC |
| 42227 | u | ST | P | EM | NL |
| 42228 | m | NX | P | EC | EC |
| 42229 | u | ST | P | EM | NL |
| 42230 | u | ST | P | EM | NL |
| 42231 | *h | FD | FG | GW | LA |
| 42232 | *h | FD | FG | GW | LA |
| 42233 | *h | FD | FG | GW | LA |
| 42234 | c | XC | P | XC | EC |
| 42235 | m | NX | A | EC | EC |
| 42236 | *h | FD | P | GW | OO |
| 42237 | m | NX | P | EC | EC |
| 42238 | m† | NX | A | EC | EC |
| 42239 | m† | NX | A | EC | EC |
| 42240 | m | NX | A | EC | EC |
| 42241 | m | NX | A | EC | EC |
| 42242 | m | NX | A | EC | EC |
| 42243 | m | NX | A | EC | EC |
| 42244 | m | NX | A | EC | EC |
| 42245 | * | FD | A | GW | LA |
| 42247 | *h | FD | P | GW | OO |
| 42249 | *h | FD | P | GW | OO |
| 42250 | * | FD | A | GW | LA |
| 42251 | *k | FD | A | GW | OO |
| 42252 | * | FD | A | GW | LA |
| 42253 | * | FD | A | GW | LA |
| 42254 | *h | FD | P | GW | OO |
| 42255 | *d | FD | A | GW | LA |
| 42256 | * | FD | A | GW | LA |
| 42257 | * | FD | A | GW | LA |
| 42258 | *h | FD | P | GW | OO |
| 42259 | *k | FD | A | GW | LA |
| 42260 | *h | FD | A | GW | OO |
| 42261 | *h | FD | A | GW | OO |
| 42263 | * | FD | A | GW | LA |
| 42264 | *k | FD | A | GW | OO |
| 42265 | * | FD | A | GW | LA |
| 42266 | *k | FD | P | GW | OO |
| 42267 | *d | FD | A | GW | LA |
| 42268 | *d | FD | A | GW | LA |
| 42269 | * | FD | A | GW | LA |
| 42271 | *k | FD | A | GW | OO |
| 42272 | *h | FD | A | GW | OO |
| 42273 | *h | FD | A | GW | OO |
| 42275 | *d | FD | A | GW | LA |
| 42276 | * | FD | A | GW | LA |
| 42277 | * | FD | A | GW | LA |
| 42279 | *d | FD | A | GW | LA |
| 42280 | * | FD | A | GW | LA |
| 42281 | * | FD | A | GW | LA |
| 42283 | *h | FD | A | GW | OO |
| 42284 | *h | FD | A | GW | OO |
| 42285 | *h | FD | A | GW | OO |
| 42286 | m† | NX | P | EC | EC |
| 42287 | *k | FD | A | GW | OO |
| 42288 | *h | FD | A | GW | OO |
| 42289 | *h | FD | A | GW | OO |
| 42290 | c | XC | P | XC | EC |
| 42291 | *d | FD | A | GW | LA |
| 42292 | *d | FD | A | GW | LA |
| 42293 | * | FD | A | GW | LA |
| 42294 | * | FD | P | GW | OO |
| 42295 | *d | FD | A | GW | LA |
| 42296 | * | FD | A | GW | LA |
| 42297 | * | FD | A | GW | LA |
| 42299 | *d | FD | A | GW | LA |
| 42300 | * | FD | A | GW | LA |
| 42301 | * | FD | A | GW | LA |
| 42302 | *k | FD | FG | GW | LA |
| 42303 | *h | FD | FG | GW | LA |
| 42304 | *h | FD | FG | GW | LA |
| 42305 | *h | FD | FG | GW | LA |
| 42306 | m | NX | P | EC | EC |
| 42307 | m | NX | P | EC | EC |
| 42308 | *h | FD | P | GW | OO |
| 42310 | *k | FD | P | GW | OO |
| 42315 | *h | FD | P | GW | OO |
| 42316 | *h | FD | P | GW | OO |
| 42317 | *k | FD | P | GW | OO |
| 42319 | *h | FD | P | GW | OO |
| 42321 | *h | FD | P | GW | OO |
| 42322 | m | NX | P | EC | EC |
| 42323 | m | NX | A | EC | EC |
| 42324 | w | MN | P | | NL |
| 42325 | * | FD | A | GW | LA |
| 42326 | m | NX | P | EC | EC |

▲ **Mark 1s:** BR Maroon-liveried Mark 1 RMB 1882 (numbered 99311) is seen at Carlisle on 13/06/09. **Robin Ralston**

▼ BR Chocolate & Cream-liveried Mark 1 FO 3110 stands at Bristol Temple Meads on 13/06/09. **Robert Pritchard**

▲ BR Carmine & Cream-liveried Mark 1 FO 3149 is seen at Eastleigh on 23/05/09.
**Robert Pritchard**

▼ BR Maroon-liveried Mark 1 BCK 21266 at Totley Tunnel East (Sheffield) on 29/03/09.
**Robert Pritchard**

▲ **Mark 2s:** Pullman Car Company-liveried Mark 2 PFK 506 "WINDERMERE" at Carlisle on 13/06/09.                                                                          **Robin Ralston**

▼ Riviera Trains-liveried Mark 2F FO 3348 "GAINSBOROUGH" at Saughton (Edinburgh) on 13/04/09.                                                                          **Robin Ralston**

► Still in InterCity livery, West Coast Railway Company's Mark 2F FO 3362 at Carlisle on 13/06/09. **Robin Ralston**

▼ A number of Riviera Trains-operated Mark 2Fs are still in use in Virgin Trains livery. On 18/04/09 Mark 2F FO 3386 is seen at Blea Moor on the Settle & Carlisle line. **Robert Pritchard**

▼ In BR maroon livery with EWS logos, DB Schenker-owned Mark 2F FO 3400 is seen at Knottingley depot on 06/09/08. **Robert Pritchard**

▲ Non-standard Green & Cream-liveried Mark 2 SO 5229 "THE GREEN KNIGHT" stands at Long Rock sidings, Penzance on 27/06/09.　　**Stephen Widdowson**

▼ Arriva Trains "executive"-liveried Mark 2F BSO 9521 at Hereford on 21/08/09 in the formation of the Cardiff–Holyhead loco-hauled train.　　**Stephen Widdowson**

▶ Cargo-D BR Blue & Grey-liveried Mark 2F BSO 9508 at Stapleton Road (Bristol) on 11/06/09 in the formation of the First Great Western loco-hauled rake. **Robert Pritchard**

▼ Riviera Trains-liveried Mark 2A BFK 17077 at Hexham on 27/09/08. **Robert Pritchard**

▼ BR Maroon-liveried Mark 2A BFK 17102 (numbered 99680) is seen near Scarborough on 29/08/09. **Andrew Mason**

▲ **Mark 3s:** Virgin Trains silver-liveried refurbished Mark 3A RFB 10212 at Milton Keynes Central on 25/07/09 (the first day in traffic for the refurbished Virgin Mark 3 set). **Mark Beal**

▼ In "One" livery with white National Express stripe, Mark 3A RFB 10216 is seen at Chelmsford on 12/06/09. **Robert Pritchard**

▲ BR Blue & Grey-liveried Mark 3A TSO 11029 (complete with non-standard blue roof) is seen at Neasden (North London) in the formation of a Wrexham & Shropshire train on 31/05/09. Although still numbered in the 11xxx FO series, this coach has been reseated with Standard Class seats. **Robert Pritchard**

▼ The first refurbished Wrexham & Shropshire-liveried Mark 3 vehicles were released for testing in September 2009. On 07/09/09 Mark 3A TSO 12145 stands at Wrexham General. **Mark Riley**

▶ First Great Western "Dynamic Lines"-liveried Mark 3B BUO 17173 at Penzance on 16/06/09.
**Robert Pritchard**

▼ Mark 3 Sleeping cars: First Group-liveried Mark 3A SLEP 10526 at Old Linslade on 30/07/09.
**Andrew Mason**

▼ First Great Western "Dynamic Lines"-liveried Mark 3A SLEP 10590 stabled between duties at Long Rock depot, Penzance on 26/06/09.       **Stephen Widdowson**

▲ **Mark 3 HST vehicles:** National Express-liveried TRFB 40702 south of Seaham on the Durham Coast Line in a diverted service on 03/01/09.   **Robert Pritchard**

▼ Grand Central-liveried TF 41201 at Thirsk on 19/08/09.   **Robert Pritchard**

▲ First Great Western TS 42025 at Plymouth on 09/06/08. **Robert Pritchard**

▼ Cross-Country-liveried TCC 45004 at Chesterfield on 09/08/09. This vehicle was converted from loco-hauled Mark 3 TSO 12077. **Andrew Mason**

▲ **Mark 4s:** In GNER livery with a National Express white stripe, Mark 4 TSOD 12321 is seen at Retford on 17/01/09. **Robert Pritchard**

▲ **Pullman cars, saloons and other stock:** Gangwayed Brake Van 92904, in VSOE Northern Belle livery, at Crewe on 06/01/09. **Mike Stone**

▶ Royal Train Royal Household Couchette 2921 is seen just south of Colton Junction on 19/02/09. **Robert Pritchard**

▲ LNWR Dining Saloon 159, dating from 1890, is seen on display at the Eastleigh Works open weekend on 23/05/09. **Robert Pritchard**

▼ Royal Scotsman Observation Car 99965 is seen on the rear of the prestigious train at Saughton (Edinburgh) on 12/06/08. **Ian Lothian**

▲ **DVTs:** "One"-liveried Mark 3B DVT 82112 passes Marks Tey at speed leading the 08.30 London Liverpool Street–Norwich on 12/06/09.     **Robert Pritchard**

▼ Wrexham & Shropshire-liveried Mark 3B DVT 82303 passes Kings Sutton with the 16.33 London Marylebone–Wrexham General on 07/08/09.     **Mark Beal**

▲ **Service Stock:** Network Rail Driving Trailer Coach 9701 (converted from a DBSO) leads a Derby–London King's Cross test train at Loughborough on 16/03/09 (31285 is at the rear). **Paul Biggs**

▼ New Measurement Train Lecture Coach 975984 (converted from prototype HST TRUK 40000) near Beighton Junction on 08/08/09. **Robert Pritchard**

▲ HSBC-liveried EMU Translator Vehicle 975864 at Polmadie depot, Glasgow on 02/08/09. **Robin Ralston**

▼ Network Rail yellow-liveried Ultrasonic Test Coach 999605 at Bromham, Bedfordshire on 31/10/08. **Mark Beal**

| 42327 | w | **MN** | P | *EM* | NL | | 42335 | u | **MN** | P | *EM* | NL |
|-------|---|--------|---|------|----|-|-------|---|--------|---|------|----|
| 42328 | w | **MN** | P | *EM* | NL | | 42337 | w | **ST** | P | *EM* | NL |
| 42329 | w | **MN** | P | *EM* | NL | | 42338 | *h | **FD** | P | *GW* | OO |
| 42330 | m | **NX** | P | *EC* | EC | | 42339 | w | **MN** | P | *EM* | NL |
| 42331 | w | **ST** | P | *EM* | NL | | 42340 | m | **NX** | A | *EC* | EC |
| 42332 | * | **FD** | A | *GW* | LA | | 42341 | u | **MN** | P | *EM* | NL |
| 42333 | * | **FD** | A | *GW* | LA | | | | | | | |

| 42342 | (44082) | | c | **XC** | A | *XC* | EC |
|-------|---------|--|----|--------|----|------|----|
| 42343 | (44095) | | * | **FD** | A | *GW* | LA |
| 42344 | (44092) | | *k | **FD** | A | *GW* | OO |
| 42345 | (44096) | | *d | **FD** | A | *GW* | LA |
| 42346 | (41053) | | *h | **FD** | A | *GW* | OO |
| 42347 | (41054) | | *k | **FD** | A | *GW* | OO |
| 42348 | (41073) | | *k | **FD** | A | *GW* | OO |
| 42349 | (41074) | | *h | **FD** | A | *GW* | OO |
| 42350 | (41047) | | * | **FD** | A | *GW* | LA |
| 42351 | (41048) | | * | **FD** | A | *GW* | LA |
| 42353 | (42001, 41171) | | *k | **FD** | FG | *GW* | LA |
| 42354 | (42114, 41175) | | m | **NX** | A | *EC* | EC |
| 42355 | (42000, 41172) | | m | **NX** | A | *EC* | EC |
| 42356 | (42002, 41173) | | *k | **FD** | A | *GW* | OO |
| 42357 | (41002, 41174) | | m | **NX** | A | *EC* | EC |
| 42360 | (44084, 45084) | | *h | **FD** | A | *GW* | LA |
| 42361 | (44099, 42000) | | *h | **FD** | A | *GW* | LA |
| 42362 | (42011, 41178) | | *h | **FD** | A | *GW* | OO |
| 42363 | (41082) | | m† | **NX** | A | *EC* | EC |
| 42364 | (41080) | | * | **FD** | P | *GW* | OO |
| 42365 | (41107) | | *h | **FD** | P | *GW* | OO |

42366–378 have been converted from loco-hauled Mark 3 vehicles for CrossCountry and 42382/383 for First Great Western.

| 42367 | (12025) | | c | **XC** | P | *XC* | EC |
|-------|---------|--|----|--------|----|------|----|
| 42368 | (12028) | | c | **XC** | P | *XC* | EC |
| 42369 | (12050) | | c | **XC** | P | *XC* | EC |
| 42370 | (12086) | | c | **XC** | P | *XC* | EC |
| 42371 | (12052) | | §c | **XC** | P | *XC* | EC |
| 42372 | (12055) | | c | **XC** | P | *XC* | EC |
| 42373 | (12071) | | c | **XC** | P | *XC* | EC |
| 42374 | (12075) | | c | **XC** | P | *XC* | EC |
| 42375 | (12113) | | c | **XC** | P | *XC* | EC |
| 42376 | (12085) | | §c | **XC** | P | *XC* | EC |
| 42377 | (12102) | | c | **XC** | P | *XC* | EC |
| 42378 | (12123) | | c | **XC** | P | *XC* | EC |
| 42379 | (41036) | | §c | **XC** | A | *XC* | EC |
| 42380 | (41025) | | §c | **XC** | A | *XC* | EC |
| 42381 | (41058) | | *k | **FD** | P | *GW* | OO |
| 42382 | (12128) | | *h | **FD** | P | *GW* | OO |
| 42383 | (12172) | | *h | **FD** | P | *GW* | OO |

The following coaches have been converted from loco-hauled Mark 3 vehicles for Grand Central. They have a lower density seating layout (most seats arranged around tables). –/64 2T († –/60 1TD 1T 2W).

| | | | | | | |
|---|---|---|---|---|---|---|
| 42401 | (12149) | | **GC** | ST | *GC* | HT |
| 42402 | (12155) | | **GC** | ST | *GC* | HT |
| 42403 | (12033) | † | **GC** | ST | *GC* | HT |
| 42404 | (12152) | | **GC** | ST | *GC* | HT |
| 42405 | (12136) | | **GC** | ST | *GC* | HT |
| 42406 | (12112) | † | **GC** | ST | *GC* | HT |
| 42407 | (12044) | | **GC** | ST | | ZJ |
| 42408 | (12121) | | **GC** | ST | *GC* | HT |
| 42409 | (12088) | † | **GC** | ST | | ZJ |

# GJ2G (TGS)          TRAILER GUARD'S STANDARD

**44000.** Lot No. 30953 Derby 1980. 33.47 t.
**44001–44090.** Lot No. 30949 Derby 1980–82. 33.47 t.
**44091–44094.** Lot No. 30964 Derby 1982. 33.47 t.
**44097–44101.** Lot No. 30970 Derby 1982. 33.47 t.

As built and m –/65 1T.
* Refurbished First Great Western vehicles. Grammer seating and toilet removed for trolley store. –/67 (unless h).
c Refurbished CrossCountry vehicles with Primarius seating. –/67 1T.
h "High density" FGW vehicles. –/71.
m Refurbished East Coast vehicles with Primarius seating.
s Fitted with centre luggage stack (EMT) –/63 1T.
t Fitted with centre luggage stack –/61 1T.

| | | | | | | | | | | | |
|---|---|---|---|---|---|---|---|---|---|---|---|
| 44000 | *h | **FD** | P | *GW* | OO | 44023 | *h | **FD** | A | *GW* | OO |
| 44001 | * | **FD** | A | *GW* | LA | 44024 | *h | **FD** | A | *GW* | OO |
| 44002 | *h | **FD** | A | *GW* | OO | 44025 | * | **FD** | A | *GW* | LA |
| 44003 | *h | **FD** | A | *GW* | OO | 44026 | *h | **FD** | A | *GW* | OO |
| 44004 | *h | **FD** | A | *GW* | LA | 44027 | s | **ST** | P | *EM* | NL |
| 44005 | *h | **FD** | A | *GW* | LA | 44028 | * | **FD** | A | *GW* | LA |
| 44007 | *h | **FD** | A | *GW* | LA | 44029 | * | **FD** | A | *GW* | LA |
| 44008 | *h | **FD** | A | *GW* | OO | 44030 | *h | **FD** | A | *GW* | OO |
| 44009 | *h | **FD** | A | *GW* | LA | 44031 | m | **NX** | A | *EC* | EC |
| 44010 | *h | **FD** | A | *GW* | LA | 44032 | * | **FD** | A | *GW* | LA |
| 44011 | * | **FD** | A | *GW* | LA | 44033 | *h | **FD** | A | *GW* | OO |
| 44012 | c | **XC** | A | *XC* | EC | 44034 | * | **FD** | A | *GW* | LA |
| 44013 | *h | **FD** | A | *GW* | OO | 44035 | * | **FD** | A | *GW* | LA |
| 44014 | *h | **FD** | A | *GW* | OO | 44036 | *h | **FD** | A | *GW* | OO |
| 44015 | * | **FD** | A | *GW* | LA | 44037 | *h | **FD** | A | *GW* | OO |
| 44016 | *h | **FD** | A | *GW* | OO | 44038 | * | **FD** | A | *GW* | LA |
| 44017 | c | **XC** | A | *XC* | EC | 44039 | * | **FD** | A | *GW* | LA |
| 44018 | * | **FD** | A | *GW* | LA | 44040 | * | **FD** | A | *GW* | LA |
| 44019 | m | **NX** | A | *EC* | EC | 44041 | s | **MN** | P | *EM* | NL |
| 44020 | *h | **FD** | A | *GW* | OO | 44042 | *h | **FD** | P | *GW* | OO |
| 44021 | c | **XC** | P | *XC* | EC | 44043 | *h | **FD** | A | *GW* | OO |
| 44022 | *h | **FD** | A | *GW* | OO | 44044 | s | **MN** | P | *EM* | NL |

| | | | | | | | | | | | |
|---|---|---|---|---|---|---|---|---|---|---|---|
| 44045 | m | **NX** | A | *EC* | EC | | 44071 | s | **MN** | P | *EM* | NL |

44045 m **NX** A *EC* EC
44046 s **ST** P *EM* NL
44047 s **ST** P *EM* NL
44048 s **MN** P *EM* NL
44049 * **FD** A *GW* LA
44050 m **NX** P *EC* EC
44051 s **MN** P *EM* NL
44052 c **XC** P *XC* EC
44054 s **MN** P *EM* NL
44055 *h **FD** FG *GW* LA
44056 m **NX** A *EC* EC
44057 m **NX** P *EC* EC
44058 m **NX** A *EC* EC
44059 * **FD** A *GW* LA
44060 *h **FD** P *GW* OO
44061 m **NX** A *EC* EC
44063 m **NX** A *EC* EC
44064 *h **FD** A *GW* OO
44065 t **V** ST LM
44066 * **FD** A *GW* LA
44067 *h **FD** A *GW* OO
44068 *h **FD** FG *GW* LA
44069 *h **FD** P *GW* OO
44070 s **MN** P *EM* NL

44071 s **MN** P *EM* NL
44072 c **XC** P *XC* EC
44073 s **MN** P *EM* NL
44074 *h **FD** FG *GW* LA
44075 m **NX** P *EC* EC
44076 *h **FD** FG *GW* LA
44077 m **NX** A *EC* EC
44078 *h **FD** P *GW* OO
44079 *h **FD** P *GW* OO
44080 m **NX** A *EC* EC
44081 *h **FD** FG *GW* LA
44083 *h **FD** P *GW* OO
44085 s **ST** P *EM* NL
44086 * **FD** A *GW* LA
44088 t **V** ST LM
44089 t **V** ST LM
44090 *h **FD** P *GW* OO
44091 *h **FD** P *GW* OO
44093 *h **FD** A *GW* OO
44094 m **NX** A *EC* EC
44097 *h **FD** P *GW* OO
44098 m **NX** A *EC* EC
44100 *h **FD** FG *GW* PM
44101 *h **FD** P *GW* OO

# GH3G (TCC)  TRAILER COMPOSITE CATERING

**45001–45005.** Lot No. 30877 Derby 1975–77. 34.3 t. Converted from Mark 3A TSO. Refurbished CrossCountry vehicles with Primarius seating. Galley for the preparation of hot food and stowage space for two trolleys between First and Standard Class sections. One toilet removed. 30/10 1T.

45001 (12004) c **XC** P *XC* EC
45002 (12106) c **XC** P *XC* EC
45003 (12076) c **XC** P *XC* EC
45004 (12077) c **XC** P *XC* EC
45005 (12080) c **XC** P *XC* EC

# 2.3. HST SET FORMATIONS

## FIRST GREAT WESTERN

The largest operator of HSTs is First Great Western with 54 sets to cover 50 diagrams. There are 16 "low density" sets, designed for working longer distance West Country and Swansea services. The rest of the sets are "high density" for other services. 19 TS vehicles are being converted to mini buffet vehicles and this programme was due for completion by late April. The sets are shown here as they should be formed from that time but the allocation of some 401xx vehicles is still to be decided and until they remaining TSRMB conversions are completed 407xx vehicles which are due to go off lease have been retained short-term. Sets that contain 401xx vehicles will mostly run as 7-car formations.

**Number of sets:** 54.
**Maximum number of daily diagrams:** 50.
**Formations:** 8-cars or 7-cars (with 401xx TSRMB vehicle).
**Allocation:** Laira (Plymouth) or Old Oak Common (London).
**Other maintenance and servicing depots:** Landore (Swansea), St. Philip's Marsh (Bristol), Long Rock (Penzance).
**Operation:** London Paddington–Exeter/Plymouth/Penzance, Bristol, Cardiff/Swansea/West Wales, Oxford/Hereford/Malvern/Gloucester.

| Set | H | G | F | E | D | C | B | A | density |
|-----|-----|-----|-----|-----|-----|-----|-----|-----|---------|
| LA01 | 41023 | 41024 | 40755 | 42034 | 42033 | 42007 | 42035 | 44011 | L |
| LA02 | 41031 | 41032 | 40727 | 42046 | 42045 | 42207 | 42047 | 44015 | L |
| LA03 | 41037 | 41038 | 40757 | 42055 | 42343 | 42292 | 42056 | 44018 | L |
| LA04 | 41051 | 41052 | 40710 | 42077 | 42076 | 42004 | 42078 | 44025 | L |
| LA05 | 41093 | 41094 | 40707 | 42185 | 42184 | 42183 | 42107 | 44001 | L |
| LA06 | 41103 | 41104 | 40713 | 42208 | 42054 | 42206 | 42209 | 44066 | L |
| LA07 | 41121 | 41122 | 40722 | 42252 | 42019 | 42345 | 42253 | 44028 | L |
| LA08 | 41123 | 41124 | 40739 | 42256 | 42263 | 42255 | 42257 | 44029 | L |
| LA09 | 41129 | 41130 | 40716 | 42072 | 42325 | 42267 | 42269 | 44032 | L |
| LA10 | 41133 | 41134 | 40721 | 42276 | 42332 | 42275 | 42277 | 44034 | L |
| LA11 | 41116 | 41135 | 40703 | 42280 | 42265 | 42279 | 42281 | 44035 | L |
| LA12 | 41003 | 41136 | 40752 | 42144 | 42143 | 42268 | 42145 | 44049 | L |
| LA13 | 41141 | 41142 | 40734 | 42333 | 42075 | 42291 | 42293 | 44038 | L |
| LA14 | 41143 | 41144 | 40733 | 42296 | 42350 | 42295 | 42297 | 44039 | L |
| LA15 | 41145 | 41146 | 40715 | 42300 | 42351 | 42299 | 42301 | 44040 | L |
| LA16 | 41157 | 41158 | 40743 | 42245 | 42129 | 42200 | 42250 | 44086 | L |
| OC30 | 41007 | 41008 | 40807 | 42079 | 42236 | 42264 | 42080 | 44026 | H |
| OC31 | 41127 | 41128 | 40804 | 42060 | 42197 | 42347 | 42061 | 44020 | H |
| OC32 | 41017 | 41018 | 40801 | 42025 | 42362 | 42024 | 42026 | 44008 | H |
| OC33 | 41027 | 41028 | 40806 | 42040 | 42039 | 42348 | 42041 | 44013 | H |
| OC34 | 41101 | 41102 | 40803 | 42203 | 42027 | 42201 | 42204 | 44064 | H |
| OC35 | 41105 | 41106 | 40808 | 42213 | 42212 | 42211 | 42214 | 44067 | H |
| OC36 | 41004 | 41110 | 40809 | 42346 | 42349 | 42138 | 42089 | 44003 | H |
| OC37 | 41131 | 41132 | 40802 | 42272 | 42073 | 42271 | 42273 | 44033 | H |

| | | | | | | | | |
|---|---|---|---|---|---|---|---|---|
| OC38 | 41137 | 41138 | 40810 | 42284 | 42003 | 42202 | 42285 | 44036 H |
| OC39 | 41179 | 41180 | 40811 | 42196 | 42098 | 42251 | 42283 | 44093 H |
| OC40 | 41181 | 41149 | 40106 | | 42166 | 42174 | *42170* | 44079 H |
| OC41 | 41109 | 41182 | 40107 | | 42222 | 42224 | *42223* | 44101 H |
| OC42 | 41168 | 41183 | 40108 | | 42315 | 42317 | *42316* | 44090 H |
| OC43 | 41186 | 41147 | 40109 | | 42258 | 42266 | *42254* | 44000 H |
| OC44 | 41191 | 41192 | 40110 | | 42115 | 42218 | *42084* | 44097 H |
| OC45 | 41119 | 41187 | 40111 | | 42247 | 42173 | *42249* | 44078 H |
| OC46 | 41096 | 41161 | 40112 | 42294 | 42178 | 42195 | *42338* | 44042 H |
| OC47 | 41081 | 41108 | 40113 | 42095 | 42308 | 42217 | *42090* | 44060 H |
| OC48 | 41184 | 41189 | 40114 | 42365 | 42085 | 42310 | 42087 | 44069 H |
| OC49 | 41148 | 41169 | 40115 | 42320 | 42319 | 42356 | 42321 | 44091 H |
| OC50 | 41153 | 41176 | 40116 | | 42102 | 42381 | 42101 | 44083 H |
| OC51 | 41005 | 41006 | 401 | 42071 | 42070 | 42069 | 42118 | 44023 H |
| OC52 | 41029 | 41030 | 401 | 42043 | 42042 | 42008 | 42044 | 44014 H |
| OC53 | 41033 | 41034 | 401 | 42049 | 42048 | 42066 | 42050 | 44016 H |
| OC54 | 41055 | 41056 | 401 | 42083 | 42074 | 42081 | 42126 | 44043 H |
| OC55 | 41065 | 41089 | 401 | 42067 | 42221 | 42062 | 42068 | 44022 H |
| OC56 | 41125 | 41126 | 401 | 42260 | 42216 | 42344 | 42261 | 44030 H |
| OC57 | 41139 | 41140 | 401 | 42288 | 42099 | 42287 | 42289 | 44037 H |
| LA60 | 41114 | 41162 | 40900 | 42231 | 42232 | 42353 | 42233 | 44074 H |
| LA61 | 41086 | 41160 | 40901 | 42304 | 42303 | 42302 | 42305 | 44068 H |
| LA62 | 41085 | 41167 | 40902 | 42167 | 42168 | 42103 | 42169 | 44055 H |
| LA63 | 41045 | 41059 | 40903 | 42175 | 42176 | 42105 | 42177 | 44081 H |
| LA64 | 41163 | 41166 | 40904 | 42094 | 42093 | 42092 | 42108 | 44076 H |
| LA71 | 41009 | 41010 | 40204 | 42013 | 42360 | 42012 | 42014 | 44004 H |
| LA72 | 41011 | 41012 | 40205 | 42016 | 42005 | 42015 | 42361 | 44005 H |
| LA73 | 41015 | 41016 | 40207 | 42006 | 42096 | 42021 | 42023 | 44007 H |
| LA74 | 41019 | 41020 | 40221 | 42028 | 42009 | 42259 | 42029 | 44009 H |
| LA75 | 41021 | 41022 | 40210 | 42031 | 42010 | 42030 | 42032 | 44010 H |

Spares:

| | | | | | | |
|---|---|---|---|---|---|---|
| OO: | 40718 | 41155 | 42364 | 42382 | 42383 | 44002 | 44024 |
| LA: | 40231 | 44059 | | | | | |
| PM: | 44100 | | | | | | |

**Note:** TS vehicles shown in *italics* are due to be converted to 401xx TSMB vehicles.

407xx buffets still in use at the time of writing (to come off lease): 40709, 40724, 40725, 40726, 40738, 40744. These are generally covering for 401xx vehicles in sets OC51–OC57.

# NETWORK RAIL: NEW MEASUREMENT TRAIN

The Network Rail "New Measurement Train" is used to test and evaluate Britain's main railway lines.

975984   977994   977993   975814   977984

**Spare:** 977995

# NATIONAL EXPRESS EAST COAST

East Coast operates 13 refurbished HST sets on the ECML. As well as serving non-electrified destinations such as Hull and Inverness the East Coast HSTs also work alongside Class 91s and Mark 4 sets on services to Leeds, Newcastle and Edinburgh. All sets have now been refurbished at Wabtec, Doncaster to "Mallard" standard. The M1 etc numbering below refers to the order of this refurbishment.

**Number of sets:** 13.
**Maximum number of daily diagrams:** 11.
**Formations:** 9-cars.
**Allocation:** Craigentinny (Edinburgh).
**Other maintenance depot:** Neville Hill (Leeds).
**Operation:** London King's Cross–Leeds/Harrogate/Skipton/Hull/Newcastle/Edinburgh/Aberdeen/Inverness.

| Set | M | L | J | G | F | E | D | C | B | Ref |
|-----|------|------|-------|-------|-------|-------|-------|-------|-------|------|
| EC51 | 41120 | 41150 | 40748 | 42215 | 42091 | 42146 | 42150 | 42154 | 44094 | M11 |
| EC52 | 41039 | 41040 | 40735 | 42323 | 42189 | 42057 | 42058 | 42059 | 44019 | M3 |
| EC53 | 41090 | 41044 | 40737 | 42340 | 42127 | 42063 | 42064 | 42065 | 44045 | M9 |
| EC54 | 41087 | 41088 | 40706 | 42104 | 42161 | 42171 | 42172 | 42219 | 44056 | M10 |
| EC55 | 41091 | 41092 | 40704 | 42179 | 42188 | 42180 | 42181 | 42106 | 44058 | M4 |
| EC56 | 41170 | 41118 | 40720 | 42241 | 42363 | 42242 | 42243 | 42244 | 44098 | M8 |
| EC57 | 41151 | 41152 | 40740 | 42226 | 42128 | 42182 | 42186 | 42190 | 44080 | M12 |
| EC58 | 41097 | 41098 | 40750 | 42158 | 42238 | 42191 | 42192 | 42193 | 44061 | M2 |
| EC59 | 41099 | 41100 | 40711 | 42235 | 42239 | 42240 | 42198 | 42199 | 44063 | M5 |
| EC60 | 41066 | 41164 | 40742 | 42122 | 42116 | 42357 | 42134 | 42355 | 44031 | M13 |
| EC61 | 41115 | 41165 | 40702 | 42117 | 42159 | 42160 | 42109 | 42110 | 44057 | M1 |
| EC62 | 41185 | 41095 | 40701 | 42306 | 42326 | 42330 | 42237 | 42307 | 44075 | M7 |
| EC63 | 41159 | 41083 | 40708 | 42163 | 42286 | 42228 | 42130 | 42322 | 44050 | M6 |

Spares:
EC:   40705  40805  41190  42354  44077

# GRAND CENTRAL

Grand Central started running services from Sunderland to London in December 2007 and up to three sets are normally formed up for use, although three coaches are still awaiting delivery following refurbishment at Marcroft (41203, 42407 and 42409).

**Number of sets:** 3.
**Maximum number of daily diagrams:** 2.
**Formations:** 5-cars.
**Allocation:** Heaton (Newcastle).
**Operation:** London King's Cross–Sunderland

| Set | TF | TRSB | TS(D) | TS | TS | |
|-----|-------|-------|-------|--------|--------|--|
| GC01 | 41204 | 40424 | 42403 | 42402 | 42401 | |
| GC02 | 41205 | 40426 | 42406 | 42405 | 42404 | |
| GC03 | 41206 | 40433 | 42408 | 41202* | 41201* | * declassified |

## EAST MIDLANDS TRAINS

East Midlands Trains HSTs are concentrated on the Nottingham corridor during the day, with early morning and evening services to Leeds for servicing at Neville Hill. Sets are currently being refurbished at Neville Hill and could be misformed during this time. Refurbished sets shown as R1 etc. below. Set NL03 was involved in an accident at Neville Hill and coaches from this set are normally formed in other sets as part of the refurbishment programme.

**Number of sets:** 11.
**Maximum number of daily diagrams:** 9.
**Formations:** 8-cars.
**Allocation:** Neville Hill (Leeds).
**Other maintenance depot:** Derby Etches Park.
**Operation:** London St. Pancras–Nottingham, Sheffield/Leeds.

| Set | J | G | F | E | D | C | B | A | |
|-----|-----|-----|-----|-----|-----|-----|-----|-----|-----|
| NL01 | 41057 | 41084 | 40730 | 42335 | 42111 | 42112 | 42113 | 44041 | |
| NL02 | 41112 | 41067 | 40754 | 42194 | 42229 | 42227 | 42225 | 44027 | R3 |
| NL03 | 41061 | 41068 | | 42337 | 42119 | 42120 | 42121 | 44054 | |
| NL04 | 41077 | 41064 | 40749 | 42151 | 42164 | 42165 | 42153 | 44047 | |
| NL05 | 41062 | 41154 | 40741 | 42327 | 42123 | 42205 | 42210 | 44073 | |
| NL06 | 41156 | 41041 | 40746 | 42132 | 42131 | 42331 | 42133 | 44046 | R2 |
| NL07 | 41111 | 41070 | 40751 | 42339 | 42135 | 42136 | 42137 | 44044 | |
| NL08 | 41071 | 41072 | 40753 | 42329 | 42139 | 42140 | 42141 | 44048 | |
| NL10 | 41075 | 41076 | 40756 | 42328 | 42341 | 42148 | 42149 | 44051 | |
| NL11 | 41117 | 41046 | 40728 | 42220 | 42100 | 42230 | 42124 | 44085 | R1 |
| NL12 | 41079 | 41069 | 40700 | 42155 | 42156 | 42157 | 42152 | 44070 | |

Spares:
NL:  41063  41078  41113  42125  44071
Accident damaged (NL):  40729  42324

## CROSSCOUNTRY

CrossCountry reintroduced regular HST diagrams on its services from the December 2008 timetable.

**Number of sets:** 5.
**Maximum number of daily diagrams:** 4.
**Formations:** 7-cars (one TS normally spare).
**Allocation:** Craigentinny (Edinburgh).
**Other maintenance depots:** Laira (Plymouth) or Neville Hill (Leeds).
**Operation:** Edinburgh–Leeds–Plymouth is the core route with some services extending to Dundee or Penzance.

| Set | A | B | C | D | E | F | G | H |
|-----|-----|-----|-----|-----|-----|-----|-----|-----|
| XC01 | 41193 | 45001 | 42368 | 42369 | 42370 | 42367 | 42366 | 44021 |
| XC02 | 41194 | 45002 | 42375 | 42374 | 42373 | 42372 | 42371 | 44072 |
| XC03 | 41195 | 45003 | 42290 | 42234 | 42378 | 42377 | 42376 | 44052 |
| XC04 | 41026 | 45004 | 42038 | 42097 | 42037 | 42036 | 42380 | 44012 |
| XC05 | 41035 | 45005 | 42051 | 42342 | 42053 | 42052 | 42379 | 44017 |

# 2.4. SALOONS

Several specialist passenger carrying vehicles, normally referred to as saloons are permitted to run on the National Rail system. Many of these are to pre-nationalisation designs.

## WCJS FIRST SALOON

Built 1892 by LNWR, Wolverton. Originally dining saloon mounted on six-wheel bogies. Rebuilt with new underframe with four-wheel bogies in 1927. Rebuilt 1960 as observation saloon with DMU end. Gangwayed at other end. The interior has a saloon, kitchen, guards vestibule and observation lounge. Gresley bogies. 19/– 1T. 28.5 t. 75 m.p.h.

**Non-standard livery:** London & North Western Railway.

41      (484, 45018)    x   **0**    WC  *WC*    CS

## LNWR DINING SALOON

Built 1890 by LNWR, Wolverton. Mounted on the underframe of LMS GUV 37908 in the 1980s. Contains kitchen and dining area seating 12 at tables for two. Gresley bogies. 10/–. 75 m.p.h. 25.4 t.

**Non-standard livery:** London & North Western Railway.

159     (5159)    x   **0**    WC  *WC*    CS

## GNR FIRST CLASS SALOON

Built 1912 by GNR, Doncaster. Contains entrance vestibule, lavatory, two separate saloons, library and luggage space. Gresley bogies. 19/– 1T. 75 m.p.h. 29.4 t.

**Non-standard livery:** Teak.

807     (4807)    x   **0**    WC  *WC*    CS

## LNER GENERAL MANAGERS SALOON

Built 1945 by LNER, York. Gangwayed at one end with a veranda at the other. The interior has a dining saloon seating 12, kitchen, toilet, office and nine seat lounge. 21/– 1T. B4 bogies. 75 m.p.h. ETH3. 35.7 t.

1999    (902260)    **M**    GS  *GS*    CS        DINING CAR No. 2

# GENERAL MANAGER'S SALOON

Renumbered 1989 from London Midland Region departmental series. Formerly the LMR General Manager's saloon. Rebuilt from LMS period 1 BFK M 5033 M to dia. 1654 and mounted on the underframe of BR suburban BS M 43232. Screw couplings have been removed. B4 bogies. 100 m.p.h. ETH2X.

LMS Lot No. 326 Derby 1927. 27.5 t.

| 6320 | (5033, DM 395707) x | **M** | 62 | *62* | SK |
|------|---------------------|-------|----|------|----|

# GWR FIRST CLASS SALOON

Built 1930 by GWR, Swindon. Contains saloons at either end with body end observation windows, staff compartment, central kitchen and pantry/bar. Numbered DE321011 when in departmental service with British Railways. 20/– 1T. GWR bogies. 75 m.p.h. 34 t.

GWR Lot No. 1431 1930.

| 9004 | **CH** | RA | *WC* | CS |
|------|--------|----|------|----|

# LMS INSPECTION SALOON

Built as engineers' inspection saloon. Non-gangwayed. Observation windows at each end. The interior layout consists of two saloons interspersed by a central lavatory/kitchen/guards section. B5 bogies. 80 m.p.h. 31.5 t.

**Non-standard livery:** EWS dark maroon.

LMS Lot No. 1356 Wolverton 1944.

| 45020 | **0** | DB | *DB* | TO |
|-------|-------|----|------|----|

# "QUEEN OF SCOTS" SERVICE CARS

Converted from BR Mark 1 BSKs. Commonwealth bogies. 100 m.p.h. ETH2.

**Non-standard livery:** London & North Western Railway.

**99035.** Lot No. 30699 Wolverton 1962–63.
**99886.** Lot No. 30721 Wolverton 1963.

| 99035 | (35322) | x | **0** | WC | *WC* | CS | SERVICE CAR No. 2 |
|-------|---------|---|-------|----|------|----|--------------------|
| 99886 | (35407) | x | **0** | WC | *WC* | CS | SERVICE CAR No. 1 |

# VSOE SUPPORT CAR

Converted 199? from Courier vehicle converted from Mark 1 BSK 1986–87. Toilet retained and former compartment area replaced with train manager's office, crew locker room, linen store and dry goods store. The former luggage area has been adapted for use as an engineers' compartment and workshop. Commonwealth bogies. 100 m.p.h. ETH2.

Lot No. 30721 Wolverton 1963. 37 t.

| | | | | | |
|---|---|---|---|---|---|
| 99545 (35466, 80207) | **PC** | VS | *VS* | SL | BAGGAGE CAR No. 11 |

# ROYAL SCOTSMAN SALOONS

Built 1960 by Metro-Cammell as Pullman Parlour First (§ Pullman Kitchen First) for East Coast Main Line services. Rebuilt 1990 as sleeping cars with four twin sleeping rooms (*§ three twin sleeping rooms and two single sleeping rooms at each end). Commonwealth bogies. 38.5 t.

| | | | | | |
|---|---|---|---|---|---|
| 99961 (324 AMBER) * | **M** | GS | *GS* | CS | STATE CAR 1 |
| 99962 (329 PEARL) | **M** | GS | *GS* | CS | STATE CAR 2 |
| 99963 (331 TOPAZ) | **M** | GS | *GS* | CS | STATE CAR 3 |
| 99964 (313 FINCH) § | **M** | GS | *GS* | CS | STATE CAR 4 |

Built 1960 by Metro-Cammell as Pullman Kitchen First for East Coast Main Line services. Rebuilt 1990 as observation car with open verandah seating 32. Commonwealth bogies. 38.5 t.

| | | | | | |
|---|---|---|---|---|---|
| 99965 (319 SNIPE) | **M** | GS | *GS* | CS | OBSERVATION CAR |

Built 1960 by Metro-Cammell as Pullman Kitchen First for East Coast Main Line services. Rebuilt 1993 as dining car. Commonwealth bogies. 38.5 t.

| | | | | | |
|---|---|---|---|---|---|
| 99967 (317 RAVEN) | **M** | GS | *GS* | CS | DINING CAR |

Mark 3A. Converted from SLEP at Carnforth Railway Restoration and Engineering Services in 1997. BT10 bogies. Attendant's and adjacent two sleeping compartments converted to generator room containing a 160 kW Volvo unit. In 99968 four sleeping compartments remain for staff use with another converted for use as a staff shower and toilet. The remaining five sleeping compartments have been replaced by two passenger cabins. In 99969 seven sleeping compartments remain for staff use. A further sleeping compartment, along with one toilet, have been converted to store rooms. The other two sleeping compartments have been combined to form a crew mess. ETH7X. 41.5 t.

Lot. No. 30960 Derby 1981–3.

| | | | | | |
|---|---|---|---|---|---|
| 99968 (10541) | **M** | GS | *GS* | CS | STATE CAR 5 |
| 99969 (10556) | **M** | GS | *GS* | CS | SERVICE CAR |

## RAILFILMS "LMS CLUB CAR"

Converted from BR Mark 1 TSO at Carnforth Railway Restoration and Engineering Services in 1994. Contains kitchen, pantry and two dining saloons. 20/– 1T. Commonwealth bogies. 100 m.p.h. ETH 4.

Lot. No. 30724 York 1963. 37 t.

99993 (5067)　　　　　**M**　RA　*WC*　CS　　　　LMS CLUB CAR

## BR INSPECTION SALOON

Mark 1. Short frames. Non-gangwayed. Observation windows at each end. The interior layout consists of two saloons interspersed by a central lavatory/kitchen/guards/luggage section. 90 m.p.h.

BR Wagon Lot No. 3095 Swindon 1957. B4 bogies. 30.5 t.

999506　　　　　**M**　WC　*WC*　CS

# 2.5. PULLMAN CAR COMPANY SERIES

Pullman cars have never generally been numbered as such, although many
have carried numbers, instead they have carried titles. However, a scheme
of schedule numbers exists which generally lists cars in chronological order.
In this section those numbers are shown followed by the car's title. Cars
described as "kitchen" contain a kitchen in addition to passenger
accommodation and have gas cooking unless otherwise stated. Cars described
as "parlour" consist entirely of passenger accommodation. Cars described
as "brake" contain a compartment for the use of the guard and a luggage
compartment in addition to passenger accommodation.

## PULLMAN PARLOUR FIRST

Built 1927 by Midland Carriage & Wagon Company. Gresley bogies. 26/– 2T.
ETH 2. 41 t.

213  MINERVA          **PC**  VS  *VS*  SL

## PULLMAN PARLOUR FIRST

Built 1928 by Metropolitan Carriage & Wagon Company. Gresley bogies.
24/– 2T. ETH 4. 40 t.

239  AGATHA           **PC**  VS        SL
243  LUCILLE          **PC**  VS  *VS*  SL

## PULLMAN KITCHEN FIRST

Built 1925 by BRCW. Rebuilt by Midland Carriage & Wagon Company in 1928.
Gresley bogies. 20/– 1T. ETH 4. 41 t.

245  IBIS             **PC**  VS  *VS*  SL

## PULLMAN PARLOUR FIRST

Built 1928 by Metropolitan Carriage & Wagon Company. Gresley bogies.
24/– 2T. ETH 4.

254  ZENA             **PC**  VS  *VS*  SL

## PULLMAN KITCHEN FIRST

Built 1928 by Metropolitan Carriage & Wagon Company. Gresley bogies.
20/– 1T. ETH 4. 42 t.

255  IONE             **PC**  VS  *VS*  SL

## PULLMAN KITCHEN COMPOSITE

Built 1932 by Metropolitan Carriage & Wagon Company. Originally included in 6-Pul EMU. Electric cooking. EMU bogies. 12/16 1T.

| 264 | RUTH | | **PC** | VS | | SL |
|-----|------|---|--------|----|---|----|

## PULLMAN KITCHEN FIRST

Built 1932 by Metropolitan Carriage & Wagon Company. Originally included in "Brighton Belle" EMUs but now used as hauled stock. Electric cooking. B5 (SR) bogies (§ EMU bogies). 20/– 1T. ETH 2. 44 t.

| 280 | AUDREY | | **PC** | VS | *VS* | SL |
|-----|--------|---|--------|----|------|----|
| 281 | GWEN | | **PC** | VS | *VS* | SL |
| 283 | MONA | § | **PC** | VS | | SL |
| 284 | VERA | | **PC** | VS | *VS* | SL |

## PULLMAN PARLOUR THIRD

Built 1932 by Metropolitan Carriage & Wagon Company. Originally included in "Brighton Belle" EMUs. EMU bogies. –/56 2T.

| 286 | CAR No. 86 | **PC** | VS | | SL |
|-----|-----------|--------|----|---|----|

## PULLMAN BRAKE THIRD

Built 1932 by Metropolitan Carriage & Wagon Company. Originally driving motor cars in "Brighton Belle" EMUs. Traction and control equipment removed for use as hauled stock. EMU bogies. –/48 1T.

| 292 | CAR No. 92 | **PC** | VS | SL |
|-----|-----------|--------|----|----|
| 293 | CAR No. 93 | **PC** | VS | SL |

## PULLMAN PARLOUR FIRST

Built 1951 by Birmingham Railway Carriage & Wagon Company. Gresley bogies. 32/– 2T. ETH 3. 39 t.

| 301 | PERSEUS | **PC** | VS | *VS* | SL |
|-----|---------|--------|----|------|----|

Built 1952 by Pullman Car Company, Preston Park using underframe and bogies from 176 RAINBOW, the body of which had been destroyed by fire. Gresley bogies. 26/– 2T. ETH 4. 38 t.

| 302 | PHOENIX | **PC** | VS | *VS* | SL |
|-----|---------|--------|----|------|----|

## PULLMAN PARLOUR FIRST

Built 1951 by Birmingham Railway Carriage & Wagon Company. Gresley
bogies. 32/– 2T. ETH 3. 39 t.

308  CYGNUS                    **PC**  VS  *VS*  SL

## PULLMAN FIRST BAR

Built 1951 by Birmingham Railway Carriage & Wagon Company. Rebuilt 1999
by Blake Fabrications, Edinburgh with original timber-framed body replaced
by a new fabricated steel body. Contains kitchen, bar, dining saloon and coupé.
Electric cooking. Gresley bogies. 14/– 1T. ETH 3.

310  PEGASUS                   **PC**  RA  *RA*  EH

Also carries "THE TRIANON BAR" branding.

## PULLMAN KITCHEN SECOND

Built 1960–1961 by Metro-Cammell for East Coast Main Line services.
Commonwealth bogies. –/30 1T. 40 t.

335  CAR No. 335          x   **PC**  VT  *VT*  TM

## PULLMAN PARLOUR SECOND

Built 1960–1961 by Metro-Cammell for East Coast Main Line services.
Commonwealth bogies. 348, 350 and 352 are used as FOs. –/42 2T. 38.5 t.

| 348 | CAR No. 348 | x | **M** | WC | *WC* | CS |
| 349 | CAR No. 349 | x | **PC** | VT | *VT* | TM |
| 350 | CAR No. 350 | x | **M** | WC | *WC* | CS |
| 352 | CAR No. 352 | x | **M** | WC | *WC* | CS |
| 353 | CAR No. 353 | x | **PC** | VT | *VT* | TM |

## PULLMAN SECOND BAR

Built 1960–1961 by Metro-Cammell for East Coast Main Line services.
Commonwealth bogies. –/24 + 17 bar seats. 38.5 t.

354  THE HADRIAN BAR  x  **PC**  WC  *WC*  CS

# 2.6. LOCOMOTIVE SUPPORT COACHES

These carriages have been adapted from Mark 1 BCK, BFK, BSK, NNX and Mark 2 BFK for use as support carriages for heritage steam locomotives. Some seating is retained for the use of personnel supporting the locos operation with the remainder of the carriage adapted for storage, workshop, dormitory and catering purposes. These carriages can spend considerable periods of time off the national railway system when the locos they support are not being used on that system. After the depot code, the loco(s) each carriage is usually used to support is given. Operator codes are not included in this section. Seating capacities refer to the original vehicle as running in normal service.

## AB11 (BFK)                           CORRIDOR BRAKE FIRST

Mark 1. 24/– 1T. Commonwealth bogies. ETH 2.

**14007.** Lot No. 30382 Swindon 1959. 35 t.
**17013–17019.** Lot No. 30668 Swindon 1961. 36 t.
**17025.** Lot No. 30718 Swindon 1963. Metal window frames. 36 t.

| | | | | | |
|---|---|---|---|---|---|
| 14007 | (14007, 17007) | x **M** | B1 | BH | LNER 61264 |
| 17013 | (14013) | x **PC** | JH | SH | LNER 60019 | BUTARUS |
| 17019 | (14019) | x **M** | 92 | CS | BR 70013/SR 30777 |
| 17025 | (14025) | v **M** | PO | CS | LMS 45690 |

## AB1Z (BFK)                           CORRIDOR BRAKE FIRST

Mark 2. Pressure ventilated. 24/– 1T. B4 bogies. ETH 4.

Lot No. 30756 Derby 1966. 31.5 t.

| | | | | | |
|---|---|---|---|---|---|
| 17041 | (14041) | **M** | DG | BQ | BR 71000 |

## AB1A (BFK)                           CORRIDOR BRAKE FIRST

Mark 2A. Pressure ventilated. 24/– 1T. B4 bogies. ETH 4.

Lot No. 30786 Derby 1968. 32 t.

| | | | | | | |
|---|---|---|---|---|---|---|
| 17096 | (14096) | **PC** | MN | SL | SR 35028 | MERCATOR |

## AB31 (BCK)                  CORRIDOR BRAKE COMPOSITE

Mark 1. Two First Class and three Standard Class compartments. 12/18 2T (* 12/24 2T). ETH 2.

**21096.** Lot No. 30185 Metro-Cammell 1956. BR Mark 1 bogies. 32.5 t.
**21232.** Lot No. 30574 GRCW 1960. B4 bogies. 34 t.
**21249.** Lot No. 30669 Swindon 1962. Commonwealth bogies. 34 t.
**21268.** Lot No. 30732 Derby 1964. Commonwealth bogies. 37 t.

**Note:** 21249 is currently undergoing restoration for use with 60163 "TORNADO".

| | | | | |
|---|---|---|---|---|
| 21096 | | x **M** | A4 | NY | LNER 60007 |

| 21232 | x | **M** | 62 | SK | LMS 46233 |
|---|---|---|---|---|---|
| 21249 | x | **M** | A1 | Darlington New build 60163 |
| 21268 | * | **M** | BS | SH | LMS 46100 |

## AB21 (BSK)     CORRIDOR BRAKE STANDARD

Mark 1. Four compartments. Metal window frames and melamine interior panelling. –/24 1T. ETH2.

**35333.** Lot No. 30699 Wolverton 1962–63. Commonwealth bogies. 37 t.
**35449.** Lot No. 30728 Wolverton 1963. Commonwealth bogies. 37 t.
**35453–35486.** Lot No. 30721 Wolverton 1963. Commonwealth bogies. 37 t.

| 35333 | x | **CH** | 24 | DI | GWR 6024 |
|---|---|---|---|---|---|
| 35449 | x | **M** | BE | BQ | LMS 45231 |
| 35453 | x | **CH** | GW | DI | GWR 5051 |
| 35461 | x | **CH** | JH | TM | GWR 5029 |
| 35463 | v | **M** | WC | CS | GWR 5972/LMS 46115/LMS 48151 |
| 35465 | x | **CC** | LW | CQ | LMS 46201 |
| 35468 | v | **M** | NM | YK | National Railway Museum locomotives |
| 35470 | v | **CH** | VT | TM | Tyseley Locomotive Works-based locomotives |
| 35476 | x | **M** | 62 | SK | LMS 46233 |
| 35479 | v | **CH** | SV | KR | Severn Valley Railway-based locomotives |
| 35486 | x | **M** | JC | TN | LNER 60009/61994 |

## AB1C (BFK)     CORRIDOR BRAKE FIRST

Mark 2C. Pressure ventilated. Renumbered when declassified. –/24 1T. B4 bogies. ETH 4.

Lot No. 30796 Derby 1969–70. 32.5 t.

| 35508 | (14128, 17128) | **M** | IR | BQ | LMS 44871/45407 |
|---|---|---|---|---|---|

## AB1A (BFK)     CORRIDOR BRAKE FIRST

Mark 2A. Pressure ventilated. Renumbered when declassified. –/24 1T. B4 bogies. Cage removed from brake compartment. ETH 4.

Lot No. 30786 Derby 1968. 32 t.

| 35517 | (14088, 17088) | **M** | IR | BQ | LMS 44871/45407 |
|---|---|---|---|---|---|
| 35518 | (14097, 17097) | **G** | 67 | SH | SR 34067 |

## NNX     COURIER VEHICLE

Mark 1. Converted 1986–7 from BSKs. One compartment and toilet retained for courier use. One set of roller shutter doors inserted on each side. ETH 2.

**80204/17.** Lot No. 30699 Wolverton 1962. Commonwealth bogies. 37 t.
**80220.** Lot No. 30573 Gloucester 1960. B4 bogies. 33 t.

| 80204 | (35297) | **M** | WC | CS | GWR 5972/LMS 46115/LMS 48151 |
|---|---|---|---|---|---|
| 80217 | (35299) | **M** | WC | CS | GWR 5972/LMS 46115/LMS 48151 |
| 80220 | (35276) | **M** | NE | NY | LNER 62005 |

# 2.7. 99xxx RANGE NUMBER CONVERSION TABLE

The following table is presented to help readers identify vehicles which may carry numbers in the 99xxx range, the former private owner number series which is no longer in general use.

| 99xxx | BR No. | 99xxx | BR No. | 99xxx | BR No. |
|-------|--------|-------|--------|-------|--------|
| 99040 | 21232 | 99349 | Pullman 349 | 99673 | 550 |
| 99041 | 35476 | 99350 | Pullman 350 | 99674 | 551 |
| 99052 | Saloon 41 | 99352 | Pullman 352 | 99675 | 552 |
| 99121 | 3105 | 99353 | Pullman 353 | 99676 | 553 |
| 99122 | 3106 | 99354 | Pullman 354 | 99677 | 586 |
| 99125 | 3113 | 99361 | Pullman 335 | 99678 | 504 |
| 99127 | 3117 | 99371 | 3128 | 99679 | 506 |
| 99128 | 3130 | 99530 | Pullman 301 | 99680 | 17102 |
| 99131 | 1999 | 99531 | Pullman 302 | 99710 | 18767 |
| 99141 | 17041 | 99532 | Pullman 308 | 99716 | 18808 |
| 99241 | 35449 | 99534 | Pullman 245 | 99718 | 18862 |
| 99304 | 21256 | 99535 | Pullman 213 | 99721 | 18756 |
| 99311 | 1882 | 99536 | Pullman 254 | 99722 | 18806 |
| 99312 | 35463 | 99537 | Pullman 280 | 99723 | 35459 |
| 99316 | 13321 | 99539 | Pullman 255 | 99792 | 17019 |
| 99317 | 3766 | 99541 | Pullman 243 | 99880 | 159 |
| 99318 | 4912 | 99543 | Pullman 284 | 99881 | 807 |
| 99319 | 17168 | 99546 | Pullman 281 | 99953 | 35468 |
| 99326 | 4954 | 99547 | Pullman 292 | 99970 | Pullman 232 |
| 99327 | 5044 | 99548 | Pullman 293 | 99972 | Pullman 318 |
| 99328 | 5033 | 99670 | 546 | 99973 | 324 |
| 99329 | 4931 | 99671 | 548 | 99974 | Pullman 328 |
| 99348 | Pullman 348 | 99672 | 549 | | |

# 2.8. MARK 4 SET FORMATIONS

The National Express East Coast Mark 4 sets generally run in fixed formations since their refurbishment at Bombardier, Wakefield (2003–05). These rakes are listed below. Class 91 locomotives are positioned next to Coach B.

| Set | B | C | D | E | F | H | K | L | M | DVT |
|---|---|---|---|---|---|---|---|---|---|---|
| BN01 | 12207 | 12417 | 12415 | 12414 | 12307 | 10307 | 11298 | 11301 | 11401 | 82207 |
| BN02 | 12232 | 12402 | 12450 | 12448 | 12302 | 10302 | 11299 | 11302 | 11402 | 82202 |
| BN03 | 12201 | 12401 | 12459 | 12478 | 12301 | 10320 | 11277 | 11303 | 11403 | 82219 |
| BN04 | 12202 | 12480 | 12421 | 12518 | 12327 | 10303 | 11278 | 11304 | 11404 | 82209 |
| BN05 | 12209 | 12486 | 12520 | 12522 | 12300 | 10326 | 11219 | 11305 | 11405 | 82210 |
| BN06 | 12208 | 12406 | 12420 | 12422 | 12313 | 10309 | 11279 | 11306 | 11406 | 82208 |
| BN07 | 12231 | 12411 | 12405 | 12489 | 12329 | 10323 | 11280 | 11307 | 11407 | 82204 |
| BN08 | 12205 | 12481 | 12485 | 12407 | 12328 | 10300 | 11229 | 11308 | 11408 | 82211 |
| BN09 | 12230 | 12513 | 12483 | 12514 | 12308 | 10331 | 11281 | 11309 | 11409 | 82215 |
| BN10 | 12214 | 12419 | 12488 | 12443 | 12305 | 10304 | 11282 | 11310 | 11410 | 82205 |
| BN11 | 12203 | 12437 | 12436 | 12484 | 12315 | 10308 | 11283 | 11311 | 11411 | 82218 |
| BN12 | 12212 | 12431 | 12404 | 12426 | 12330 | 10333 | 11284 | 11312 | 11412 | 82212 |
| BN13 | 12228 | 12469 | 12430 | 12424 | 12311 | 10313 | 11285 | 11313 | 11413 | 82213 |
| BN14 | 12229 | 12410 | 12526 | 12423 | 12312 | 10332 | 11201 | 11314 | 11414 | 82206 |
| BN15 | 12226 | 12442 | 12409 | 12515 | 12309 | 10306 | 11286 | 11315 | 11415 | 82214 |
| BN16 | 12213 | 12428 | 12445 | 12433 | 12304 | 10315 | 11287 | 11316 | 11416 | 82225 |
| BN17 | 12223 | 12444 | 12427 | 12432 | 12303 | 10324 | 11288 | 11317 | 11417 | 82222 |
| BN18 | 12215 | 12453 | 12468 | 12467 | 12324 | 10305 | 11289 | 11318 | 11418 | 82220 |
| BN19 | 12211 | 12434 | 12400 | 12470 | 12310 | 10318 | 11290 | 11319 | 11419 | 82201 |
| BN20 | 12224 | 12477 | 12439 | 12440 | 12326 | 10321 | 11241 | 11320 | 11420 | 82200 |
| BN21 | 12222 | 12461 | 12441 | 12476 | 12323 | 10330 | 11244 | 11321 | 11421 | 82227 |
| BN22 | 12210 | 12452 | 12460 | 12473 | 12316 | 10301 | 11291 | 11322 | 11422 | 82230 |
| BN23 | 12225 | 12454 | 12456 | 12455 | 12318 | 10325 | 11292 | 11323 | 11423 | 82226 |
| BN24 | 12219 | 12447 | 12425 | 12403 | 12319 | 10328 | 11293 | 11324 | 11424 | 82229 |
| BN25 | 12217 | 12446 | 12519 | 12464 | 12322 | 10312 | 11294 | 11325 | 11425 | 82216 |
| BN26 | 12220 | 12474 | 12465 | 12429 | 12325 | 10311 | 11295 | 11326 | 11426 | 82223 |
| BN27 | 12216 | 12449 | 12466 | 12538 | 12317 | 10319 | 11237 | 11327 | 11427 | 82228 |
| BN28 | 12218 | 12458 | 12463 | 12533 | 12320 | 10310 | 11273 | 11328 | 11428 | 82217 |
| BN29 | 12204 | 12462 | 12457 | 12438 | 12321 | 10317 | 11998 | 11329 | 11429 | 82231 |
| BN30 | 12227 | 12471 | 12534 | 12472 | 12331 | 10329 | 11999 | 11330 | 11430 | 82203 |
| Spare | 12200 | | | | | | | | | 82224 |

# 2.9. SERVICE STOCK

Most vehicles in this section are numbered in the former BR departmental number series. They are used for internal purposes within the railway industry, i.e. they do not generate revenue from outside the industry.

## BARRIER, ESCORT & TRANSLATOR VEHICLES

These vehicles are used to move multiple unit, HST and other vehicles around the national railway system.

**Desiro EMU Barrier Vehicles.** Mark 1. Converted from GUVs with bodies removed and B4 bogies for use as Eurostar barrier vehicles but modified in 2003 by LNWR, Crewe for current use.

**6321.** Lot No. 30343 York 1957. 40 t.
**6322/23.** Lot No. 30616 Pressed Steel 1959–60. 40 t.
**6324.** Lot No. 30403 Glasgow 1958–60. 40 t.
**6325.** Lot No. 30417 Pressed Steel 1958–59. 40 t.

| 6321 | (86515, 96385) | **B** | SM | *FL* | NN |
|------|----------------|-------|-----|------|-----|
| 6322 | (86859, 96386) | **B** | SM | *FL* | NN |
| 6323 | (86973, 96387) | **B** | SM | *FL* | NN |
| 6324 | (86562, 96388) | **B** | SM | *FL* | NN |
| 6325 | (86135, 96389) | **B** | SM | *FL* | NN |

**HST Barrier Vehicles.** Mark 1/2A. Renumbered from BR departmental series, or converted from various types. B4 bogies (* Commonwealth bogies).

**6330.** Mark 2A. Lot No. 30786 Derby 1968. 32 t.
**6336/38/44.** Mark 1. Lot No. 30715 Gloucester 1962. 31 t.
**6340.** Mark 1. Lot No. 30669 Swindon 1962. 36 t.
**6346.** Mark 2A. Lot No. 30777 Derby 1967. 31.5 t.
**6348.** Mark 1. Lot No. 30163 Pressed Steel 1957. 31.5 t.

**Non-standard livery:** 6340, 6344, 6346 All over dark blue.

| 6330 | (14084, 975629) | | **FB** | A | *GW* | LA |
|------|-----------------|---|--------|---|------|-----|
| 6336 | (81591, 92185)  |   | **FB** | A | *GW* | LA |
| 6338 | (81581, 92180)  |   | **FB** | A | *GW* | LA |
| 6340 | (21251, 975678) | * | **0**  | A | *EC* | EC |
| 6344 | (81263, 92080)  | * | **0**  | A | *EC* | EC |
| 6346 | (9422)          |   | **0**  | A | *EC* | EC |
| 6348 | (81233, 92963)  |   | **FB** | A | *GW* | LA |

**Mark 4 Barrier Vehicles.** Mark 2A/2C. Converted from *FK or BSO. B4 bogies.

**6352/3.** Mark 2A. Lot No. 30774 Derby 1968. 33 t.
**6354/5.** Mark 2C. Lot No. 30820 Derby 1970. 32 t.
**6358/9.** Mark 2A. Lot No. 30788 Derby 1968. 31.5 t.

| 6352 | (13465, 19465) | * | **GN** | H | *EC* | BN |
|------|----------------|---|--------|---|------|-----|
| 6353 | (13478, 19478) | * | **GN** | H | *EC* | BN |
| 6354 | (9459)         |   | **GN** | H | *EC* | BN |

| 6355 | (9477) | **GN** | H | *EC* | BN |
| 6358 | (9432) | **GN** | H | *EC* | BN |
| 6359 | (9429) | **GN** | H | *EC* | BN |

**EMU Translator Vehicles.** Mark 1. Converted 1992 from BG. BR Mark 1 bogies.

**6364.** Mark 1. Lot No. 30039 Derby 1954. 32 t.
**6365.** Mark 1. Lot No. 30323 Pressed Steel 1957. 32 t.

| 6364 | (80565) | **RR** | LM | *LM* | SO |
| 6365 | (81296, 84296) | **RR** | LM | *LM* | SO |

**EMU Translator Vehicles.** Mark 1. Converted 1980 from RUO. Commonwealth bogies.

Lot No. 30647 Wolverton 1959–61. 36 t.

| 6376 | (1021, 975973) | **P** | P | *GB* | WB |
| 6377 | (1042, 975975) | **P** | P | *GB* | WB |
| 6378 | (1054, 975971) | **P** | P | *GB* | WB |
| 6379 | (1059, 975972) | **P** | P | *GB* | WB |

**HST Barrier Vehicles.** Mark 1. Converted from BG in 1994–95. B4 bogies.

**6392.** Lot No. 30715 Gloucester 1962. 29.5 t.
**6393/97.** Lot No. 30716 Gloucester 1962. 29.5 t.
**6394.** Lot No. 30162 Pressed Steel 1956–57. 30.5 t.
**6395.** Lot No. 30484 Pressed Steel 1958. 30.5 t.
**6398/99.** Lot No. 30400 Pressed Steel 1957–58. 30.5 t.

| 6392 | (81588, 92183) | **MA** | P | *EM* | NL |
| 6393 | (81609, 92196) | **P** | P | *EC* | EC |
| 6394 | (80878, 92906) | **P** | P | *EC* | EC |
| 6395 | (81506, 92148) | **P** | EM | *EM* | NL |
| 6397 | (81600, 92190) | **MA** | P | *EM* | NL |
| 6398 | (81471, 92126) | **MA** | EM | *EM* | NL |
| 6399 | (81367, 92994) | **MA** | EM | *EM* | NL |

**Escort Coaches.** Converted from Mark 2A BSO. These vehicles use the same bodyshell as the Mark 2A BFK. B4 bogies.

**9419.** Lot No.30777 Derby 1970. 31.5 t.
**9428.** Lot No.30820 Derby 1970. 31.5 t.

| 9419 | | **DS** | DR | *DR* | KM |
| 9428 | | **DS** | DR | *DR* | KM |

**Eurostar Barrier Vehicles.** Mark 1. Converted from GUVs. Bodies removed. B4 bogies.

**96380–96382.** Lot No. 30417 Pressed Steel 1958–59. 40 t.
**96383.** Lot No. 30565 Pressed Steel 1959. 40 t.
**96384.** Lot No. 30616 Pressed Steel 1959–60. 40 t.

| 96380 | (86386, 6380) | **B** | EU | *EU* | TI |
| 96381 | (86187, 6381) | **B** | EU | *EU* | TI |
| 96382 | (86295, 6382) | **B** | EU | *EU* | TI |
| 96383 | (86664, 6383) | **B** | EU | *EU* | TI |
| 96384 | (86955, 6384) | **B** | EU | *EU* | TI |

**EMU Translator Vehicles.** Converted from Mark 1 TSO, RSOs, RUOs, BSKs and GUVs (NP/NL).

**975864.** Lot No. 30054 Eastleigh 1951–54. Commonwealth bogies.
**975867.** Lot No. 30014 York 1950–51. Commonwealth bogies.
**975875.** Lot No. 30143 Charles Roberts 1954–55. Commonwealth bogies.
**975974/975978.** Lot No. 30647 Wolverton 1959–61. Commonwealth bogies.
**977087.** Lot No. 30229 Metro–Cammell 1955–57. Commonwealth bogies.
**977942/948.** Lot No. 30417 Pressed Steel 1958–59. B5 bogies.
**977943/949.** Lot No. 30565 Pressed Steel 1959. B5 bogies.

**Non-standard livery:** 975974 and 975978 Plain grey.

| | | | | | |
|---|---|---|---|---|---|
| 975864 | (3849) | **HB** | H | *FL* | LD |
| 975867 | (1006) | **HB** | H | *FL* | LD |
| 975875 | (34643) | **HB** | H | *FL* | LD |
| 975974 | (1030) | **0** | A | *ME* | BD |
| 975978 | (1025) | **0** | A | *ME* | BD |
| 977087 | (34971) | **HB** | H | *FL* | LD |
| 977942 | (86467, 80251) | **E** | DB | *DB* | EH |
| 977943 | (86718, 80252) | **E** | DB | *DB* | EH |
| 977948 | (86733, 94028) | **E** | DB | *DB* | EH |
| 977949 | (86377, 94025) | **E** | DB | *DB* | EH |

# LABORATORY, TESTING & INSPECTION COACHES

These coaches are used for research, development, testing and inspection on the national railway system. Many are fitted with sophisticated technical equipment.

**Staff Coaches.** Mark 2F. Converted from BR Mark 2F FO later converted to RFB and TSO. B4 bogies.

**1256.** Lot No. 30845 Derby 1973.
**5981.** Lot No. 30860 Derby 1973–74.

| | | | | | |
|---|---|---|---|---|---|
| 1256 | (3296) | **Y** | NR | *SO* | ZA |
| 5981 | | **Y** | NR | *SO* | ZA |

**Generator Vans.** Mark 1. Converted from BR Mark 1 BGs. B5 bogies.

**6260.** Lot No. 30400 Pressed Steel 1957–58.
**6261.** Lot No. 30323 Pressed Steel 1957.
**6262.** Lot No. 30228 Metro-Cammell 1957–58.
**6263.** Lot No. 30163 Pressed Steel 1957.
**6264.** Lot No. 30173 York 1956.

| | | | | | |
|---|---|---|---|---|---|
| 6260 | (81450, 92116) | **NR** | NR | | LU |
| 6261 | (81284, 92988) | **Y** | NR | *SO* | ZA |
| 6262 | (81064, 92928) | **Y** | NR | *SO* | ZA |
| 6263 | (81231, 92961) | **Y** | NR | *SO* | ZA |
| 6264 | (80971, 92923) | **Y** | NR | *SO* | ZA |

**Staff Coach.** Mark 2D. Converted from BR Mark 2D BSO. B4 bogies.

**9481.** Lot No. 30824 Derby 1971.

| | | | | |
|---|---|---|---|---|
| 9481 | **Y** | NR | *SO* | ZA |

**Driving Trailer Coaches.** Converted 2008 at Serco, Derby from Mark 2F DBSOs. Modified to work in Blue Star push-pull mode. Disc brakes. B4 bogies.

**9701–08.** Lot No. 30861 Derby 1974. Converted to DBSO Glasgow 1974.
**9714.** Lot No. 30861 Derby 1974. Converted to DBSO Glasgow 1986.

| | | | | | |
|---|---|---|---|---|---|
| 9701 | (9528) | **Y** | NR | *SO* | ZA |
| 9702 | (9510) | **Y** | NR | *SO* | ZA |
| 9703 | (9517) | **Y** | NR | *SO* | ZA |
| 9708 | (9530) | **Y** | NR | *SO* | ZA |
| 9714 | (9536) | **Y** | NR | *SO* | ZA |

**Ultrasonic Test Coach.** Converted from BR Mark 2E FO then converted to exhibition van. Lot No. 30843 Derby 1972–73. B4 bogies.

| | | | | | |
|---|---|---|---|---|---|
| 99666 | (3250) | **Y** | NR | *SO* | ZA |

**Inspection Saloon.** Converted from Class 202 DEMU TRB at Stewarts Lane for use as a BR Southern Region General Manager's Saloon. Overhauled at FM Rail, Derby in 2004/05 for use as a New Trains Project Saloon. Can be used in push-pull mode with suitably equipped locomotives. Eastleigh 1958. SR Mk. 4 bogies.

| | | | | | | |
|---|---|---|---|---|---|---|
| 975025 | (60755) | **G** | NR | *SO* | ZA | CAROLINE |

**Structure Gauging Train Coach.** Originally used as a Driving Trailer. Converted from BR Mark 1 BSK. Lot No. 30699 Wolverton 1961–63. B4 bogies.

| | | | | | |
|---|---|---|---|---|---|
| 975081 | (35313) | **Y** | NR | *SO* | ZA |

**Overhead Line Equipment Test Coach ("MENTOR").** Converted from BR Mark 1 BSK Lot No. 30142 Gloucester 1954–5. Fitted with pantograph. B4 bogies.

| | | | | | |
|---|---|---|---|---|---|
| 975091 | (34615) | **Y** | NR | *SO* | ZA |

**Structure Gauging Train Dormitory and Generator Coach.** Converted from BR Mark 1 BCK Lot No. 30732 Derby 1962–4. B4 bogies.

| | | | | | |
|---|---|---|---|---|---|
| 975280 | (21263) | **Y** | NR | *SO* | ZA |

**Test Coach.** Converted from BR Mark 1 BSK Lot No. 30699 Wolverton 1961–63. Commonwealth bogies.

| | | | | | |
|---|---|---|---|---|---|
| 975397 | (35386) | **SO** | SO | *SO* | ZA |

**New Measurement Train Conference Coach.** Converted from prototype HST TF Lot No. 30848 Derby 1972. BT10 bogies.

| | | | | | |
|---|---|---|---|---|---|
| 975814 | (11000,41000) | **Y** | NR | *SO* | EC |

**New Measurement Train Lecture Coach.** Converted from prototype HST TRUB Lot No. 30849 Derby 1972–3. BT10 bogies.

| | | | | | |
|---|---|---|---|---|---|
| 975984 | (10000, 40000) | **Y** | NR | *SO* | EC |

**Track Recording Train Dormitory Coach**. Converted from BR Mark 2 BSO. Lot No 30757 Derby 1965–66. B4 bogies.

977337 (9395)                    **Y**    NR    *SO*    ZA

**Radio Equipment Survey Coaches**. Converted from BR Mark 2E TSO. Lot No. 30844 Derby 1972–73. B4 bogies.

977868 (5846)                    **Y**    NR    *SO*    ZA
977869 (5858)                    **Y**    NR    *SO*    ZA

**Test Train Staff Coach**. Converted from Royal Household couchette Lot No. 30889, which in turn had been converted from BR Mark 2B BFK Lot No. 30790 Derby 1969. B5 bogies.

977969 (14112, 2906)             **Y**    NR    *SO*    ZA

**Hot Box Detection Coach**. Converted from BR Mark 2F FO converted to Class 488/2 EMU TFOH. Lot No. 30859 Derby 1973–74. B4 bogies.

977983 (3407, 72503)             **Y**    NR    *SO*    ZA

**New Measurement Train Staff Coach**. Converted from HST TRFK. Lot No. 30884 Derby 1976–77. BT10 bogies.

977984  (40501)                  **Y**    P     *SO*    EC

**Test Train Coach**. Converted from BR Mark 2F TSO converted to Class 488/3 EMU TSO. Lot No. 30860 Derby 1973–74. B4 bogies.

977985  (6019, 72715)            **Y**    NR    *SO*    ZA

**Track Recording Train Coach**. Converted from BR Mark 2D FO subsequently declassified to SO and then converted to exhibition van. Lot No. 30821 Derby 1971.

977986  (3189, 99664)            **Y**    NR    *SO*    ZA

**New Measurement Train Overhead Line Equipment Test Coach**. Converted from HST TGS. Lot No. 30949 Derby 1982. Fitted with pantograph. BT10 bogies.

977993  (44053)                  **Y**    P     *SO*    EC

**New Measurement Train Track Recording Coach**. Converted from HST TGS. Lot No. 30949 Derby 1982. BT10 bogies.

977994  (44087)                  **Y**    P     *SO*    EC

**New Measurement Train Coach**. Converted from HST TRFM. Lot No. 30921 Derby 1978–79. BT10 bogies. Fitted with generator.

977995  (40719, 40619)           **Y**    P     *SO*    EC

**New Measurement Train Coach**. Converted from HST TGS for Hitachi. Lot No. 30949 Derby 1982. BT10 bogies.

977996  (44062)                  **Y**    P             LM

**Radio Equipment Survey Coach**. Converted from Mark 2F TSO converted to Class 488/3 EMU TSOLH. Lot No. 30860 Derby 1973–74. 33.5 t.

977997  (72613, 6126)            **Y**    NR    *SO*    ZA

**Track Recording Coach.** Converted from BR Inspection Saloon. BR Wagon Lot No. 3379. Swindon 1960. B4 bogies.

| | | | | | |
|---|---|---|---|---|---|
| 999508 | | **Y** | SO | *SO* | ZA |

**Track Recording Coach.** Purpose built Mark 2. B4 bogies.

| | | | | | |
|---|---|---|---|---|---|
| 999550 | | **Y** | NR | *SO* | ZA |

**Ultrasonic Test Coaches.** Converted from Class 421 EMU MBSO and Class 432 EMU MSO.

**999602/605.** Lot No. 30862 York 1974. 55.5 t. SR Mk. 6 bogies.
**999606.** Lot No. 30816. York 1970. ? bogies.

| | | | | | |
|---|---|---|---|---|---|
| 999602 | (62483) | **Y** | NR | *SO* | ZA |
| 999605 | (62482) | **Y** | NR | *SO* | ZA |
| 999606 | (62356) | **Y** | NR | *SO* | ZA |

# TEST TRAIN BRAKE FORCE RUNNERS

Converted from Class 488/3 ex-Gatwick Express locomotive-hauled stock (formerly Mark 2 coaches). These vehicles are included in test trains to provide brake force and are not used for any other purposes.

**72612–72639.** Lot No. 30860 Derby 1973–74. 33.5 t.
**72708.** Lot No. 30860 Derby 1973–74. 33.5 t.

| | | | | | |
|---|---|---|---|---|---|
| 72612 | (6156) | **RK** | NR | *SO* | ZA |
| 72616 | (6007) | **Y** | NR | *SO* | ZA |
| 72630 | (6094) | **Y** | NR | *SO* | ZA |
| 72631 | (6096) | **Y** | NR | *SO* | ZA |
| 72639 | (6070) | **Y** | NR | *SO* | ZA |

# BREAKDOWN TRAIN COACHES

These coaches are formed in trains used for the recovery of derailed railway vehicles and were converted from BR Mark 1 BCK, BG and BSK. The current use of each vehicle is given. 975611–613 were previously converted to trailer luggage vans in 1968. BR Mark 1 bogies.

**975087.** Lot No. 30032 Wolverton 1951–52.
**975477/494.** Lot No. 30233 GRCW 1955–57.
**975471.** Lot No. 30095 Wolverton 1953–55.
**975481/574.** Lot No. 30141 GRCW 1954–55.
**975573.** Lot No. 30156 Wolverton 1954–55.
**975611–613.** Lot No. 30162 Pressed Steel 1954–57.
**977088/235.** Lot No. 30229 Metro-Cammell 1955–57.
**977107.** Lot No. 30425 Metro-Cammell 1956–58.

r refurbished

| | | | | | | | |
|---|---|---|---|---|---|---|---|
| 975087 | (34289) | r | **NR** | NR | | SP | Generator Van |
| 975471 | (34543) | r | **NR** | NR | | SP | Staff & Tool Coach |
| 975477 | (35108) | r | **NR** | NR | | SP | Staff Coach |
| 975481 | (34606) | r | **Y** | NR | | SP | Generator Van |
| 975494 | (35082) | r | **Y** | NR | *DB* | MG | Generator Van |

| 975573 | (34729) | r | **Y** | NR | *DB* | MG | Staff Coach |
| 975574 | (34599) | r | **Y** | NR | *DB* | BS | Staff Coach |
| 975611 | (80915, 68201) | r | **Y** | NR | *DB* | BS | Generator Van |
| 975612 | (80922, 68203) | r | **Y** | NR | *DB* | MG | Tool Van |
| 975613 | (80918, 68202) | r | **Y** | NR | *DB* | BS | Tool Van |
| 977088 | (34990) | | **Y** | NR | *DB* | SP | Generator Van |
| 977107 | (21202) | | **Y** | NR | *DB* | SP | Staff Coach |
| 977235 | (34989, 083172) | | **Y** | NR | *DB* | SP | Tool Van |

# INFRASTRUCTURE MAINTENANCE COACHES

### Snowblower Train Coaches

These coaches worked with Snowblower ADB 968501. They were converted from BR Mark 1 BSK. The former use of each vehicle is given. Commonwealth bogies.

**975464.** Lot No. 30386 Charles Roberts 1956–58.
**975486.** Lot No. 30025 Wolverton 1950–52.

| 975464 | (35171) | **Y** | NR | | SP | | Staff & dormitory coach |
| 975486 | (34100) | **Y** | NR | | SP | | Tool van |

### De-Icing Coaches

These coaches are used for removing ice from the conductor rail of DC lines. They were converted from Class 489 DMLVs that had originally been Class 414/3 DMBSOs.

Lot No. 30452 Ashford/Eastleigh 1959. Mk. 4 bogies.

| 68501 | (61281) | **Y** | NR | *GB* | TW |
| 68504 | (61286) | **Y** | NR | *GB* | TW |
| 68505 | (61299) | **Y** | NR | *GB* | TW |
| 68508 | (61272) | **Y** | NR | *GB* | TW |

### Miscellaneous Infrastructure Coaches

These coaches are used for various infrastructure projects on the National Rail network. They were converted from BR Mark 1 BSK & BG and BR Mark 3 SLEP. The current use of each vehicle is given.

**80211.** Lot No. 30699 Wolverton 1961–63. Commonwealth bogies.
**975463.** Lot No. 30156 Wolverton 1954–55. BR Mark 1 bogies.
**975482.** Lot No. 30141 GRCW 1954–55. BR Mark 1 bogies.
**975498.** Lot No. 30074 Wolverton 1953–54. BR Mark 1 bogies.
**977989.** Lot No. 30960 Derby 1981–83. BT 10 bogies.
**977990.** Lot No. 30228 Metro-Cammell 1957-58. B4 bogies.
**977991.** Lot No. 30323 Pressed steel 1957. B4 bogies.

| 80211 | (35296) | **Y** | NR | *SO* | ZA | Staff & Tool Van |
| 975463 | (34721) | **Y** | NR | *SO* | ZA | Staff Coach |
| 975482 | (34602) | **Y** | NR | *SO* | ZA | Generator Van |
| 975498 | (34367) | **Y** | NR | *SO* | ZA | Tool Van |
| 977989 | (10536) | **M** | NR | | ZA | Staff & Dormitory Coach |
| 977990 | (81165, 92937) | **NR** | NR | | SP | Tool Van |
| 977991 | (81308, 92991) | **NR** | NR | | SP | Tool Van |

# INTERNAL USER VEHICLES

These vehicles are confined to yards and depots or do not normally move at all.
Details are given of the internal user number (if allocated), type, former identity,
current use and location. Many of those listed no longer see regular use.

| | | | |
|---|---|---|---|
| 024909 | BR BSOT 9106 | Staff accommodation | Preston Station |
| 025000 | BR BSO 9423 | Staff accommodation | Preston Station |
| 041379 | LMS CCT 35527 | Stores van | Leeman Road EY, York |
| 041898 | BR BG 84608 | Stores van | Leeman Road EY, York |
| 041947 | BR GUV 93425 | Stores van | IL |
| 041963 | LMS milk tank 44047 | Storage tank | DR |
| 042154 | BR GUV 93975 | Stores van | Ipswich Upper Yard |
| 061061 | BR CCT 94135 | Stores van | Oxford station |
| 061223 | BR GUV 93714 | Stores van | Oxford station |
| 083439 | BR CCT 94752 | Stores van | WD |
| 083602 | BR CCT 94494 | Stores van | Three Bridges station |
| 083637 | BR NW 99203 | Stores van | SL |
| 083644 | BR Ferry Van 889201 | Stores van | EH |
| 083664 | BR Ferry Van 889203 | Stores van | EH |
| 095030 | BR GUV 96140 | Stores van | EC |
| - | BR FO 3186 | Instruction Coach | DY |
| - | BR FO 3381 | Instruction Coach | HE |
| - | BR TSO 5636 | Instruction Coach | PM |
| - | BR HSBV 6396 | Stores van | MA |
| - | BR RFB 10256 | Instruction Coach | Yoker |
| - | BR RFB 10260 | Instruction Coach | Yoker |
| - | BR BFK 17156 | Instruction Coach | DY |
| - | BR TSOLH 72614 | Instruction Coach | DY |
| - | BR TSOLH 72615 | Instruction Coach | DY |
| - | BR TSOL 72707 | Instruction Coach | DY |
| - | BR BG 92901 | Stores van | WB |
| - | BR NL 94003 | Stores van | OO |
| - | BR NL 94006 | Stores van | OO |
| - | BR NK 94101 | Stores van | GL |
| - | BR NK 94121 | Stores van | TO |
| - | BR CCT 94181 | Stores van | SL |
| - | BR NB 94438 | Stores van | TO |
| - | BR GUV 96139 | Stores van | MA |
| - | BR Ferry Van 889017 | Stores van | SL |
| - | BR Ferry Van 889200 | Stores van | SL |
| - | BR Ferry Van 889202 | Stores van | SL |
| - | BR TSO 975403 | Cinema Coach | PM |

**Notes:** CCT = Covered Carriage Truck (a 4-wheeled van similar to a GUV)
GUV = General Utility Van
NB = High Security Brake Van (converted from BG)
NK= High Security General Utility Van
NL = Newspaper Van (converted from a GUV)
NW = Bullion Van (converted from a BSK)

# 2.10. COACHING STOCK AWAITING DISPOSAL

This list contains the last known locations of coaching stock awaiting disposal. The definition of which vehicles are "awaiting disposal" is somewhat vague, but generally speaking these are vehicles of types not now in normal service or vehicles which have been damaged by fire, vandalism or collision.

| | | | | | | | |
|---|---|---|---|---|---|---|---|
| 1204 | SN | 10682 | LM | 94155 | SP | 94326 | TY |
| 1205 | ZA | 10709 | ZN | 94160 | MH | 94331 | ** |
| 1644 | CS | 10710 | LM | 94166 | BS | 94332 | TY |
| 1650 | CS | 10727 | LM | 94168 | SP | 94333 | TY |
| 1652 | CS | 10731 | LM | 94170 | CD | 94334 | CD |
| 1655 | CS | 12096 | ZN | 94176 | BS | 94335 | TY |
| 1663 | CS | 13306 | CS | 94177 | TO | 94336 | TY |
| 1670 | CS | 13320 | CS | 94190 | SP | 94337 | WE |
| 2127 | CS | 13323 | CS | 94191 | SP | 94338 | WE |
| 3181 | CD | 13508 | CS | 94192 | ME | 94340 | CD |
| 4860 | CS | 17161 | CE | 94195 | BS | 94343 | MH |
| 4932 | CS | 18837 | CS | 94196 | ME | 94344 | TO |
| 4997 | CS | 18893 | CS | 94197 | BS | 94400 | ** |
| 5299 | CS | 19013 | CS | 94199 | ME | 94401 | ME |
| 5600 | CS | 34525 | CS | 94203 | SP | 94406 | MH |
| 5647 | CD | 40417 | ZK | 94207 | TO | 94408 | TY |
| 5727 | CS | 40425 | ZK | 94208 | TO | 94410 | WE |
| 5756 | CS | 41043 | ZB | 94209 | ** | 94411 | ** |
| 5779 | ZH | 80403 | CS | 94213 | ME | 94412 | ME |
| 5812 | IS | 80404 | CS | 94214 | MH | 94413 | ME |
| 5897 | IS | 84364 | DW | 94217 | MH | 94416 | ME |
| 6178 | HM | 84519 | CD | 94221 | ME | 94420 | MH |
| 6335 | LA | 92111 | CD | 94222 | MH | 94422 | TO |
| 6339 | EC | 92114 | ZA | 94224 | CD | 94423 | BS |
| 6345 | EC | 92159 | KT | 94225 | MH | 94427 | WE |
| 6360 | NL | 92193 | ** | 94227 | TE | 94428 | ME |
| 6361 | NL | 92303 | CD | 94229 | MH | 94429 | TE |
| 6523 | CS | 92400 | CD | 94302 | TY | 94431 | MH |
| 6805 | ZG | 92908 | CS | 94303 | TY | 94432 | ME |
| 6808 | ZG | 92929 | CD | 94304 | MH | 94433 | MH |
| 6811 | ZG | 92936 | CD | 94306 | TY | 94434 | TY |
| 6817 | ZG | 92939 | ZA | 94307 | ** | 94435 | TO |
| 6828 | ZG | 93723 | BY | 94308 | MH | 94440 | ME |
| 6829 | ZG | 94103 | ** | 94310 | WE | 94445 | WE |
| 9482 | NL | 94104 | TO | 94311 | WE | 94450 | WE |
| 10201 | LM | 94106 | MH | 94313 | WE | 94451 | WE |
| 10222 | ZN | 94116 | TY | 94316 | TO | 94458 | ** |
| 10540 | LM | 94137 | ME | 94317 | TO | 94462 | CD |
| 10547 | IS | 94147 | ME | 94318 | ** | 94463 | TY |
| 10554 | LM | 94150 | SP | 94322 | MH | 94470 | TO |
| 10681 | LM | 94153 | WE | 94323 | TY | 94476 | CD |

| | | | | | | |
|---|---|---|---|---|---|---|
| 94479 | TO | 94538 | EH | 96191 | CS | 975685 Portobello |
| 94481 | ** | 94539 | MH | 96192 | CS | 975686 Portobello |
| 94482 | MH | 94540 | TJ | 96210 | CS | 975687 Portobello |
| 94488 | CD | 94541 | ME | 96218 | CS | 975688 Portobello |
| 94490 | MH | 94542 | TY | 96371 | WB | 975699 Preston |
| 94492 | WE | 94543 | ME | 96372 | ZN | 975700 Preston |
| 94495 | TY | 94544 | MH | 96373 | ZN | 975714 Preston |
| 94497 | ME | 94545 | TE | 96374 | ZN | 975724 Preston |
| 94498 | MH | 94546 | TY | 96375 | ZN | 975734 Preston |
| 94499 | CD | 94547 | MH | 96602 | LM | 975744 Preston |
| 94501 | TO | 94548 | TY | 96603 | LM | 975976 ZG |
| 94504 | TY | 95300 | MH | 96604 | LM | 975977 ZG |
| 94512 | TY | 95301 | MH | 96605 | LM | 975991 CD |
| 94514 | ME | 95400 | MH | 96606 | LM | 977077 ** |
| 94515 | EH | 95410 | MH | 96607 | LM | 977085 BH |
| 94517 | CD | 95727 | WE | 96608 | LM | 977095 CS |
| 94518 | ME | 95754 | TY | 96609 | LM | 977111 ** |
| 94519 | ME | 95758 | SP | 99014 | ** | 977112 ** |
| 94520 | TY | 95761 | WE | 99015 | ** | 977163 AP |
| 94521 | CD | 95763 | BS | 99019 | ZR | 977165 AP |
| 94522 | TY | 96100 | TM | 200715 | IS | 977166 AP |
| 94525 | TY | 96101 | LM | 787395 | IS | 977167 AP |
| 94526 | TY | 96110 | CS | 889005 | Bedford | 977359 ZN |
| 94527 | TY | 96132 | CS | 889400 | ZA | 977399 NL |
| 94528 | ME | 96135 | CS | 975000 | ZA | 977618 BY |
| 94529 | CD | 96164 | CS | 975290 | ZA | 977855 ZA |
| 94530 | ME | 96165 | CS | 975454 | TO | 977905 EH |
| 94531 | TY | 96170 | CS | 975484 | CS | 977974 ZA |
| 94532 | ** | 96175 | CS | 975639 | CS | |
| 94534 | ME | 96178 | CS | 975681 | Portobello | |
| 94536 | ME | 96182 | CS | 975682 | Portobello | DS 70220 ** |

** Other locations:

| | | | |
|---|---|---|---|
| 92193 | Preston Carriage Sidings | 94481 | Cardiff Tidal Yard |
| 94103 | Cardiff Tidal Yard | 94532 | Long Marston Aerodrome |
| 94209 | Cardiff Tidal Yard | 99014 | Horsham Yard |
| 94307 | Cardiff Tidal Yard | 99015 | Horsham Yard |
| 94318 | Cardiff Tidal Yard | 977077 | Ripple Lane Yard |
| 94331 | Cardiff Tidal Yard | 977111 | Ripple Lane Yard |
| 94400 | Cardiff Tidal Yard | 977112 | Ripple Lane Yard |
| 94411 | Cardiff Tidal Yard | DS70220 | Western Trading Estate |
| 94458 | Cardiff Tidal Yard | | Siding, North Acton |

# 3. DIESEL MULTIPLE UNITS

# INTRODUCTION

## DMU CLASSES

DMU Classes are listed in class number order. Principal details and dimensions are quoted for each class in metric and/or imperial units as considered appropriate bearing in mind common usage in the UK.

All dimensions and weights are quoted for vehicles in an "as new" condition with all necessary supplies (e.g. oil, water, sand) on board. Dimensions are quoted in the order Length – Width. All lengths quoted are over buffers or couplers as appropriate. Where two lengths are quoted, the first refers to outer vehicles in a set and the second to inner vehicles. All width dimensions quoted are maxima.

## NUMERICAL LISTINGS

DMUs are listed in numerical order of set – using current numbers as allocated by the RSL. Individual "loose" vehicles are listed in numerical order after vehicles formed into fixed formations. Where sets or vehicles have been renumbered in recent years, former numbering detail is shown in parentheses. Each entry is laid out as in the following example:

| RSL Set No. | Detail | Livery | Owner | Operator | Depot | Formation | | Name |
|---|---|---|---|---|---|---|---|---|
| 142 073 | v | AV | A | AW | CF | 55723 | 55769 | Myfanwy |

**Detail Differences.** Detail differences which currently affect the areas and types of train which vehicles may work are shown, plus differences in interior layout. Where such differences occur within a class, these are shown either in the heading information or alongside the individual set or vehicle number. The following standard abbreviations are used:

e   European Railway Traffic Management System (ERTMS) signalling equipment fitted.
r   Radio Electric Token Block signalling equipment fitted.

Use of the above abbreviations indicates the equipment fitted is normally operable. Meaning of non-standard abbreviations is detailed ion individual class headings.

**Set Formations.** Regular set formations are shown where these are normally maintained. Readers should note set formations might be temporarily varied from time to time to suit maintenance and/or operational requirements. Vehicles shown as "spare" are not formed in any regular set formation.

**Codes.** Codes are used to denote the livery, owner, operation and depot of each unit. Details of these will be found in section 5 of this book. Where a unit or spare car is off-lease, the operator column will be left blank.

**Names**. Only names carried with official sanction are listed. As far as possible names are shown in UPPER/lower case characters as actually shown on the name carried on the vehicle(s). Unless otherwise shown, complete units are regarded as named rather than just the individual car(s) which carry the name.

# GENERAL INFORMATION

## CLASSIFICATION AND NUMBERING

First generation ("Heritage") DMUs are classified in the series 100–139.
Second generation DMUs are classified in the series 140–199.
Diesel-electric multiple units are classified in the series 200–249.
Service units are classified in the series 930–999.
First and second generation individual cars are numbered in the series 50000–59999 and 79000–79999.

DEMU individual cars are numbered in the series 60000–60999, except for a few former EMU vehicles which retain their EMU numbers.

Service stock individual cars are numbered in the series 975000–975999 and 977000–977999, although this series is not exclusively used for DMU vehicles.

## OPERATING CODES

These codes are used by train operating company staff to describe the various different types of vehicles and normally appear on data panels on the inner (i.e. non driving) ends of vehicles.

The first part of the code describes whether or not the car has a motor or a driving cab as follows:

DM  Driving motor.
M    Motor
DT  Driving trailer
T    Trailer

The next letter is a "B" for cars with a brake compartment.

This is followed by the saloon details:

F    First
S    Standard
C    Composite

so denotes a semi-open vehicle (part compartments, part open). All other vehicles are assumed to consist solely of open saloons.

L denotes a vehicle with a toilet.

Finally vehicles with a buffet are suffixed RB or RMB for a miniature buffet.

Where two vehicles of the same type are formed within the same unit, the above codes may be suffixed by (A) and (B) to differentiate between the vehicles.

A composite is a vehicle containing both first and standard class accommodation, whilst a brake vehicle is a vehicle containing separate specific accommodation for the conductor.

**Special Note:** Where vehicles have been declassified, the correct operating code which describes the actual vehicle layout is quoted in this publication.

# BUILD DETAILS

**Lot Numbers**
Vehicles ordered under the auspices of BR were allocated a lot (batch) number when ordered and these are quoted in class headings and sub-headings.

**Builders**
These are shown in class headings. Abbreviations used are found in section 6.7.

Information on sub-contracting works which built parts of vehicles e.g. the underframes etc. is not shown.

# ACCOMMODATION

The information given in class headings and sub-headings is in the form F/S nT (or TD) nW. For example 12/54 1T 1W denotes 12 first class and 54 standard class seats, one toilet and one space for a wheelchair. A number in brackets (i.e. (2)) denotes tip-up seats (in addition to the fixed seats). Tip-up seats in vestibules do not count. The seating layout of open saloons is shown as 2+1, 2+2 or 3+2 as the case may be. Where units have first class accommodation as well as standard and the layout is different for each class then these are shown separately prefixed by "1:" and "2:". TD denotes a toilet suitable for use by a disabled person.

▲ Two Parry People Movers vehicles now work shuttle services on the short Stourbridge branch. On 15/06/09 139 002 carries full London Midland livery as it leaves Stourbridge Town with the 17.16 to Stourbridge Junction. **Robert Pritchard**

▼ Chiltern Railways "Bubble car" 121 020 arrives at Princes Risborough with the 09.40 from Aylesbury on 16/07/09. **Robert Pritchard**

▲ Northern-liveried 142 025 arrives at Metrocentre with the 11.44 Hexham–Middlesbrough on 21/10/08. **Robert Pritchard**

▼ First Great Western "Local Lines"-liveried 143 612 leaves Dawlish Warren with the 16.45 Exeter Central–Paignton on 04/07/09. **Colin Marsden**

▲ Northern-liveried 144 008 arrives at Althorpe with the 08.25 Sheffield–Scunthorpe on 16/03/09. **Andrew Wills**

▼ Network West Midlands-liveried 150 126 leads a Centro-liveried 150 away from its Birmingham Moor Street stop with a Shirley service on 02/06/09. **Cliff Beeton**

Northern-liveried 150 140 leaves Sheffield with the 17.53 Hope Valley stopping service to Manchester Piccadilly on 29/06/08.

**Gordon Clarke**

▲ First Great Western "Local Lines"-liveried 153 329 stands at Plymouth with the 09.34 to Gunnislake on 09/06/08. **Robert Pritchard**

▼ London Midland-liveried 153 371 passes Woburn Sands with the 10.01 Bletchley–Bedford on 08/08/09. **Mark Beal**

Northern-liveried 155 346, with promotional vinyls for the Calder Valley Line, leaves Halifax with the 15.54 Manchester Victoria–Leeds on 14/04/07. **Gavin Morrison**

▲ East Midlands Trains-liveried 156 414 passes Unstone, near Dronfield, with the 15.44 Nottingham–Liverpool on 24/08/08. **Robert Pritchard**

▼ In the new Scotland's Railways "Saltire" livery, 156 512, passes Fauldhouse with the 13.15 Glasgow Central–Edinburgh via Shotts on 25/07/09. **Ian Lothian**

Refurbished East Midlands Trains 158 852, in Stagecoach livery, passes Wash near Chinley with the 13.57 Norwich–Liverpool Lime Street on 30/05/09. **Andrew Wills**

▲ First Great Western's 158 769 passes Norton Bavant, near Warminster, with the 10.30 Cardiff Central–Portsmouth Harbour on 02/01/09. **Andrew Mist**

▼ 159 010 leads 159 011 just west of Axminster (on a section of line to be double-tracked) with the 16.20 London Waterloo–Exeter St Davids on 07/07/09. **Robert Pritchard**

▲ Chiltern Railways-liveried 165 005 passes Neasden shortly after departure from London Marylebone with the 17.00 to Aylesbury via Princes Risborough on 31/05/09. **Robert Pritchard**

▼ First Great Western "Dynamic Lines"-liveried 166 214 arrives at Guildford with the 08.04 Reading–Redhill on 30/05/09. **Alex Dasi-Sutton**

▲ Chiltern Railways-liveried 168 001 passes Kings Sutton with the 16.36 London Marylebone–Stratford-upon-Avon on 07/08/09. **Mark Beal**

▼ In "One" livery with white National Express stripe, 170 206 arrives at Marks Tey with the 07.38 London Liverpool Street–Lowestoft on 12/06/09. **Robert Pritchard**

▲ With a threatening sky behind, Strathclyde PTE-liveried 170 476 passes Greenhill Lower Junction with the 18.44 Falkirk Grahamston–Glasgow Queen Street on 24/07/09. **Ian Lothian**

▼ Arriva Trains-liveried 175 107 passes Moore near Warrington with the 07.45 Llandudno–Manchester Piccadilly on 04/06/09. **Andrew Wills**

▲ Grand Central-liveried 180 112 passes Brafferton, north of Darlington, with a crew training run from York to Heaton on 31/08/09, just before the class entered service on the Sunderland–King's Cross route.          **Grand Central**

▼ Now back on the main line, "Hastings" DEMU 1001 works a 1Z82 06.31 Hastings–Nottingham "Midland Forester" charter at East Goscote (near Melton Mowbray) on 04/07/09. DMSO 60118 "Tunbridge Wells" is leading.          **Bill Atkinson**

TransPennine Express "Desiro" 185 133 passes Millhouses, Sheffield with the 17.42 Doncaster–Manchester Airport on 24/06/09.

**Robert Pritchard**

▲ CrossCountry-liveried 220 023 is seen near Dore & Totley with the 14.05 Edinburgh–Plymouth on 19/07/08. **Robert Pritchard**

▼ Virgin Trains-liveried 221 112 "Ferdinand Magellan" arrives at Warrington Bank Quay with the 06.52 Edinburgh–Birmingham New Street on 19/03/09. **Robert Pritchard**

▲ Stagecoach-liveried 222 002 arrives at Sheffield with an e.c.s. working from Derby (to form a service to London St. Pancras) on 12/07/09. **Robert Pritchard**

▼ Network Rail Track Assessment Unit 950 001 works a 2Q08 09.44 Ipswich–Norwich test train at West House Crossing on the Sizewell branch on 11/03/09.
**Aubrey Evans**

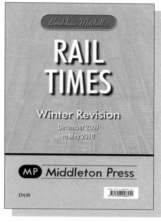

# 3.1. DIESEL MECHANICAL & DIESEL HYDRAULIC UNITS

## 3.1.1. FIRST GENERATION UNITS

### CLASS 121           PRESSED STEEL SUBURBAN

First generation units used by Chiltern Railways on selected Aylesbury–Princes Risborough services (121 020) and by Arriva Trains Wales on Cardiff Queen Street–Cardiff Bay shuttles (121 032).

**Construction:** Steel.
**Engines:** Two Leyland 1595 of 112 kW (150 h.p.) at 1800 r.p.m.
**Transmission:** Mechanical. Cardan shaft and freewheel to a four-speed epicyclic gearbox and final drive.
**Bogies:** DD10.
**Brakes:** Vacuum.
**Couplers:** Screw.
**Dimensions:** 20.45 x 2.82 m.
**Gangways:** Non gangwayed single cars with cabs at each end.
**Wheel arrangement:** 1-A + A-1.
**Doors:** Manually-operated slam.
**Maximum Speed:** 70 m.p.h.
**Seating Layout:** 3+2 facing.
**Multiple Working:** "Blue Square" coupling code. First Generation vehicles cannot be coupled to Second Generation units.

**55020/55032. DMBS.** Lot No. 30518 1960/1961. –/65. 38.0 t.

**Non-standard livery:** 121 020 All over Chiltern blue with a silver stripe.

**Notes:** Fitted with central door locking.

121 020 formerly in departmental use as unit 960 002 (977722).

121 032 formerly in departmental use as 977842, and more recently in preservation at The Railway Age, Crewe.

| | | | | | |
|---|---|---|---|---|---|
| 121 020 | **0** | CR | *CR* | AL | 55020 |
| 121 032 | **AV** | AW | *AW* | CF | 55032 |

## 3.1.2 PARRY PEOPLE MOVERS

## CLASS 139                                                          PPM-60

Gas/flywheel hybrid drive Railcars used on the Stourbridge Junction–Stourbridge Town branch.

**Body construction:** Stainless steel framework.
**Chassis construction:** Welded mild steel box section.
**Primary Drive:** Ford MVH420 2.3 litre 64 kW (86 h.p.) LPG fuel engine driving through Newage marine gearbox, Tandler bevel box and 4 "V" belt driver to flywheel.
**Flywheel Energy Store:** 500 kg, 1 m diameter, normal operational speed range 1000–1500 r.p.m.
**Final transmission:** 4 "V" belt driver from flywheel to Tandler bevel box, Linde hydrostatic transmission and spiral bevel gearbox at No. 2 end axle.
**Braking:** Normal service braking by regeneration to flywheel (1 m/s/s); emergency/parking braking by sprung-on, air-off disc brakes (3 m/s/s).
**Maximum Speed:** 45 m.p.h.
**Dimensions:** 8.7 x 2.4 m.
**Doors:** Deans powered doors, double-leaf folding (one per side).
**Seating Layout:** 1+1 unidirectional/facing.
**Multiple Working:** Not applicable.

39001–39002. **DMS.** Main Road Sheet Metal, Leyland 2007–08. –/20 1W. 12.5 t.

| 139 001 | **LM** | P | *LM* | SJ | 39001 |
| 139 002 | **LM** | P | *LM* | SJ | 39002 |

## 3.1.3. SECOND GENERATION UNITS

All units in this section have air brakes and are equipped with public address, with transmission equipment on driving vehicles and flexible diaphragm gangways. Except where otherwise stated, transmission is Voith 211r hydraulic with a cardan shaft to a Gmeinder GM190 final drive.

## CLASS 142     PACER     BREL DERBY/LEYLAND

DMS–DMSL.

**Construction:** Steel underframe, aluminium alloy body and roof. Built from Leyland National bus parts on four-wheeled underframes.
**Engines:** One Cummins LT10-R of 165 kW (225 h.p.) at 1950 r.p.m.
**Couplers:** BSI at outer ends, bar within unit.
**Dimensions:** 15.55 x 2.80 m.

| | |
|---|---|
| **Gangways:** Within unit only. | **Wheel Arrangement:** 1-A + A-1. |
| **Doors:** Twin-leaf inward pivoting. | **Maximum Speed:** 75 m.p.h. |

**Seating Layout:** 3+2 mainly unidirectional bus/bench style unless stated.
**Multiple Working:** Within class and with Classes 143, 144, 150, 153, 155, 156, 158 and 159.

**55542–55591. DMS.** Lot No. 31003 1985–1986. –/62 (c –/46(6) 2W, s –/56, t –/53 or 55 1W, u –/52 or 54 1W). 24.5 t.
**55592–55641. DMSL.** Lot No. 31004 1985–1986. –/59 1T (c –/44(6) 1T 2W, s –/50 1T, u –/60 1T). 25.0 t.
**55701–55746. DMS.** Lot No. 31013 1986–1987. –/62 (c –/46(6) 2W, s –/56, t –/53 or 55 1W, u –/52 or 54 1W). 24.5 t.
**55747–55792. DMSL.** Lot No. 31014 1986–1987. –/59 1T (c –/44(6) 1T 2W, s –/50 1T, u –/60 1T). 25.0 t.

**Notes:**

c Refurbished Arriva Trains Wales units. Fitted with 2+2 individual Chapman seating.
s Fitted with 2+2 individual high-back seating.
t Former First North Western facelifted units – DMS fitted with a luggage/bicycle rack and wheelchair space.
u Merseytravel units – Fitted with 3+2 individual low-back seating.

The following units are on sub-lease from Northern to First Great Western: 142 001/009/029/030/063/064/068.

| 142 001 | t | **NW** | A | *GW* | EX | 55542 | 55592 |
|---|---|---|---|---|---|---|---|
| 142 002 | c | **AV** | A | *AW* | CF | 55543 | 55593 |
| 142 003 | | **NO** | A | *NO* | NH | 55544 | 55594 |
| 142 004 | t | **NO** | A | *NO* | NH | 55545 | 55595 |
| 142 005 | t | **NO** | A | *NO* | NH | 55546 | 55596 |
| 142 006 | c | **AV** | A | *AW* | CF | 55547 | 55597 |
| 142 007 | t | **NO** | A | *NO* | NH | 55548 | 55598 |
| 142 009 | t | **NW** | A | *GW* | EX | 55550 | 55600 |
| 142 010 | c | **AV** | A | *AW* | CF | 55551 | 55601 |
| 142 011 | t | **NO** | A | *NO* | NH | 55552 | 55602 |
| 142 012 | t | **NO** | A | *NO* | NH | 55553 | 55603 |
| 142 013 | | **NO** | A | *NO* | NH | 55554 | 55604 |
| 142 014 | t | **NO** | A | *NO* | NH | 55555 | 55605 |
| 142 015 | s | **NO** | A | *NO* | HT | 55556 | 55606 |
| 142 016 | s | **NO** | A | *NO* | HT | 55557 | 55607 |
| 142 017 | s | **NO** | A | *NO* | HT | 55558 | 55608 |
| 142 018 | s | **NO** | A | *NO* | HT | 55559 | 55609 |
| 142 019 | s | **NO** | A | *NO* | HT | 55560 | 55610 |
| 142 020 | s | **NO** | A | *NO* | HT | 55561 | 55611 |
| 142 021 | s | **NO** | A | *NO* | HT | 55562 | 55612 |
| 142 022 | s | **NO** | A | *NO* | HT | 55563 | 55613 |
| 142 023 | t | **NO** | A | *NO* | HT | 55564 | 55614 |
| 142 024 | s | **NO** | A | *NO* | HT | 55565 | 55615 |
| 142 025 | s | **NO** | A | *NO* | HT | 55566 | 55616 |
| 142 026 | s | **NO** | A | *NO* | HT | 55567 | 55617 |
| 142 027 | t | **NO** | A | *NO* | HT | 55568 | 55618 |
| 142 028 | t | **NO** | A | *NO* | NH | 55569 | 55619 |
| 142 029 | | **NW** | A | *GW* | EX | 55570 | 55620 |
| 142 030 | | **NW** | A | *GW* | EX | 55571 | 55621 |
| 142 031 | t | **NO** | A | *NO* | NH | 55572 | 55622 |
| 142 032 | t | **NO** | A | *NO* | NH | 55573 | 55623 |
| 142 033 | t | **NO** | A | *NO* | NH | 55574 | 55624 |

| | | | | | | | | |
|---|---|---|---|---|---|---|---|---|
| 142 034 | t | **N0** | A | *N0* | HT | 55575 | 55625 | |
| 142 035 | t | **N0** | A | *N0* | NH | 55576 | 55626 | |
| 142 036 | t | **N0** | A | *N0* | NH | 55577 | 55627 | |
| 142 037 | t | **N0** | A | *N0* | NH | 55578 | 55628 | |
| 142 038 | t | **N0** | A | *N0* | NH | 55579 | 55629 | |
| 142 039 | t | **N0** | A | *N0* | NH | 55580 | 55630 | |
| 142 040 | t | **N0** | A | *N0* | NH | 55581 | 55631 | |
| 142 041 | u | **N0** | A | *N0* | NH | 55582 | 55632 | |
| 142 042 | u | **N0** | A | *N0* | NH | 55583 | 55633 | |
| 142 043 | u | **N0** | A | *N0* | NH | 55584 | 55634 | |
| 142 044 | u | **N0** | A | *N0* | NH | 55585 | 55635 | |
| 142 045 | u | **N0** | A | *N0* | NH | 55586 | 55636 | |
| 142 046 | u | **N0** | A | *N0* | NH | 55587 | 55637 | |
| 142 047 | u | **N0** | A | *N0* | NH | 55588 | 55638 | |
| 142 048 | u | **N0** | A | *N0* | NH | 55589 | 55639 | |
| 142 049 | u | **N0** | A | *N0* | NH | 55590 | 55640 | |
| 142 050 | s | **N0** | A | *N0* | HT | 55591 | 55641 | |
| 142 051 | u | **N0** | A | *N0* | NH | 55701 | 55747 | |
| 142 052 | u | **N0** | A | *N0* | NH | 55702 | 55748 | |
| 142 053 | u | **N0** | A | *N0* | NH | 55703 | 55749 | |
| 142 054 | u | **N0** | A | *N0* | NH | 55704 | 55750 | |
| 142 055 | u | **N0** | A | *N0* | NH | 55705 | 55751 | |
| 142 056 | u | **N0** | A | *N0* | NH | 55706 | 55752 | |
| 142 057 | u | **N0** | A | *N0* | NH | 55707 | 55753 | |
| 142 058 | u | **N0** | A | *N0* | NH | 55708 | 55754 | |
| 142 060 | t | **N0** | A | *N0* | NH | 55710 | 55756 | |
| 142 061 | t | **N0** | A | *N0* | NH | 55711 | 55757 | |
| 142 062 | t | **N0** | A | *N0* | NH | 55712 | 55758 | |
| 142 063 | t | **NW** | A | *GW* | EX | 55713 | 55759 | |
| 142 064 | t | **NW** | A | *GW* | EX | 55714 | 55760 | |
| 142 065 | s | **N0** | A | *N0* | HT | 55715 | 55761 | |
| 142 066 | s | **N0** | A | *N0* | HT | 55716 | 55762 | |
| 142 067 | | **N0** | A | *N0* | NH | 55717 | 55763 | |
| 142 068 | t | **NW** | A | *GW* | EX | 55718 | 55764 | |
| 142 069 | c | **AV** | A | *AW* | CF | 55719 | 55765 | |
| 142 070 | t | **N0** | A | *N0* | HT | 55720 | 55766 | |
| 142 071 | s | **N0** | A | *N0* | HT | 55721 | 55767 | |
| 142 072 | c | **AV** | A | *AW* | CF | 55722 | 55768 | |
| 142 073 | c | **AV** | A | *AW* | CF | 55723 | 55769 | Myfanwy |
| 142 074 | c | **AV** | A | *AW* | CF | 55724 | 55770 | |
| 142 075 | c | **AV** | A | *AW* | CF | 55725 | 55771 | |
| 142 076 | c | **AV** | A | *AW* | CF | 55726 | 55772 | |
| 142 077 | c | **AV** | A | *AW* | CF | 55727 | 55773 | |
| 142 078 | s | **N0** | A | *N0* | HT | 55728 | 55774 | |
| 142 079 | s | **N0** | A | *N0* | HT | 55729 | 55775 | |
| 142 080 | c | **AV** | A | *AW* | CF | 55730 | 55776 | |
| 142 081 | c | **AV** | A | *AW* | CF | 55731 | 55777 | |
| 142 082 | c | **AV** | A | *AW* | CF | 55732 | 55778 | |
| 142 083 | c | **AV** | A | *AW* | CF | 55733 | 55779 | |
| 142 084 | s | **N0** | A | *N0* | HT | 55734 | 55780 | |
| 142 085 | c | **AV** | A | *AW* | CF | 55735 | 55781 | |

| 142 086 | s | **NO** | A | *NO* | HT | 55736 | 55782 |
| 142 087 | s | **NO** | A | *NO* | HT | 55737 | 55783 |
| 142 088 | s | **NO** | A | *NO* | HT | 55738 | 55784 |
| 142 089 | s | **NO** | A | *NO* | HT | 55739 | 55785 |
| 142 090 | s | **NO** | A | *NO* | HT | 55740 | 55786 |
| 142 091 | s | **NO** | A | *NO* | HT | 55741 | 55787 |
| 142 092 | s | **NO** | A | *NO* | HT | 55742 | 55788 |
| 142 093 | s | **AV** | A | *NO* | HT | 55743 | 55789 |
| 142 094 | s | **AV** | A | *NO* | HT | 55744 | 55790 |
| 142 095 | s | **NO** | A | *NO* | HT | 55745 | 55791 |
| 142 096 | s | **NO** | A | *NO* | HT | 55746 | 55792 |

# CLASS 143    PACER    ALEXANDER/BARCLAY

DMS–DMSL. Similar design to Class 142, but bodies built by W. Alexander with Barclay underframes.

**Construction:** Steel underframe, aluminium alloy body and roof. Alexander bus bodywork on four-wheeled underframes.
**Engines:** One Cummins LT10-R of 165 kW (225 h.p.) at 1950 r.p.m.
**Couplers:** BSI at outer ends, bar within unit.
**Dimensions:** 15.45 x 2.80 m.

| **Gangways:** Within unit only. | **Wheel Arrangement:** 1-A + A-1. |
| **Doors:** Twin-leaf inward pivoting. | **Maximum Speed:** 75 m.p.h. |

**Seating Layout:** 2+2 high-back Chapman seating, mainly unidirectional.
**Multiple Working:** Within class and with Classes 142, 144, 150, 153, 155, 156, 158 and 159.

**DMS.** Lot No. 31005 Andrew Barclay 1985–1986. –/48(6) 2W. 24.0 t.
**DMSL.** Lot No. 31006 Andrew Barclay 1985–1986. –/44(6) 1T 2W. 24.5 t.

| 143 601 | **AV** | BC | *AW* | CF | 55642 | 55667 |               |
| 143 602 | **AV** | P  | *AW* | CF | 55651 | 55668 |               |
| 143 603 | **FI** | P  | *GW* | EX | 55658 | 55669 |               |
| 143 604 | **AV** | P  | *AW* | CF | 55645 | 55670 |               |
| 143 605 | **AV** | P  | *AW* | CF | 55646 | 55671 |               |
| 143 606 | **AV** | P  | *AW* | CF | 55647 | 55672 |               |
| 143 607 | **AV** | P  | *AW* | CF | 55648 | 55673 |               |
| 143 608 | **AV** | P  | *AW* | CF | 55649 | 55674 |               |
| 143 609 | **AV** | CC | *AW* | CF | 55650 | 55675 | Sir Tom Jones |
| 143 610 | **AV** | BC | *AW* | CF | 55643 | 55676 |               |
| 143 611 | **FI** | P  | *GW* | EX | 55652 | 55677 |               |
| 143 612 | **FI** | P  | *GW* | EX | 55653 | 55678 |               |
| 143 614 | **AV** | BC | *AW* | CF | 55655 | 55680 |               |
| 143 616 | **AV** | P  | *AW* | CF | 55657 | 55682 |               |
| 143 617 | **FI** | RI | *GW* | EX | 55644 | 55683 |               |
| 143 618 | **FI** | RI | *GW* | EX | 55659 | 55684 |               |
| 143 619 | **FI** | RI | *GW* | EX | 55660 | 55685 |               |
| 143 620 | **FI** | P  | *GW* | EX | 55661 | 55686 |               |
| 143 621 | **FI** | P  | *GW* | EX | 55662 | 55687 |               |
| 143 622 | **AV** | P  | *AW* | CF | 55663 | 55688 |               |
| 143 623 | **AV** | P  | *AW* | CF | 55664 | 55689 |               |

| | | | | | | |
|---|---|---|---|---|---|---|
| 143 624 | **AV** | P | *AW* | CF | 55665 | 55690 |
| 143 625 | **AV** | P | *AW* | CF | 55666 | 55691 |

## CLASS 144   PACER   ALEXANDER/BREL DERBY

DMS–DMSL or DMS–MS–DMSL. As Class 143, but underframes built by BREL.

**Construction:** Steel underframe, aluminium alloy body and roof. Alexander bus bodywork on four-wheeled underframes.
**Engines:** One Cummins LT10-R of 165 kW (225 h.p.) at 1950 r.p.m.
**Couplers:** BSI at outer ends, bar within unit.
**Dimensions:** 15.45/15.43 x 2.80 m.
**Gangways:** Within unit only.                    **Wheel Arrangement:** 1-A + A-1.
**Doors:** Twin-leaf inward pivoting.              **Maximum Speed:** 75 m.p.h.
**Seating Layout:** 2+2 high-back Richmond seating, mainly unidirectional.
**Multiple Working:** Within class and with Classes 142, 143, 150, 153, 155, 156, 158 and 159.

**DMS.** Lot No. 31015 BREL Derby 1986–1987. –/45(3) 1W 24.0 t.
**MS.** Lot No. BREL Derby 31037 1987. –/58. 23.5 t.
**DMSL.** Lot No. BREL Derby 31016 1986–1987. –/42(3) 1T. 24.5 t.

**Note:** The centre cars of the 3-car units are owned by West Yorkshire PTE, although managed by Porterbrook Leasing Company.

| | | | | | | | |
|---|---|---|---|---|---|---|---|
| 144 001 | **NO** | P | *NO* | NL | 55801 | | 55824 |
| 144 002 | **NO** | P | *NO* | NL | 55802 | | 55825 |
| 144 003 | **NO** | P | *NO* | NL | 55803 | | 55826 |
| 144 004 | **NO** | P | *NO* | NL | 55804 | | 55827 |
| 144 005 | **NO** | P | *NO* | NL | 55805 | | 55828 |
| 144 006 | **NO** | P | *NO* | NL | 55806 | | 55829 |
| 144 007 | **NO** | P | *NO* | NL | 55807 | | 55830 |
| 144 008 | **NO** | P | *NO* | NL | 55808 | | 55831 |
| 144 009 | **NO** | P | *NO* | NL | 55809 | | 55832 |
| 144 010 | **NO** | P | *NO* | NL | 55810 | | 55833 |
| 144 011 | **NO** | P | *NO* | NL | 55811 | | 55834 |
| 144 012 | **NO** | P | *NO* | NL | 55812 | | 55835 |
| 144 013 | **NO** | P | *NO* | NL | 55813 | | 55836 |
| 144 014 | **NO** | P | *NO* | NL | 55814 | 55850 | 55837 |
| 144 015 | **NO** | P | *NO* | NL | 55815 | 55851 | 55838 |
| 144 016 | **NO** | P | *NO* | NL | 55816 | 55852 | 55839 |
| 144 017 | **NO** | P | *NO* | NL | 55817 | 55853 | 55840 |
| 144 018 | **NO** | P | *NO* | NL | 55818 | 55854 | 55841 |
| 144 019 | **NO** | P | *NO* | NL | 55819 | 55855 | 55842 |
| 144 020 | **NO** | P | *NO* | NL | 55820 | 55856 | 55843 |
| 144 021 | **NO** | P | *NO* | NL | 55821 | 55857 | 55844 |
| 144 022 | **NO** | P | *NO* | NL | 55822 | 55858 | 55845 |
| 144 023 | **NO** | P | *NO* | NL | 55823 | 55859 | 55846 |

**Name:** 144 001 THE PENISTONE LINE PARTNERSHIP

## CLASS 150/0     SPRINTER     BREL YORK

DMSL–MS–DMS. Prototype Sprinter.

**Construction:** Steel.
**Engines:** One Cummins NT-855-R4 of 213 kW (285 h.p.) at 2100 r.p.m.
**Bogies:** BX8P (powered), BX8T (non-powered).
**Couplers:** BSI at outer end of driving vehicles, bar non-driving ends.
**Dimensions:** 20.06/20.18 x 2.82 m.
**Gangways:** Within unit only.     **Wheel Arrangement:** 2-B + 2-B + B-2.
**Doors:** Twin-leaf sliding.     **Maximum Speed:** 75 m.p.h.
**Seating Layout:** 3+2 (mainly unidirectional).
**Multiple Working:** Within class and with Classes 142, 143, 144, 153, 155, 156, 158, 159, 170 and 172.

**DMSL.** Lot No. 30984 1984. –/72 1T. 35.4 t.
**MS.** Lot No. 30986 1984. –/92. 34.1 t.
**DMS.** Lot No. 30985 1984. –/76. 29.5 t.

| | | | | | | | |
|---|---|---|---|---|---|---|---|
| 150 001 | **CI** | A | *LM* | TS | 55200 | 55400 | 55300 |
| 150 002 | **CI** | A | *LM* | TS | 55201 | 55401 | 55301 |

## CLASS 150/1     SPRINTER     BREL YORK

DMSL–DMS or DMSL–DMSL–DMS or DMSL–DMS–DMS.

**Construction:** Steel.
**Engines:** One Cummins NT855R5 of 213 kW (285 h.p.) at 2100 r.p.m.
**Bogies:** BP38 (powered), BT38 (non-powered).
**Couplers:** BSI.
**Dimensions:** 19.74 x 2.82 m.
**Gangways:** Within unit only.     **Wheel Arrangement:** 2-B (+ 2–B) + B-2.
**Doors:** Twin-leaf sliding.     **Maximum Speed:** 75 m.p.h.
**Seating Layout:** 3+2 facing as built but Centro units were reseated with mainly unidirectional seating.
**Multiple Working:** Within class and with Classes 142, 143, 144, 153, 155, 156, 158, 159, 170 and 172.

**DMSL.** Lot No. 31011 1985–1986. –/72 1T (c –/59 1TD (except 52144 which is –/62 1TD), t –/71 1T, u –/71 1T). 38.3 t.
**DMS.** Lot No. 31012 1985–1986. –/76 (c –/65, t –/73, u –/70). 38.1 t.

**Notes:** The centre cars of 3-car units are Class 150/2 vehicles. For details see Class 150/2.

c 3+2 Chapman seating.

| | | | | | | | |
|---|---|---|---|---|---|---|---|
| 150 003 | u | **WM** | A | *LM* | TS | 52103 | 57210 | 57103 |
| 150 005 | u | **CI** | A | *LM* | TS | 52105 | 52210 | 57105 |
| 150 007 | u | **CI** | A | *LM* | TS | 52107 | 52202 | 57107 |
| 150 009 | u | **CI** | A | *LM* | TS | 52109 | 57202 | 57109 |
| 150 010 | u | **WM** | A | *LM* | TS | 52110 | 57226 | 57110 |
| 150 011 | u | **CI** | A | *LM* | TS | 52111 | 52204 | 57111 |

| | | | | | | | | |
|---|---|---|---|---|---|---|---|---|
| 150 012 | u | **CI** | A | *LM* | TS | 52112 | 57206 | 57112 |
| 150 013 | u | **CI** | A | *LM* | TS | 52113 | 52226 | 57113 |
| 150 014 | u | **CI** | A | *LM* | TS | 52114 | 57204 | 57114 |
| 150 015 | u | **CI** | A | *LM* | TS | 52115 | 52206 | 57115 |
| 150 016 | u | **CI** | A | *LM* | TS | 52116 | 57212 | 57116 |
| 150 017 | u | **CI** | A | *LM* | TS | 52117 | 57209 | 57117 |
| 150 018 | u | **WM** | A | *LM* | TS | 52118 | 52220 | 57118 |
| 150 019 | u | **CI** | A | *LM* | TS | 52119 | 57220 | 57119 |
| | | | | | | | | |
| 150 101 | u | **CI** | A | *LM* | TS | 52101 | 57101 | |
| 150 102 | u | **CI** | A | *LM* | TS | 52102 | 57102 | |
| 150 104 | u | **CI** | A | *LM* | TS | 52104 | 57104 | |
| 150 106 | u | **CI** | A | *LM* | TS | 52106 | 57106 | |
| 150 108 | u | **CI** | A | *LM* | TS | 52108 | 57108 | |
| 150 120 | t | **SL** | A | *LO* | WN | 52120 | 57120 | Gospel Oak–Barking 2000 |
| 150 121 | u | **SL** | A | *GW* | PM | 52121 | 57121 | |
| 150 122 | u | **CI** | A | *LM* | TS | 52122 | 57122 | |
| 150 123 | t | **SL** | A | *LO* | WN | 52123 | 57123 | Willesden TMD |
| 150 124 | u | **CI** | A | *LM* | TS | 52124 | 57124 | |
| 150 125 | u | **CI** | A | *LM* | TS | 52125 | 57125 | |
| 150 126 | u | **WM** | A | *LM* | TS | 52126 | 57126 | |
| 150 127 | t | **SL** | A | *GW* | PM | 52127 | 57127 | |
| 150 128 | t | **SL** | A | *LO* | WN | 52128 | 57128 | Bedford-Bamberg 30 |
| 150 129 | t | **SL** | A | *LO* | WN | 52129 | 57129 | MARSTON VALE |
| 150 130 | t | **SL** | A | *LO* | WN | 52130 | 57130 | Bedford–Bletchley 150 |
| 150 131 | t | **SL** | A | *LO* | WN | 52131 | 57131 | LESLIE CRABBE |
| 150 132 | u | **WM** | A | *LM* | TS | 52132 | 57132 | |
| 150 133 | c | **NO** | A | *NO* | NH | 52133 | 57133 | |
| 150 134 | c | **NO** | A | *NO* | NH | 52134 | 57134 | |
| 150 135 | c | **NO** | A | *NO* | NH | 52135 | 57135 | |
| 150 136 | c | **NO** | A | *NO* | NH | 52136 | 57136 | |
| 150 137 | c | **NO** | A | *NO* | NH | 52137 | 57137 | |
| 150 138 | c | **NO** | A | *NO* | NH | 52138 | 57138 | |
| 150 139 | c | **NO** | A | *NO* | NH | 52139 | 57139 | |
| 150 140 | c | **NO** | A | *NO* | NH | 52140 | 57140 | |
| 150 141 | c | **NO** | A | *NO* | NH | 52141 | 57141 | |
| 150 142 | c | **NO** | A | *NO* | NH | 52142 | 57142 | |
| 150 143 | c | **NO** | A | *NO* | NH | 52143 | 57143 | |
| 150 144 | c | **NO** | A | *NO* | NH | 52144 | 57144 | |
| 150 145 | c | **NO** | A | *NO* | NH | 52145 | 57145 | |
| 150 146 | c | **NO** | A | *NO* | NH | 52146 | 57146 | |
| 150 147 | c | **NO** | A | *NO* | NH | 52147 | 57147 | |
| 150 148 | c | **NO** | A | *NO* | NH | 52148 | 57148 | |
| 150 149 | c | **NO** | A | *NO* | NH | 52149 | 57149 | |
| 150 150 | c | **NO** | A | *NO* | NH | 52150 | 57150 | |

# CLASS 150/2          SPRINTER          BREL YORK

DMSL–DMS.

**Construction:** Steel.
**Engines:** One Cummins NT855R5 of 213 kW (285 h.p.) at 2100 r.p.m.
**Bogies:** BP38 (powered), BT38 (non-powered).
**Couplers:** BSI.
**Dimensions:** 19.74 x 2.82 m.
**Gangways:** Throughout.                    **Wheel Arrangement:** 2-B + B-2.
**Doors:** Twin-leaf sliding.                **Maximum Speed:** 75 m.p.h.
**Seating Layout:** 3+2 mainly unidirectional seating as built, but most units have now been refurbished with new 2+2 seating (see notes below).
**Multiple Working:** Within class and with Classes 142, 143, 144, 153, 155, 156, 158, 159, 170 and 172.

**DMSL.** Lot No. 31017 1986–1987. –/73 1T (c –/62 1TD, p –/60(4) 1T, u –/71 1T), v –/60(8) 1T, w –/60(8) 1T). 37.5 t.
**DMS.** Lot No. 31018 1986–1987. –/76 (c –/70, p –/56(10) 1W, u –/70), v –/56(15) 2W, w –/56(17) 2W, z –/68). 36.5 t.

**Northern promotional vinyls:** 150 271 Rugby League (Northern Rail Cup).
150 272 R&B Festival week, Colne.

**Notes:**

c  3+2 Chapman seating (former First North Western units).
p  Refurbished Arriva Trains Wales units with 2+2 Primarius seating.
v  Units refurbished for Valley Lines with 2+2 Chapman seating.
w  Units refurbished for First Great Western with 2+2 Chapman seating.

The following units are on sub-lease from Arriva Trains Wales to First Great Western: 150 267/278/279/281.

| | | | | | | |
|---|---|---|---|---|---|---|
| 150 201 | c | **NO** | A | *NO* | NH | 52201 | 57201 |
| 150 203 | c | **NO** | A | *NO* | NH | 52203 | 57203 |
| 150 205 | c | **NO** | A | *NO* | NH | 52205 | 57205 |
| 150 207 | c | **NO** | A | *NO* | NH | 52207 | 57207 |
| 150 208 | p | **AV** | P | *AW* | CF | 52208 | 57208 |
| 150 211 | c | **NO** | A | *NO* | NH | 52211 | 57211 |
| 150 213 | p | **AV** | P | *AW* | CF | 52213 | 57213 |
| 150 214 | u | **CI** | A | *LM* | TS | 52214 | 57214 |
| 150 215 | c | **NO** | A | *NO* | NH | 52215 | 57215 |
| 150 216 | u | **CI** | A | *LM* | TS | 52216 | 57216 |
| 150 217 | p | **AV** | P | *AW* | CF | 52217 | 57217 |
| 150 218 | c | **NO** | A | *NO* | NH | 52218 | 57218 |
| 150 219 | w | **FI** | P | *GW* | PM | 52219 | 57219 |
| 150 221 | w | **FI** | P | *GW* | PM | 52221 | 57221 |
| 150 222 | c | **NO** | A | *NO* | NH | 52222 | 57222 |
| 150 223 | c | **NO** | A | *NO* | NH | 52223 | 57223 |
| 150 224 | c | **NO** | A | *NO* | NH | 52224 | 57224 |
| 150 225 | c | **NO** | A | *NO* | NH | 52225 | 57225 |
| 150 227 | p | **AV** | P | *AW* | CF | 52227 | 57227 |

LDS  10/10

| 150 228 |   | NO | P | NO | NH | 52228 | 57228 |
| 150 229 | p | AV | P | AW | CF | 52229 | 57229 |
| 150 230 | w | AV | P | AW | CF | 52230 | 57230 |
| 150 231 | p | AV | P | AW | CF | 52231 | 57231 |
| 150 232 | w | FI | P | GW | PM | 52232 | 57232 |
| 150 233 | w | FI | P | GW | PM | 52233 | 57233 |
| 150 234 | w | FI | P | GW | PM | 52234 | 57234 |
| 150 235 | p | AV | P | AW | CF | 52235 | 57235 |
| 150 236 | w | AV | P | AW | CF | 52236 | 57236 |
| 150 237 | p | AV | P | AW | CF | 52237 | 57237 |
| 150 238 | w | FI | P | GW | PM | 52238 | 57238 |
| 150 239 | w | FI | P | GW | PM | 52239 | 57239 |
| 150 240 | w | AV | P | AW | CF | 52240 | 57240 |
| 150 241 | w | AV | P | AW | CF | 52241 | 57241 |
| 150 242 | w | AV | P | AW | CF | 52242 | 57242 |
| 150 243 | w | FI | P | GW | PM | 52243 | 57243 |
| 150 244 | w | FI | P | GW | PM | 52244 | 57244 |
| 150 245 | p | AV | P | AW | CF | 52245 | 57245 |
| 150 246 | w | FI | P | GW | PM | 52246 | 57246 |
| 150 247 | w | FI | P | GW | PM | 52247 | 57247 |
| 150 248 | w | FI | P | GW | PM | 52248 | 57248 |
| 150 249 | w | FI | P | GW | PM | 52249 | 57249 |
| 150 250 | p | AV | P | AW | CF | 52250 | 57250 |
| 150 251 | w | AV | P | AW | CF | 52251 | 57251 |
| 150 252 | p | AV | P | AW | CF | 52252 | 57252 |
| 150 253 | w | AV | P | AW | CF | 52253 | 57253 |
| 150 254 | w | AV | P | AW | CF | 52254 | 57254 |
| 150 255 | p | AV | P | AW | CF | 52255 | 57255 |
| 150 256 | p | AV | P | AW | CF | 52256 | 57256 |
| 150 257 | p | AV | P | AW | CF | 52257 | 57257 |
| 150 258 | p | AV | P | AW | CF | 52258 | 57258 |
| 150 259 | p | AV | P | AW | CF | 52259 | 57259 |
| 150 260 | p | AV | P | AW | CF | 52260 | 57260 |
| 150 261 | w | FI | P | GW | PM | 52261 | 57261 |
| 150 262 | p | AV | P | AW | CF | 52262 | 57262 |
| 150 263 | w | FI | P | GW | PM | 52263 | 57263 |
| 150 264 | p | AV | P | AW | CF | 52264 | 57264 |
| 150 265 | w | FI | P | GW | PM | 52265 | 57265 |
| 150 266 | w | FI | P | GW | PM | 52266 | 57266 |
| 150 267 | v | AV | P | GW | PM | 52267 | 57267 |
| 150 268 |   | NO | P | NO | NH | 52268 | 57268 |
| 150 269 |   | NO | P | NO | NH | 52269 | 57269 |
| 150 270 |   | NO | P | NO | NH | 52270 | 57270 |
| 150 271 |   | NO | P | NO | NH | 52271 | 57271 |
| 150 272 |   | NO | P | NO | NH | 52272 | 57272 |
| 150 273 |   | NO | P | NO | NH | 52273 | 57273 | Driver John Axon G.C. |
| 150 274 |   | NO | P | NO | NH | 52274 | 57274 |
| 150 275 |   | NO | P | NO | NH | 52275 | 57275 |
| 150 276 |   | NO | P | NO | NH | 52276 | 57276 |
| 150 277 |   | NO | P | NO | NH | 52277 | 57277 |
| 150 278 | v | AV | P | GW | PM | 52278 | 57278 |

| | | | | | | |
|---|---|---|---|---|---|---|
| 150 279 | v | **AV** | P | *GW* | PM | 52279 | 57279 |
| 150 280 | v | **AV** | P | *AW* | CF | 52280 | 57280 |
| 150 281 | v | **AV** | P | *GW* | PM | 52281 | 57281 |
| 150 282 | v | **AV** | P | *AW* | CF | 52282 | 57282 |
| 150 283 | p | **AV** | P | *AW* | CF | 52283 | 57283 |
| 150 284 | p | **AV** | P | *AW* | CF | 52284 | 57284 |
| 150 285 | p | **AV** | P | *AW* | CF | 52285 | 57285 |

# CLASS 153   SUPER SPRINTER   LEYLAND BUS

DMSL. Converted by Hunslet-Barclay, Kilmarnock from Class 155 2-car units.

**Construction:** Steel underframe, aluminium alloy body and roof. Built from Leyland National bus parts on bogied underframes.
**Engine:** One Cummins NT855R5 of 213 kW (285 h.p.) at 2100 r.p.m.
**Bogies:** One P3-10 (powered) and one BT38 (non-powered).
**Couplers:** BSI.
**Dimensions:** 23.21 x 2.70 m.
**Gangways:** Throughout.                        **Wheel Arrangement:** 2-B.
**Doors:** Single-leaf sliding plug.              **Maximum Speed:** 75 m.p.h.
**Seating Layout:** 2+2 facing/unidirectional.
**Multiple Working:** Within class and with Classes 142, 143, 144, 150, 155, 156, 158, 159, 170 and 172.

**52301–52335. DMSL.** Lot No. 31026 1987–1988. Converted under Lot No. 31115 1991–1992. –/72(3) 1T 1W. (* –/66(3) 1T 1W, s –/72 1T 1W, t –/72(2) 1T 1W). 41.2 t.
**57301–57335. DMSL.** Lot No. 31027 1987–1988. Converted under Lot No. 31115 1991–1992. –/72(3) 1T 1W. (* –/66(3) 1T 1W). 41.2 t.

**Notes:** Cars numbered in the 573xx series were renumbered by adding 50 to their original number so that the last two digits correspond with the set number.

* Refurbished East Anglia area units with a bicycle rack.
c Chapman seating.
d Richmond seating.
Units not shown as c or d were reseated using original Class 158 seats.

| | | | | | | |
|---|---|---|---|---|---|---|
| 153 301 | d | **NO** | A | *NO* | NL | 52301 |
| 153 302 | | **EM** | A | *EM* | NM | 52302 |
| 153 303 | | **AV** | A | *AW* | CF | 52303 |
| 153 304 | d | **NO** | A | *NO* | NL | 52304 |
| 153 305 | d | **FI** | A | *GW* | EX | 52305 |
| 153 306 | cr | **1** | P | *EA* | NC | 52306 |
| 153 307 | d | **NO** | A | *NO* | NL | 52307 |
| 153 308 | | **EM** | A | *EM* | NM | 52308 |
| 153 309 | cr | **AR** | P | *EA* | NC | 52309 |
| 153 310 | c | **EM** | P | *EM* | NM | 52310 |
| 153 311 | c* | **EM** | P | *EM* | NM | 52311 |
| 153 312 | s | **AV** | A | *AW* | CF | 52312 |
| 153 313 | cs | **EM** | P | *EM* | NM | 52313 |
| 153 314 | cr | **1** | P | *EA* | NC | 52314 |
| 153 315 | ds | **NO** | A | *NO* | NL | 52315 |

handwritten annotations: "SvD 3/11", "GERARD FIENNES (SvD)", "SvD 1/11", "SvD 11/11"

| | | | | | | |
|---|---|---|---|---|---|---|
| 153 316 | c | **NO** | P | *NO* | NL | 52316 |
| 153 317 | d | **NO** | A | *NO* | NL | 52317 |
| 153 318 | d | **FI** | A | *GW* | EX | 52318 |
| 153 319 | d | **EM** | A | *EM* | NM | 52319 |
| 153 320 | | **AV** | P | *AW* | CF | 52320 |
| 153 321 | c | **EM** | P | *EM* | NM | 52321 |
| 153 322 | cr | **AR** | P | *EA* | NC | 52322 | BENJAMIN BRITTEN SUD 1/11 3/11 |
| 153 323 | | **AV** | P | *AW* | CF | 52323 |
| 153 324 | c | **NO** | P | *NO* | NL | 52324 |
| 153 325 | c | **LM** | P | *LM* | TS | 52325 |
| 153 326 | c* | **EM** | P | *EM* | NM | 52326 |
| 153 327 | | **AV** | A | *AW* | CF | 52327 |
| 153 328 | ds | **NO** | A | *NO* | NL | 52328 |
| 153 329 | c | **FI** | P | *GW* | EX | 52329 |
| 153 330 | cs | **NO** | P | *NO* | NL | 52330 |
| 153 331 | d | **NO** | A | *NO* | NL | 52331 |
| 153 332 | c | **NO** | P | *NO* | NL | 52332 |
| 153 333 | cs | **LM** | P | *LM* | TS | 52333 |
| 153 334 | ct | **LM** | P | *LM* | TS | 52334 |
| 153 335 | cr | **AR** | P | *EA* | NC | 52335 | MICHAEL PALIN SUD 4/11 |
| 153 351 | d | **NO** | A | *NO* | NL | 57351 |
| 153 352 | d | **NO** | A | *NO* | NL | 57352 |
| 153 353 | | **AV** | A | *AW* | CF | 57353 |
| 153 354 | c | **LM** | P | *LM* | TS | 57354 |
| 153 355 | | **EM** | A | *EM* | NM | 57355 |
| 153 356 | c | **LM** | P | *LM* | TS | 57356 | P|Boro |
| 153 357 | d | **EM** | A | *EM* | NM | 57357 |
| 153 358 | c | **NO** | P | *NO* | NL | 57358 |
| 153 359 | c | **NO** | P | *NO* | NL | 57359 |
| 153 360 | c | **NO** | P | *NO* | NL | 57360 |
| 153 361 | cs | **FI** | P | *GW* | EX | 57361 |
| 153 362 | | **AV** | A | *AW* | CF | 57362 | Dylan Thomas 1914–1953 |
| 153 363 | cs | **NO** | P | *NO* | NL | 57363 |
| 153 364 | c | **LM** | P | *LM* | TS | 57364 |
| 153 365 | c | **LM** | P | *LM* | TS | 57365 |
| 153 366 | c | **LM** | P | *LM* | TS | 57366 |
| 153 367 | c | **AV** | P | *AW* | CF | 57367 |
| 153 368 | d | **FI** | A | *GW* | EX | 57368 |
| 153 369 | c | **FI** | P | *GW* | EX | 57369 |
| 153 370 | d | **FI** | A | *GW* | EX | 57370 |
| 153 371 | c | **LM** | P | *LM* | TS | 57371 |
| 153 372 | d | **FI** | A | *GW* | EX | 57372 |
| 153 373 | d | **FI** | A | *GW* | EX | 57373 |
| 153 374 | | **EM** | A | *EM* | NM | 57374 |
| 153 375 | c | **LM** | P | *LM* | TS | 57375 |
| 153 376 | c | **CT** | P | *EM* | NM | 57376 |
| 153 377 | d | **FI** | A | *GW* | EX | 57377 |
| 153 378 | d | **NO** | A | *NO* | NL | 57378 |
| 153 379 | c | **CT** | P | *EM* | NM | 57379 |
| 153 380 | d | **FI** | A | *GW* | EX | 57380 |
| 153 381 | c | **EM** | P | *EM* | NM | 57381 |

| 153 382 | d | **FI** | A | *GW* | EX | 57382 |
| 153 383 | c | **EM** | P | *EM* | NM | 57383 |
| 153 384 | c | **CT** | P | *EM* | NM | 57384 |
| 153 385 | c | **EM** | P | *EM* | NM | 57385 |

# CLASS 155  SUPER SPRINTER  LEYLAND BUS

DMSL–DMS.

**Construction:** Steel underframe, aluminium alloy body and roof. Built from Leyland National bus parts on bogied underframes.
**Engines:** One Cummins NT855R5 of 213 kW (285 h.p.) at 2100 r.p.m.
**Bogies:** One P3-10 (powered) and one BT38 (non-powered).
**Couplers:** BSI.
**Dimensions:** 23.21 x 2.70 m.
**Gangways:** Throughout.                **Wheel Arrangement:** 2-B + B-2.
**Doors:** Single-leaf sliding plug.        **Maximum Speed:** 75 m.p.h.
**Seating Layout:** 2+2 facing/unidirectional Chapman seating.
**Multiple Working:** Within class and with Classes 142, 143, 144, 150, 153, 156, 158, 159, 170 and 172.

**DMSL.** Lot No. 31057 1988. –/76 1TD 1W. 39.0 t.
**DMS.** Lot No. 31058 1988. –/80. 38.6 t.

**Northern promotional vinyls:**

155 341–347 Leeds–Bradford–Manchester route (the "Calder Valley").

**Note:** These units are owned by West Yorkshire PTE, although managed by Porterbrook Leasing Company.

| 155 341 | **NO** | P | *NO* | NL | 52341 | 57341 |
| 155 342 | **NO** | P | *NO* | NL | 52342 | 57342 |
| 155 343 | **NO** | P | *NO* | NL | 52343 | 57343 |
| 155 344 | **NO** | P | *NO* | NL | 52344 | 57344 |
| 155 345 | **NO** | P | *NO* | NL | 52345 | 57345 |
| 155 346 | **NO** | P | *NO* | NL | 52346 | 57346 |
| 155 347 | **NO** | P | *NO* | NL | 52347 | 57347 |

# CLASS 156 SUPER SPRINTER METRO-CAMMELL

DMSL–DMS.

**Construction:** Steel.
**Engines:** One Cummins NT855R5 of 213 kW (285 h.p.) at 2100 r.p.m.
**Bogies:** One P3-10 (powered) and one BT38 (non-powered).
**Couplers:** BSI.
**Dimensions:** 23.03 x 2.73 m.
**Gangways:** Throughout.                **Wheel Arrangement:** 2-B + B-2.
**Doors:** Single-leaf sliding.            **Maximum Speed:** 75 m.p.h.
**Seating Layout:** 2+2 facing/unidirectional.
**Multiple Working:** Within class and with Classes 142, 143, 144, 150, 153, 155, 158, 159, 170 and 172.

**DMSL.** Lot No. 31028 1988–1989. –/74 (†* –/72, c, t –/70, u –/68) 1TD 1W. 38.6 t.
**DMS.** Lot No. 31029 1987–1989. –/76 (d –/78, † –/74, t, u –/72) 36.1 t.

**Advertising livery:** 156 402 Chapelfield Shopping Centre (white & blue).

### Northern promotional vinyls:

156 448 Hadrians Wall Country (Newcastle–Carlisle line).
156 461 Ravenglass & Eskdale Railway.
156 469 Bishop Auckland branch.
156 484 Settle & Carlisle line.
156 490 National Railway Museum.

### Notes:

c  Chapman seating.
d  Richmond seating.

| | | | | | | | |
|---|---|---|---|---|---|---|---|
| 156 401 | c* | **EM** | P | *EM* | DY | 52401 | 57401 |
| 156 402 | cr | **AL** | P | *EA* | NC | 52402 | 57402 |
| 156 403 | c* | **EM** | P | *EM* | DY | 52403 | 57403 |
| 156 404 | c* | **EM** | P | *EM* | DY | 52404 | 57404 |
| 156 405 | c* | **EM** | P | *EM* | DY | 52405 | 57405 |
| 156 406 | c* | **EM** | P | *EM* | DY | 52406 | 57406 |
| 156 407 | cr | **1** | P | *EA* | NC | 52407 | 57407 | Sud 6/11 |
| 156 408 | c* | **EM** | P | *EM* | DY | 52408 | 57408 |
| 156 409 | cr | **1** | P | *EA* | NC | 52409 | 57409 |
| 156 410 | c* | **EM** | P | *EM* | DY | 52410 | 57410 |
| 156 411 | c* | **EM** | P | *EM* | DY | 52411 | 57411 |
| 156 412 | cr | **CT** | P | *EA* | NC | 52412 | 57412 | Sud 3/11 |
| 156 413 | c* | **EM** | P | *EM* | DY | 52413 | 57413 |
| 156 414 | c* | **EM** | P | *EM* | DY | 52414 | 57414 |
| 156 415 | c* | **EM** | P | *EM* | DY | 52415 | 57415 |
| 156 416 | cr | **1** | P | *EA* | NC | 52416 | 57416 |
| 156 417 | cr | **1** | P | *EA* | NC | 52417 | 57417 |
| 156 418 | cr | **CT** | P | *EA* | NC | 52418 | 57418 | Sud 4/11 |
| 156 419 | cr | **NX** | P | *EA* | NC | 52419 | 57419 | Sud 3/11 |
| 156 420 | c | **NO** | P | *NO* | NH | 52420 | 57420 |
| 156 421 | c | **NO** | P | *NO* | NH | 52421 | 57421 |
| 156 422 | cr | **1** | P | *EA* | NC | 52422 | 57422 | Sud 2/11 |
| 156 423 | c | **NO** | P | *NO* | NH | 52423 | 57423 |
| 156 424 | c | **NO** | P | *NO* | NH | 52424 | 57424 |
| 156 425 | c | **NO** | P | *NO* | NH | 52425 | 57425 |
| 156 426 | c | **NO** | P | *NO* | NH | 52426 | 57426 |
| 156 427 | c | **NO** | P | *NO* | NH | 52427 | 57427 |
| 156 428 | c | **NO** | P | *NO* | NH | 52428 | 57428 |
| 156 429 | c | **NO** | P | *NO* | NH | 52429 | 57429 |
| 156 430 | t | **SC** | A | *SR* | CK | 52430 | 57430 |
| 156 431 | t | **SR** | A | *SR* | CK | 52431 | 57431 |
| 156 432 | t | **SR** | A | *SR* | CK | 52432 | 57432 |
| 156 433 | t | **SR** | A | *SR* | CK | 52433 | 57433 |
| 156 434 | t | **SR** | A | *SR* | CK | 52434 | 57434 |
| 156 435 | t | **SR** | A | *SR* | CK | 52435 | 57435 |
| 156 436 | † | **SC** | A | *SR* | CK | 52436 | 57436 |

| 156 437 | t | **SR** | A | *SR* | CK | 52437 | 57437 |
|---|---|---|---|---|---|---|---|
| 156 438 | d | **NO** | A | *NO* | HT | 52438 | 57438 |
| 156 439 | t | **SR** | A | *SR* | CK | 52439 | 57439 |
| 156 440 | c | **NO** | P | *NO* | NH | 52440 | 57440 |
| 156 441 | c | **NO** | P | *NO* | NH | 52441 | 57441 |
| 156 442 | t | **SC** | A | *SR* | CK | 52442 | 57442 |
| 156 443 | d | **NO** | A | *NO* | HT | 52443 | 57443 |
| 156 444 | d | **NO** | A | *NO* | HT | 52444 | 57444 |
| 156 445 | u | **SC** | A | *SR* | CK | 52445 | 57445 |
| 156 446 | rt | **FS** | A | *SR* | CK | 52446 | 57446 |
| 156 447 | ru | **FS** | A | *SR* | CK | 52447 | 57447 |
| 156 448 | d | **NO** | A | *NO* | HT | 52448 | 57448 |
| 156 449 | u | **FS** | A | *SR* | CK | 52449 | 57449 |
| 156 450 | ru | **FS** | A | *SR* | CK | 52450 | 57450 |
| 156 451 | d | **NO** | A | *NO* | HT | 52451 | 57451 |
| 156 452 | c | **NO** | P | *NO* | NH | 52452 | 57452 |
| 156 453 | ru | **FS** | A | *SR* | CK | 52453 | 57453 |
| 156 454 | d | **NO** | A | *NO* | HT | 52454 | 57454 |
| 156 455 | c | **NO** | P | *NO* | NH | 52455 | 57455 |
| 156 456 | rt | **FS** | A | *SR* | CK | 52456 | 57456 |
| 156 457 | rt | **FS** | A | *SR* | CK | 52457 | 57457 |
| 156 458 | rt | **FS** | A | *SR* | CK | 52458 | 57458 |
| 156 459 | c | **NO** | P | *NO* | NH | 52459 | 57459 |
| 156 460 | c | **NO** | P | *NO* | NH | 52460 | 57460 |
| 156 461 | c | **NO** | P | *NO* | NH | 52461 | 57461 |
| 156 462 | | **FS** | A | *SR* | CK | 52462 | 57462 |
| 156 463 | d | **NO** | A | *NO* | HT | 52463 | 57463 |
| 156 464 | c | **NO** | P | *NO* | NH | 52464 | 57464 |
| 156 465 | ru | **FS** | A | *SR* | CK | 52465 | 57465 |
| 156 466 | c | **NO** | P | *NO* | NH | 52466 | 57466 |
| 156 467 | r | **FS** | A | *SR* | CK | 52467 | 57467 |
| 156 468 | d | **NO** | A | *NO* | NH | 52468 | 57468 |
| 156 469 | d | **NO** | A | *NO* | HT | 52469 | 57469 |
| 156 470 | d | **NO** | A | *NO* | NH | 52470 | 57470 |
| 156 471 | d | **NO** | A | *NO* | NH | 52471 | 57471 |
| 156 472 | d | **NO** | A | *NO* | NH | 52472 | 57472 |
| 156 473 | d | **NO** | A | *NO* | NH | 52473 | 57473 |
| 156 474 | rt | **FS** | A | *SR* | CK | 52474 | 57474 |
| 156 475 | d | **NO** | A | *NO* | HT | 52475 | 57475 |
| 156 476 | rt | **FS** | A | *SR* | CK | 52476 | 57476 |
| 156 477 | t | **FS** | A | *SR* | CK | 52477 | 57477 |
| 156 478 | rt | **FS** | A | *SR* | CK | 52478 | 57478 |
| 156 479 | d | **NO** | A | *NO* | HT | 52479 | 57479 |
| 156 480 | d | **NO** | A | *NO* | HT | 52480 | 57480 |
| 156 481 | d | **NO** | A | *NO* | HT | 52481 | 57481 |
| 156 482 | d | **NO** | A | *NO* | NH | 52482 | 57482 |
| 156 483 | d | **NO** | A | *NO* | NH | 52483 | 57483 |
| 156 484 | d | **NO** | A | *NO* | HT | 52484 | 57484 |
| 156 485 | ru | **FS** | A | *SR* | CK | 52485 | 57485 |
| 156 486 | d | **NO** | A | *NO* | NH | 52486 | 57486 |
| 156 487 | d | **NO** | A | *NO* | NH | 52487 | 57487 |

| 156 488 | d | **NO** | A | *NO* | NH | 52488 | 57488 |
| 156 489 | d | **NO** | A | *NO* | NH | 52489 | 57489 |
| 156 490 | d | **NO** | A | *NO* | HT | 52490 | 57490 |
| 156 491 | d | **NO** | A | *NO* | NH | 52491 | 57491 |
| 156 492 | rt† | **FS** | A | *SR* | CK | 52492 | 57492 |
| 156 493 | rt | **FS** | A | *SR* | CK | 52493 | 57493 |
| 156 494 | u | **SR** | A | *SR* | CK | 52494 | 57494 |
| 156 495 | u | **SC** | A | *SR* | CK | 52495 | 57495 |
| 156 496 | ru | **FS** | A | *SR* | CK | 52496 | 57496 |
| 156 497 | d | **NO** | A | *NO* | NH | 52497 | 57497 |
| 156 498 | d | **NO** | A | *NO* | NH | 52498 | 57498 |
| 156 499 | rt | **FS** | A | *SR* | CK | 52499 | 57499 |
| 156 500 | u | **SR** | A | *SR* | CK | 52500 | 57500 |
| 156 501 | | **SC** | A | *SR* | CK | 52501 | 57501 |
| 156 502 | | **SR** | A | *SR* | CK | 52502 | 57502 |
| 156 503 | | **SR** | A | *SR* | CK | 52503 | 57503 |
| 156 504 | | **SC** | A | *SR* | CK | 52504 | 57504 |
| 156 505 | | **SR** | A | *SR* | CK | 52505 | 57505 |
| 156 506 | | **SC** | A | *SR* | CK | 52506 | 57506 |
| 156 507 | | **SR** | A | *SR* | CK | 52507 | 57507 |
| 156 508 | | **SC** | A | *SR* | CK | 52508 | 57508 |
| 156 509 | | **SR** | A | *SR* | CK | 52509 | 57509 |
| 156 510 | | **SR** | A | *SR* | CK | 52510 | 57510 |
| 156 511 | | **SR** | A | *SR* | CK | 52511 | 57511 |
| 156 512 | | **SR** | A | *SR* | CK | 52512 | 57512 |
| 156 513 | | **SC** | A | *SR* | CK | 52513 | 57513 |
| 156 514 | | **SC** | A | *SR* | CK | 52514 | 57514 |

**Names:**

| 156 409 | Cromer Pier Seaside Special |
| 156 416 | Saint Edmund |
| 156 420 | LA' AL RATTY Ravenglass & Eskdale Railway |
| 156 444 | Councillor Bill Cameron |
| 156 466 | Gracie Fields |

# CLASS 158/0                                                    BREL

DMSL(B)–DMSL(A) or DMCL–DMSL or DMSL–MSL–DMSL.

**Construction:** Welded aluminium.
**Engines:** 158 701–158 813/158 880–158 890/158 950–158 959: One Cummins NTA855R of 260 kW (350 h.p.) at 1900 r.p.m.
158 815–158 862: One Perkins 2006-TWH of 260 kW (350 h.p.) at 1900 r.p.m.
158 863–158 872: One Cummins NTA855R of 300 kW (400 h.p.) at 2100 r.p.m.
**Bogies:** One BREL P4 (powered) and one BREL T4 (non-powered) per car.
**Couplers:** BSI.
**Dimensions:** 22.57 x 2.70 m.
**Gangways:** Throughout.                    **Wheel Arrangement:** 2-B + B-2.
**Doors:** Twin-leaf swing plug.            **Maximum Speed:** 90 m.p.h.
**Seating Layout:** 2+2 facing/unidirectional in all Standard and First Class except 2+1 in South West Trains First Class.

**Multiple Working:** Within class and with Classes 142, 143, 144, 150, 153, 155, 156, 159, 170 and 172.

**DMSL(B).** Lot No. 31051 BREL Derby 1989–1992. –/68 1TD 1W. († –/72 1TD 1W, c, w –/66 1TD 1W, t –/64 1TD 1W). 38.5 t.
**MSL.** Lot No. 31050 BREL Derby 1991. –/66(3) 1T. 38.5 t.
**DMSL(A).** Lot No. 31052 BREL Derby 1989–1992. –/70 1T († –/74, c, w –/68 1T, * –/64(2) 1T plus cycle stowage area, t –/66 1T). 38.5 t.

The above details refer to the "as built" condition. The following DMSL(B) have now been converted to DMCL as follows:

**52701–52736/52738–52741 (ScotRail).** 15/53 1TD 1W (* refurbished sets 14/46(6) 1TD 1W plus cycle stowage area).
**52773/774. (Former TransPennine Express 2-car units).** 16/48 1TD 1W.
**52786/52789 (Former South West Trains units).** 13/44 1TD 1W.

**Non-standard livery:** 158 782, 158 786 & 158 789 Unbranded Northern dark blue.

**Northern promotional vinyls:**

158 784 PTEG: 40 years.
158 787, 158 792–796 Sheffield–Leeds fast service.
158 790 Rugby League (Northern Rail Cup).
158 860 Keighley & Brontë Country.
158 901–910 Leeds–Bradford–Manchester route (the "Calder Valley").

**Notes:**

\* Refurbished ScotRail units fitted with Grammer seating, additional luggage racks and cycle stowage areas.
   ScotRail units 158 726–741 are fitted with Richmond seating.
† Refurbished East Midlands Trains units with Primarius seating.
c Chapman seating.
s Former TransPennine and Central Trains units refurbished with new shape seat cushions.
t Arriva Trains Wales and Northern units with some seats removed for additional luggage space.
u Refurbished former South West Trains units with Class 159-style interiors, including First Class seating.
w Refurbished First Great Western units. Units 158 745–751 & 158 762 (most formed into 3-car sets) have been fitted with Richmond seating.

The following units are on sub-lease from Northern to ScotRail: 158 782/786/789/867–871.

All ScotRail 158s are "fitted" for RETB. When a unit arrives at Inverness the cab display unit is clipped on and plugged in. Similarly Arriva Trains Wales units have RETB plugged in at Shrewsbury for working the Cambrian Lines.

| | | | | | | |
|---|---|---|---|---|---|---|
| 158 701 | * | **FS** | P | *SR* | IS | 52701 57701 |
| 158 702 | * | **FS** | P | *SR* | IS | 52702 57702 |
| 158 703 | * | **FS** | P | *SR* | IS | 52703 57703 |
| 158 704 | * | **FS** | P | *SR* | IS | 52704 57704 |
| 158 705 | * | **FS** | P | *SR* | IS | 52705 57705 |
| 158 706 | * | **FS** | P | *SR* | IS | 52706 57706 |

| 158 707 | * | FS | P | SR | IS | 52707 | 57707 | |
| 158 708 | * | FS | P | SR | IS | 52708 | 57708 | |
| 158 709 | * | FS | P | SR | IS | 52709 | 57709 | |
| 158 710 | * | FS | P | SR | IS | 52710 | 57710 | |
| 158 711 | * | FS | P | SR | IS | 52711 | 57711 | |
| 158 712 | * | FS | P | SR | IS | 52712 | 57712 | |
| 158 713 | * | FS | P | SR | IS | 52713 | 57713 | |
| 158 714 | * | FS | P | SR | IS | 52714 | 57714 | |
| 158 715 | * | FS | P | SR | IS | 52715 | 57715 | |
| 158 716 | * | FS | P | SR | IS | 52716 | 57716 | |
| 158 717 | * | FS | P | SR | IS | 52717 | 57717 | |
| 158 718 | * | FS | P | SR | IS | 52718 | 57718 | |
| 158 719 | * | FS | P | SR | IS | 52719 | 57719 | |
| 158 720 | * | FS | P | SR | IS | 52720 | 57720 | |
| 158 721 | * | FS | P | SR | IS | 52721 | 57721 | |
| 158 722 | * | FS | P | SR | IS | 52722 | 57722 | |
| 158 723 | * | FS | P | SR | IS | 52723 | 57723 | |
| 158 724 | * | FS | P | SR | IS | 52724 | 57724 | |
| 158 725 | * | FS | P | SR | IS | 52725 | 57725 | |
| 158 726 | | FS | P | SR | HA | 52726 | 57726 | |
| 158 727 | | FS | P | SR | HA | 52727 | 57727 | |
| 158 728 | | FS | P | SR | HA | 52728 | 57728 | |
| 158 729 | | FS | P | SR | HA | 52729 | 57729 | |
| 158 730 | | FS | P | SR | HA | 52730 | 57730 | |
| 158 731 | | FS | P | SR | HA | 52731 | 57731 | |
| 158 732 | | FS | P | SR | HA | 52732 | 57732 | |
| 158 733 | | FS | P | SR | HA | 52733 | 57733 | |
| 158 734 | | FS | P | SR | HA | 52734 | 57734 | |
| 158 735 | | FS | P | SR | HA | 52735 | 57735 | |
| 158 736 | | FS | P | SR | HA | 52736 | 57736 | |
| 158 738 | | FS | P | SR | HA | 52738 | 57738 | |
| 158 739 | | FS | P | SR | HA | 52739 | 57739 | |
| 158 740 | | FS | P | SR | HA | 52740 | 57740 | |
| 158 741 | | FS | P | SR | HA | 52741 | 57741 | |
| 158 745 | w | FI | P | GW | PM | 52745 | 57745 | |
| 158 752 | | NO | P | NO | NL | 52752 | 58716 | 57752 |
| 158 753 | | NO | P | NO | NL | 52753 | 58710 | 57753 |
| 158 754 | | NO | P | NO | NL | 52754 | 58708 | 57754 |
| 158 755 | | NO | P | NO | NL | 52755 | 58702 | 57755 |
| 158 756 | | NO | P | NO | NL | 52756 | 58712 | 57756 |
| 158 757 | | NO | P | NO | NL | 52757 | 58706 | 57757 |
| 158 758 | | NO | P | NO | NL | 52758 | 58714 | 57758 |
| 158 759 | | NO | P | NO | NL | 52759 | 58713 | 57759 |
| 158 763 | w | FI | P | GW | PM | 52763 | 57763 | |
| 158 766 | w | FI | P | GW | PM | 52766 | 57766 | |
| 158 767 | w | FI | P | GW | PM | 52767 | 57767 | |
| 158 769 | w | FI | P | GW | PM | 52769 | 57769 | |
| 158 770 | † | ST | P | EM | NM | 52770 | 57770 | |
| 158 773 | s | TC | P | EM | NM | 52773 | 57773 | |
| 158 774 | s | TC | P | EM | NM | 52774 | 57774 | |
| 158 777 | † | ST | P | EM | NM | 52777 | 57777 | |

| 158 780 | † | ST | A | EM | NM | 52780 | 57780 | | |
| 158 782 | s | 0 | A | SR | HA | 52782 | 57782 | | |
| 158 783 | † | ST | A | EM | NM | 52783 | 57783 | | |
| 158 784 | st | NO | A | NO | NL | 52784 | 57784 | | |
| 158 785 | † | ST | A | EM | NM | 52785 | 57785 | | |
| 158 786 | u | 0 | A | SR | HA | 52786 | 57786 | | |
| 158 787 | s | NO | A | NO | NL | 52787 | 57787 | | |
| 158 788 | † | ST | A | EM | NM | 52788 | 57788 | | |
| 158 789 | u | 0 | A | SR | HA | 52789 | 57789 | | |
| 158 790 | st | NO | A | NO | NL | 52790 | 57790 | | |
| 158 791 | st | NO | A | NO | NL | 52791 | 57791 | | |
| 158 792 | s | NO | A | NO | NL | 52792 | 57792 | | |
| 158 793 | s | NO | A | NO | NL | 52793 | 57793 | | |
| 158 794 | s | NO | A | NO | NL | 52794 | 57794 | | |
| 158 795 | s | NO | A | NO | NL | 52795 | 57795 | | |
| 158 796 | s | NO | A | NO | NL | 52796 | 57796 | | |
| 158 797 | st | NO | A | NO | NL | 52797 | 57797 | | |
| 158 798 | w | FI | P | GW | PM | 52798 | 58715 | 57798 | Eery 7/11 |
| 158 799 | † | ST | P | EM | NM | 52799 | 57799 | | |
| 158 806 | † | ST | P | EM | NM | 52806 | 57806 | | |
| 158 810 | † | ST | P | EM | NM | 52810 | 57810 | | |
| 158 812 | † | ST | P | EM | NM | 52812 | 57812 | | |
| 158 813 | † | ST | P | EM | NM | 52813 | 57813 | | |
| 158 815 | c | NO | A | NO | NL | 52815 | 57815 | | |
| 158 816 | c | NO | A | NO | NL | 52816 | 57816 | | |
| 158 817 | c | NO | A | NO | NL | 52817 | 57817 | | |
| 158 818 | c | AV | A | AW | MN | 52818 | 57818 | | |
| 158 819 | ce | WB | A | AW | MN | 52819 | 57819 | | |
| 158 820 | ce | AV | A | AW | MN | 52820 | 57820 | | |
| 158 821 | ce | AV | A | AW | MN | 52821 | 57821 | | |
| 158 822 | ce | AV | A | AW | MN | 52822 | 57822 | | |
| 158 823 | ce | AV | A | AW | MN | 52823 | 57823 | | |
| 158 824 | ce | AV | A | AW | MN | 52824 | 57824 | | |
| 158 825 | c | WB | A | AW | MN | 52825 | 57825 | | |
| 158 826 | c | WB | A | AW | MN | 52826 | 57826 | | |
| 158 827 | ce | WB | A | AW | MN | 52827 | 57827 | | |
| 158 828 | c | AV | A | AW | MN | 52828 | 57828 | | |
| 158 829 | ce | AV | A | AW | MN | 52829 | 57829 | | |
| 158 830 | c | WB | A | AW | MN | 52830 | 57830 | | |
| 158 831 | c | WB | A | AW | MN | 52831 | 57831 | | |
| 158 832 | ce | WB | A | AW | MN | 52832 | 57832 | | |
| 158 833 | c | WB | A | AW | MN | 52833 | 57833 | | |
| 158 834 | ce | WB | A | AW | MN | 52834 | 57834 | | |
| 158 835 | c | WB | A | AW | MN | 52835 | 57835 | | |
| 158 836 | ce | WB | A | AW | MN | 52836 | 57836 | | |
| 158 837 | ce | AV | A | AW | MN | 52837 | 57837 | | |
| 158 838 | ce | WB | A | AW | MN | 52838 | 57838 | | |
| 158 839 | ce | WB | A | AW | MN | 52839 | 57839 | | |
| 158 840 | c | AV | A | AW | MN | 52840 | 57840 | | |
| 158 841 | c | WB | A | AW | MN | 52841 | 57841 | | |
| 158 842 | c | NO | A | NO | NL | 52842 | 57842 | | |

| | | | | | | | |
|---|---|---|---|---|---|---|---|
| 158 843 | c | **NO** | A | *NO* | NL | 52843 | 57843 |
| 158 844 | t | **NO** | A | *NO* | NL | 52844 | 57844 |
| 158 845 | t | **NO** | A | *NO* | NL | 52845 | 57845 |
| 158 846 | † | **ST** | A | *EM* | NM | 52846 | 57846 |
| 158 847 | † | **ST** | A | *EM* | NM | 52847 | 57847 |
| 158 848 | t | **NO** | A | *NO* | NL | 52848 | 57848 |
| 158 849 | t | **NO** | A | *NO* | NL | 52849 | 57849 |
| 158 850 | t | **NO** | A | *NO* | NL | 52850 | 57850 |
| 158 851 | t | **NO** | A | *NO* | NL | 52851 | 57851 |
| 158 852 | † | **ST** | A | *EM* | NM | 52852 | 57852 |
| 158 853 | t | **NO** | A | *NO* | NL | 52853 | 57853 |
| 158 854 | † | **ST** | A | *EM* | NM | 52854 | 57854 |
| 158 855 | s | **NO** | A | *NO* | NL | 52855 | 57855 |
| 158 856 | † | **ST** | A | *EM* | NM | 52856 | 57856 |
| 158 857 | † | **ST** | A | *EM* | NM | 52857 | 57857 |
| 158 858 | † | **ST** | A | *EM* | NM | 52858 | 57858 |
| 158 859 | s | **NO** | A | *NO* | NL | 52859 | 57859 |
| 158 860 | s | **NO** | A | *NO* | NL | 52860 | 57860 |
| 158 861 | s | **NO** | A | *NO* | NL | 52861 | 57861 |
| 158 862 | † | **ST** | A | *EM* | NM | 52862 | 57862 |
| 158 863 | c | **WT** | A | *EM* | NM | 52863 | 57863 |
| 158 864 | c | **WT** | A | *EM* | NM | 52864 | 57864 |
| 158 865 | c | **WT** | A | *EM* | NM | 52865 | 57865 |
| 158 866 | c | **WT** | A | *EM* | NM | 52866 | 57866 |
| 158 867 | c | **WT** | A | *SR* | HA | 52867 | 57867 |
| 158 868 | c | **WT** | A | *SR* | HA | 52868 | 57868 |
| 158 869 | c | **WT** | A | *SR* | HA | 52869 | 57869 |
| 158 870 | c | **WT** | A | *SR* | HA | 52870 | 57870 |
| 158 871 | c | **WT** | A | *SR* | HA | 52871 | 57871 |
| 158 872 | c | **NO** | A | *NO* | NL | 52872 | 57872 |

**Names:**

| | |
|---|---|
| 158 702 | BBC Scotland 75 years |
| 158 707 | Far North Line 125th ANNIVERSARY |
| 158 715 | Haymarket |
| 158 720 | Inverness & Nairn Railway – 150 years |
| 158 784 | Barbara Castle |
| 158 791 | County of Nottinghamshire |
| 158 796 | Fred Trueman Cricketing Legend |
| 158 860 | Ian Dewhirst |

**Class 158/8. Refurbished South West Trains units.** Converted from former TransPennine Express units at Wabtec, Doncaster in 2007. 2+1 seating in First Class. Details as Class 158/0 except:

**DMCL.** Lot No. 31051 BREL Derby 1989–1992. 13/44 1TD 1W. 38.5 t.
**DMSL.** Lot No. 31052 BREL Derby 1989–1992. –/70 1T. 38.5 t.

| | | | | | | | |
|---|---|---|---|---|---|---|---|
| 158 880 | (158 737) | **ST** | P | *SW* | SA | 52737 | 57737 |
| 158 881 | (158 742) | **ST** | P | *SW* | SA | 52742 | 57742 |
| 158 882 | (158 743) | **ST** | P | *SW* | SA | 52743 | 57743 |
| 158 883 | (158 744) | **ST** | P | *SW* | SA | 52744 | 57744 |

| 158 884 | (158 772) | **ST** | P | *SW* | SA | 52772 | 57772 |
| 158 885 | (158 775) | **ST** | P | *SW* | SA | 52775 | 57775 |
| 158 886 | (158 779) | **ST** | P | *SW* | SA | 52779 | 57779 |
| 158 887 | (158 781) | **ST** | P | *SW* | SA | 52781 | 57781 |
| 158 888 | (158 802) | **ST** | P | *NO* | NL | 52802 | 57802 |
| 158 889 | (158 808) | **ST** | P | *SW* | SA | 52808 | 57808 |
| 158 890 | (158 814) | **ST** | P | *SW* | SA | 52814 | 57814 |

## CLASS 158/9                                                    BREL

DMSL–DMS. Units leased by West Yorkshire PTE but managed by HSBC Rail. Details as Class 158/0 except for seating and toilets.

**DMSL.** Lot No. 31051 BREL Derby 1990–1992. –/70 1TD 1W. 38.5 t.
**DMS.** Lot No. 31052 BREL Derby 1990–1992. –/72 and parcels area. 38.5 t.

| 158 901 | **NO** | H | *NO* | NL | 52901 | 57901 | |
| 158 902 | **NO** | H | *NO* | NL | 52902 | 57902 | |
| 158 903 | **NO** | H | *NO* | NL | 52903 | 57903 | |
| 158 904 | **NO** | H | *NO* | NL | 52904 | 57904 | |
| 158 905 | **NO** | H | *NO* | NL | 52905 | 57905 | |
| 158 906 | **NO** | H | *NO* | NL | 52906 | 57906 | |
| 158 907 | **NO** | H | *NO* | NL | 52907 | 57907 | |
| 158 908 | **NO** | H | *NO* | NL | 52908 | 57908 | |
| 158 909 | **NO** | H | *NO* | NL | 52909 | 57909 | |
| 158 910 | **NO** | H | *NO* | NL | 52910 | 57910 | William Wilberforce |

## CLASS 158/0                                                    BREL

DMSL–DMSL–DMSL. Refurbished units reformed in 2008 for First Great Western. For vehicle details see above.

| 158 950 | w | **FI** | P | *GW* | PM | 57751 | 52761 | 57761 |
| 158 951 | w | **FI** | P | *GW* | PM | 52751 | 52764 | 57764 |
| 158 952 | w | **FI** | P | *GW* | PM | 57748 | 52762 | 57762 |
| 158 953 | w | **FI** | P | *GW* | PM | 52748 | 52750 | 57750 |
| 158 954 | w | **FI** | P | *GW* | PM | 57747 | 52760 | 57760 |
| 158 955 | w | **FI** | P | *GW* | PM | 52747 | 52765 | 57765 |
| 158 956 | w | **FI** | P | *GW* | PM | 57749 | 52768 | 57768 |
| 158 957 | w | **FI** | P | *GW* | PM | 52749 | 52771 | 57771 |
| 158 958 | w | **FI** | P | *GW* | PM | 57746 | 52776 | 57776 |
| 158 959 | w | **FI** | P | *GW* | PM | 52746 | 52778 | 57778 |

# CLASS 159/0          BREL

DMCL–MSL–DMSL. Built as Class 158. Converted before entering passenger service to Class 159 by Rosyth Dockyard.

**Construction:** Welded aluminium.
**Engines:** One Cummins NTA855R of 300 kW (400 h.p.) at 2100 r.p.m.
**Bogies:** One BREL P4 (powered) and one BREL T4 (non-powered) per car.
**Couplers:** BSI.
**Dimensions:** 22.16 x 2.70 m.
**Gangways:** Throughout.      **Wheel Arrangement:** 2-B + B-2 + B-2.
**Doors:** Twin-leaf swing plug.      **Maximum Speed:** 90 m.p.h.
**Seating Layout:** 1: 2+1 facing, 2: 2+2 facing/unidirectional.
**Multiple Working:** Within class and with Classes 142, 143, 144, 150, 153, 155, 156, 158 and 170.

**DMCL.** Lot No. 31051 BREL Derby 1992–1993. 23/28 1TD 1W. 38.5 t.
**MSL.** Lot No. 31050 BREL Derby 1992–1993. –/70(6) 1T. 38.5 t.
**DMSL.** Lot No. 31052 BREL Derby 1992–1993. –/72 1T. 38.5 t.

| | | | | | | | | |
|---|---|---|---|---|---|---|---|---|
| 159 001 | **ST** | P | *SW* | SA | 52873 | 58718 | 57873 | CITY OF EXETER |
| 159 002 | **ST** | P | *SW* | SA | 52874 | 58719 | 57874 | CITY OF SALISBURY |
| 159 003 | **ST** | P | *SW* | SA | 52875 | 58720 | 57875 | TEMPLECOMBE |
| 159 004 | **ST** | P | *SW* | SA | 52876 | 58721 | 57876 | BASINGSTOKE AND DEANE |
| 159 005 | **ST** | P | *SW* | SA | 52877 | 58722 | 57877 | |
| 159 006 | **ST** | P | *SW* | SA | 52878 | 58723 | 57878 | |
| 159 007 | **ST** | P | *SW* | SA | 52879 | 58724 | 57879 | |
| 159 008 | **ST** | P | *SW* | SA | 52880 | 58725 | 57880 | |
| 159 009 | **ST** | P | *SW* | SA | 52881 | 58726 | 57881 | |
| 159 010 | **ST** | P | *SW* | SA | 52882 | 58727 | 57882 | |
| 159 011 | **ST** | P | *SW* | SA | 52883 | 58728 | 57883 | |
| 159 012 | **ST** | P | *SW* | SA | 52884 | 58729 | 57884 | |
| 159 013 | **ST** | P | *SW* | SA | 52885 | 58730 | 57885 | |
| 159 014 | **ST** | P | *SW* | SA | 52886 | 58731 | 57886 | |
| 159 015 | **ST** | P | *SW* | SA | 52887 | 58732 | 57887 | |
| 159 016 | **ST** | P | *SW* | SA | 52888 | 58733 | 57888 | |
| 159 017 | **ST** | P | *SW* | SA | 52889 | 58734 | 57889 | |
| 159 018 | **ST** | P | *SW* | SA | 52890 | 58735 | 57890 | |
| 159 019 | **ST** | P | *SW* | SA | 52891 | 58736 | 57891 | |
| 159 020 | **ST** | P | *SW* | SA | 52892 | 58737 | 57892 | |
| 159 021 | **ST** | P | *SW* | SA | 52893 | 58738 | 57893 | |
| 159 022 | **ST** | P | *SW* | SA | 52894 | 58739 | 57894 | |

# CLASS 159/1                                    BREL

DMCL–MSL–DMSL. Units converted from Class 158s at Wabtec, Doncaster in 2006–07 for South West Trains.

Details as Class 158/0 except:
**Seating Layout:** 1: 2+1 facing, 2: 2+2 facing/unidirectional.

**DMCL.** Lot No. 31051 BREL Derby 1989–1992. 24/28 1TD 1W. 38.5 t.
**MSL.** Lot No. 31050 BREL Derby 1989–1992. –/70 1T. 38.5 t.
**DMSL.** Lot No. 31052 BREL Derby 1989–1992. –/72 1T.38.5 t.

| | | | | | | | |
|---|---|---|---|---|---|---|---|
| 159 101 | (158 800) | **ST** | P | *SW* | SA | 52800 | 58717 | 57800 |
| 159 102 | (158 803) | **ST** | P | *SW* | SA | 52803 | 58703 | 57803 |
| 159 103 | (158 804) | **ST** | P | *SW* | SA | 52804 | 58704 | 57804 |
| 159 104 | (158 805) | **ST** | P | *SW* | SA | 52805 | 58705 | 57805 |
| 159 105 | (158 807) | **ST** | P | *SW* | SA | 52807 | 58707 | 57807 |
| 159 106 | (158 809) | **ST** | P | *SW* | SA | 52809 | 58709 | 57809 |
| 159 107 | (158 811) | **ST** | P | *SW* | SA | 52811 | 58711 | 57811 |
| 159 108 | (158 801) | **ST** | P | *SW* | SA | 52801 | 58701 | 57801 |

# CLASS 165/0          NETWORK TURBO          BREL

DMSL–DMS and DMSL–MS–DMS. Chiltern Railways units. Refurbished 2003–2005 with First Class seats removed and air conditioning fitted.

**Construction:** Welded aluminium.
**Engines:** One Perkins 2006-TWH of 260 kW (350 h.p.) at 1900 r.p.m.
**Bogies:** BREL P3-17 (powered), BREL T3-17 (non-powered).
**Couplers:** BSI.
**Dimensions:** 23.50/23.25 x 2.81 m.
**Gangways:** Within unit only.          **Wheel Arrangement:** 2-B (+ B-2) + B-2.
**Doors:** Twin-leaf swing plug.          **Maximum Speed:** 75 m.p.h.
**Seating Layout:** 2+2/3+2 facing/unidirectional.
**Multiple Working:** Within class and with Classes 166 and 168.

Fitted with tripcocks for working over London Underground tracks between Harrow-on-the-Hill and Amersham.

**58801–58822/58873–58878. DMSL.** Lot No. 31087 BREL York 1990. –/82(7) 1T 2W. 40.1 t.
**58823–58833. DMSL.** Lot No. 31089 BREL York 1991–1992. –/82(7) 1T 2W. 40.1 t.
**MS.** Lot No. 31090 BREL York 1991–1992. –/106. 37.0 t.
**DMS.** Lot No. 31088 BREL York 1991–1992. –/94. 39.4 t.

| | | | | | | |
|---|---|---|---|---|---|---|
| 165 001 | **CR** | A | *CR* | AL | 58801 | 58834 |
| 165 002 | **CR** | A | *CR* | AL | 58802 | 58835 |
| 165 003 | **CR** | A | *CR* | AL | 58803 | 58836 |
| 165 004 | **CR** | A | *CR* | AL | 58804 | 58837 |
| 165 005 | **CR** | A | *CR* | AL | 58805 | 58838 |
| 165 006 | **CR** | A | *CR* | AL | 58806 | 58839 |
| 165 007 | **CR** | A | *CR* | AL | 58807 | 58840 |
| 165 008 | **CR** | A | *CR* | AL | 58808 | 58841 |

| 165 009 | **CR** | A | *CR* | AL | 58809 |       | 58842 |
| 165 010 | **CR** | A | *CR* | AL | 58810 |       | 58843 |
| 165 011 | **CR** | A | *CR* | AL | 58811 |       | 58844 |
| 165 012 | **CR** | A | *CR* | AL | 58812 |       | 58845 |
| 165 013 | **CR** | A | *CR* | AL | 58813 |       | 58846 |
| 165 014 | **CR** | A | *CR* | AL | 58814 |       | 58847 |
| 165 015 | **CR** | A | *CR* | AL | 58815 |       | 58848 |
| 165 016 | **CR** | A | *CR* | AL | 58816 |       | 58849 |
| 165 017 | **CR** | A | *CR* | AL | 58817 |       | 58850 |
| 165 018 | **CR** | A | *CR* | AL | 58818 |       | 58851 |
| 165 019 | **CR** | A | *CR* | AL | 58819 |       | 58852 |
| 165 020 | **CR** | A | *CR* | AL | 58820 |       | 58853 |
| 165 021 | **CR** | A | *CR* | AL | 58821 |       | 58854 |
| 165 022 | **CR** | A | *CR* | AL | 58822 |       | 58855 |
| 165 023 | **CR** | A | *CR* | AL | 58873 |       | 58867 |
| 165 024 | **CR** | A | *CR* | AL | 58874 |       | 58868 |
| 165 025 | **CR** | A | *CR* | AL | 58875 |       | 58869 |
| 165 026 | **CR** | A | *CR* | AL | 58876 |       | 58870 |
| 165 027 | **CR** | A | *CR* | AL | 58877 |       | 58871 |
| 165 028 | **CR** | A | *CR* | AL | 58878 |       | 58872 |
| 165 029 | **CR** | A | *CR* | AL | 58823 | 55404 | 58856 |
| 165 030 | **CR** | A | *CR* | AL | 58824 | 55405 | 58857 |
| 165 031 | **CR** | A | *CR* | AL | 58825 | 55406 | 58858 |
| 165 032 | **CR** | A | *CR* | AL | 58826 | 55407 | 58859 |
| 165 033 | **CR** | A | *CR* | AL | 58827 | 55408 | 58860 |
| 165 034 | **CR** | A | *CR* | AL | 58828 | 55409 | 58861 |
| 165 035 | **CR** | A | *CR* | AL | 58829 | 55410 | 58862 |
| 165 036 | **CR** | A | *CR* | AL | 58830 | 55411 | 58863 |
| 165 037 | **CR** | A | *CR* | AL | 58831 | 55412 | 58864 |
| 165 038 | **CR** | A | *CR* | AL | 58832 | 55413 | 58865 |
| 165 039 | **CR** | A | *CR* | AL | 58833 | 55414 | 58866 |

# CLASS 165/1          NETWORK TURBO          BREL

First Great Western units. DMCL–MS–DMS or DMCL–DMS.

**Construction:** Welded aluminium.
**Engines:** One Perkins 2006-TWH of 260 kW (350 h.p.) at 1900 r.p.m.
**Bogies:** BREL P3-17 (powered), BREL T3-17 (non-powered).
**Couplers:** BSI.
**Dimensions:** 23.50/23.25 x 2.81 m.
**Gangways:** Within unit only.               **Wheel Arrangement:** 2-B (+ B-2) + B-2.
**Doors:** Twin-leaf swing plug.              **Maximum Speed:** 90 m.p.h.
**Seating Layout:** 1: 2+2 facing, 2: 3+2 facing/unidirectional.
**Multiple Working:** Within class and with Classes 166 and 168.

**58953–58969. DMCL.** Lot No. 31098 BREL York 1992. 16/66 1T. 38.0 t.
**58879–58898. DMCL.** Lot No. 31096 BREL York 1992. 16/72 1T. 38.0 t.
**MS.** Lot No. 31099 BREL 1992. –/106. 37.0 t.
**DMS.** Lot No. 31097 BREL 1992. –/98. 37.0 t.

| 165 101 | FD | A | GW | RG | 58953 | 55415 | 58916 |
| 165 102 | FD | A | GW | RG | 58954 | 55416 | 58917 |
| 165 103 | FD | A | GW | RG | 58955 | 55417 | 58918 |
| 165 104 | FD | A | GW | RG | 58956 | 55418 | 58919 |
| 165 105 | FD | A | GW | RG | 58957 | 55419 | 58920 |
| 165 106 | FD | A | GW | RG | 58958 | 55420 | 58921 |
| 165 107 | FD | A | GW | RG | 58959 | 55421 | 58922 |
| 165 108 | FD | A | GW | RG | 58960 | 55422 | 58923 |
| 165 109 | FD | A | GW | RG | 58961 | 55423 | 58924 |
| 165 110 | FD | A | GW | RG | 58962 | 55424 | 58925 |
| 165 111 | FD | A | GW | RG | 58963 | 55425 | 58926 |
| 165 112 | FD | A | GW | RG | 58964 | 55426 | 58927 |
| 165 113 | FD | A | GW | RG | 58965 | 55427 | 58928 |
| 165 114 | FD | A | GW | RG | 58966 | 55428 | 58929 |
| 165 116 | FD | A | GW | RG | 58968 | 55430 | 58931 |
| 165 117 | FD | A | GW | RG | 58969 | 55431 | 58932 |
| 165 118 | FD | A | GW | RG | 58879 |       | 58933 |
| 165 119 | FD | A | GW | RG | 58880 |       | 58934 |
| 165 120 | FD | A | GW | RG | 58881 |       | 58935 |
| 165 121 | FD | A | GW | RG | 58882 |       | 58936 |
| 165 122 | FD | A | GW | RG | 58883 |       | 58937 |
| 165 123 | FD | A | GW | RG | 58884 |       | 58938 |
| 165 124 | FD | A | GW | RG | 58885 |       | 58939 |
| 165 125 | FD | A | GW | RG | 58886 |       | 58940 |
| 165 126 | FD | A | GW | RG | 58887 |       | 58941 |
| 165 127 | FD | A | GW | RG | 58888 |       | 58942 |
| 165 128 | FD | A | GW | RG | 58889 |       | 58943 |
| 165 129 | FD | A | GW | RG | 58890 |       | 58944 |
| 165 130 | FD | A | GW | RG | 58891 |       | 58945 |
| 165 131 | FD | A | GW | RG | 58892 |       | 58946 |
| 165 132 | FD | A | GW | RG | 58893 |       | 58947 |
| 165 133 | FD | A | GW | RG | 58894 |       | 58948 |
| 165 134 | FD | A | GW | RG | 58895 |       | 58949 |
| 165 135 | FD | A | GW | RG | 58896 |       | 58950 |
| 165 136 | FD | A | GW | RG | 58897 |       | 58951 |
| 165 137 | FD | A | GW | RG | 58898 |       | 58952 |

# CLASS 166   NETWORK EXPRESS TURBO   ABB

DMCL(A)–MS–DMCL(B). First Great Western units, built for Paddington–Oxford/ Newbury services. Air conditioned and with additional luggage space compared to the Class 165s.

**Construction:** Welded aluminium.
**Engines:** One Perkins 2006-TWH of 260 kW (350 h.p.) at 1900 r.p.m.
**Bogies:** BREL P3-17 (powered), BREL T3-17 (non-powered).
**Couplers:** BSI.
**Dimensions:** 23.50 x 2.81 m.
**Gangways:** Within unit only.          **Wheel Arrangement:** 2-B + B-2 + B-2.
**Doors:** Twin-leaf swing plug.          **Maximum Speed:** 90 m.p.h.
**Seating Layout:** 1: 2+2 facing, 2: 2+2/3+2 facing/unidirectional.

**Multiple Working:** Within class and with Classes 165 and 168.

**DMCL (A).** Lot No. 31116 ABB York 1992–1993. 16/68 1T. 39.6 t.
**MS.** Lot No. 31117 ABB York 1992–1993. –/91. 38.0 t.
**DMCL (B).** Lot No. 31116 ABB York 1992–1993. 16/68 1T. 39.6 t.

| | | | | | | | |
|---|---|---|---|---|---|---|---|
| 166 201 | **FD** | A | *GW* | RG | 58101 | 58601 | 58122 |
| 166 202 | **FD** | A | *GW* | RG | 58102 | 58602 | 58123 |
| 166 203 | **FD** | A | *GW* | RG | 58103 | 58603 | 58124 |
| 166 204 | **FD** | A | *GW* | RG | 58104 | 58604 | 58125 |
| 166 205 | **FD** | A | *GW* | RG | 58105 | 58605 | 58126 |
| 166 206 | **FD** | A | *GW* | RG | 58106 | 58606 | 58127 |
| 166 207 | **FD** | A | *GW* | RG | 58107 | 58607 | 58128 |
| 166 208 | **FD** | A | *GW* | RG | 58108 | 58608 | 58129 |
| 166 209 | **FD** | A | *GW* | RG | 58109 | 58609 | 58130 |
| 166 210 | **FD** | A | *GW* | RG | 58110 | 58610 | 58131 |
| 166 211 | **FD** | A | *GW* | RG | 58111 | 58611 | 58132 |
| 166 212 | **FD** | A | *GW* | RG | 58112 | 58612 | 58133 |
| 166 213 | **FD** | A | *GW* | RG | 58113 | 58613 | 58134 |
| 166 214 | **FD** | A | *GW* | RG | 58114 | 58614 | 58135 |
| 166 215 | **FD** | A | *GW* | RG | 58115 | 58615 | 58136 |
| 166 216 | **FD** | A | *GW* | RG | 58116 | 58616 | 58137 |
| 166 217 | **FD** | A | *GW* | RG | 58117 | 58617 | 58138 |
| 166 218 | **FD** | A | *GW* | RG | 58118 | 58618 | 58139 |
| 166 219 | **FD** | A | *GW* | RG | 58119 | 58619 | 58140 |
| 166 220 | **FD** | A | *GW* | RG | 58120 | 58620 | 58141 |
| 166 221 | **FD** | A | *GW* | RG | 58121 | 58621 | 58142 |

# CLASS 168    CLUBMAN    ADTRANZ/BOMBARDIER

Air conditioned.

**Construction:** Welded aluminium bodies with bolt-on steel ends.
**Engines:** One MTU 6R183TD13H of 315 kW (422 h.p.) at 1900 r.p.m.
**Transmission:** Hydraulic. Voith T211rzze to ZF final drive.
**Bogies:** One Adtranz P3–23 and one BREL T3–23 per car.
**Couplers:** BSI at outer ends, bar within unit.
**Dimensions:** Class 168/0: 24.1/23.61 x 2.69 m. Others: 23.62/23.61 x 2.69 m.
**Gangways:** Within unit only.    **Wheel Arrangement:** 2-B (+ B-2 + B-2) + B-2.
**Doors:** Twin-leaf swing plug.    **Maximum Speed:** 100 m.p.h.
**Seating Layout:** 2+2 facing/unidirectional.
**Multiple Working:** Within class and with Classes 165 and 166.

Fitted with tripcocks for working over London Underground tracks between Harrow-on-the-Hill and Amersham.

**Class 168/0.** Original Design. DMSL(A)–MS–MSL–DMSL(B) or DMSL(A)–MSL–MS–DMSL(B).

**58151–58155. DMSL(A).** Adtranz Derby 1997–1998. –/57 1TD 1W. 44.0 t.
**58651–58655. MSL.** Adtranz Derby 1998. –/73 1T. 41.0 t.
**58451–58455. MS.** Adtranz Derby 1998. –/77. 41.0 t.
**58251–58255. DMSL(B).** Adtranz Derby 1998. –/68 1T. 43.6 t.

**Note:** 58451–58455 were numbered 58656–58660 for a time when used in 168 106–168 110.

| | | | | | | | | |
|---|---|---|---|---|---|---|---|---|
| 168 001 | **CR** | P | *CR* | AL | 58151 | 58451 | 58651 | 58251 |
| 168 002 | **CR** | P | *CR* | AL | 58152 | 58652 | 58452 | 58252 |
| 168 003 | **CR** | P | *CR* | AL | 58153 | 58653 | 58453 | 58253 |
| 168 004 | **CR** | P | *CR* | AL | 58154 | 58654 | 58454 | 58254 |
| 168 005 | **CR** | P | *CR* | AL | 58155 | 58655 | 58455 | 58255 |

**Class 168/1.** These units are effectively Class 170s. DMSL(A)–MSL–MS–DMSL(B), DMSL(A)–MS–MSL–DMSL(B) or DMSL(A)–MS–DMSL(B).

**58156–58163. DMSL(A).** Adtranz Derby 2000. –/57 1TD 2W. 45.2 t.
**58456–58460. MS.** Bombardier Derby 2002. –/76. 41.8 t.
**58756–58757. MSL.** Bombardier Derby 2002. –/73 1T. 42.9 t.
**58461–58463. MS.** Adtranz Derby 2000. –/76. 42.4 t.
**58256–58263. DMSL(B).** Adtranz Derby 2000. –/69 1T. 45.2 t.

**Notes:** 58461–58463 have been renumbered from 58661–58663.

| | | | | | | | | |
|---|---|---|---|---|---|---|---|---|
| 168 106 | **CR** | P | *CR* | AL | 58156 | 58456 | 58756 | 58256 |
| 168 107 | **CR** | P | *CR* | AL | 58157 | 58757 | 58457 | 58257 |
| 168 108 | **CR** | P | *CR* | AL | 58158 | | 58458 | 58258 |
| 168 109 | **CR** | P | *CR* | AL | 58159 | | 58459 | 58259 |
| 168 110 | **CR** | P | *CR* | AL | 58160 | | 58460 | 58260 |
| 168 111 | **CR** | H | *CR* | AL | 58161 | | 58461 | 58261 |
| 168 112 | **CR** | H | *CR* | AL | 58162 | | 58462 | 58262 |
| 168 113 | **CR** | H | *CR* | AL | 58163 | | 58463 | 58263 |

**Class 168/2.** These units are effectively Class 170s. DMSL(A)–(MS)–MS–DMSL(B).

**58164–58169. DMSL(A).** Bombardier Derby 2003–2004. –/57 1TD 2W. 45.4 t.
**58365–58367. MS.** Bombardier Derby 2006. –/76. 43.3 t.
**58464/58468/58469. MS.** Bombardier Derby 2003–2004. –/76. 44.0 t.
**58465–58467. MS.** Bombardier Derby 2006. –/76. 43.3 t.
**58264–58269. DMSL(B).** Bombardier Derby 2003–2004. –/69 1T. 45.5 t.

| | | | | | | | | |
|---|---|---|---|---|---|---|---|---|
| 168 214 | **CR** | P | *CR* | AL | 58164 | | 58464 | 58264 |
| 168 215 | **CR** | P | *CR* | AL | 58165 | 58465 | 58365 | 58265 |
| 168 216 | **CR** | P | *CR* | AL | 58166 | 58366 | 58466 | 58266 |
| 168 217 | **CR** | P | *CR* | AL | 58167 | 58367 | 58467 | 58267 |
| 168 218 | **CR** | P | *CR* | AL | 58168 | | 58468 | 58268 |
| 168 219 | **CR** | P | *CR* | AL | 58169 | | 58469 | 58269 |

# CLASS 170 TURBOSTAR ADTRANZ/BOMBARDIER

Various formations. Air conditioned.

**Construction:** Welded aluminium bodies with bolt-on steel ends.
**Engines:** One MTU 6R183TD13H of 315 kW (422 h.p.) at 1900 r.p.m.
**Transmission:** Hydraulic. Voith T211rzze to ZF final drive.
**Bogies:** One Adtranz P3–23 and one BREL T3–23 per car.
**Couplers:** BSI at outer ends, bar within later build units.
**Dimensions:** 23.62/23.61 x 2.69 m.
**Gangways:** Within unit only.     **Wheel Arrangement:** 2-B (+ B-2) + B-2.
**Doors:** Twin-leaf sliding plug.     **Maximum Speed:** 100 m.p.h.
**Seating Layout:** 1: 2+1 facing/unidirectional. 2: 2+2 unidirectional/facing.
**Multiple Working:** Within class and with Classes 150, 153, 155, 156, 158, 159 and 172.

**Class 170/1. CrossCountry (former Midland Mainline) units.** Lazareni seating. DMSL–MS–DMCL/DMSL–DMCL.

**DMSL.** Adtranz Derby 1998–1999. –/59 1TD 2W. 45.0 t.
**MS.** Adtranz Derby 2001. –/80. 43.0 t.
**DMCL.** Adtranz Derby 1998–1999. 9/52 1T. 44.8 t

| | | | | | | | |
|---|---|---|---|---|---|---|---|
| 170 101 | **XC** | P | *XC* | TS | 50101 | 55101 | 79101 |
| 170 102 | **XC** | P | *XC* | TS | 50102 | 55102 | 79102 |
| 170 103 | **XC** | P | *XC* | TS | 50103 | 55103 | 79103 |
| 170 104 | **XC** | P | *XC* | TS | 50104 | 55104 | 79104 |
| 170 105 | **XC** | P | *XC* | TS | 50105 | 55105 | 79105 |
| 170 106 | **XC** | P | *XC* | TS | 50106 | 55106 | 79106 |
| 170 107 | **XC** | P | *XC* | TS | 50107 | 55107 | 79107 |
| 170 108 | **XC** | P | *XC* | TS | 50108 | 55108 | 79108 |
| 170 109 | **XC** | P | *XC* | TS | 50109 | 55109 | 79109 |
| 170 110 | **XC** | P | *XC* | TS | 50110 | 55110 | 79110 |
| 170 111 | **XC** | P | *XC* | TS | 50111 | | 79111 |
| 170 112 | **XC** | P | *XC* | TS | 50112 | | 79112 |
| 170 113 | **XC** | P | *XC* | TS | 50113 | | 79113 |
| 170 114 | **XC** | P | *XC* | TS | 50114 | | 79114 |
| 170 115 | **XC** | P | *XC* | TS | 50115 | | 79115 |
| 170 116 | **XC** | P | *XC* | TS | 50116 | | 79116 |
| 170 117 | **XC** | P | *XC* | TS | 50117 | | 79117 |

**Class 170/2. National Express East Anglia 3-car units.** Chapman seating. DMCL–MSL–DMSL.

**DMCL.** Adtranz Derby 1999. 7/39 1TD 2W. 45.0 t.
**MSL.** Adtranz Derby 1999. –/68 1T. Guard's office. 45.3 t.
**DMSL.** Adtranz Derby 1999. –/66 1T. 43.4 t.

| | | | | | | | | |
|---|---|---|---|---|---|---|---|---|
| 170 201 | r | **1** | P | *EA* | NC | 50201 | 56201 | 79201 |
| 170 202 | r | **1** | P | *EA* | NC | 50202 | 56202 | 79202 |
| 170 203 | r | **1** | P | *EA* | NC | 50203 | 56203 | 79203 |
| 170 204 | r | **1** | P | *EA* | NC | 50204 | 56204 | 79204 |
| 170 205 | r | **1** | P | *EA* | NC | 50205 | 56205 | 79205 |

| 170 206 | r | 1 | P | EA | NC | 50206 | 56206 | 79206 | Skaw 3/12 |
| 170 207 | r | 1 | P | EA | NC | 50207 | 56207 | 79207 | |
| 170 208 | r | 1 | P | EA | NC | 50208 | 56208 | 79208 | |

**Class 170/2. National Express East Anglia 2-car units.** Chapman seating. DMSL–DMCL.

**DMSL.** Bombardier Derby 2002. –/57 1TD 2W. 45.7 t.
**DMCL.** Bombardier Derby 2002. 9/53 1T. 45.7 t.

| 170 270 | r | 1 | P | EA | NC | 50270 | 79270 | |
| 170 271 | r | AN | P | EA | NC | 50271 | 79271 | |
| 170 272 | r | AN | P | EA | NC | 50272 | 79272 | |
| 170 273 | r | AN | P | EA | NC | 50273 | 79273 | NM 3/12 |

**Class 170/3. TransPennine Express units.** Chapman seating. DMCL–DMSL. 170 309 renumbered from 170 399.

**50301–50308/50399. DMCL.** Adtranz Derby 2000–2001. 8/43 1TD 2W. 45.8 t.
**79301–79308/79399. DMSL.** Adtranz Derby 2000–2001. –/65 1T. 45.8 t.

| 170 301 | FT | P | TP | XW | 50301 | 79301 |
| 170 302 | FT | P | TP | XW | 50302 | 79302 |
| 170 303 | FT | P | TP | XW | 50303 | 79303 |
| 170 304 | FT | P | TP | XW | 50304 | 79304 |
| 170 305 | FT | P | TP | XW | 50305 | 79305 |
| 170 306 | FT | P | TP | XW | 50306 | 79306 |
| 170 307 | FT | P | TP | XW | 50307 | 79307 |
| 170 308 | FT | P | TP | XW | 50308 | 79308 |
| 170 309 | FT | P | TP | XW | 50399 | 79399 |

**Class 170/3. Units built for Hull Trains. Now in use with ScotRail and dedicated to Edinburgh/Glasgow–Inverness services.** Chapman seating. DMCL–MSLRB–DMSL.

**DMCL.** Bombardier Derby 2004. 7/41 1TD 2W. 46.5 t.
**MSLRB.** Bombardier Derby 2004. –/53 1T. Buffet and guard's office 44.7 t.
**DMSL.** Bombardier Derby 2004. –/67 1T. 46.3 t.

| 170 393 | FS | P | SR | HA | 50393 | 56393 | 79393 |
| 170 394 | FS | P | SR | HA | 50394 | 56394 | 79394 |
| 170 395 | FS | P | SR | HA | 50395 | 56395 | 79395 |
| 170 396 | FS | P | SR | HA | 50396 | 56396 | 79396 |

**Class 170/3. CrossCountry units.** Lazareni seating. DMSL–MS–DMCL.

**DMSL.** Bombardier Derby 2002. –/59 1TD 2W. 45.4 t.
**MS.** Bombardier Derby 2002. –/80. 43.0 t.
**DMCL.** Bombardier Derby 2002. 9/52 1T. 45.8 t.

| 170 397 | XC | P | XC | TS | 50397 | 56397 | 79397 |
| 170 398 | XC | P | XC | TS | 50398 | 56398 | 79398 |

**Class 170/4. ScotRail "express" units.** Chapman seating. DMCL–MS–DMCL.

**DMCL(A).** Adtranz Derby 1999–2001. 9/43 1TD 2W. 45.2 t.
**MS.** Adtranz Derby 1999–2001. –/76. 42.5 t.
**DMCL(B).** Adtranz Derby 1999–2001. 9/49 1T. 45.2 t.

| 170 401 | **FS** | P | *SR* | HA | 50401 | 56401 | 79401 | |
|---|---|---|---|---|---|---|---|---|
| 170 402 | **FS** | P | *SR* | HA | 50402 | 56402 | 79402 | |
| 170 403 | **FS** | P | *SR* | HA | 50403 | 56403 | 79403 | |
| 170 404 | **FS** | P | *SR* | HA | 50404 | 56404 | 79404 | |
| 170 405 | **FS** | P | *SR* | HA | 50405 | 56405 | 79405 | |
| 170 406 | **FS** | P | *SR* | HA | 50406 | 56406 | 79406 | |
| 170 407 | **FS** | P | *SR* | HA | 50407 | 56407 | 79407 | |
| 170 408 | **FS** | P | *SR* | HA | 50408 | 56408 | 79408 | |
| 170 409 | **FS** | P | *SR* | HA | 50409 | 56409 | 79409 | |
| 170 410 | **FS** | P | *SR* | HA | 50410 | 56410 | 79410 | |
| 170 411 | **FS** | P | *SR* | HA | 50411 | 56411 | 79411 | |
| 170 412 | **FS** | P | *SR* | HA | 50412 | 56412 | 79412 | |
| 170 413 | **FS** | P | *SR* | HA | 50413 | 56413 | 79413 | |
| 170 414 | **FS** | P | *SR* | HA | 50414 | 56414 | 79414 | |
| 170 415 | **FS** | P | *SR* | HA | 50415 | 56415 | 79415 | |
| 170 416 | **FS** | H | *SR* | HA | 50416 | 56416 | 79416 | |
| 170 417 | **FS** | H | *SR* | HA | 50417 | 56417 | 79417 | |
| 170 418 | **FS** | H | *SR* | HA | 50418 | 56418 | 79418 | |
| 170 419 | **FS** | H | *SR* | HA | 50419 | 56419 | 79419 | |
| 170 420 | **FS** | H | *SR* | HA | 50420 | 56420 | 79420 | |
| 170 421 | **FS** | H | *SR* | HA | 50421 | 56421 | 79421 | |
| 170 422 | **FS** | H | *SR* | HA | 50422 | 56422 | 79422 | |
| 170 423 | **FS** | H | *SR* | HA | 50423 | 56423 | 79423 | |
| 170 424 | **FS** | H | *SR* | HA | 50424 | 56424 | 79424 | |

**Class 170/4. ScotRail "express" units.** Chapman seating. DMCL–MS–DMCL.

**DMCL.** Bombardier Derby 2003–2005. 9/43 1TD 2W. 46.8 t.
**MS.** Bombardier Derby 2003–2005. –/76. 43.7 t.
**DMCL.** Bombardier Derby 2003–2005. 9/49 1T. 46.5 t.

**Note:** 170 431 & 170 432 have new uprated engines fitted: MTU 6H1800R83 of 360 kW (483 h.p.) at 1800 r.p.m.

| 170 425 | | **FS** | P | *SR* | HA | 50425 | 56425 | 79425 | |
|---|---|---|---|---|---|---|---|---|---|
| 170 426 | | **FS** | P | *SR* | HA | 50426 | 56426 | 79426 | |
| 170 427 | | **FS** | P | *SR* | HA | 50427 | 56427 | 79427 | |
| 170 428 | | **FS** | P | *SR* | HA | 50428 | 56428 | 79428 | |
| 170 429 | | **FS** | P | *SR* | HA | 50429 | 56429 | 79429 | |
| 170 430 | | **FS** | P | *SR* | HA | 50430 | 56430 | 79430 | |
| 170 431 | * | **FS** | P | *SR* | HA | 50431 | 56431 | 79431 | |
| 170 432 | * | **FS** | P | *SR* | HA | 50432 | 56432 | 79432 | |
| 170 433 | | **FS** | P | *SR* | HA | 50433 | 56433 | 79433 | Investor in People |
| 170 434 | | **SR** | P | *SR* | HA | 50434 | 56434 | 79434 | |

**Class 170/4. ScotRail units.** Originally built as Standard Class only units. 170 450–455 retro-fitted with First Class in 2008. Chapman seating. DMSL–MS–DMSL or † DMCL–MS–DMCL.

**DMSL.** Bombardier Derby 2004–2005. –/55 1TD 2W († 9/47 1TD 2W). 46.3 t.
**MS.** Bombardier Derby 2004–2005. –/76. 43.4 t.
**DMSL.** Bombardier Derby 2004–2005. –/67 1T († 9/49 1T 1W). 46.4 t.

| 170 450 | † | **FS** | P | *SR* | HA | 50450 | 56450 | 79450 |
|---|---|---|---|---|---|---|---|---|

| 170 451 | † | **FS** | P | *SR* | HA | 50451 | 56451 | 79451 |
|---------|---|--------|---|------|----|-------|-------|-------|
| 170 452 | † | **FS** | P | *SR* | HA | 50452 | 56452 | 79452 |
| 170 453 | † | **FS** | P | *SR* | HA | 50453 | 56453 | 79453 |
| 170 454 | † | **FS** | P | *SR* | HA | 50454 | 56454 | 79454 |
| 170 455 | † | **FS** | P | *SR* | HA | 50455 | 56455 | 79455 |
| 170 456 |   | **FS** | P | *SR* | HA | 50456 | 56456 | 79456 |
| 170 457 |   | **FS** | P | *SR* | HA | 50457 | 56457 | 79457 |
| 170 458 |   | **FS** | P | *SR* | HA | 50458 | 56458 | 79458 |
| 170 459 |   | **FS** | P | *SR* | HA | 50459 | 56459 | 79459 |
| 170 460 |   | **FS** | P | *SR* | HA | 50460 | 56460 | 79460 |
| 170 461 |   | **FS** | P | *SR* | HA | 50461 | 56461 | 79461 |

**Class 170/4. ScotRail units.** Standard Class only units. Chapman seating.
DMSL–MS–DMSL.

**50470–50471. DMSL(A).** Adtranz Derby 2001. –/55 1TD 2W. 45.1 t.
**50472–50478. DMSL(A).** Bombardier Derby 2004–2005. –/57 1TD 2W. 46.3 t.
**56470–56471. MS.** Adtranz Derby 2001. –/76. 42.4 t.
**56472–56478. MS.** Bombardier Derby 2004–2005. –/76. 43.4 t.
**79470–79471. DMSL(B).** Adtranz Derby 2001. –/67 1T. 45.1 t.
**79472–79478. DMSL(B).** Bombardier Derby 2004–2005. –/67 1T. 46.4 t.

| 170 470 | **SC** | P | *SR* | HA | 50470 | 56470 | 79470 |
|---------|--------|---|------|----|-------|-------|-------|
| 170 471 | **SC** | P | *SR* | HA | 50471 | 56471 | 79471 |
| 170 472 | **SP** | P | *SR* | HA | 50472 | 56472 | 79472 |
| 170 473 | **SP** | P | *SR* | HA | 50473 | 56473 | 79473 |
| 170 474 | **SP** | P | *SR* | HA | 50474 | 56474 | 79474 |
| 170 475 | **SP** | P | *SR* | HA | 50475 | 56475 | 79475 |
| 170 476 | **SP** | P | *SR* | HA | 50476 | 56476 | 79476 |
| 170 477 | **SP** | P | *SR* | HA | 50477 | 56477 | 79477 |
| 170 478 | **SP** | P | *SR* | HA | 50478 | 56478 | 79478 |

**Class 170/5. London Midland and CrossCountry 2-car units.** Lazareni seating.
DMSL–DMSL or * DMSL–DMCL (CrossCountry).

**DMSL(A).** Adtranz Derby 1999–2000. –/55 1TD 2W (* –/59 1TD 2W). 45.8 t.
**DMSL(B).** Adtranz Derby 1999–2000. –/67 1T (* DMCL 9/52 1T). 45.9 t.

| 170 501 | **LM** | P | *LM* | TS | 50501 | 79501 |
|---------|--------|---|------|----|-------|-------|
| 170 502 | **LM** | P | *LM* | TS | 50502 | 79502 |
| 170 503 | **LM** | P | *LM* | TS | 50503 | 79503 |
| 170 504 | **LM** | P | *LM* | TS | 50504 | 79504 |
| 170 505 | **LM** | P | *LM* | TS | 50505 | 79505 |
| 170 506 | **LM** | P | *LM* | TS | 50506 | 79506 |
| 170 507 | **LM** | P | *LM* | TS | 50507 | 79507 |
| 170 508 | **LM** | P | *LM* | TS | 50508 | 79508 |
| 170 509 | **LM** | P | *LM* | TS | 50509 | 79509 |
| 170 510 | **LM** | P | *LM* | TS | 50510 | 79510 |
| 170 511 | **LM** | P | *LM* | TS | 50511 | 79511 |
| 170 512 | **LM** | P | *LM* | TS | 50512 | 79512 |
| 170 513 | **LM** | P | *LM* | TS | 50513 | 79513 |
| 170 514 | **LM** | P | *LM* | TS | 50514 | 79514 |
| 170 515 | **LM** | P | *LM* | TS | 50515 | 79515 |
| 170 516 | **LM** | P | *LM* | TS | 50516 | 79516 |

| 170 517 |   | **LM** | P | *LM* | TS | 50517 | 79517 |
| 170 518 | * | **XC** | P | *XC* | TS | 50518 | 79518 |
| 170 519 | * | **XC** | P | *XC* | TS | 50519 | 79519 |
| 170 520 | * | **XC** | P | *XC* | TS | 50520 | 79520 |
| 170 521 | * | **XC** | P | *XC* | TS | 50521 | 79521 |
| 170 522 | * | **XC** | P | *XC* | TS | 50522 | 79522 |
| 170 523 | * | **XC** | P | *XC* | TS | 50523 | 79523 |

**Class 170/6. London Midland and CrossCountry 3-car units**. Lazareni seating. DMSL–MS–DMSL or * DMSL–MS–DMCL (Cross-Country).

**DMSL(A).** Adtranz Derby 2000. –/55 1TD 2W (* –/59 1TD 2W). 45.8 t.
**MS.** Adtranz Derby 2000. –/74 (* –/80). 42.4 t.
**DMSL(B).** Adtranz Derby 2000. –/67 1T (* DMCL 9/52 1T). 45.9 t.

| 170 630 |   | **LM** | P | *LM* | TS | 50630 | 56630 | 79630 |
| 170 631 |   | **LM** | P | *LM* | TS | 50631 | 56631 | 79631 |
| 170 632 |   | **LM** | P | *LM* | TS | 50632 | 56632 | 79632 |
| 170 633 |   | **LM** | P | *LM* | TS | 50633 | 56633 | 79633 |
| 170 634 |   | **LM** | P | *LM* | TS | 50634 | 56634 | 79634 |
| 170 635 |   | **LM** | P | *LM* | TS | 50635 | 56635 | 79635 |
| 170 636 | * | **XC** | P | *XC* | TS | 50636 | 56636 | 79636 |
| 170 637 | * | **XC** | P | *XC* | TS | 50637 | 56637 | 79637 |
| 170 638 | * | **XC** | P | *XC* | TS | 50638 | 56638 | 79638 |
| 170 639 | * | **XC** | P | *XC* | TS | 50639 | 56639 | 79639 |

# CLASS 171     TURBOSTAR     BOMBARDIER

DMCL–DMSL or DMCL–MS–MS–DMCL. Southern units. Air conditioned. Chapman seating.

**Construction:** Welded aluminium bodies with bolt-on steel ends.
**Engines:** One MTU 6R183TD13H of 315 kW (422 h.p.) at 1900 r.p.m.
**Transmission:** Hydraulic. Voith T211rzze to ZF final drive.
**Bogies:** One Adtranz P3–23 and one BREL T3–23 per car.
**Couplers:** Dellner 12 at outer ends, bar within unit (Class 171/8s).
**Dimensions:** 23.62/23.61 x 2.69 m.
**Gangways:** Within unit only.     **Wheel Arrangement:** 2-B (+ B-2 + B-2) + B-2.
**Doors:** Twin-leaf swing plug.     **Maximum Speed:** 100 m.p.h.
**Seating Layout:** 1: 2+1 facing/unidirectional. 2: 2+2 facing/unidirectional.
**Multiple Working:** Within class and with EMU Classes 375 and 377 in an emergency.

**Class 171/7. 2-car units.** DMCL–DMSL.

**50721–50726. DMCL.** Bombardier Derby 2003. 9/43 1TD 2W. 47.6 t.
**50727–50729. DMCL.** Bombardier Derby 2005. 9/43 1TD 2W. 46.3 t.
**50392. DMCL.** Bombardier Derby 2003. 9/43 1TD 2W. 46.6 t.
**79721–79726. DMSL.** Bombardier Derby 2003. –/64 1T. 47.8 t.
**79727–79729. DMSL.** Bombardier Derby 2005. –/64 1T. 46.2 t.
**79392. DMSL.** Bombardier Derby 2003. –/64 1T. 46.5 t.

**Notes:** 171 721–726 were built as Class 170s (170 721–726), but renumbered as Class 171s on fitting with Dellner couplers.

171 730 was formerly South West Trains unit 170 392, before transferring to Southern in 2007.

| | | | | | | | |
|---|---|---|---|---|---|---|---|
| 171 721 | **SN** | P | *SN* | SU | 50721 | 79721 |
| 171 722 | **SN** | P | *SN* | SU | 50722 | 79722 |
| 171 723 | **SN** | P | *SN* | SU | 50723 | 79723 |
| 171 724 | **SN** | P | *SN* | SU | 50724 | 79724 |
| 171 725 | **SN** | P | *SN* | SU | 50725 | 79725 |
| 171 726 | **SN** | P | *SN* | SU | 50726 | 79726 |
| 171 727 | **SN** | P | *SN* | SU | 50727 | 79727 |
| 171 728 | **SN** | P | *SN* | SU | 50728 | 79728 |
| 171 729 | **SN** | P | *SN* | SU | 50729 | 79729 |
| 171 730 | **SN** | P | *SN* | SU | 50392 | 79392 |

**Class 171/8. 4-car units.** DMCL(A)–MS–MS–DMCL(B).

**DMCL(A).** Bombardier Derby 2004. 9/43 1TD 2W. 46.5 t.
**MS.** Bombardier Derby 2004. –/74. 43.7 t.
**DMCL(B).** Bombardier Derby 2004. 9/50 1T. 46.5 t.

| | | | | | | | | |
|---|---|---|---|---|---|---|---|---|
| 171 801 | **SN** | P | *SN* | SU | 50801 | 54801 | 56801 | 79801 |
| 171 802 | **SN** | P | *SN* | SU | 50802 | 54802 | 56802 | 79802 |
| 171 803 | **SN** | P | *SN* | SU | 50803 | 54803 | 56803 | 79803 |
| 171 804 | **SN** | P | *SN* | SU | 50804 | 54804 | 56804 | 79804 |
| 171 805 | **SN** | P | *SN* | SU | 50805 | 54805 | 56805 | 79805 |
| 171 806 | **SN** | P | *SN* | SU | 50806 | 54806 | 56806 | 79806 |

# CLASS 172     TURBOSTAR     BOMBARDIER

New generation Turbostars on order for London Overground, Chiltern Railways and London Midland. Air conditioned. Full details awaited.

**Construction:** Welded aluminium bodies with bolt-on steel ends.
**Engines:** One MTU 6H1800R83 of 360 kW (483 h.p.) at 1800 r.p.m.
**Transmission:** Mechanical. Supplied by ZG, Germany.
**Bogies:** B5000 type "lightweight" bogies.
**Couplers:** BSI.
**Dimensions:** 23.27/23.36 x 2.75 m.
**Gangways:** London Overground & Chiltern units: Within unit only. London Midland units: Throughout.
**Wheel Arrangement:**
**Doors:** Twin-leaf swing plug.
**Maximum Speed:** 75 m.p.h. (London Midland units 100 m.p.h.)
**Seating Layout:** 2+2 facing/unidirectional.
**Multiple Working:** Within class and with Classes 150, 153, 155, 156, 158, 159 and 170.

**Class 172/0. London Overground units.** DMS–DMS. On order for use on the Gospel Oak–Barking line. Due for delivery spring 2010.

**59311–59318. DMS.** Bombardier Derby 2009–2010.     2W.   . t.
**59411–59418. DMS.** Bombardier Derby 2009–2010.     .   . t.

| 172 001 | A | 59311 | 59411 |
|---------|---|-------|-------|
| 172 002 | A | 59312 | 59412 |
| 172 003 | A | 59313 | 59413 |
| 172 004 | A | 59314 | 59414 |
| 172 005 | A | 59315 | 59415 |
| 172 006 | A | 59316 | 59416 |
| 172 007 | A | 59317 | 59417 |
| 172 008 | A | 59318 | 59418 |

**Class 172/1. Chiltern Railways units**. DMSL–DMS. On order. Due for delivery from summer 2010.

**59111–59114. DMSL**. Bombardier Derby 2009–2010.    1TD 2W.    . t.
**59211–59214. DMS**. Bombardier Derby 2009–2010.    .    . t.

| 172 101 | A | 59111 | 59211 |
|---------|---|-------|-------|
| 172 102 | A | 59112 | 59212 |
| 172 103 | A | 59113 | 59213 |
| 172 104 | A | 59114 | 59214 |

**Class 172/2. London Midland 2-car units**. DMSL–DMS. On order for use on West Midlands suburban services. Due for delivery from summer 2010.

**50211–50222. DMSL**. Bombardier Derby 2009–2010. –/53(4) 1TD 2W.    . t.
**79211–79222. DMS**. Bombardier Derby 2009–2010. –/68(3).    . t.

| 172 211 | P | 50211 | 79211 |
|---------|---|-------|-------|
| 172 212 | P | 50212 | 79212 |
| 172 213 | P | 50213 | 79213 |
| 172 214 | P | 50214 | 79214 |
| 172 215 | P | 50215 | 79215 |
| 172 216 | P | 50216 | 79216 |
| 172 217 | P | 50217 | 79217 |
| 172 218 | P | 50218 | 79218 |
| 172 219 | P | 50219 | 79219 |
| 172 220 | P | 50220 | 79220 |
| 172 221 | P | 50221 | 79221 |
| 172 222 | P | 50222 | 79222 |

**Class 172/3. London Midland 3-car units**. DMSL–MS–DMS. On order for use on West Midlands suburban services. Due for delivery from summer 2010.

**50331–50345. DMSL**. Bombardier Derby 2009–2010. –/53(4) 1TD 2W.    . t.
**56331–56345. MS**. Bombardier Derby 2009–2010. –/72.    . t.
**79331–79345. DMS**. Bombardier Derby 2009–2010. –/68(3).    . t.

| 172 331 | P | 50331 | 56331 | 79331 |
|---------|---|-------|-------|-------|
| 172 332 | P | 50332 | 56332 | 79332 |
| 172 333 | P | 50333 | 56333 | 79333 |
| 172 334 | P | 50334 | 56334 | 79334 |
| 172 335 | P | 50335 | 56335 | 79335 |
| 172 336 | P | 50336 | 56336 | 79336 |
| 172 337 | P | 50337 | 56337 | 79337 |
| 172 338 | P | 50338 | 56338 | 79338 |
| 172 339 | P | 50339 | 56339 | 79339 |

| 172 340 | P | | 50340 | 56340 | 79340 |
| 172 341 | P | | 50341 | 56341 | 79341 |
| 172 342 | P | | 50342 | 56342 | 79342 |
| 172 343 | P | | 50343 | 56343 | 79343 |
| 172 344 | P | | 50344 | 56344 | 79344 |
| 172 345 | P | | 50345 | 56345 | 79345 |

# CLASS 175      CORADIA 1000      ALSTOM

Air conditioned.

**Construction:** Steel.
**Engines:** One Cummins N14 of 335 kW (450 h.p.).
**Transmission:** Hydraulic. Voith T211rzze to ZF Voith final drive.
**Bogies:** ACR (Alstom FBO) – LTB-MBS1, TB-MB1, MBS1-LTB.
**Couplers:** Scharfenberg outer ends and bar within unit (Class 175/1).
**Dimensions:** 23.7 x 2.73 m.
**Gangways:** Within unit only.      **Wheel Arrangement:** 2-B (+ B-2) + B-2.
**Doors:** Single-leaf swing plug.      **Maximum Speed:** 100 m.p.h.
**Seating Layout:** 2+2 facing/unidirectional.
**Multiple Working:** Within class and with Class 180.

**Class 175/0.** DMSL–DMSL. 2-car units.

**DMSL(A).** Alstom Birmingham 1999–2000. –/54 1TD 2W. 48.8 t.
**DMSL(B).** Alstom Birmingham 1999–2000. –/64 1T. 50.7 t.

| 175 001 | **AV** | A | *AW* | CH | 50701 | 79701 |
| 175 002 | **AV** | A | *AW* | CH | 50702 | 79702 |
| 175 003 | **AV** | A | *AW* | CH | 50703 | 79703 |
| 175 004 | **AV** | A | *AW* | CH | 50704 | 79704 |
| 175 005 | **AV** | A | *AW* | CH | 50705 | 79705 |
| 175 006 | **AV** | A | *AW* | CH | 50706 | 79706 |
| 175 007 | **AV** | A | *AW* | CH | 50707 | 79707 |
| 175 008 | **AV** | A | *AW* | CH | 50708 | 79708 |
| 175 009 | **AV** | A | *AW* | CH | 50709 | 79709 |
| 175 010 | **AV** | A | *AW* | CH | 50710 | 79710 |
| 175 011 | **AV** | A | *AW* | CH | 50711 | 79711 |

**Class 175/1.** DMSL–MSL–DMSL. 3-car units.

**DMSL(A).** Alstom Birmingham 1999–2001. –/54 1TD 2W. 50.7 t.
**MSL.** Alstom Birmingham 1999–2001. –/68 1T. 47.5 t.
**DMSL(B).** Alstom Birmingham 1999–2001. –/64 1T. 49.5 t.

| 175 101 | **AV** | A | *AW* | CH | 50751 | 56751 | 79751 |
| 175 102 | **AV** | A | *AW* | CH | 50752 | 56752 | 79752 |
| 175 103 | **AV** | A | *AW* | CH | 50753 | 56753 | 79753 |
| 175 104 | **AV** | A | *AW* | CH | 50754 | 56754 | 79754 |
| 175 105 | **AV** | A | *AW* | CH | 50755 | 56755 | 79755 |
| 175 106 | **AV** | A | *AW* | CH | 50756 | 56756 | 79756 |
| 175 107 | **AV** | A | *AW* | CH | 50757 | 56757 | 79757 |
| 175 108 | **AV** | A | *AW* | CH | 50758 | 56758 | 79758 |
| 175 109 | **AV** | A | *AW* | CH | 50759 | 56759 | 79759 |
| 175 110 | **AV** | A | *AW* | CH | 50760 | 56760 | 79760 |

| 175 111 | **AV** | A | *AW* | CH | 50761 | 56761 | 79761 |
| 175 112 | **AV** | A | *AW* | CH | 50762 | 56762 | 79762 |
| 175 113 | **AV** | A | *AW* | CH | 50763 | 56763 | 79763 |
| 175 114 | **AV** | A | *AW* | CH | 50764 | 56764 | 79764 |
| 175 115 | **AV** | A | *AW* | CH | 50765 | 56765 | 79765 |
| 175 116 | **AV** | A | *AW* | CH | 50766 | 56766 | 79766 |

# CLASS 180       CORADIA 1000       ALSTOM

Air conditioned.

**Construction:** Steel.
**Engines:** One Cummins QSK19 of 560 kW (750 h.p.) at 2100 r.p.m.
**Transmission:** Hydraulic. Voith T312br to Voith final drive.
**Bogies:** ACR (Alstom FBO): LTB1-MBS2, TB1-MB2, TB1-MB2, TB2-MB2, MBS2-LTB1.
**Couplers:** Scharfenberg outer ends, bar within unit.
**Dimensions:** 23.71/23.03 x 2.73 m.
**Gangways:** Within unit only.
**Wheel Arrangement:** 2-B + B-2 + B-2 + B-2 + B-2.
**Doors:** Single-leaf swing plug.       **Maximum Speed:** 125 m.p.h.
**Seating Layout:** 1: 2+1 facing/unidirectional, 2: 2+2 facing/unidirectional.
**Multiple Working:** Within class and with Class 175.

**DMSL(A).** Alstom Birmingham 2000–2001. –/46 2W 1TD. 51.7 t.
**MFL.** Alstom Birmingham 2000–2001. 42/– 1T 1W + catering point. 49.6 t.
**MSL.** Alstom Birmingham 2000–2001. –/68 1T. 49.5 t.
**MSLRB.** Alstom Birmingham 2000–2001. –/56 1T. 50.3 t.
**DMSL(B).** Alstom Birmingham 2000–2001. –/56 1T. 51.4 t.

**Notes:** 180 103/106/108 are on sub-lease from East Coast. 180 102/104 are also allocated for use by East Coast.

A total of five sets, 180 101/105/107/112/114 are ultimately to be used by Grand Central.

180 107 is on sub-lease to First Hull Trains. Ultimately it will form part of the Grand Central fleet and the Hull Trains fleet will comprise 180 109/110/111/113.

| 180 101 | **FG** | A | | ZH | 50901 | 54901 | 55901 | 56901 | 59901 |
| 180 102 | **FG** | A | | BN | 50902 | 54902 | 55902 | 56902 | 59902 |
| 180 103 | **FB** | A | *NO* | NH | 50903 | 54903 | 55903 | 56903 | 59903 |
| 180 104 | **FG** | A | | BN | 50904 | 54904 | 55904 | 56904 | 59904 |
| 180 105 | **FG** | A | *GC* | HT | 50905 | 54905 | 55905 | 56905 | 59905 |
| 180 106 | **FB** | A | *NO* | NH | 50906 | 54906 | 55906 | 56906 | 59906 |
| 180 107 | **FG** | A | *HT* | XW | 50907 | 54907 | 55907 | 56907 | 59907 |
| 180 108 | **FB** | A | *NO* | NH | 50908 | 54908 | 55908 | 56908 | 59908 |
| 180 109 | **FG** | A | *HT* | XW | 50909 | 54909 | 55909 | 56909 | 59909 |
| 180 110 | **FG** | A | *HT* | XW | 50910 | 54910 | 55910 | 56910 | 59910 |
| 180 111 | **FG** | A | *HT* | XW | 50911 | 54911 | 55911 | 56911 | 59911 |
| 180 112 | **GC** | A | *GC* | HT | 50912 | 54912 | 55912 | 56912 | 59912 |
| 180 113 | **FD** | A | *HT* | XW | 50913 | 54913 | 55913 | 56913 | 59913 |
| 180 114 | **GC** | A | *GC* | HT | 50914 | 54914 | 55914 | 56914 | 59914 |

**Name (carried on DMSL(A)):** 180 112     JAMES HERRIOT

# CLASS 185        DESIRO UK        SIEMENS

Air conditioned. Grammer seating.

**Construction:** Aluminium.
**Engines:** One Cummins QSK19 of 560 kW (750 h.p.) at 2100 r.p.m.
**Transmission:** Voith.
**Bogies:** Siemens.
**Couplers:** Dellner 12.
**Dimensions:** 23.76/23.75 x 2.66 m.
**Gangways:** Within unit only.            **Wheel Arrangement:** 2-B + 2-B + B-2.
**Doors:** Double-leaf sliding plug.        **Maximum Speed:** 100 m.p.h.
**Seating Layout:** 1: 2+1 facing/unidirectional, 2: 2+2 facing/unidirectional.
**Multiple Working:** Within class only.

**DMCL.** Siemens Uerdingen 2005–2006. 15/18(8) 2W 1TD + catering point. 55.4 t.
**MSL.** Siemens Uerdingen 2005–2006. –/72 1T. 52.7 t.
**DMS.** Siemens Uerdingen 2005–2006. –/64(4). 54.9 t.

| | | | | | | | |
|---|---|---|---|---|---|---|---|
| 185 101 | FT | H | TP | AK | 51101 | 53101 | 54101 |
| 185 102 | FT | H | TP | AK | 51102 | 53102 | 54102 |
| 185 103 | FT | H | TP | AK | 51103 | 53103 | 54103 |
| 185 104 | FT | H | TP | AK | 51104 | 53104 | 54104 |
| 185 105 | FT | H | TP | AK | 51105 | 53105 | 54105 |
| 185 106 | FT | H | TP | AK | 51106 | 53106 | 54106 |
| 185 107 | FT | H | TP | AK | 51107 | 53107 | 54107 |
| 185 108 | FT | H | TP | AK | 51108 | 53108 | 54108 |
| 185 109 | FT | H | TP | AK | 51109 | 53109 | 54109 |
| 185 110 | FT | H | TP | AK | 51110 | 53110 | 54110 |
| 185 111 | FT | H | TP | AK | 51111 | 53111 | 54111 |
| 185 112 | FT | H | TP | AK | 51112 | 53112 | 54112 |
| 185 113 | FT | H | TP | AK | 51113 | 53113 | 54113 |
| 185 114 | FT | H | TP | AK | 51114 | 53114 | 54114 |
| 185 115 | FT | H | TP | AK | 51115 | 53115 | 54115 |
| 185 116 | FT | H | TP | AK | 51116 | 53116 | 54116 |
| 185 117 | FT | H | TP | AK | 51117 | 53117 | 54117 |
| 185 118 | FT | H | TP | AK | 51118 | 53118 | 54118 |
| 185 119 | FT | H | TP | AK | 51119 | 53119 | 54119 |
| 185 120 | FT | H | TP | AK | 51120 | 53120 | 54120 |
| 185 121 | FT | H | TP | AK | 51121 | 53121 | 54121 |
| 185 122 | FT | H | TP | AK | 51122 | 53122 | 54122 |
| 185 123 | FT | H | TP | AK | 51123 | 53123 | 54123 |
| 185 124 | FT | H | TP | AK | 51124 | 53124 | 54124 |
| 185 125 | FT | H | TP | AK | 51125 | 53125 | 54125 |
| 185 126 | FT | H | TP | AK | 51126 | 53126 | 54126 |
| 185 127 | FT | H | TP | AK | 51127 | 53127 | 54127 |
| 185 128 | FT | H | TP | AK | 51128 | 53128 | 54128 |
| 185 129 | FT | H | TP | AK | 51129 | 53129 | 54129 |
| 185 130 | FT | H | TP | AK | 51130 | 53130 | 54130 |
| 185 131 | FT | H | TP | AK | 51131 | 53131 | 54131 |
| 185 132 | FT | H | TP | AK | 51132 | 53132 | 54132 |

| | | | | | | | |
|---|---|---|---|---|---|---|---|
| 185 133 | **FT** | H | *TP* | AK | 51133 | 53133 | 54133 |
| 185 134 | **FT** | H | *TP* | AK | 51134 | 53134 | 54134 |
| 185 135 | **FT** | H | *TP* | AK | 51135 | 53135 | 54135 |
| 185 136 | **FT** | H | *TP* | AK | 51136 | 53136 | 54136 |
| 185 137 | **FT** | H | *TP* | AK | 51137 | 53137 | 54137 |
| 185 138 | **FT** | H | *TP* | AK | 51138 | 53138 | 54138 |
| 185 139 | **FT** | H | *TP* | AK | 51139 | 53139 | 54139 |
| 185 140 | **FT** | H | *TP* | AK | 51140 | 53140 | 54140 |
| 185 141 | **FT** | H | *TP* | AK | 51141 | 53141 | 54141 |
| 185 142 | **FT** | H | *TP* | AK | 51142 | 53142 | 54142 |
| 185 143 | **FT** | H | *TP* | AK | 51143 | 53143 | 54143 |
| 185 144 | **FT** | H | *TP* | AK | 51144 | 53144 | 54144 |
| 185 145 | **FT** | H | *TP* | AK | 51145 | 53145 | 54145 |
| 185 146 | **FT** | H | *TP* | AK | 51146 | 53146 | 54146 |
| 185 147 | **FT** | H | *TP* | AK | 51147 | 53147 | 54147 |
| 185 148 | **FT** | H | *TP* | AK | 51148 | 53148 | 54148 |
| 185 149 | **FT** | H | *TP* | AK | 51149 | 53149 | 54149 |
| 185 150 | **FT** | H | *TP* | AK | 51150 | 53150 | 54150 |
| 185 151 | **FT** | H | *TP* | AK | 51151 | 53151 | 54151 |

# 3.2. DIESEL ELECTRIC UNITS

## CLASS 201/202 PRESERVED "HASTINGS" UNIT BR

DMBS–TSL–TSL–TSRB–TSL–DMBS.

Preserved unit made up from two Class 201 short-frame cars and three Class 202 long-frame cars. The "Hastings" units were made with narrow body-profiles for use on the section between Tonbridge and Battle which had tunnels of restricted loading gauge. These tunnels were converted to single track operation in the 1980s thus allowing standard loading gauge stock to be used. The set also contains a Class 411 EMU trailer (not Hastings line gauge) and a Class 422 EMU buffet car.

**Construction:** Steel.
**Engine:** One English Electric 4SRKT Mk. 2 of 450 kW (600 h.p.) at 850 r.p.m.
**Main Generator:** English Electric EE824.
**Traction Motors:** Two English Electric EE507 mounted on the inner bogie.
**Bogies:** SR Mk. 4. (Former EMU TSL vehicles have Commonwealth bogies).
**Couplers:** Drophead buckeye.
**Dimensions:** 18.40 x 2.50 m (60000), 20.35 x 2.50 m (60116/60118/60529), 18.36 x 2.50 m (60501), 20.35 x 2.82 (69337), 20.30 x 2.82 (70262).
**Gangways:** Within unit only.
**Doors:** Manually operated slam.
**Brakes:** Electro-pneumatic and automatic air.
**Maximum Speed:** 75 m.p.h.
**Seating Layout:** 2+2 facing.
**Multiple Working:** Other ex-BR Southern Region DEMU vehicles.

**60000. DMBS.** Lot No. 30329 Eastleigh 1957. –/22. 55.0 t.
**60116. DMBS.** Lot No. 30395 Eastleigh 1957. –/31. 56.0 t.
**60118. DMBS.** Lot No. 30395 Eastleigh 1957. –/30. 56.0 t.
**60501. TSL.** Lot No. 30331 Eastleigh 1957. –/52 2T. 29.5 t.
**60529. TSL.** Lot No. 30397 Eastleigh 1957. –/60 2T. 30.5 t.
**69337. TSRB (ex-Class 422 EMU).** Lot No. 30805 York 1970. –/40. 35.0 t.
**70262. TSL (ex-Class 411/5 EMU).** Lot No. 30455 Eastleigh 1958. –/64 2T. 31.5 t.

| 201 001 | **G** | HD *HD* | SE | 60116 | 60529 | 70262 | 69337 | 60501 | 60118 |
|---------|-------|---------|-----|-------|-------|-------|-------|-------|-------|
| Spare   | **G** | HD *HD* | SE | 60000 | | | | | |

**Names:**

60000 Hastings
60116 Mountfield
60118 Tunbridge Wells

# CLASS 220      VOYAGER      BOMBARDIER

DMS–MS–MS–DMF.

**Construction:** Steel.
**Engine:** Cummins QSK19 of 560 kW (750 h.p.) at 1800 r.p.m.
**Transmission:** Two Alstom Onix 800 three-phase traction motors of 275 kW.
**Braking:** Rheostatic and electro-pneumatic.
**Bogies:** Bombardier B5005.
**Couplers:** Dellner 12 at outer ends, bar within unit.
**Dimensions:** 23.85/23.00(602xx) x 2.73 m.
**Gangways:** Within unit only.
**Wheel Arrangement:** 1A-A1 + 1A-A1 + 1A-A1 + 1A-A1.
**Doors:** Single-leaf swing plug.
**Maximum Speed:** 125 m.p.h.
**Seating Layout:** 1: 2+1 facing/unidirectional, 2: 2+2 mainly unidirectional.
**Multiple Working:** Within class and with Classes 221 and 222 (in an emergency).
Also can be controlled from Class 57/3 locomotives.

**DMS.** Bombardier Brugge/Wakefield 2000–2001. –/42 1TD 1W. 51.1 t.
**MS (A).** Bombardier Brugge/Wakefield 2000–2001. –/66. 45.9 t.
**MS (B).** Bombardier Brugge/Wakefield 2000–2001. –/66 1TD. 46.7 t.
**DMF.** Bombardier Brugge/Wakefield 2000–2001. 26/– 1TD 1W. 50.9 t.

| | | | | | | | |
|---|---|---|---|---|---|---|---|
| 220 001 | **XC** | HX | *XC* | CZ | 60301 | 60701 | 60201 | 60401 |
| 220 002 | **XC** | HX | *XC* | CZ | 60302 | 60702 | 60202 | 60402 |
| 220 003 | **XC** | HX | *XC* | CZ | 60303 | 60703 | 60203 | 60403 |
| 220 004 | **XC** | HX | *XC* | CZ | 60304 | 60704 | 60204 | 60404 |
| 220 005 | **XC** | HX | *XC* | CZ | 60305 | 60705 | 60205 | 60405 |
| 220 006 | **XC** | HX | *XC* | CZ | 60306 | 60706 | 60206 | 60406 |
| 220 007 | **XC** | HX | *XC* | CZ | 60307 | 60707 | 60207 | 60407 |
| 220 008 | **XC** | HX | *XC* | CZ | 60308 | 60708 | 60208 | 60408 |
| 220 009 | **XC** | HX | *XC* | CZ | 60309 | 60709 | 60209 | 60409 |
| 220 010 | **XC** | HX | *XC* | CZ | 60310 | 60710 | 60210 | 60410 |
| 220 011 | **XC** | HX | *XC* | CZ | 60311 | 60711 | 60211 | 60411 |
| 220 012 | **XC** | HX | *XC* | CZ | 60312 | 60712 | 60212 | 60412 |
| 220 013 | **XC** | HX | *XC* | CZ | 60313 | 60713 | 60213 | 60413 |
| 220 014 | **XC** | HX | *XC* | CZ | 60314 | 60714 | 60214 | 60414 |
| 220 015 | **XC** | HX | *XC* | CZ | 60315 | 60715 | 60215 | 60415 |
| 220 016 | **XC** | HX | *XC* | CZ | 60316 | 60716 | 60216 | 60416 |
| 220 017 | **XC** | HX | *XC* | CZ | 60317 | 60717 | 60217 | 60417 |
| 220 018 | **XC** | HX | *XC* | CZ | 60318 | 60718 | 60218 | 60418 |
| 220 019 | **XC** | HX | *XC* | CZ | 60319 | 60719 | 60219 | 60419 |
| 220 020 | **XC** | HX | *XC* | CZ | 60320 | 60720 | 60220 | 60420 |
| 220 021 | **XC** | HX | *XC* | CZ | 60321 | 60721 | 60221 | 60421 |
| 220 022 | **XC** | HX | *XC* | CZ | 60322 | 60722 | 60222 | 60422 |
| 220 023 | **XC** | HX | *XC* | CZ | 60323 | 60723 | 60223 | 60423 |
| 220 024 | **XC** | HX | *XC* | CZ | 60324 | 60724 | 60224 | 60424 |
| 220 025 | **XC** | HX | *XC* | CZ | 60325 | 60725 | 60225 | 60425 |
| 220 026 | **XC** | HX | *XC* | CZ | 60326 | 60726 | 60226 | 60426 |
| 220 027 | **XC** | HX | *XC* | CZ | 60327 | 60727 | 60227 | 60427 |
| 220 028 | **XC** | HX | *XC* | CZ | 60328 | 60728 | 60228 | 60428 |

| 220 029 | **XC** | HX | *XC* | CZ | 60329 | 60729 | 60229 | 60429 |
| 220 030 | **XC** | HX | *XC* | CZ | 60330 | 60730 | 60230 | 60430 |
| 220 031 | **XC** | HX | *XC* | CZ | 60331 | 60731 | 60231 | 60431 |
| 220 032 | **XC** | HX | *XC* | CZ | 60332 | 60732 | 60232 | 60432 |
| 220 033 | **XC** | HX | *XC* | CZ | 60333 | 60733 | 60233 | 60433 |
| 220 034 | **XC** | HX | *XC* | CZ | 60334 | 60734 | 60234 | 60434 |

# CLASS 221    SUPER VOYAGER    BOMBARDIER

* DMS–MS–(MS)–MSRMB–DMF (Virgin Trains units) or DMS–MS–MS–MS–DMF (CrossCountry units). Built as tilting units but tilt now isolated on CrossCountry sets.

**Construction:** Steel.
**Engine:** Cummins QSK19 of 560 kW (750 h.p.) at 1800 r.p.m.
**Transmission:** Two Alstom Onix 800 three-phase traction motors of 275 kW.
**Braking:** Rheostatic and electro-pneumatic.
**Bogies:** Bombardier HVP.
**Couplers:** Dellner 12 at outer ends, bar within unit.
**Dimensions:** 23.67 x 2.73 m.
**Gangways:** Within unit only.
**Wheel Arrangement:** 1A-A1 + 1A-A1 + 1A-A1 (+ 1A-A1) + 1A-A1.
**Doors:** Single-leaf swing plug.
**Maximum Speed:** 125 m.p.h.
**Seating Layout:** 1: 2+1 facing/unidirectional, 2: 2+2 mainly unidirectional.
**Multiple Working:** Within class and with Classes 220 and 222 (in an emergency). Also can be controlled from Class 57/3 locomotives.

**DMS.** Bombardier Brugge/Wakefield 2001–2002. –/42 1TD 1W. 58.5 t (* 58.9 t.)
**60751–794 MS (* MSRMB).** Bombardier Brugge/Wakefield 2001–2002. –/66 (* –/52). 54.1 t (* 55.9 t.)
**60951–994. MS.** Bombardier Brugge/Wakefield 2001–2002. –/66 1TD (* –/68 1TD). 54.8 t (* 54.3 t.)
**60851–890. MS.** Bombardier Brugge/Wakefield 2001–2002. –/62 1TD (* –/68 1TD). 54.4 t (* 55.0 t.)
**DMF.** Bombardier Brugge/Wakefield 2001–2002. 26/– 1TD 1W. 58.9 t (* 59.1 t.)

**Note:** * Virgin Trains units. MSRMB moved adjacent to the DMF. The seating in this vehicle (2+2 facing) can be used by First or Standard Class passengers depending on demand.

| 221 101 | * | **VT** | HX | *VW* | CZ | 60351 | 60951 | 60851 | 60751 | 60451 |
| 221 102 | * | **VT** | HX | *VW* | CZ | 60352 | 60952 | 60852 | 60752 | 60452 |
| 221 103 | * | **VT** | HX | *VW* | CZ | 60353 | 60953 | 60853 | 60753 | 60453 |
| 221 104 | * | **VT** | HX | *VW* | CZ | 60354 | 60954 | 60854 | 60754 | 60454 |
| 221 105 | * | **VT** | HX | *VW* | CZ | 60355 | 60955 | 60855 | 60755 | 60455 |
| 221 106 | * | **VT** | HX | *VW* | CZ | 60356 | 60956 | 60856 | 60756 | 60456 |
| 221 107 | * | **VT** | HX | *VW* | CZ | 60357 | 60957 | 60857 | 60757 | 60457 |
| 221 108 | * | **VT** | HX | *VW* | CZ | 60358 | 60958 | 60858 | 60758 | 60458 |
| 221 109 | * | **VT** | HX | *VW* | CZ | 60359 | 60959 | 60859 | 60759 | 60459 |
| 221 110 | * | **VT** | HX | *VW* | CZ | 60360 | 60960 | 60860 | 60760 | 60460 |
| 221 111 | * | **VT** | HX | *VW* | CZ | 60361 | 60961 | 60861 | 60761 | 60461 |

| | | | | | | | | | |
|---|---|---|---|---|---|---|---|---|---|
| 221 112 | * | **VT** | HX | *VW* | CZ | 60362 | 60962 | 60862 | 60762 | 60462 |
| 221 113 | * | **VT** | HX | *VW* | CZ | 60363 | 60963 | 60863 | 60763 | 60463 |
| 221 114 | * | **VT** | HX | *VW* | CZ | 60364 | 60764 | 60964 | 60864 | 60464 |
| 221 115 | * | **VT** | HX | *VW* | CZ | 60365 | 60765 | 60965 | 60865 | 60465 |
| 221 116 | * | **VT** | HX | *VW* | CZ | 60366 | 60766 | 60966 | 60866 | 60466 |
| 221 117 | * | **VT** | HX | *VW* | CZ | 60367 | 60767 | 60967 | 60867 | 60467 |
| 221 118 | * | **VT** | HX | *VW* | CZ | 60368 | 60768 | 60968 | 60868 | 60468 |
| 221 119 | | **XC** | HX | *XC* | CZ | 60369 | 60769 | 60969 | 60869 | 60469 |
| 221 120 | | **XC** | HX | *XC* | CZ | 60370 | 60770 | 60970 | 60870 | 60470 |
| 221 121 | | **XC** | HX | *XC* | CZ | 60371 | 60771 | 60971 | 60871 | 60471 |
| 221 122 | | **XC** | HX | *XC* | CZ | 60372 | 60772 | 60972 | 60872 | 60472 |
| 221 123 | | **XC** | HX | *XC* | CZ | 60373 | 60773 | 60973 | 60873 | 60473 |
| 221 124 | | **XC** | HX | *XC* | CZ | 60374 | 60774 | 60974 | 60874 | 60474 |
| 221 125 | | **XC** | HX | *XC* | CZ | 60375 | 60775 | 60975 | 60875 | 60475 |
| 221 126 | | **XC** | HX | *XC* | CZ | 60376 | 60776 | 60976 | 60876 | 60476 |
| 221 127 | | **XC** | HX | *XC* | CZ | 60377 | 60777 | 60977 | 60877 | 60477 |
| 221 128 | | **XC** | HX | *XC* | CZ | 60378 | 60778 | 60978 | 60878 | 60478 |
| 221 129 | | **XC** | HX | *XC* | CZ | 60379 | 60779 | 60979 | 60879 | 60479 |
| 221 130 | | **XC** | HX | *XC* | CZ | 60380 | 60780 | 60980 | 60880 | 60480 |
| 221 131 | | **XC** | HX | *XC* | CZ | 60381 | 60781 | 60981 | 60881 | 60481 |
| 221 132 | | **XC** | HX | *XC* | CZ | 60382 | 60782 | 60982 | 60882 | 60482 |
| 221 133 | | **XC** | HX | *XC* | CZ | 60383 | 60783 | 60983 | 60883 | 60483 |
| 221 134 | | **XC** | HX | *XC* | CZ | 60384 | 60784 | 60984 | 60884 | 60484 |
| 221 135 | | **XC** | HX | *XC* | CZ | 60385 | 60785 | 60985 | 60885 | 60485 |
| 221 136 | | **XC** | HX | *XC* | CZ | 60386 | 60786 | 60986 | 60886 | 60486 |
| 221 137 | | **XC** | HX | *XC* | CZ | 60387 | 60787 | 60987 | 60887 | 60487 |
| 221 138 | | **XC** | HX | *XC* | CZ | 60388 | 60788 | 60988 | 60888 | 60488 |
| 221 139 | | **XC** | HX | *XC* | CZ | 60389 | 60789 | 60989 | 60889 | 60489 |
| 221 140 | | **XC** | HX | *XC* | CZ | 60390 | 60790 | 60990 | 60890 | 60490 |
| 221 141 | | **XC** | HX | *XC* | CZ | 60391 | 60791 | 60991 | | 60491 |
| 221 142 | * | **VT** | HX | *VW* | CZ | 60392 | 60992 | | 60792 | 60492 |
| 221 143 | * | **VT** | HX | *VW* | CZ | 60393 | 60993 | | 60793 | 60493 |
| 221 144 | * | **VT** | HX | *VW* | CZ | 60394 | 60994 | | 60794 | 60494 |

**Names (carried on MS No. 609xx):**

| | | | |
|---|---|---|---|
| 221 101 | Louis Bleriot | 221 109 | Marco Polo |
| 221 102 | John Cabot | 221 110 | James Cook |
| 221 103 | Christopher Columbus | 221 111 | Roald Amundsen |
| 221 104 | Sir John Franklin | 221 112 | Ferdinand Magellan |
| 221 105 | William Baffin | 221 113 | Sir Walter Raleigh |
| 221 106 | Willem Barents | 221 142 | Matthew Flinders |
| 221 107 | Sir Martin Frobisher | 221 143 | Auguste Picard |
| 221 108 | Sir Ernest Shackleton | 221 144 | BOMBARDIER Voyager |

# CLASS 222          MERIDIAN          BOMBARDIER

**Construction:** Steel.
**Engine:** Cummins QSK19 of 560 kW (750 h.p.) at 1800 r.p.m.
**Transmission:** Two Alstom Onix 800 three-phase traction motors of 275 kW.
**Braking:** Rheostatic and electro-pneumatic.
**Bogies:** Bombardier B5005.
**Couplers:** Dellner at outer ends, bar within unit.
**Dimensions:** 23.85/23.00 x 2.73 m.
**Gangways:** Within unit only.          **Wheel Arrangement:** All cars 1A-A1.
**Doors:** Single-leaf swing plug.          **Maximum Speed:** 125 m.p.h.
**Seating Layout:** 1: 2+1, 2: 2+2 facing/unidirectional.
**Multiple Working:** Within class and with Classes 220 and 221 (in an emergency).

**222 001–222 006.** 7-car units. DMF–MF–MF–MSRMB–MS–MS–DMS.

**Note:** The 7-car units were built as 9-car units, before being reduced to 8-car sets and then later to 7-car sets to strengthen all 4-car units to 5-cars. 222 007 was built as a 9-car unit but has now been reduced to a 5-car unit.

**DMF.** Bombardier Brugge 2004–2005. 22/– 1TD 1W. 52.8 t.
**MF.** Bombardier Brugge 2004–2005. 42/– 1T. 46.8 t.
**MSRMB.** Bombardier Brugge 2004–2005. –/62. 48.0 t.
**MS.** Bombardier Brugge 2004–2005. –/68 1T. 47.0 t.
**DMS.** Bombardier Brugge 2004–2005. –/38 1TD 1W. 49.4 t.

| 222 001 | **ST** | H | *EM* | DY | 60241 | 60445 | 60341 | 60621 |
|         |        |   |      |    | 60561 | 60551 | 60161 |       |
| 222 002 | **ST** | H | *EM* | DY | 60242 | 60346 | 60342 | 60622 |
|         |        |   |      |    | 60562 | 60544 | 60162 |       |
| 222 003 | **ST** | H | *EM* | DY | 60243 | 60446 | 60343 | 60623 |
|         |        |   |      |    | 60563 | 60553 | 60163 | TORNADO |
| 222 004 | **ST** | H | *EM* | DY | 60244 | 60345 | 60344 | 60624 |
|         |        |   |      |    | 60564 | 60554 | 60164 |       |
| 222 005 | **ST** | H | *EM* | DY | 60245 | 60347 | 60443 | 60625 |
|         |        |   |      |    | 60565 | 60555 | 60165 |       |
| 222 006 | **ST** | H | *EM* | DY | 60246 | 60447 | 60441 | 60626 |
|         |        |   |      |    | 60566 | 60556 | 60166 |       |

**222 007–222 023.** 5-car units. DMF–MC–MSRMB–MS–DMS.

**DMF.** Bombardier Brugge 2003–2004. 22/– 1TD 1W. 52.8 t.
**MC.** Bombardier Brugge 2003–2004. 28/22 1T. 48.6 t.
**MSRMB.** Bombardier Brugge 2003–2004. –/62. 49.6 t.
**MS.** Bombardier Brugge 2004–2005. –/68 1T. 47.0 t.
**DMS.** Bombardier Brugge 2003–2004. –/40 1TD 1W. 51.0 t.

| 222 007 | **ST** | H | *EM* | DY | 60247 | 60442 | 60627 | 60567 | 60167 |
| 222 008 | **ST** | H | *EM* | DY | 60248 | 60918 | 60628 | 60545 | 60168 |
| 222 009 | **ST** | H | *EM* | DY | 60249 | 60919 | 60629 | 60557 | 60169 |
| 222 010 | **ST** | H | *EM* | DY | 60250 | 60920 | 60630 | 60546 | 60170 |
| 222 011 | **ST** | H | *EM* | DY | 60251 | 60921 | 60631 | 60531 | 60171 |
| 222 012 | **ST** | H | *EM* | DY | 60252 | 60922 | 60632 | 60532 | 60172 |

| 222 013 | **ST** | H | *EM* | DY | 60253 | 60923 | 60633 | 60533 | 60173 |
|---------|--------|---|------|----|-------|-------|-------|-------|-------|
| 222 014 | **ST** | H | *EM* | DY | 60254 | 60924 | 60634 | 60534 | 60174 |
| 222 015 | **ST** | H | *EM* | DY | 60255 | 60925 | 60635 | 60535 | 60175 |
| 222 016 | **ST** | H | *EM* | DY | 60256 | 60926 | 60636 | 60536 | 60176 |
| 222 017 | **ST** | H | *EM* | DY | 60257 | 60927 | 60637 | 60537 | 60177 |
| 222 018 | **ST** | H | *EM* | DY | 60258 | 60928 | 60638 | 60444 | 60178 |
| 222 019 | **ST** | H | *EM* | DY | 60259 | 60929 | 60639 | 60547 | 60179 |
| 222 020 | **ST** | H | *EM* | DY | 60260 | 60930 | 60640 | 60543 | 60180 |
| 222 021 | **ST** | H | *EM* | DY | 60261 | 60931 | 60641 | 60552 | 60181 |
| 222 022 | **ST** | H | *EM* | DY | 60262 | 60932 | 60642 | 60542 | 60182 |
| 222 023 | **ST** | H | *EM* | DY | 60263 | 60933 | 60643 | 60541 | 60183 |

**222 101–222 104. 4-car units formerly operated by Hull Trains.** DMF–MC–MSRMB–DMS.

**DMF.** Bombardier Brugge 2005. 22/– 1TD 1W. 52.8 t.
**MC.** Bombardier Brugge 2005. 11/46 1T. 47.1 t.
**MSRMB.** Bombardier Brugge 2005. –/62. 48.0 t.
**DMS.** Bombardier Brugge 2005. –/40 1TD 1W. 49.4 t.

| 222 101 | **ST** | H | *EM* | DY | 60271 | 60571 | 60681 | 60191 |
|---------|--------|---|------|----|-------|-------|-------|-------|
| 222 102 | **ST** | H | *EM* | DY | 60272 | 60572 | 60682 | 60192 |
| 222 103 | **ST** | H | *EM* | DY | 60273 | 60573 | 60683 | 60193 |
| 222 104 | **ST** | H | *EM* | DY | 60274 | 60574 | 60684 | 60194 |

# 3.3. SERVICE DMUS

This section lists vehicles not used for passenger-carrying purposes. Vehicles are numbered in the special service stock number series.

## CLASS 950                   TRACK ASSESSMENT UNIT

DM–DM. Purpose built service unit based on the Class 150/1 design. Gangwayed within unit.

**Construction:** Steel.
**Engine:** One Cummins NT-855-RT5 of 213 kW (285 h.p.) at 2100 r.p.m. per power car.
**Transmission:** Hydraulic. Voith T211r with cardan shafts to Gmeinder GM190 final drive.
**Maximum Speed:** 75 m.p.h.              **Couplers:** BSI automatic.
**Bogies:** BP38 (powered), BT38 (non-powered).
**Brakes:** Electro-pneumatic.           **Dimensions:** 20.06 x 2.82 m.
**Doors:** Manually operated slam & power operated sliding.
**Multiple Working:** Classes 142, 143, 144, 150, 153, 155, 156, 158, 159 and 170.

**999600. DM.** Lot No. 4060 BREL York 1987. 35.0 t.
**999601. DM.** Lot No. 4061 BREL York 1987. 35.0 t.

| | | | | | | |
|---|---|---|---|---|---|---|
| 950 001 | **Y** | NR | *SO* | ZA | 999600 | 999601 |

## CLASS 960              SANDITE & SERVICE UNITS

DMB. Converted from Class 121s. Non gangwayed.

**For details see Page 210.**

960 014 is a Chiltern Route Learning Unit and is also hired to other operators.

**977723. DMB.** Lot No. 30518 Pressed Steel 1960. 38.0 t.
**977858–60/66/73. DMB.** Lot No. 30518 Pressed Steel 1960. 38.0 t.

| | | | | | | |
|---|---|---|---|---|---|---|
| 960 010 | **M**  | NR | *CR* | AL | 977858 | (55024) |
| 960 013 | **N**  | NR |      | AL | 977866 | (55030) |
| 960 014 | **BG** | CR | *CR* | AL | 977873 | (55022) |
| 960 021 | **RO** | NR |      | AL | 977723 | (55021) |

# CLASS 960                         SANDITE UNIT

DMB. Converted 1991 from Class 122. Non gangwayed.

**Construction:** Steel.
**Engines:** Two Leyland 1595 of 112 kW (150 h.p.) at 1800 r.p.m.
**Transmission:** Mechanical. Cardan shaft and freewheel to a four-speed epicyclic gearbox with a further cardan shaft to the final drive, each engine driving the inner axle of one bogie.
**Maximum Speed:** 70 m.p.h.
**Bogies:** DD10.                   **Couplings:** Screw.
**Brakes:** Twin pipe vacuum.      **Multiple Working:** Blue Square.
**Doors:** Manually operated slam.    **Dimensions:** 20.45 x 2.82 m.

**975042. DMB.** Lot No. 30419 Gloucester 1958. 36.5 t.

960 015    **Y**    NR      AL      975042   (55019)


# CLASS 960              WATER-JETTING UNIT

DMB–MS–DMB. Converted 2003–2004 from Class 117. Non gangwayed.

**Construction:** Steel.
**Engines:** Two Leyland 1595 of 112 kW (150 h.p.) at 1800 r.p.m.
**Transmission:** Mechanical. Cardan shaft and freewheel to a four-speed epicyclic gearbox with a further cardan shaft to the final drive, each engine driving the inner axle of one bogie.
**Maximum Speed:** 70 m.p.h.
**Bogies:** DD10.                   **Couplings:** Screw.
**Brakes:** Twin pipe vacuum.      **Multiple Working:** Blue Square.
**Doors:** Manually operated slam.    **Dimensions:** 20.45 x 2.84 m.

**977987/977988. DMB.** Lot No. 30546/30548 Pressed Steel 1959–1960. 36.5 t.
**977992. MS.** Lot No. 30548 Pressed Steel 1959–1960. 36.5 t.

960 301    **G**    CR  *CR*   AL     977987   (51371)    977992 (51375)
                                        977988   (51413)


# CLASS 960              DRIVER TRAINING UNIT

Converted from a Class 121.

**For details see Page 210.**

**977968. DMB.** Lot No. 30518 Pressed Steel 1960. 38.0 t.

-      **Y**    CS  *CS*   RU     977968   (55029)

# 3.4. DMUS AWAITING DISPOSAL

The list below comprises vehicles awaiting disposal which are stored on the National Railway network.

**IMPORTANT NOTE:** DMUs still intact but already at scrapyards, unless specifically there for storage purposes, are not included in this list.

**Class 101**

| Spare | **RR** | X | SN | 51432 | 51498 |

**Class 960**

Converted from Class 121. 960 302/303 converted for use as Severn Tunnel Emergency Train units, but not actually used as such.

| 960 011 | **RK** | NR | TM | 977859 | (55025) |
| 960 302 | **Y** | AW | CF | 977975 | (55027) |
| 960 303 | **Y** | AW | CF | 977976 | (55031) |

# 4. ELECTRIC MULTIPLE UNITS

# INTRODUCTION

## EMU CLASSES

Principal details and dimensions are quoted for each class in metric and/or imperial units as considered appropriate bearing in mind common UK usage.

All dimensions and weights are quoted for vehicles in an "as new" condition with all necessary supplies on board. Dimensions are quoted in the order length x overall width. All lengths quoted are over buffers or couplers as appropriate. Where two lengths are quoted, the first refers to outer vehicles in a set and the second to inner vehicles.

Bogie Types are quoted in the format motored/non-motored (e.g BP20/BT13 denotes BP20 motored bogies and BT non-motored bogies).

Unless noted to the contrary, all vehicles listed have bar couplers at non-driving ends.

Vehicles ordered under the auspices of BR were allocated a Lot (batch) number when ordered and these are quoted in class headings and sub-headings. Vehicles ordered since 1995 have no Lot Numbers, but the manufacturer and location that they were built is given.

## NUMERICAL LISTINGS

25 kV AC 50 Hz overhead Electric Multiple Units (EMUs) and dual voltage EMUs are listed in numerical order of set numbers. Individual "loose" vehicles are listed in numerical order after vehicles formed into fixed formations.

750 V DC third rail EMUs are listed in numerical order of class number, then in numerical order of set number. Some of these use the former Southern Region four-digit set numbers. These are derived from theoretical six digit set numbers which are the four-digit set number prefixed by the first two numbers of the class.

Where sets or vehicles have been renumbered in recent years, former numbering detail is shown alongside current detail. Each entry is laid out as in the following example:

| Set No. | Detail | Livery | Owner | Operator | Allocation | Formation | | | |
|---------|--------|--------|-------|----------|------------|-----------|---|---|---|
| 319 436 | * | **FU** | P | *FU* | BF | 77361 | 62926 | 71807 | 77360 |

**Detail Differences**. Only detail differences which currently affect the areas and types of train which vehicles may work are shown. All other detail differences are specifically excluded. Where such differences occur within a class or part class, these are shown alongside the individual set or vehicle number. Meaning of abbreviations are detailed in individual class headings.

**Set Formations.** Set formations shown are those normally maintained. Readers should note some set formations might be temporarily varied from time to time to suit maintenance and/or operational requirements. Vehicles shown as "Spare" are not formed in any regular set formation.

**Codes.** Codes are used to denote the livery, owner, operator and depot of each unit. Details of these will be found in section 6 of this book. Where a unit or spare car is off-lease, the operator column will be left blank.

**Names.** Only names carried with official sanction are listed. As far as possible names are shown in UPPER/lower case characters as actually shown on the name carried on the vehicle(s). Unless otherwise shown, complete units are regarded as named rather than just the individual car(s) which carry the name.

# GENERAL INFORMATION

## CLASSIFICATION AND NUMBERING

25 kV AC 50 Hz overhead and "Versatile" EMUs are classified in the series 300–399.

750 V DC  third rail EMUs are classified in the series 400–599.

Service units are classified in the series 900–949.

EMU individual cars are numbered in the series 61000–78999, except for vehicles used on the Isle of Wight – which are numbered in a separate series, and for the Class 378s, 380s and 395s, which take up new 38xxx and 39xxx series'.

Any vehicle constructed or converted to replace another vehicle following accident damage and carrying the same number as the original vehicle is denoted by the suffix" in this publication.

## OPERATING CODES

These codes are used by train operating company staff to describe the various different types of vehicles and normally appear on data panels on the inner (i.e. non driving) ends of vehicles.

A "B" prefix indicates a battery vehicle.
A "P" prefix indicates a trailer vehicle on which is mounted the pantograph, instead of the default case where the pantograph is mounted on a motor vehicle.

The first part of the code describes whether or not the car has a motor or a driving cab as follows:

DM Driving motor.
M   Motor
DT  Driving trailer
T    Trailer

The next letter is a "B" for cars with a brake compartment.

This is followed by the saloon details:

F   First
S   Standard
C   Composite

The next letter denotes the style of accommodation as follows:

O   Open
K   Side compartment with lavatory
so  Semi-open (part compartments, part open). All other vehicles are
    assumed to consist solely of open saloons.

Finally vehicles with a buffet are suffixed RB or RMB for a miniature buffet.

Where two vehicles of the same type are formed within the same unit, the above codes may be suffixed by (A) and (B) to differentiate between the vehicles.

A composite is a vehicle containing both First and Standard Class accommodation, whilst a brake vehicle is a vehicle containing separate specific accommodation for the conductor.

# BUILD DETAILS

### Lot Numbers

Vehicles ordered under the auspices of BR were allocated a Lot (batch) number when ordered and these are quoted in class headings and sub-headings.

### Builders

These are shown in class headings. Abbreviations used are found in section 6.7.

Information on sub-contracting works which built parts of vehicles e.g. the underframes etc. is not shown.

# ACCOMMODATION

The information given in class headings and sub-headings is in the form F/S nT (or TD) nW. For example 12/54 1T 1W denotes 12 First Class and 54 Standard Class seats, one toilet and one space for a wheelchair. A number in brackets (i.e. (2)) denotes tip-up seats (in addition to the fixed seats). Tip-up seats in vestibules do not count. The seating layout of open saloons is shown as 2+1, 2+2 or 3+2 as the case may be. Where units have first class accommodation as well as standard and the layout is different for each class then these are shown separately prefixed by "1:" and "2:". Compartments are three seats a side in First Class and mostly four a side in Standard Class in EMUs. TD denotes a toilet suitable for use by a disabled person.

# RAILWAY TIMETABLE ON CD-ROM

The **ELECTRONIC TIMETABLE CD-ROM** contains full railway timetable information* for most European countries, including Great Britain, France, Germany, Belgium, Netherlands, Luxembourg, Italy, Switzerland, Austria etc.

**Simply specify the following:**
- **Date of travel**
- **Destination station**
- **Departure station**
- **Preferred time of travel (arrival or departure)**

**LASTS FOR 12 MONTHS**

**The journey planner facility will calculate your rail travel options.**
- **Specify a particular route or routes for your journey.**
- **Print a full itinerary for each journey option.**
- **Print full arrival/departure listings for any station.**
- **Print a diagrammatic map of your route for each journey option.**
- **Simple reverse facility for calculating your return journey.**

\* In most countries where a timetable change occurs during the period of validity, information is included only up to the date of timetable change. Regular updates can be downloaded over the internet, by choosing 'file', 'update' and following the instructions given.

The system is not restricted to international travel and also works for entirely domestic journeys within any country selected.

Capable of running in English, French, German or Italian languages. Minimum system requirements: Windows 98 or later, 486/33 MHz, 8MB RAM.

**PRICE: £12.95 (post free to UK and Europe, please add £1.00 postage to rest of World).**

***TODAY'S RAILWAYS SUBSCRIBER PRICE: £10.95***

**Note:** The electronic timetable is released in December every year. Our mail order department will be able to take advance orders from the beginning of November for each forthcoming timetable.

**Telephone, fax or send your order to the Platform 5 Mail Order Department. See page 384 of this book for details.**

# 4.1. 25 kV AC 50 Hz OVERHEAD & DUAL VOLTAGE UNITS

**Note:** Except where otherwise stated, all units in this section operate on 25 kV AC 50 Hz overhead only.

## CLASS 313                                        BREL YORK

Inner suburban units.

**Formation:** DMSO–PTSO–BDMSO.
**Systems:** 25 kV AC overhead/750 V DC third rail.
**Construction:** Steel underframe, aluminium alloy body and roof.
**Traction Motors:** Four GEC G310AZ of 82.125 kW.
**Wheel Arrangement:** Bo-Bo + 2-2 + Bo-Bo.
**Braking:** Disc & rheostatic.                **Dimensions:** 20.33/20.18 x 2.82 m.
**Bogies:** BX1.                                **Couplers:** Tightlock.
**Gangways:** Within unit + end doors.          **Control System:** Camshaft.
**Doors:** Sliding.                             **Maximum Speed:** 75 m.p.h.
**Seating Layout:** 313/0: Refurbished with high back seats (3+2 facing layout).
313/1 Low back seats, mainly 2+2 facing.
**Multiple Working:** Within class.

**DMSO.** Lot No. 30879 1976–1977. –/74 (313/1 –/66). 36.0 t.
**PTSO.** Lot No. 30880 1976–1977. –/83 (313/1 –/70 1W). 31.0 t.
**BDMSO.** Lot No. 30885 1976–1977. –/74 (313/1 –/66). 37.5 t.

**Class 313/0. Standard Design.**

| | | | | | | | |
|---|---|---|---|---|---|---|---|
| 313 018 | **FU** | H | *FC* | HE | 62546 | 71230 | 62610 |
| 313 024 | **FU** | H | *FC* | HE | 62552 | 71236 | 62616 |
| 313 025 | **FU** | H | *FC* | HE | 62553 | 71237 | 62617 |
| 313 026 | **FU** | H | *FC* | HE | 62554 | 71238 | 62618 |
| 313 027 | **FU** | H | *FC* | HE | 62555 | 71239 | 62619 |
| 313 028 | **FU** | H | *FC* | HE | 62556 | 71240 | 62620 |
| 313 029 | **FU** | H | *FC* | HE | 62557 | 71241 | 62621 |
| 313 030 | **FU** | H | *FC* | HE | 62558 | 71242 | 62622 |
| 313 031 | **FU** | H | *FC* | HE | 62559 | 71243 | 62623 |
| 313 032 | **FU** | H | *FC* | HE | 62560 | 71244 | 62643 |
| 313 033 | **FU** | H | *FC* | HE | 62561 | 71245 | 62625 |
| 313 035 | **FU** | H | *FC* | HE | 62563 | 71247 | 62627 |
| 313 036 | **FU** | H | *FC* | HE | 62564 | 71248 | 62628 |
| 313 037 | **FU** | H | *FC* | HE | 62565 | 71249 | 62629 |
| 313 038 | **FU** | H | *FC* | HE | 62566 | 71250 | 62630 |
| 313 039 | **FU** | H | *FC* | HE | 62567 | 71251 | 62631 |
| 313 040 | **FU** | H | *FC* | HE | 62568 | 71252 | 62632 |
| 313 041 | **FU** | H | *FC* | HE | 62569 | 71253 | 62633 |
| 313 042 | **FU** | H | *FC* | HE | 62570 | 71254 | 62634 |
| 313 043 | **FU** | H | *FC* | HE | 62571 | 71255 | 62635 |
| 313 044 | **FU** | H | *FC* | HE | 62572 | 71256 | 62636 |

| | | | | | | | |
|---|---|---|---|---|---|---|---|
| 313 045 | **FU** | H | *FC* | HE | 62573 | 71257 | 62637 |
| 313 046 | **FU** | H | *FC* | HE | 62574 | 71258 | 62638 |
| 313 047 | **FU** | H | *FC* | HE | 62575 | 71259 | 62639 |
| 313 048 | **FU** | H | *FC* | HE | 62576 | 71260 | 62640 |
| 313 049 | **FU** | H | *FC* | HE | 62577 | 71261 | 62641 |
| 313 050 | **FU** | H | *FC* | HE | 62578 | 71262 | 62649 |
| 313 051 | **FU** | H | *FC* | HE | 62579 | 71263 | 62624 |
| 313 052 | **FU** | H | *FC* | HE | 62580 | 71264 | 62644 |
| 313 053 | **FU** | H | *FC* | HE | 62581 | 71265 | 62645 |
| 313 054 | **FU** | H | *FC* | HE | 62582 | 71266 | 62646 |
| 313 055 | **FU** | H | *FC* | HE | 62583 | 71267 | 62647 |
| 313 056 | **FU** | H | *FC* | HE | 62584 | 71268 | 62648 |
| 313 057 | **FU** | H | *FC* | HE | 62585 | 71269 | 62642 |
| 313 058 | **FU** | H | *FC* | HE | 62586 | 71270 | 62650 |
| 313 059 | **FU** | H | *FC* | HE | 62587 | 71271 | 62651 |
| 313 060 | **FU** | H | *FC* | HE | 62588 | 71272 | 62652 |
| 313 061 | **FU** | H | *FC* | HE | 62589 | 71273 | 62653 |
| 313 062 | **FU** | H | *FC* | HE | 62590 | 71274 | 62654 |
| 313 063 | **FU** | H | *FC* | HE | 62591 | 71275 | 62655 |
| 313 064 | **FU** | H | *FC* | HE | 62592 | 71276 | 62656 |

**Class 313/1. Extra shoegear for London Overground services.** Units are being replaced by Class 378s, with the first 19 due to transfer to Southern and will be renumbered 313/2 (see below).

| | | | | | | | |
|---|---|---|---|---|---|---|---|
| 313 101 | **SL** | H | | ZN | 62529 | 71213 | 62593 |
| 313 102 | **SL** | H | | ZN | 62530 | 71214 | 62594 |
| 313 103 | **SL** | H | | ZN | 62531 | 71215 | 62595 |
| 313 106 | **SL** | H | *LO* | WN | 62534 | 71218 | 62598 |
| 313 107 | **SL** | H | | ZN | 62535 | 71219 | 62599 |
| 313 108 | **SL** | H | | ZN | 62536 | 71220 | 62600 |
| 313 109 | **SL** | H | | BI | 62537 | 71221 | 62601 |
| 313 110 | **SL** | H | *LO* | WN | 62538 | 71222 | 62602 |
| 313 111 | **SL** | H | *LO* | WN | 62539 | 71223 | 62603 |
| 313 112 | **SL** | H | | ZN | 62540 | 71224 | 62604 |
| 313 113 | **SL** | H | *LO* | WN | 62541 | 71225 | 62605 |
| 313 114 | **SL** | H | *LO* | WN | 62542 | 71226 | 62606 |
| 313 115 | **SL** | H | *LO* | WN | 62543 | 71227 | 62607 |
| 313 116 | **SL** | H | *LO* | WN | 62544 | 71228 | 62608 |
| 313 117 | **SL** | H | *LO* | WN | 62545 | 71229 | 62609 |
| 313 119 | **SL** | H | *LO* | WN | 62547 | 71231 | 62611 |
| 313 120 | **SL** | H | *LO* | WN | 62548 | 71232 | 62612 |
| 313 121 | **SL** | H | *LO* | WN | 62549 | 71233 | 62613 |
| 313 122 | **SL** | H | *LO* | WN | 62550 | 71234 | 62614 |
| 313 123 | **SL** | H | *LO* | WN | 62551 | 71235 | 62615 |
| 313 134 | **SL** | H | *LO* | WN | 62562 | 71246 | 62626 |

**Names (carried on PTSO):**

| | |
|---|---|
| 313 111 | London TravelWatch |
| 313 120 | PARLIAMENT HILL |
| 313 134 | The Hackney Empire |

**Class 313/2. Units for Southern.** 19 units are due to transfer to Southern (initially unrefurbished) and are being renumbered in the 313/2 series.

| | | | | | | |
|---|---|---|---|---|---|---|
| 313 201 | (313 101) | | | | | |
| 313 202 | (313 102) | | | | | |
| 313 203 | (313 103) | | | | | |
| 313 204 | (313 104) | **SN** | H | BI | 62532 | 71216 | 62596 |
| 313 205 | (313 105) | **SN** | H | BI | 62533 | 71217 | 62597 |
| 313 206 | (313 106) | | | | | |
| 313 207 | (313 107) | | | | | |
| 313 208 | (313 108) | | | | | |
| 313 209 | (313 109) | | | | | |
| 313 210 | (313 110) | | | | | |
| 313 211 | (313 111) | | | | | |
| 313 212 | (313 112) | | | | | |
| 313 213 | (313 113) | | | | | |
| 313 214 | (313 114) | | | | | |
| 313 215 | (313 115) | | | | | |
| 313 216 | (313 116) | | | | | |
| 313 217 | (313 117) | | | | | |
| 313 219 | (313 119) | | | | | |
| 313 220 | (313 120) | | | | | |

# CLASS 314 BREL YORK

Inner suburban units.

**Formation:** DMSO–PTSO–DMSO.
**Construction:** Steel underframe, aluminium alloy body and roof.
**Traction Motors:** Four GEC G310AZ (* Brush TM61-53) of 82.125 kW.
**Wheel Arrangement:** Bo-Bo + 2-2 + Bo-Bo.
**Braking:** Disc & rheostatic.  **Dimensions:** 20.33/20.18 x 2.82 m.
**Bogies:** BX1.  **Couplers:** Tightlock.
**Gangways:** Within unit + end doors.  **Control System:** Thyristor.
**Doors:** Sliding.  **Maximum Speed:** 70 m.p.h.
**Seating Layout:** 3+2 low-back facing.
**Multiple Working:** Within class and with Class 315.

**DMSO.** Lot No. 30912 1979. –/68. 34.5 t.
**64588**[II]. **DMSO.** Lot No. 30908 1978–1980. Rebuilt Railcare Glasgow 1996 from Class 507 No. 64426. The original 64588 has been scrapped. –/74. 34.5 t.
**PTSO.** Lot No. 30913 1979. –/76. 33.0 t.

| | | | | | | | | |
|---|---|---|---|---|---|---|---|---|
| 314 201 | * | **SC** | A | *SR* | GW | 64583 | 71450 | 64584 | |
| 314 202 | * | **SC** | A | *SR* | GW | 64585 | 71451 | 64586 | |
| 314 203 | * | **SC** | A | *SR* | GW | 64587 | 71452 | 64588[II] | European Union |
| 314 204 | * | **SC** | A | *SR* | GW | 64589 | 71453 | 64590 | |
| 314 205 | * | **SC** | A | *SR* | GW | 64591 | 71454 | 64592 | |
| 314 206 | * | **SC** | A | *SR* | GW | 64593 | 71455 | 64594 | |
| 314 207 | | **SC** | A | *SR* | GW | 64595 | 71456 | 64596 | |
| 314 208 | | **SC** | A | *SR* | GW | 64597 | 71457 | 64598 | |
| 314 209 | | **SC** | A | *SR* | GW | 64599 | 71458 | 64600 | |
| 314 210 | | **SC** | A | *SR* | GW | 64601 | 71459 | 64602 | |

| 314 211 | **SC** | A | *SR* | GW | 64603 | 71460 | 64604 |
| 314 212 | **SC** | A | *SR* | GW | 64605 | 71461 | 64606 |
| 314 213 | **SC** | A | *SR* | GW | 64607 | 71462 | 64608 |
| 314 214 | **SC** | A | *SR* | GW | 64609 | 71463 | 64610 |
| 314 215 | **SC** | A | *SR* | GW | 64611 | 71464 | 64612 |
| 314 216 | **SC** | A | *SR* | GW | 64613 | 71465 | 64614 |

# CLASS 315                                              BREL YORK

Inner suburban units.

**Formation:** DMSO–TSO–PTSO–DMSO.
**Construction:** Steel underframe, aluminium alloy body and roof.
**Traction Motors:** Four Brush TM61-53 (\* GEC G310AZ) of 82.125 kW.
**Wheel Arrangement:** Bo-Bo + 2-2 + 2-2 + Bo-Bo.
**Braking:** Disc & rheostatic.          **Dimensions:** 20.33/20.18 x 2.82 m.
**Bogies:** BX1.                          **Couplers:** Tightlock.
**Gangways:** Within unit + end doors.   **Control System:** Thyristor.
**Doors:** Sliding.                       **Maximum Speed:** 75 m.p.h.
**Seating Layout:** 3+2 low-back facing.
**Multiple Working:** Within class and with Class 314.
**DMSO.** Lot No. 30902 1980–1981. –/74. 35.0 t.
**TSO.** Lot No. 30904 1980–1981. –/86. 25.5 t.
**PTSO.** Lot No. 30903 1980–1981. –/84. 32.0 t.

| 315 801 | **1** | H | *EA* | IL | 64461 | 71281 | 71389 | 64462 |
| 315 802 | **1** | H | *EA* | IL | 64463 | 71282 | 71390 | 64464 |
| 315 803 | **1** | H | *EA* | IL | 64465 | 71283 | 71391 | 64466 |
| 315 804 | **1** | H | *EA* | IL | 64467 | 71284 | 71392 | 64468 |
| 315 805 | **1** | H | *EA* | IL | 64469 | 71285 | 71393 | 64470 |
| 315 806 | **1** | H | *EA* | IL | 64471 | 71286 | 71394 | 64472 |
| 315 807 | **1** | H | *EA* | IL | 64473 | 71287 | 71395 | 64474 |
| 315 808 | **1** | H | *EA* | IL | 64475 | 71288 | 71396 | 64476 |
| 315 809 | **1** | H | *EA* | IL | 64477 | 71289 | 71397 | 64478 |
| 315 810 | **1** | H | *EA* | IL | 64479 | 71290 | 71398 | 64480 |
| 315 811 | **1** | H | *EA* | IL | 64481 | 71291 | 71399 | 64482 |
| 315 812 | **1** | H | *EA* | IL | 64483 | 71292 | 71400 | 64484 |
| 315 813 | **1** | H | *EA* | IL | 64485 | 71293 | 71401 | 64486 |
| 315 814 | **1** | H | *EA* | IL | 64487 | 71294 | 71402 | 64488 |
| 315 815 | **1** | H | *EA* | IL | 64489 | 71295 | 71403 | 64490 |
| 315 816 | **1** | H | *EA* | IL | 64491 | 71296 | 71404 | 64492 |
| 315 817 | **1** | H | *EA* | IL | 64493 | 71297 | 71405 | 64494 |
| 315 818 | **1** | H | *EA* | IL | 64495 | 71298 | 71406 | 64496 |
| 315 819 | **1** | H | *EA* | IL | 64497 | 71299 | 71407 | 64498 |
| 315 820 | **1** | H | *EA* | IL | 64499 | 71300 | 71408 | 64500 |
| 315 821 | **1** | H | *EA* | IL | 64501 | 71301 | 71409 | 64502 |
| 315 822 | **1** | H | *EA* | IL | 64503 | 71302 | 71410 | 64504 |
| 315 823 | **1** | H | *EA* | IL | 64505 | 71303 | 71411 | 64506 |
| 315 824 | **1** | H | *EA* | IL | 64507 | 71304 | 71412 | 64508 |
| 315 825 | **1** | H | *EA* | IL | 64509 | 71305 | 71413 | 64510 |
| 315 826 | **1** | H | *EA* | IL | 64511 | 71306 | 71414 | 64512 |

| | | | | | | | | |
|---|---|---|---|---|---|---|---|---|
| 315 827 | | 1 | H | *EA* | IL | 64513 | 71307 | 71415 | 64514 |
| 315 828 | | 1 | H | *EA* | IL | 64515 | 71308 | 71416 | 64516 |
| 315 829 | | 1 | H | *EA* | IL | 64517 | 71309 | 71417 | 64518 |
| 315 830 | | 1 | H | *EA* | IL | 64519 | 71310 | 71418 | 64520 |
| 315 831 | | 1 | H | *EA* | IL | 64521 | 71311 | 71419 | 64522 |
| 315 832 | | 1 | H | *EA* | IL | 64523 | 71312 | 71420 | 64524 |
| 315 833 | | 1 | H | *EA* | IL | 64525 | 71313 | 71421 | 64526 |
| 315 834 | | 1 | H | *EA* | IL | 64527 | 71314 | 71422 | 64528 |
| 315 835 | | 1 | H | *EA* | IL | 64529 | 71315 | 71423 | 64530 |
| 315 836 | | 1 | H | *EA* | IL | 64531 | 71316 | 71424 | 64532 |
| 315 837 | | 1 | H | *EA* | IL | 64533 | 71317 | 71425 | 64534 |
| 315 838 | | 1 | H | *EA* | IL | 64535 | 71318 | 71426 | 64536 |
| 315 839 | | 1 | H | *EA* | IL | 64537 | 71319 | 71427 | 64538 |
| 315 840 | | 1 | H | *EA* | IL | 64539 | 71320 | 71428 | 64540 |
| 315 841 | | 1 | H | *EA* | IL | 64541 | 71321 | 71429 | 64542 |
| 315 842 | * | 1 | H | *EA* | IL | 64543 | 71322 | 71430 | 64544 |
| 315 843 | * | 1 | H | *EA* | IL | 64545 | 71323 | 71431 | 64546 |
| 315 844 | * | 1 | H | *EA* | IL | 64547 | 71324 | 71432 | 64548 |
| 315 845 | * | 1 | H | *EA* | IL | 64549 | 71325 | 71433 | 64550 |
| 315 846 | * | 1 | H | *EA* | IL | 64551 | 71326 | 71434 | 64552 |
| 315 847 | * | 1 | H | *EA* | IL | 64553 | 71327 | 71435 | 64554 |
| 315 848 | * | 1 | H | *EA* | IL | 64555 | 71328 | 71436 | 64556 |
| 315 849 | * | 1 | H | *EA* | IL | 64557 | 71329 | 71437 | 64558 |
| 315 850 | * | 1 | H | *EA* | IL | 64559 | 71330 | 71438 | 64560 |
| 315 851 | * | 1 | H | *EA* | IL | 64561 | 71331 | 71439 | 64562 |
| 315 852 | * | 1 | H | *EA* | IL | 64563 | 71332 | 71440 | 64564 |
| 315 853 | * | 1 | H | *EA* | IL | 64565 | 71333 | 71441 | 64566 |
| 315 854 | * | 1 | H | *EA* | IL | 64567 | 71334 | 71442 | 64568 |
| 315 855 | * | 1 | H | *EA* | IL | 64569 | 71335 | 71443 | 64570 |
| 315 856 | * | 1 | H | *EA* | IL | 64571 | 71336 | 71444 | 64572 |
| 315 857 | * | 1 | H | *EA* | IL | 64573 | 71337 | 71445 | 64574 |
| 315 858 | * | 1 | H | *EA* | IL | 64575 | 71338 | 71446 | 64576 |
| 315 859 | * | 1 | H | *EA* | IL | 64577 | 71339 | 71447 | 64578 |
| 315 860 | * | 1 | H | *EA* | IL | 64579 | 71340 | 71448 | 64580 |
| 315 861 | * | 1 | H | *EA* | IL | 64581 | 71341 | 71449 | 64582 |

**Names (carried on DMSO):**

| | |
|---|---|
| 315 817 | Transport for London |
| 315 829 | London Borough of Havering Celebrating 40 years |
| 315 845 | Herbie Woodward |
| 315 857 | Stratford Connections |

# CLASS 317                                      BREL YORK/DERBY

Outer suburban units.

**Formation:** Various, see sub-class headings.
**Construction:** Steel.
**Traction Motors:** Four GEC G315BZ of 247.5 kW.
**Wheel Arrangement:** 2-2 + Bo-Bo + 2-2 + 2-2.
**Braking:** Disc.                        **Dimensions:** 20.13/20.18 x 2.82 m.

**Bogies:** BP20 (MSO), BT13 (others).    **Couplers:** Tightlock.
**Gangways:** Throughout    **Control System:** Thyristor.
**Doors:** Sliding.    **Maximum Speed:** 100 m.p.h.
**Seating Layout:** Various, see sub-class headings.
**Multiple Working:** Within class & with Classes 318, 319, 320, 321, 322 and 323.

**Class 317/1.** Pressure ventilated.

**Formation:** DTSO–MSO–TCO–DTSO.
**Seating Layout:** 1: 2+2 facing, 2: 3+2 facing.

**DTSO(A)** Lot No. 30955 York 1981–1982. –/74. 29.5 t.
**MSO.** Lot No. 30958 York 1981–1982. –/79. 49.0 t.
**TCO.** Lot No. 30957 Derby 1981–1982. 22/46 2T. 29.0 t.
**DTSO(B)** Lot No. 30956 York 1981–1982. –/71. 29.5 t.

| | | | | | | | | |
|---|---|---|---|---|---|---|---|---|
| 317 337 | **FU** | A | *FC* | HE | 77036 | 62671 | 71613 | 77084 |
| 317 338 | **FU** | A | *FC* | HE | 77037 | 62698 | 71614 | 77085 |
| 317 339 | **FU** | A | *FC* | HE | 77038 | 62699 | 71615 | 77086 |
| 317 340 | **FU** | A | *FC* | HE | 77039 | 62700 | 71616 | 77087 |
| 317 341 | **FU** | A | *FC* | HE | 77040 | 62701 | 71617 | 77088 |
| 317 342 | **FU** | A | *FC* | HE | 77041 | 62702 | 71618 | 77089 |
| 317 343 | **FU** | A | *FC* | HE | 77042 | 62703 | 71619 | 77090 |
| 317 344 | **WP** | A | *FC* | HE | 77029 | 62690 | 71620 | 77091 |
| 317 345 | **FU** | A | *FC* | HE | 77044 | 62705 | 71621 | 77092 |
| 317 346 | **FU** | A | *FC* | HE | 77045 | 62706 | 71622 | 77093 |
| 317 347 | **FU** | A | *FC* | HE | 77046 | 62707 | 71623 | 77094 |
| 317 348 | **FU** | A | *FC* | HE | 77047 | 62708 | 71624 | 77095 |

**Names (carried on TCO):**

| 317 345 | Driver John Webb | 317 348 | Richard A Jenner |
|---|---|---|---|

**Class 317/5.** Pressure ventilated. Units renumbered from Class 317/1 in 2005 for West Anglia Metro services. Refurbished with new upholstery and Passenger Information Systems. Details as Class 317/1.

| | | | | | | | | |
|---|---|---|---|---|---|---|---|---|
| 317 501 | **NX** | A | *EA* | IL | 77024 | 62661 | 71577 | 77048 |
| 317 502 | **NX** | A | *EA* | IL | 77001 | 62662 | 71578 | 77049 |
| 317 503 | **NX** | A | *EA* | IL | 77002 | 62663 | 71579 | 77050 |
| 317 504 | **NX** | A | *EA* | IL | 77003 | 62664 | 71580 | 77051 |
| 317 505 | **NX** | A | *EA* | IL | 77004 | 62665 | 71581 | 77052 |
| 317 506 | **NX** | A | *EA* | IL | 77005 | 62666 | 71582 | 77053 |
| 317 507 | **NX** | A | *EA* | IL | 77006 | 62667 | 71583 | 77054 |
| 317 508 | **NX** | A | *EA* | IL | 77010 | 62697 | 71587 | 77058 |
| 317 509 | **NX** | A | *EA* | IL | 77011 | 62672 | 71588 | 77059 |
| 317 510 | **NX** | A | *EA* | IL | 77012 | 62673 | 71589 | 77060 |
| 317 511 | **1** | A | *EA* | IL | 77014 | 62675 | 71591 | 77062 |
| 317 512 | **1** | A | *EA* | IL | 77015 | 62676 | 71592 | 77063 |
| 317 513 | **NX** | A | *EA* | IL | 77016 | 62677 | 71593 | 77064 |
| 317 514 | **NX** | A | *EA* | IL | 77017 | 62678 | 71594 | 77065 |
| 317 515 | **NX** | A | *EA* | IL | 77019 | 62680 | 71596 | 77067 |

**Name (carried on TCO):**

317 507    University of Cambridge 800 Years 1209–2009

**Class 317/6.** Convection heating. Units converted from Class 317/2 by Railcare Wolverton 1998–99 with new seating layouts.

**Formation:** DTSO–MSO–TSO–DTCO.
**Seating Layout:** 2+2 facing.

**77200–77219. DTSO.** Lot No. 30994 York 1985–1986. –/64. 29.5 t.
**77280–77283. DTSO.** Lot No. 31007 York 1987. –/64. 29.5 t.
**62846–62865. MSO.** Lot No. 30996 York 1985–1986. –/70. 49.0 t.
**62886–62889. MSO.** Lot No. 31009 York 1987. –/70. 49.0 t.
**71734–71753. TSO.** Lot No. 30997 York 1985–1986. –/62 2T. 29.0 t.
**71762–71765. TSO.** Lot No. 31010 York 1987. –/62 2T. 29.0 t.
**77220–77239. DTCO.** Lot No. 30995 York 1985–1986. 24/48. 29.5 t.
**77284–77287. DTCO.** Lot No. 31008 York 1987. 24/48. 29.5 t.

| | | | | | | | | | |
|---|---|---|---|---|---|---|---|---|---|
| 317 649 | **WN** | A | *EA* | IL | 77200 | 62846 | 71734 | 77220 | |
| 317 650 | **WN** | A | *EA* | IL | 77201 | 62847 | 71735 | 77221 | |
| 317 651 | **WN** | A | *EA* | IL | 77202 | 62848 | 71736 | 77222 | |
| 317 652 | **1** | A | *EA* | IL | 77203 | 62849 | 71739 | 77223 | |
| 317 653 | **1** | A | *EA* | IL | 77204 | 62850 | 71738 | 77224 | |
| 317 654 | **1** | A | *EA* | IL | 77205 | 62851 | 71737 | 77225 | Richard Wells |
| 317 655 | **1** | A | *EA* | IL | 77206 | 62852 | 71740 | 77226 | |
| 317 656 | **1** | A | *EA* | IL | 77207 | 62853 | 71742 | 77227 | |
| 317 657 | **1** | A | *EA* | IL | 77208 | 62854 | 71741 | 77228 | |
| 317 658 | **1** | A | *EA* | IL | 77209 | 62855 | 71743 | 77229 | |
| 317 659 | **1** | A | *EA* | IL | 77210 | 62856 | 71744 | 77230 | |
| 317 660 | **1** | A | *EA* | IL | 77211 | 62857 | 71745 | 77231 | |
| 317 661 | **1** | A | *EA* | IL | 77212 | 62858 | 71746 | 77232 | |
| 317 662 | **1** | A | *EA* | IL | 77213 | 62859 | 71747 | 77233 | |
| 317 663 | **1** | A | *EA* | IL | 77214 | 62860 | 71748 | 77234 | |
| 317 664 | **1** | A | *EA* | IL | 77215 | 62861 | 71749 | 77235 | |
| 317 665 | **1** | A | *EA* | IL | 77216 | 62862 | 71750 | 77236 | |
| 317 666 | **1** | A | *EA* | IL | 77217 | 62863 | 71752 | 77237 | |
| 317 667 | **1** | A | *EA* | IL | 77218 | 62864 | 71751 | 77238 | |
| 317 668 | **1** | A | *EA* | IL | 77219 | 62865 | 71753 | 77239 | |
| 317 669 | **1** | A | *EA* | IL | 77280 | 62886 | 71762 | 77284 | |
| 317 670 | **1** | A | *EA* | IL | 77281 | 62887 | 71763 | 77285 | |
| 317 671 | **1** | A | *EA* | IL | 77282 | 62888 | 71764 | 77286 | |
| 317 672 | **1** | A | *EA* | IL | 77283 | 62889 | 71765 | 77287 | |

**Class 317/7.** Units converted from Class 317/1 by Railcare Wolverton 2000 for Stansted Express services between London Liverpool Street and Stansted. Air conditioning. Fitted with luggage stacks.

**Formation:** DTSO–MSO–TSO–DTCO.
**Seating Layout:** 1: 2+1 facing, 2: 2+2 facing.

**DTSO** Lot No. 30955 York 1981–1982. –/52 + catering point. 31.4 t.
**MSO.** Lot No. 30958 York 1981–1982. –/62. 51.3 t.
**TSO.** Lot No. 30957 Derby 1981–1982. –/42 1W 1T 1TD. 30.2 t.
**DTCO** Lot No. 30956 York 1981–1982. 22/16 + catering point. 31.6 t.

| | | | | | | | | |
|---|---|---|---|---|---|---|---|---|
| 317 708 | **NX** | A | *EA* | IL | 77007 | 62668 | 71584 | 77055 |
| 317 709 | **NX** | A | *EA* | IL | 77008 | 62669 | 71585 | 77056 |

| 317 710 | NX | A | EA | IL | 77009 | 62670 | 71586 | 77057 |
| 317 714 | NX | A | EA | IL | 77013 | 62674 | 71590 | 77061 |
| 317 719 | NX | A | EA | IL | 77018 | 62679 | 71595 | 77066 |
| 317 722 | NX | A | EA | IL | 77021 | 62682 | 71598 | 77069 |
| 317 723 | SX | A | EA | IL | 77022 | 62683 | 71599 | 77070 |
| 317 729 | NX | A | EA | IL | 77028 | 62689 | 71605 | 77076 |
| 317 732 | NX | A | EA | IL | 77031 | 62692 | 71608 | 77079 |

**Names (carried on DTCO):**

317 709   Len Camp                    | 317 723   The Tottenham Flyer

**Class 317/8.** Pressure Ventilated. Units refurbished and renumbered from Class 317/1 in 2005–2006 at Wabtec, Doncaster for use on Stansted Express services. Fitted with luggage stacks.

**Formation:** DTSO–MSO–TCO–DTSO.
**Seating Layout:** 1: 2+2 facing, 2: 3+2 facing.

**DTSO(A)** Lot No. 30955 York 1981–1982. –/66. 29.5 t.
**MSO.** Lot No. 30958 York 1981–1982. –/71. 49.0 t.
**TCO.** Lot No. 30957 Derby 1981–1982. 20/42 2T. 29.0 t.
**DTSO(B)** Lot No. 30956 York 1981–1982. –/66. 29.5 t.

| 317 881 | NX | A | EA | IL | 77020 | 62681 | 71597 | 77068 | |
| 317 882 | SU | A | EA | IL | 77023 | 62684 | 71600 | 77071 | |
| 317 883 | SU | A | EA | IL | 77000 | 62685 | 71601 | 77072 | |
| 317 884 | SU | A | EA | IL | 77025 | 62686 | 71602 | 77073 | |
| 317 885 | SU | A | EA | IL | 77026 | 62687 | 71603 | 77074 | |
| 317 886 | SU | A | EA | IL | 77027 | 62688 | 71604 | 77075 | |
| 317 887 | NX | A | EA | IL | 77043 | 62704 | 71606 | 77077 | |
| 317 888 | NX | A | EA | IL | 77030 | 62691 | 71607 | 77078 | |
| 317 889 | NX | A | EA | IL | 77032 | 62693 | 71609 | 77080 | |
| 317 890 | NX | A | EA | IL | 77033 | 62694 | 71610 | 77081 | |
| 317 891 | NX | A | EA | IL | 77034 | 62695 | 71611 | 77082 | |
| 317 892 | NX | A | EA | IL | 77035 | 62696 | 71612 | 77083 | Ilford Depot |

# CLASS 318                                    BREL YORK

Outer suburban units.

**Formation:** DTSO–MSO–DTSO.
**Construction:** Steel.
**Traction Motors:** Four Brush TM 2141 of 268 kW.
**Wheel Arrangement:** 2-2 + Bo-Bo + 2-2.
**Braking:** Disc.                          **Dimensions:** 19.83/19.92 x 2.82 m.
**Bogies:** BP20 (MSO), BT13 (others).    **Couplers:** Tightlock.
**Gangways:** Within unit.                 **Control System:** Thyristor.
**Doors:** Sliding.                        **Maximum Speed:** 90 m.p.h.
**Seating Layout:** 3+2 facing.
**Multiple Working:** Within class & with Classes 317, 319, 320, 321, 322 and 323.

**77240–77259. DTSO.** Lot No. 30999 1985–1986. –/64 1T. 30.0 t.
**77288. DTSO.** Lot No. 31020 1987. –/64 1T. 30.0 t.

**62866–62885. MSO.** Lot No. 30998 1985–1986. –/77. 50.9 t.
**62890. MSO.** Lot No. 31019 1987. –/77. 50.9 t.
**77260–77279. DTSO.** Lot No. 31000 1985–1986. –/72. 29.6 t.
**77289. DTSO.** Lot No. 31021 1987. –/72. 29.6 t.

| | | | | | | | | |
|---|---|---|---|---|---|---|---|---|
| 318 250 | **SC** | H | *SR* | GW | 77240 | 62866 | 77260 | |
| 318 251 | **SC** | H | *SR* | GW | 77241 | 62867 | 77261 | |
| 318 252 | **SC** | H | *SR* | GW | 77242 | 62868 | 77262 | |
| 318 253 | **SC** | H | *SR* | GW | 77243 | 62869 | 77263 | |
| 318 254 | **SC** | H | *SR* | GW | 77244 | 62870 | 77264 | |
| 318 255 | **SC** | H | *SR* | GW | 77245 | 62871 | 77265 | |
| 318 256 | **SC** | H | *SR* | GW | 77246 | 62872 | 77266 | |
| 318 257 | **SC** | H | *SR* | GW | 77247 | 62873 | 77267 | |
| 318 258 | **SC** | H | *SR* | GW | 77248 | 62874 | 77268 | |
| 318 259 | **SC** | H | *SR* | GW | 77249 | 62875 | 77269 | Citizens' Network |
| 318 260 | **SC** | H | *SR* | GW | 77250 | 62876 | 77270 | |
| 318 261 | **SC** | H | *SR* | GW | 77251 | 62877 | 77271 | |
| 318 262 | **SC** | H | *SR* | GW | 77252 | 62878 | 77272 | |
| 318 263 | **SC** | H | *SR* | GW | 77253 | 62879 | 77273 | |
| 318 264 | **SC** | H | *SR* | GW | 77254 | 62880 | 77274 | |
| 318 265 | **SC** | H | *SR* | GW | 77255 | 62881 | 77275 | |
| 318 266 | **SC** | H | *SR* | GW | 77256 | 62882 | 77276 | STRATHCLYDER |
| 318 267 | **SC** | H | *SR* | GW | 77257 | 62883 | 77277 | |
| 318 268 | **SC** | H | *SR* | GW | 77258 | 62884 | 77278 | |
| 318 269 | **SC** | H | *SR* | GW | 77259 | 62885 | 77279 | |
| 318 270 | **SC** | H | *SR* | GW | 77288 | 62890 | 77289 | |

# CLASS 319                                                          BREL YORK

Express and outer suburban units.

**Formation:** Various, see sub-class headings.
**Systems:** 25 kV AC overhead/750 V DC third rail.
**Construction:** Steel.
**Traction Motors:** Four GEC G315BZ of 268 kW.
**Wheel Arrangement:** 2-2 + Bo-Bo + 2-2 + 2-2.
**Braking:** Disc.    **Dimensions:** 20.17/20.16 x 2.82 m.
**Bogies:** P7-4 (MSO), T3-7 (others).    **Couplers:** Tightlock.
**Gangways:** Within unit + end doors.    **Control System:** GTO chopper.
**Doors:** Sliding.    **Maximum Speed:** 100 m.p.h.
**Seating Layout:** Various, see sub-class headings.
**Multiple Working:** Within class & with Classes 317, 318, 320, 321, 322 and 323.

**Class 319/0.** DTSO–MSO–TSO–DTSO.

**Seating Layout:** 3+2 facing.

**DTSO(A).** Lot No. 31022 (odd nos.) 1987–1988. –/82. 28.2 t.
**MSO.** Lot No. 31023 1987–1988. –/82. 49.2 t.
**TSO.** Lot No. 31024 1987–1988. –/77 2T. 31.0 t.
**DTSO(B).** Lot No. 31025 (even nos.) 1987–1988. –/78. 28.1 t.

| | | | | | | | | |
|---|---|---|---|---|---|---|---|---|
| 319 001 | **FU** | P | *FC* | BF | 77291 | 62891 | 71772 | 77290 |
| 319 002 | **FU** | P | *FC* | BF | 77293 | 62892 | 71773 | 77292 |

| 319 003 | **FU** | P | *FC* | BF | 77295 | 62893 | 71774 | 77294 |
| 319 004 | **FU** | P | *FC* | BF | 77297 | 62894 | 71775 | 77296 |
| 319 005 | **FU** | P | *FC* | BF | 77299 | 62895 | 71776 | 77298 |
| 319 006 | **FU** | P | *FC* | BF | 77301 | 62896 | 71777 | 77300 |
| 319 007 | **FU** | P | *FC* | BF | 77303 | 62897 | 71778 | 77302 |
| 319 008 | **SN** | P | *FC* | BF | 77305 | 62898 | 71779 | 77304 |
| 319 009 | **SN** | P | *FC* | BF | 77307 | 62899 | 71780 | 77306 |
| 319 010 | **FU** | P | *FC* | BF | 77309 | 62900 | 71781 | 77308 |
| 319 011 | **SN** | P | *FC* | BF | 77311 | 62901 | 71782 | 77310 |
| 319 012 | **SN** | P | *FC* | BF | 77313 | 62902 | 71783 | 77312 |
| 319 013 | **SN** | P | *FC* | BF | 77315 | 62903 | 71784 | 77314 |

**Names (carried on TSO):**

319 011    John Ruskin College    | 319 013    The Surrey Hills

**Class 319/2.** DTSO–MSO–TSO–DTCO. Units converted from Class 319/0 for express services from London to Brighton.

**Seating Layout:** 1: 2+1 facing, 2: 2+2 facing.

**DTSO.** Lot No. 31022 (odd nos.) 1987–1988. –/64. 28.2 t.
**MSO.** Lot No. 31023 1987–1988. –/60 2T. (including 12 seats in a "snug" under the pantograph area). External sliding doors sealed adjacent to this area. 49.2 t.
**TSO.** Lot No. 31024 1987–1988. –/52 1T 1TD. 31.0 t.
**DTCO.** Lot No. 31025 (even nos.) 1987–1988. 18/36. 28.1 t.

| 319 214 | **SN** | P | *FC* | BF | 77317 | 62904 | 71785 | 77316 |          |
| 319 215 | **SN** | P | *FC* | BF | 77319 | 62905 | 71786 | 77318 | London   |
| 319 216 | **SN** | P | *FC* | BF | 77321 | 62906 | 71787 | 77320 |          |
| 319 217 | **SN** | P | *FC* | BF | 77323 | 62907 | 71788 | 77322 | Brighton |
| 319 218 | **SN** | P | *FC* | BF | 77325 | 62908 | 71789 | 77324 | Croydon  |
| 319 219 | **SN** | P | *FC* | BF | 77327 | 62909 | 71790 | 77326 |          |
| 319 220 | **SN** | P | *FC* | BF | 77329 | 62910 | 71791 | 77328 |          |

**Class 319/3.** DTSO–MSO–TSO–DTSO. Converted from Class 319/1 by replacing first class seats with standard class seats. Used mainly on the Luton–Sutton/Wimbledon routes.

**Seating Layout:** 3+2 facing.
**Dimensions:** 19.33 x 2.82 m.

**Advertising livery:** 319 364 & 319 365 Thameslink Programme (multi-coloured horizontal stripes with pink ends).

* Sets refurbished by First Capital Connect. This programme is ongoing.

**DTSO(A).** Lot No. 31063 1990. –/70. 29.0 t.
**MSO.** Lot No. 31064 1990. –/78. 50.6 t.
**TSO.** Lot No. 31065 1990. –/74 2T. 31.0 t.
**DTSO(B).** Lot No. 31066 1990. –/78 (* –/75). 29.7 t.

| 319 361 | * | **FU** | P | *FC* | BF | 77459 | 63043 | 71929 | 77458 |
| 319 362 | * | **FU** | P | *FC* | BF | 77461 | 63044 | 71930 | 77460 |
| 319 363 | * | **FU** | P | *FC* | BF | 77463 | 63045 | 71931 | 77462 |
| 319 364 | * | **AL** | P | *FC* | BF | 77465 | 63046 | 71932 | 77464 |
| 319 365 | * | **AL** | P | *FC* | BF | 77467 | 63047 | 71933 | 77466 |

| 319 366 | * | **FU** | P | *FC* | BF | 77469 | 63048 | 71934 | 77468 |
| 319 367 | * | **FU** | P | *FC* | BF | 77471 | 63049 | 71935 | 77470 |
| 319 368 | * | **FU** | P | *FC* | BF | 77473 | 63050 | 71936 | 77472 |
| 319 369 | * | **FU** | P | *FC* | BF | 77475 | 63051 | 71937 | 77474 |
| 319 370 | * | **FU** | P | *FC* | BF | 77477 | 63052 | 71938 | 77476 |
| 319 371 | * | **FU** | P | *FC* | BF | 77479 | 63053 | 71939 | 77478 |
| 319 372 |   | **FU** | P | *FC* | BF | 77481 | 63054 | 71940 | 77480 |
| 319 373 |   | **FU** | P | *FC* | BF | 77483 | 63055 | 71941 | 77482 |
| 319 374 | * | **FU** | P | *FC* | BF | 77485 | 63056 | 71942 | 77484 |
| 319 375 | * | **FU** | P | *FC* | BF | 77487 | 63057 | 71943 | 77486 |
| 319 376 |   | **TW** | P | *FC* | BF | 77489 | 63058 | 71944 | 77488 |
| 319 377 | * | **FU** | P | *FC* | BF | 77491 | 63059 | 71945 | 77490 |
| 319 378 | * | **FU** | P | *FC* | BF | 77493 | 63060 | 71946 | 77492 |
| 319 379 | * | **FU** | P | *FC* | BF | 77495 | 63061 | 71947 | 77494 |
| 319 380 |   | **TW** | P | *FC* | BF | 77497 | 63062 | 71948 | 77496 |
| 319 381 | * | **FU** | P | *FC* | BF | 77973 | 63093 | 71979 | 77974 |
| 319 382 | * | **FU** | P | *FC* | BF | 77975 | 63094 | 71980 | 77976 |
| 319 383 | * | **FU** | P | *FC* | BF | 77977 | 63095 | 71981 | 77978 |
| 319 384 |   | **TW** | P | *FC* | BF | 77979 | 63096 | 71982 | 77980 |
| 319 385 | * | **FU** | P | *FC* | BF | 77981 | 63097 | 71983 | 77982 |
| 319 386 |   | **TW** | P | *FC* | BF | 77983 | 63098 | 71984 | 77984 |

**Names (carried on TSO):**

| 319 364 | Transforming Blackfriars |
| 319 365 | Transforming Farringdon |
| 319 374 | Bedford Cauldwell TMD |

**Class 319/4.** DTCO–MSO–TSO–DTSO. Converted from Class 319/0. Refurbished with carpets. DTSO(A) converted to composite. Used mainly on the Bedford–Gatwick–Brighton route.

**Seating Layout:** 1: 2+1 facing 2: 2+2/3+2 facing.

* Sets refurbished by First Capital Connect with some seats removed for additional luggage space. This programme is ongoing.

**77331–77381. DTCO.** Lot No. 31022 (odd nos.) 1987–1988. 12/54 (* 12/51). 28.2 t.
**77431–77457. DTCO.** Lot No. 31038 (odd nos.) 1988. 12/54 (* 12/51). 28.2 t.
**62911–62936. MSO.** Lot No. 31023 1987–1988. –/77 (* –/74). 49.2 t.
**62961–62974. MSO.** Lot No. 31039 1988. –/77 (* –/74). 49.2 t.
**71792–71817. TSO.** Lot No. 31024 1987–1988. –/72 2T (* –/67 2T). 31.0 t.
**71866–71879. TSO.** Lot No. 31040 1988. –/72 2T (* –67 2T). 31.0 t.
**77330–77380. DTSO.** Lot No. 31025 (even nos.) 1987–1988. –/74 (* –/71 1W). 28.1 t.
**77430–77456. DTSO.** Lot No. 31041 (even nos.) 1988. –/74 (* –/71 1W). 28.1 t.

| 319 421 | * | **FU** | P | *FC* | BF | 77331 | 62911 | 71792 | 77330 |
| 319 422 | * | **FU** | P | *FC* | BF | 77333 | 62912 | 71793 | 77332 |
| 319 423 | * | **FU** | P | *FC* | BF | 77335 | 62913 | 71794 | 77334 |
| 319 424 | * | **FU** | P | *FC* | BF | 77337 | 62914 | 71795 | 77336 |
| 319 425 | * | **FU** | P | *FC* | BF | 77339 | 62915 | 71796 | 77338 |
| 319 426 | * | **FU** | P | *FC* | BF | 77341 | 62916 | 71797 | 77340 |
| 319 427 | * | **FU** | P | *FC* | BF | 77343 | 62917 | 71798 | 77342 |

| 319 428 | * | **FU** | P | *FC* | BF | 77345 | 62918 | 71799 | 77344 |
| 319 429 |   | **FU** | P | *FC* | BF | 77347 | 62919 | 71800 | 77346 |
| 319 430 |   | **TL** | P | *FC* | BF | 77349 | 62920 | 71801 | 77348 |
| 319 431 |   | **FU** | P | *FC* | BF | 77351 | 62921 | 71802 | 77350 |
| 319 432 | * | **FU** | P | *FC* | BF | 77353 | 62922 | 71803 | 77352 |
| 319 433 | * | **FU** | P | *FC* | BF | 77355 | 62923 | 71804 | 77354 |
| 319 434 | * | **FU** | P | *FC* | BF | 77357 | 62924 | 71805 | 77356 |
| 319 435 | * | **FU** | P | *FC* | BF | 77359 | 62925 | 71806 | 77358 |
| 319 436 | * | **FU** | P | *FC* | BF | 77361 | 62926 | 71807 | 77360 |
| 319 437 | * | **FU** | P | *FC* | BF | 77363 | 62927 | 71808 | 77362 |
| 319 438 |   | **FU** | P | *FC* | BF | 77365 | 62928 | 71809 | 77364 |
| 319 439 |   | **FU** | P | *FC* | BF | 77367 | 62929 | 71810 | 77366 |
| 319 440 | * | **FU** | P | *FC* | BF | 77369 | 62930 | 71811 | 77368 |
| 319 441 | * | **FU** | P | *FC* | BF | 77371 | 62931 | 71812 | 77370 |
| 319 442 | * | **FU** | P | *FC* | BF | 77373 | 62932 | 71813 | 77372 |
| 319 443 |   | **FU** | P | *FC* | BF | 77375 | 62933 | 71814 | 77374 |
| 319 444 |   | **FU** | P | *FC* | BF | 77377 | 62934 | 71815 | 77376 |
| 319 445 |   | **FU** | P | *FC* | BF | 77379 | 62935 | 71816 | 77378 |
| 319 446 | * | **FU** | P | *FC* | BF | 77381 | 62936 | 71817 | 77380 |
| 319 447 |   | **FU** | P | *FC* | BF | 77431 | 62961 | 71866 | 77430 |
| 319 448 | * | **FU** | P | *FC* | BF | 77433 | 62962 | 71867 | 77432 |
| 319 449 | * | **FU** | P | *FC* | BF | 77435 | 62963 | 71868 | 77434 |
| 319 450 | * | **FU** | P | *FC* | BF | 77437 | 62964 | 71869 | 77436 |
| 319 451 | * | **FU** | P | *FC* | BF | 77439 | 62965 | 71870 | 77438 |
| 319 452 | * | **FU** | P | *FC* | BF | 77441 | 62966 | 71871 | 77440 |
| 319 453 | * | **FU** | P | *FC* | BF | 77443 | 62967 | 71872 | 77442 |
| 319 454 | * | **FU** | P | *FC* | BF | 77445 | 62968 | 71873 | 77444 |
| 319 455 | * | **FU** | P | *FC* | BF | 77447 | 62969 | 71874 | 77446 |
| 319 456 | * | **FU** | P | *FC* | BF | 77449 | 62970 | 71875 | 77448 |
| 319 457 | * | **FU** | P | *FC* | BF | 77451 | 62971 | 71876 | 77450 |
| 319 458 | * | **FU** | P | *FC* | BF | 77453 | 62972 | 71877 | 77452 |
| 319 459 | * | **FU** | P | *FC* | BF | 77455 | 62973 | 71878 | 77454 |
| 319 460 | * | **FU** | P | *FC* | BF | 77457 | 62974 | 71879 | 77456 |

**Names (carried on TSO):**

| 319 425 | Transforming Travel |
| 319 435 | Adrian Jackson-Robbins Chairman 1987–2007 Association of Public Transport Users |
| 319 446 | St Pancras International |
| 319 449 | King's Cross Thameslink |

# CLASS 320                                                    BREL YORK

Suburban units.

**Formation:** DTSO–MSO–DTSO.
**Construction:** Steel
**Traction Motors:** Four Brush TM2141B of 268 kW.
**Wheel Arrangement:** 2-2 + Bo-Bo + 2-2.
**Braking:** Disc.                          **Dimensions:** 19.33 x 2.82 m.
**Bogies:** P7-4 (MSO), T3-7 (others).     **Couplers:** Tightlock.

**Gangways:** Within unit.      **Control System:** Thyristor.
**Doors:** Sliding.      **Maximum Speed:** 75 m.p.h.
**Seating Layout:** 3+2 facing.
**Multiple Working:** Within class & with Classes 317, 318, 319, 321, 322 and 323.

**DTSO (A).** Lot No. 31060 1990. –/76 1W. 29.1 t.
**MSO.** Lot No. 31062 1990. –/76 1W. 51.8 t.
**DTSO (B).** Lot No. 31061 1990. –/75. 30.0 t.

| | | | | | | | |
|---|---|---|---|---|---|---|---|
| 320 301 | **SC** | H | *SR* | GW | 77899 | 63021 | 77921 |
| 320 302 | **SC** | H | *SR* | GW | 77900 | 63022 | 77922 |
| 320 303 | **SC** | H | *SR* | GW | 77901 | 63023 | 77923 |
| 320 304 | **SC** | H | *SR* | GW | 77902 | 63024 | 77924 |
| 320 305 | **SC** | H | *SR* | GW | 77903 | 63025 | 77925 |
| 320 306 | **SC** | H | *SR* | GW | 77904 | 63026 | 77926 |
| 320 307 | **SC** | H | *SR* | GW | 77905 | 63027 | 77927 |
| 320 308 | **SC** | H | *SR* | GW | 77906 | 63028 | 77928 |
| 320 309 | **SC** | H | *SR* | GW | 77907 | 63029 | 77929 |
| 320 310 | **SC** | H | *SR* | GW | 77908 | 63030 | 77930 |
| 320 311 | **SC** | H | *SR* | GW | 77909 | 63031 | 77931 |
| 320 312 | **SC** | H | *SR* | GW | 77910 | 63032 | 77932 |
| 320 313 | **SC** | H | *SR* | GW | 77911 | 63033 | 77933 |
| 320 314 | **SC** | H | *SR* | GW | 77912 | 63034 | 77934 |
| 320 315 | **SC** | H | *SR* | GW | 77913 | 63035 | 77935 |
| 320 316 | **SC** | H | *SR* | GW | 77914 | 63036 | 77936 |
| 320 317 | **SC** | H | *SR* | GW | 77915 | 63037 | 77937 |
| 320 318 | **SC** | H | *SR* | GW | 77916 | 63038 | 77938 |
| 320 319 | **SC** | H | *SR* | GW | 77917 | 63039 | 77939 |
| 320 320 | **SC** | H | *SR* | GW | 77918 | 63040 | 77940 |
| 320 321 | **SC** | H | *SR* | GW | 77919 | 63041 | 77941 |
| 320 322 | **SC** | H | *SR* | GW | 77920 | 63042 | 77942 |

**Names (carried on MSO):**

| | |
|---|---|
| 320 305 | GLASGOW SCHOOL OF ART 1845 150 1995 |
| 320 306 | Model Rail Scotland |
| 320 308 | High Road 20th Anniversary 2000 |
| 320 309 | Radio Clyde 25th Anniversary |
| 320 311 | Royal College of Physicians and Surgeons of Glasgow |
| 320 312 | Sir William A Smith Founder of the Boys' Brigade |
| 320 321 | The Rt. Hon. John Smith, QC, MP |
| 320 322 | Festive Glasgow Orchid |

# CLASS 321          BREL YORK

Outer suburban units.

**Formation:** DTCO (DTSO on Class 321/9)–MSO–TSO–DTSO.
**Construction:** Steel.
**Traction Motors:** Four Brush TM2141C (268 kW).
**Wheel Arrangement:** 2-2 + Bo-Bo + 2-2 + 2-2.
**Braking:** Disc.      **Dimensions:** 19.95 x 2.82 m.
**Bogies:** P7-4 (MSO), T3-7 (others).      **Couplers:** Tightlock.

**Gangways:** Within unit.                    **Control System:** Thyristor.
**Doors:** Sliding.                           **Maximum Speed:** 100 m.p.h..
**Seating Layout:** 1: 2+2 facing, 2: 3+2 facing.
**Multiple Working:** Within class & with Classes 317, 318, 319, 320, 322 and 323.

**Class 321/3.**

**DTCO.** Lot No. 31053 1988–1990. 16/57. 29.7 t.
**MSO.** Lot No. 31054 1988–1990. –/82. 51.5 t.
**TSO.** Lot No. 31055 1988–1990. –/75 2T. 29.1 t.
**DTSO.** Lot No. 31056 1988–1990. –/78. 29.7 t.

| | | | | | | | | |
|---|---|---|---|---|---|---|---|---|
| 321 301 | NX | H | EA | IL | 78049 | 62975 | 71880 | 77853 |
| 321 302 | NX | H | EA | IL | 78050 | 62976 | 71881 | 77854 |
| 321 303 | NX | H | EA | IL | 78051 | 62977 | 71882 | 77855 |
| 321 304 | NX | H | EA | IL | 78052 | 62978 | 71883 | 77856 |
| 321 305 | NX | H | EA | IL | 78053 | 62979 | 71884 | 77857 |
| 321 306 | NX | H | EA | IL | 78054 | 62980 | 71885 | 77858 |
| 321 307 | NX | H | EA | IL | 78055 | 62981 | 71886 | 77859 |
| 321 308 | NX | H | EA | IL | 78056 | 62982 | 71887 | 77860 |
| 321 309 | NX | H | EA | IL | 78057 | 62983 | 71888 | 77861 |
| 321 310 | NX | H | EA | IL | 78058 | 62984 | 71889 | 77862 |
| 321 311 | NX | H | EA | IL | 78059 | 62985 | 71890 | 77863 |
| 321 312 | NX | H | EA | IL | 78060 | 62986 | 71891 | 77864 |
| 321 313 | NX | H | EA | IL | 78061 | 62987 | 71892 | 77865 |
| 321 314 | NX | H | EA | IL | 78062 | 62988 | 71893 | 77866 |
| 321 315 | NX | H | EA | IL | 78063 | 62989 | 71894 | 77867 |
| 321 316 | NX | H | EA | IL | 78064 | 62990 | 71895 | 77868 |
| 321 317 | NX | H | EA | IL | 78065 | 62991 | 71896 | 77869 |
| 321 318 | NX | H | EA | IL | 78066 | 62992 | 71897 | 77870 |
| 321 319 | NX | H | EA | IL | 78067 | 62993 | 71898 | 77871 |
| 321 320 | NX | H | EA | IL | 78068 | 62994 | 71899 | 77872 |
| 321 321 | NX | H | EA | IL | 78069 | 62995 | 71900 | 77873 |
| 321 322 | GE | H | EA | IL | 78070 | 62996 | 71901 | 77874 |
| 321 323 | NX | H | EA | IL | 78071 | 62997 | 71902 | 77875 |
| 321 324 | NX | H | EA | IL | 78072 | 62998 | 71903 | 77876 |
| 321 325 | GE | H | EA | IL | 78073 | 62999 | 71904 | 77877 |
| 321 326 | NX | H | EA | IL | 78074 | 63000 | 71905 | 77878 |
| 321 327 | GE | H | EA | IL | 78075 | 63001 | 71906 | 77879 |
| 321 328 | GE | H | EA | IL | 78076 | 63002 | 71907 | 77880 |
| 321 329 | GE | H | EA | IL | 78077 | 63003 | 71908 | 77881 |
| 321 330 | GE | H | EA | IL | 78078 | 63004 | 71909 | 77882 |
| 321 331 | GE | H | EA | IL | 78079 | 63005 | 71910 | 77883 |
| 321 332 | GE | H | EA | IL | 78080 | 63006 | 71911 | 77884 |
| 321 333 | GE | H | EA | IL | 78081 | 63007 | 71912 | 77885 |
| 321 334 | GE | H | EA | IL | 78082 | 63008 | 71913 | 77886 |
| 321 335 | GE | H | EA | IL | 78083 | 63009 | 71914 | 77887 |
| 321 336 | GE | H | EA | IL | 78084 | 63010 | 71915 | 77888 |
| 321 337 | GE | H | EA | IL | 78085 | 63011 | 71916 | 77889 |
| 321 338 | GE | H | EA | IL | 78086 | 63012 | 71917 | 77890 |
| 321 339 | GE | H | EA | IL | 78087 | 63013 | 71918 | 77891 |
| 321 340 | GE | H | EA | IL | 78088 | 63014 | 71919 | 77892 |

| 321 341 | **GE** | H | *EA* | IL | 78089 | 63015 | 71920 | 77893 |
|---------|--------|---|------|----|-------|-------|-------|-------|
| 321 342 | **GE** | H | *EA* | IL | 78090 | 63016 | 71921 | 77894 |
| 321 343 | **GE** | H | *EA* | IL | 78091 | 63017 | 71922 | 77895 |
| 321 344 | **GE** | H | *EA* | IL | 78092 | 63018 | 71923 | 77896 |
| 321 345 | **GE** | H | *EA* | IL | 78093 | 63019 | 71924 | 77897 |
| 321 346 | **GE** | H | *EA* | IL | 78094 | 63020 | 71925 | 77898 |
| 321 347 | **GE** | H | *EA* | IL | 78131 | 63105 | 71991 | 78280 |
| 321 348 | **GE** | H | *EA* | IL | 78132 | 63106 | 71992 | 78281 |
| 321 349 | **GE** | H | *EA* | IL | 78133 | 63107 | 71993 | 78282 |
| 321 350 | **GE** | H | *EA* | IL | 78134 | 63108 | 71994 | 78283 |
| 321 351 | **GE** | H | *EA* | IL | 78135 | 63109 | 71995 | 78284 |
| 321 352 | **GE** | H | *EA* | IL | 78136 | 63110 | 71996 | 78285 |
| 321 353 | **GE** | H | *EA* | IL | 78137 | 63111 | 71997 | 78286 |
| 321 354 | **GE** | H | *EA* | IL | 78138 | 63112 | 71998 | 78287 |
| 321 355 | **GE** | H | *EA* | IL | 78139 | 63113 | 71999 | 78288 |
| 321 356 | **GE** | H | *EA* | IL | 78140 | 63114 | 72000 | 78289 |
| 321 357 | **GE** | H | *EA* | IL | 78141 | 63115 | 72001 | 78290 |
| 321 358 | **GE** | H | *EA* | IL | 78142 | 63116 | 72002 | 78291 |
| 321 359 | **GE** | H | *EA* | IL | 78143 | 63117 | 72003 | 78292 |
| 321 360 | **GE** | H | *EA* | IL | 78144 | 63118 | 72004 | 78293 |
| 321 361 | **GE** | H | *EA* | IL | 78145 | 63119 | 72005 | 78294 |
| 321 362 | **GE** | H | *EA* | IL | 78146 | 63120 | 72006 | 78295 |
| 321 363 | **GE** | H | *EA* | IL | 78147 | 63121 | 72007 | 78296 |
| 321 364 | **GE** | H | *EA* | IL | 78148 | 63122 | 72008 | 78297 |
| 321 365 | **GE** | H | *EA* | IL | 78149 | 63123 | 72009 | 78298 |
| 321 366 | **GE** | H | *EA* | IL | 78150 | 63124 | 72010 | 78299 |

**Names (carried on TSO):**

| 321 312 | Southend-on-Sea |
|---------|-----------------|
| 321 313 | University of Essex |
| 321 321 | NSPCC ESSEX FULL STOP |
| 321 334 | Amsterdam |
| 321 336 | GEOFFREY FREEMAN ALLEN |
| 321 343 | RSA RAILWAY STUDY ASSOCIATION |
| 321 351 | GURKHA |
| 321 361 | Phoenix |

**Class 321/4.**

**DTCO.** Lot No. 31067 1989–1990. 28/40. 29.8 t.
**MSO.** Lot No. 31068 1989–1990. –/79. 51.6 t.
**TSO.** Lot No. 31069 1989–1990. –/74 2T. 29.2 t.
**DTSO.** Lot No. 31070 1989–1990. –/78. 29.8 t.

**Note:** The DTCOs of 321 438–321 448 units have had 12 First Class seats declassified.

| 321 401 | **FU** | H | *FC* | HE | 78095 | 63063 | 71949 | 77943 |
|---------|--------|---|------|----|-------|-------|-------|-------|
| 321 402 | **FU** | H | *FC* | HE | 78096 | 63064 | 71950 | 77944 |
| 321 403 | **FU** | H | *FC* | HE | 78097 | 63065 | 71951 | 77945 |
| 321 404 | **FU** | H | *FC* | HE | 78098 | 63066 | 71952 | 77946 |
| 321 405 | **SL** | H | *FC* | HE | 78099 | 63067 | 71953 | 77947 |
| 321 406 | **FU** | H | *FC* | HE | 78100 | 63068 | 71954 | 77948 |

| 321 407 | SL | H |    | ZG | 78101 | 63069 | 71955 | 77949 |
| 321 408 | SL | H |    | ZG | 78102 | 63070 | 71956 | 77950 |
| 321 409 | SL | H |    | ZG | 78103 | 63071 | 71957 | 77951 |
| 321 410 | SL | H |    | HE | 78104 | 63072 | 71958 | 77952 |
| 321 411 | LM | H | LM | NN | 78105 | 63073 | 71959 | 77953 |
| 321 412 | LM | H | LM | NN | 78106 | 63074 | 71960 | 77954 |
| 321 413 | SL | H | LM | NN | 78107 | 63075 | 71961 | 77955 |
| 321 414 | SL | H | LM | NN | 78108 | 63076 | 71962 | 77956 |
| 321 415 | SL | H | LM | NN | 78109 | 63077 | 71963 | 77957 |
| 321 416 | SL | H | LM | NN | 78110 | 63078 | 71964 | 77958 |
| 321 417 | SL | H | LM | NN | 78111 | 63079 | 71965 | 77959 |
| 321 418 | SL | H |    | ZG | 78112 | 63080 | 71968 | 77962 |
| 321 419 | SL | H |    | ZG | 78113 | 63081 | 71967 | 77961 |
| 321 420 | SL | H |    | ZG | 78114 | 63082 | 71966 | 77960 |
| 321 421 | SL | H | EA | IL | 78115 | 63083 | 71969 | 77963 |
| 321 422 | SL | H | EA | IL | 78116 | 63084 | 71970 | 77964 |
| 321 423 | SL | H | EA | IL | 78117 | 63085 | 71971 | 77965 |
| 321 424 | NX | H | EA | IL | 78118 | 63086 | 71972 | 77966 |
| 321 425 | SL | H | EA | IL | 78119 | 63087 | 71973 | 77967 |
| 321 426 | NX | H | EA | IL | 78120 | 63088 | 71974 | 77968 |
| 321 427 | NX | H | EA | IL | 78121 | 63089 | 71975 | 77969 |
| 321 428 | NX | H | EA | IL | 78122 | 63090 | 71976 | 77970 |
| 321 429 | NX | H | EA | IL | 78123 | 63091 | 71977 | 77971 |
| 321 430 | NX | H | EA | IL | 78124 | 63092 | 71978 | 77972 |
| 321 431 | SL | H |    | ZG | 78151 | 63125 | 72011 | 78300 |
| 321 432 | SL | H |    | ZG | 78152 | 63126 | 72012 | 78301 |
| 321 433 | SL | H |    | ZG | 78153 | 63127 | 72013 | 78302 |
| 321 434 | SL | H | EA | IL | 78154 | 63128 | 72014 | 78303 |
| 321 435 | SL | H | EA | IL | 78155 | 63129 | 72015 | 78304 |
| 321 436 | SL | H | EA | IL | 78156 | 63130 | 72016 | 78305 |
| 321 437 | SL | H | EA | IL | 78157 | 63131 | 72017 | 78306 |
| 321 438 | GE | H | EA | IL | 78158 | 63132 | 72018 | 78307 |
| 321 439 | GE | H | EA | IL | 78159 | 63133 | 72019 | 78308 |
| 321 440 | GE | H | EA | IL | 78160 | 63134 | 72020 | 78309 |
| 321 441 | GE | H | EA | IL | 78161 | 63135 | 72021 | 78310 |
| 321 442 | GE | H | EA | IL | 78162 | 63136 | 72022 | 78311 |
| 321 443 | GE | H | EA | IL | 78125 | 63099 | 71985 | 78274 |
| 321 444 | GE | H | EA | IL | 78126 | 63100 | 71986 | 78275 |
| 321 445 | GE | H | EA | IL | 78127 | 63101 | 71987 | 78276 |
| 321 446 | 1  | H | EA | IL | 78128 | 63102 | 71988 | 78277 |
| 321 447 | GE | H | EA | IL | 78129 | 63103 | 71989 | 78278 |
| 321 448 | GE | H | EA | IL | 78130 | 63104 | 71990 | 78279 |

**Names (carried on TSO):**

| 321 403 | Stewart Fleming Signalman King's Cross |
| 321 428 | The Essex Commuter |
| 321 444 | Essex Lifeboats |
| 321 446 | George Mullings |

**Class 321/9.** DTSO(A)–MSO–TSO–DTSO(B).

**DTSO(A).** Lot No. 31108 1991. –/70(8). 29.2 t.
**MSO.** Lot No. 31109 1991. –/79. 51.1 t.
**TSO.** Lot No. 31110 1991. –/74 2T. 29.0 t.
**DTSO(B).** Lot No. 31111 1991. –/70(7) 1W. 29.2 t.

| 321 901 | **YR** | H | *NO* | NL | 77990 | 63153 | 72128 | 77993 |
| 321 902 | **YR** | H | *NO* | NL | 77991 | 63154 | 72129 | 77994 |
| 321 903 | **YR** | H | *NO* | NL | 77992 | 63155 | 72130 | 77995 |

# CLASS 322                                              BREL YORK

Units built for use on Stansted Airport services, now in use with ScotRail.

**Formation:** DTSO–MSO–TSO–DTSO.
**Construction:** Steel.
**Traction Motors:** Four Brush TM2141C (268 kW).
**Wheel Arrangement:** 2-2 + Bo-Bo + 2-2 + 2-2.
**Braking:** Disc.                          **Dimensions:** 19.95/19.92 x 2.82 m.
**Bogies:** P7-4 (MSO), T3-7 (others).      **Couplers:** Tightlock.
**Gangways:** Within unit.                  **Control System:** Thyristor.
**Doors:** Sliding.                         **Maximum Speed:** 100 m.p.h.
**Seating Layout:** 3+2 facing.
**Multiple Working:** Within class & with Classes 317, 318, 319, 320, 321 and 323.

**DTSO(A).** Lot No. 31094 1990. –/58. 29.3 t.
**MSO.** Lot No. 31092 1990. –/83. 51.5 t.
**TSO.** Lot No. 31093 1990. –/76 2T. 28.8 t.
**DTSO(B).** Lot No. 31091 1990. –/74(2) 1W. 29.1 t.

| 322 481 | **FS** | H | *SR* | GW | 78163 | 63137 | 72023 | 77985 |
| 322 482 | **FS** | H | *SR* | GW | 78164 | 63138 | 72024 | 77986 |
| 322 483 | **FS** | H | *SR* | GW | 78165 | 63139 | 72025 | 77987 |
| 322 484 | **FS** | H | *SR* | GW | 78166 | 63140 | 72026 | 77988 |
| 322 485 | **FS** | H | *SR* | GW | 78167 | 63141 | 72027 | 77989 |

**Name (carried on DTSO(A)):**

322 481    North Berwick Flyer 1850–2000

# CLASS 323    HUNSLET TRANSPORTATION PROJECTS

Suburban units.

**Formation:** DMSO–PTSO–DMSO.
**Construction:** Welded aluminium alloy.
**Traction Motors:** Four Holec DMKT 52/24 asynchronous of 146 kW.
**Wheel Arrangement:** Bo-Bo + 2-2 + Bo-Bo.
**Braking:** Disc.                          **Dimensions:** 23.37/23.44 x 2.80 m.
**Bogies:** SRP BP62 (DMSO), BT52 (PTSO). **Couplers:** Tightlock.
**Gangways:** Within unit.                  **Control System:** GTO Inverter.
**Doors:** Sliding plug.                     **Maximum Speed:** 90 m.p.h.
**Seating Layout:** 3+2 facing/unidirectional.

**Multiple Working:** Within class & with Classes 317, 318, 319, 320, 321 and 322.

**DMSO(A).** Lot No. 31112 Hunslet 1992–1993. –/98 (* –/82). 41.0 t.
**TSO.** Lot No. 31113 Hunslet 1992–1993. –/88(5) 1T 2W. (* –/80 1T 2W). 39.4 t.
**DMSO(B).** Lot No. 31114 Hunslet 1992–1993. –/98 (* –/82). 41.0 t.

| | | | | | | | |
|---|---|---|---|---|---|---|---|
| 323 201 | **LM** | P | *LM* | SO | 64001 | 72201 | 65001 |
| 323 202 | **LM** | P | *LM* | SO | 64002 | 72202 | 65002 |
| 323 203 | **LM** | P | *LM* | SO | 64003 | 72203 | 65003 |
| 323 204 | **LM** | P | *LM* | SO | 64004 | 72204 | 65004 |
| 323 205 | **LM** | P | *LM* | SO | 64005 | 72205 | 65005 |
| 323 206 | **LM** | P | *LM* | SO | 64006 | 72206 | 65006 |
| 323 207 | **LM** | P | *LM* | SO | 64007 | 72207 | 65007 |
| 323 208 | **LM** | P | *LM* | SO | 64008 | 72208 | 65008 |
| 323 209 | **LM** | P | *LM* | SO | 64009 | 72209 | 65009 |
| 323 210 | **LM** | P | *LM* | SO | 64010 | 72210 | 65010 |
| 323 211 | **LM** | P | *LM* | SO | 64011 | 72211 | 65011 |
| 323 212 | **LM** | P | *LM* | SO | 64012 | 72212 | 65012 |
| 323 213 | **LM** | P | *LM* | SO | 64013 | 72213 | 65013 |
| 323 214 | **LM** | P | *LM* | SO | 64014 | 72214 | 65014 |
| 323 215 | **LM** | P | *LM* | SO | 64015 | 72215 | 65015 |
| 323 216 | **LM** | P | *LM* | SO | 64016 | 72216 | 65016 |
| 323 217 | **LM** | P | *LM* | SO | 64017 | 72217 | 65017 |
| 323 218 | **LM** | P | *LM* | SO | 64018 | 72218 | 65018 |
| 323 219 | **LM** | P | *LM* | SO | 64019 | 72219 | 65019 |
| 323 220 | **LM** | P | *LM* | SO | 64020 | 72220 | 65020 |
| 323 221 | **LM** | P | *LM* | SO | 64021 | 72221 | 65021 |
| 323 222 | **LM** | P | *LM* | SO | 64022 | 72222 | 65022 |
| 323 223 | * **NO** | P | *NO* | LG | 64023 | 72223 | 65023 |
| 323 224 | * **NO** | P | *NO* | LG | 64024 | 72224 | 65024 |
| 323 225 | * **NO** | P | *NO* | LG | 64025 | 72225 | 65025 |
| 323 226 | **NO** | P | *NO* | LG | 64026 | 72226 | 65026 |
| 323 227 | **NO** | P | *NO* | LG | 64027 | 72227 | 65027 |
| 323 228 | **NO** | P | *NO* | LG | 64028 | 72228 | 65028 |
| 323 229 | **NO** | P | *NO* | LG | 64029 | 72229 | 65029 |
| 323 230 | **NO** | P | *NO* | LG | 64030 | 72230 | 65030 |
| 323 231 | **FS** | P | *NO* | LG | 64031 | 72231 | 65031 |
| 323 232 | **NO** | P | *NO* | LG | 64032 | 72232 | 65032 |
| 323 233 | **NO** | P | *NO* | LG | 64033 | 72233 | 65033 |
| 323 234 | **NO** | P | *NO* | LG | 64034 | 72234 | 65034 |
| 323 235 | **NO** | P | *NO* | LG | 64035 | 72235 | 65035 |
| 323 236 | **NO** | P | *NO* | LG | 64036 | 72236 | 65036 |
| 323 237 | **NO** | P | *NO* | LG | 64037 | 72237 | 65037 |
| 323 238 | **NO** | P | *NO* | LG | 64038 | 72238 | 65038 |
| 323 239 | **NO** | P | *NO* | LG | 64039 | 72239 | 65039 |
| 323 240 | **LM** | P | *LM* | SO | 64040 | 72340 | 65040 |
| 323 241 | **LM** | P | *LM* | SO | 64041 | 72341 | 65041 |
| 323 242 | **LM** | P | *LM* | SO | 64042 | 72342 | 65042 |
| 323 243 | **LM** | P | *LM* | SO | 64043 | 72343 | 65043 |

# CLASS 325                                                       ABB DERBY

Postal units based on Class 319s. Compatible with diesel or electric locomotive haulage.

**Formation:** DTPMV–MPMV–TPMV–DTPMV.
**System:** 25 kV AC overhead/750 V DC third rail.
**Construction:** Steel.
**Traction Motors:** Four GEC G315BZ of 268 kW.
**Wheel Arrangement:** 2-2 + Bo-Bo + 2-2 + 2-2.
**Braking:** Disc.                            **Dimensions:** 19.33 x 2.82 m.
**Bogies:** P7-4 (MSO), T3-7 (others).        **Couplers:** Drop-head buckeye.
**Gangways:** None.                           **Control System:** GTO Chopper.
**Doors:** Roller shutter.                    **Maximum Speed:** 100 m.p.h.
**Multiple Working:** Within class.

**DTPMV.** Lot No. 31144 1995. 29.1 t.
**MPMV.** Lot No. 31145 1995. 49.5 t.
**TPMV.** Lot No. 31146 1995. 30.7 t.

| | | | | | | | |
|---|---|---|---|---|---|---|---|
| 325 001 | **RM** | RM *GB* | WB | 68300 | 68340 | 68360 | 68301 |
| 325 002 | **RM** | RM *GB* | WB | 68302 | 68341 | 68361 | 68303 |
| 325 003 | **RM** | RM *GB* | WB | 68304 | 68342 | 68362 | 68305 |
| 325 004 | **RM** | RM *GB* | WB | 68306 | 68343 | 68363 | 68307 |
| 325 005 | **RM** | RM *GB* | WB | 68308 | 68344 | 68364 | 68309 |
| 325 006 | **RM** | RM *GB* | WB | 68310 | 68345 | 68365 | 68311 |
| 325 007 | **RM** | RM *GB* | WB | 68312 | 68346 | 68366 | 68313 |
| 325 008 | **RM** | RM *GB* | WB | 68314 | 68347 | 68367 | 68315 |
| 325 009 | **RM** | RM *GB* | WB | 68316 | 68349 | 68368 | 68317 |
| 325 010 | **RM** | RM | ZI | 68318 | 68348 | 68369 | 68319 |
| 325 011 | **RM** | RM *GB* | WB | 68320 | 68350 | 68370 | 68321 |
| 325 012 | **RM** | RM *GB* | WB | 68322 | 68351 | 68371 | 68323 |
| 325 013 | **RM** | RM *GB* | WB | 68324 | 68352 | 68372 | 68325 |
| 325 014 | **RM** | RM *GB* | WB | 68326 | 68353 | 68373 | 68327 |
| 325 015 | **RM** | RM *GB* | WB | 68328 | 68354 | 68374 | 68329 |
| 325 016 | **RM** | RM *GB* | WB | 68330 | 68355 | 68375 | 68331 |

**Names (carried on one side of each DTPMV):**

325 002     Royal Mail North Wales & North West
325 006     John Grierson
325 008     Peter Howarth CBE

# CLASS 332     HEATHROW EXPRESS     SIEMENS

Dedicated Heathrow Express units. Five units were increased from 4-car to 5-car in 2002. Usually operate in coupled pairs.

**Formations:** Various.
**Construction:** Steel.
**Traction Motors:** Two Siemens monomotors asynchronous of 350 kW.
**Wheel Arrangement:** B-B + 2-2 + 2-2 (+ 2-2) + B-B.

**Braking:** Disc.
**Bogies:** CAF.
**Gangways:** Within unit.
**Doors:** Sliding plug.
**Heating & ventilation:** Air conditioning.
**Seating Layout:** 1: 2+1 facing, 2: 2+2 mainly unidirectional.
**Multiple Working:** Within class.

**Dimensions:** 23.63/23.35 x 2.75 m.
**Couplers:** Scharfenberg 10L.
**Control System:** IGBT Inverter.
**Maximum Speed:** 100 m.p.h.

**332 001–332 007.** DMFO–TSO–PTSO–(TSO)–DMSO.

**DMFO.** CAF 1997–1998. 26/–. 48.8 t.
**72400–72413. TSO.** CAF 1997–1998. –/56 35.8 t.
**72414–72418. TSO.** CAF 2002. –/56 35.8 t.
**PTSO.** CAF 1997–1998. –/44 1TD 1W. 45.6 t.
**DMSO.** CAF 1997–1998. –/48. 48.8 t.
**DMLFO.** CAF 1997–1998. 14/– 1W. 48.8 t.

**Advertising livery:** Vehicles 78401, 78402, 78405, 78406, 78408, 78410, 78412
Royal Bank of Scotland (deep blue).

| 332 001 | **HE** | HE *HE* | OH | 78400 | 72412 | 63400 | | 78401 |
| 332 002 | **HE** | HE *HE* | OH | 78402 | 72409 | 63401 | | 78403 |
| 332 003 | **HE** | HE *HE* | OH | 78404 | 72407 | 63402 | | 78405 |
| 332 004 | **HE** | HE *HE* | OH | 78406 | 72405 | 63403 | | 78407 |
| 332 005 | **HE** | HE *HE* | OH | 78408 | 72411 | 63404 | 72417 | 78409 |
| 332 006 | **HE** | HE *HE* | OH | 78410 | 72410 | 63405 | 72415 | 78411 |
| 332 007 | **HE** | HE *HE* | OH | 78412 | 72401 | 63406 | 72414 | 78413 |

**332 008–332 014.** DMSO–TSO–PTSO–(TSO)–DMLFO.

**Advertising livery:** Vehicles 78414, 78416, 78419, 78421, 78423, 78425, 78427
Royal Bank of Scotland (deep blue).

| 332 008 | **HE** | HE *HE* | OH | 78414 | 72413 | 63407 | 72418 | 78415 |
| 332 009 | **HE** | HE *HE* | OH | 78416 | 72400 | 63408 | 72416 | 78417 |
| 332 010 | **HE** | HE *HE* | OH | 78418 | 72402 | 63409 | | 78419 |
| 332 011 | **HE** | HE *HE* | OH | 78420 | 72403 | 63410 | | 78421 |
| 332 012 | **HE** | HE *HE* | OH | 78422 | 72404 | 63411 | | 78423 |
| 332 013 | **HE** | HE *HE* | OH | 78424 | 72408 | 63412 | | 78425 |
| 332 014 | **HE** | HE *HE* | OH | 78426 | 72406 | 63413 | | 78427 |

# CLASS 333                                          SIEMENS

West Yorkshire area suburban units.

**Formation:** DMSO–PTSO–TSO–DMSO.
**Construction:** Steel.
**Traction Motors:** Two Siemens monomotors asynchronous of 350 kW.
**Wheel Arrangement:** B-B + 2-2 + 2-2 + B-B.
**Braking:** Disc.
**Dimensions:** 23.74 (outer ends)/23.35 (TSO) x 2.75 m.
**Bogies:** CAF.
**Gangways:** Within unit.
**Doors:** Sliding plug.

**Couplers:** Dellner 10L.
**Control System:** IGBT Inverter.
**Maximum Speed:** 100 m.p.h.

**Heating & ventilation:** Air conditioning.
**Seating Layout:** 3+2 facing/unidirectional.
**Multiple Working:** Within class.

**DMSO(A).** (Odd Nos.) CAF 2001. –/90. 50.6 t.
**PTSO.** CAF 2001. –/73(6) 1TD 2W. 46.0 t.
**TSO.** CAF 2002–2003. –/100. 38.5 t.
**DMSO(B).** (Even Nos.) CAF 2001. –/90. 50.0 t.

**Notes:** 333 001–333 008 were made up to 4-car units from 3-car units in 2002.

333 009–333 016 were made up to 4-car units from 3-car units in 2003.

| | | | | | | | | |
|---|---|---|---|---|---|---|---|---|
| 333 001 | **YR** | A | *NO* | NL | 78451 | 74461 | 74477 | 78452 |
| 333 002 | **YR** | A | *NO* | NL | 78453 | 74462 | 74478 | 78454 |
| 333 003 | **YR** | A | *NO* | NL | 78455 | 74463 | 74479 | 78456 |
| 333 004 | **YR** | A | *NO* | NL | 78457 | 74464 | 74480 | 78458 |
| 333 005 | **YR** | A | *NO* | NL | 78459 | 74465 | 74481 | 78460 |
| 333 006 | **YR** | A | *NO* | NL | 78461 | 74466 | 74482 | 78462 |
| 333 007 | **YR** | A | *NO* | NL | 78463 | 74467 | 74483 | 78464 |
| 333 008 | **YR** | A | *NO* | NL | 78465 | 74468 | 74484 | 78466 |
| 333 009 | **YR** | A | *NO* | NL | 78467 | 74469 | 74485 | 78468 |
| 333 010 | **YR** | A | *NO* | NL | 78469 | 74470 | 74486 | 78470 |
| 333 011 | **YR** | A | *NO* | NL | 78471 | 74471 | 74487 | 78472 |
| 333 012 | **YR** | A | *NO* | NL | 78473 | 74472 | 74488 | 78474 |
| 333 013 | **YR** | A | *NO* | NL | 78475 | 74473 | 74489 | 78476 |
| 333 014 | **YR** | A | *NO* | NL | 78477 | 74474 | 74490 | 78478 |
| 333 015 | **YR** | A | *NO* | NL | 78479 | 74475 | 74491 | 78480 |
| 333 016 | **YR** | A | *NO* | NL | 78481 | 74476 | 74492 | 78482 |

**Name:**

333 007    Alderman J Arthur Godwin First Lord Mayor of Bradford 1907

# CLASS 334 JUNIPER ALSTOM BIRMINGHAM

Outer suburban units.

**Formation:** DMSO–PTSO–DMSO.
**Construction:** Steel.
**Traction Motors:** Two Alstom ONIX 800 asynchronous of 270 kW.
**Wheel Arrangement:** 2-Bo + 2-2 + Bo-2.
**Braking:** Disc.                         **Dimensions:** 21.01/19.94 x 2.80 m.
**Bogies:** Alstom LTB3/TBP3.              **Couplers:** Tightlock.
**Gangways:** Within unit.                 **Control System:** IGBT Inverter.
**Doors:** Sliding plug.                   **Maximum Speed:** 90 m.p.h.
**Heating & ventilation:** Pressure heating and ventilation.
**Seating Layout:** 2+2 facing/unidirectional (3+2 in PTSO).
**Multiple Working:** Within class.

**64101–64140. DMSO.** Alstom Birmingham 1999–2001. –/64. 42.6 t.
**PTSO.** Alstom Birmingham 1999–2001. –/55 1TD 1W. 39.4 t.
**65101–65140. DMSO.** Alstom Birmingham 1999–2001. –/64. 42.6 t.

| 334 001 | **SP** | H | *SR* | GW | 64101 | 74301 | 65101 | Donald Dewar |
| 334 002 | **SP** | H | *SR* | GW | 64102 | 74302 | 65102 | |
| 334 003 | **SP** | H | *SR* | GW | 64103 | 74303 | 65103 | |
| 334 004 | **SP** | H | *SR* | GW | 64104 | 74304 | 65104 | |
| 334 005 | **SP** | H | *SR* | GW | 64105 | 74305 | 65105 | |
| 334 006 | **SP** | H | *SR* | GW | 64106 | 74306 | 65106 | |
| 334 007 | **SP** | H | *SR* | GW | 64107 | 74307 | 65107 | |
| 334 008 | **SP** | H | *SR* | GW | 64108 | 74308 | 65108 | |
| 334 009 | **SP** | H | *SR* | GW | 64109 | 74309 | 65109 | |
| 334 010 | **SP** | H | *SR* | GW | 64110 | 74310 | 65110 | |
| 334 011 | **SP** | H | *SR* | GW | 64111 | 74311 | 65111 | |
| 334 012 | **SP** | H | *SR* | GW | 64112 | 74312 | 65112 | |
| 334 013 | **SP** | H | *SR* | GW | 64113 | 74313 | 65113 | |
| 334 014 | **SP** | H | *SR* | GW | 64114 | 74314 | 65114 | |
| 334 015 | **SP** | H | *SR* | GW | 64115 | 74315 | 65115 | |
| 334 016 | **SP** | H | *SR* | GW | 64116 | 74316 | 65116 | |
| 334 017 | **SP** | H | *SR* | GW | 64117 | 74317 | 65117 | |
| 334 018 | **SP** | H | *SR* | GW | 64118 | 74318 | 65118 | |
| 334 019 | **SP** | H | *SR* | GW | 64119 | 74319 | 65119 | |
| 334 020 | **SP** | H | *SR* | GW | 64120 | 74320 | 65120 | |
| 334 021 | **SP** | H | *SR* | GW | 64121 | 74321 | 65121 | Larkhall |
| 334 022 | **SP** | H | *SR* | GW | 64122 | 74322 | 65122 | |
| 334 023 | **SP** | H | *SR* | GW | 64123 | 74323 | 65123 | |
| 334 024 | **SP** | H | *SR* | GW | 64124 | 74324 | 65124 | |
| 334 025 | **SP** | H | *SR* | GW | 64125 | 74325 | 65125 | |
| 334 026 | **SP** | H | *SR* | GW | 64126 | 74326 | 65126 | |
| 334 027 | **SP** | H | *SR* | GW | 64127 | 74327 | 65127 | |
| 334 028 | **SP** | H | *SR* | GW | 64128 | 74328 | 65128 | |
| 334 029 | **SP** | H | *SR* | GW | 64129 | 74329 | 65129 | |
| 334 030 | **SP** | H | *SR* | GW | 64130 | 74330 | 65130 | |
| 334 031 | **SP** | H | *SR* | GW | 64131 | 74331 | 65131 | |
| 334 032 | **SP** | H | *SR* | GW | 64132 | 74332 | 65132 | |
| 334 033 | **SP** | H | *SR* | GW | 64133 | 74333 | 65133 | |
| 334 034 | **SP** | H | *SR* | GW | 64134 | 74334 | 65134 | |
| 334 035 | **SP** | H | *SR* | GW | 64135 | 74335 | 65135 | |
| 334 036 | **SP** | H | *SR* | GW | 64136 | 74336 | 65136 | |
| 334 037 | **SP** | H | *SR* | GW | 64137 | 74337 | 65137 | |
| 334 038 | **SP** | H | *SR* | GW | 64138 | 74338 | 65138 | |
| 334 039 | **SP** | H | *SR* | GW | 64139 | 74339 | 65139 | |
| 334 040 | **SP** | H | *SR* | GW | 64140 | 74340 | 65140 | |

# CLASS 350                    DESIRO UK                    SIEMENS

Outer suburban and long distance units.

**Formation:** DMCO–TCO–PTSO–DMCO.
**Systems:** 25 kV AC overhead (350/1s built with 750 V DC).
**Construction:** Welded aluminium.
**Traction Motors:** 4 Siemens 1TB2016-0GB02 asynchronous of 250 kW.
**Wheel Arrangement:** Bo-Bo + 2-2 + 2-2 + Bo-Bo.

**Braking:** Disc & regenerative.
**Bogies:** SGP SF5000.
**Gangways:** Throughout.
**Doors:** Sliding plug.
**Heating & ventilation:** Air conditioning.
**Seating Layout:** 1: 2+2 facing, 2: 2+2 facing/unidirectional (3+2 in 350/2s).
**Multiple Working:** Within class.

**Dimensions:** 20.34 x 2.79 m.
**Couplers:** Dellner 12.
**Control System:** IGBT Inverter.
**Maximum Speed:** 100 m.p.h.

**Class 350/1.** Original build units owned by Angel Trains. Formerly part of an aborted South West Trains 5-car Class 450/2 order. 2+2 seating.

**DMSO(A).** Siemens Uerdingen 2004–2005. –/60. 48.7 t.
**TCO.** Siemens Uerdingen/Praha 2004–2005. 24/32 1T. 36.2 t.
**PTSO.** Siemens Uerdingen/Praha 2004–2005. –/48(9) 1TD 2W. 45.2 t.
**DMSO(B).** Siemens Uerdingen 2004–2005. –/60. 49.2 t.

| | | | | | | | | |
|---|---|---|---|---|---|---|---|---|
| 350 101 | **LM** | A | *LM* | NN | 63761 | 66811 | 66861 | 63711 |
| 350 102 | **LM** | A | *LM* | NN | 63762 | 66812 | 66862 | 63712 |
| 350 103 | **LM** | A | *LM* | NN | 63765 | 66813 | 66863 | 63713 |
| 350 104 | **LM** | A | *LM* | NN | 63764 | 66814 | 66864 | 63714 |
| 350 105 | **LM** | A | *LM* | NN | 63763 | 66815 | 66888 | 63715 |
| 350 106 | **LM** | A | *LM* | NN | 63766 | 66816 | 66866 | 63716 |
| 350 107 | **LM** | A | *LM* | NN | 63767 | 66817 | 66867 | 63717 |
| 350 108 | **LM** | A | *LM* | NN | 63768 | 66818 | 66865 | 63718 |
| 350 109 | **LM** | A | *LM* | NN | 63769 | 66819 | 66869 | 63719 |
| 350 110 | **LM** | A | *LM* | NN | 63770 | 66820 | 66870 | 63720 |
| 350 111 | **LM** | A | *LM* | NN | 63771 | 66821 | 66871 | 63721 |
| 350 112 | **LM** | A | *LM* | NN | 63772 | 66822 | 66872 | 63722 |
| 350 113 | **LM** | A | *LM* | NN | 63773 | 66823 | 66873 | 63723 |
| 350 114 | **LM** | A | *LM* | NN | 63774 | 66824 | 66874 | 63724 |
| 350 115 | **LM** | A | *LM* | NN | 63775 | 66825 | 66875 | 63725 |
| 350 116 | **LM** | A | *LM* | NN | 63776 | 66826 | 66876 | 63726 |
| 350 117 | **LM** | A | *LM* | NN | 63777 | 66827 | 66877 | 63727 |
| 350 118 | **LM** | A | *LM* | NN | 63778 | 66828 | 66878 | 63728 |
| 350 119 | **LM** | A | *LM* | NN | 63779 | 66829 | 66879 | 63729 |
| 350 120 | **LM** | A | *LM* | NN | 63780 | 66830 | 66880 | 63730 |
| 350 121 | **LM** | A | *LM* | NN | 63781 | 66831 | 66881 | 63731 |
| 350 122 | **LM** | A | *LM* | NN | 63782 | 66832 | 66882 | 63732 |
| 350 123 | **LM** | A | *LM* | NN | 63783 | 66833 | 66883 | 63733 |
| 350 124 | **LM** | A | *LM* | NN | 63784 | 66834 | 66884 | 63734 |
| 350 125 | **LM** | A | *LM* | NN | 63785 | 66835 | 66885 | 63735 |
| 350 126 | **LM** | A | *LM* | NN | 63786 | 66836 | 66886 | 63736 |
| 350 127 | **LM** | A | *LM* | NN | 63787 | 66837 | 66887 | 63737 |
| 350 128 | **LM** | A | *LM* | NN | 63788 | 66838 | 66888 | 63738 |
| 350 129 | **LM** | A | *LM* | NN | 63789 | 66839 | 66889 | 63739 |
| 350 130 | **LM** | A | *LM* | NN | 63790 | 66840 | 66890 | 63740 |

**Class 350/2.** Owned by Porterbrook Leasing. 3+2 seating.

**DMSO(A).** Siemens Uerdingen 2008–2009. –/70. 43.7 t.
**TCO.** Siemens Praha 2008–2009. 24/42 1T. 35.3 t.
**PTSO.** Siemens Praha 2008–2009. –/61(9) 1TD 2W. 42.9 t.
**DMSO(B).** Siemens Uerdingen 2008–2009. –/70. 44.2 t.

| 350 231 | LM | P | *LM* | NN | 61431 | 65231 | 67531 | 61531 |
| 350 232 | LM | P | *LM* | NN | 61432 | 65232 | 67532 | 61532 |
| 350 233 | LM | P | *LM* | NN | 61433 | 65233 | 67533 | 61533 |
| 350 234 | LM | P | *LM* | NN | 61434 | 65234 | 67534 | 61534 |
| 350 235 | LM | P | *LM* | NN | 61435 | 65235 | 67535 | 61535 |
| 350 236 | LM | P | *LM* | NN | 61436 | 65236 | 67536 | 61536 |
| 350 237 | LM | P | *LM* | NN | 61437 | 65237 | 67537 | 61537 |
| 350 238 | LM | P | *LM* | NN | 61438 | 65238 | 67538 | 61538 |
| 350 239 | LM | P | *LM* | NN | 61439 | 65239 | 67539 | 61539 |
| 350 240 | LM | P | *LM* | NN | 61440 | 65240 | 67540 | 61540 |
| 350 241 | LM | P | *LM* | NN | 61441 | 65241 | 67541 | 61541 |
| 350 242 | LM | P | *LM* | NN | 61442 | 65242 | 67542 | 61542 |
| 350 243 | LM | P | *LM* | NN | 61443 | 65243 | 67543 | 61543 |
| 350 244 | LM | P | *LM* | NN | 61444 | 65244 | 67544 | 61544 |
| 350 245 | LM | P | *LM* | NN | 61445 | 65245 | 67545 | 61545 |
| 350 246 | LM | P | *LM* | NN | 61446 | 65246 | 67546 | 61546 |
| 350 247 | LM | P | *LM* | NN | 61447 | 65247 | 67546 | 61547 |
| 350 248 | LM | P | *LM* | NN | 61448 | 65248 | 67548 | 61548 |
| 350 249 | LM | P | *LM* | NN | 61449 | 65249 | 67549 | 61549 |
| 350 250 | LM | P | *LM* | NN | 61450 | 65250 | 67550 | 61550 |
| 350 251 | LM | P | *LM* | NN | 61451 | 65251 | 67551 | 61551 |
| 350 252 | LM | P | *LM* | NN | 61452 | 65252 | 67552 | 61552 |
| 350 253 | LM | P | *LM* | NN | 61453 | 65253 | 67553 | 61553 |
| 350 254 | LM | P | *LM* | NN | 61454 | 65254 | 67554 | 61554 |
| 350 255 | LM | P | *LM* | NN | 61455 | 65255 | 67555 | 61555 |
| 350 256 | LM | P | *LM* | NN | 61456 | 65256 | 67556 | 61556 |
| 350 257 | LM | P | *LM* | NN | 61457 | 65257 | 67557 | 61557 |
| 350 258 | LM | P | *LM* | NN | 61458 | 65258 | 67558 | 61558 |
| 350 259 | LM | P | *LM* | NN | 61459 | 65259 | 67559 | 61559 |
| 350 260 | LM | P | *LM* | NN | 61460 | 65260 | 67560 | 61560 |
| 350 261 | LM | P | *LM* | NN | 61461 | 65261 | 67561 | 61561 |
| 350 262 | LM | P | *LM* | NN | 61462 | 65262 | 67562 | 61562 |
| 350 263 | LM | P | *LM* | NN | 61463 | 65263 | 67563 | 61563 |
| 350 264 | LM | P | *LM* | NN | 61464 | 65264 | 67564 | 61564 |
| 350 265 | LM | P | *LM* | NN | 61465 | 65265 | 67565 | 61565 |
| 350 266 | LM | P | *LM* | NN | 61466 | 65266 | 67566 | 61566 |
| 350 267 | LM | P | *LM* | NN | 61467 | 65267 | 67567 | 61567 |

# CLASS 357 ELECTROSTAR
## ADTRANZ/BOMBARDIER DERBY

Provision for 750 V DC supply if required.

**Formation:** DMSO–MSO–PTSO–DMSO.
**Construction:** Welded aluminium alloy underframe, sides and roof with steel ends. All sections bolted together.
**Traction Motors:** Two Adtranz asynchronous of 250 kW.
**Wheel Arrangement:** 2-Bo + 2-Bo + 2-2 + Bo-2.
**Braking:** Disc & regenerative.  **Dimensions:** 20.40/19.99 x 2.80 m.
**Bogies:** Adtranz P3-25/T3-25.  **Couplers:** Tightlock.
**Gangways:** Within unit.  **Control System:** IGBT Inverter.

**Doors:** Sliding plug.      **Maximum Speed:** 100 m.p.h.
**Heating & ventilation:** Air conditioning.
**Seating Layout:** 3+2 facing/unidirectional.
**Multiple Working:** Within class.

**Class 357/0.** Owned by Porterbrook Leasing.

**DMSO(A).** Adtranz Derby 1999–2001. –/71. 40.7 t.
**MSO.** Adtranz Derby 1999–2001. –/78. 36.7 t.
**PTSO.** Adtranz Derby 1999–2001. –/58(4) 1TD 2W. 39.5 t.
**DMSO(B).** Adtranz Derby 1999–2001. –/71. 40.7 t.

**Advertising livery:**
357 010 c2c "green train" (green with purple doors).

| | | | | | | | | |
|---|---|---|---|---|---|---|---|---|
| 357 001 | NC | P | C2 | EM | 67651 | 74151 | 74051 | 67751 |
| 357 002 | C2 | P | C2 | EM | 67652 | 74152 | 74052 | 67752 |
| 357 003 | NC | P | C2 | EM | 67653 | 74153 | 74053 | 67753 |
| 357 004 | NC | P | C2 | EM | 67654 | 74154 | 74054 | 67754 |
| 357 005 | C2 | P | C2 | EM | 67655 | 74155 | 74055 | 67755 |
| 357 006 | C2 | P | C2 | EM | 67656 | 74156 | 74056 | 67756 |
| 357 007 | C2 | P | C2 | EM | 67657 | 74157 | 74057 | 67757 |
| 357 008 | C2 | P | C2 | EM | 67658 | 74158 | 74058 | 67758 |
| 357 009 | C2 | P | C2 | EM | 67659 | 74159 | 74059 | 67759 |
| 357 010 | AL | P | C2 | EM | 67660 | 74160 | 74060 | 67760 |
| 357 011 | C2 | P | C2 | EM | 67661 | 74161 | 74061 | 67761 |
| 357 012 | C2 | P | C2 | EM | 67662 | 74162 | 74062 | 67762 |
| 357 013 | C2 | P | C2 | EM | 67663 | 74163 | 74063 | 67763 |
| 357 014 | C2 | P | C2 | EM | 67664 | 74164 | 74064 | 67764 |
| 357 015 | C2 | P | C2 | EM | 67665 | 74165 | 74065 | 67765 |
| 357 016 | C2 | P | C2 | EM | 67666 | 74166 | 74066 | 67766 |
| 357 017 | C2 | P | C2 | EM | 67667 | 74167 | 74067 | 67767 |
| 357 018 | C2 | P | C2 | EM | 67668 | 74168 | 74068 | 67768 |
| 357 019 | C2 | P | C2 | EM | 67669 | 74169 | 74069 | 67769 |
| 357 020 | C2 | P | C2 | EM | 67670 | 74170 | 74070 | 67770 |
| 357 021 | C2 | P | C2 | EM | 67671 | 74171 | 74071 | 67771 |
| 357 022 | C2 | P | C2 | EM | 67672 | 74172 | 74072 | 67772 |
| 357 023 | C2 | P | C2 | EM | 67673 | 74173 | 74073 | 67773 |
| 357 024 | C2 | P | C2 | EM | 67674 | 74174 | 74074 | 67774 |
| 357 025 | C2 | P | C2 | EM | 67675 | 74175 | 74075 | 67775 |
| 357 026 | C2 | P | C2 | EM | 67676 | 74176 | 74076 | 67776 |
| 357 027 | C2 | P | C2 | EM | 67677 | 74177 | 74077 | 67777 |
| 357 028 | C2 | P | C2 | EM | 67678 | 74178 | 74078 | 67778 |
| 357 029 | C2 | P | C2 | EM | 67679 | 74179 | 74079 | 67779 |
| 357 030 | NC | P | C2 | EM | 67680 | 74180 | 74080 | 67780 |
| 357 031 | NC | P | C2 | EM | 67681 | 74181 | 74081 | 67781 |
| 357 032 | NC | P | C2 | EM | 67682 | 74182 | 74082 | 67782 |
| 357 033 | NC | P | C2 | EM | 67683 | 74183 | 74083 | 67783 |
| 357 034 | NC | P | C2 | EM | 67684 | 74184 | 74084 | 67784 |
| 357 035 | NC | P | C2 | EM | 67685 | 74185 | 74085 | 67785 |
| 357 036 | NC | P | C2 | EM | 67686 | 74186 | 74086 | 67786 |
| 357 037 | NC | P | C2 | EM | 67687 | 74187 | 74087 | 67787 |
| 357 038 | NC | P | C2 | EM | 67688 | 74188 | 74088 | 67788 |

3/11

| 357 039 | NC | P | C2 | EM | 67689 | 74189 | 74089 | 67789 |
| 357 040 | NC | P | C2 | EM | 67690 | 74190 | 74090 | 67790 |
| 357 041 | NC | P | C2 | EM | 67691 | 74191 | 74091 | 67791 |
| 357 042 | C2 | P | C2 | EM | 67692 | 74192 | 74092 | 67792 |
| 357 043 | C2 | P | C2 | EM | 67693 | 74193 | 74093 | 67793 |
| 357 044 | NC | P | C2 | EM | 67694 | 74194 | 74094 | 67794 |
| 357 045 | C2 | P | C2 | EM | 67695 | 74195 | 74095 | 67795 |
| 357 046 | C2 | P | C2 | EM | 67696 | 74196 | 74096 | 67796 |

**Names (carried on DMSO(A) and DMSO(B) (one plate on each)):**

| 357 001 | BARRY FLAXMAN |
| 357 002 | ARTHUR LEWIS STRIDE 1841–1922 |
| 357 003 | JASON LEONARD |
| 357 004 | TONY AMOS |
| 357 011 | JOHN LOWING |
| 357 028 | London, Tilbury & Southend Railway 1854–2004 |
| 357 029 | THOMAS WHITELEGG 1840–1922 |
| 357 030 | ROBERT HARBEN WHITELEGG 1871–1957 |

**Class 357/2.** Owned by Angel Trains.

**DMSO(A).** Bombardier Derby 2001–2002. –/71. 40.7 t.
**MSO.** Bombardier Derby 2001–2002. –/78. 36.7 t.
**PTSO.** Bombardier Derby 2001–2002. –/58(4) 1TD 2W. 39.5 t.
**DMSO(B).** Bombardier Derby 2001–2002. –/71. 40.7 t.

| 357 201 | C2 | A | C2 | EM | 68601 | 74701 | 74601 | 68701 |
| 357 202 | C2 | A | C2 | EM | 68602 | 74702 | 74602 | 68702 |
| 357 203 | NC | A | C2 | EM | 68603 | 74703 | 74603 | 68703 |
| 357 204 | C2 | A | C2 | EM | 68604 | 74704 | 74604 | 68704 |
| 357 205 | C2 | A | C2 | EM | 68605 | 74705 | 74605 | 68705 |
| 357 206 | C2 | A | C2 | EM | 68606 | 74706 | 74606 | 68706 |
| 357 207 | C2 | A | C2 | EM | 68607 | 74707 | 74607 | 68707 |
| 357 208 | C2 | A | C2 | EM | 68608 | 74708 | 74608 | 68708 |
| 357 209 | C2 | A | C2 | EM | 68609 | 74709 | 74609 | 68709 |
| 357 210 | C2 | A | C2 | EM | 68610 | 74710 | 74610 | 68710 |
| 357 211 | C2 | A | C2 | EM | 68611 | 74711 | 74611 | 68711 |
| 357 212 | C2 | A | C2 | EM | 68612 | 74712 | 74612 | 68712 |
| 357 213 | C2 | A | C2 | EM | 68613 | 74713 | 74613 | 68713 |
| 357 214 | C2 | A | C2 | EM | 68614 | 74714 | 74614 | 68714 |
| 357 215 | C2 | A | C2 | EM | 68615 | 74715 | 74615 | 68715 |
| 357 216 | C2 | A | C2 | EM | 68616 | 74716 | 74616 | 68716 |
| 357 217 | C2 | A | C2 | EM | 68617 | 74717 | 74617 | 68717 |
| 357 218 | C2 | A | C2 | EM | 68618 | 74718 | 74618 | 68718 |
| 357 219 | NC | A | C2 | EM | 68619 | 74719 | 74619 | 68719 |
| 357 220 | C2 | A | C2 | EM | 68620 | 74720 | 74620 | 68720 |
| 357 221 | C2 | A | C2 | EM | 68621 | 74721 | 74621 | 68721 |
| 357 222 | C2 | A | C2 | EM | 68622 | 74722 | 74622 | 68722 |
| 357 223 | C2 | A | C2 | EM | 68623 | 74723 | 74623 | 68723 |
| 357 224 | C2 | A | C2 | EM | 68624 | 74724 | 74624 | 68724 |
| 357 225 | C2 | A | C2 | EM | 68625 | 74725 | 74625 | 68725 |
| 357 226 | C2 | A | C2 | EM | 68626 | 74726 | 74626 | 68726 |

| 357 227 | **C2** | A | *C2* | EM | 68627 | 74727 | 74627 | 68727 |
| 357 228 | **C2** | A | *C2* | EM | 68628 | 74728 | 74628 | 68728 |

**Names (carried on DMSO(A) and DMSO(B) (one plate on each)):**

| 357 201 | KEN BIRD | | 357 207 | JOHN PAGE |
| 357 202 | KENNY MITCHELL | | 357 208 | DAVE DAVIS |
| 357 203 | HENRY PUMFRETT | | 357 209 | JAMES SNELLING |
| 357 204 | DEREK FOWERS | | 357 213 | UPMINSTER I.E.C.C. |
| 357 205 | JOHN D'SILVA | | 357 217 | ALLAN BURNELL |
| 357 206 | MARTIN AUNGIER | | | |

## CLASS 360/0              DESIRO UK              SIEMENS

Outer suburban/express units.

**Formation:** DMCO–PTSO–TSO–DMCO.
**Construction:** Welded aluminium.
**Traction Motors:** 4 Siemens 1TB2016-0GB02 asynchronous of 250 kW.
**Wheel Arrangement:** Bo-Bo + 2-2 + 2-2 + Bo-Bo.
**Braking:** Disc & regenerative.          **Dimensions:** 20.34 x 2.80 m.
**Bogies:** SGP SF5000.                    **Couplers:** Dellner 12.
**Gangways:** Within unit.                 **Control System:** IGBT Inverter.
**Doors:** Sliding plug.                   **Maximum Speed:** 100 m.p.h.
**Heating & ventilation:** Air conditioning.
**Seating Layout:** 1: 2+2 facing, 2: 3+2 facing/unidirectional.
**Multiple Working:** Within class.
**DMCO(A).** Siemens Uerdingen 2002–2003. 8/59. 45.0 t.
**PTSO.** Siemens Wien (Vienna) 2002–2003. –/60(9) 1TD 2W. 43.0 t.
**TSO.** Siemens Wien (Vienna) 2002–2003. –/78. 35.0 t.
**DMCO(B).** Siemens Uerdingen 2002–2003. 8/59. 45.0 t.

| 360 101 | **FB** | A | *EA* | IL | 65551 | 72551 | 74551 | 68551 |
| 360 102 | **FB** | A | *EA* | IL | 65552 | 72552 | 74552 | 68552 |
| 360 103 | **FB** | A | *EA* | IL | 65553 | 72553 | 74553 | 68553 |
| 360 104 | **FB** | A | *EA* | IL | 65554 | 72554 | 74554 | 68554 |
| 360 105 | **FB** | A | *EA* | IL | 65555 | 72555 | 74555 | 68555 |
| 360 106 | **FB** | A | *EA* | IL | 65556 | 72556 | 74556 | 68556 |
| 360 107 | **FB** | A | *EA* | IL | 65557 | 72557 | 74557 | 68557 |
| 360 108 | **FB** | A | *EA* | IL | 65558 | 72558 | 74558 | 68558 |
| 360 109 | **FB** | A | *EA* | IL | 65559 | 72559 | 74559 | 68559 |
| 360 110 | **FB** | A | *EA* | IL | 65560 | 72560 | 74560 | 68560 |
| 360 111 | **FB** | A | *EA* | IL | 65561 | 72561 | 74561 | 68561 |
| 360 112 | **FB** | A | *EA* | IL | 65562 | 72562 | 74562 | 68562 |
| 360 113 | **FB** | A | *EA* | IL | 65563 | 72563 | 74563 | 68563 |
| 360 114 | **FB** | A | *EA* | IL | 65564 | 72564 | 74564 | 68564 |
| 360 115 | **NX** | A | *EA* | IL | 65565 | 72565 | 74565 | 68565 |
| 360 116 | **FB** | A | *EA* | IL | 65566 | 72566 | 74566 | 68566 |
| 360 117 | **FB** | A | *EA* | IL | 65567 | 72567 | 74567 | 68567 |
| 360 118 | **FB** | A | *EA* | IL | 65568 | 72568 | 74568 | 68568 |
| 360 119 | **FB** | A | *EA* | IL | 65569 | 72569 | 74569 | 68569 |
| 360 120 | **FB** | A | *EA* | IL | 65570 | 72570 | 74570 | 68570 |
| 360 121 | **FB** | A | *EA* | IL | 65571 | 72571 | 74571 | 68571 |

# CLASS 360/2          DESIRO UK          SIEMENS

4-car Class 350 testbed units rebuilt for use by Heathrow Express on Paddington–Heathrow Airport stopping services ("Heathrow Connect").

Original 4-car sets 360 201–360 204 were made up to 5-cars during 2007 using additional TSOs. A fifth unit (360 205) was delivered in late 2005 as a 5-car set.

**Formation:** DMSO–PTSO–TSO–TSO–DMSO.
**Construction:** Welded aluminium.
**Traction Motors:** 4 Siemens 1TB2016-0GB02 asynchronous of 250 kW.
**Wheel Arrangement:** Bo-Bo + 2-2 + 2-2 + 2-2 + Bo-Bo.
**Braking:** Disc & regenerative.          **Dimensions:** 20.34 x 2.80 m.
**Bogies:** SGP SF5000.                     **Couplers:** Dellner 12.
**Gangways:** Within unit.                  **Control System:** IGBT Inverter.
**Doors:** Sliding plug.                    **Maximum Speed:** 100 m.p.h.
**Heating & ventilation:** Air conditioning.
**Seating Layout:** 3+2 facing/unidirectional.
**Multiple Working:** Within class.

**DMSO(A).** Siemens Uerdingen 2002–2006. –/63. 44.8 t.
**PTSO.** Siemens Uerdingen 2002–2006. –/57(9) 1TD 2W. 44.2 t.
**TSO.** Siemens Uerdingen 2005–2006. –/74. 35.3 t.
**TSO.** Siemens Uerdingen 2002–2006. –/74. 34.1 t.
**DMSO(B).** Siemens Uerdingen 2002–2006. –/63. 44.4 t.

| 360 201 | **HC** | HE *HC* | OH | 78431 | 63421 | 72431 | 72421 | 78441 |
| 360 202 | **HC** | HE *HC* | OH | 78432 | 63422 | 72432 | 72422 | 78442 |
| 360 203 | **HC** | HE *HC* | OH | 78433 | 63423 | 72433 | 72423 | 78443 |
| 360 204 | **HC** | HE *HC* | OH | 78434 | 63424 | 72434 | 72424 | 78444 |
| 360 205 | **HC** | HE *HC* | OH | 78435 | 63425 | 72435 | 72425 | 78445 |

# CLASS 365  NETWORKER EXPRESS  ABB YORK

Outer suburban units.

**Formations:** DMCO–TSO–PTSO–DMCO.
**Systems:** 25 kV AC overhead but with 750 V DC third rail capability (units marked * were formerly used on DC lines in the South-East).
**Construction:** Welded aluminium alloy.
**Traction Motors:** Four GEC-Alsthom G354CX asynchronous of 157 kW.
**Wheel Arrangement:** Bo-Bo + 2-2 + 2-2 + Bo-Bo.
**Braking:** Disc & rheostatic.
**Dimensions:** 20.89/20.06 x 2.81 m.
**Bogies:** ABB P3-16/T3-16.              **Couplers:** Tightlock.
**Gangways:** Within unit.                **Control System:** GTO Inverter.
**Doors:** Sliding plug.                  **Maximum Speed:** 100 m.p.h.
**Seating Layout:** 1: 2+2 facing, 2: 2+2 facing.
**Multiple Working:** Within class only.

**DMCO(A).** Lot No. 31133 1994–1995. 12/56. 41.7 t.
**TSO.** Lot No. 31134 1994–1995. –/65 1TD (* –/64 1TD). 32.9 t.

**PTSO**. Lot No. 31135 1994–1995. –/68 1T. 34.6 t.
**DMCO(B)**. Lot No. 31136 1994–1995. 12/56. 41.7 t.

**Note:** Vehicle 65960 of 365 526 is stored at ZC, whilst the others are at ZN.

**Advertising liveries:**

365 510 Cambridge & Ely; Cathedral cities (blue & white with various images).
365 519 Peterborough; environment capital (blue & white with various images).
365 531 Nelson's County; Norfolk (blue & white with various images).
365 540 Garden cities of Hertfordshire (blue & white with various images).

| | | | | | | | | |
|---|---|---|---|---|---|---|---|---|
| 365 501 | * | **FU** | H | *FC* | HE | 65894 | 72241 | 72240 | 65935 |
| 365 502 | * | **FU** | H | *FC* | HE | 65895 | 72243 | 72242 | 65936 |
| 365 503 | * | **FU** | H | *FC* | HE | 65896 | 72245 | 72244 | 65937 |
| 365 504 | * | **FU** | H | *FC* | HE | 65897 | 72247 | 72246 | 65938 |
| 365 505 | * | **FU** | H | *FC* | HE | 65898 | 72249 | 72248 | 65939 |
| 365 506 | * | **FU** | H | *FC* | HE | 65899 | 72251 | 72250 | 65940 |
| 365 507 | * | **FU** | H | *FC* | HE | 65900 | 72253 | 72252 | 65941 |
| 365 508 | * | **FU** | H | *FC* | HE | 65901 | 72255 | 72254 | 65942 |
| 365 509 | * | **FU** | H | *FC* | HE | 65902 | 72257 | 72256 | 65943 |
| 365 510 | * | **AL** | H | *FC* | HE | 65903 | 72259 | 72258 | 65944 |
| 365 511 | * | **FU** | H | *FC* | HE | 65904 | 72261 | 72260 | 65945 |
| 365 512 | * | **FU** | H | *FC* | HE | 65905 | 72263 | 72262 | 65946 |
| 365 513 | * | **FU** | H | *FC* | HE | 65906 | 72265 | 72264 | 65947 |
| 365 514 | * | **FU** | H | *FC* | HE | 65907 | 72267 | 72266 | 65948 |
| 365 515 | * | **FU** | H | *FC* | HE | 65908 | 72269 | 72268 | 65949 |
| 365 516 | * | **FU** | H | *FC* | HE | 65909 | 72271 | 72270 | 65950 |
| 365 517 | | **FU** | H | *FC* | HE | 65910 | 72273 | 72272 | 65951 |
| 365 518 | | **FU** | H | *FC* | HE | 65911 | 72275 | 72274 | 65952 |
| 365 519 | | **AL** | H | *FC* | HE | 65912 | 72277 | 72276 | 65953 |
| 365 520 | | **FU** | H | *FC* | HE | 65913 | 72279 | 72278 | 65954 |
| 365 521 | | **FU** | H | *FC* | HE | 65914 | 72281 | 72280 | 65955 |
| 365 522 | | **FU** | H | *FC* | HE | 65915 | 72283 | 72282 | 65956 |
| 365 523 | | **FU** | H | *FC* | HE | 65916 | 72285 | 72284 | 65957 |
| 365 524 | | **FU** | H | *FC* | HE | 65917 | 72287 | 72286 | 65958 |
| 365 525 | | **FU** | H | *FC* | HE | 65918 | 72289 | 72288 | 65959 |
| 365 526 | | **N** | H | | ZN | 65919 | 72291 | 72290 | 65960 |
| 365 527 | | **FU** | H | *FC* | HE | 65920 | 72293 | 72292 | 65961 |
| 365 528 | | **FU** | H | *FC* | HE | 65921 | 72295 | 72294 | 65962 |
| 365 529 | | **FU** | H | *FC* | HE | 65922 | 72297 | 72296 | 65963 |
| 365 530 | | **FU** | H | *FC* | HE | 65923 | 72299 | 72298 | 65964 |
| 365 531 | | **AL** | H | *FC* | HE | 65924 | 72301 | 72300 | 65965 |
| 365 532 | | **FU** | H | *FC* | HE | 65925 | 72303 | 72302 | 65966 |
| 365 533 | | **FU** | H | *FC* | HE | 65926 | 72305 | 72304 | 65967 |
| 365 534 | | **FU** | H | *FC* | HE | 65927 | 72307 | 72306 | 65968 |
| 365 535 | | **FU** | H | *FC* | HE | 65928 | 72309 | 72308 | 65969 |
| 365 536 | | **FU** | H | *FC* | HE | 65929 | 72311 | 72310 | 65970 |
| 365 537 | | **FU** | H | *FC* | HE | 65930 | 72313 | 72312 | 65971 |
| 365 538 | | **FU** | H | *FC* | HE | 65931 | 72315 | 72314 | 65972 |
| 365 539 | | **FU** | H | *FC* | HE | 65932 | 72317 | 72316 | 65973 |
| 365 540 | | **AL** | H | *FC* | HE | 65933 | 72319 | 72318 | 65974 |
| 365 541 | | **FU** | H | *FC* | HE | 65934 | 72321 | 72320 | 65975 |

**Names (carried on each DMCO):**

| | |
|---|---|
| 365 513 | Hornsey Depot |
| 365 514 | Captain George Vancouver |
| 365 518 | The Fenman |
| 365 527 | Robert Stripe Passengers' Champion |
| 365 530 | The Intalink Partnership |
| 365 536 | Rufus Barnes Chief Executive of London TravelWatch for 25 years |

# CLASS 375 ELECTROSTAR
## ADTRANZ/BOMBARDIER DERBY

Express and outer suburban units.

**Formations:** Various.
**Systems:** 25 kV AC overhead/750 V DC third rail (some third rail only with provision for retro-fitting of AC equipment).
**Construction:** Welded aluminium alloy underframe, sides and roof with steel ends. All sections bolted together.
**Traction Motors:** Two Adtranz asynchronous of 250 kW.
**Wheel Arrangement:** 2-Bo (+ 2-Bo) + 2-2 + Bo-2.

| | |
|---|---|
| **Braking:** Disc & regenerative. | **Dimensions:** 20.40/19.99 x 2.80 m. |
| **Bogies:** Adtranz P3-25/T3-25. | **Couplers:** Dellner 12. |
| **Gangways:** Throughout. | **Control System:** IGBT Inverter. |
| **Doors:** Sliding plug. | **Maximum Speed:** 100 m.p.h. |

**Heating & ventilation:** Air conditioning.
**Seating Layout:** 1: 2+2 facing/unidirectional (seats behind drivers cab in each DMCO). 2: 2+2 facing/unidirectional (except 375/9 – 3+2 facing/unidirectional).
**Multiple Working:** Within class and with Classes 376, 377 and 378.
**Class 375/3.** Express units. 750 V DC only. DMCO–TSO–DMCO.

**DMCO(A).** Bombardier Derby 2001–2002. 12/48. 43.8 t.
**TSO.** Bombardier Derby 2001–2002. –/56 1TD 2W. 35.5 t.
**DMCO(B).** Bombardier Derby 2001–2002. 12/48. 43.8 t.

| | | | | | | |
|---|---|---|---|---|---|---|
| 375 301 | **CN** | H | *SE* | RM | 67921 | 74351 | 67931 |
| 375 302 | **CN** | H | *SE* | RM | 67922 | 74352 | 67932 |
| 375 303 | **CN** | H | *SE* | RM | 67923 | 74353 | 67933 |
| 375 304 | **CN** | H | *SE* | RM | 67924 | 74354 | 67934 |
| 375 305 | **CN** | H | *SE* | RM | 67925 | 74355 | 67935 |
| 375 306 | **CN** | H | *SE* | RM | 67926 | 74356 | 67936 |
| 375 307 | **CN** | H | *SE* | RM | 67927 | 74357 | 67937 |
| 375 308 | **CN** | H | *SE* | RM | 67928 | 74358 | 67938 |
| 375 309 | **CN** | H | *SE* | RM | 67929 | 74359 | 67939 |
| 375 310 | **CN** | H | *SE* | RM | 67930 | 74360 | 67940 |

**Name (carried on TSO):**

375 304    Medway Valley Line 1856–2006

**Class 375/6.** Express units. 25 kV AC/750 V DC. DMCO–MSO–PTSO–DMCO.

**DMCO(A).** Adtranz Derby 1999–2001. 12/48. 46.2 t.
**MSO.** Adtranz Derby 1999–2001. –/66 1T. 40.5 t.
**PTSO.** Adtranz Derby 1999–2001. –/56 1TD 2W. 40.7 t.
**DMCO(B).** Adtranz Derby 1999–2001. 12/48. 46.2 t.

| | | | | | | | | |
|---|---|---|---|---|---|---|---|---|
| 375 601 | **CN** | H | *SE* | RM | 67801 | 74251 | 74201 | 67851 |
| 375 602 | **CN** | H | *SE* | RM | 67802 | 74252 | 74202 | 67852 |
| 375 603 | **CN** | H | *SE* | RM | 67803 | 74253 | 74203 | 67853 |
| 375 604 | **CN** | H | *SE* | RM | 67804 | 74254 | 74204 | 67854 |
| 375 605 | **CN** | H | *SE* | RM | 67805 | 74255 | 74205 | 67855 |
| 375 606 | **CN** | H | *SE* | RM | 67806 | 74256 | 74206 | 67856 |
| 375 607 | **CN** | H | *SE* | RM | 67807 | 74257 | 74207 | 67857 |
| 375 608 | **CN** | H | *SE* | RM | 67808 | 74258 | 74208 | 67858 |
| 375 609 | **CN** | H | *SE* | RM | 67809 | 74259 | 74209 | 67859 |
| 375 610 | **CN** | H | *SE* | RM | 67810 | 74260 | 74210 | 67860 |
| 375 611 | **CN** | H | *SE* | RM | 67811 | 74261 | 74211 | 67861 |
| 375 612 | **CN** | H | *SE* | RM | 67812 | 74262 | 74212 | 67862 |
| 375 613 | **CN** | H | *SE* | RM | 67813 | 74263 | 74213 | 67863 |
| 375 614 | **CN** | H | *SE* | RM | 67814 | 74264 | 74214 | 67864 |
| 375 615 | **CN** | H | *SE* | RM | 67815 | 74265 | 74215 | 67865 |
| 375 616 | **CN** | H | *SE* | RM | 67816 | 74266 | 74216 | 67866 |
| 375 617 | **CN** | H | *SE* | RM | 67817 | 74267 | 74217 | 67867 |
| 375 618 | **CN** | H | *SE* | RM | 67818 | 74268 | 74218 | 67868 |
| 375 619 | **CN** | H | *SE* | RM | 67819 | 74269 | 74219 | 67869 |
| 375 620 | **CN** | H | *SE* | RM | 67820 | 74270 | 74220 | 67870 |
| 375 621 | **CN** | H | *SE* | RM | 67821 | 74271 | 74221 | 67871 |
| 375 622 | **CN** | H | *SE* | RM | 67822 | 74272 | 74222 | 67872 |
| 375 623 | **CN** | H | *SE* | RM | 67823 | 74273 | 74223 | 67873 |
| 375 624 | **CN** | H | *SE* | RM | 67824 | 74274 | 74224 | 67874 |
| 375 625 | **CN** | H | *SE* | RM | 67825 | 74275 | 74225 | 67875 |
| 375 626 | **CN** | H | *SE* | RM | 67826 | 74276 | 74226 | 67876 |
| 375 627 | **CN** | H | *SE* | RM | 67827 | 74277 | 74227 | 67877 |
| 375 628 | **CN** | H | *SE* | RM | 67828 | 74278 | 74228 | 67878 |
| 375 629 | **CN** | H | *SE* | RM | 67829 | 74279 | 74229 | 67879 |
| 375 630 | **CN** | H | *SE* | RM | 67830 | 74280 | 74230 | 67880 |

**Names (carried on one side of each MSO or PTSO):**

| | | | | |
|---|---|---|---|---|
| 375 608 | Bromley Travelwise | | 375 619 | Driver John Neve |
| 375 610 | Royal Tunbridge Wells | | 375 623 | Hospice in the Weald |
| 375 611 | Dr. William Harvey | | | |

**Class 375/7.** Express units. 750 V DC only. DMCO–MSO–TSO–DMCO.

**DMCO(A).** Bombardier Derby 2001–2002. 12/48. 43.8 t.
**MSO.** Bombardier Derby 2001–2002. –/66 1T. 36.4 t.
**TSO.** Bombardier Derby 2001–2002. –/56 1TD 2W. 34.1 t.
**DMCO(B).** Bombardier Derby 2001–2002. 12/48. 43.8 t.

| | | | | | | | | |
|---|---|---|---|---|---|---|---|---|
| 375 701 | **CN** | H | *SE* | RM | 67831 | 74281 | 74231 | 67881 |
| 375 702 | **CN** | H | *SE* | RM | 67832 | 74282 | 74232 | 67882 |
| 375 703 | **CN** | H | *SE* | RM | 67833 | 74283 | 74233 | 67883 |

| | | | | | | | | |
|---|---|---|---|---|---|---|---|---|
| 375 704 | **CN** | H | *SE* | RM | 67834 | 74284 | 74234 | 67884 |
| 375 705 | **CN** | H | *SE* | RM | 67835 | 74285 | 74235 | 67885 |
| 375 706 | **CN** | H | *SE* | RM | 67836 | 74286 | 74236 | 67886 |
| 375 707 | **CN** | H | *SE* | RM | 67837 | 74287 | 74237 | 67887 |
| 375 708 | **CN** | H | *SE* | RM | 67838 | 74288 | 74238 | 67888 |
| 375 709 | **CN** | H | *SE* | RM | 67839 | 74289 | 74239 | 67889 |
| 375 710 | **CN** | H | *SE* | RM | 67840 | 74290 | 74240 | 67890 |
| 375 711 | **CN** | H | *SE* | RM | 67841 | 74291 | 74241 | 67891 |
| 375 712 | **CN** | H | *SE* | RM | 67842 | 74292 | 74242 | 67892 |
| 375 713 | **CN** | H | *SE* | RM | 67843 | 74293 | 74243 | 67893 |
| 375 714 | **CN** | H | *SE* | RM | 67844 | 74294 | 74244 | 67894 |
| 375 715 | **CN** | H | *SE* | RM | 67845 | 74295 | 74245 | 67895 |

**Names (carried on one side of each MSO or TSO):**

| | |
|---|---|
| 375 701 | Kent Air Ambulance Explorer |
| 375 703 | Dickens Traveller |

**Class 375/8.** Express units. 750 V DC only. DMCO–MSO–TSO–DMCO.

**DMCO(A).** Bombardier Derby 2004. 12/48. 43.3 t.
**MSO.** Bombardier Derby 2004. –/66 1T. 39.8 t.
**TSO.** Bombardier Derby 2004. –/52 1TD 2W. 35.9 t.
**DMCO(B).** Bombardier Derby 2004. 12/52. 43.3 t.

| | | | | | | | | |
|---|---|---|---|---|---|---|---|---|
| 375 801 | **CN** | H | *SE* | RM | 73301 | 79001 | 78201 | 73701 |
| 375 802 | **CN** | H | *SE* | RM | 73302 | 79002 | 78202 | 73702 |
| 375 803 | **CN** | H | *SE* | RM | 73303 | 79003 | 78203 | 73703 |
| 375 804 | **CN** | H | *SE* | RM | 73304 | 79004 | 78204 | 73704 |
| 375 805 | **CN** | H | *SE* | RM | 73305 | 79005 | 78205 | 73705 |
| 375 806 | **CN** | H | *SE* | RM | 73306 | 79006 | 78206 | 73706 |
| 375 807 | **CN** | H | *SE* | RM | 73307 | 79007 | 78207 | 73707 |
| 375 808 | **CN** | H | *SE* | RM | 73308 | 79008 | 78208 | 73708 |
| 375 809 | **CN** | H | *SE* | RM | 73309 | 79009 | 78209 | 73709 |
| 375 810 | **CN** | H | *SE* | RM | 73310 | 79010 | 78210 | 73710 |
| 375 811 | **CN** | H | *SE* | RM | 73311 | 79011 | 78211 | 73711 |
| 375 812 | **CN** | H | *SE* | RM | 73312 | 79012 | 78212 | 73712 |
| 375 813 | **CN** | H | *SE* | RM | 73313 | 79013 | 78213 | 73713 |
| 375 814 | **CN** | H | *SE* | RM | 73314 | 79014 | 78214 | 73714 |
| 375 815 | **CN** | H | *SE* | RM | 73315 | 79015 | 78215 | 73715 |
| 375 816 | **CN** | H | *SE* | RM | 73316 | 79016 | 78216 | 73716 |
| 375 817 | **CN** | H | *SE* | RM | 73317 | 79017 | 78217 | 73717 |
| 375 818 | **CN** | H | *SE* | RM | 73318 | 79018 | 78218 | 73718 |
| 375 819 | **CN** | H | *SE* | RM | 73319 | 79019 | 78219 | 73719 |
| 375 820 | **CN** | H | *SE* | RM | 73320 | 79020 | 78220 | 73720 |
| 375 821 | **CN** | H | *SE* | RM | 73321 | 79021 | 78221 | 73721 |
| 375 822 | **CN** | H | *SE* | RM | 73322 | 79022 | 78222 | 73722 |
| 375 823 | **CN** | H | *SE* | RM | 73323 | 79023 | 78223 | 73723 |
| 375 824 | **CN** | H | *SE* | RM | 73324 | 79024 | 78224 | 73724 |
| 375 825 | **CN** | H | *SE* | RM | 73325 | 79025 | 78225 | 73725 |
| 375 826 | **CN** | H | *SE* | RM | 73326 | 79026 | 78226 | 73726 |
| 375 827 | **CN** | H | *SE* | RM | 73327 | 79027 | 78227 | 73727 |
| 375 828 | **CN** | H | *SE* | RM | 73328 | 79028 | 78228 | 73728 |

| 375 829 | **CN** | H | *SE* | RM | 73329 | 79029 | 78229 | 73729 |
| 375 830 | **CN** | H | *SE* | RM | 73330 | 79030 | 78230 | 73730 |

**Name (carried on one side of each MSO or TSO):**

375 830    City of London

**Class 375/9.** Outer suburban units. 750 V DC only. DMCO–MSO–TSO–DMCO.

**DMCO(A).** Bombardier Derby 2003–2004. 12/59. 43.4 t.
**MSO.** Bombardier Derby 2003–2004. –/73 1T. 39.3 t.
**TSO.** Bombardier Derby 2003–2004. –/59 1TD 2W. 35.6 t.
**DMCO(B).** Bombardier Derby 2003–2004. 12/59. 43.4 t.

| 375 901 | **CN** | H | *SE* | RM | 73331 | 79031 | 79061 | 73731 |
| 375 902 | **CN** | H | *SE* | RM | 73332 | 79032 | 79062 | 73732 |
| 375 903 | **CN** | H | *SE* | RM | 73333 | 79033 | 79063 | 73733 |
| 375 904 | **CN** | H | *SE* | RM | 73334 | 79034 | 79064 | 73734 |
| 375 905 | **CN** | H | *SE* | RM | 73335 | 79035 | 79065 | 73735 |
| 375 906 | **CN** | H | *SE* | RM | 73336 | 79036 | 79066 | 73736 |
| 375 907 | **CN** | H | *SE* | RM | 73337 | 79037 | 79067 | 73737 |
| 375 908 | **CN** | H | *SE* | RM | 73338 | 79038 | 79068 | 73738 |
| 375 909 | **CN** | H | *SE* | RM | 73339 | 79039 | 79069 | 73739 |
| 375 910 | **CN** | H | *SE* | RM | 73340 | 79040 | 79070 | 73740 |
| 375 911 | **CN** | H | *SE* | RM | 73341 | 79041 | 79071 | 73741 |
| 375 912 | **CN** | H | *SE* | RM | 73342 | 79042 | 79072 | 73742 |
| 375 913 | **CN** | H | *SE* | RM | 73343 | 79043 | 79073 | 73743 |
| 375 914 | **CN** | H | *SE* | RM | 73344 | 79044 | 79074 | 73744 |
| 375 915 | **CN** | H | *SE* | RM | 73345 | 79045 | 79075 | 73745 |
| 375 916 | **CN** | H | *SE* | RM | 73346 | 79046 | 79076 | 73746 |
| 375 917 | **CN** | H | *SE* | RM | 73347 | 79047 | 79077 | 73747 |
| 375 918 | **CN** | H | *SE* | RM | 73348 | 79048 | 79078 | 73748 |
| 375 919 | **CN** | H | *SE* | RM | 73349 | 79049 | 79079 | 73749 |
| 375 920 | **CN** | H | *SE* | RM | 73350 | 79050 | 79080 | 73750 |
| 375 921 | **CN** | H | *SE* | RM | 73351 | 79051 | 79081 | 73751 |
| 375 922 | **CN** | H | *SE* | RM | 73352 | 79052 | 79082 | 73752 |
| 375 923 | **CN** | H | *SE* | RM | 73353 | 79053 | 79083 | 73753 |
| 375 924 | **CN** | H | *SE* | RM | 73354 | 79054 | 79084 | 73754 |
| 375 925 | **CN** | H | *SE* | RM | 73355 | 79055 | 79085 | 73755 |
| 375 926 | **CN** | H | *SE* | RM | 73356 | 79056 | 79086 | 73756 |
| 375 927 | **CN** | H | *SE* | RM | 73357 | 79057 | 79087 | 73757 |

# CLASS 376    ELECTROSTAR    BOMBARDIER DERBY

Inner suburban units.

**Formation:** DMSO–MSO–TSO–MSO–DMSO.
**System:** 750 V DC third rail.
**Construction:** Welded aluminium alloy underframe, sides and roof with steel ends. All sections bolted together.
**Traction Motors:** Two Bombardier asynchronous of 250 kW.
**Wheel Arrangement:** 2-Bo + 2-Bo + 2-2 + Bo-2 + Bo-2.
**Braking:** Disc & regenerative.          **Dimensions:** 20.40/19.99 x 2.80 m.

**Bogies:** Bombardier P3-25/T3-25.          **Couplers:** Dellner 12.
**Gangways:** Within unit.                    **Control System:** IGBT Inverter.
**Doors:** Sliding.                           **Maximum Speed:** 75 m.p.h.
**Heating & ventilation:** Pressure heating and ventilation.
**Seating Layout:** 2+2 low density facing.
**Multiple Working:** Within class and with Classes 375, 377 and 378.

**DMSO(A).** Bombardier Derby 2004–2005. –/36(6) 1W. 42.1 t.
**MSO.** Bombardier Derby 2004–2005. –/48. 36.2 t.
**TSO.** Bombardier Derby 2004–2005. –/48. 36.3 t.
**DMSO(B).** Bombardier Derby 2004–2005. –/36(6) 1W. 42.1 t.

| | | | | | | | | | |
|---|---|---|---|---|---|---|---|---|---|
| 376 001 | **CN** | H | *SE* | SG | 61101 | 63301 | 64301 | 63501 | 61601 |
| 376 002 | **CN** | H | *SE* | SG | 61102 | 63302 | 64302 | 63502 | 61602 |
| 376 003 | **CN** | H | *SE* | SG | 61103 | 63303 | 64303 | 63503 | 61603 |
| 376 004 | **CN** | H | *SE* | SG | 61104 | 63304 | 64304 | 63504 | 61604 |
| 376 005 | **CN** | H | *SE* | SG | 61105 | 63305 | 64305 | 63505 | 61605 |
| 376 006 | **CN** | H | *SE* | SG | 61106 | 63306 | 64306 | 63506 | 61606 |
| 376 007 | **CN** | H | *SE* | SG | 61107 | 63307 | 64307 | 63507 | 61607 |
| 376 008 | **CN** | H | *SE* | SG | 61108 | 63308 | 64308 | 63508 | 61608 |
| 376 009 | **CN** | H | *SE* | SG | 61109 | 63309 | 64309 | 63509 | 61609 |
| 376 010 | **CN** | H | *SE* | SG | 61110 | 63310 | 64310 | 63510 | 61610 |
| 376 011 | **CN** | H | *SE* | SG | 61111 | 63311 | 64311 | 63511 | 61611 |
| 376 012 | **CN** | H | *SE* | SG | 61112 | 63312 | 64312 | 63512 | 61612 |
| 376 013 | **CN** | H | *SE* | SG | 61113 | 63313 | 64313 | 63513 | 61613 |
| 376 014 | **CN** | H | *SE* | SG | 61114 | 63314 | 64314 | 63514 | 61614 |
| 376 015 | **CN** | H | *SE* | SG | 61115 | 63315 | 64315 | 63515 | 61615 |
| 376 016 | **CN** | H | *SE* | SG | 61116 | 63316 | 64316 | 63516 | 61616 |
| 376 017 | **CN** | H | *SE* | SG | 61117 | 63317 | 64317 | 63517 | 61617 |
| 376 018 | **CN** | H | *SE* | SG | 61118 | 63318 | 64318 | 63518 | 61618 |
| 376 019 | **CN** | H | *SE* | SG | 61119 | 63319 | 64319 | 63519 | 61619 |
| 376 020 | **CN** | H | *SE* | SG | 61120 | 63320 | 64320 | 63520 | 61620 |
| 376 021 | **CN** | H | *SE* | SG | 61121 | 63321 | 64321 | 63521 | 61621 |
| 376 022 | **CN** | H | *SE* | SG | 61122 | 63322 | 64322 | 63522 | 61622 |
| 376 023 | **CN** | H | *SE* | SG | 61123 | 63323 | 64323 | 63523 | 61623 |
| 376 024 | **CN** | H | *SE* | SG | 61124 | 63324 | 64324 | 63524 | 61624 |
| 376 025 | **CN** | H | *SE* | SG | 61125 | 63325 | 64325 | 63525 | 61625 |
| 376 026 | **CN** | H | *SE* | SG | 61126 | 63326 | 64326 | 63526 | 61626 |
| 376 027 | **CN** | H | *SE* | SG | 61127 | 63327 | 64327 | 63527 | 61627 |
| 376 028 | **CN** | H | *SE* | SG | 61128 | 63328 | 64328 | 63528 | 61628 |
| 376 029 | **CN** | H | *SE* | SG | 61129 | 63329 | 64329 | 63529 | 61629 |
| 376 030 | **CN** | H | *SE* | SG | 61130 | 63330 | 64330 | 63530 | 61630 |
| 376 031 | **CN** | H | *SE* | SG | 61131 | 63331 | 64331 | 63531 | 61631 |
| 376 032 | **CN** | H | *SE* | SG | 61132 | 63332 | 64332 | 63532 | 61632 |
| 376 033 | **CN** | H | *SE* | SG | 61133 | 63333 | 64333 | 63533 | 61633 |
| 376 034 | **CN** | H | *SE* | SG | 61134 | 63334 | 64334 | 63534 | 61634 |
| 376 035 | **CN** | H | *SE* | SG | 61135 | 63335 | 64335 | 63535 | 61635 |
| 376 036 | **CN** | H | *SE* | SG | 61136 | 63336 | 64336 | 63536 | 61636 |

# CLASS 377    ELECTROSTAR    BOMBARDIER DERBY

Express and outer suburban units.

**Formations:** Various.
**Systems:** 25 kV AC overhead/750 V DC third rail or third rail only with provision for retro-fitting of AC equipment.
**Construction:** Welded aluminium alloy underframe, sides and roof with steel ends. All sections bolted together.
**Traction Motors:** Two Bombardier asynchronous of 250 kW.
**Wheel Arrangement:** 2-Bo (+ 2-Bo) + 2-2 + Bo-2.

| | |
|---|---|
| **Braking:** Disc & regenerative. | **Dimensions:** 20.39/19.99 x 2.80 m. |
| **Bogies:** Bombardier P3-25/T3-25. | **Couplers:** Dellner 12. |
| **Gangways:** Throughout. | **Control System:** IGBT Inverter. |
| **Doors:** Sliding plug. | **Maximum Speed:** 100 m.p.h. |

**Heating & ventilation:** Air conditioning.
**Seating Layout:** Various.
**Multiple Working:** Within class and with Classes 375, 376 and 378.

**Class 377/1.** 750 V DC only. DMCO–MSO–TSO–DMCO.
**Seating layout:** 1: 2+2 facing/unidirectional, 2: 2+2 facing/unidirectional (377 101–377 119), 3+2 and 2+2 facing/unidirectional (377 120–377 164) (3+2 seating in middle cars only 377 140–377 164).

**DMCO(A).** Bombardier Derby 2002–2003. 12/48 (s 12/56). 44.8 t.
**MSO.** Bombardier Derby 2002–2003. –/62 (s –/70, t –/69). 1T. 39.0 t.
**TSO.** Bombardier Derby 2002–2003. –/52 (s –/60, t –/57). 1TD 2W. 35.4 t.
**DMCO(B).** Bombardier Derby 2002–2003. 12/48 (s 12/56). 43.4 t.

| | | | | | | | | |
|---|---|---|---|---|---|---|---|---|
| 377 101 | | **SN** | P | *SN* | Bl | 78501 | 77101 | 78901 | 78701 |
| 377 102 | | **SN** | P | *SN* | Bl | 78502 | 77102 | 78902 | 78702 |
| 377 103 | | **SN** | P | *SN* | Bl | 78503 | 77103 | 78903 | 78703 |
| 377 104 | | **SN** | P | *SN* | Bl | 78504 | 77104 | 78904 | 78704 |
| 377 105 | | **SN** | P | *SN* | Bl | 78505 | 77105 | 78905 | 78705 |
| 377 106 | | **SN** | P | *SN* | Bl | 78506 | 77106 | 78906 | 78706 |
| 377 107 | | **SN** | P | *SN* | Bl | 78507 | 77107 | 78907 | 78707 |
| 377 108 | | **SN** | P | *SN* | Bl | 78508 | 77108 | 78908 | 78708 |
| 377 109 | | **SN** | P | *SN* | Bl | 78509 | 77109 | 78909 | 78709 |
| 377 110 | | **SN** | P | *SN* | Bl | 78510 | 77110 | 78910 | 78710 |
| 377 111 | | **SN** | P | *SN* | Bl | 78511 | 77111 | 78911 | 78711 |
| 377 112 | | **SN** | P | *SN* | Bl | 78512 | 77112 | 78912 | 78712 |
| 377 113 | | **SN** | P | *SN* | Bl | 78513 | 77113 | 78913 | 78713 |
| 377 114 | | **SN** | P | *SN* | Bl | 78514 | 77114 | 78914 | 78714 |
| 377 115 | | **SN** | P | *SN* | Bl | 78515 | 77115 | 78915 | 78715 |
| 377 116 | | **SN** | P | *SN* | Bl | 78516 | 77116 | 78916 | 78716 |
| 377 117 | | **SN** | P | *SN* | Bl | 78517 | 77117 | 78917 | 78717 |
| 377 118 | | **SN** | P | *SN* | Bl | 78518 | 77118 | 78918 | 78718 |
| 377 119 | | **SN** | P | *SN* | Bl | 78519 | 77119 | 78919 | 78719 |
| 377 120 | s | **SN** | P | *SN* | SU | 78520 | 77120 | 78920 | 78720 |
| 377 121 | s | **SN** | P | *SN* | SU | 78521 | 77121 | 78921 | 78721 |
| 377 122 | s | **SN** | P | *SN* | SU | 78522 | 77122 | 78922 | 78722 |
| 377 123 | s | **SN** | P | *SN* | SU | 78523 | 77123 | 78923 | 78723 |

| | | | | | | | | |
|---|---|---|---|---|---|---|---|---|
| 377 124 | s | **SN** | P | *SN* | SU | 78524 | 77124 | 78924 | 78724 |
| 377 125 | s | **SN** | P | *SN* | SU | 78525 | 77125 | 78925 | 78725 |
| 377 126 | s | **SN** | P | *SN* | SU | 78526 | 77126 | 78926 | 78726 |
| 377 127 | s | **SN** | P | *SN* | SU | 78527 | 77127 | 78927 | 78727 |
| 377 128 | s | **SN** | P | *SN* | SU | 78528 | 77128 | 78928 | 78728 |
| 377 129 | s | **SN** | P | *SN* | SU | 78529 | 77129 | 78929 | 78729 |
| 377 130 | s | **SN** | P | *SN* | SU | 78530 | 77130 | 78930 | 78730 |
| 377 131 | s | **SN** | P | *SN* | SU | 78531 | 77131 | 78931 | 78731 |
| 377 132 | s | **SN** | P | *SN* | SU | 78532 | 77132 | 78932 | 78732 |
| 377 133 | s | **SN** | P | *SN* | SU | 78533 | 77133 | 78933 | 78733 |
| 377 134 | s | **SN** | P | *SN* | SU | 78534 | 77134 | 78934 | 78734 |
| 377 135 | s | **SN** | P | *SN* | SU | 78535 | 77135 | 78935 | 78735 |
| 377 136 | s | **SN** | P | *SN* | SU | 78536 | 77136 | 78936 | 78736 |
| 377 137 | s | **SN** | P | *SN* | SU | 78537 | 77137 | 78937 | 78737 |
| 377 138 | s | **SN** | P | *SN* | SU | 78538 | 77138 | 78938 | 78738 |
| 377 139 | s | **SN** | P | *SN* | SU | 78539 | 77139 | 78939 | 78739 |
| 377 140 | t | **SN** | P | *SN* | SU | 78540 | 77140 | 78940 | 78740 |
| 377 141 | t | **SN** | P | *SN* | SU | 78541 | 77141 | 78941 | 78741 |
| 377 142 | t | **SN** | P | *SN* | SU | 78542 | 77142 | 78942 | 78742 |
| 377 143 | t | **SN** | P | *SN* | SU | 78543 | 77143 | 78943 | 78743 |
| 377 144 | t | **SN** | P | *SN* | SU | 78544 | 77144 | 78944 | 78744 |
| 377 145 | t | **SN** | P | *SN* | SU | 78545 | 77145 | 78945 | 78745 |
| 377 146 | t | **SN** | P | *SN* | SU | 78546 | 77146 | 78946 | 78746 |
| 377 147 | t | **SN** | P | *SN* | SU | 78547 | 77147 | 78947 | 78747 |
| 377 148 | t | **SN** | P | *SN* | SU | 78548 | 77148 | 78948 | 78748 |
| 377 149 | t | **SN** | P | *SN* | SU | 78549 | 77149 | 78949 | 78749 |
| 377 150 | t | **SN** | P | *SN* | SU | 78550 | 77150 | 78950 | 78750 |
| 377 151 | t | **SN** | P | *SN* | SU | 78551 | 77151 | 78951 | 78751 |
| 377 152 | t | **SN** | P | *SN* | SU | 78552 | 77152 | 78952 | 78752 |
| 377 153 | t | **SN** | P | *SN* | SU | 78553 | 77153 | 78953 | 78753 |
| 377 154 | t | **SN** | P | *SN* | SU | 78554 | 77154 | 78954 | 78754 |
| 377 155 | t | **SN** | P | *SN* | SU | 78555 | 77155 | 78955 | 78755 |
| 377 156 | t | **SN** | P | *SN* | SU | 78556 | 77156 | 78956 | 78756 |
| 377 157 | t | **SN** | P | *SN* | SU | 78557 | 77157 | 78957 | 78757 |
| 377 158 | t | **SN** | P | *SN* | BI | 78558 | 77158 | 78958 | 78758 |
| 377 159 | t | **SN** | P | *SN* | BI | 78559 | 77159 | 78959 | 78759 |
| 377 160 | t | **SN** | P | *SN* | BI | 78560 | 77160 | 78960 | 78760 |
| 377 161 | t | **SN** | P | *SN* | BI | 78561 | 77161 | 78961 | 78761 |
| 377 162 | t | **SN** | P | *SN* | BI | 78562 | 77162 | 78962 | 78762 |
| 377 163 | t | **SN** | P | *SN* | BI | 78563 | 77163 | 78963 | 78763 |
| 377 164 | t | **SN** | P | *SN* | BI | 78564 | 77164 | 78964 | 78764 |

**Class 377/2.** 25 kV AC/750 V DC. DMCO–MSO–PTSO–DMCO. These dual-voltage units are used on the East Croydon–Milton Keynes cross-London service.
**Seating layout:** 1: 2+2 facing/unidirectional, 2: 2+2 and 3+2 facing/unidirectional (3+2 seating in middle cars only).

**DMCO(A).** Bombardier Derby 2003–2004. 12/48. 44.2 t.
**MSO.** Bombardier Derby 2003–2004. –/69 1T. 39.8 t.
**PTSO.** Bombardier Derby 2003–2004. –/57 1TD 2W. 40.1 t.
**DMCO(B).** Bombardier Derby 2003–2004. 12/48. 44.2 t.

| 377 201 | | **SN** | P | *SN* | BI | 78571 | 77171 | 78971 | 78771 |
| 377 202 | | **SN** | P | *SN* | SU | 78572 | 77172 | 78972 | 78772 |
| 377 203 | | **SN** | P | *SN* | BI | 78573 | 77173 | 78973 | 78773 |
| 377 204 | | **SN** | P | *SN* | BI | 78574 | 77174 | 78974 | 78774 |
| 377 205 | | **SN** | P | *SN* | SU | 78575 | 77175 | 78975 | 78775 |
| 377 206 | | **SN** | P | *SN* | BI | 78576 | 77176 | 78976 | 78776 |
| 377 207 | | **SN** | P | *SN* | BI | 78577 | 77177 | 78977 | 78777 |
| 377 208 | | **SN** | P | *SN* | SU | 78578 | 77178 | 78978 | 78778 |
| 377 209 | | **SN** | P | *SN* | SU | 78579 | 77179 | 78979 | 78779 |
| 377 210 | | **SN** | P | *SN* | SU | 78580 | 77180 | 78980 | 78780 |
| 377 211 | | **SN** | P | *SN* | SU | 78581 | 77181 | 78981 | 78781 |
| 377 212 | | **SN** | P | *SN* | SU | 78582 | 77182 | 78982 | 78782 |
| 377 213 | | **SN** | P | *SN* | SU | 78583 | 77183 | 78983 | 78783 |
| 377 214 | | **SN** | P | *SN* | SU | 78584 | 77184 | 78984 | 78784 |
| 377 215 | | **SN** | P | *SN* | SU | 78585 | 77185 | 78985 | 78785 |

**Class 377/3.** 750 V DC only. DMCO–TSO–DMCO.
**Seating Layout:** 1: 2+2 facing/unidirectional, 2: 2+2 facing/unidirectional.

**Notes:** Units built as Class 375, but renumbered in the Class 377/3 range when fitted with Dellner couplers.

† Wi-fi high-speed internet connection equipment fitted. Units generally used on Victoria–Brighton fast services.

**DMCO(A).** Bombardier Derby 2001–2002. 12/48. 43.5 t.
**TSO.** Bombardier Derby 2001–2002. –/56 1TD 2W. 35.4 t.
**DMCO(B).** Bombardier Derby 2001–2002. 12/48. 43.5 t.

| 377 301 | (375 311) | | **SN** | P | *SN* | BI | 68201 | 74801 | 68401 |
| 377 302 | (375 312) | | **SN** | P | *SN* | BI | 68202 | 74802 | 68402 |
| 377 303 | (375 313) | | **SN** | P | *SN* | BI | 68203 | 74803 | 68403 |
| 377 304 | (375 314) | † | **SN** | P | *SN* | BI | 68204 | 74804 | 68404 |
| 377 305 | (375 315) | † | **SN** | P | *SN* | BI | 68205 | 74805 | 68405 |
| 377 306 | (375 316) | | **SN** | P | *SN* | BI | 68206 | 74806 | 68406 |
| 377 307 | (375 317) | | **SN** | P | *SN* | BI | 68207 | 74807 | 68407 |
| 377 308 | (375 318) | | **SN** | P | *SN* | BI | 68208 | 74808 | 68408 |
| 377 309 | (375 319) | | **SN** | P | *SN* | BI | 68209 | 74809 | 68409 |
| 377 310 | (375 320) | | **SN** | P | *SN* | BI | 68210 | 74810 | 68410 |
| 377 311 | (375 321) | | **SN** | P | *SN* | BI | 68211 | 74811 | 68411 |
| 377 312 | (375 322) | | **SN** | P | *SN* | BI | 68212 | 74812 | 68412 |
| 377 313 | (375 323) | † | **SN** | P | *SN* | BI | 68213 | 74813 | 68413 |
| 377 314 | (375 324) | | **SN** | P | *SN* | BI | 68214 | 74814 | 68414 |
| 377 315 | (375 325) | † | **SN** | P | *SN* | BI | 68215 | 74815 | 68415 |
| 377 316 | (375 326) | † | **SN** | P | *SN* | BI | 68216 | 74816 | 68416 |
| 377 317 | (375 327) | † | **SN** | P | *SN* | BI | 68217 | 74817 | 68417 |
| 377 318 | (375 328) | | **SN** | P | *SN* | BI | 68218 | 74818 | 68418 |
| 377 319 | (375 329) | | **SN** | P | *SN* | BI | 68219 | 74819 | 68419 |
| 377 320 | (375 330) | † | **SN** | P | *SN* | BI | 68220 | 74820 | 68420 |
| 377 321 | (375 331) | † | **SN** | P | *SN* | BI | 68221 | 74821 | 68421 |
| 377 322 | (375 332) | † | **SN** | P | *SN* | BI | 68222 | 74822 | 68422 |
| 377 323 | (375 333) | | **SN** | P | *SN* | BI | 68223 | 74823 | 68423 |
| 377 324 | (375 334) | † | **SN** | P | *SN* | BI | 68224 | 74824 | 68424 |

| 377 325 | (375 335) | † | **SN** | P | *SN* | Bl | 68225 | 74825 | 68425 |
| 377 326 | (375 336) | † | **SN** | P | *SN* | Bl | 68226 | 74826 | 68426 |
| 377 327 | (375 337) | † | **SN** | P | *SN* | Bl | 68227 | 74827 | 68427 |
| 377 328 | (375 338) | † | **SN** | P | *SN* | Bl | 68228 | 74828 | 68428 |

**Class 377/4.** 750 V DC only. DMCO–MSO–TSO–DMCO.
**Seating Layout:** 1: 2+2 facing/two seats longitudinal, 2: 2+2 and 3+2 facing/
unidirectional (3+2 seating in middle cars only).

**DMCO(A).** Bombardier Derby 2004–2005. 10/48. 43.1 t.
**MSO.** Bombardier Derby 2004–2005. –/69 1T. 39.3 t.
**TSO.** Bombardier Derby 2004–2005. –/56 1TD 2W. 35.3 t.
**DMCO(B).** Bombardier Derby 2004–2005. 10/48. 43.2 t.

| 377 401 | **SN** | P | *SN* | Bl | 73401 | 78801 | 78601 | 73801 |
| 377 402 | **SN** | P | *SN* | Bl | 73402 | 78802 | 78602 | 73802 |
| 377 403 | **SN** | P | *SN* | Bl | 73403 | 78803 | 78603 | 73803 |
| 377 404 | **SN** | P | *SN* | Bl | 73404 | 78804 | 78604 | 73804 |
| 377 405 | **SN** | P | *SN* | Bl | 73405 | 78805 | 78605 | 73805 |
| 377 406 | **SN** | P | *SN* | Bl | 73406 | 78806 | 78606 | 73806 |
| 377 407 | **SN** | P | *SN* | Bl | 73407 | 78807 | 78607 | 73807 |
| 377 408 | **SN** | P | *SN* | Bl | 73408 | 78808 | 78608 | 73808 |
| 377 409 | **SN** | P | *SN* | Bl | 73409 | 78809 | 78609 | 73809 |
| 377 410 | **SN** | P | *SN* | Bl | 73410 | 78810 | 78610 | 73810 |
| 377 411 | **SN** | P | *SN* | Bl | 73411 | 78811 | 78611 | 73811 |
| 377 412 | **SN** | P | *SN* | Bl | 73412 | 78812 | 78612 | 73812 |
| 377 413 | **SN** | P | *SN* | Bl | 73413 | 78813 | 78613 | 73813 |
| 377 414 | **SN** | P | *SN* | Bl | 73414 | 78814 | 78614 | 73814 |
| 377 415 | **SN** | P | *SN* | Bl | 73415 | 78815 | 78615 | 73815 |
| 377 416 | **SN** | P | *SN* | Bl | 73416 | 78816 | 78616 | 73816 |
| 377 417 | **SN** | P | *SN* | Bl | 73417 | 78817 | 78617 | 73817 |
| 377 418 | **SN** | P | *SN* | Bl | 73418 | 78818 | 78618 | 73818 |
| 377 419 | **SN** | P | *SN* | Bl | 73419 | 78819 | 78619 | 73819 |
| 377 420 | **SN** | P | *SN* | Bl | 73420 | 78820 | 78620 | 73820 |
| 377 421 | **SN** | P | *SN* | Bl | 73421 | 78821 | 78621 | 73821 |
| 377 422 | **SN** | P | *SN* | Bl | 73422 | 78822 | 78622 | 73822 |
| 377 423 | **SN** | P | *SN* | Bl | 73423 | 78823 | 78623 | 73823 |
| 377 424 | **SN** | P | *SN* | Bl | 73424 | 78824 | 78624 | 73824 |
| 377 425 | **SN** | P | *SN* | Bl | 73425 | 78825 | 78625 | 73825 |
| 377 426 | **SN** | P | *SN* | Bl | 73426 | 78826 | 78626 | 73826 |
| 377 427 | **SN** | P | *SN* | Bl | 73427 | 78827 | 78627 | 73827 |
| 377 428 | **SN** | P | *SN* | Bl | 73428 | 78828 | 78628 | 73828 |
| 377 429 | **SN** | P | *SN* | Bl | 73429 | 78829 | 78629 | 73829 |
| 377 430 | **SN** | P | *SN* | Bl | 73430 | 78830 | 78630 | 73830 |
| 377 431 | **SN** | P | *SN* | Bl | 73431 | 78831 | 78631 | 73831 |
| 377 432 | **SN** | P | *SN* | Bl | 73432 | 78832 | 78632 | 73832 |
| 377 433 | **SN** | P | *SN* | Bl | 73433 | 78833 | 78633 | 73833 |
| 377 434 | **SN** | P | *SN* | Bl | 73434 | 78834 | 78634 | 73834 |
| 377 435 | **SN** | P | *SN* | Bl | 73435 | 78835 | 78635 | 73835 |
| 377 436 | **SN** | P | *SN* | Bl | 73436 | 78836 | 78636 | 73836 |
| 377 437 | **SN** | P | *SN* | Bl | 73437 | 78837 | 78637 | 73837 |
| 377 438 | **SN** | P | *SN* | Bl | 73438 | 78838 | 78638 | 73838 |

| 377 439 | **SN** | P | *SN* | BI | 73439 | 78839 | 78639 | 73839 |
|---------|--------|---|------|----|-------|-------|-------|-------|
| 377 440 | **SN** | P | *SN* | BI | 73440 | 78840 | 78640 | 73840 |
| 377 441 | **SN** | P | *SN* | BI | 73441 | 78841 | 78641 | 73841 |
| 377 442 | **SN** | P | *SN* | BI | 73442 | 78842 | 78642 | 73842 |
| 377 443 | **SN** | P | *SN* | BI | 73443 | 78843 | 78643 | 73843 |
| 377 444 | **SN** | P | *SN* | BI | 73444 | 78844 | 78644 | 73844 |
| 377 445 | **SN** | P | *SN* | BI | 73445 | 78845 | 78645 | 73845 |
| 377 446 | **SN** | P | *SN* | BI | 73446 | 78846 | 78646 | 73846 |
| 377 447 | **SN** | P | *SN* | BI | 73447 | 78847 | 78647 | 73847 |
| 377 448 | **SN** | P | *SN* | BI | 73448 | 78848 | 78648 | 73848 |
| 377 449 | **SN** | P | *SN* | BI | 73449 | 78849 | 78649 | 73849 |
| 377 450 | **SN** | P | *SN* | BI | 73450 | 78850 | 78650 | 73850 |
| 377 451 | **SN** | P | *SN* | BI | 73451 | 78851 | 78651 | 73851 |
| 377 452 | **SN** | P | *SN* | BI | 73452 | 78852 | 78652 | 73852 |
| 377 453 | **SN** | P | *SN* | BI | 73453 | 78853 | 78653 | 73853 |
| 377 454 | **SN** | P | *SN* | BI | 73454 | 78854 | 78654 | 73854 |
| 377 455 | **SN** | P | *SN* | BI | 73455 | 78855 | 78655 | 73855 |
| 377 456 | **SN** | P | *SN* | BI | 73456 | 78856 | 78656 | 73856 |
| 377 457 | **SN** | P | *SN* | BI | 73457 | 78857 | 78657 | 73857 |
| 377 458 | **SN** | P | *SN* | BI | 73458 | 78858 | 78658 | 73858 |
| 377 459 | **SN** | P | *SN* | BI | 73459 | 78859 | 78659 | 73859 |
| 377 460 | **SN** | P | *SN* | BI | 73460 | 78860 | 78660 | 73860 |
| 377 461 | **SN** | P | *SN* | BI | 73461 | 78861 | 78661 | 73861 |
| 377 462 | **SN** | P | *SN* | BI | 73462 | 78862 | 78662 | 73862 |
| 377 463 | **SN** | P | *SN* | BI | 73463 | 78863 | 78663 | 73863 |
| 377 464 | **SN** | P | *SN* | BI | 73464 | 78864 | 78664 | 73864 |
| 377 465 | **SN** | P | *SN* | BI | 73465 | 78865 | 78665 | 73865 |
| 377 466 | **SN** | P | *SN* | BI | 73466 | 78866 | 78666 | 73866 |
| 377 467 | **SN** | P | *SN* | BI | 73467 | 78867 | 78667 | 73867 |
| 377 468 | **SN** | P | *SN* | BI | 73468 | 78868 | 78668 | 73868 |
| 377 469 | **SN** | P | *SN* | BI | 73469 | 78869 | 78669 | 73869 |
| 377 470 | **SN** | P | *SN* | BI | 73470 | 78870 | 78670 | 73870 |
| 377 471 | **SN** | P | *SN* | BI | 73471 | 78871 | 78671 | 73871 |
| 377 472 | **SN** | P | *SN* | BI | 73472 | 78872 | 78672 | 73872 |
| 377 473 | **SN** | P | *SN* | BI | 73473 | 78873 | 78673 | 73873 |
| 377 474 | **SN** | P | *SN* | BI | 73474 | 78874 | 78674 | 73874 |
| 377 475 | **SN** | P | *SN* | BI | 73475 | 78875 | 78675 | 73875 |

**Class 377/5.** 25 kV AC/750 V DC. DMCO–MSO–PTSO–DMCO. Dual voltage First Capital Connect units (sub-leased from Southern). Details as Class 377/2 unless stated.

**DMCO(A).** Bombardier Derby 2008–2009. 10/48. 43.1 t.
**MSO.** Bombardier Derby 2008–2009. –/69 1T. 39.3 t.
**PTSO.** Bombardier Derby 2008–2009. –/53 1TD 2W. 35.3 t.
**DMCO(B).** Bombardier Derby 2008–2009. 10/48. 43.1 t.

| 377 501 | **FU** | P | *FC* | BF | 73501 | 75901 | 74901 | 73601 |
|---------|--------|---|------|----|-------|-------|-------|-------|
| 377 502 | **FU** | P | *FC* | BF | 73502 | 75902 | 74902 | 73602 |
| 377 503 | **FB** | P | *FC* | BF | 73503 | 75903 | 74903 | 73603 |
| 377 504 | **FU** | P | *FC* | BF | 73504 | 75904 | 74904 | 73604 |
| 377 505 | **FU** | P | *FC* | BF | 73505 | 75905 | 74905 | 73605 |

| 377 506 | FU | P  | *FC* | BF |    | 73506 | 75906 | 74906 | 73606 |
| 377 507 | FU | P  | *FC* | BF |    | 73507 | 75907 | 74907 | 73607 |
| 377 508 | FU | P  | *FC* | BF |    | 73508 | 75908 | 74908 | 73608 |
| 377 509 | FU | P  | *FC* | BF |    | 73509 | 75909 | 74909 | 73609 |
| 377 510 | FU | P  | *FC* | BF |    | 73510 | 75910 | 74910 | 73610 |
| 377 511 | FU | P  | *FC* | BF |    | 73511 | 75911 | 74911 | 73611 |
| 377 512 | FU | P  | *FC* | BF |    | 73512 | 75912 | 74912 | 73612 |
| 377 513 | FU | SN | *FC* | BF |    | 73513 | 75913 | 74913 | 73613 |
| 377 514 | FB | SN | *FC* | BF |    | 73514 | 75914 | 74914 | 73614 |
| 377 515 | FB | SN | *FC* | BF |    | 73515 | 75915 | 74915 | 73615 |
| 377 516 | FU | SN | *FC* | BF |    | 73516 | 75916 | 74916 | 73616 |
| 377 517 | FU | SN | *FC* | BF |    | 73517 | 75917 | 74917 | 73617 |
| 377 518 | FU | SN | *FC* | BF |    | 73518 | 75918 | 74918 | 73618 |
| 377 519 | FB | SN | *FC* | BF |    | 73519 | 75919 | 74919 | 73619 |
| 377 520 | FU | SN | *FC* | BF |    | 73520 | 75920 | 74920 | 73620 |
| 377 521 | FU | SN | *FC* | BF |    | 73521 | 75921 | 74921 | 73621 |
| 377 522 | FB | SN | *FC* | BF |    | 73522 | 75922 | 74922 | 73622 |
| 377 523 | FB | SN | *FC* | BF |    | 73523 | 75923 | 74923 | 73623 |

# CLASS 378  CAPITALSTAR  BOMBARDIER DERBY

57 new Class 378 suburban Electrostars (designated Capitalstars by TfL) are currently being delivered for the London Overground network.

**Formation:** DMSO–(MSO)–PTSO–DMSO or DMSO–MSO–TSO–DMSO.
**System:** Class 378/0 and Class 378/2 25 kV AC overhead and 750 V DC third rail. Class 378/1 750 V DC third rail only.
**Construction:** Welded aluminium alloy underframe, sides and roof with steel ends. All sections bolted together.
**Traction Motors:** Two Bombardier asynchronous of 250 kW.
**Wheel Arrangement:** 2-Bo (+ 2-Bo) + 2-2 + Bo-2.
**Braking:** Disc & regenerative.          **Dimensions:** 20.46/20.14 x 2.80 m.
**Bogies:** Bombardier P3-25/T3-25.        **Couplers:** Dellner 12.
**Gangways:** Within unit + end doors.     **Control System:** IGBT Inverter.
**Doors:** Sliding.                        **Maximum Speed:** 75 m.p.h.
**Heating & ventilation:** Air conditioning.
**Seating Layout:** Longitudinal ("tube style") low density.
**Multiple Working:** Within class and with Classes 375, 376 and 377.

**Class 378/0.** 25 kV AC/750 V DC. DMSO–PTSO–DMSO. Initial order of 24 3-car sets for North London Railway services. These units will be renumbered in the 378 2xx series when extra (MSO) vehicles (*382xx* series) are added later in 2010.

**DMSO(A).** Bombardier Derby 2008–2010. –/36. 43.2 t.
**MSO.** Bombardier Derby 2008–2010. –/40. 39.8 t.
**PTSO.** Bombardier Derby 2008–2010. –/34(6) 2W. 39.0 t.
**DMSO(B).** Bombardier Derby 2008–2010. –/36. 42.8 t.

| 378 001 | LO | QW |    |    | 38001 | *38201* | 38301 | 38101 |
| 378 002 | LO | QW |    |    | 38002 | *38202* | 38302 | 38102 |
| 378 003 | LO | QW |    |    | 38003 | *38203* | 38303 | 38103 |
| 378 004 | LO | QW |    |    | 38004 | *38204* | 38304 | 38104 |
| 378 005 | LO | QW | *LO* | WN | 38005 | *38205* | 38305 | 38105 |

| 378 006 | LO | QW |    | WN | 38006 | *38206* | 38306 | 38106 |
| 378 007 | LO | QW | *LO* | WN | 38007 | *38207* | 38307 | 38107 |
| 378 008 | LO | QW | *LO* | WN | 38008 | *38208* | 38308 | 38108 |
| 378 009 | LO | QW | *LO* | WN | 38009 | *38209* | 38309 | 38109 |
| 378 010 | LO | QW | *LO* | WN | 38010 | *38210* | 38310 | 38110 |
| 378 011 | LO | QW | *LO* | WN | 38011 | *38211* | 38311 | 38111 |
| 378 012 | LO | QW | *LO* | WN | 38012 | *38212* | 38312 | 38112 |
| 378 013 | LO | QW | *LO* | WN | 38013 | *38213* | 38313 | 38113 |
| 378 014 | LO | QW | *LO* | WN | 38014 | *38214* | 38314 | 38114 |
| 378 015 | LO | QW | *LO* | WN | 38015 | *38215* | 38315 | 38115 |
| 378 016 | LO | QW | *LO* | WN | 38016 | *38216* | 38316 | 38116 |
| 378 017 | LO | QW | *LO* | WN | 38017 | *38217* | 38317 | 38117 |
| 378 018 | LO | QW | *LO* | WN | 38018 | *38218* | 38318 | 38118 |
| 378 019 | LO | QW |    |    | 38019 | *38219* | 38319 | 38119 |
| 378 020 | LO | QW |    |    | 38020 | *38220* | 38320 | 38120 |
| 378 021 | LO | QW |    |    | 38021 | *38221* | 38321 | 38121 |
| 378 022 | LO | QW |    |    | 38022 | *38222* | 38322 | 38122 |
| 378 023 | LO | QW |    |    | 38023 | *38223* | 38323 | 38123 |
| 378 024 | LO | QW |    |    | 38024 | *38224* | 38324 | 38124 |

**Class 378/1.** 750 V DC. DMSO–MSO–TSO–DMSO. Third rail only units for East London Railway services from summer 2010. Provision for retro-fitting as dual voltage if required.

**DMSO(A).** Bombardier Derby 2009–2010. –/36. 43.5 t.
**MSO.** Bombardier Derby 2009–2010. –/40. 39.4 t.
**TSO.** Bombardier Derby 2009–2010. –/34(6) 2W. 34.3 t.
**DMSO(B).** Bombardier Derby 2009–2010. –/36. 43.1 t.

| 378 135 | LO | QW |    | 38035 | 38235 | 38335 | 38135 |
| 378 136 | LO | QW | NG | 38036 | 38236 | 38336 | 38136 |
| 378 137 | LO | QW | NG | 38037 | 38237 | 38337 | 38137 |
| 378 138 | LO | QW | NG | 38038 | 38238 | 38338 | 38138 |
| 378 139 | LO | QW | NG | 38039 | 38239 | 38339 | 38139 |
| 378 140 | LO | QW | NG | 38040 | 38240 | 38340 | 38140 |
| 378 141 | LO | QW | NG | 38041 | 38241 | 38341 | 38141 |
| 378 142 | LO | QW | NG | 38042 | 38242 | 38342 | 38142 |
| 378 143 | LO | QW | NG | 38043 | 38243 | 38343 | 38143 |
| 378 144 | LO | QW | NG | 38044 | 38244 | 38344 | 38144 |
| 378 145 | LO | QW | NG | 38045 | 38245 | 38345 | 38145 |
| 378 146 | LO | QW | NG | 38046 | 38246 | 38346 | 38146 |
| 378 147 | LO | QW | NG | 38047 | 38247 | 38347 | 38147 |
| 378 148 | LO | QW | NG | 38048 | 38248 | 38348 | 38148 |
| 378 149 | LO | QW | NG | 38049 | 38249 | 38349 | 38149 |
| 378 150 | LO | QW | NG | 38050 | 38250 | 38350 | 38150 |
| 378 151 | LO | QW | NG | 38051 | 38251 | 38351 | 38151 |
| 378 152 | LO | QW | NG | 38052 | 38252 | 38352 | 38152 |
| 378 153 | LO | QW | NG | 38053 | 38253 | 38353 | 38153 |
| 378 154 | LO | QW |    | 38054 | 38254 | 38354 | 38154 |

**Class 378/2.** 25 kV AC/750 V DC. DMSO–MSO–PTSO–DMSO. Details as Class 378/0. Extra ten 4-car dual voltage units for NLR or ELR services. Note that 378 001–024 will be renumbered into the 378 2xx series in 2010 (by addition of 200 to their original numbers) when they receive extra MSO vehicles. A further three dual voltage units have been ordered, number series to be confirmed (expected to be 378 255–257).

| 378 225 | **LO** | QW | 38025 | 38225 | 38325 | 38125 |
|---------|--------|----|-------|-------|-------|-------|
| 378 226 | **LO** | QW | 38026 | 38226 | 38326 | 38126 |
| 378 227 | **LO** | QW | 38027 | 38227 | 38327 | 38127 |
| 378 228 | **LO** | QW | 38028 | 38228 | 38328 | 38128 |
| 378 229 | **LO** | QW | 38029 | 38229 | 38329 | 38129 |
| 378 230 | **LO** | QW | 38030 | 38230 | 38330 | 38130 |
| 378 231 | **LO** | QW | 38031 | 38231 | 38331 | 38131 |
| 378 232 | **LO** | QW | 38032 | 38232 | 38332 | 38132 |
| 378 233 | **LO** | QW | 38033 | 38233 | 38333 | 38133 |
| 378 234 | **LO** | QW | 38034 | 38234 | 38334 | 38134 |

# CLASS 379   ELECTROSTAR   BOMBARDIER DERBY

30 new 4-car Class 379 Bombardier EMUs are on order for the National Express East Anglia franchise (principally London Liverpool Street–Stansted Airport services), with the first due to be delivered in 2011. Funding will be provided by Lloyds Banking Group. Numbering series is to be finalised.

# CLASS 380      DESIRO UK                SIEMENS

38 new Class 380 Siemens EMUs are on order for the ScotRail franchise (Strathclyde area services), with the first due to be delivered in summer 2010. There will be 22 3-car units and 16 4-car units.

**Formation:** DMSO–PTSO–DMSO or DMSO–PTSO–TSO–DMSO.
**System:** 25 kV AC overhead.
**Construction:** Welded aluminium with steel ends.
**Traction Motors:** Four Siemens ITB2016-0GB02 asynchronous of 250 kW.
**Wheel Arrangement:** Bo-Bo + 2-2 (+2-2) + Bo-Bo

| | |
|---|---|
| **Braking:** Disc & regenerative. | **Dimensions:** 23.0 x 2.80 m. |
| **Bogies:** SGP SF5000. | **Couplers:** Voith. |
| **Gangways:** Throughout. | **Control System:** IGBT Inverter. |
| **Doors:** Sliding plug. | **Maximum Speed:** 100 m.p.h. |

**Heating & ventilation:** Air conditioning.
**Seating Layout:** 2+2 facing/unidirectional.
**Multiple Working:** Within class.

**DMSO(A).** Siemens Uerdingen (Krefeld) 2009–2010.          .    . t.
**PTSO.** Siemens Uerdingen (Krefeld) 2009–2010.          .    . t.
**TSO.** Siemens Uerdingen (Krefeld) 2009–2010.        .    . t.
**DMSO(B).** Siemens Uerdingen (Krefeld) 2009–2010.          .    . t.

**Class 380/0.** 3-car units.

| | | | | | |
|---|---|---|---|---|---|
| 380 001 | **SR** | H | 38501 | 38601 | 38701 |
| 380 002 | **SR** | H | 38502 | 38602 | 38702 |
| 380 003 | **SR** | H | 38503 | 38603 | 38703 |
| 380 004 | **SR** | H | 38504 | 38604 | 38704 |
| 380 005 | **SR** | H | 38505 | 38605 | 38705 |
| 380 006 | **SR** | H | 38506 | 38606 | 38706 |
| 380 007 | **SR** | H | 38507 | 38607 | 38707 |
| 380 008 | **SR** | H | 38508 | 38608 | 38708 |
| 380 009 | **SR** | H | 38509 | 38609 | 38709 |
| 380 010 | **SR** | H | 38510 | 38610 | 38710 |
| 380 011 | **SR** | H | 38511 | 38611 | 38711 |
| 380 012 | **SR** | H | 38512 | 38612 | 38712 |
| 380 013 | **SR** | H | 38513 | 38613 | 38713 |
| 380 014 | **SR** | H | 38514 | 38614 | 38714 |
| 380 015 | **SR** | H | 38515 | 38615 | 38715 |
| 380 016 | **SR** | H | 38516 | 38616 | 38716 |
| 380 017 | **SR** | H | 38517 | 38617 | 38717 |
| 380 018 | **SR** | H | 38518 | 38618 | 38718 |
| 380 019 | **SR** | H | 38519 | 38619 | 38719 |
| 380 020 | **SR** | H | 38520 | 38620 | 38720 |
| 380 021 | **SR** | H | 38521 | 38621 | 38721 |
| 380 022 | **SR** | H | 38522 | 38622 | 38722 |

**Class 380/1.** 4-car units.

| | | | | | | |
|---|---|---|---|---|---|---|
| 380 101 | **SR** | H | 38551 | 38651 | 38851 | 38751 |
| 380 102 | **SR** | H | 38552 | 38652 | 38852 | 38752 |
| 380 103 | **SR** | H | 38553 | 38653 | 38853 | 38753 |
| 380 104 | **SR** | H | 38554 | 38654 | 38854 | 38754 |
| 380 105 | **SR** | H | 38555 | 38655 | 38855 | 38755 |
| 380 106 | **SR** | H | 38556 | 38656 | 38856 | 38756 |
| 380 107 | **SR** | H | 38557 | 38657 | 38857 | 38757 |
| 380 108 | **SR** | H | 38558 | 38658 | 38858 | 38758 |
| 380 109 | **SR** | H | 38559 | 38659 | 38859 | 38759 |
| 380 110 | **SR** | H | 38560 | 38660 | 38860 | 38760 |
| 380 111 | **SR** | H | 38561 | 38661 | 38861 | 38761 |
| 380 112 | **SR** | H | 38562 | 38662 | 38862 | 38762 |
| 380 113 | **SR** | H | 38563 | 38663 | 38863 | 38763 |
| 380 114 | **SR** | H | 38564 | 38664 | 38864 | 38764 |
| 380 115 | **SR** | H | 38565 | 38665 | 38865 | 38765 |
| 380 116 | **SR** | H | 38566 | 38666 | 38866 | 38766 |

# CLASS 390   PENDOLINO   ALSTOM BIRMINGHAM

Tilting West Coast Main Line units.

**Formation:** DMRFO–MFO–PTFO–MFO–TSO–MSO–PTSRMB–MSO–DMSO.
**Construction:** Welded aluminium alloy.
**Traction Motors:** Two Alstom ONIX 800 of 425 kW.
**Wheel Arrangement:** 1A-A1 + 1A-A1 + 2-2 + 1A-A1 + 2-2 + 1A-A1 + 1A-A1.
**Braking:** Disc, rheostatic & regenerative.
**Dimensions:** 24.80/23.90 x 2.73 m.
**Bogies:** Fiat-SIG.                       **Couplers:** Dellner 12.
**Gangways:** Within unit.                  **Control System:** IGBT Inverter.
**Doors:** Sliding plug.                    **Maximum Speed:** 125 m.p.h.
**Heating & ventilation:** Air conditioning.
**Seating Layout:** 1: 2+1 facing/unidirectional, 2: 2+2 facing/unidirectional.
**Multiple Working:** Within class. Can also be controlled from Class 57/3 locos.

**DMRFO:** Alstom Birmingham 2001–2005. 18/–. 55.6 t.
**MFO(A):** Alstom Birmingham 2001–2005. 37/–(2) 1TD 1W. 52.0 t.
**PTFO:** Alstom Birmingham 2001–2005. 44/– 1T. 50.1 t.
**MFO(B):** Alstom Birmingham 2001–2005. 46/– 1T. 51.8 t.
**TSO:** Alstom Birmingham 2001–2005. –/76 1T. 45.5 t.
**MSO(A):** Alstom Birmingham 2001–2005. –/62(4) 1TD 1W. 50.0 t.
**PTSRMB:** Alstom Birmingham 2001–2005. –/48. 52.0 t.
**MSO(B):** Alstom Birmingham 2001–2005. –/62(2) 1TD 1W. 51.7 t.
**DMSO:** Alstom Birmingham 2001–2005. –/46 1T. 51.0 t.

**Notes:** Units up to 390 034 were delivered as 8-car sets, without the TSO (688xx). During 2004 and early 2005 these units had their 9th cars added.

390 033 was written off following accident damage in the Lambrigg accident of February 2007. It has been sold to Virgin and is now shown in the "EMUs awaiting disposal" section of this book.

| | | | | | | | | | |
|---|---|---|---|---|---|---|---|---|---|
| 390 001 | **VT** | A | *VW* | MA | 69101 | 69401 | 69501 | 69601 | 68801 |
| | | | | | 69701 | 69801 | 69901 | 69201 | |
| 390 002 | **VT** | A | *VW* | MA | 69102 | 69402 | 69502 | 69602 | 68802 |
| | | | | | 69702 | 69802 | 69902 | 69202 | |
| 390 003 | **VT** | A | *VW* | MA | 69103 | 69403 | 69503 | 69603 | 68803 |
| | | | | | 69703 | 69803 | 69903 | 69203 | |
| 390 004 | **VT** | A | *VW* | MA | 69104 | 69404 | 69504 | 69604 | 68804 |
| | | | | | 69704 | 69804 | 69904 | 69204 | |
| 390 005 | **VT** | A | *VW* | MA | 69105 | 69405 | 69505 | 69605 | 68805 |
| | | | | | 69705 | 69805 | 69905 | 69205 | |
| 390 006 | **VT** | A | *VW* | MA | 69106 | 69406 | 69506 | 69606 | 68806 |
| | | | | | 69706 | 69806 | 69906 | 69206 | |
| 390 007 | **VT** | A | *VW* | MA | 69107 | 69407 | 69507 | 69607 | 68807 |
| | | | | | 69707 | 69807 | 69907 | 69207 | |
| 390 008 | **VT** | A | *VW* | MA | 69108 | 69408 | 69508 | 69608 | 68808 |
| | | | | | 69708 | 69808 | 69908 | 69208 | |
| 390 009 | **VT** | A | *VW* | MA | 69109 | 69409 | 69509 | 69609 | 68809 |
| | | | | | 69709 | 69809 | 69909 | 69209 | |

▲ First Capital Connect "Urban Lights"-liveried 313 038 and 313 032 pass Welwyn North with the 16.45 Letchworth Sidings–London King's Cross e.c.s. working on 01/06/07.                                                    **Robert Pritchard**

▼ All suburban EMUs in the Glasgow area still retain Strathclyde PTE livery at the time of writing. On 17/03/09 314 205 approaches Cathcart with the 17.08 Glasgow Central–Neilston limited stop service on 21/08/09.    **Robin Ralston**

▲ In unbranded "One" livery with National Express stripe, 315 833 arrives at Chingford with the 10.03 from London Liverpool Street on 12/07/09. **Andrew Mist**

▼ First Capital Connect "Urban Lights"-liveried 317 341 approaches Harringay on 25/07/09 with the 08.36 London King's Cross–Peterborough. **Brian Morrison**

▲ Also in FCC livery, 319 438 and 319 455 pass Coulsdon South on the glorious morning of 19/06/09 with the 06.23 Brighton–Bedford via Redhill Thameslink route service. **Robert Pritchard**

▼ Strathclyde PTE-liveried 320 313 arrives at Hyndland with the 13.27 Milngavie–High Street (Glasgow) on 07/05/09. **Robert Pritchard**

▲ National Express-liveried 321 303 approaches Brentwood with the 14.00 Braintree–London Liverpool Street on 24/04/09. **Anthony Guppy**

▼ London Midland-liveried 323 207 pauses at Tame Bridge Parkway with a Walsall–Birmingham New Street service on 02/06/09. **Cliff Beeton**

▲ Royal Mail-liveried 325 012 passes Heamies Farm, near Norton Bridge, with a northbound afternoon Mail service on 12/05/09. **Dave Gommersall**

▼ West Yorkshire PTE/Northern-liveried 333 015 shows off its new livery (now carried by all 333s) as it approaches Bingley with the 09.02 Skipton–Bradford Forster Square on 20/04/09. **Andrew Wills**

▲ Strathclyde PTE-liveried 334 036 and 334 013 pass Dalry with the 16.18 Glasgow Central–Largs on 02/05/09.                    **Robin Ralston**

▼ London Midland-liveried 350 247 at Longport with the 14.50 London Euston–Crewe on 19/04/09.                    **Cliff Beeton**

▲ c2c Rail-liveried 357 006 passes Ripple Lane with the 12.35 London Fenchurch Street–Grays on 30/06/09. **Anthony Guppy**

▼ National Express-liveried 360 115 is seen south of Kelvedon with the 10.50 Clacton–London Liverpool Street on 11/09/09. **Anthony Guppy**

▲ Southeastern's 375 825 and 375 903 pass Paddock Wood with the 10.53 London Charing Cross–Ramsgate/Margate on 05/09/09. **Chris Wilson**

▼ In FCC livery, 377 510 arrives at East Croydon with the 14.10 Bedford–Brighton on 25/09/09. These units are now working alongside Class 319s on this route.
**Alisdair Anderson**

▲ The first London Overground Class 378s entered service in summer 2009. On 01/10/09 378 018 leaves Hampstead Heath with the 12.27 Richmond–Stratford North London Line service. **Anthony Guppy**

▼ Virgin Pendolino 390 051 "Virgin Ambassador" passes Millmeece with the 14.46 London Euston–Glasgow Central on 10/06/08. **Andrew Mist**

▲ One of the Hitachi Class 395s, 395 010, passes the c2c station at Rainham with the 14.37 St Pancras International–Ebbsfleet on 18/08/09.     **Anthony Guppy**

▼ Two slam door Class 421 units remain in use on the Lymington branch but are due to be withdrawn in spring 2010. On 01/06/09 BR Blue & Grey-liveried 1497 is seen passing through the New Forest shortly after departure from Brockenhurst with the 15.59 to Lymington Pier.     **Robert Pritchard**

▲ Southern uses 17 former South West Trains Class 442s on services from Brighton/Eastbourne to London as an extension of Gatwick Express services. On 04/06/09 442 411 and 442 406 pass Stoats Nest Junction with the 16.50 Gatwick Airport–London Victoria as a Southern Class 377 heads south. **Robert Pritchard**

▼ South West Trains white-liveried 444 045 arrives at Southampton Airport Parkway with the 08.50 Poole–London Waterloo on 23/05/09. **Robert Pritchard**

▲ South West Trains blue-liveried 450 113 arrives at Guildford with the 08.08 from Aldershot on 30/05/09. **Alex Dasi-Sutton**

▼ South West Trains red-liveried 5716 arrives at Surbiton with the 18.10 London Waterloo–Guildford via Woking on 31/05/09. **Robert Pritchard**

▲ Southern-liveried 456 004 is seen near Wandsworth Common with the 10.49 London Victoria–London Bridge on 24/03/09. **Alex Dasi-Sutton**

▼ South West Trains white-liveried 8007 and 8023 leave Putney with the 10.54 Reading–London Waterloo on 31/05/09. **Robert Pritchard**

▲ Gatwick Express-liveried 460 001 is seen near Coulsdon South with the 08.20 Gatwick Airport–London Victoria on 19/06/09.　　**Robert Pritchard**

▼ Southeastern-liveried 465 036 arrives at St Johns with the 14.17 Hayes–London Cannon Street on 31/05/09.　　**Robert Pritchard**

▲ Merseyrail-liveried 508 111 stands at Ellesmere Port with the 15.49 to Liverpool Central on 26/03/09. **Robert Pritchard**

▼ Eurostar 3202/01 passes Rainham at speed on 18/06/09 with the 11.13 Paris Nord–St Pancras International. **Robert Pritchard**

▲ Sheffield tram 110, carrying the now standard Stagecoach blue colours, leaves Meadowhall with a yellow route service to Middlewood on 06/12/08. The M1 Motorway viaduct can be seen to the right. **Robert Pritchard**

▼ The first of the new Manchester Metrolink trams, built by Bombardier in Austria, arrived in the summer of 2009. Here 3001 is displayed to the media at Queen's Road depot on 15/07/09. **Paul Jackson**

| | | | | | | | | | |
|---|---|---|---|---|---|---|---|---|---|
| 390 010 | **VT** | A | *VW* | MA | 69110 | 69410 | 69510 | 69610 | 68810 |
| | | | | | 69710 | 69810 | 69910 | 69210 | |
| 390 011 | **VT** | A | *VW* | MA | 69111 | 69411 | 69511 | 69611 | 68811 |
| | | | | | 69711 | 69811 | 69911 | 69211 | |
| 390 012 | **VT** | A | *VW* | MA | 69112 | 69412 | 69512 | 69612 | 68812 |
| | | | | | 69712 | 69812 | 69912 | 69212 | |
| 390 013 | **VT** | A | *VW* | MA | 69113 | 69413 | 69513 | 69613 | 68813 |
| | | | | | 69713 | 69813 | 69913 | 69213 | |
| 390 014 | **VT** | A | *VW* | MA | 69114 | 69414 | 69514 | 69614 | 68814 |
| | | | | | 69714 | 69814 | 69914 | 69214 | |
| 390 015 | **VT** | A | *VW* | MA | 69115 | 69415 | 69515 | 69615 | 68815 |
| | | | | | 69715 | 69815 | 69915 | 69215 | |
| 390 016 | **VT** | A | *VW* | MA | 69116 | 69416 | 69516 | 69616 | 68816 |
| | | | | | 69716 | 69816 | 69916 | 69216 | |
| 390 017 | **VT** | A | *VW* | MA | 69117 | 69417 | 69517 | 69617 | 68817 |
| | | | | | 69717 | 69817 | 69917 | 69217 | |
| 390 018 | **VT** | A | *VW* | MA | 69118 | 69418 | 69518 | 69618 | 68818 |
| | | | | | 69718 | 69818 | 69918 | 69218 | |
| 390 019 | **VT** | A | *VW* | MA | 69119 | 69419 | 69519 | 69619 | 68819 |
| | | | | | 69719 | 69819 | 69919 | 69219 | |
| 390 020 | **VT** | A | *VW* | MA | 69120 | 69420 | 69520 | 69620 | 68820 |
| | | | | | 69720 | 69820 | 69920 | 69220 | |
| 390 021 | **VT** | A | *VW* | MA | 69121 | 69421 | 69521 | 69621 | 68821 |
| | | | | | 69721 | 69821 | 69921 | 69221 | |
| 390 022 | **VT** | A | *VW* | MA | 69122 | 69422 | 69522 | 69622 | 68822 |
| | | | | | 69722 | 69822 | 69922 | 69222 | |
| 390 023 | **VT** | A | *VW* | MA | 69123 | 69423 | 69523 | 69623 | 68823 |
| | | | | | 69723 | 69823 | 69923 | 69223 | |
| 390 024 | **VT** | A | *VW* | MA | 69124 | 69424 | 69524 | 69624 | 68824 |
| | | | | | 69724 | 69824 | 69924 | 69224 | |
| 390 025 | **VT** | A | *VW* | MA | 69125 | 69425 | 69525 | 69625 | 68825 |
| | | | | | 69725 | 69825 | 69925 | 69225 | |
| 390 026 | **VT** | A | *VW* | MA | 69126 | 69426 | 69526 | 69626 | 68826 |
| | | | | | 69726 | 69826 | 69926 | 69226 | |
| 390 027 | **VT** | A | *VW* | MA | 69127 | 69427 | 69527 | 69627 | 68827 |
| | | | | | 69727 | 69827 | 69927 | 69227 | |
| 390 028 | **VT** | A | *VW* | MA | 69128 | 69428 | 69528 | 69628 | 68828 |
| | | | | | 69728 | 69828 | 69928 | 69228 | |
| 390 029 | **VT** | A | *VW* | MA | 69129 | 69429 | 69529 | 69629 | 68829 |
| | | | | | 69729 | 69829 | 69929 | 69229 | |
| 390 030 | **VT** | A | *VW* | MA | 69130 | 69430 | 69530 | 69630 | 68830 |
| | | | | | 69730 | 69830 | 69930 | 69230 | |
| 390 031 | **VT** | A | *VW* | MA | 69131 | 69431 | 69531 | 69631 | 68831 |
| | | | | | 69731 | 69831 | 69931 | 69231 | |
| 390 032 | **VT** | A | *VW* | MA | 69132 | 69432 | 69532 | 69632 | 68832 |
| | | | | | 69732 | 69832 | 69932 | 69232 | |
| 390 034 | **VT** | A | *VW* | MA | 69134 | 69434 | 69534 | 69634 | 68834 |
| | | | | | 69734 | 69834 | 69934 | 69234 | |
| 390 035 | **VT** | A | *VW* | MA | 69135 | 69435 | 69535 | 69635 | 68835 |
| | | | | | 69735 | 69835 | 69935 | 69235 | |

| | | | | | | | | | |
|---|---|---|---|---|---|---|---|---|---|
| 390 036 | **VT** | A | *VW* | MA | 69136 | 69436 | 69536 | 69636 | 68836 |
| | | | | | 69736 | 69836 | 69936 | 69236 | |
| 390 037 | **VT** | A | *VW* | MA | 69137 | 69437 | 69537 | 69637 | 68837 |
| | | | | | 69737 | 69837 | 69937 | 69237 | |
| 390 038 | **VT** | A | *VW* | MA | 69138 | 69438 | 69538 | 69638 | 68838 |
| | | | | | 69738 | 69838 | 69938 | 69238 | |
| 390 039 | **VT** | A | *VW* | MA | 69139 | 69439 | 69539 | 69639 | 68839 |
| | | | | | 69739 | 69839 | 69939 | 69239 | |
| 390 040 | **VT** | A | *VW* | MA | 69140 | 69440 | 69540 | 69640 | 68840 |
| | | | | | 69740 | 69840 | 69940 | 69240 | |
| 390 041 | **VT** | A | *VW* | MA | 69141 | 69441 | 69541 | 69641 | 68841 |
| | | | | | 69741 | 69841 | 69941 | 69241 | |
| 390 042 | **VT** | A | *VW* | MA | 69142 | 69442 | 69542 | 69642 | 68842 |
| | | | | | 69742 | 69842 | 69942 | 69242 | |
| 390 043 | **VT** | A | *VW* | MA | 69143 | 69443 | 69543 | 69643 | 68843 |
| | | | | | 69743 | 69843 | 69943 | 69243 | |
| 390 044 | **VT** | A | *VW* | MA | 69144 | 69444 | 69544 | 69644 | 68844 |
| | | | | | 69744 | 69844 | 69944 | 69244 | |
| 390 045 | **VT** | A | *VW* | MA | 69145 | 69445 | 69545 | 69645 | 68845 |
| | | | | | 69745 | 69845 | 69945 | 69245 | |
| 390 046 | **VT** | A | *VW* | MA | 69146 | 69446 | 69546 | 69646 | 68846 |
| | | | | | 69746 | 69846 | 69946 | 69246 | |
| 390 047 | **VT** | A | *VW* | MA | 69147 | 69447 | 69547 | 69647 | 68847 |
| | | | | | 69747 | 69847 | 69947 | 69247 | |
| 390 048 | **VT** | A | *VW* | MA | 69148 | 69448 | 69548 | 69648 | 68848 |
| | | | | | 69748 | 69848 | 69948 | 69248 | |
| 390 049 | **VT** | A | *VW* | MA | 69149 | 69449 | 69549 | 69649 | 68849 |
| | | | | | 69749 | 69849 | 69949 | 69249 | |
| 390 050 | **VT** | A | *VW* | MA | 69150 | 69450 | 69550 | 69650 | 68850 |
| | | | | | 69750 | 69850 | 69950 | 69250 | |
| 390 051 | **VT** | A | *VW* | MA | 69151 | 69451 | 69551 | 69651 | 68851 |
| | | | | | 69751 | 69851 | 69951 | 69251 | |
| 390 052 | **VT** | A | *VW* | MA | 69152 | 69452 | 69552 | 69652 | 68852 |
| | | | | | 69752 | 69852 | 69952 | 69252 | |
| 390 053 | **VT** | A | *VW* | MA | 69153 | 69453 | 69553 | 69653 | 68853 |
| | | | | | 69753 | 69853 | 69953 | 69253 | |

**Names (carried on MFO No. 696xx):**

| | | | |
|---|---|---|---|
| 390 001 | Virgin Pioneer | 390 027 | Virgin Buccaneer |
| 390 002 | Virgin Angel | 390 028 | City of Preston |
| 390 003 | Virgin Hero | 390 029 | City of Stoke-on-Trent |
| 390 004 | Virgin Scot | 390 030 | City of Edinburgh |
| 390 005 | City of Wolverhampton | 390 031 | City of Liverpool |
| 390 006 | Tate Liverpool | 390 032 | City of Birmingham |
| 390 007 | Virgin Lady | 390 034 | City of Carlisle |
| 390 008 | Virgin King | 390 035 | City of Lancaster |
| 390 009 | Treaty of Union | 390 036 | City of Coventry |
| 390 010 | A Decade of Progress | 390 037 | Virgin Difference |
| 390 011 | City of Lichfield | 390 038 | City of London |
| 390 012 | Virgin Star | 390 039 | Virgin Quest |
| 390 013 | Virgin Spirit | 390 040 | Virgin Pathfinder |
| 390 014 | City of Manchester | 390 041 | City of Chester |
| 390 015 | Virgin Crusader | 390 042 | City of Bangor/Dinas Bangor |
| 390 016 | Virgin Champion | 390 043 | Virgin Explorer |
| 390 017 | Virgin Prince | 390 044 | Virgin Lionheart |
| 390 018 | Virgin Princess | 390 045 | 101 Squadron |
| 390 019 | Virgin Warrior | 390 046 | Virgin Soldiers |
| 390 020 | Virgin Cavalier | 390 047 | CLIC Sargent |
| 390 021 | Virgin Dream | 390 048 | Virgin Harrier |
| 390 022 | Penny the Pendolino | 390 049 | Virgin Express |
| 390 023 | Virgin Glory | 390 050 | Virgin Invader |
| 390 024 | Virgin Venturer | 390 051 | Virgin Ambassador |
| 390 025 | Virgin Stagecoach | 390 052 | Virgin Knight |
| 390 026 | Virgin Enterprise | 390 053 | Mission Accomplished |

# CLASS 395   HS1 DOMESTIC SETS   HITACHI JAPAN

New 6-car dual-voltage units for Southeastern domestic services from St Pancras International to Ashford/Dover/Margate via Ramsgate and Faversham.

**Formation:** PDTSO–MSO–MSO–MSO–MSO–PDTSO.
**Systems:** 25 kV AC overhead/750 V DC third rail.
**Construction:** Aluminium.
**Traction Motors:** Hitachi asynchronous of 210 kW.
**Wheel Arrangement:** 2-2 + Bo-Bo + Bo-Bo + Bo-Bo + Bo-Bo + 2-2.
**Braking:** Disc, rheostatic & capability for regenerative braking.
**Dimensions:** 20.88/20.0 x 2.81 m.    **Couplers:** Scharfenberg.
**Bogies:** Hitachi.                     **Control System:** IGBT Inverter.
**Gangways:** Within unit.               **Maximum Speed:** 140 m.p.h.
**Doors:** Single-leaf sliding.          **Multiple Working:** Within class only.
**Heating & ventilation:** Air conditioning.
**Seating Layout:** 2+2 facing/unidirectional (mainly unidirectional).

**PDTSO(A):** Hitachi Kasado, Japan 2006–2009. –/28(12) 1TD 2W. 46.7 t.
**MSO:** Hitachi Kasado, Japan 2006–2009. –/66. 45.0 t.–45.7 t.
**PDTSO(B):** Hitachi Kasado, Japan 2006–2009. –/48 1T. 46.7 t.

| 395 001 | **SB** | H | *SE* | AD | 39011 | 39012 | 39013 | 39014 | 39015 | 39016 |
| 395 002 | **SB** | H | *SE* | AD | 39021 | 39022 | 39023 | 39024 | 39025 | 39026 |
| 395 003 | **SB** | H | *SE* | AD | 39031 | 39032 | 39033 | 39034 | 39035 | 39036 |
| 395 004 | **SB** | H | *SE* | AD | 39041 | 39042 | 39043 | 39044 | 39045 | 39046 |
| 395 005 | **SB** | H | *SE* | AD | 39051 | 39052 | 39053 | 39054 | 39055 | 39056 |
| 395 006 | **SB** | H | *SE* | AD | 39061 | 39062 | 39063 | 39064 | 39065 | 39066 |
| 395 007 | **SB** | H | *SE* | AD | 39071 | 39072 | 39073 | 39074 | 39075 | 39076 |
| 395 008 | **SB** | H | *SE* | AD | 39081 | 39082 | 39083 | 39084 | 39085 | 39086 |
| 395 009 | **SB** | H | *SE* | AD | 39091 | 39092 | 39093 | 39094 | 39095 | 39096 |
| 395 010 | **SB** | H | *SE* | AD | 39101 | 39102 | 39103 | 39104 | 39105 | 39106 |
| 395 011 | **SB** | H | *SE* | AD | 39111 | 39112 | 39113 | 39114 | 39115 | 39116 |
| 395 012 | **SB** | H | *SE* | AD | 39121 | 39122 | 39123 | 39124 | 39125 | 39126 |
| 395 013 | **SB** | H | *SE* | AD | 39131 | 39132 | 39133 | 39134 | 39135 | 39136 |
| 395 014 | **SB** | H | *SE* | AD | 39141 | 39142 | 39143 | 39144 | 39145 | 39146 |
| 395 015 | **SB** | H | *SE* | AD | 39151 | 39152 | 39153 | 39154 | 39155 | 39156 |
| 395 016 | **SB** | H | *SE* | AD | 39161 | 39162 | 39163 | 39164 | 39165 | 39166 |
| 395 017 | **SB** | H | *SE* | AD | 39171 | 39172 | 39173 | 39174 | 39175 | 39176 |
| 395 018 | **SB** | H | *SE* | AD | 39181 | 39182 | 39183 | 39184 | 39185 | 39186 |
| 395 019 | **SB** | H | *SE* | AD | 39191 | 39192 | 39193 | 39194 | 39195 | 39196 |
| 395 020 | **SB** | H | *SE* | AD | 39201 | 39202 | 39203 | 39204 | 39205 | 39206 |
| 395 021 | **SB** | H | *SE* | AD | 39211 | 39212 | 39213 | 39214 | 39215 | 39216 |
| 395 022 | **SB** | H | *SE* | AD | 39221 | 39222 | 39223 | 39224 | 39225 | 39226 |
| 395 023 | **SB** | H | *SE* | AD | 39231 | 39232 | 39233 | 39234 | 39235 | 39236 |
| 395 024 | **SB** | H | *SE* | AD | 39241 | 39242 | 39243 | 39244 | 39245 | 39246 |
| 395 025 | **SB** | H | *SE* | AD | 39251 | 39252 | 39253 | 39254 | 39255 | 39256 |
| 395 026 | **SB** | H | *SE* | AD | 39261 | 39262 | 39263 | 39264 | 39265 | 39266 |
| 395 027 | **SB** | H | *SE* | AD | 39271 | 39272 | 39273 | 39274 | 39275 | 39276 |
| 395 028 | **SB** | H | *SE* | AD | 39281 | 39282 | 39283 | 39284 | 39285 | 39286 |
| 395 029 | **SB** | H | *SE* | AD | 39291 | 39292 | 39293 | 39294 | 39295 | 39296 |

**Names (carried on end cars):**

| 395 001 | Dame Kelly Holmes | 395 006 | Daley Thompson |
| 395 003 | Sir Steve Redgrave | 395 016 | Jamie Staff |
| 395 004 | Sir Chris Hoy | | |

# 4.2. 750 V DC THIRD RAIL EMUs

These classes use the third rail system at 750 V DC (unless stated). Outer couplers are buckeyes on units built before 1982 with bar couplers within the units. Newer units generally have Dellner outer couplers.

## CLASS 421                                                        BR YORK

Specially converted Phase 2 3-car "Cig" sets for use on the Lymington branch line. Central Door Locking system fitted and wheelchair space created. Toilets removed. Due to be withdrawn from traffic spring 2010.

**Formation:** DTCso–MBSO–DTCso.
**Construction:** Steel.
**Traction Motors:** Four EE507 of 185 kW.
**Wheel Arrangement:** 2-2 + Bo-Bo + 2-2.
**Braking:** Tread.
**Bogies:** Mark 6 motor bogies (MBSO). B5 (SR) bogies (trailer cars).
**Couplers:** Buckeye.
**Gangways:** Throughout.
**Doors:** Slam.
**Dimensions:** 20.18 x 2.82 m.
**Multiple Working:** Within class.
**Control System:** 1963-type.
**Maximum Speed:** 90 m.p.h.
**Seating Layout:** 1: Compartments, 2: 2+2 facing (plus one four-a-side compartment per DTC).

**76764/76773. DTCso(A).** Lot No. 30814 1971. 18/36. 35.5 t.
**62402/62411. MBSO.** Lot No. 30816 1971. –/56 1W + 3 tip-up seats. 49 t.
**76835/76844. DTCso(B).** Lot No. 30815 1971. 18/36. 35 t.

| | | | | | | | | | |
|---|---|---|---|---|---|---|---|---|---|
| 1497 | (1883) | **BG** | SW | *SW* | BM | 76764 | 62402 | 76835 | Freshwater |
| 1498 | (1888) | **G** | SW | *SW* | BM | 76773 | 62411 | 76844 | Farringford |

## CLASS 442   WESSEX EXPRESS   BREL DERBY

Stock built for Waterloo–Bournemouth–Weymouth services. Withdrawn from service with South West Trains in early 2007. 17 sets have been refurbished at Railcare, Wolverton for use by Southern principally on Victoria–Gatwick Airport–Brighton services (in 10-car formations).

**Formation:** As built: DTFso–TSO–MBRMB–TSO–DTSO * refurbished Southern: DTSO(A)–TSO–MBC–TSO(W)–DTSO(B).
**Construction:** Steel.
**Traction Motors:** Four EE546 of 300 kW recovered from Class 432s.
**Wheel Arrangement:** 2-2 + 2-2 + Bo-Bo + 2-2 + 2-2.
**Braking:** Disc.
**Bogies:** Two BREL P7 motor bogies (MBSO). T4 bogies (trailer cars).
**Couplers:** Buckeye.
**Gangways:** Throughout.
**Doors:** Sliding plug.
**Dimensions:** 23.15/23.00 x 2.74 m.
**Control System:** 1986-type.
**Maximum Speed:** 100 m.p.h.
**Heating & Ventilation:** Air conditioning.
**Seating Layout (unrefurbished):** 1: 2+2 facing/compartments, 2: 2+2 facing/unidirectional.
**Seating Layout (refurbished):** 1: 2+1 facing, 2: 2+2 mainly unidirectional.
**Multiple Working:** Within class and with locos of Classes 33/1 & 73 in an emergency.

Details of refurbished Southern units (*):

**DTSO(A).** Lot No. 31030 Derby 1988–1989. –/74. 38.5 t.
**TSO.** Lot No. 31032 Derby 1988–1989. –/76 2T. 37.5 t.
**MBC.** Lot No. 31034 Derby 1988–1989. 24/28. 55.0 t.
**TSO(W).** Lot No. 31033 Derby 1988–1989. –/66(4) 1TD 1T 2W. 37.8 t.
**DTSO(B).** Lot No. 31031 Derby 1988–1989. –/74. 37.3 t.

Details of unrefurbished units:

**DTFso.** Lot No. 31030 Derby 1988–1989. 50/– 1T. (36 in six compartments and 14 in one saloon). 39.0 t.
**TSO(A).** Lot No. 31032 Derby 1988–1989. –/80 2T. 35.3 t.
**MBRMB.** Lot No. 31034 Derby 1988–1989. –/30+17 ("snug") 1W. 54.7 t.
**TSO(B).** Lot No. 31033 Derby 1988–1989. –/76(2) 1TD 1T 1W. 35.4 t.
**DTSO.** Lot No. 31031 Derby 1988–1989. –/78 1T. 35.7 t.

| | | | | | | | | | |
|---|---|---|---|---|---|---|---|---|---|
| 442 401 | * | **GV** | A | *SN* | BI | 77382 | 71818 | 62937 | 71842 | 77406 |
| 442 402 | * | **GV** | A | *SN* | BI | 77383 | 71819 | 62938 | 71843 | 77407 |
| 442 403 | * | **GV** | A | *SN* | BI | 77384 | 71820 | 62941 | 71844 | 77408 |
| 442 404 | * | **GV** | A | *SN* | BI | 77385 | 71821 | 62939 | 71845 | 77409 |
| 442 405 | * | **GV** | A | *SN* | BI | 77386 | 71822 | 62944 | 71846 | 77410 |
| 442 406 | * | **GV** | A | *SN* | BI | 77389 | 71823 | 62942 | 71847 | 77411 |
| 442 407 | * | **GV** | A | *SN* | BI | 77388 | 71824 | 62943 | 71848 | 77412 |
| 442 408 | * | **GV** | A | *SN* | BI | 77387 | 71825 | 62945 | 71849 | 77413 |
| 2409 | | **ST** | A | | AF | 77390 | 71826 | 62946 | 71850 | 77414 |
| 442 410 | * | **GV** | A | *SN* | BI | 77391 | 71827 | 62948 | 71851 | 77415 |
| 442 411 | * | **GV** | A | *SN* | BI | 77392 | 71828 | 62940 | 71858 | 77422 |
| 442 412 | * | **GV** | A | *SN* | SI | 77393 | 71829 | 62947 | 71853 | 77417 |
| 442 413 | * | **GV** | A | *SN* | BI | 77394 | 71830 | 62949 | 71854 | 77418 |
| 442 414 | * | **GV** | A | *SN* | BI | 77395 | 71831 | 62950 | 71855 | 77419 |
| 2415 | | **GV** | A | | ZN | 77396 | 71832 | 62951 | 71856 | 77420 |
| 2416 | | **ST** | A | | AF | 77397 | 71833 | 62952 | 71857 | 77421 |
| 442 417 | * | **GV** | A | *SN* | BI | 77398 | 71834 | 62953 | 71852 | 77416 |
| 2418 | | **ST** | A | *SN* | BI | 77399 | 71835 | 62954 | 71859 | 77423 |
| 442 419 | * | **GV** | A | *SN* | BI | 77400 | 71836 | 62955 | 71860 | 77424 |
| 2420 | | **ST** | A | | AF | 77401 | 71837 | 62956 | 71861 | 77425 |
| 442 421 | * | **GV** | A | *SN* | BI | 77402 | 71838 | 62957 | 71862 | 77426 |
| 2422 | | **ST** | A | | AF | 77403 | 71839 | 62958 | 71863 | 77427 |
| 2423 | | **ST** | A | *SN* | BI | 77404 | 71840 | 62959 | 71864 | 77428 |
| 442 424 | * | **GV** | A | *SN* | BI | 77405 | 71841 | 62960 | 71865 | 77429 |

# CLASS 444          DESIRO UK          SIEMENS

Express units.

**Formation:** DMCO–TSO–TSO–TSORMB–DMSO.
**Construction:** Aluminium.
**Traction Motors:** 4 Siemens 1TB2016-0GB02 asynchronous of 250 kW.
**Wheel Arrangement:** Bo-Bo + 2-2 + 2-2 + 2-2 + Bo-Bo.
**Braking:** Disc & rheostatic.          **Dimensions:** 23.57 x 2.80 m.
**Bogies:** SGP SF5000.          **Couplers:** Dellner 12.
**Gangways:** Throughout.          **Control System:** IGBT Inverter.

**Doors:** Single-leaf sliding plug.　　**Maximum Speed:** 100 m.p.h.
**Heating & Ventilation:** Air conditioning.
**Seating Layout:** 1: 2+1 facing/unidirectional, 2: 2+2 facing/unidirectional.
**Multiple Working:** Within class and with Class 450.

**DMSO.** Siemens Wien (Vienna)/Uerdingen 2003–2004. –/76. 51.3 t.
**TSO 67101–67145.** Siemens Wien (Vienna)/Uerdingen 2003–2004. –/76 1T. 40.3 t.
**TSO 67151–67195.** Siemens Wien (Vienna)/Uerdingen 2003–2004. –/76 1T. 36.8 t.
**TSORMB.** Siemens Wien (Vienna)/Uerdingen 2003–2004. –/47 1T 1TD 2W. 42.1 t.
**DMCO.** Siemens Wien (Vienna)/Uerdingen 2003–2004. 35/24. 51.3 t.

| | | | | | | | | | |
|---|---|---|---|---|---|---|---|---|---|
| 444 001 | **ST** | A | *SW* | NT | 63801 | 67101 | 67151 | 67201 | 63851 |
| 444 002 | **ST** | A | *SW* | NT | 63802 | 67102 | 67152 | 67202 | 63852 |
| 444 003 | **ST** | A | *SW* | NT | 63803 | 67103 | 67153 | 67203 | 63853 |
| 444 004 | **ST** | A | *SW* | NT | 63804 | 67104 | 67154 | 67204 | 63854 |
| 444 005 | **ST** | A | *SW* | NT | 63805 | 67105 | 67155 | 67205 | 63855 |
| 444 006 | **ST** | A | *SW* | NT | 63806 | 67106 | 67156 | 67206 | 63856 |
| 444 007 | **ST** | A | *SW* | NT | 63807 | 67107 | 67157 | 67207 | 63857 |
| 444 008 | **ST** | A | *SW* | NT | 63808 | 67108 | 67158 | 67208 | 63858 |
| 444 009 | **ST** | A | *SW* | NT | 63809 | 67109 | 67159 | 67209 | 63859 |
| 444 010 | **ST** | A | *SW* | NT | 63810 | 67110 | 67160 | 67210 | 63860 |
| 444 011 | **ST** | A | *SW* | NT | 63811 | 67111 | 67161 | 67211 | 63861 |
| 444 012 | **ST** | A | *SW* | NT | 63812 | 67112 | 67162 | 67212 | 63862 |
| 444 013 | **ST** | A | *SW* | NT | 63813 | 67113 | 67163 | 67213 | 63863 |
| 444 014 | **ST** | A | *SW* | NT | 63814 | 67114 | 67164 | 67214 | 63864 |
| 444 015 | **ST** | A | *SW* | NT | 63815 | 67115 | 67165 | 67215 | 63865 |
| 444 016 | **ST** | A | *SW* | NT | 63816 | 67116 | 67166 | 67216 | 63866 |
| 444 017 | **ST** | A | *SW* | NT | 63817 | 67117 | 67167 | 67217 | 63867 |
| 444 018 | **ST** | A | *SW* | NT | 63818 | 67118 | 67168 | 67218 | 63868 |
| 444 019 | **ST** | A | *SW* | NT | 63819 | 67119 | 67169 | 67219 | 63869 |
| 444 020 | **ST** | A | *SW* | NT | 63820 | 67120 | 67170 | 67220 | 63870 |
| 444 021 | **ST** | A | *SW* | NT | 63821 | 67121 | 67171 | 67221 | 63871 |
| 444 022 | **ST** | A | *SW* | NT | 63822 | 67122 | 67172 | 67222 | 63872 |
| 444 023 | **ST** | A | *SW* | NT | 63823 | 67123 | 67173 | 67223 | 63873 |
| 444 024 | **ST** | A | *SW* | NT | 63824 | 67124 | 67174 | 67224 | 63874 |
| 444 025 | **ST** | A | *SW* | NT | 63825 | 67125 | 67175 | 67225 | 63875 |
| 444 026 | **ST** | A | *SW* | NT | 63826 | 67126 | 67176 | 67226 | 63876 |
| 444 027 | **ST** | A | *SW* | NT | 63827 | 67127 | 67177 | 67227 | 63877 |
| 444 028 | **ST** | A | *SW* | NT | 63828 | 67128 | 67178 | 67228 | 63878 |
| 444 029 | **ST** | A | *SW* | NT | 63829 | 67129 | 67179 | 67229 | 63879 |
| 444 030 | **ST** | A | *SW* | NT | 63830 | 67130 | 67180 | 67230 | 63880 |
| 444 031 | **ST** | A | *SW* | NT | 63831 | 67131 | 67181 | 67231 | 63881 |
| 444 032 | **ST** | A | *SW* | NT | 63832 | 67132 | 67182 | 67232 | 63882 |
| 444 033 | **ST** | A | *SW* | NT | 63833 | 67133 | 67183 | 67233 | 63883 |
| 444 034 | **ST** | A | *SW* | NT | 63834 | 67134 | 67184 | 67234 | 63884 |
| 444 035 | **ST** | A | *SW* | NT | 63835 | 67135 | 67185 | 67235 | 63885 |
| 444 036 | **ST** | A | *SW* | NT | 63836 | 67136 | 67186 | 67236 | 63886 |
| 444 037 | **ST** | A | *SW* | NT | 63837 | 67137 | 67187 | 67237 | 63887 |
| 444 038 | **ST** | A | *SW* | NT | 63838 | 67138 | 67188 | 67238 | 63888 |
| 444 039 | **ST** | A | *SW* | NT | 63839 | 67139 | 67189 | 67239 | 63889 |
| 444 040 | **ST** | A | *SW* | NT | 63840 | 67140 | 67190 | 67240 | 63890 |
| 444 041 | **ST** | A | *SW* | NT | 63841 | 67141 | 67191 | 67241 | 63891 |

| 444 042 | **ST** | A | *SW* | NT | 63842 | 67142 | 67192 | 67242 | 63892 |
| 444 043 | **ST** | A | *SW* | NT | 63843 | 67143 | 67193 | 67243 | 63893 |
| 444 044 | **ST** | A | *SW* | NT | 63844 | 67144 | 67194 | 67244 | 63894 |
| 444 045 | **ST** | A | *SW* | NT | 63845 | 67145 | 67195 | 67245 | 63895 |

**Names (carried on TSORMB):**

444 001   NAOMI HOUSE
444 012   DESTINATION WEYMOUTH
444 018   THE FAB 444

# CLASS 450            DESIRO UK            SIEMENS

Outer suburban units.

**Formation:** DMSO–TCO–TSO–DMSO (DMSO–TSO–TCO–DMSO 450 111–127).
**Construction:** Aluminium.
**Traction Motors:** 4 Siemens 1TB2016-0GB02 asynchronous of 250 kW.
**Wheel Arrangement:** Bo-Bo + 2-2 + 2-2 + Bo-Bo.
**Braking:** Disc & rheostatic.          **Dimensions:** 20.34 x 2.79 m.
**Bogies:** SGP SF5000.                  **Couplers:** Dellner 12.
**Gangways:** Throughout.                **Control System:** IGBT Inverter.
**Doors:** Sliding plug.                 **Maximum Speed:** 100 m.p.h.
**Heating & Ventilation:** Air conditioning.
**Seating Layout:** 1: 2+2 facing/unidirectional, 2: 3+2 facing/unidirectional.
**Multiple Working:** Within class and with Class 444.

**Class 450/0. Standard units.**

**DMSO(A).** Siemens Uerdingen/Wien (Vienna) 2002–2006. –/70. 48.0 t.
**TCO.** Siemens Uerdingen/Wien (Vienna) 2002–2006. 24/32(4) 1T. 35.8 t.
**TSO.** Siemens Uerdingen/Wien (Vienna) 2002–2006. –/61(9) 1TD 2W. 39.8 t.
**DMSO(B).** Siemens Uerdingen/Wien (Vienna) 2002–2006. –/70. 48.6 t.

| 450 001 | **SD** | A | *SW* | NT | 63201 | 64201 | 68101 | 63601 |
| 450 002 | **SD** | A | *SW* | NT | 63202 | 64202 | 68102 | 63602 |
| 450 003 | **SD** | A | *SW* | NT | 63203 | 64203 | 68103 | 63603 |
| 450 004 | **SD** | A | *SW* | NT | 63204 | 64204 | 68104 | 63604 |
| 450 005 | **SD** | A | *SW* | NT | 63205 | 64205 | 68105 | 63605 |
| 450 006 | **SD** | A | *SW* | NT | 63206 | 64206 | 68106 | 63606 |
| 450 007 | **SD** | A | *SW* | NT | 63207 | 64207 | 68107 | 63607 |
| 450 008 | **SD** | A | *SW* | NT | 63208 | 64208 | 68108 | 63608 |
| 450 009 | **SD** | A | *SW* | NT | 63209 | 64209 | 68109 | 63609 |
| 450 010 | **SD** | A | *SW* | NT | 63210 | 64210 | 68110 | 63610 |
| 450 011 | **SD** | A | *SW* | NT | 63211 | 64211 | 68111 | 63611 |
| 450 012 | **SD** | A | *SW* | NT | 63212 | 64212 | 68112 | 63612 |
| 450 013 | **SD** | A | *SW* | NT | 63213 | 64213 | 68113 | 63613 |
| 450 014 | **SD** | A | *SW* | NT | 63214 | 64214 | 68114 | 63614 |
| 450 015 | **SD** | A | *SW* | NT | 63215 | 64215 | 68115 | 63615 |
| 450 016 | **SD** | A | *SW* | NT | 63216 | 64216 | 68116 | 63616 |
| 450 017 | **SD** | A | *SW* | NT | 63217 | 64217 | 68117 | 63617 |
| 450 018 | **SD** | A | *SW* | NT | 63218 | 64218 | 68118 | 63618 |
| 450 019 | **SD** | A | *SW* | NT | 63219 | 64219 | 68119 | 63619 |
| 450 020 | **SD** | A | *SW* | NT | 63220 | 64220 | 68120 | 63620 |

| 450 021 | **SD** | A | *SW* | NT | 63221 | 64221 | 68121 | 63621 |
| 450 022 | **SD** | A | *SW* | NT | 63222 | 64222 | 68122 | 63622 |
| 450 023 | **SD** | A | *SW* | NT | 63223 | 64223 | 68123 | 63623 |
| 450 024 | **SD** | A | *SW* | NT | 63224 | 64224 | 68124 | 63624 |
| 450 025 | **SD** | A | *SW* | NT | 63225 | 64225 | 68125 | 63625 |
| 450 026 | **SD** | A | *SW* | NT | 63226 | 64226 | 68126 | 63626 |
| 450 027 | **SD** | A | *SW* | NT | 63227 | 64227 | 68127 | 63627 |
| 450 028 | **SD** | A | *SW* | NT | 63228 | 64228 | 68128 | 63628 |
| 450 029 | **SD** | A | *SW* | NT | 63229 | 64229 | 68129 | 63629 |
| 450 030 | **SD** | A | *SW* | NT | 63230 | 64230 | 68130 | 63630 |
| 450 031 | **SD** | A | *SW* | NT | 63231 | 64231 | 68131 | 63631 |
| 450 032 | **SD** | A | *SW* | NT | 63232 | 64232 | 68132 | 63632 |
| 450 033 | **SD** | A | *SW* | NT | 63233 | 64233 | 68133 | 63633 |
| 450 034 | **SD** | A | *SW* | NT | 63234 | 64234 | 68134 | 63634 |
| 450 035 | **SD** | A | *SW* | NT | 63235 | 64235 | 68135 | 63635 |
| 450 036 | **SD** | A | *SW* | NT | 63236 | 64236 | 68136 | 63636 |
| 450 037 | **SD** | A | *SW* | NT | 63237 | 64237 | 68137 | 63637 |
| 450 038 | **SD** | A | *SW* | NT | 63238 | 64238 | 68138 | 63638 |
| 450 039 | **SD** | A | *SW* | NT | 63239 | 64239 | 68139 | 63639 |
| 450 040 | **SD** | A | *SW* | NT | 63240 | 64240 | 68140 | 63640 |
| 450 041 | **SD** | A | *SW* | NT | 63241 | 64241 | 68141 | 63641 |
| 450 042 | **SD** | A | *SW* | NT | 63242 | 64242 | 68142 | 63642 |
| 450 071 | **SD** | A | *SW* | NT | 63271 | 64271 | 68171 | 63671 |
| 450 072 | **SD** | A | *SW* | NT | 63272 | 64272 | 68172 | 63672 |
| 450 073 | **SD** | A | *SW* | NT | 63273 | 64273 | 68173 | 63673 |
| 450 074 | **SD** | A | *SW* | NT | 63274 | 64274 | 68174 | 63674 |
| 450 075 | **SD** | A | *SW* | NT | 63275 | 64275 | 68175 | 63675 |
| 450 076 | **SD** | A | *SW* | NT | 63276 | 64276 | 68176 | 63676 |
| 450 077 | **SD** | A | *SW* | NT | 63277 | 64277 | 68177 | 63677 |
| 450 078 | **SD** | A | *SW* | NT | 63278 | 64278 | 68178 | 63678 |
| 450 079 | **SD** | A | *SW* | NT | 63279 | 64279 | 68179 | 63679 |
| 450 080 | **SD** | A | *SW* | NT | 63280 | 64280 | 68180 | 63680 |
| 450 081 | **SD** | A | *SW* | NT | 63281 | 64281 | 68181 | 63681 |
| 450 082 | **SD** | A | *SW* | NT | 63282 | 64282 | 68182 | 63682 |
| 450 083 | **SD** | A | *SW* | NT | 63283 | 64283 | 68183 | 63683 |
| 450 084 | **SD** | A | *SW* | NT | 63284 | 64284 | 68184 | 63684 |
| 450 085 | **SD** | A | *SW* | NT | 63285 | 64285 | 68185 | 63685 |
| 450 086 | **SD** | A | *SW* | NT | 63286 | 64286 | 68186 | 63686 |
| 450 087 | **SD** | A | *SW* | NT | 63287 | 64287 | 68187 | 63687 |
| 450 088 | **SD** | A | *SW* | NT | 63288 | 64288 | 68188 | 63688 |
| 450 089 | **SD** | A | *SW* | NT | 63289 | 64289 | 68189 | 63689 |
| 450 090 | **SD** | A | *SW* | NT | 63290 | 64290 | 68190 | 63690 |
| 450 091 | **SD** | A | *SW* | NT | 63291 | 64291 | 68191 | 63691 |
| 450 092 | **SD** | A | *SW* | NT | 63292 | 64292 | 68192 | 63692 |
| 450 093 | **SD** | A | *SW* | NT | 63293 | 64293 | 68193 | 63693 |
| 450 094 | **SD** | A | *SW* | NT | 63294 | 64294 | 68194 | 63694 |
| 450 095 | **SD** | A | *SW* | NT | 63295 | 64295 | 68195 | 63695 |
| 450 096 | **SD** | A | *SW* | NT | 63296 | 64296 | 68196 | 63696 |
| 450 097 | **SD** | A | *SW* | NT | 63297 | 64297 | 68197 | 63697 |
| 450 098 | **SD** | A | *SW* | NT | 63298 | 64298 | 68198 | 63698 |
| 450 099 | **SD** | A | *SW* | NT | 63299 | 64299 | 68199 | 63699 |

| 450 100 | **SD** | A | *SW* | NT | 63300 | 64300 | 68200 | 63700 |
|---------|--------|---|------|----|-------|-------|-------|-------|
| 450 101 | **SD** | A | *SW* | NT | 63701 | 66851 | 66801 | 63751 |
| 450 102 | **SD** | A | *SW* | NT | 63702 | 66852 | 66802 | 63752 |
| 450 103 | **SD** | A | *SW* | NT | 63703 | 66853 | 66803 | 63753 |
| 450 104 | **SD** | A | *SW* | NT | 63704 | 66854 | 66804 | 63754 |
| 450 105 | **SD** | A | *SW* | NT | 63705 | 66855 | 66805 | 63755 |
| 450 106 | **SD** | A | *SW* | NT | 63706 | 66856 | 66806 | 63756 |
| 450 107 | **SD** | A | *SW* | NT | 63707 | 66857 | 66807 | 63757 |
| 450 108 | **SD** | A | *SW* | NT | 63708 | 66858 | 66808 | 63758 |
| 450 109 | **SD** | A | *SW* | NT | 63709 | 66859 | 66809 | 63759 |
| 450 110 | **SD** | A | *SW* | NT | 63710 | 66860 | 66810 | 63760 |
| 450 111 | **SD** | A | *SW* | NT | 63901 | 66921 | 66901 | 63921 |
| 450 112 | **SD** | A | *SW* | NT | 63902 | 66922 | 66902 | 63922 |
| 450 113 | **SD** | A | *SW* | NT | 63903 | 66923 | 66903 | 63923 |
| 450 114 | **SD** | A | *SW* | NT | 63904 | 66924 | 66904 | 63924 |
| 450 115 | **SD** | A | *SW* | NT | 63905 | 66925 | 66905 | 63925 |
| 450 116 | **SD** | A | *SW* | NT | 63906 | 66926 | 66906 | 63926 |
| 450 117 | **SD** | A | *SW* | NT | 63907 | 66927 | 66907 | 63927 |
| 450 118 | **SD** | A | *SW* | NT | 63908 | 66928 | 66908 | 63928 |
| 450 119 | **SD** | A | *SW* | NT | 63909 | 66929 | 66909 | 63929 |
| 450 120 | **SD** | A | *SW* | NT | 63910 | 66930 | 66910 | 63930 |
| 450 121 | **SD** | A | *SW* | NT | 63911 | 66931 | 66911 | 63931 |
| 450 122 | **SD** | A | *SW* | NT | 63912 | 66932 | 66912 | 63932 |
| 450 123 | **SD** | A | *SW* | NT | 63913 | 66933 | 66913 | 63933 |
| 450 124 | **SD** | A | *SW* | NT | 63914 | 66934 | 66914 | 63934 |
| 450 125 | **SD** | A | *SW* | NT | 63915 | 66935 | 66915 | 63935 |
| 450 126 | **SD** | A | *SW* | NT | 63916 | 66936 | 66916 | 63936 |
| 450 127 | **SD** | A | *SW* | NT | 63917 | 66937 | 66917 | 63937 |

**Names (carried on DMSO(B)):**

| 450 015 | DESIRO |
|---------|--------|
| 450 042 | TRELOAR COLLEGE |
| 450 114 | FAIRBRIDGE investing in the future |

**Class 450/5. "High density" units.** 28 units converted at Bournemouth for Waterloo–Windsor/Weybridge/Hounslow services. First Class removed and modified seating layout with more standing room. Details as Class 450/0 except:

**Formation:** DMSO–TSO–TSO–DMSO.

**DMSO(A).** Siemens Uerdingen/Wien (Vienna) 2002–2004. –/64. 48.0 t.
**TSO(A).** Siemens Uerdingen/Wien (Vienna) 2002–2004. –/56(4) 1T. 35.5 t.
**TSO(B).** Siemens Uerdingen/Wien (Vienna) 2002–2004. –/56(9) 1TD 2W. 39.8 t.
**DMSO(B).** Siemens Uerdingen/Wien (Vienna) 2002–2004. –/64. 48.6 t.

| 450 543 | (450 043) | **SD** | A | *SW* | NT | 63243 | 64243 | 68143 | 63643 |
|---------|-----------|--------|---|------|----|-------|-------|-------|-------|
| 450 544 | (450 044) | **SD** | A | *SW* | NT | 63244 | 64244 | 68144 | 63644 |
| 450 545 | (450 045) | **SD** | A | *SW* | NT | 63245 | 64245 | 68145 | 63645 |
| 450 546 | (450 046) | **SD** | A | *SW* | NT | 63246 | 64246 | 68146 | 63646 |
| 450 547 | (450 047) | **SD** | A | *SW* | NT | 63247 | 64247 | 68147 | 63647 |
| 450 548 | (450 048) | **SD** | A | *SW* | NT | 63248 | 64248 | 68148 | 63648 |
| 450 549 | (450 049) | **SD** | A | *SW* | NT | 63249 | 64249 | 68149 | 63649 |
| 450 550 | (450 050) | **SD** | A | *SW* | NT | 63250 | 64250 | 68150 | 63650 |

| | | | | | | | | |
|---|---|---|---|---|---|---|---|---|
| 450 551 | (450 051) | **SD** | A | *SW* | NT | 63251 | 64251 | 68151 | 63651 |
| 450 552 | (450 052) | **SD** | A | *SW* | NT | 63252 | 64252 | 68152 | 63652 |
| 450 553 | (450 053) | **SD** | A | *SW* | NT | 63253 | 64253 | 68153 | 63653 |
| 450 554 | (450 054) | **SD** | A | *SW* | NT | 63254 | 64254 | 68154 | 63654 |
| 450 555 | (450 055) | **SD** | A | *SW* | NT | 63255 | 64255 | 68155 | 63655 |
| 450 556 | (450 056) | **SD** | A | *SW* | NT | 63256 | 64256 | 68156 | 63656 |
| 450 557 | (450 057) | **SD** | A | *SW* | NT | 63257 | 64257 | 68157 | 63657 |
| 450 558 | (450 058) | **SD** | A | *SW* | NT | 63258 | 64258 | 68158 | 63658 |
| 450 559 | (450 059) | **SD** | A | *SW* | NT | 63259 | 64259 | 68159 | 63659 |
| 450 560 | (450 060) | **SD** | A | *SW* | NT | 63260 | 64260 | 68160 | 63660 |
| 450 561 | (450 061) | **SD** | A | *SW* | NT | 63261 | 64261 | 68161 | 63661 |
| 450 562 | (450 062) | **SD** | A | *SW* | NT | 63262 | 64262 | 68162 | 63662 |
| 450 563 | (450 063) | **SD** | A | *SW* | NT | 63263 | 64263 | 68163 | 63663 |
| 450 564 | (450 064) | **SD** | A | *SW* | NT | 63264 | 64264 | 68164 | 63664 |
| 450 565 | (450 065) | **SD** | A | *SW* | NT | 63265 | 64265 | 68165 | 63665 |
| 450 566 | (450 066) | **SD** | A | *SW* | NT | 63266 | 64266 | 68166 | 63666 |
| 450 567 | (450 067) | **SD** | A | *SW* | NT | 63267 | 64267 | 68167 | 63667 |
| 450 568 | (450 068) | **SD** | A | *SW* | NT | 63268 | 64268 | 68168 | 63668 |
| 450 569 | (450 069) | **SD** | A | *SW* | NT | 63269 | 64269 | 68169 | 63669 |
| 450 570 | (450 070) | **SD** | A | *SW* | NT | 63270 | 64270 | 68170 | 63670 |

# CLASS 455                                          BR YORK

Inner suburban units.

**Formation**: DTSO–MSO–TSO–DTSO.
**Construction**: Steel. Class 455/7 TSO have a steel underframe and an aluminium alloy body & roof.
**Traction Motors**: Four GEC507-20J of 185 kW, some recovered from Class 405s.
**Wheel Arrangement**: 2-2 + Bo-Bo + 2-2 + 2-2.
**Braking**: Disc.                    **Dimensions**: 19.92/19.83 x 2.82 m.
**Bogies**: P7 (motor) and T3 (455/8 & 455/9) BX1 (455/7) trailer.
**Gangways**: Within unit + end doors (sealed on Southern units).
**Couplers**: Tightlock.                **Control System**: 1982-type, camshaft.
**Doors**: Sliding.                    **Maximum Speed**: 75 m.p.h.
**Heating & Ventilation**: Various.
**Seating Layout**: All units refurbished. SWT units: 2+2 high-back unidirectional/facing seating. Southern units: 3+2 high back mainly facing seating.
**Multiple Working**: Within class and with Class 456.

**Class 455/7. South West Trains units.** Second series with TSOs originally in Class 508s. Pressure heating & ventilation.

**DTSO**. Lot No. 30976 1984–1985. –/50(4) 1W. 30.8 t.
**MSO**. Lot No. 30975 1984–1985. –/68. 45.7 t.
**TSO**. Lot No. 30944 1979–1980. –/68. 26.1 t.

| | | | | | | | | |
|---|---|---|---|---|---|---|---|---|
| 5701 | **SS** | P | *SW* | WD | 77727 | 62783 | 71545 | 77728 |
| 5702 | **SS** | P | *SW* | WD | 77729 | 62784 | 71547 | 77730 |
| 5703 | **SS** | P | *SW* | WD | 77731 | 62785 | 71540 | 77732 |
| 5704 | **SS** | P | *SW* | WD | 77733 | 62786 | 71548 | 77734 |
| 5705 | **SS** | P | *SW* | WD | 77735 | 62787 | 71565 | 77736 |
| 5706 | **SS** | P | *SW* | WD | 77737 | 62788 | 71534 | 77738 |

| 5707 | **SS** | P | *SW* | WD | 77739 | 62789 | 71536 | 77740 |
|------|--------|---|------|----|-------|-------|-------|-------|
| 5708 | **SS** | P | *SW* | WD | 77741 | 62790 | 71560 | 77742 |
| 5709 | **SS** | P | *SW* | WD | 77743 | 62791 | 71532 | 77744 |
| 5710 | **SS** | P | *SW* | WD | 77745 | 62792 | 71566 | 77746 |
| 5711 | **SS** | P | *SW* | WD | 77747 | 62793 | 71542 | 77748 |
| 5712 | **SS** | P | *SW* | WD | 77749 | 62794 | 71546 | 77750 |
| 5713 | **SS** | P | *SW* | WD | 77751 | 62795 | 71567 | 77752 |
| 5714 | **SS** | P | *SW* | WD | 77753 | 62796 | 71539 | 77754 |
| 5715 | **SS** | P | *SW* | WD | 77755 | 62797 | 71535 | 77756 |
| 5716 | **SS** | P | *SW* | WD | 77757 | 62798 | 71564 | 77758 |
| 5717 | **SS** | P | *SW* | WD | 77759 | 62799 | 71528 | 77760 |
| 5718 | **SS** | P | *SW* | WD | 77761 | 62800 | 71557 | 77762 |
| 5719 | **SS** | P | *SW* | WD | 77763 | 62801 | 71558 | 77764 |
| 5720 | **SS** | P | *SW* | WD | 77765 | 62802 | 71568 | 77766 |
| 5721 | **SS** | P | *SW* | WD | 77767 | 62803 | 71553 | 77768 |
| 5722 | **SS** | P | *SW* | WD | 77769 | 62804 | 71533 | 77770 |
| 5723 | **SS** | P | *SW* | WD | 77771 | 62805 | 71526 | 77772 |
| 5724 | **SS** | P | *SW* | WD | 77773 | 62806 | 71561 | 77774 |
| 5725 | **SS** | P | *SW* | WD | 77775 | 62807 | 71541 | 77776 |
| 5726 | **SS** | P | *SW* | WD | 77777 | 62808 | 71556 | 77778 |
| 5727 | **SS** | P | *SW* | WD | 77779 | 62809 | 71562 | 77780 |
| 5728 | **SS** | P | *SW* | WD | 77781 | 62810 | 71527 | 77782 |
| 5729 | **SS** | P | *SW* | WD | 77783 | 62811 | 71550 | 77784 |
| 5730 | **SS** | P | *SW* | WD | 77785 | 62812 | 71551 | 77786 |
| 5731 | **SS** | P | *SW* | WD | 77787 | 62813 | 71555 | 77788 |
| 5732 | **SS** | P | *SW* | WD | 77789 | 62814 | 71552 | 77790 |
| 5733 | **SS** | P | *SW* | WD | 77791 | 62815 | 71549 | 77792 |
| 5734 | **SS** | P | *SW* | WD | 77793 | 62816 | 71531 | 77794 |
| 5735 | **SS** | P | *SW* | WD | 77795 | 62817 | 71563 | 77796 |
| 5736 | **SS** | P | *SW* | WD | 77797 | 62818 | 71554 | 77798 |
| 5737 | **SS** | P | *SW* | WD | 77799 | 62819 | 71544 | 77800 |
| 5738 | **SS** | P | *SW* | WD | 77801 | 62820 | 71529 | 77802 |
| 5739 | **SS** | P | *SW* | WD | 77803 | 62821 | 71537 | 77804 |
| 5740 | **SS** | P | *SW* | WD | 77805 | 62822 | 71530 | 77806 |
| 5741 | **SS** | P | *SW* | WD | 77807 | 62823 | 71559 | 77808 |
| 5742 | **SS** | P | *SW* | WD | 77809 | 62824 | 71543 | 77810 |
| 5750 | **SS** | P | *SW* | WD | 77811 | 62825 | 71538 | 77812 |

**Class 455/8. Southern units.** First series. Pressure heating & ventilation. Fitted with in-cab air conditioning systems meaning that the end door has been sealed.

**DTSO**. Lot No. 30972 York 1982–1984. –/74. 33.6 t.
**MSO**. Lot No. 30973 York 1982–1984. –/84. 37.9 t.
**TSO**. Lot No. 30974 York 1982–1984. –/75(3) 2W. 34.0 t.

| 455 801 | **SN** | H | *SN* | SU | 77627 | 62709 | 71657 | 77580 |
|---------|--------|---|------|----|-------|-------|-------|-------|
| 455 802 | **SN** | H | *SN* | SU | 77581 | 62710 | 71664 | 77582 |
| 455 803 | **SN** | H | *SN* | SU | 77583 | 62711 | 71639 | 77584 |
| 455 804 | **SN** | H | *SN* | SU | 77585 | 62712 | 71640 | 77586 |
| 455 805 | **SN** | H | *SN* | SU | 77587 | 62713 | 71641 | 77588 |
| 455 806 | **SN** | H | *SN* | SU | 77589 | 62714 | 71642 | 77590 |
| 455 807 | **SN** | H | *SN* | SU | 77591 | 62715 | 71643 | 77592 |

| 455 808 | **SN** | H | *SN* | SU | 77637 | 62716 | 71644 | 77594 |
| 455 809 | **SN** | H | *SN* | SU | 77623 | 62717 | 71648 | 77602 |
| 455 810 | **SN** | H | *SN* | SU | 77597 | 62718 | 71646 | 77598 |
| 455 811 | **SN** | H | *SN* | SU | 77599 | 62719 | 71647 | 77600 |
| 455 812 | **SN** | H | *SN* | SU | 77595 | 62720 | 71645 | 77626 |
| 455 813 | **SN** | H | *SN* | SU | 77603 | 62721 | 71649 | 77604 |
| 455 814 | **SN** | H | *SN* | SU | 77605 | 62722 | 71650 | 77606 |
| 455 815 | **SN** | H | *SN* | SU | 77607 | 62723 | 71651 | 77608 |
| 455 816 | **SN** | H | *SN* | SU | 77609 | 62724 | 71652 | 77633 |
| 455 817 | **SN** | H | *SN* | SU | 77611 | 62725 | 71653 | 77612 |
| 455 818 | **SN** | H | *SN* | SU | 77613 | 62726 | 71654 | 77632 |
| 455 819 | **SN** | H | *SN* | SU | 77615 | 62727 | 71637 | 77616 |
| 455 820 | **SN** | H | *SN* | SU | 77617 | 62728 | 71656 | 77618 |
| 455 821 | **SN** | H | *SN* | SU | 77619 | 62729 | 71655 | 77620 |
| 455 822 | **SN** | H | *SN* | SU | 77621 | 62730 | 71658 | 77622 |
| 455 823 | **SN** | H | *SN* | SU | 77601 | 62731 | 71659 | 77596 |
| 455 824 | **SN** | H | *SN* | SU | 77593 | 62732 | 71660 | 77624 |
| 455 825 | **SN** | H | *SN* | SU | 77579 | 62733 | 71661 | 77628 |
| 455 826 | **SN** | H | *SN* | SU | 77630 | 62734 | 71662 | 77629 |
| 455 827 | **SN** | H | *SN* | SU | 77610 | 62735 | 71663 | 77614 |
| 455 828 | **SN** | H | *SN* | SU | 77631 | 62736 | 71638 | 77634 |
| 455 829 | **SN** | H | *SN* | SU | 77635 | 62737 | 71665 | 77636 |
| 455 830 | **SN** | H | *SN* | SU | 77625 | 62743 | 71666 | 77638 |
| 455 831 | **SN** | H | *SN* | SU | 77639 | 62739 | 71667 | 77640 |
| 455 832 | **SN** | H | *SN* | SU | 77641 | 62740 | 71668 | 77642 |
| 455 833 | **SN** | H | *SN* | SU | 77643 | 62741 | 71669 | 77644 |
| 455 834 | **SN** | H | *SN* | SU | 77645 | 62742 | 71670 | 77646 |
| 455 835 | **SN** | H | *SN* | SU | 77647 | 62738 | 71671 | 77648 |
| 455 836 | **SN** | H | *SN* | SU | 77649 | 62744 | 71672 | 77650 |
| 455 837 | **SN** | H | *SN* | SU | 77651 | 62745 | 71673 | 77652 |
| 455 838 | **SN** | H | *SN* | SU | 77653 | 62746 | 71674 | 77654 |
| 455 839 | **SN** | H | *SN* | SU | 77655 | 62747 | 71675 | 77656 |
| 455 840 | **SN** | H | *SN* | SU | 77657 | 62748 | 71676 | 77658 |
| 455 841 | **SN** | H | *SN* | SU | 77659 | 62749 | 71677 | 77660 |
| 455 842 | **SN** | H | *SN* | SU | 77661 | 62750 | 71678 | 77662 |
| 455 843 | **SN** | H | *SN* | SU | 77663 | 62751 | 71679 | 77664 |
| 455 844 | **SN** | H | *SN* | SU | 77665 | 62752 | 71680 | 77666 |
| 455 845 | **SN** | H | *SN* | SU | 77667 | 62753 | 71681 | 77668 |
| 455 846 | **SN** | H | *SN* | SU | 77669 | 62754 | 71682 | 77670 |

**Class 455/8. South West Trains units.** First series. Pressure heating & ventilation.

**DTSO.** Lot No. 30972 York 1982–1984. –50(4) 1W. 29.5 t.
**MSO.** Lot No. 30973 York 1982–1984. –/84 –/68. 45.6 t.
**TSO.** Lot No. 30974 York 1982–1984. –/84 –/68. 27.1 t.

| 5847 | **SS** | P | *SW* | WD | 77671 | 62755 | 71683 | 77672 |
| 5848 | **SS** | P | *SW* | WD | 77673 | 62756 | 71684 | 77674 |
| 5849 | **SS** | P | *SW* | WD | 77675 | 62757 | 71685 | 77676 |
| 5850 | **SS** | P | *SW* | WD | 77677 | 62758 | 71686 | 77678 |
| 5851 | **SS** | P | *SW* | WD | 77679 | 62759 | 71687 | 77680 |
| 5852 | **SS** | P | *SW* | WD | 77681 | 62760 | 71688 | 77682 |

| 5853 | **SS** | P | *SW* | WD | 77683 | 62761 | 71689 | 77684 |
| 5854 | **SS** | P | *SW* | WD | 77685 | 62762 | 71690 | 77686 |
| 5855 | **SS** | P | *SW* | WD | 77687 | 62763 | 71691 | 77688 |
| 5856 | **SS** | P | *SW* | WD | 77689 | 62764 | 71692 | 77690 |
| 5857 | **SS** | P | *SW* | WD | 77691 | 62765 | 71693 | 77692 |
| 5858 | **SS** | P | *SW* | WD | 77693 | 62766 | 71694 | 77694 |
| 5859 | **SS** | P | *SW* | WD | 77695 | 62767 | 71695 | 77696 |
| 5860 | **SS** | P | *SW* | WD | 77697 | 62768 | 71696 | 77698 |
| 5861 | **SS** | P | *SW* | WD | 77699 | 62769 | 71697 | 77700 |
| 5862 | **SS** | P | *SW* | WD | 77701 | 62770 | 71698 | 77702 |
| 5863 | **SS** | P | *SW* | WD | 77703 | 62771 | 71699 | 77704 |
| 5864 | **SS** | P | *SW* | WD | 77705 | 62772 | 71700 | 77706 |
| 5865 | **SS** | P | *SW* | WD | 77707 | 62773 | 71701 | 77708 |
| 5866 | **SS** | P | *SW* | WD | 77709 | 62774 | 71702 | 77710 |
| 5867 | **SS** | P | *SW* | WD | 77711 | 62775 | 71703 | 77712 |
| 5868 | **SS** | P | *SW* | WD | 77713 | 62776 | 71704 | 77714 |
| 5869 | **SS** | P | *SW* | WD | 77715 | 62777 | 71705 | 77716 |
| 5870 | **SS** | P | *SW* | WD | 77717 | 62778 | 71706 | 77718 |
| 5871 | **SS** | P | *SW* | WD | 77719 | 62779 | 71707 | 77720 |
| 5872 | **SS** | P | *SW* | WD | 77721 | 62780 | 71708 | 77722 |
| 5873 | **SS** | P | *SW* | WD | 77723 | 62781 | 71709 | 77724 |
| 5874 | **SS** | P | *SW* | WD | 77725 | 62782 | 71710 | 77726 |

**Class 455/9. South West Trains units.** Third series. Convection heating.
**Dimensions:** 19.96/20.18 x 2.82 m.

**DTSO.** Lot No. 30991 York 1985. –/50(4) 1W. 30.7 t.
**MSO.** Lot No. 30992 York 1985. –/68. 46.3 t.
**TSO.** Lot No. 30993 York 1985. –/68. 28.3 t.
**TSO†.** Lot No. 30932 Derby 1981. –/68. 26.5 t.

**Note:** † Prototype vehicle 67400 converted from a Class 210 DEMU.

| 5901 | | **SS** | P | *SW* | WD | 77813 | 62826 | 71714 | 77814 |
| 5902 | | **SS** | P | *SW* | WD | 77815 | 62827 | 71715 | 77816 |
| 5903 | | **SS** | P | *SW* | WD | 77817 | 62828 | 71716 | 77818 |
| 5904 | | **SS** | P | *SW* | WD | 77819 | 62829 | 71717 | 77820 |
| 5905 | | **SS** | P | *SW* | WD | 77821 | 62830 | 71725 | 77822 |
| 5906 | | **SS** | P | *SW* | WD | 77823 | 62831 | 71719 | 77824 |
| 5907 | | **SS** | P | *SW* | WD | 77825 | 62832 | 71720 | 77826 |
| 5908 | | **SS** | P | *SW* | WD | 77827 | 62833 | 71721 | 77828 |
| 5909 | | **SS** | P | *SW* | WD | 77829 | 62834 | 71722 | 77830 |
| 5910 | | **SS** | P | *SW* | WD | 77831 | 62835 | 71723 | 77832 |
| 5911 | | **SS** | P | *SW* | WD | 77833 | 62836 | 71724 | 77834 |
| 5912 | † | **SS** | P | *SW* | WD | 77835 | 62837 | 67400 | 77836 |
| 5913 | | **SS** | P | *SW* | WD | 77837 | 62838 | 71726 | 77838 |
| 5914 | | **SS** | P | *SW* | WD | 77839 | 62839 | 71727 | 77840 |
| 5915 | | **SS** | P | *SW* | WD | 77841 | 62840 | 71728 | 77842 |
| 5916 | | **SS** | P | *SW* | WD | 77843 | 62841 | 71729 | 77844 |
| 5917 | | **SS** | P | *SW* | WD | 77845 | 62842 | 71730 | 77846 |
| 5918 | | **SS** | P | *SW* | WD | 77847 | 62843 | 71732 | 77848 |
| 5919 | | **SS** | P | *SW* | WD | 77849 | 62844 | 71718 | 77850 |
| 5920 | | **SS** | P | *SW* | WD | 77851 | 62845 | 71733 | 77852 |

# CLASS 456                                                          BREL YORK

Inner suburban units.

**Formation:** DMSO–DTSO.
**Construction:** Steel underframe, aluminium alloy body & roof.
**Traction Motors:** Two GEC507-20J of 185 kW, some recovered from Class 405s.
**Wheel Arrangement:** 2-Bo + 2-2.         **Dimensions:** 20.61 x 2.82 m.
**Braking:** Disc.                          **Couplers:** Tightlock.
**Bogies:** P7 (motor) and T3 (trailer).   **Control System:** GTO Chopper.
**Gangways:** Within unit.                  **Maximum Speed:** 75 m.p.h.
**Doors:** Sliding.                         **Seating Layout:** 3+2 facing.
**Heating & Ventilation:** Convection heating.
**Multiple Working:** Within class and with Class 455.

**DMSO.** Lot No. 31073 1990–1991. –/79. 41.1 t.
**DTSO.** Lot No. 31074 1990–1991. –/73. 31.4 t.

**Advertising livery:** 456 006 TfL/City of London (blue & green with various images).

| 456 001 | **SN** | P | *SN* | SU | 64735 | 78250 | |
| 456 002 | **SN** | P | *SN* | SU | 64736 | 78251 | |
| 456 003 | **SN** | P | *SN* | SU | 64737 | 78252 | |
| 456 004 | **SN** | P | *SN* | SU | 64738 | 78253 | |
| 456 005 | **SN** | P | *SN* | SU | 64739 | 78254 | |
| 456 006 | **AL** | P | *SN* | SU | 64740 | 78255 | |
| 456 007 | **SN** | P | *SN* | SU | 64741 | 78256 | |
| 456 008 | **SN** | P | *SN* | SU | 64742 | 78257 | |
| 456 009 | **SN** | P | *SN* | SU | 64743 | 78258 | |
| 456 010 | **SN** | P | *SN* | SU | 64744 | 78259 | |
| 456 011 | **SN** | P | *SN* | SU | 64745 | 78260 | |
| 456 012 | **SN** | P | *SN* | SU | 64746 | 78261 | |
| 456 013 | **SN** | P | *SN* | SU | 64747 | 78262 | |
| 456 014 | **SN** | P | *SN* | SU | 64748 | 78263 | |
| 456 015 | **SN** | P | *SN* | SU | 64749 | 78264 | |
| 456 016 | **SN** | P | *SN* | SU | 64750 | 78265 | |
| 456 017 | **SN** | P | *SN* | SU | 64751 | 78266 | |
| 456 018 | **SN** | P | *SN* | SU | 64752 | 78267 | |
| 456 019 | **SN** | P | *SN* | SU | 64753 | 78268 | |
| 456 020 | **SN** | P | *SN* | SU | 64754 | 78269 | |
| 456 021 | **SN** | P | *SN* | SU | 64755 | 78270 | |
| 456 022 | **SN** | P | *SN* | SU | 64756 | 78271 | |
| 456 023 | **SN** | P | *SN* | SU | 64757 | 78272 | |
| 456 024 | **SN** | P | *SN* | SU | 64758 | 78273 | Sir Cosmo Bonsor |

# CLASS 458   JUNIPER   ALSTOM BIRMINGHAM

Outer suburban units.

**Formation:** DMCO–TSO–MSO–DMCO.
**Construction:** Steel.
**Traction Motors:** Two Alstom ONIX 800 asynchronous of 270 kW.
**Wheel Arrangement:** 2-Bo + 2-2 + Bo-2 + Bo-2.
**Braking:** Disc & regenerative.     **Dimensions:** 21.16/19.94 x 2.80 m.
**Bogies:** ACR.                          **Couplers:** Scharfenberg AAR.
**Gangways:** Throughout (not in use). **Control System:** IGBT Inverter.
**Doors:** Sliding plug.               **Maximum Speed:** 100 m.p.h.
**Heating & Ventilation:** Air conditioning. **Multiple Working:** Within class.
**Seating Layout:** 1: 2+2 facing, 2: 3+2 facing/unidirectional.

**DMCO(A).** Alstom 1998–2000. 12/63. 46.4 t.
**TSO.** Alstom 1998–2000. –/54(6) 1TD 2W. 34.6 t.
**MSO.** Alstom 1998–2000. –/75 1T. 42.1 t.
**DMCO(B).** Alstom 1998–2000. 12/63. 46.4 t.

| | | | | | | | | |
|---|---|---|---|---|---|---|---|---|
| 8001 | **ST** | P | *SW* | WD | 67601 | 74001 | 74101 | 67701 |
| 8002 | **ST** | P | *SW* | WD | 67602 | 74002 | 74102 | 67702 |
| 8003 | **ST** | P | *SW* | WD | 67603 | 74003 | 74103 | 67703 |
| 8004 | **ST** | P | *SW* | WD | 67604 | 74004 | 74104 | 67704 |
| 8005 | **ST** | P | *SW* | WD | 67605 | 74005 | 74105 | 67705 |
| 8006 | **ST** | P | *SW* | WD | 67606 | 74006 | 74106 | 67706 |
| 8007 | **ST** | P | *SW* | WD | 67607 | 74007 | 74107 | 67707 |
| 8008 | **ST** | P | *SW* | WD | 67608 | 74008 | 74108 | 67708 |
| 8009 | **ST** | P | *SW* | WD | 67609 | 74009 | 74109 | 67709 |
| 8010 | **ST** | P | *SW* | WD | 67610 | 74010 | 74110 | 67710 |
| 8011 | **ST** | P | *SW* | WD | 67611 | 74011 | 74111 | 67711 |
| 8012 | **ST** | P | *SW* | WD | 67612 | 74012 | 74112 | 67712 |
| 8013 | **ST** | P | *SW* | WD | 67613 | 74013 | 74113 | 67713 |
| 8014 | **ST** | P | *SW* | WD | 67614 | 74014 | 74114 | 67714 |
| 8015 | **ST** | P | *SW* | WD | 67615 | 74015 | 74115 | 67715 |
| 8016 | **ST** | P | *SW* | WD | 67616 | 74016 | 74116 | 67716 |
| 8017 | **ST** | P | *SW* | WD | 67617 | 74017 | 74117 | 67717 |
| 8018 | **ST** | P | *SW* | WD | 67618 | 74018 | 74118 | 67718 |
| 8019 | **ST** | P | *SW* | WD | 67619 | 74019 | 74119 | 67719 |
| 8020 | **ST** | P | *SW* | WD | 67620 | 74020 | 74120 | 67720 |
| 8021 | **ST** | P | *SW* | WD | 67621 | 74021 | 74121 | 67721 |
| 8022 | **ST** | P | *SW* | WD | 67622 | 74022 | 74122 | 67722 |
| 8023 | **ST** | P | *SW* | WD | 67623 | 74023 | 74123 | 67723 |
| 8024 | **ST** | P | *SW* | WD | 67624 | 74024 | 74124 | 67724 |
| 8025 | **ST** | P | *SW* | WD | 67625 | 74025 | 74125 | 67725 |
| 8026 | **ST** | P | *SW* | WD | 67626 | 74026 | 74126 | 67726 |
| 8027 | **ST** | P | *SW* | WD | 67627 | 74027 | 74127 | 67727 |
| 8028 | **ST** | P | *SW* | WD | 67628 | 74028 | 74128 | 67728 |
| 8029 | **ST** | P | *SW* | WD | 67629 | 74029 | 74129 | 67729 |
| 8030 | **ST** | P | *SW* | WD | 67630 | 74030 | 74130 | 67730 |

# CLASS 460        GEC-ALSTHOM JUNIPER

Only the last two digits of the unit number are carried on the front ends of these units. Used on London Victoria–Gatwick Airport express services.

**Formation:** DMLFO–TFO–TCO–MSO–MSO–TSO–MSO–DMSO.
**Construction:** Steel.
**Traction Motors:** Two Alstom ONIX 800 asynchronous of 270 kW.
**Wheel Arrangement:** 2-Bo + 2-2 + 2-2 +Bo-2 + 2-Bo + 2-2 + Bo-2 + Bo-2.
**Braking:** Disc & regenerative.     **Dimensions:** 21.01/19.94 x 2.80 m.
**Bogies:** ACR.
**Couplers:** Scharfenberg 330 at outer ends and between cars 4 and 5.
**Gangways:** Within unit.     **Control System:** IGBT Inverter.
**Doors:** Sliding plug.     **Maximum Speed:** 100 m.p.h.
**Heating & Ventilation:** Air conditioning.
**Seating Layout:** 1: 2+1 facing, 2: 2+2 facing/unidirectional.
**Multiple Working:** Within class.

**DMLFO.** Alstom 1998–1999. 10/– 42.7 t.
**TFO.** Alstom 1998–1999. 25/– 1TD 1W. 34.5 t.
**TCO.** Alstom 1998–1999. 8/38 1T. 35.6 t.
**MSO(A).** Alstom 1998–1999. –/58. 42.8 t.
**MSO(B).** Alstom 1998–1999. –/58. 42.5 t.
**TSO.** Alstom 1998–1999. –/33 1TD 1T 1W. 35.2 t.
**MSO(C).** Alstom 1998–1999. –/58. 40.5 t.
**DMSO.** Alstom 1998–1999. –/54. 45.4 t.

**Advertising liveries:**

| | |
|---|---|
| 460 002   Emirates Airlines (Australia) | 460 004   Emirates Airlines (General) |
| 460 003   Emirates Airlines (China) | 460 006   Emirates Airlines (Africa) |

| 460 001 | **GV** | P | *SN* | SL | 67901 | 74401 | 74411 | 74421 |
|---|---|---|---|---|---|---|---|---|
|  |  |  |  |  | 74431 | 74441 | 74451 | 67911 |
| 460 002 | **AL** | P | *SN* | SL | 67902 | 74402 | 74412 | 74422 |
|  |  |  |  |  | 74432 | 74442 | 74452 | 67912 |
| 460 003 | **AL** | P | *SN* | SL | 67903 | 74403 | 74413 | 74423 |
|  |  |  |  |  | 74433 | 74443 | 74453 | 67913 |
| 460 004 | **AL** | P | *SN* | SL | 67904 | 74404 | 74414 | 74424 |
|  |  |  |  |  | 74434 | 74444 | 74454 | 67914 |
| 460 005 | **GV** | P | *SN* | SL | 67905 | 74405 | 74415 | 74425 |
|  |  |  |  |  | 74435 | 74445 | 74455 | 67915 |
| 460 006 | **AL** | P | *SN* | SL | 67906 | 74406 | 74416 | 74426 |
|  |  |  |  |  | 74436 | 74446 | 74456 | 67916 |
| 460 007 | **GV** | P | *SN* | SL | 67907 | 74407 | 74417 | 74427 |
|  |  |  |  |  | 74437 | 74447 | 74457 | 67917 |
| 460 008 | **GV** | P | *SN* | SL | 67908 | 74408 | 74418 | 74428 |
|  |  |  |  |  | 74438 | 74448 | 74458 | 67918 |

# CLASS 465        NETWORKER

Inner/outer suburban units.
**Formation:** DMSO–TSO–TSO–DMSO.

**Construction:** Welded aluminium alloy.
**Traction Motors:** Four Brush TIM970 (Classes 465/0 and 465/1) or GEC-Alsthom G352BY (Classes 465/2 and 465/9) or † Hitachi asynchronous of 280 kW.
**Wheel Arrangement:** Bo-Bo + 2-2 + 2-2 + Bo-Bo.
**Braking:** Disc & rheostatic and † regenerative.
**Bogies:** BREL P3/T3 (Classes 465/0 and 465/1), SRP BP62/BT52 (Classes 465/2 and 465/9).                           **Dimensions:** 20.89/20.06 x 2.81 m.
**Control System:** 1992-type GTO Inverter. † IGBT Inverter.
**Gangways:** Within unit.                    **Couplers:** Tightlock.
**Doors:** Sliding plug.                       **Maximum Speed:** 75 m.p.h.
**Seating Layout:** 3+2 facing/unidirectional.
**Multiple Working:** Within class and with Class 466.

**64759–64808. DMSO(A).** Lot No. 31100 BREL York 1991–1993. –/86. 39.2 t.
**64809–64858. DMSO(B).** Lot No. 31100 BREL York 1991–1993. –/86. 39.2 t.
**65734–65749. DMSO(A).** Lot No. 31103 Metro-Cammell 1991–1993. –/86. 39.2 t.
**65784–65799. DMSO(B).** Lot No. 31103 Metro-Cammell 1991–1993. –/86. 39.2 t.
**65800–65846. DMSO(A).** Lot No. 31130 ABB York 1993–1994. –/86. 39.2 t.
**65847–65893. DMSO(B).** Lot No. 31130 ABB York 1993–1994. –/86. 39.2 t.
**72028–72126 (even nos.) TSO.** Lot No. 31102 BREL York 1991–1993. –/90. 27.2 t.
**72029–72127 (odd nos.) TSO.** Lot No. 31101 BREL York 1991–1993. –/86 1T. 28.0 t.
**72787–72817 (odd nos.) TSO.** Lot No. 31104 Metro-Cammell 1991–1992. –/86 1T. 28.0 t.
**72788–72818 (even nos.) TSO.** Lot No. 31105 Metro-Cammell 1991–1992. –/90. 27.2 t.
**72900–72992 (even nos.) TSO.** Lot No. 31102 ABB York 1993–1994. –/90. 27.2 t.
**72901–72993 (odd nos.) TSO.** Lot No. 31101 ABB York 1993–1994. –/86 1T. 28.0 t.

**Class 465/0.** Built by BREL/ABB.

| | | | | | | | | |
|---|---|---|---|---|---|---|---|---|
| 465 001 | † | **CN** | H | *SE* | SG | 64759 | 72028 | 72029 | 64809 |
| 465 002 | † | **CN** | H | *SE* | SG | 64760 | 72030 | 72031 | 64810 |
| 465 003 | † | **CN** | H | *SE* | SG | 64761 | 72032 | 72033 | 64811 |
| 465 004 | † | **CN** | H | *SE* | SG | 64762 | 72034 | 72035 | 64812 |
| 465 005 | † | **CN** | H | *SE* | SG | 64763 | 72036 | 72037 | 64813 |
| 465 006 | † | **CN** | H | *SE* | SG | 64764 | 72038 | 72039 | 64814 |
| 465 007 | † | **CN** | H | *SE* | SG | 64765 | 72040 | 72041 | 64815 |
| 465 008 | † | **CN** | H | *SE* | SG | 64766 | 72042 | 72043 | 64816 |
| 465 009 | † | **CN** | H | *SE* | SG | 64767 | 72044 | 72045 | 64817 |
| 465 010 | † | **CN** | H | *SE* | SG | 64768 | 72046 | 72047 | 64818 |
| 465 011 | † | **CN** | H | *SE* | SG | 64769 | 72048 | 72049 | 64819 |
| 465 012 | † | **CN** | H | *SE* | SG | 64770 | 72050 | 72051 | 64820 |
| 465 013 | † | **CN** | H | *SE* | SG | 64771 | 72052 | 72053 | 64821 |
| 465 014 | † | **CN** | H | *SE* | SG | 64772 | 72054 | 72055 | 64822 |
| 465 015 | † | **CN** | H | *SE* | SG | 64773 | 72056 | 72057 | 64823 |
| 465 016 | † | **CN** | H | *SE* | SG | 64774 | 72058 | 72059 | 64824 |
| 465 017 | † | **CN** | H | *SE* | SG | 64775 | 72060 | 72061 | 64825 |
| 465 018 | † | **CN** | H | *SE* | SG | 64776 | 72062 | 72063 | 64826 |
| 465 019 | † | **CN** | H | *SE* | SG | 64777 | 72064 | 72065 | 64827 |
| 465 020 | † | **CN** | H | *SE* | SG | 64778 | 72066 | 72067 | 64828 |
| 465 021 | † | **CN** | H | *SE* | SG | 64779 | 72068 | 72069 | 64829 |
| 465 022 | † | **CN** | H | *SE* | SG | 64780 | 72070 | 72071 | 64830 |
| 465 023 | † | **CN** | H | *SE* | SG | 64781 | 72072 | 72073 | 64831 |
| 465 024 | † | **CN** | H | *SE* | SG | 64782 | 72074 | 72075 | 64832 |

| | | | | | | | | |
|---|---|---|---|---|---|---|---|---|
| 465 025 | † | CN | H | SE | SG | 64783 | 72076 | 72077 | 64833 |
| 465 026 | | CN | H | SE | SG | 64784 | 72078 | 72079 | 64834 |
| 465 027 | † | CN | H | SE | SG | 64785 | 72080 | 72081 | 64835 |
| 465 028 | | CN | H | SE | SG | 64786 | 72082 | 72083 | 64836 |
| 465 029 | | CN | H | SE | SG | 64787 | 72084 | 72085 | 64837 |
| 465 030 | | CN | H | SE | SG | 64788 | 72086 | 72087 | 64838 |
| 465 031 | | CN | H | SE | SG | 64789 | 72088 | 72089 | 64839 |
| 465 032 | | CN | H | SE | SG | 64790 | 72090 | 72091 | 64840 |
| 465 033 | | CN | H | SE | SG | 64791 | 72092 | 72093 | 64841 |
| 465 034 | | CN | H | SE | SG | 64792 | 72094 | 72095 | 64842 |
| 465 035 | | CN | H | SE | SG | 64793 | 72096 | 72097 | 64843 |
| 465 036 | | CN | H | SE | SG | 64794 | 72098 | 72099 | 64844 |
| 465 037 | | CN | H | SE | SG | 64795 | 72100 | 72101 | 64845 |
| 465 038 | | CN | H | SE | SG | 64796 | 72102 | 72103 | 64846 |
| 465 039 | | CN | H | SE | SG | 64797 | 72104 | 72105 | 64847 |
| 465 040 | | CN | H | SE | SG | 64798 | 72106 | 72107 | 64848 |
| 465 041 | | CN | H | SE | SG | 64799 | 72108 | 72109 | 64849 |
| 465 042 | | CN | H | SE | SG | 64800 | 72110 | 72111 | 64850 |
| 465 043 | † | CN | H | SE | SG | 64801 | 72112 | 72113 | 64851 |
| 465 044 | | CN | H | SE | SG | 64802 | 72114 | 72115 | 64852 |
| 465 045 | † | CN | H | SE | SG | 64803 | 72116 | 72117 | 64853 |
| 465 046 | | CN | H | SE | SG | 64804 | 72118 | 72119 | 64854 |
| 465 047 | | CN | H | SE | SG | 64805 | 72120 | 72121 | 64855 |
| 465 048 | | CN | H | SE | SG | 64806 | 72122 | 72123 | 64856 |
| 465 049 | | CN | H | SE | SG | 64807 | 72124 | 72125 | 64857 |
| 465 050 | † | CN | H | SE | SG | 64808 | 72126 | 72127 | 64858 |

**Class 465/1.** Built by BREL/ABB. Similar to Class 465/0 but with detail differences.

| | | | | | | | | |
|---|---|---|---|---|---|---|---|---|
| 465 151 | † | CN | H | SE | SG | 65800 | 72900 | 72901 | 65847 |
| 465 152 | † | CN | H | SE | SG | 65801 | 72902 | 72903 | 65848 |
| 465 153 | † | CN | H | SE | SG | 65802 | 72904 | 72905 | 65849 |
| 465 154 | † | CN | H | SE | SG | 65803 | 72906 | 72907 | 65850 |
| 465 155 | † | CN | H | SE | SG | 65804 | 72908 | 72909 | 65851 |
| 465 156 | † | CN | H | SE | SG | 65805 | 72910 | 72911 | 65852 |
| 465 157 | † | CN | H | SE | SG | 65806 | 72912 | 72913 | 65853 |
| 465 158 | † | CN | H | SE | SG | 65807 | 72914 | 72915 | 65854 |
| 465 159 | † | CN | H | SE | SG | 65808 | 72916 | 72917 | 65855 |
| 465 160 | † | CN | H | SE | SG | 65809 | 72918 | 72919 | 65856 |
| 465 161 | † | CN | H | SE | SG | 65810 | 72920 | 72921 | 65857 |
| 465 162 | † | CN | H | SE | SG | 65811 | 72922 | 72923 | 65858 |
| 465 163 | † | CN | H | SE | SG | 65812 | 72924 | 72925 | 65859 |
| 465 164 | † | CN | H | SE | SG | 65813 | 72926 | 72927 | 65860 |
| 465 165 | † | CN | H | SE | SG | 65814 | 72928 | 72929 | 65861 |
| 465 166 | † | CN | H | SE | SG | 65815 | 72930 | 72931 | 65862 |
| 465 167 | † | CN | H | SE | SG | 65816 | 72932 | 72933 | 65863 |
| 465 168 | † | CN | H | SE | SG | 65817 | 72934 | 72935 | 65864 |
| 465 169 | † | CN | H | SE | SG | 65818 | 72936 | 72937 | 65865 |
| 465 170 | † | CN | H | SE | SG | 65819 | 72938 | 72939 | 65866 |
| 465 171 | † | CN | H | SE | SG | 65820 | 72940 | 72941 | 65867 |
| 465 172 | † | CN | H | SE | SG | 65821 | 72942 | 72943 | 65868 |
| 465 173 | † | CN | H | SE | SG | 65822 | 72944 | 72945 | 65869 |

| | | | | | | | | |
|---|---|---|---|---|---|---|---|---|
| 465 174 | † | **CN** | H | *SE* | SG | 65823 | 72946 | 72947 | 65870 |
| 465 175 | | **CN** | H | *SE* | SG | 65824 | 72948 | 72949 | 65871 |
| 465 176 | † | **CN** | H | *SE* | SG | 65825 | 72950 | 72951 | 65872 |
| 465 177 | † | **CN** | H | *SE* | SG | 65826 | 72952 | 72953 | 65873 |
| 465 178 | † | **CN** | H | *SE* | SG | 65827 | 72954 | 72955 | 65874 |
| 465 179 | † | **CN** | H | *SE* | SG | 65828 | 72956 | 72957 | 65875 |
| 465 180 | † | **CN** | H | *SE* | SG | 65829 | 72958 | 72959 | 65876 |
| 465 181 | † | **CN** | H | *SE* | SG | 65830 | 72960 | 72961 | 65877 |
| 465 182 | † | **CN** | H | *SE* | SG | 65831 | 72962 | 72963 | 65878 |
| 465 183 | † | **CN** | H | *SE* | SG | 65832 | 72964 | 72965 | 65879 |
| 465 184 | † | **CN** | H | *SE* | SG | 65833 | 72966 | 72967 | 65880 |
| 465 185 | † | **CN** | H | *SE* | SG | 65834 | 72968 | 72969 | 65881 |
| 465 186 | † | **CN** | H | *SE* | SG | 65835 | 72970 | 72971 | 65882 |
| 465 187 | † | **CN** | H | *SE* | SG | 65836 | 72972 | 72973 | 65883 |
| 465 188 | † | **CN** | H | *SE* | SG | 65837 | 72974 | 72975 | 65884 |
| 465 189 | † | **CN** | H | *SE* | SG | 65838 | 72976 | 72977 | 65885 |
| 465 190 | † | **CN** | H | *SE* | SG | 65839 | 72978 | 72979 | 65886 |
| 465 191 | † | **CN** | H | *SE* | SG | 65840 | 72980 | 72981 | 65887 |
| 465 192 | † | **CN** | H | *SE* | SG | 65841 | 72982 | 72983 | 65888 |
| 465 193 | † | **CN** | H | *SE* | SG | 65842 | 72984 | 72985 | 65889 |
| 465 194 | † | **CN** | H | *SE* | SG | 65843 | 72986 | 72987 | 65890 |
| 465 195 | † | **CN** | H | *SE* | SG | 65844 | 72988 | 72989 | 65891 |
| 465 196 | † | **CN** | H | *SE* | SG | 65845 | 72990 | 72991 | 65892 |
| 465 197 | † | **CN** | H | *SE* | SG | 65846 | 72992 | 72993 | 65893 |

**Class 465/2.** Built by Metro-Cammell.
**Dimensions**: 20.80/20.15 x 2.81 m.

| | | | | | | | | |
|---|---|---|---|---|---|---|---|---|
| 465 235 | **CN** | A | *SE* | SG | 65734 | 72787 | 72788 | 65784 |
| 465 236 | **CN** | A | *SE* | SG | 65735 | 72789 | 72790 | 65785 |
| 465 237 | **CN** | A | *SE* | SG | 65736 | 72791 | 72792 | 65786 |
| 465 238 | **CN** | A | *SE* | SG | 65737 | 72793 | 72794 | 65787 |
| 465 239 | **CN** | A | *SE* | SG | 65738 | 72795 | 72796 | 65788 |
| 465 240 | **CN** | A | *SE* | SG | 65739 | 72797 | 72798 | 65789 |
| 465 241 | **CN** | A | *SE* | SG | 65740 | 72799 | 72800 | 65790 |
| 465 242 | **CN** | A | *SE* | SG | 65741 | 72801 | 72802 | 65791 |
| 465 243 | **CN** | A | *SE* | SG | 65742 | 72803 | 72804 | 65792 |
| 465 244 | **CN** | A | *SE* | SG | 65743 | 72805 | 72806 | 65793 |
| 465 245 | **CN** | A | *SE* | SG | 65744 | 72807 | 72808 | 65794 |
| 465 246 | **CN** | A | *SE* | SG | 65745 | 72809 | 72810 | 65795 |
| 465 247 | **CN** | A | *SE* | SG | 65746 | 72811 | 72812 | 65796 |
| 465 248 | **CN** | A | *SE* | SG | 65747 | 72813 | 72814 | 65797 |
| 465 249 | **CN** | A | *SE* | SG | 65748 | 72815 | 72816 | 65798 |
| 465 250 | **CN** | A | *SE* | SG | 65749 | 72817 | 72818 | 65799 |

**Class 465/9.** Built by Metro-Cammell. Refurbished 2005 for longer distance services, with the addition of First Class seats. Details as Class 465/0 unless stated.
**Formation:** DMCO–TSO(A)–TSO(B)–DMCO.
**Seating Layout:** 1: 2+2 facing/unidirectional, 2: 3+2 facing/unidirectional.

**65700–65733. DMCO(A).** Lot No. 31103 Metro-Cammell 1991–1993. 12/68. 39.2 t.
**72719–72785 (odd nos.) TSO(A).** Lot No. 31104 Metro-Cammell 1991–1992.
–/76 1T 2W. 30.3 t.

**72720–72786 (even nos.) TSO(B).** Lot No. 31105 Metro-Cammell 1991–1992. -/90. 29.5 t.
**65750–65783. DMCO(B).** Lot No. 31103 Metro-Cammell 1991–1993. 12/68. 39.2 t.

| | | | | | | | | |
|---|---|---|---|---|---|---|---|---|
| 465 901 | (465 201) | **CN** | A | *SE* | SG | 65700 | 72719 | 72720 | 65750 |
| 465 902 | (465 202) | **CN** | A | *SE* | SG | 65701 | 72721 | 72722 | 65751 |
| 465 903 | (465 203) | **CN** | A | *SE* | SG | 65702 | 72723 | 72724 | 65752 |
| 465 904 | (465 204) | **CN** | A | *SE* | SG | 65703 | 72725 | 72726 | 65753 |
| 465 905 | (465 205) | **CN** | A | *SE* | SG | 65704 | 72727 | 72728 | 65754 |
| 465 906 | (465 206) | **CN** | A | *SE* | SG | 65705 | 72729 | 72730 | 65755 |
| 465 907 | (465 207) | **CN** | A | *SE* | SG | 65706 | 72731 | 72732 | 65756 |
| 465 908 | (465 208) | **CN** | A | *SE* | SG | 65707 | 72733 | 72734 | 65757 |
| 465 909 | (465 209) | **CN** | A | *SE* | SG | 65708 | 72735 | 72736 | 65758 |
| 465 910 | (465 210) | **CN** | A | *SE* | SG | 65709 | 72737 | 72738 | 65759 |
| 465 911 | (465 211) | **CN** | A | *SE* | SG | 65710 | 72739 | 72740 | 65760 |
| 465 912 | (465 212) | **CN** | A | *SE* | SG | 65711 | 72741 | 72742 | 65761 |
| 465 913 | (465 213) | **CN** | A | *SE* | SG | 65712 | 72743 | 72744 | 65762 |
| 465 914 | (465 214) | **CN** | A | *SE* | SG | 65713 | 72745 | 72746 | 65763 |
| 465 915 | (465 215) | **CN** | A | *SE* | SG | 65714 | 72747 | 72748 | 65764 |
| 465 916 | (465 216) | **CN** | A | *SE* | SG | 65715 | 72749 | 72750 | 65765 |
| 465 917 | (465 217) | **CN** | A | *SE* | SG | 65716 | 72751 | 72752 | 65766 |
| 465 918 | (465 218) | **CN** | A | *SE* | SG | 65717 | 72753 | 72754 | 65767 |
| 465 919 | (465 219) | **CN** | A | *SE* | SG | 65718 | 72755 | 72756 | 65768 |
| 465 920 | (465 220) | **CN** | A | *SE* | SG | 65719 | 72757 | 72758 | 65769 |
| 465 921 | (465 221) | **CN** | A | *SE* | SG | 65720 | 72759 | 72760 | 65770 |
| 465 922 | (465 222) | **CN** | A | *SE* | SG | 65721 | 72761 | 72762 | 65771 |
| 465 923 | (465 223) | **CN** | A | *SE* | SG | 65722 | 72763 | 72764 | 65772 |
| 465 924 | (465 224) | **CN** | A | *SE* | SG | 65723 | 72765 | 72766 | 65773 |
| 465 925 | (465 225) | **CN** | A | *SE* | SG | 65724 | 72767 | 72768 | 65774 |
| 465 926 | (465 226) | **CN** | A | *SE* | SG | 65725 | 72769 | 72770 | 65775 |
| 465 927 | (465 227) | **CN** | A | *SE* | SG | 65726 | 72771 | 72772 | 65776 |
| 465 928 | (465 228) | **CN** | A | *SE* | SG | 65727 | 72773 | 72774 | 65777 |
| 465 929 | (465 229) | **CN** | A | *SE* | SG | 65728 | 72775 | 72776 | 65778 |
| 465 930 | (465 230) | **CN** | A | *SE* | SG | 65729 | 72777 | 72778 | 65779 |
| 465 931 | (465 231) | **CN** | A | *SE* | SG | 65730 | 72779 | 72780 | 65780 |
| 465 932 | (465 232) | **CN** | A | *SE* | SG | 65731 | 72781 | 72782 | 65781 |
| 465 933 | (465 233) | **CN** | A | *SE* | SG | 65732 | 72783 | 72784 | 65782 |
| 465 934 | (465 234) | **CN** | A | *SE* | SG | 65733 | 72785 | 72786 | 65783 |

**Name:** 465 903    Remembrance

## CLASS 466    NETWORKER    GEC-ALSTHOM

Inner/outer suburban units.

**Formation:** DMSO–DTSO.
**Construction:** Welded aluminium alloy.
**Traction Motors:** Two GEC-Alsthom G352AY asynchronous of 280 kW.
**Wheel Arrangement:** Bo-Bo + 2-2.   **Couplers:** Tightlock.
**Braking:** Disc & rheostatic.    **Control System:** 1992-type GTO Inverter.
**Dimensions:** 20.80 x 2.80 m.    **Maximum Speed:** 75 m.p.h.
**Bogies:** BREL P3/T3.    **Doors:** Sliding plug.

**Gangways:** Within unit.  **Seating Layout:** 3+2 facing/unidirectional.
**Multiple Working:** Within class and with Class 465.

**DMSO.** Lot No. 31128 Birmingham 1993–1994. –/86. 40.6 t.
**DTSO.** Lot No. 31129 Birmingham 1993–1994. –/82 1T. 31.4 t.

| | | | | | | |
|---|---|---|---|---|---|---|
| 466 001 | CN | A | SE | SG | 64860 | 78312 |
| 466 002 | CN | A | SE | SG | 64861 | 78313 |
| 466 003 | CN | A | SE | SG | 64862 | 78314 |
| 466 004 | CN | A | SE | SG | 64863 | 78315 |
| 466 005 | CN | A | SE | SG | 64864 | 78316 |
| 466 006 | CN | A | SE | SG | 64865 | 78317 |
| 466 007 | CN | A | SE | SG | 64866 | 78318 |
| 466 008 | CN | A | SE | SG | 64867 | 78319 |
| 466 009 | CN | A | SE | SG | 64868 | 78320 |
| 466 010 | CN | A | SE | SG | 64869 | 78321 |
| 466 011 | CN | A | SE | SG | 64870 | 78322 |
| 466 012 | CN | A | SE | SG | 64871 | 78323 |
| 466 013 | CN | A | SE | SG | 64872 | 78324 |
| 466 014 | CN | A | SE | SG | 64873 | 78325 |
| 466 015 | CN | A | SE | SG | 64874 | 78326 |
| 466 016 | CN | A | SE | SG | 64875 | 78327 |
| 466 017 | CN | A | SE | SG | 64876 | 78328 |
| 466 018 | CN | A | SE | SG | 64877 | 78329 |
| 466 019 | CN | A | SE | SG | 64878 | 78330 |
| 466 020 | CN | A | SE | SG | 64879 | 78331 |
| 466 021 | CN | A | SE | SG | 64880 | 78332 |
| 466 022 | CN | A | SE | SG | 64881 | 78333 |
| 466 023 | CN | A | SE | SG | 64882 | 78334 |
| 466 024 | CN | A | SE | SG | 64883 | 78335 |
| 466 025 | CN | A | SE | SG | 64884 | 78336 |
| 466 026 | CN | A | SE | SG | 64885 | 78337 |
| 466 027 | CN | A | SE | SG | 64886 | 78338 |
| 466 028 | CN | A | SE | SG | 64887 | 78339 |
| 466 029 | CN | A | SE | SG | 64888 | 78340 |
| 466 030 | CN | A | SE | SG | 64889 | 78341 |
| 466 031 | CN | A | SE | SG | 64890 | 78342 |
| 466 032 | CN | A | SE | SG | 64891 | 78343 |
| 466 033 | CN | A | SE | SG | 64892 | 78344 |
| 466 034 | CN | A | SE | SG | 64893 | 78345 |
| 466 035 | CN | A | SE | SG | 64894 | 78346 |
| 466 036 | CN | A | SE | SG | 64895 | 78347 |
| 466 037 | CN | A | SE | SG | 64896 | 78348 |
| 466 038 | CN | A | SE | SG | 64897 | 78349 |
| 466 039 | CN | A | SE | SG | 64898 | 78350 |
| 466 040 | CN | A | SE | SG | 64899 | 78351 |
| 466 041 | CN | A | SE | SG | 64900 | 78352 |
| 466 042 | CN | A | SE | SG | 64901 | 78353 |
| 466 043 | CN | A | SE | SG | 64902 | 78354 |

# CLASS 483                               METRO-CAMMELL

Built 1938 onwards for LTE. Converted 1989–1990 for the Isle of Wight Line.

**Formation:** DMSO–DMSO.
**System:** 660 V DC third rail.
**Construction:** Steel.
**Traction Motors:** Two Crompton Parkinson/GEC/BTH LT100 of 125 kW.
**Braking:** Tread.             **Dimensions:** 16.15 x 2.69 m.
**Bogies:** LT design.         **Couplers:** Wedglock.
**Gangways:** None. End doors.
**Control System:** Pneumatic Camshaft Motor (PCM).
**Doors:** Sliding.            **Maximum Speed:** 45 m.p.h.
**Seating Layout:** Longitudinal or 2+2 facing/unidirectional.
**Multiple Working:** Within class.

**Notes:** The last three numbers of the unit number only are carried.

Former London Underground numbers are shown in parentheses.

**DMSO (A).** Lot No. 31071. –/40. 27.4 t.
**DMSO (B).** Lot No. 31072. –/42. 27.4 t.

| | | | | | | | | |
|---|---|---|---|---|---|---|---|---|
| 483 002 | **LT** | SW | *SW* | RY | 122 | (10221) | 225 | (11142) |
| 483 004 | **LT** | SW | *SW* | RY | 124 | (10205) | 224 | (11205) |
| 483 006 | **LT** | SW | *SW* | RY | 126 | (10297) | 226 | (11297) |
| 483 007 | **LT** | SW | *SW* | RY | 127 | (10291) | 227 | (11291) |
| 483 008 | **LT** | SW | *SW* | RY | 128 | (10255) | 228 | (11255) |
| 483 009 | **LT** | SW | *SW* | RY | 129 | (10289) | 229 | (11229) |

# CLASS 507                                   BREL YORK

Suburban units.

**Formation:** BDMSO–TSO–DMSO.
**Construction:** Steel underframe, aluminium alloy body and roof.
**Traction Motors:** Four GEC G310AZ of 82.125 kW.
**Wheel Arrangement:** Bo-Bo + 2-2 + Bo-Bo.
**Braking:** Disc & rheostatic.      **Dimensions:** 20.18 x 2.82 m.
**Bogies:** BX1.               **Couplers:** Tightlock.
**Gangways:** Within unit + end doors.   **Control System:** Camshaft.
**Doors:** Sliding.            **Maximum Speed:** 75 m.p.h.
**Seating Layout:** All refurbished with 2+2 high-back facing seating.
**Multiple Working:** Within class and with Class 508.

**BDMSO.** Lot No. 30906 1978–1980. –/56(3) 1W. 37.0 t.
**TSO.** Lot No. 30907 1978–1980. –/74. 25.5 t.
**DMSO.** Lot No. 30908 1978–1980. –/56(3) 1W. 35.5 t.

| | | | | | | | | |
|---|---|---|---|---|---|---|---|---|
| 507 001 | **ME** | A | *ME* | BD | 64367 | 71342 | 64405 | |
| 507 002 | **ME** | A | *ME* | BD | 64368 | 71343 | 64406 | |
| 507 003 | **ME** | A | *ME* | BD | 64369 | 71344 | 64407 | |
| 507 004 | **ME** | A | *ME* | BD | 64388 | 71345 | 64408 | Bob Paisley |
| 507 005 | **ME** | A | *ME* | BD | 64371 | 71346 | 64409 | |

| 507 006 | **ME** | A | *ME* | BD | 64372 | 71347 | 64410 | |
| 507 007 | **ME** | A | *ME* | BD | 64373 | 71348 | 64411 | |
| 507 008 | **ME** | A | *ME* | BD | 64374 | 71349 | 64412 | |
| 507 009 | **ME** | A | *ME* | BD | 64375 | 71350 | 64413 | Dixie Dean |
| 507 010 | **ME** | A | *ME* | BD | 64376 | 71351 | 64414 | |
| 507 011 | **ME** | A | *ME* | BD | 64377 | 71352 | 64415 | |
| 507 012 | **ME** | A | *ME* | BD | 64378 | 71353 | 64416 | |
| 507 013 | **ME** | A | *ME* | BD | 64379 | 71354 | 64417 | |
| 507 014 | **ME** | A | *ME* | BD | 64380 | 71355 | 64418 | |
| 507 015 | **ME** | A | *ME* | BD | 64381 | 71356 | 64419 | |
| 507 016 | **ME** | A | *ME* | BD | 64382 | 71357 | 64420 | |
| 507 017 | **ME** | A | *ME* | BD | 64383 | 71358 | 64421 | |
| 507 018 | **ME** | A | *ME* | BD | 64384 | 71359 | 64422 | |
| 507 019 | **ME** | A | *ME* | BD | 64385 | 71360 | 64423 | |
| 507 020 | **ME** | A | *ME* | BD | 64386 | 71361 | 64424 | John Peel |
| 507 021 | **ME** | A | *ME* | BD | 64387 | 71362 | 64425 | Red Rum |
| 507 023 | **ME** | A | *ME* | BD | 64389 | 71364 | 64427 | |
| 507 024 | **ME** | A | *ME* | BD | 64390 | 71365 | 64428 | |
| 507 025 | **ME** | A | *ME* | BD | 64391 | 71366 | 64429 | |
| 507 026 | **ME** | A | *ME* | BD | 64392 | 71367 | 64430 | |
| 507 027 | **ME** | A | *ME* | BD | 64393 | 71368 | 64431 | |
| 507 028 | **ME** | A | *ME* | BD | 64394 | 71369 | 64432 | |
| 507 029 | **ME** | A | *ME* | BD | 64395 | 71370 | 64433 | |
| 507 030 | **ME** | A | *ME* | BD | 64396 | 71371 | 64434 | |
| 507 031 | **ME** | A | *ME* | BD | 64397 | 71372 | 64435 | |
| 507 032 | **ME** | A | *ME* | BD | 64398 | 71373 | 64436 | |
| 507 033 | **ME** | A | *ME* | BD | 64399 | 71374 | 64437 | |

# CLASS 508                                                BREL YORK

Suburban units.

**Formation:** DMSO–TSO–BDMSO.
**Construction:** Steel underframe, aluminium alloy body and roof.
**Traction Motors:** Four GEC G310AZ of 82.125 kW.
**Wheel Arrangement:** Bo-Bo + 2-2 + Bo-Bo.
**Braking:** Disc & rheostatic.          **Dimensions:** 20.18 x 2.82 m.
**Bogies:** BX1.                          **Couplers:** Tightlock.
**Gangways:** Within unit + end doors.  **Control System:** Camshaft.
**Doors:** Sliding.                       **Maximum Speed:** 75 m.p.h.
**Seating Layout:** All Merseyrail units refurbished with 2+2 high-back facing seating. 508/2 and 508/3 units have 3+2 low-back facing seating.
**Multiple Working:** Within class and with Class 507.

**DMSO.** Lot No. 30979 1979–1980. –/56(3) 1W. 36.0 t.
**TSO.** Lot No. 30980 1979–1980. –/74. 26.5 t.
**BDMSO.** Lot No. 30981 1979–1980. –/56(3) 1W. 36.5 t.

**Class 508/1.** Merseyrail units.

| 508 103 | **ME** | A | *ME* | BD | 64651 | 71485 | 64694 |
| 508 104 | **ME** | A | *ME* | BD | 64652 | 71486 | 64695 |
| 508 108 | **ME** | A | *ME* | BD | 64656 | 71490 | 64699 |
| 508 110 | **ME** | A | *ME* | BD | 64658 | 71492 | 64701 |

| | | | | | | | | |
|---|---|---|---|---|---|---|---|---|
| 508 111 | **ME** | A | *ME* | BD | 64659 | 71493 | 64702 | |
| 508 112 | **ME** | A | *ME* | BD | 64660 | 71494 | 64703 | |
| 508 114 | **ME** | A | *ME* | BD | 64662 | 71496 | 64705 | |
| 508 115 | **ME** | A | *ME* | BD | 64663 | 71497 | 64706 | |
| 508 117 | **ME** | A | *ME* | BD | 64665 | 71499 | 64708 | |
| 508 120 | **ME** | A | *ME* | BD | 64668 | 71502 | 64711 | |
| 508 122 | **ME** | A | *ME* | BD | 64670 | 71504 | 64713 | |
| 508 123 | **ME** | A | *ME* | BD | 64671 | 71505 | 64714 | |
| 508 124 | **ME** | A | *ME* | BD | 64672 | 71506 | 64715 | |
| 508 125 | **ME** | A | *ME* | BD | 64673 | 71507 | 64716 | |
| 508 126 | **ME** | A | *ME* | BD | 64674 | 71508 | 64717 | |
| 508 127 | **ME** | A | *ME* | BD | 64675 | 71509 | 64718 | |
| 508 128 | **ME** | A | *ME* | BD | 64676 | 71510 | 64719 | |
| 508 130 | **ME** | A | *ME* | BD | 64678 | 71512 | 64721 | |
| 508 131 | **ME** | A | *ME* | BD | 64679 | 71513 | 64722 | |
| 508 134 | **ME** | A | *ME* | BD | 64682 | 71516 | 64725 | |
| 508 136 | **ME** | A | *ME* | BD | 64684 | 71518 | 64727 | Capital of Culture |
| 508 137 | **ME** | A | *ME* | BD | 64685 | 71519 | 64728 | |
| 508 138 | **ME** | A | *ME* | BD | 64686 | 71520 | 64729 | |
| 508 139 | **ME** | A | *ME* | BD | 64687 | 71521 | 64730 | |
| 508 140 | **ME** | A | *ME* | BD | 64688 | 71522 | 64731 | |
| 508 141 | **ME** | A | *ME* | BD | 64689 | 71523 | 64732 | |
| 508 143 | **ME** | A | *ME* | BD | 64691 | 71525 | 64734 | |

**Class 508/2.** Units facelifted for the South Eastern lines by Wessex Traincare/ Alstom, Eastleigh 1998–1999.

**DMSO.** Lot No. 30979 1979–1980. –/66. 36.0 t.
**TSO.** Lot No. 30980 1979–1980. –/79 1W. 26.5 t.
**BDMSO.** Lot No. 30981 1979–1980. –/74. 36.5 t.

| | | | | | | | |
|---|---|---|---|---|---|---|---|
| 508 201 | (508 101) | **CX** | A | AF | 64649 | 71483 | 64692 |
| 508 202 | (508 105) | **CX** | A | AF | 64653 | 71487 | 64696 |
| 508 203 | (508 106) | **CN** | A | SL | 64654 | 71488 | 64697 |
| 508 204 | (508 107) | **CX** | A | AF | 64655 | 71489 | 64698 |
| 508 205 | (508 109) | **CN** | A | GI | 64657 | 71491 | 64700 |
| 508 206 | (508 113) | **CX** | A | AF | 64661 | 71495 | 64704 |
| 508 207 | (508 116) | **CN** | A | GI | 64664 | 71498 | 64707 |
| 508 208 | (508 119) | **CN** | A | SL | 64667 | 71501 | 64710 |
| 508 209 | (508 121) | **CX** | A | AF | 64669 | 71503 | 64712 |
| 508 210 | (508 129) | **CN** | A | SL | 64677 | 71515 | 64720 |
| 508 211 | (508 132) | **CN** | A | GI | 64680 | 71514 | 64723 |
| 508 212 | (508 133) | **CX** | A | GI | 64681 | 71511 | 64724 |

**Class 508/3.** Units facelifted units for use on Euston–Watford Junction services by Alstom, Eastleigh 2002–2003.

**DMSO.** Lot No. 30979 1979–1980. –/68 1W. 36.0 t.
**TSO.** Lot No. 30980 1979–1980. –/86. 26.5 t.
**BDMSO.** Lot No. 30981 1979–1980. –/68 1W. 36.5 t.

| | | | | | | | |
|---|---|---|---|---|---|---|---|
| 508 301 | (508 102) | **SL** | A | ZG | 64650 | 71484 | 64693 |
| 508 302 | (508 135) | **SL** | A | ZG | 64683 | 71517 | 64726 |
| 508 303 | (508 142) | **SL** | A | ZG | 64690 | 71524 | 64733 |

# 4.3. EUROSTAR UNITS (CLASS 373)

Eurostar units were built for and are normally used on services between Britain and Continental Europe via the Channel Tunnel. Apart from such workings units may be used as follows:

SNCF-owned units 3203/04, 3225/26 and 3227/28 have been removed from the Eurostar pool and only operate SNCF-internal services between Paris and Lille. In addition six of the former Regional Eurostar sets are now on hire to SNCF for use on Paris–Lille services and also a Paris–Douai/Valanciennes turn.

Each train consists of two 10-car units coupled, with a motor car at each driving end (the sets built for Regional Eurostar services are 8-car). All units are articulated with an extra motor bogie on the coach adjacent to the motor car.

Sets marked "r" have been refurbished. This now includes all sets used by Eurostar, but not 3101/02 (in store) or the sets used by SNCF.

**Formation:** DM–MSO–4TSO–RB–2TFO–TBFO or DM–MSO–3TSO–RB–TFO–TBFO. Gangwayed within pair of units. Air conditioned.
**Construction:** Steel.
**Supply Systems:** 25 kV AC 50 Hz overhead or 3000 V DC overhead  (* also equipped for 1500 V DC overhead operation).
**Control System:** GTO–GTO Inverter on UK 750 V DC and 25 kV AC, GTO Chopper on SNCB 3000 V DC.
**Wheel Arrangement:** Bo–Bo + Bo–2–2–2–2–2–2–2–2.
**Length:** 22.15 m (DM), 21.85 m (MS & TBF), 18.70 m (other cars).
**Couplers:** Schaku 10S at outer ends, Schaku 10L at inner end of each DM and outer ends of each sub set.
**Maximum Speed:** 186 m.p.h. (300 km/h).
**Built:** 1992–1993 by GEC-Alsthom/Brush/ANF/De Dietrich/BN Construction/ACEC.
**Note:** DM vehicles carry the set numbers indicated below.

**Class 373/0. 10-Car sets.** Built for services starting from/terminating in London Waterloo (now St Pancras). Individual vehicles in each set are allocated numbers 373xxx0 + 373xxx1 + 373xxx2 + 373xxx3 + 373xxx4 + 373xxx5 + 373xxx6 + 373xxx7 + 373xxx8 + 373xxx9, where 3xxx denotes the set number.

**Non-standard livery (0):** Grey with silver ends, TGV symbol & green/blue doors.

**373xxx0 series. DM.** Lot No. 31118 1992–1995. 68.5 t.
**373xxx1 series. MSO.** Lot No. 31119 1992–1995. –/48 2T. 44.6 t.
**373xxx2 series. TSO.** Lot No. 31120 1992–1995. –/58 1T (r –/56 1T). 28.1 t.
**373xxx3 series. TSO.** Lot No. 31121 1992–1995. –/58 2T (r –/56 2T). 29.7 t.
**373xxx4 series. TSO.** Lot No. 31122 1992–1995. –/58 1T (r –/56 1T). 28.3 t.
**373xxx5 series. TSO.** Lot No. 31123 1992–1995. –/58 2T (r –/56 2T). 29.2 t.
**373xxx6 series. RB.** Lot No.31124 1992–1995. 31.1 t.
**373xxx7 series. TFO.** Lot No. 31125 1992–1995. 39/– 1T. 29.6 t.
**373xxx8 series. TFO.** Lot No. 31126 1992–1995. 39/– 1T. 32.2 t.
**373xxx9 series. TBFO.** Lot No. 31127 1992–1995. 25/– 1TD. 39.4 t.

| | | | | | | | | | |
|---|---|---|---|---|---|---|---|---|---|
| 3001 r | **EU** | EU | _EU_ | TI | Tread Lightly | 3004 r | **EU** | EU | _EU_ | TI |
| 3002 r | **EU** | EU | _EU_ | TI | Voyage Vert | 3005 r | **EU** | EU | _EU_ | TI |
| 3003 r | **EU** | EU | _EU_ | TI | | 3006 r | **EU** | EU | _EU_ | TI |

| Set | | | | | Name | Set | | | | | Name |
|---|---|---|---|---|---|---|---|---|---|---|---|
| 3007 r | **EU** | EU | *EU* | TI | Waterloo Sunset | 3205 r | **EU** | SF | *EU* | LY | |
| 3008 r | **EU** | EU | *EU* | TI | Waterloo Sunset | 3206 r | **EU** | SF | *EU* | LY | |
| 3009 r | **EU** | EU | *EU* | TI | | 3207 r* | **EU** | SF | *EU* | LY | MICHEL HOLLARD |
| 3010 r | **EU** | EU | *EU* | TI | | 3208 r* | **EU** | SF | *EU* | LY | MICHEL HOLLARD |
| 3011 r | **EU** | EU | *EU* | TI | | 3209 r* | **EU** | SF | *EU* | LY | THE DA VINCI CODE |
| 3012 r | **EU** | EU | *EU* | TI | | 3210 r* | **EU** | SF | *EU* | LY | THE DA VINCI CODE |
| 3013 r | **EU** | EU | *EU* | TI | LONDON 2012 | 3211 r | **EU** | SF | *EU* | LY | |
| 3014 r | **EU** | EU | *EU* | TI | LONDON 2012 | 3212 r | **EU** | SF | *EU* | LY | |
| 3015 r | **EU** | EU | *EU* | TI | | 3213 r* | **EU** | SF | *EU* | LY | |
| 3016 r | **EU** | EU | *EU* | TI | | 3214 r* | **EU** | SF | *EU* | LY | |
| 3017 r | **EU** | EU | *EU* | TI | | 3215 r* | **EU** | SF | *EU* | LY | |
| 3018 r | **EU** | EU | *EU* | TI | | 3216 r* | **EU** | SF | *EU* | LY | |
| 3019 r | **EU** | EU | *EU* | TI | | 3217 r* | **EU** | SF | *EU* | LY | |
| 3020 r | **EU** | EU | *EU* | TI | | 3218 r* | **EU** | SF | *EU* | LY | |
| 3021 r | **EU** | EU | *EU* | TI | | 3219 r | **EU** | SF | *EU* | LY | |
| 3022 r | **EU** | EU | *EU* | TI | | 3220 r | **EU** | SF | *EU* | LY | |
| 3101 | **EU** | SB | | TI | | 3221 r* | **EU** | SF | *EU* | LY | |
| 3102 | **EU** | SB | | TI | | 3222 r* | **EU** | SF | *EU* | LY | |
| 3103 r | **EU** | SB | *EU* | FF | | 3223 r* | **EU** | SF | *EU* | LY | |
| 3104 r | **EU** | SB | *EU* | FF | | 3224 r* | **EU** | SF | *EU* | LY | |
| 3105 r | **EU** | SB | *EU* | FF | | 3225 | **0** | SF | *SF* | LY | |
| 3106 r | **EU** | SB | *EU* | FF | | 3226 | **0** | SF | *SF* | LY | |
| 3107 r | **EU** | SB | *EU* | FF | | 3227 | **0** | SF | *SF* | LY | |
| 3108 r | **EU** | SB | *EU* | FF | | 3228 | **0** | SF | *SF* | LY | |
| 3201 r* | **EU** | SF | *EU* | LY | | 3229 r* | **EU** | SF | *EU* | LY | |
| 3202 r* | **EU** | SF | *EU* | LY | | 3230 r* | **EU** | SF | *EU* | LY | |
| 3203 | **0** | SF | *SF* | LY | | 3231 r | **EU** | SF | *EU* | LY | |
| 3204 | **0** | SF | *SF* | LY | | 3232 r | **EU** | SF | *EU* | LY | |

**Class 373/2. 8-Car sets. Built for Regional Eurostar services, now on long-term hire to SNCF.** Individual vehicles in each set are allocated numbers 373xxx0 + 373xxx1 + 373xxx2 + 373xxx3 + 373xxx5 + 373xxx6 + 373xxx7 + 373xxx9, where 3xxx denotes the set number.

**3733xx0 series. DM.** 68.5 t.
**3733xx1 series. MSO.** –/48 1T. 44.6 t.
**3733xx2 series. TSO.** –/58 2T. 28.1 t.
**3733xx3 series. TSO.** –/58 1T. 29.7 t.
**3733xx5 series. TSO.** –/58 1T. 29.2 t.
**3733xx6 series. RB.** 31.1 t.
**3733xx7 series. TFO.** 39/– 1T. 29.6 t.
**3733xx9 series. TBFO.** 18/– 1TD. 39.4 t.

| Set | | | | | | Set | | | | | Name |
|---|---|---|---|---|---|---|---|---|---|---|---|
| 3301 | **EU** | EU | *SF* | LY | | 3308 | **EU** | EU | | TI | |
| 3302 | **EU** | EU | *SF* | LY | | 3309 | **EU** | EU | *SF* | LY | |
| 3303 | **EU** | EU | *SF* | LY | | 3310 | **EU** | EU | *SF* | LY | |
| 3304 | **EU** | EU | *SF* | LY | | 3311 | **EU** | EU | *SF* | LY | |
| 3305 | **EU** | EU | *SF* | LY | | 3312 | **EU** | EU | *SF* | LY | |
| 3306 | **EU** | EU | *SF* | LY | | 3313 | **EU** | EU | *SF* | LY | ENTENTE CORDIALE |
| 3307 | **EU** | EU | *SF* | LY | | 3314 | **EU** | EU | *SF* | LY | ENTENTE CORDIALE |

**Spare DM:**

| | | | | |
|---|---|---|---|---|
| 3999 | **EU** | EU | *EU* | TI |

# 4.4. INTERNAL USE EMUS

### Class 423 "Vep" Service Units

The following units are used by Bombardier as tractor units at Chart Leacon. They are fitted with special couplers for moving intermediate EMU vehicles.

| | | | | | | | |
|---|---|---|---|---|---|---|---|
| 3905 | **CX** | BT | AF | 76398 | 62266 | 70904 | 76397 |
| 3918 | **CX** | BT | AF | 76528 | 62321 | 70950 | 76527 |

### Class 930 Service Unit

The following unit (converted from a Class 405) is in use by East Midlands Trains at Derby as a Staff Coach (975600) and as a Training Room (975601).

| | | | | | | |
|---|---|---|---|---|---|---|
| 930 010 | **B/RK** | EM | DY | 975600 | (10988) | 975601 (10843) |

# 4.5. EMUS AWAITING DISPOSAL

The list below comprises vehicles awaiting disposal which are stored on the National Railway network.

**IMPORTANT NOTE:** EMUs still intact but already at scrapyards, unless specifically there for storage purposes, are not included in this list.

### 25 kV AC 50 Hz OVERHEAD UNITS:

**Note:** 390 033 was written off following the Lambrigg accident of 2007 and some of the remaining vehicles may be used for training purposes.

| | | | | | | | | |
|---|---|---|---|---|---|---|---|---|
| 390 033 | **VT** | VI | LM | 69133 | 69433 | 69533 | 68833 | 69833 |

**Spare car:**

| | | | | | |
|---|---|---|---|---|---|
| Cl. 309 | **RR** | WC | CS | 71758 |

### 750 V DC THIRD RAIL UNITS:

**Non-standard liveries:**
1304, 1881, 1884 & 3536 – Old Stagecoach (as **N** but with an orange stripe).
930 101 – Used for paint trials.

| | | | | | | | |
|---|---|---|---|---|---|---|---|
| 1881 | **O** | KN | ZG | 76762 | 62400 | 71080 | 76833 |
| 1884 | **O** | KN | ZG | 76767 | | | 76838 |
| 930 101 | **O** | NR | AF | 977207 | (61658) | 977609 | (65414) |

**Spare cars:**

**Non-standard liveries:**
70293 – Used for paint trials.
76112 – Silver (prototype Class 424 "Networker Classic" conversion).

| | | | | | | |
|---|---|---|---|---|---|---|
| Cl. 411 | **O** | H | ZI | 70293 | | |
| Cl. 424 | **O** | BT | ZD | 76112 | | |
| Cl. 930 | **RO** | NR | AF | 975598 | (10989) | 975605 (10940) |
| | **RO** | NR | SE | 977364 | (10400) | |

# 5. UK LIGHT RAIL & METRO SYSTEMS

This section lists the rolling stock of the various light rail and metro systems in the UK. Passenger carrying vehicles only are covered (not works vehicles). This listing does not cover the London Underground network.

# 5.1. BLACKPOOL & FLEETWOOD TRAMWAY

Until the opening of Manchester Metrolink, the Blackpool Tramway was the only urban/inter-urban tramway system left in Britain. The infrastructure is owned by Blackpool Corporation, and the tramway is operated by Blackpool Transport Services Ltd., using a mixture of trams dating back to the 1930s, as well as some newer vehicles dating from the 1980s. The line normally runs for 11½ miles from Fleetwood in the north to Starr Gate in the south, but is closed between Fleetwood and Ash Street and Starr Gate and Pleasure Beach, for modernisation. These sections will reopen in 2012, complete with a new fleet of 16 Bombardier trams.

**System:** 550 V DC overhead (600 V DC from 2012).
**Depot & Workshops:** Rigby Road, Blackpool.
**Standard livery:** Cream & green except where stated otherwise.

All cars are single-deck unless stated otherwise. For advertising liveries predominate colours are given.

(S) – Stored out of service.

The status of individual trams is flexible and is varied to meet traffic requirements and seasonal demand.

## OPEN BOAT CARS                                     A1-1A

Used during the summer season!
**Built:** 1934 by English Electric. 12 built.
**Traction Motors:** Two EE327 of 30 kW.
**Seats:** 56 (* 52).

| | | |
|---|---|---|
| 600 | 604 * | 607 (S)  **Yellow & Green** |
| 602  *  **Yellow & Black** | 605 *    **Green & Cream** | |

**Named:** 600 "THE DUCHESS OF CORNWALL".

## BRUSH CARS                                          A1-1A

Most of the Brush Railcoaches are now mothballed and only four remained in use at the time of writing.
**Built:** 1937 by Brush, Loughborough. 20 built.
**Traction Motors:** Two EE305 of 40 kW.
**Seats:** 48 (* 46).

**Advertising liveries:**

621 – Hot Ice Show, Pleasure Beach (blue)
622 – Pontins (blue & yellow)
626 – Blackpool Zoo & Dinosaur Safari (white, black & green)
627 – Buccaneer Family Bar (black)
630 – Karting 2000 (yellow & purple)
631 – Walls ice cream (red)
637 – Blackpool Zoo (green & white)

| | | | | | | | |
|---|---|---|---|---|---|---|---|
| 621 (S) | **AL** | 625 (S) | | 630 | **AL** | | |
| 622 | **AL** | 626 *(S) | **AL** | 631 | **AL** | | |
| 623 | **Green & Cream** | 627 (S) | **AL** | 637 (S) | **AL** | | |

## CENTENARY CLASS                      A1-1A

The newest trams in use, these are used all year round.
**Built:** 1984–1987. Body by East Lancs. Coachbuilders, Blackburn. Driver-only operated.
**Traction Motors:** Two EE305 of 40 kW.
**Seats:** 53.                    † Rebuilt from GEC car 651.
**Advertising liveries:**

641 – Orion Bingo, Cleveleys (blue)
644 – Farmer Parrs Animal World/Fleetwood Market (yellow)
645 – jet2.com (red)
646 – Paul Gaunt Furniture (blue)
647 – B&M Bargain Stores (black, blue & yellow)

| | | | | | | | |
|---|---|---|---|---|---|---|---|
| 641 | **AL** | 643 | **Black** | 645 | **AL** | 647 | **AL** |
| 642 | **Yellow** | 644 | **AL** | 646 | **AL** | 648 † | **White** |

## PROGRESS TWIN CARS              A1-1A + 2-2

These cars mainly see use during the "illuminations" season.
**Built:** Motor cars (671–676) rebuilt 1958–1960 from English Electric Railcoaches by Blackpool Corporation Transport. Driving trailers (681–687) built 1960 by Metro-Cammell.
**Traction Motors:** Two EE305 of 40 kW.     **Seats:** 53 + 61.

| | | | | | |
|---|---|---|---|---|---|
| 671+681 | (S) **Green/yellow** | 673+683 | **Turquoise/yellow** | 675+685 | **Red/yellow** |
| 672+682 | **Orange/yellow** | 674+684 | **Blue/yellow** | 676+686 | (S) |

## ENGLISH ELECTRIC RAILCOACHES           A1-1A

**Built:** Rebuilt 1958–1960 from EE Railcoaches. Originally ran with trailers.
**Traction Motors:** Two EE305 of 40 kW.     **Seats:** 48.
**Advertising livery:**

678 – Radiowave (black & blue)

| | | | | |
|---|---|---|---|---|
| 678 (S) | **AL** | 680 | (S) | **Blue** |

# "BALLOON" DOUBLE DECKERS     A1-1A

The "Balloon" cars are still the mainstay of the fleet during the summer months and are also used in lesser numbers during the winter.
**Built:** 1934–1935 by English Electric. 700–712 were originally built with open tops and 706 has now reverted to that condition.
**Traction Motors:** Two EE305 of 40 kW.     **Seats:** 94 (*† 92, ‡ 90, ¶ 88).

**Notes:** 717 is named "PHILLIP R THORPE"
719 is named "DONNA'S DREAM HOUSE"
* Rebuilt with a new flat front end design and air-conditioned cabs. Known as "Millennium Class".
o Rebuilt as an open-topped double-decker seating 92. Named "PRINCESS ALICE". Also carries original number 243.

**Advertising liveries:**

704 – Eclipse at the Globe, Pleasure Beach (black & orange)
707 – Coral Island – The Jewel on the Mile (black)
709 – Blackpool Sealife Centre (blue/yellow)
721 – Pleasure Beach Resort (black/gold)
724 – Lyndene Hotel (blue)
726 – HM Coastguard (blue & yellow)

| | | | | | | | |
|---|---|---|---|---|---|---|---|
| 700 | | **Green & Cream** | 709 | * | **AL** | 718 | * | **Yellow/blue** |
| 701 | ‡ | **Yellow** | 710 | (S) | **Yellow/purple** | 719 | | **Light blue** |
| 702 | (S) | ¶ | 711 | † | **Yellow/green** | 720 | | |
| 703 | (S) | | 712 | | | 721 | | **AL** |
| 704 | (S) | **AL** | 713 | | **Yellow/purple** | 723 | † | |
| 706 | o | | 715 | | **Yellow/blue** | 724 | * | **AL** |
| 707 | * | **AL** | 716 | (S) | | 726 | | **AL** |
| 708 | (S) | ‡ | 717 | | | | | |

# JUBILEE CLASS DOUBLE DECKERS

**Built:** Rebuilt 1979/1982 from Balloon cars 725 and 714 respectively. Standard bus ends, Westinghouse Chopper control and stairs at each end. 761 has one door per side whereas 762 has two. Suitable for driver-only operation.
**Traction Motors:** Two EE305 of 40 kW.     **Seats:** 104 (*86).
**Note:** 762 is named "STUART L PILLAR"
**Advertising liveries:**

761 – Wynsors World of Shoes (orange)
762 – www.reblackpool.com (Green/various)

761    **AL**         | 762 * **AL**

## ILLUMINATED CARS

| | | | |
|---|---|---|---|
| 732 (S) | The Rocket | Rebuilt: 1961 | Seats: 47 |
| 733 | Western Train loco & tender | Rebuilt: 1962 | Seats: 35 |
| 734 | Western Train coach | Rebuilt: 1962 | Seats: 60 |
| 736 | "Warship" HMS Blackpool | Rebuilt: 1965 | Seats: 71 |
| 737 | Illuminated Trawler – "Fisherman's Friend" | Rebuilt: 2001 | Seats: 48 |

## VINTAGE CARS

These trams are used for special services as well as for occasional normal services, particularly during the "illuminations" season.

**Note:** 147 is named "MICHAEL AIREY"

| | | |
|---|---|---|
| Stockport 5 | Open-top double-decker | Built: 1901 |
| Blackpool & Fleetwood 40 | Single deck "box car" | Built: 1914 |
| Bolton 66 | Bogie double-decker | Built: 1901 |
| Blackpool 143 | Open balcony standard double-decker | Built: 1924 |
| Blackpool 147 | Standard double-decker | Built: 1924 |
| Blackpool 304 | Coronation Class single decker | Built: 1952 |
| Sheffield "Roberts Car" 513 | Double-decker | Built: 1950 |
| Blackpool 619 | Single deck Replica Vanguard | Rebuilt: 1987 |
| Blackpool 660 | Coronation Class single decker | Built: 1953 |

# 5.2. SHEFFIELD SUPERTRAM

This system opened in 1994 and has three lines radiating from Sheffield City Centre. These run to Halfway in the south east, with a spur from Gleadless Townend to Herdings Park, to Middlewood in the north with a spur from Hillsborough to Malin Bridge and to Meadowhall Interchange in the north east, adjacent to the large shopping complex. The total route mileage is 18 miles. The system is a mixture of on-street and segregated running.

The cars are owned by South Yorkshire Light Rail Ltd., a subsidiary of South Yorkshire PTE. The operating company, South Yorkshire Supertram Ltd. is leased to Stagecoach who operate the system as Stagecoach Supertram.

Because of severe gradients in Sheffield (up to 1 in 10) all axles are powered on the vehicles, which have low-floor outer sections.

**System:** 750 DC overhead.
**Depot & Workshops:** Nunnery.
**Standard livery:** All over blue with red & orange ends.

**Advertising livery:**

120 – East Midlands Trains (blue).

# EIGHT-AXLE ARTICULATED UNITS                    B–B–B–B

**Built:** 1993–1994 by Duewag, Dusseldorf, Germany.
**Traction Motors:** Four monomotor drives of 250 kW.
**Seats:** 80 + 6 tip-up.
**Weight:** 52 t.
**Dimensions:** 34.75 x 2.65 m.
**Couplers:** Not equipped.
**Doors:** Sliding plug.
**Braking:** Rheostatic, regenerative, disc and emergency track.
**Max. Speed:** 50 m.p.h.

| | | | | | |
|---|---|---|---|---|---|
| 101 | 106 | 110 | 114 | 118 | 122 |
| 102 | 107 | 111 | 115 | 119 | 123 |
| 103 | 108 | 112 | 116 | 120 **AL** | 124 |
| 104 | 109 | 113 | 117 | 121 | 125 |
| 105 | | | | | |

# 5.3. DOCKLANDS LIGHT RAILWAY

This system now runs for a total of 19 route miles, with more extensions in the pipeline. Lines run from termini at Bank and Tower Gateway in central London to Lewisham, Stratford, Beckton and Woolwich Arsenal. Another extension currently under construction will be from Canning Town to Stratford (due to open mid 2010). The first line was opened in 1987 from Tower Gateway to Island Gardens.

Originally owned by London Transport, it is now owned by DLR Ltd. and operated by Serco Docklands. Cars are normally "driven" automatically using the Alcatel "Seltrack" moving block signalling system.

**Notes:** Original P86 and P89 Class vehicles 01–21 were withdrawn from service in 1991 (01–11) and 1995 (12–21) and sold for use in Essen, Germany.

55 new cars from Bombardier in Germany are currently being delivered. These new cars will ultimately enable 3-car trains to operate on all routes as well as providing additional vehicles required for extensions to the network. Longer term they will meet higher projected passenger demand during the 2012 Olympics and beyond.

**System:** 750 V DC third rail (bottom contact).
**Depots:** Beckton (main depot) and Poplar.
**Livery:** Red with a curving blue stripe to represent the River Thames.

## CLASS B90      B–2–B

**Built:** 1991–1992 by BN Construction, Brugge, Belgium. Chopper control.
**Traction Motors:** Two Brush of 140 kW.
**Seats:** 52 + 4 tip-up.      **Weight:** 37 t.
**Dimensions:** 28.80 x 2.65 m.      **Braking:** Rheostatic.
**Couplers:** Scharfenberg.      **Max. Speed:** 50 m.p.h.
**Doors:** Sliding. End doors for staff use.

| | | | | | |
|---|---|---|---|---|---|
| 22 | 26 | 30 | 34 | 38 | 42 |
| 23 | 27 | 31 | 35 | 39 | 43 |
| 24 | 28 | 32 | 36 | 40 | 44 |
| 25 | 29 | 33 | 37 | 41 | |

## CLASS B92      B–2–B

**Built:** 1992–1995 by BN Construction, Brugge, Belgium. Chopper control.
**Traction Motors:** Two Brush of 140 kW.
**Seats:** 52 + 4 tip-up.      **Weight:** 37 t.
**Dimensions:** 28.80 x 2.65 m.      **Braking:** Rheostatic.
**Couplers:** Scharfenberg.      **Max. Speed:** 50 m.p.h.
**Doors:** Sliding. End doors for staff use.

| | | | | | |
|---|---|---|---|---|---|
| 45 | 53 | 61 | 69 | 77 | 85 |
| 46 | 54 | 62 | 70 | 78 | 86 |
| 47 | 55 | 63 | 71 | 79 | 87 |
| 48 | 56 | 64 | 72 | 80 | 88 |
| 49 | 57 | 65 | 73 | 81 | 89 |
| 50 | 58 | 66 | 74 | 82 | 90 |
| 51 | 59 | 67 | 75 | 83 | 91 |
| 52 | 60 | 68 | 76 | 84 | |

## CLASS B2K      B–2–B

**Built:** 2002–2003 by Bombardier Transportation, Brugge, Belgium.
**Traction Motors:** Two Brush of 140 kW.
**Seats:** 52 + 4 tip-up.      **Weight:** 37 t.
**Dimensions:** 28.80 x 2.65 m.      **Braking:** Rheostatic.
**Couplers:** Scharfenberg.      **Max. Speed:** 50 m.p.h.
**Doors:** Sliding. End doors for staff use.

| | | | | | |
|---|---|---|---|---|---|
| 92 | 96 | 01 | 05 | 09 | 13 |
| 93 | 97 | 02 | 06 | 10 | 14 |
| 94 | 98 | 03 | 07 | 11 | 15 |
| 95 | 99 | 04 | 08 | 12 | 16 |

## CLASS B07      B–2–B

55 new vehicles now being delivered. 24 cars were ordered in 2005 (101–124) and 31 extra cars were ordered in 2006 ready for the London 2012 Olympic Games (125–155).

**Built:** 2007–2010 by Bombardier Transportation, Bautzen, Germany.
**Traction Motors:** Two Brush of 140 kW.

| | |
|---|---|
| **Seats:** 52 + 4 tip-up. | **Weight:** 37 t. |
| **Dimensions:** | **Braking:** Rheostatic. |
| **Couplers:** Scharfenberg. | **Max. Speed:** 50 m.p.h. |

**Doors:** Sliding. End doors for staff use.

| | | | | | |
|---|---|---|---|---|---|
| 101 | 111 | 120 | 129 | 138 | 147 |
| 102 | 112 | 121 | 130 | 139 | 148 |
| 103 | 113 | 122 | 131 | 140 | 149 |
| 104 | 114 | 123 | 132 | 141 | 150 |
| 105 | 115 | 124 | 133 | 142 | 151 |
| 106 | 116 | 125 | 134 | 143 | 152 |
| 107 | 117 | 126 | 135 | 144 | 153 |
| 108 | 118 | 127 | 136 | 145 | 154 |
| 109 | 119 | 128 | 137 | 146 | 155 |
| 110 | | | | | |

# 5.4. LONDON TRAMLINK

This system runs through central Croydon via a one-way loop, with lines radiating out to Wimbledon, New Addington and Beckenham Junction/Elmers End, the total route mileage being 18½ miles. It opened in 2000 and is now operated by Transport for London.

**System:** 750 V DC overhead.
**Depot & Workshops:** Therapia Lane, Croydon.

# SIX AXLE ARTICULATED CARS          Bo–2–Bo

**Built:** 1998–1999 by Bombardier-Wien Schienenfahrzeuge, Austria.
**Traction Motors:** Four of 120 kW each.

| | |
|---|---|
| **Seats:** 70. | **Dimensions:** 30.1 x 2.65 m. |
| **Couplers:** Scharfenberg. | **Doors:** Sliding plug. |
| **Weight:** 36.3 t. | **Max. Speed:** 50 m.p.h. |

**Braking:** Disc, regenerative and magnetic track.

**Livery:** Light grey & lime green with a blue solebar.

| | | | | | |
|---|---|---|---|---|---|
| 2530 | 2534 | 2538 | 2542 | 2546 | 2550 |
| 2531 | 2535 | 2539 | 2543 | 2547 | 2551 |
| 2532 | 2536 | 2540 | 2544 | 2548 | 2552 |
| 2533 | 2537 | 2541 | 2545 | 2549 | 2553 |

**Name:** 2535 STEPHEN PARASCANDOLO 1980–2007

# 5.5. GREATER MANCHESTER METROLINK

Metrolink was the first modern tramway system in the UK, combining on-street running with longer distance running over former BR lines. The system opened in 1992 from Bury to Altrincham through the streets of Manchester, with a spur to Piccadilly station. A second line opened in 2000 from Cornbrook to Eccles extending the total route mileage to 23 miles.

Further extensions ("Phase 3a") are under construction to Rochdale station via Oldham to the north of Manchester (involving converting the former National Rail line to light rail use), Droylsden to the east (on a line which will eventually reach Ashton-under-Lyne) and St. Werburgh's Road, Chorlton to the south (on a line which will eventually reach Manchester Airport). A short spur off the Eccles line to mediacity:uk is also under construction (to open in 2010). "Phase 3b" will consist of Oldham and Rochdale town centre sections, and the extension of above lines to Ashton-under-Lyne, Manchester Airport and East Didsbury.

The system is operated by Stagecoach Metrolink.

**System:** 750 V DC overhead.
**Depot & Workshops:** Queens Road, Manchester. A second depot is under construction at Trafford to service the expanding fleet.

## SIX-AXLE ARTICULATED CARS              Bo–2–Bo

**Built:** 1991–1992 by Firema, Italy. Chopper control.
**Traction Motors:** Four GEC of 130 kW.
**Seats:** 82 + 4 tip-up.
**Dimensions:** 29.0 x 2.65 m.          **Couplers:** Scharfenberg.
**Doors:** Sliding.                      **Weight:** 45 t.
**Braking:** Rheostatic, regenerative, disc and emergency track.
**Max. Speed:** 50 m.p.h.

**Livery:** White, dark grey & blue with light blue doors.

\* Fitted with front-end valances, retractable couplers and controllable magnetic track brakes for running to Eccles.

| | | | | | |
|---|---|---|---|---|---|
| 1001 | * | | 1014 | | THE GREAT MANCHESTER RUNNER |
| 1002 | * | DA VINCI | 1015 | * | BURMA STAR |
| 1003 | * | | 1016 | * | |
| 1004 | | THE ROBERT OWEN | 1017 | | BURY HOSPICE |
| 1005 | * | THE RAILWAY MISSION | 1018 | | |
| 1006 | | | 1019 | | |
| 1007 | * | EAST LANCASHIRE RAILWAY | 1020 | * | LANCASHIRE FUSILIER |
| 1008 | | | 1021 | | |
| 1009 | | VIRGIN MEGASTORES | 1022 | * | POPPY APPEAL |
| 1010 | * | | 1023 | | |
| 1011 | * | SYSTEM ONE | 1024 | | |
| 1012 | * | | 1025 | * | |
| 1013 | | | 1026 | | |

## SIX-AXLE ARTICULATED CARS                   Bo–2–Bo

**Built:** 1999 by Ansaldo, Italy. Chopper control. Fitted with front-end valances, retractable couplers and controllable magnetic track brakes for running to Eccles. Can also be used on the Bury–Altrincham route.
**Traction Motors:** Four GEC of 130 kW.
**Seats:** 82 + 4 tip-up.
**Dimensions:** 29.0 x 2.65 m.                    **Couplers:** Scharfenberg.
**Doors:** Sliding.                               **Weight:** 45 t.
**Braking:** Rheostatic, regenerative, disc and magnetic track.
**Max. Speed:** 50 m.p.h.

**Livery:** White, dark grey & blue with light blue doors.

| | | | |
|---|---|---|---|
| 2001 | (S) | 2004 | |
| 2002 | | 2005 | WHSMITH WEST ONE |
| 2003 | TRAVELLER 2000 | 2006 | |

## SIX-AXLE ARTICULATED CARS                   Bo–2–Bo

The first of 40 new trams are now being delivered for Metrolink from the Bombardier B5000 "Flexity Swift" family. The first eight cars are being used on existing routes from late 2009/early 2010. The remaining 32 cars are for the extensions mentioned above.
**Built:** 2009–2011 by Bombardier, Wien, Austria.
**Traction Motors:** Four Bombardier 3-phase asynchronous of 120 kW.
**Seats:** 52.
**Dimensions:** 28.4 x 2.65 m.                    **Couplers:** Scharfenberg.
**Doors:** Sliding.                               **Weight:** 39.7 t.
**Braking:** Rheostatic, regenerative, disc and magnetic track.
**Max. Speed:** 50 m.p.h.

**Livery:** New Manchester Metrolink silver & yellow.

| | | | | |
|---|---|---|---|---|
| 3001 | 3003 | 3005 | 3007 | 3008 |
| 3002 | 3004 | 3006 | | |
| 3009 | 3016 | 3023 | 3029 | 3035 |
| 3010 | 3017 | 3024 | 3030 | 3036 |
| 3011 | 3018 | 3025 | 3031 | 3037 |
| 3012 | 3019 | 3026 | 3032 | 3038 |
| 3013 | 3020 | 3027 | 3033 | 3039 |
| 3014 | 3021 | 3028 | 3034 | 3040 |
| 3015 | 3022 | | | |

# 5.6. NOTTINGHAM EXPRESS TRANSIT

This is the newest light rail system in the UK, opened in 2004. Line 1 runs for 8¾ miles from Station Street, Nottingham (alongside Nottingham station) to Hucknall, including a short spur to Phoenix Park. There is around three miles of on-street running through Nottingham. Extensions are planned to Clifton (Line 2) to the south of Nottingham and Chilwell via Beeston to the west (Line 3).

The system is operated by the Arrow Light Rail Ltd. consortium (Transdev, Nottingham City Transport, Carillion, Bombardier, Innsfree and Galaxy).

**System:** 750 V DC overhead.
**Depot & Workshops:** Wilkinson Street.

## SIX-AXLE ARTICULATED CARS                          Bo–2–Bo

**Built:** 2002–2003 by Bombardier, Derby Litchurch Lane Works. Branded "Bombardier Incentros".
**Traction Motors:** 8 Asynchronous.

| | |
|---|---|
| **Seats:** 54 + 4 tip-up | **Dimensions:** 33.0 x 2.4 m |
| **Couplers:** Not equipped. | **Doors:** Sliding plug. |
| **Weight:** 36.7 t. | **Max. Speed:** 50 m.p.h. |

**Braking:** Disc, regenerative and magnetic track for emergency use.

**Standard livery:** Black, silver & green unless stated.
**Advertising livery:**

201 – Nottinghamcontemporary.org (yellow/light blue & white).

| | | | | |
|---|---|---|---|---|
| 201 | **AL** | Torvill and Dean | 209 | Sid Standard |
| 202 | | DH Lawrence | 210 | Sir Jesse Boot |
| 203 | | Bendigo Thompson | 211 | Robin Hood |
| 204 | | Erica Beardsmore | 212 | William Booth |
| 205 | | Lord Byron | 213 | Mary Potter |
| 206 | | Angela Alcock | 214 | Dennis McCarthy |
| 207 | | Mavis Worthington | 215 | Brian Clough |
| 208 | | Dinah Minton | | |

# 5.7. MIDLAND METRO

This system opened in 1999 and has one 12½ mile line from Birmingham Snow Hill to Wolverhampton along the former GWR line to Wolverhampton Low Level. On the approach to Wolverhampton it deviates from the former railway alignment to run on-street to the St. George's terminus. It is operated by Travel West Midlands Ltd. Extensions are proposed from Snow Hill through Birmingham to Five Ways and from Wednesbury to Brierley Hill and Dudley.

**System:** 750 V DC overhead.     **Depot & Workshops:** Wednesbury.

## SIX-AXLE ARTICULATED CARS                Bo–2–Bo

**Built:** 1998–1999 by Ansaldo Transporti, Italy.
**Traction Motors:** Four.                          **Seats:** 52 + 4 tip-up.
**Dimensions:** 24.00 x 2.65 m.                    **Couplers:** Not equipped.
**Doors:** Sliding plug.                            **Weight:** 35.6 t.
**Braking:** Rheostatic, regenerative, disc and magnetic track.
**Max. Speed:** 43 m.p.h.

**Standard livery:** Dark blue & light grey with green stripe, yellow doors & red front end.

**MW:** New Network West Midlands tram livery (silver & pink).
**Note:** 01 is currently stored out of use and used for spares.

| | | | | | |
|---|---|---|---|---|---|
| 01 | (S) | SIR FRANK WHITTLE | 09 | **MW** | JEFF ASTLE |
| 02 | | | 10 | **MW** | JOHN STANLEY WEBB |
| 03 | | RAY LEWIS | 11 | | THERESA STEWART |
| 04 | | | 12 | | |
| 05 | **MW** | SISTER DORA | 13 | | ANTHONY NOLAN |
| 06 | | ALAN GARNER | 14 | | JIM EAMES |
| 07 | **MW** | BILLY WRIGHT | 15 | | AGENORIA |
| 08 | | JOSEPH CHAMBERLAIN | 16 | | GERWYN JOHN |

# 5.8. TYNE & WEAR METRO

The Tyne & Wear Metro system covers 48 route miles and can be described as the UK's first modern light rail system. However it is not a true light rail system, but more of a hybrid system, with elements of light rail, underground metro and outer suburban heavy rail operations.

The initial network opened between 1980 and 1984 consisting of a line from South Shields via Gateshead and Newcastle Central station to Bank Foot (later extended to Newcastle Airport in 1991) and the North Tyneside loop (over former BR lines) serving North Shields, Tynemouth and Whitley Bay with a terminus at St. James in Newcastle city centre. A more recent extension came from Pelaw to Sunderland and South Hylton in 2002, making use of existing heavy rail infrastructure between Heworth and Sunderland.

The system is owned and operated by Nexus  – the Tyne & Wear PTE.

**System:** 1500 V DC overhead.     **Depot & Workshops:** South Gosforth.

# SIX-AXLE ARTICULATED UNITS B–2–B

**Built:** 1978–1981 by Metropolitan Cammell, Birmingham (Prototype cars 4001 and 4002 were built by Metropolitan Cammell in 1976 and rebuilt 1984–1987 by Hunslet TPL, Leeds).
**Traction Motors:** Two Siemens of 187 kW each.

| | |
|---|---|
| **Seats:** 68. | **Dimensions:** 27.80 x 2.65 m. |
| **Couplers:** BSI. | **Doors:** Sliding plug. |
| **Weight:** 39.0 t. | **Maximum Speed:** 50 m.p.h. |

**Standard livery:** Red & yellow unless otherwise indicated.
**B** Blue & yellow
**G** Green & yellow.
**O (4001)** Original 1975 Tyne & Wear Metro livery of yellow & cream.
**O (4027)** Original North Eastern Railway style (red & white).
**Advertising liveries:**

4002 – Tyne & Wear Metro (orange & black).
4020 – Modern Apprenticeships (white, red & blue).
4038 – Talktofrank.com (white).
4040 – Cut your $CO_2$ day (blue & white).
4042 – Metro Radio (blue & pink).
4045 – Newcastle Racecourse (green).
4049 – Kidd & Spoor Harper Solicitors (blue).
4055 – European Regional Development Fund (blue & yellow).
4075 – Tyne & Wear Public Services (purple & white).
4080 – South Shields market (white).

| | | | | | | | | | |
|---|---|---|---|---|---|---|---|---|---|
| 4001 | O | 4019 | | 4037 | | 4055 | AL | 4073 | |
| 4002 | AL | 4020 | AL | 4038 | AL | 4056 | | 4074 | |
| 4003 | | 4021 | | 4039 | B | 4057 | | 4075 | AL |
| 4004 | G | 4022 | | 4040 | AL | 4058 | B | 4076 | B |
| 4005 | | 4023 | G | 4041 | | 4059 | | 4077 | |
| 4006 | | 4024 | B | 4042 | AL | 4060 | | 4078 | |
| 4007 | | 4025 | G | 4043 | | 4061 | | 4079 | |
| 4008 | | 4026 | | 4044 | | 4062 | G | 4080 | AL |
| 4009 | | 4027 | O | 4045 | AL | 4063 | | 4081 | B |
| 4010 | | 4028 | | 4046 | | 4064 | | 4082 | |
| 4011 | | 4029 | B | 4047 | B | 4065 | | 4083 | B |
| 4012 | | 4030 | | 4048 | | 4066 | B | 4084 | |
| 4013 | | 4031 | B | 4049 | AL | 4067 | | 4085 | |
| 4014 | | 4032 | | 4050 | | 4068 | | 4086 | |
| 4015 | | 4033 | | 4051 | G | 4069 | | 4087 | |
| 4016 | B | 4034 | | 4052 | | 4070 | | 4088 | |
| 4017 | | 4035 | B | 4053 | B | 4071 | | 4089 | |
| 4018 | G | 4036 | G | 4054 | B | 4072 | B | 4090 | |

**Names:**

| | | | |
|---|---|---|---|
| 4026 | George Stephenson | 4065 | DAME Catherine Cookson |
| 4041 | HARRY COWANS | 4073 | Danny Marshall |
| 4060 | Thomas Bewick | 4077 | Robert Stephenson |
| 4064 | Michael Campbell | 4078 | Ellen Wilkinson |

# 5.9. EDINBURGH TRAMS

A new tramway is under construction in Edinburgh, with the first of the new trams now complete. It is planned that the delayed opening of the tramway will be in early 2012, with trams arriving for testing in 2011. The route will run for 11½ miles from Newhaven to Edinburgh Airport via Leith and central Edinburgh, including the famous Princes Street and Waverley and Haymarket stations. The trams will be the longest to operate in the UK, with seven low-floor articulated sections resting on four bogies.

**System:** 750 V DC overhead.
**Depot & Workshops:** Gogar.
**Livery:** White, red & black.

# EIGHT-AXLE ARTICULATED CARS                      Bo-Bo-2-Bo

**Built:** 2009–2010 by CAF, Irun, Spain.
**Traction Motors:** 12 CAF of 80 kW.          **Seats:** 80.
**Dimensions:** 42.8 x 2.65 m.                  **Couplers:**
**Doors:** Sliding plug.                        **Weight:**
**Braking:**
**Max. Speed:** 50 m.p.h.

| | | | | |
|---|---|---|---|---|
| 251 | 257 | 263 | 268 | 273 |
| 252 | 258 | 264 | 269 | 274 |
| 253 | 259 | 265 | 270 | 275 |
| 254 | 260 | 266 | 271 | 276 |
| 255 | 261 | 267 | 272 | 277 |
| 256 | 262 | | | |

# 5.10. GLASGOW SUBWAY

This circular 4 ft. gauge underground line is the smallest metro system in the UK, running for just over six miles. It is generally referred to as the "Subway" or the "Clockwork Orange". Operated by Strathclyde PTE the system has 15 stations. The entire passenger railway is underground, contained in twin tunnels, allowing for clockwise operation on the "outer" circle and anti-clockwise operation on the "inner" circle.

Trains are formed of 3-cars – either three power cars or two power cars sandwiching one of the newer trailer cars.

**System:** 600 V DC third rail.
**Depot & Workshops:** Broomloan.
**Livery:** Strathclyde PTE carmine & cream unless stated.

## SINGLE POWER CARS
Bo–Bo

**Built:** 1977–1979 by Metro-Cammell, Birmingham. Refurbished 1993–1995 by ABB Derby.
**Traction Motors:** Four GEC G312AZ of 35.6 kW each.
**Seats:** 36.
**Couplers:** Wedglock.
**Weight:** 19.6 t.
**Dimensions:** 12.81 m x 2.34 m.
**Doors:** Sliding.
**Maximum Speed:** 33.5 m.p.h.

| | | | | |
|---|---|---|---|---|
| 101 | 108 | 115 | 122 | 128 |
| 102 | 109 | 116 | 123 | 129 |
| 103 | 110 | 117 | 124 | 130 |
| 104 | 111 | 118 | 125 | 131 |
| 105 | 112 | 119 | 126 | 132 |
| 106 | 113 | 120 | 127 | 133 |
| 107 | 114 | 121 | | |

## INTERMEDIATE TRAILERS
2–2

**Built:** 1992 by Hunslet Barclay, Kilmarnock.
**Seats:** 40.
**Couplers:** Wedglock.
**Weight:** 17.2 t.
**Dimensions:** 12.70 m x 2.34 m.
**Doors:** Sliding.
**Maximum Speed:** 33.5 m.p.h.

**Advertising liveries:**

201 – Scottish Sun (white/red/black)
203 – Radio Clyde (red).
204 – SPT Zonecard ticket (blue).
205 – Robert Burns (different images of the famous poet).
208 – Glasgow 2014 – "back the bid" (blue with various images).

| | | | | | | | |
|---|---|---|---|---|---|---|---|
| 201 | **AL** | 203 | **AL** | 205 | **AL** | 207 | | 208 | **AL** |
| 202 | | 204 | **AL** | 206 | | | |

# Keep right up to date with....

# Today's
## Railways

**UK**

## The UK railway magazine from Platform 5 Publishing.

Read all the very latest news from Britain and Ireland and unrivalled coverage of UK rolling stock news, every month.

**On sale 2nd Monday of EVERY MONTH**

Subscribe to Today's Railways UK TODAY!

### Never miss an issue!
- Your copy delivered to your door at no extra cost.
- Recieve every issue hot off the press.
- No price increase for the duration of your subscription.
- Exclusive reduced prices on selected books and videos from the Platform 5 Mail Order Department

Today's Railways UK subscriptions:
☎: (+44) 0114 255 8000   Fax: (+44) 0114 255 2471

# Subscription order form

To subscribe, please complete the form below (or a copy) and return it with your remittance to:

**Today's Railways UK (Dept. LCS), 3 Wyvern House, Sark Road, SHEFFIELD, S2 4HG, ENGLAND.**

**BLOCK CAPITALS PLEASE**

(All prices include postage and packing.)

---

**Today's Railways UK: Subscription (12 issues)**

☐ UK £45.00 (post free);         ☐ Overseas Airmail £54.60.

JAN   FEB   MAR   APR   MAY   JUN   JUL   AUG   SEP   OCT   NOV   DEC

Please circle start issue required

---

**Name:** ..............................................................................................

**Address:** ..........................................................................................

.........................................................................................................

.................................................. **Postcode:** ...................................

**Daytime Tel. No:** ..............................................................................

**E-mail:** .............................................................................................

---

I enclose my cheque/UK postal order for £ .........................................

made payable to '**PLATFORM 5 PUBLISHING LTD.**'

**Please debit my Visa/Mastercard/Maestro**

**Card No:** ................................................. **Expiry Date:** ..................

**Card Issue No./Date (Maestro only):** .................. **Security No.:** ............

**for £** ............................................................ **Date:** ........................

**Signature:** .........................................................................................

---

or if ordering by debit/credit card, telephone our subscription department on the numbers opposite.

**Special note:** Subscriptions may begin with the current issue or the next to be published. Subscriptions cannot be backdated.

# 6. CODES

## 6.1. LIVERY CODES

Livery codes are used to denote the various liveries carried. It is impossible to list every livery variation which currently exists. In particular items ignored for this publication include:

- Minor colour variations.
- Omission of logos.
- All numbering, lettering and brandings.

Descriptions quoted are thus a general guide only. Logos as appropriate for each livery are normally deemed to be carried.

The colour of the lower half of the bodyside is stated first. Minor variations to these liveries are ignored.

*Code Description*

| | |
|---|---|
| **1** | "One" (metallic grey with a broad black bodyside stripe. White National Express interim stripe as branding). |
| **AB** | Arriva Trains "executive" dark & light blue. |
| **AI** | Aggregate Industries (green, light grey & blue). |
| **AL** | Advertising/promotional livery (see class heading for details). |
| **AN** | Anglia Railways Class 170s (white & turquoise with blue vignette). |
| **AR** | Anglia Railways (turquoise blue with a white stripe). |
| **AV** | Arriva Trains (turquoise blue with white doors & a cream "swish"). |
| **AZ** | Advenza Freight (deep blue with green Advenza brandings). |
| **B** | BR blue. |
| **BA** | British American Railway Services (dark green). |
| **BG** | BR blue & grey lined out in white. |
| **BL** | BR Revised blue with yellow cabs, grey roof, large numbers & logo. |
| **BP** | Blue Pullman ("Nanking" blue & white). |
| **BS** | Serco Railtest blue (deep blue with white Serco brandings). |
| **C2** | c2c Rail (blue with metallic grey doors & pink c2c branding). |
| **CC** | BR Carmine & Cream. |
| **CD** | Cotswold Rail (silver with blue & red logo). |
| **CE** | BR Civil Engineers (yellow & grey with black cab doors & window surrounds). |
| **CH** | BR Western Region/GWR (chocolate & cream lined out in gold). |
| **CI** | Centro {Class 150} (light green with a broad blue lower bodyside band & blue cab end sections). |
| **CN** | Southeastern (white with black window surrounds & grey lower band). |
| **CR** | Chiltern Railways (blue & white with a thin red stripe). |
| **CS** | Colas Rail (yellow, orange & black). |
| **CT** | Central Trains (two-tone green with yellow doors. Blue flash & red stripe at vehicle ends). |
| **CU** | Corus (silver with red logos). |
| **CX** | Connex (white with yellow lower body & blue solebar). |
| **DB** | DB Schenker (Deutsch Bahn red with grey roof & solebar). |
| **DG** | BR Departmental (dark grey with black cab doors & window surrounds). |

**DR** Direct Rail Services (dark blue with light blue or dark grey roof).
**DS** Revised Direct Rail Services (dark blue, light blue & green. "Compass" logo).
**E** English Welsh & Scottish Railway (maroon bodyside & roof with a broad gold bodyside band).
**EB** Eurotunnel (two-tone grey with a broad blue stripe).
**EG** "EWS grey" (as **F** but with large yellow & red EWS logo).
**EL** Electric Traction Services (silver & red).
**EP** European Passenger Services (two-tone grey with dark blue roof).
**EM** East Midlands Trains {Connect} (blue with red & orange swish at unit ends).
**EU** Eurostar (white with dark blue & yellow stripes).
**F** BR Trainload Freight (two-tone grey with black cab doors & window surrounds. Various logos).
**FA** Fastline Freight (grey & black with white & orange stripes).
**FB** First Group dark blue.
**FD** First Great Western & First Hull Trains "Dynamic Lines" (dark blue with thin multi-coloured lines on the lower bodyside).
**FE** Railfreight Distribution International (two tone-grey with black cab doors & dark blue roof).
**FER** Fertis (light grey with a dark grey roof & solebar).
**FF** Freightliner grey (two-tone grey with black cab doors & window surrounds. Freightliner logo).
**FG** First Group Inter-City (indigo blue with a white roof & gold, pink & white stripes).
**FH** Revised Freightliner {Class 70} (dark green with yellow cab ends & a grey stripe/buffer beam).
**FI** First Great Western "Local Lines" DMU (varying blue with local visitor attractions applied to the lower bodyside).
**FL** Freightliner (dark green with yellow cabs).
**FP** Old First Great Western (green & ivory with thin green & broad gold stripes).
**FO** BR Railfreight (grey bodysides, yellow cabs & red lower bodyside stipe, large BR logo).
**FR** Fragonset Railways (black with silver roof & a red bodyside band lined out in white).
**FS** First Group (indigo blue with pink & white stripes).
**FT** First TransPennine Express "Dynamic Lines" (varying blue with thin multi-coloured lines on the lower bodyside).
**FU** First Group "Urban Lights" (varying blue with pink, white and blue markings on the lower bodyside).
**FY** Foster Yeoman (blue & silver. Cast numberplates).
**G¹** BR Green (plain green, with white stripe on main line locomotives).
**G²** BR Southern Region/SR or BR DMU green.
**GB** GB Railfreight (blue with orange cantrail & solebar stripes, orange cabs).
**GC** Grand Central (all over black (with an orange stripe for DMUs)).
**GE** First Great Eastern (grey, green, blue & white).
**GG** BR green (two-tone green).
**GL** First Great Western locos (green with a gold stripe).
**GN** Great North Eastern Railway {modified} (dark blue with a white (was red) stripe).

**GS** Royal Scotsman/Great Scottish & Western Railway (maroon).
**GV** Gatwick Express EMU (red, white & indigo blue with mauve & blue doors).
**GW** Great Western Railway (green, lined out in black & orange).
**GX** Gatwick Express InterCity (dark grey/white/burgundy/white).
**GY** Eurotunnel (grey & yellow).
**HA** Hanson Quarry Products (dark blue/silver with oxide red roof).
**HB** HSBC Rail (Oxford blue & white).
**HC** Heathrow Connect (grey with a broad deep blue bodyside band & orange doors).
**HE** Heathrow Express (grey & indigo blue with black window surrounds).
**HN** Harry Needle Railroad Company (orange & grey, lined out in black).
**IC** BR InterCity (dark grey/white/red/white).
**IM** BR InterCity Mainline (dark grey/white/red/light grey & yellow lower cabsides except shunters).
**K** Black.
**LH** BR Loadhaul (black with orange cabsides).
**LM** London Midland (white/grey & green with broad black stripe around the windows).
**LN** LNER Tourist (green & cream).
**LO** London Overground (all over white with a blue solebar & black window surrounds).
**LT** London Transport maroon & cream.
**M** BR maroon (maroon lined out in straw & black).
**MA** Maintrain/East Midlands Trains blue.
**ME** Merseyrail (metallic silver with yellow doors).
**ML** BR Mainline Freight (aircraft blue with a silver stripe).
**MM** Old Midland Mainline (teal green with grey lower body sides & three tangerine stripes).
**MN** Midland Mainline (thin tangerine stripe on the lower bodyside, ocean blue, grey & white).
**MT** First GBRf Metronet (blue with orange cabsides).
**N** BR Network South East (white & blue with red lower bodyside stripe, grey solebar & cab ends).
**NC** National Express/c2c (white with blue doors).
**NO** Northern (deep blue, lilac & white). Some units have area-specific promotional vinyls (see class headings for details).
**NR** Network Rail (blue with a red stripe).
**NW** North Western Trains (blue with gold cantrail stripe & star).
**NX** National Express (white with grey ends).
**O** Non standard livery (see class heading for details).
**P** Porterbrook Leasing Company (white or grey & purple).
**PC** Pullman Car Company (umber & cream with gold lettering lined out in gold).
**RG** BR Parcels (dark grey & red).
**RK** Railtrack (green & blue).
**RM** Royal Mail (red with yellow stripes above solebar).
**RO** Old Railtrack (orange with white & grey stripes).
**RP** Royal Train (claret, lined out in red & black).
**RR** Regional Railways (dark blue & grey with light blue & white stripes, three narrow dark blue stripes at vehicle ends).
**RT** RT Rail (black, lined out in red).
**RV** Riviera Trains (Oxford blue & cream lined out in gold {blue only for locos}).

| | |
|---|---|
| **RX** | Rail Express Systems (dark grey & red with or without blue markings). |
| **RZ** | Royal Train revised (plain claret, no lining). |
| **SB** | Southeastern High Speed (all over blue with black window surrounds). |
| **SC** | Strathclyde PTE (carmine & cream lined out in black & gold). |
| **SD** | South West Trains outer suburban {Class 450 style} (deep blue with red doors & orange & red cab sides). |
| **SL** | Silverlink (indigo blue with white stripe, green lower body & yellow doors). |
| **SP** | Strathclyde PTE {Class 334 style} (carmine & cream, with a turquoise stripe). |
| **SN** | Southern (white & dark green with light green semi-circles at one end of each vehicle. Light grey band at solebar level). |
| **SO** | Serco Railtest (red & grey). |
| **SR** | ScotRail – Scotland's Railways (dark blue with Scottish Saltire flag & white/light blue flashes). |
| **SS** | South West Trains inner suburban {Class 455 style} (red with blue & orange flashes at unit ends). |
| **ST** | Stagecoach {long-distance stock} (white & dark blue with dark blue window surrounds and red & orange swishes at unit ends). |
| **SU** | Revised Stansted Express (light blue with a dark blue lower bodyside stripe & light grey doors). |
| **SX** | Stansted Express (two-tone metallic blue with grey doors). |
| **TC** | Revised TransPennine Express (all over plum). |
| **TL** | New Thameslink (silver with blue window surrounds & ends). |
| **TW** | Modified Thameslink (dark blue with broad white lower bodyside stripe). |
| **U** | Plain white or grey undercoat. |
| **V** | Virgin Trains (red with black doors extending into bodysides, three white lower bodysides stripes). |
| **VP** | Virgin Trains shunters (black with a large black & white chequered flag on the bodyside). |
| **VN** | Venice Simplon Orient Express "Northern Belle" (crimson lake & cream lined out in gold). |
| **VT** | Virgin Trains silver (silver, with black window surrounds, white cantrail stripe & red roof. Red swept down at unit ends. Black & white striped doors on units). |
| **WA** | Wabtec Rail (black). |
| **WB** | Wales & Borders Alphaline (metallic silver with blue doors). |
| **WC** | West Coast Railway Company maroon (57601 carries a black bodyside stripe). |
| **WM** | Network West Midlands (light blue with green lower bodyside stripe and white stripe at cantrail level). |
| **WN** | Old West Anglia Great Northern (white with blue, grey & orange stripes). |
| **WP** | West Anglia Great Northern (deep purple with white or light purple doors). |
| **WS** | Wrexham & Shropshire (two-tone grey & silver). |
| **WT** | Wessex Trains Alphaline (metallic silver with maroon or pink doors). |
| **WX** | Heart of Wessex Line promotional livery (cerise pink). |
| **XC** | CrossCountry (two-tone silver with deep crimson ends and pink doors). |
| **Y** | Network Rail yellow. |
| **YR** | West Yorkshire PTE/Northern EMUs (red, lilac & grey). |

# 6.2. OWNER CODES

The following codes are used to define the ownership details of the locomotives or rolling stock listed in this book. Codes shown indicate either the legal owner or "responsible custodian" of each vehicle.

*Code   Owner*

| | |
|---|---|
| 20 | Class 20189 |
| 24 | 6024 Preservation Society |
| 40 | The Class 40 Preservation Society |
| 47 | The Stratford 47 Group |
| 50 | Class 50 Alliance |
| 62 | The Princess Royal Locomotive Trust |
| 67 | Tangmere Locomotive Company |
| 70 | 7029 Clun Castle |
| 92 | City of Wells Supporters Association |
| 2L | Class 20 Locomotive Society |
| A | Angel Trains |
| A1 | A1 Steam Locomotive Trust |
| A4 | The A4 Locomotive Society |
| AI | Aggregate Industries |
| AM | Alstom |
| AW | Arriva Trains Wales |
| BA | British American Railway Services |
| B1 | Thompson B1 Locomotive Society |
| BC | Bridgend County Borough Council/Rhondda Cynon Taff District Council |
| BD | Boden Rail Engineering |
| BE | Bert Hitchins |
| BK | The Scottish Railway Preservation Society |
| BN | Beacon Rail |
| BS | Bressingham Steam Museum |
| BT | Bombardier Transportation |
| BU | The Bulgarian Railway Company |
| CC | Cardiff City Council |
| CD | Cotswold Rail |
| CG | Cargo-D |
| CR | Chiltern Railways |
| CS | Colas Rail |
| DB | DB Schenker / DB Regio |
| DG | Duke of Gloucester Steam Locomotive Trust |
| DM | Dartmoor Railway |
| DR | Direct Rail Services |
| DT | The Diesel Traction Group |
| EL | Electric Traction Services |
| EM | East Midlands Trains |
| EP | Europhoenix |
| ET | Eurotunnel |
| EU | Eurostar (UK) |
| FA | Fastline |
| FG | First Group |

| FL | Freightliner |
|----|-------------|
| GB | First GBRf |
| GS | The Great Scottish & Western Railway Company |
| GW | The Great Western Society |
| H | HSBC Rail (UK) |
| HA | Hanson Group |
| HD | Hastings Diesels |
| HE | British Airports Authority |
| HJ | Howard Johnston Engineering |
| HN | Harry Needle Railroad Company |
| HS | Hanson Traction |
| HX | Halifax Bank of Scotland |
| IR | Ian Riley Engineering |
| JC | John Cameron |
| JH | Jeremy Hosking |
| KN | Knights Rail Services |
| LM | London Midland |
| LR | Les Ross |
| LW | Arriva LNWR |
| LY | Lloyds Banking Group |
| MN | Merchant Navy Locomotive Preservation Society |
| MW | Martin Walker |
| NE | North Eastern Locomotive Preservation Group |
| NM | National Railway Museum |
| NR | Network Rail |
| NS | Nemesis Rail |
| NY | North Yorkshire Moors Railway |
| P | Porterbrook Leasing Company |
| PO | Other owner |
| PU | Pullman Rail |
| QW | QW Rail Leasing |
| RA | Railfilms |
| RE | Railway Vehicle Engineering |
| RI | Rail Assets Investments |
| RL | RMS Locotec |
| RM | Royal Mail |
| RV | Riviera Trains |
| SB | SNCB/NMBS (Société Nationale des Chemins de fer Belges/ Nationale Maatschappij der Belgische Spoorwegen) |
| SF | SNCF (Société Nationale des Chemins de fer Français) |
| SM | Siemens Transportation |
| SN | Southern |
| SO | Serco Railtest |
| ST | Sovereign Trains |
| SV | Severn Valley Railway |
| SW | South West Trains |
| TT | Type Three Traction Group |
| VI | Virgin Trains |
| VS | Venice-Simplon Orient Express |
| VT | Vintage Trains |
| WA | Wabtec Rail |

WC    West Coast Railway Company
WT    Wessex Trains
X     Sold for scrap/further use and awaiting collection or owner unknown

# 6.3. LOCOMOTIVE POOL CODES

Locomotives are split into operational groups ("pools") for diagramming and maintenance purposes. The official codes used to denote these pools are shown in this publication.

| Code | Pool |
|------|------|
| ACAC | Electric Traction Limited locomotives |
| ACXX | Electric Traction Limited locomotives for static depot use. |
| ADFL | Advenza Freight locomotives (stored). |
| ATLO | Alstom Class 08. |
| ATZZ | Alstom locomotives for disposal. |
| BREL | Boden Rail locomotives. |
| CDJD | Serco Railtest Class 08. |
| CFOL | Class 50 Operations locomotives. |
| COLO | Colas Rail locomotives. |
| DFGC | Freightliner Intermodal Class 86/5. |
| DFGH | Freightliner Heavy Haul Class 70. |
| DFGI | Freightliner Intermodal Class 70. |
| DFGM | Freightliner Intermodal Class 66. |
| DFHG | Freightliner Heavy Haul modified Class 66 (general). |
| DFHH | Freightliner Heavy Haul Class 66. |
| DFIM | Freightliner Intermodal modified Class 66. |
| DFIN | Freightliner Intermodal Class 66 (low emission). |
| DFLC | Freightliner Intermodal Class 90. |
| DFLH | Freightliner Heavy Haul Class 47. |
| DFLS | Freightliner Class 08. |
| DFNC | Freightliner Intermodal Class 86/6. |
| DFNR | Freightliner Heavy Haul modified Class 66. Infrastructure services. |
| DFRT | Freightliner Heavy Haul Class 66. Infrastructure services. |
| DFTZ | Freightliner stored Class 66. |
| DHLT | Freightliner locomotives awaiting maintenance/repair/disposal. |
| EFOO | First Great Western Class 57. |
| EFPC | First Great Western Class 43. |
| EFSH | First Great Western Class 08. |
| EHPC | CrossCountry Class 43. |
| EJLO | London Midland Class 08. |
| ELRD | East Lancashire Railway-based main line registered locomotives. |
| EMPC | East Midlands Trains Class 43. |
| EMSL | East Midlands Trains Class 08. |
| EPXX | Europhoenix Class 86. |
| ETLO | Electric Traction Limited locomotives. |
| GBCM | First GBRf Class 66. General. |

| | |
|---|---|
| GBED | First GBRf Class 73. |
| GBRT | First GBRf Class 66. Network Rail contracts. |
| GBZZ | First GBRf. Stored locomotives. |
| GCHP | Grand Central Class 43. |
| GPSS | Eurostar (UK) Class 08. |
| GBWN | First GBRf Class 73 (March Whitemoor pilot). |
| HBSH | Wabtec hire shunting locomotives. |
| HNRL | Harry Needle Railroad Company hire locomotives. |
| HNRS | Harry Needle Railroad Company stored locomotives. |
| HTLX | Hanson Traction locomotives. |
| HWSU | Southern Class 09. |
| HYWD | South West Trains Class 73 (standby use). |
| IANA | National Express East Anglia Class 90. |
| IECA | East Coast Class 91. |
| IECP | East Coast Class 43. |
| IVGA | Gatwick Express Class 73 (standby use). |
| IWCA | Virgin Trains Class 57. |
| MBDL | Non TOC-owned diesel locomotives. |
| MBED | Non TOC-owned electro-diesel locomotives. |
| MBEL | Non TOC-owned electric locomotives. |
| MOLO | Class 20s for London Underground rolling stock moves. |
| MRSO | RMS Locotec Class 08. |
| NRLO | Nemesis Rail locomotives. |
| PTXX | Europorte2 locomotives. |
| QACL | Network Rail Class 86. |
| QADD | Network Rail diesel locomotives. |
| QCAR | Network Rail New Measurement Train Class 43. |
| QETS | Network Rail Class 37. |
| QSTR | Network Rail stored locomotives. |
| RCJB | Fastline Class 66. |
| RCJZ | Fastline stored locomotives. |
| RFSH | Wabtec Rail locomotives. |
| RTLO | Riviera Trains operational fleet. |
| RTLS | Riviera Trains stored locomotives. |
| RVLO | Rail Vehicle Engineering/British American Railway Services locomotives. |
| SAXL | HSBC Rail (UK) off-lease locomotives. |
| SBXL | Porterbrook Leasing Company off-lease locomotives. |
| TTTC | Type Three Traction Group Class 37. |
| WAAN | DB Schenker Network Class 67. |
| WABN | DB Schenker Network Class 67. RETB fitted. |
| WAFN | DB Schenker Network Class 67 for hire to First Great Western. |
| WAWN | DB Schenker Network Class 67 for hire to Wrexham & Shropshire. |
| WBAI | DB Schenker Industrial Class 66. |
| WBAK | DB Schenker Construction Class 66. |
| WBAM | DB Schenker Energy Class 66. |
| WBAN | DB Schenker Network Class 66. |
| WBBI | DB Schenker Industrial Class 66. RETB fitted. |
| WBBK | DB Schenker Construction Class 66. RETB fitted. |
| WBBN | DB Schenker Network Class 66. RETB fitted. |
| WBLI | DB Schenker Industrial Class 66. Dedicated locos for Lickey Incline banking duties. |

| | |
|---|---|
| WCAI | DB Schenker Industrial Class 60. |
| WCAK | DB Schenker Construction Class 60. |
| WCAM | DB Schenker Energy Classes 59 & 60. |
| WCAN | DB Schenker Network Class 60. |
| WCBI | DB Schenker Industrial Class 60. Extended-range fuel tanks. |
| WCBK | DB Schenker Construction Class 60. Extended-range fuel tanks. |
| WCBM | DB Schenker Energy Class 60. Extended-range fuel tanks. |
| WCBN | DB Schenker Network Class 60. Extended-range fuel tanks. |
| WDAK | DB Schenker Construction Class 59. |
| WEFE | DB Schenker Network Class 90. |
| WFMU | DB Schenker Fleet Management Unit locomotives. |
| WKBN | DB Schenker Network Class 37. |
| WNSO | DB Schenker locomotives – sold awaiting collection. |
| WNTR | DB Schenker locomotives – tactical reserve. |
| WNTS | DB Schenker locomotives – tactical stored unserviceable. |
| WNWX | DB Schenker main line locomotives – for major repairs. |
| WNXX | DB Schenker locomotives – stored unserviceable. |
| WNYX | DB Schenker locomotives – authorised for component recovery. |
| WSSI | DB Schenker Industrial operational Shunters. |
| WSSK | DB Schenker Construction operational Shunters. |
| WSSM | DB Schenker Energy operational Shunters. |
| WSSN | DB Schenker Network operational Shunters. |
| WSXX | DB Schenker shunting locomotives – internal/depot use. |
| WTAE | DB Schenker Network Class 92. |
| WZGF | DB Schenker Class 56 – former hire locomotives France (stored). |
| WZTS | DB Schenker locomotives – tactical stored. |
| XHAC | Direct Rail Services Class 47. |
| XHCK | Direct Rail Services Class 57. |
| XHHP | Direct Rail Services locomotives – holding pool. |
| XHIM | Direct Rail Services locomotives – Intermodal traffic. |
| XHNC | Direct Rail Services locomotives – nuclear traffic/general. |
| XHSS | Direct Rail Services stored locomotives. |
| XYPA | Mendip Rail Class 59/1. |
| XYPO | Mendip Rail Class 59/0. |

# 6.4. OPERATOR CODES

Operator codes are used to denote the organisation that facilitates the use of that vehicle, and may not be the actual Train Operating Company which runs the train. Where no operator code is shown, vehicles are currently not in use.

| Code | Operator |
|------|----------|
| 62 | The Princess Royal Locomotive Trust |
| AW | Arriva Trains Wales |
| BK | The Scottish Railway Preservation Society |
| C2 | c2c Rail |
| CD | Cotswold Rail |
| CG | Cargo-D |
| CR | Chiltern Railways |
| CS | Colas Rail |
| DB | DB Schenker |
| DR | Direct Rail Services |
| EA | National Express East Anglia |
| EC | East Coast |
| EM | East Midlands Trains |
| EU | Eurostar (UK) |
| FC | First Capital Connect |
| FL | Freightliner |
| GB | First GBRf |
| GC | Grand Central |
| GS | The Great Scottish & Western Railway Company |
| GW | First Great Western |
| HC | Heathrow Connect |
| HD | Hastings Diesels |
| HE | Heathrow Express |
| HT | First Hull Trains |
| LO | London Overground |
| LM | London Midland |
| ME | Merseyrail |
| NO | Northern |
| NY | North Yorkshire Moors Railway |
| RA | Railfilms |
| RP | Royal Train |
| RV | Riviera Trains |
| SE | Southeastern |
| SF | SNCF (French Railways) |
| SN | Southern |
| SO | Serco Railtest |
| SR | ScotRail |
| SW | South West Trains |
| TP | TransPennine Express |
| VS | Venice-Simplon Orient Express |
| VT | Vintage Trains |
| VW | Virgin Trains |
| WC | West Coast Railway Company |

| WS | Wrexham & Shropshire |
| WT | Wessex Trains |
| XC | CrossCountry |

# 6.5. ALLOCATION & LOCATION CODES

Allocation codes are used in this publication to denote the normal maintenance base ("depots") of each operational locomotive, multiple unit or coach. However, maintenance may be carried out at other locations and may also be carried out by mobile maintenance teams.

Location codes are used to denote common storage locations whilst the full place name is used for other locations. The designation (S) denotes stored. However, when a locomotive pool code denotes that a loco is stored anyway then the (S) is not shown.

| Code | Depot | Operator |
|------|-------|----------|
| AD | Ashford | Hitachi |
| AF | Ashford Chart Leacon Works | Bombardier Transportation |
| AK | Ardwick (Manchester) | Siemens |
| AL | Aylesbury | Chiltern Railways |
| AN | Allerton (Liverpool) | DB Schenker |
| AP* | Ashford Rail Plant (Kent) | Balfour Beatty Rail Services |
| AY | Ayr | DB Schenker |
| BA | Basford Hall Yard (Crewe) | Storage location only |
| BD | Birkenhead North | Merseyrail |
| BF | Bedford Cauldwell Walk | First Capital Connect |
| BH | Barrow Hill (Chesterfield) | Barrow Hill Engine Shed Society |
| BI | Brighton Lovers Walk | Southern |
| BK | Bristol Barton Hill | DB Schenker |
| BM | Bournemouth | South West Trains |
| BN | Bounds Green (London) | East Coast |
| BR* | MoD DSDC Bicester | Ministry of Defence |
| BQ | Bury (Greater Manchester) | East Lancashire Railway |
| BS | Bescot (Walsall) | DB Schenker |
| BT | Bo'ness (West Lothian) | Bo'ness & Kinneil Railway |
| BY | Bletchley | London Midland |
| BZ | St. Blazey (Par) | DB Schenker |
| CD | Crewe Diesel | DB Schenker |
| CE | Crewe International | DB Schenker |
| CF | Cardiff Canton | Arriva Trains Wales/Pullman Rail |
| CH | Chester | Alstom |
| CJ | Clapham Yard (London) | South West Trains |
| CK | Corkerhill (Glasgow) | ScotRail |
| CO | Coquelles (France) | Eurotunnel |
| CP | Crewe Carriage | Arriva LNWR |
| CQ | Crewe (The Railway Age) | LNWR Heritage |

| CR | Crewe Gresty Lane | Direct Rail Services |
|----|----|----|
| CS | Carnforth | West Coast Railway Company |
| CZ | Central Rivers (Burton) | Bombardier Transportation |
| DC* | Didcot Yard | DB Schenker |
| DF | Derby | Railway Vehicle Engineering |
| DI | Didcot Railway Centre | Great Western Society |
| DR | Doncaster | DB Schenker |
| DW* | Doncaster West Yard | *Storage location only* |
| DY | Derby Etches Park | East Midlands Trains |
| EC | Edinburgh Craigentinny | East Coast |
| EH | Eastleigh | DB Schenker |
| EM | East Ham (London) | c2c Rail |
| EX | Exeter | First Great Western |
| FA | Fawley (Hampshire) | *Storage location only* |
| FD | Freightliner diesels nationwide | Freightliner |
| FE | Freightliner electrics nationwide | Freightliner |
| FF* | Forest (Brussels) | SNCB/NMBS |
| FN* | Locos in use in France | Euro Cargo Rail/SNCF |
| GI | Gillingham (Kent) | Southeastern |
| GL | Gloucester Horton Road | Cotswold Rail |
| GW | Glasgow Shields Road | ScotRail |
| HA | Haymarket (Edinburgh) | ScotRail |
| HE | Hornsey (London) | First Capital Connect |
| HG | Hither Green (London) | DB Schenker |
| HM | Healey Mills (Wakefield) | DB Schenker |
| HP* | Hope Cement Works | Lafarge |
| HT | Heaton (Newcastle) | Northern |
| IL | Ilford (London) | National Express East Anglia |
| IM | Immingham | DB Schenker |
| IS | Inverness | ScotRail |
| KM | Carlisle Kingmoor | Direct Rail Services |
| KR | Kidderminster | Severn Valley Railway |
| KT | MoD Kineton (Warwickshire) | Ministry of Defence |
| LA | Laira (Plymouth) | First Great Western |
| LB | Loughborough Works | Brush Traction |
| LD | Leeds Midland Road | Freightliner |
| LE | Landore (Swansea) | First Great Western |
| LG | Longsight (Manchester) | Northern |
| LH* | LH Group, Barton-under-Needwood | LH Group Services |
| LL | Edge Hill (Liverpool) | Alstom |
| LM | Long Marston (Warwickshire) | Motorail Logistics |
| LU* | MoD Ludgersall | Ministry of Defence |
| LY* | Le Landy (Paris) | SNCF |
| MA | Manchester Longsight | Alstom |
| MD | Merehead | Mendip Rail |
| ME | Mossend Yard | DB Schenker |
| MG | Margam (Port Talbot) | DB Schenker |
| MH | Millerhill (Edinburgh) | DB Schenker |
| MN | Machynlleth | Arriva Trains Wales |
| MQ* | Meldon Quarry (Okehampton) | *Storage locoation only* |
| NC | Norwich Crown Point | National Express East Anglia |

| NG | New Cross Gate (London) | London Overground |
| NH | Newton Heath (Manchester) | Northern |
| NL | Neville Hill (Leeds) | East Midlands Trains/Northern |
| NM | Nottingham Eastcroft | East Midlands Trains |
| NN | Northampton King's Heath | Siemens |
| NT | Northam (Southampton) | Siemens |
| NY | Grosmont (North Yorkshire) | North Yorkshire Moors Railway |
| OD* | Old Dalby test centre | Bombardier Transportation |
| OH | Old Oak Common Heathrow | Heathrow Express |
| OO | Old Oak Common HST | First Great Western |
| OY | Oxley (Wolverhampton) | Alstom |
| PM | St. Philip's Marsh (Bristol) | First Great Western |
| PZ | Penzance Long Rock | First Great Western |
| RG | Reading | First Great Western |
| RM | Ramsgate | Southeastern |
| RR | Doncaster Robert's Road | Fastline |
| RU | Rugby Rail Plant | Colas Rail |
| RY | Ryde (Isle of Wight) | South West Trains |
| SA | Salisbury | South West Trains |
| SE | St. Leonards (Hastings) | St. Leonards Railway Engineering |
| SG | Slade Green (London) | Southeastern |
| SH | Southall (Greater London) | Jeremy Hosking |
| SJ* | Stourbridge Junction | Parry People Movers |
| SK | Swanwick Junction (Derbyshire) | Midland Railway-Butterley |
| SL | Stewarts Lane (London) | Southern/VSOE |
| SN* | MoD Shoeburyness | Ministry of Defence |
| SO | Soho (Birmingham) | London Midland |
| SP | Springs Branch (Wigan) | DB Schenker |
| SU | Selhurst (Croydon) | Southern |
| SZ | Southampton Maritime | Freightliner |
| TE | Thornaby (Middlesbrough) | DB Schenker |
| TI | Temple Mills (London) | Eurostar |
| TJ | Tavistock Junction (Plymouth) | Colas Rail |
| TM | Tyseley Locomotive Works | Birmingham Railway Museum |
| TN | Thornton (Fife) | John Cameron |
| TO | Toton (Nottinghamshire) | DB Schenker |
| TS | Tyseley (Birmingham) | London Midland |
| TW* | Tonbridge West Yard | First GBRf |
| TY | Tyne Yard (Newcastle) | DB Schenker |
| WA | Warrington | DB Schenker |
| WB | Wembley (London) | Alstom |
| WD | Wimbledon (London) | South West Trains |
| WE | Willesden Brent sidings | *Storage location only* |
| WF | Wansford (Cambridgeshire) | Hanson Traction |
| WH* | Washwood Heath (Birmingham) | Boden Rail Engineering |
| WN | Willesden (London) | London Overground |
| WR* | Willesden Railnet PRDC | Royal Mail |
| WY* | Wembley Yard | DB Schenker |
| XW | Crofton (Wakefield) | Bombardier Transportation |
| YK | National Railway Museum (York) | Science Museum |
| YJ | Yeovil Junction Railway Centre | The Yeovil Country Railway |

| | | |
|---|---|---|
| ZA | RTC Business Park (Derby) | Serco Railtest/Delta Rail |
| ZB | Doncaster Works | Wabtec Rail |
| ZC | Crewe Works | Bombardier Transportation |
| ZD | Derby Works | Bombardier Transportation |
| ZG | Eastleigh Works | Knights Rail Services |
| ZH | Springburn Works (Glasgow) | Railcare |
| ZI | Ilford Works | Bombardier Transportation |
| ZJ | Marcroft, Stoke | Turners/DB Axiom Rail |
| ZK | Kilmarnock Works | Brush-Barclay |
| ZN | Wolverton Works | Railcare |
| ZR | York (Holgate Works) | Network Rail |

\* unofficial code.

# Subscription order form

To subscribe, please complete the form below (or a copy) and return it with your remittance to:

**Today's Railways Europe (Dept. LCS), 3 Wyvern House, Sark Road, SHEFFIELD, S2 4HG, ENGLAND.**

**BLOCK CAPITALS PLEASE**

(All prices include postage and packing.)

**Today's Railways Europe: Subscription (12 issues)**

☐ UK £45.00 (post free);   ☐ Overseas Airmail £54.60.

JAN   FEB   MAR   APR   MAY   JUN   JUL   AUG   SEP   OCT   NOV   DEC

Please circle start issue required

---

**Name:** ......................................................................................................

**Address:** ..................................................................................................

............................................................................................................

........................................................ **Postcode:** .....................................

**Daytime Tel. No:** ......................................................................................

**E-mail:** ....................................................................................................

---

I enclose my cheque/UK postal order for £ ....................................................

made payable to **'PLATFORM 5 PUBLISHING LTD.'**

**Please debit my Visa/Mastercard/Maestro**

**Card No:** .......................................................... **Expiry Date:** ..................

**Card Issue No./Date (Maestro only):** ...................... **Security No.:** ...............

**for £** .................................................. **Date:** ...........................................

**Signature:** ...............................................................................................

---

or if ordering by debit/credit card, telephone our subscription department on the numbers opposite.

**Special note:** Subscriptions may begin with the current issue or the next to be published. Subscriptions cannot be backdated.

# 6.6. ABBREVIATIONS

**The following general abbreviations are used in this book:**

| | |
|---|---|
| AC | Alternating Current (i.e. Overhead supply) |
| AFD | Air Force Department |
| BAA | British Airports Authority |
| BR | British Railways |
| BSI | Bergische Stahl Industrie |
| CRDC | Component Recovery & Disposal Centre |
| C&W | Carriage & Wagon |
| DC | Direct Current (i.e. Third Rail) |
| DEMU | Diesel Electric Multiple Unit |
| DERA | Defence Evaluation & Research Agency |
| DfT | Department for Transport |
| Dia. | Diagram number |
| DMU | Diesel Multiple Unit (general term) |
| DSDC | Defence Storage & Distribution Centre |
| DRS | Direct Rail Services |
| EMU | Electric Multiple Unit (general term) |
| GWR | Great Western Railway |
| H-B | Hunslet-Barclay |
| h.p. | Horse power |
| HNRC | Harry Needle Railroad Company |
| Hz | Hertz |
| kN | Kilonewtons |
| km/h | Kilometres per hour |
| kW | Kilowatts |
| lbf | Pounds force |
| LT | London Transport |
| LUL | London Underground Limited |
| m. | Metres |
| mm. | Millimetres |
| m.p.h. | Miles per hour |
| NPCCS | Non Passenger Carrying Coaching Stock |
| PTE | Passenger Transport Executive |
| RCH | Railway Clearing House |
| r.p.m. | Revolutions per minute |
| RR | Rolls Royce |
| RSL | Rolling Stock Library |
| SR | BR Southern Region and Southern Railway |
| t. | Tonnes |
| T | Toilet |
| TD | Toilet suitable for disabled passengers |
| TDM | Time Division Multiplex |
| TOPS | Total Operations Processing System |
| V | Volts |
| W | Wheelchair space |

# 6.7 BUILDERS

These are shown in class headings. The workshops of British Railways and the pre-nationalisation and pre-grouping companies were first transferred to a wholly-owned subsidiary called "British Rail Engineering Ltd.", abbreviated to BREL. These workshops were later privatised, BREL then becoming "BREL Ltd.". Some of the works were then taken over by ABB, which was later merged with Daimler-Benz Transportation to become "Adtranz". This company has now been taken over by Bombardier Transportation, which had taken over Procor at Horbury previously. Bombardier also builds vehicles for the British market in Brugge, Belgium.

Other workshops were the subject of separate sales, Springburn, Glasgow and Wolverton becoming "Railcare" and Eastleigh becoming "Wessex Traincare". All three were sold to GEC-Alsthom (now Alstom) but Eastleigh Works closed in 2006, although the site is now used as a storage and refurbishment location.

Part of Doncaster works was sold to RFS Engineering, which became insolvent and was bought out and renamed RFS Industries. This is now Wabtec.

The builder details in the class headings show the owner at the time of vehicle construction followed by the works as follows:

| | |
|---|---|
| Ashford | Ashford Works (now Ashford Rail Plant depot). Note that this is not the same as the current Bombardier Ashford depot which is at Chart Leacon. |
| Birmingham | The former Metro-Cammell works at Saltley, Birmingham. |
| Cowlairs | Cowlairs Works, Glasgow. |
| Derby | Derby Carriage Works (also known as Litchurch Lane). |
| Doncaster | Doncaster Works. |
| Eastleigh | Eastleigh Works |
| Swindon | Swindon Works. |
| Wolverton | Wolverton Works. |
| York | York Carriage Works. |

Other builders are:

| | |
|---|---|
| Alexander | Walter Alexander, Falkirk. |
| Barclay | Andrew Barclay, Caledonia Works, Kilmarnock (now Hunslet-Barclay). |
| BRCW | Birmingham Railway Carriage & Wagon, Smethwick. |
| CAF | Construcciones y Auxiliar de Ferrocarriles, Zaragosa, Spain. |
| Cravens | Cravens, Sheffield. |
| Gloucester | Gloucester Railway Carriage & Wagon, Gloucester. |
| Hunslet-Barclay | Hunslet-Barclay, Caledonia Works, Kilmarnock. |
| Hunslet TPL | Hunslet Transportation Projects, Leeds. |
| Lancing | SR, Lancing Works. |
| Leyland Bus | Leyland Bus, Workington. |
| Metro-Cammell | Metropolitan-Cammell, Saltley, Birmingham |
| Pressed Steel | Pressed Steel, Linwood. |
| Charles Roberts | Charles Roberts, Horbury Junction, Wakefield. |
| SGP | Simmering-Graz-Pauker, Austria (now owned by Siemens). |
| Siemens | Siemens Transportation Systems (various works in Germany and Austria). |
| SRP | Specialist Rail Products Ltd (A subsidiary of RFS). |

**S**

Geraldine Sheridan spoke to more than seventy survivors throughout the United Kingdom. She is a freelance journalist who has worked for newspapers, magazines and television.

Thomas Kenning talked to experts about Post-Traumatic Stress. He also looked at safety and compensation. He is a lawyer in Birmingham.

# *SURVIVORS*

**GERALDINE SHERIDAN
and
THOMAS KENNING**

A Pan Original
PAN BOOKS
LONDON, SYDNEY AND AUCKLAND

First published 1993 by Pan Books Ltd

a division of Pan Macmillan Publishers Limited
Cavaye Place London SW10 9PG
and Basingstoke

Associated companies throughout the world

ISBN 0 330 32853 0

1 3 5 7 9 8 6 4 2

A CIP catalogue record for this book is available from
the British Library

Typeset by Cambridge Composing (UK) Limited, Cambridge
Printed and bound in Great Britain by
Cox & Wyman Ltd, Reading, Berkshire

# CONTENTS

# FOREWORD

## by Dr James Thompson

This book is about survivors, that is to say, those who continue to live when others have died. Looked at from one point of view this is very positive, in the sense that anyone who has a brush with death is lucky to survive. However, looked at from another point of view it is profoundly negative, in that one need not have had a brush with tragedy anyway. From this perspective the word victim is more appropriate. Originally this word carried the implication that a person was being sacrificed as part of a religious rite, or was injured or destroyed in trying to seek a particular goal. This book shows vividly that survivors can be victims and that victims can be survivors.

The book doesn't harp on horror, but it certainly gives you a feeling for people's experiences and for the sadness and the terror they went through. Why are we drawn to such stories? I suppose it is because we wonder how we ourselves would have coped. Partly this allows us to have a fantasy in which we carry out heroic actions, or at the very least show a sensible appreciation of where the dangers are and find ways to overcome them. Many of us who live happy and safe lives may wonder what we would do if we were tested by a tragedy.

Many people have the feeling that calamity is a person's true touchstone. I can understand this point of view, but I disagree with it. Disasters are often entirely haphazard events to which people will respond according to random circumstances. Someone with a child next to them may carry out actions which are later described as heroic. Someone who happened to be separated from their child at the moment of impact may carry out actions which later on will seem entirely concerned with their own personal survival. Some people will be in a position to escape easily. Others will have to beg for help or will have to decide whether to put their own lives at risk in order to help others. Because of the enormous importance of these decisions, they tend to get a very high status and often serve as a judgement. We talk about these events as 'the moment of truth'. However they also carry their own falsehoods. If you want to read this book in order to find out how you yourself might respond, I think you will have to accept that you cannot get that answer, though you may understand somewhat better how other people reacted in the circumstances.

Another reason for reading this book might be that you want to learn if there are any particular ways of coping with dreadful events. As you will see, the book gives some indication of what the various survivors found helpful. It gives due weight to all of the ways in which they tried to cope and also charts their long-term progress after the disasters.

I think the best reason for reading this book is to understand about other people's needs. We live in a busy society and indeed all these disasters arose out of our wish to travel quickly from one part of the world to the other and extract the fuel we need in order to do so. One might call them the disasters of busyness and speed. Another consequence of our busyness is our willingness to have superficial relationships with those whom we briefly encounter as we go about our business. All of the survivors in this book have had to face the additional pressures of a society which is busy with other matters and has a distinct limit on the amount of time it is willing to spend in supporting those who are in distress. It has sometimes been observed that in our society everyone is sympathetic with the bereaved, so long as they are back at work within a fortnight. It would be a marvellous consequence of this book if people realized that disasters and tragedies can have long-term consequences, and that many people take a long time to get back to their usual levels of performance in society. I think that reading this book might even help people to recognize their own needs, particularly if they are attracted to it by some trouble of their own. All the data about human response to painful events shows a surprising resilience, but that resilience requires not only personal strengths, but support from one's neighbours.

In a sense this need for support is becoming more widely recognized and we are experiencing a cultural change. The dominant themes which people use in describing disaster and tragedy probably come from warfare. The two great European wars this century contributed enormous trauma to the European community, but also made a virtue of trying to cope with disasters with minimal complaint. In Britain the idea of the stiff upper lip and the thin red line of soldiers was a useful way of avoiding investing resources into dealing with the psychological distress which often follows tragedy. Nowadays the mood has shifted from the military analogy to that of quality of life. No one wants to suffer just for suffering's sake, if they know that there are procedures and resources which could make their burden lighter to bear. At the very end of this book you will find some of the organizations which are trying to offer services to survivors of disasters. Unfortunately, these provisions are quite inadequate when measured against national needs. There are two steps which could be taken to ensure a better service. The first is to ensure that in every health area there is someone within the National Health Service who has a particular interest in major stress, and has resources with which to offer a specialist service. At the moment there are only two specialist centres and both of those are on short-term grants. The second step is for employers to recognize that certain occupations subject people to higher than average stress effects. The emergency services are an obvious example of groups who would benefit from careful monitoring and appropriate support and many of these are making proper provision though as yet in a piecemeal fashion. The armed forces would probably benefit from an official veterans' association which could monitor their progress and give them assistance long after they had left the armed forces themselves.

I hope that when you read this book you will deal with the sadness which is contained in so many of these accounts and recognize the way these survivors coped with what fate had given them. If that spurs you on to helping other survivors in whatever way you can, then this book will have made its contribution to helping the process of personal survival.

James Thompson PhD, Dip.Clin Psychol,
C Psychol, FBPsS
Senior Lecturer in Psychology

# INTRODUCTION

The eighties will be remembered as a decade of disaster. There were eight within a three-year period, and they devastated the nation. Who could forget the pictures of fans crushed and fighting for life against the fences at Hillsborough or the aeroplane crashed on the side of the M1?

Long after the scenes faded from our television screens a staggering number of survivors struggled to rebuild their lives. Many found a way to cope with their post traumatic stress; for others the physical and mental scars have taken longer to heal. In this book the survivors open their hearts to tell their often harrowing stories.

The first of the eight disasters happened on the clear still evening of 6 March 1987. The cross-channel ferry, the *Herald of Free Enterprise*, cleared Zeebrugge Harbour at 6.20 p.m., on her way to Dover. Eight minutes later she capsized, killing 193 of the 454 passengers and crew on board. The ferry ended up half submerged on a sandbank and those who survived had to battle their way out.

Later the same year, on 18 November 1987, an escalator caught fire at King's Cross underground station. This developed into a violent flashover in the ticket hall. The blaze cost thirty-one lives and left many more seriously injured.

On 6 July 1988 came the world's worst offshore oil rig catastrophe as Piper Alpha was blown apart. Of the 229 men on board, 62 survived the series of blasts which ripped through the rig sending a 350-foot fireball into the sky.

Five months later, on the morning of Monday 12 December 1988, a crowded passenger train ploughed into the back of another rush-hour train near Clapham Junction, in South London. Seconds later an empty train smashed into the wreckage. The crash killed 36 people and injured more than 120.

On 21 December 1988 a Pan Am Jumbo exploded in mid-air four days before Christmas, raining fire, bodies and burning fuselage over the Scottish town of Lockerbie. All 259 passengers and crew died, and eleven people in Lockerbie were also killed.

Just eighteen days later, on 8 January 1989, there was another horrific air disaster, this time in Leicestershire. A burning Boeing 737 narrowly missed the village of Kegworth and crashed on the M1 killing 47 of the 126 people on board. Nearly all of the survivors had serious injuries.

The date of the worst disaster in sporting history was 15 April 1989. It happened at the FA Cup Semi-Final between Liverpool and Nottingham Forest at Hillsborough. Ninety-five people were crushed to death in the crowd and more than seven hundred were injured.

Four months later, on 20 August 1989, came the last of the eight disasters. The Thames pleasure cruiser, the *Marchioness*, sank following a collision with the 2,000-ton sand dredger, *Bowbelle*. Fifty-one of the 131 people on board drowned.

As the terrible events slipped from our minds, the problems were just beginning for some of the survivors. They had survived the disaster but then had to fight again to overcome the after-effects.

Recent research shows that for natural disasters such as volcanoes and floods, psychological consequences can persist for as long as three years, though most symptoms seem to abate by about sixteen months. The consequences of disasters caused by fellow human beings can persist even longer.

The majority of disaster victims do come to terms with what has happened to them but it takes time. Studies indicate that 40 to 70 per cent of survivors experience distress in the first month after a disaster. Between 24 and 40 per cent continue to experience distress after the first year. Up to 20 per cent experience chronic levels of anxiety which remain high for longer than two years.

Survivors of those eight disasters experienced an intensity of feeling they had never known before. They felt out of control for the first time in their lives, some even thought they were going mad. They experienced feelings of fear, grief, guilt and anger. Some lost interest in sex, had nightmares and lacked concentration. They suffered flashbacks to the event itself. Many survivors were forced to change their jobs, others found that their relationships broke down under the strain.

But the disasters also brought some surprising and positive effects. Many of the survivors believe they are better people for having survived and have become more socially conscious and appreciative of life. All of the survivors stared death in the face and won. Some were stronger than they would have ever believed.

They struggled to cope with their own difficulties and helped others at the same time. Strong bonds developed between the survivors and the bereaved. Strangers who sat next to each other on an aeroplane have become friends and have gone on to campaign for greater public safety.

On 30 October 1991 a new organization, called Disaster Action, was launched. The families of those who died in the disasters and the survivors themselves set out to prevent others suffering in the way they have done. Since then they have worked on issues including legal reform, corporate responsibility, compensation and post-disaster counselling.

As a result of the disasters psychologists have had a greater opportunity to study trauma. A stress clinic was set up at the Middlesex Hospital in London the day after the King's Cross fire. It has worked with the victims of many of the disasters and also with people who have experienced other kinds of trauma including rape, car crashes and combat torture.

Post Traumatic Stress Disorder has also been legally accepted as a positive psychiatric disorder for compensation purposes.

## TRAUMA PSYCHOLOGY

Experts have found that up to 50 per cent of the survivors of a major disaster suffer from the effects of the trauma seriously enough to need professional help. Most will recover within a few years but few will ever be the same again.

'Post-trauma reaction has been around for as long as men have been throwing spears at each other,' says psychiatrist Morgan O'Connell who runs residential courses for sufferers at his clinic in Portsmouth. In the past, those who were unlucky enough to suffer from it as a result of war received little sympathy. It was called shell shock, battle fatigue, some even said cowardice. Even today there are those in the medical profession who have little sympathy when they cannot see any visible scars.

It was the Americans who first formally diagnosed Post Traumatic Stress Disorder (PTSD) in 1980. Following work with veterans of the Vietnam war, the American Psychiatric Association added PTSD to the third edition of their manual for the classification of psychiatric disorders (*see* p. 275).

In the immediate aftermath of a disaster most survivors are unable fully to comprehend what has happened to them. The unreality of the situation leaves them feeling numb.

Psychiatrist Dr David Alexander visited survivors in the burns unit of the Aberdeen Royal Infirmary shortly after the destruction of the Piper Alpha Rig. He found that at first most of them felt relieved to be alive. They chatted away cheerfully, swapping stories of how they got off the burning rig.

This post-disaster euphoria soon wore off to give way to depression and anxiety. The reality of what had happened to them and their friends began to percolate through. Many began to hallucinate and suffer terrifying flashbacks to the disaster scene causing intense feelings of fear and anxiety.

'The majority of survivors will have symptoms that persist, certainly through the first week,' says District Clinical Psychologist Roderick Orner, of the County Hospital, Lincoln. 'What happens then is that over time these reactions subside and maybe within a month you are left with a smaller proportion who are still having flashbacks. Then you will have a group, depending on the involvement and personal vulnerabilities they bring to the situation, who will have more entrenched problems and who will need professional help to recover.'

The disaster survivors went through something that brought them very close to death; they glimpsed their own mortality. Suddenly and without warning, they were confronted with scenes that most of us can only imagine. They were trapped, powerless to stop it happening. Fundamental responses for self-preservation were useless in such a situation.

Psychiatrist Morgan O'Connell believes 'One or more of the special senses is overstimulated to such an extent that the computer that is the brain is unable to process the information. It is incorrectly programmed and liable to be reactivated for example by a particular smell that was present at the disaster scene.'

Other psychologists add that to see the trauma again in the mind brings on a state of helplessness in the survivors. A basic human fear of non-existence is tapped. The frighteningly vivid flashbacks are liable to penetrate their thoughts when they are triggered by something that reminds them of the disaster.

Given the close call many survivors had with death or personal injury, it is understandable that this may cause them to become more cautious about their safety in the future. Most of us do not worry too much about the risk we are taking every time we drive a car. But the shock and terror of a disaster may cause irrational fears or exaggerated feelings of danger to the extent that a normal life is impossible.

It is difficult to predict who will suffer a serious psychological reaction to trauma. The degree of suffering among the disaster survivors varied enormously. The impact of the disaster was unique to the individual involved. No two survivors were the same, each had his or her own personality, family and social background, giving them strengths and vulnerabilities. Dr Alexander believes 'there isn't a personality quality that protects you from post-trauma stress. It is nothing to do with weakness.'

The greater the intensity of the trauma and the longer the period of exposure to it the more chance there is of psychological damage. It was found that survivors who were trapped in a frightening situation for a substantial time had a severe trauma reaction.

The detail of what each survivor went through was

often very different. Even in the same disaster, survivors had to cope with their own different traumatic experiences. Those survivors who were able to help in some way during the disaster were found to benefit from this themselves. If they did not have their minds distracted by doing something then they only had their suffering to focus on. They were tortured by their own fear.

It was also found that those who were able to attribute their survival partly to their own efforts seemed to fare better. Those who had regrets about their actions during the disaster seemed to carry a degree of guilt. Many survivors felt they could or should have done more to save others. Some even punished themselves for acting in panic to save their own lives when others died.

Some survivors also had to cope with bereavement. Added to the psychological reaction to the disaster itself was the burden of having a loved one suddenly ripped from their lives. The chaos that usually accompanied the disaster scenes interfered with the grieving process. Many families were deprived of quiet time with their loved one's body. In some cases victims' bodies were badly disfigured or never found. Psychologists believe that all possible steps should be taken to allow the close family to spend some time with the body to say that last farewell. Parents whose children have been violently killed in a disaster suffer terribly. We do not expect to outlive our children; they are our immortality. Some parents carry feelings of guilt for not protecting their family from harm.

Those who survived but were injured in the disasters were found to have severe problems. They had to cope with physical as well as psychological effects. There was no escaping the constant external reminder of involvement in the disaster. They would be asked about their scars for the rest of their lives. This would mean going over it again and again. Families had to adjust to the survivor's disability. Our physical appearance and attributes affect our personality. Disfiguring burns or disabling injuries require the survivor to come to terms with a new self, adding to the strain of the trauma aftermath.

Some survivors became so obsessed with the disaster that nothing else in their lives seemed to matter. Many felt that no one who hadn't experienced the disaster could understand what they were going through. This had a tendency to isolate them from their family and friends who wondered when they were going to put the disaster behind them.

Support groups were set up following the major disasters. The regular meetings were venues for discussions about their feelings, compensation applications and safety campaigns. The mutual support helped them adjust to life after the disaster in the knowledge that they were not alone in their struggle to come to terms with harrowing experiences.

Most psychologists today prefer not to apply rigid criteria for diagnosis and treatment of PTSD. In practice they believe there is little to be gained from categorizing survivors or their problems. It is more important to focus on how to help the survivors than to define what particular condition it is that they have.

The eight disasters have meant that the country has accumulated a vast store of post-disaster expertise. Throughout the world, in recent years, there has been a huge increase in awareness of post-traumatic stress.

The survivors in this book illustrate that although there are similarities in response every individual is different. Even those who went through the same disaster found that the aftermath was not exactly the same.

This book shows how the lives of the survivors were changed by disaster. Ordinary lives were made extraordinary overnight. There are stories of great strength and bravery as people struggled to cope, sometimes with the added burdens of bereavement and injury.

The spate of disasters reminded us that the unexpected can happen. Anyone could have been a passenger on the *Herald of Free Enterprise* that night, or catching a train at King's Cross station. For most of us that nightmare will never come true. The people in this book have lived a nightmare and survived.

# CHAPTER ONE

# A FAMILY TRAGEDY

It is 6 a.m. and the sun glistens on his mountain bike as it crunches over a forest path. The rain has stopped; he heard it tapping on his window as he lay awake in the early hours of the morning. Now only the leaves are wet, dropping an occasional bead of moisture on to his head. There's no one to break the silence, nothing but a deer scampering between the trees.

Trevor Hicks, a successful, middle-aged, managing director, is alone. His marriage is over and his children are dead. Grief and trauma shatter the peace of his early morning bike rides. His mind takes him on terrifying flashbacks, out of the forest and on to the pitch at Sheffield's Hillsborough stadium where nineteen-year old Sarah and her fifteen-year-old sister Victoria lie side by side.

Trevor remembers how he carried Vicky to the ambulance, then came back to it with Sarah in his arms. There was no more space inside, the beds were full and bodies littered the floor. He had to put her down again on the pitch. In a blinding moment he pictures the ambulance moving away and recalls the agonizing decision he had to make. Should he go with Vicky or stay behind with her sister? 'It was an awful dilemma,' he says.

Both girls were crushed to death in the worst disaster in British sporting history. The tragedy happened in April 1989, after police opened 16-foot-wide gates, letting hundreds of supporters pour into the back of the caged terraces at the Liverpool–Nottingham Forest FA Cup Semi-Final.

'Football was the one common interest we had as a family,' says Trevor. He and his wife Jenny were born in the North East and had no connection with Liverpool or its football team. But they followed them all over the country, travelling to both home and away matches from their £300,000 detached home in Middlesex.

'We were very fortunate,' he says. 'We lived in a middle-class area and we were just an average family with two kids.' He treasures the memory of their 1987 holiday in Tuscany when they stayed overnight in Paris, then drove up through the Alps. Sarah loved art and had thought about being an architect so they walked around buildings in Florence. At other times they just lay on the beach.

As he talks Trevor looks at a photograph of the girls on the window-ledge of his office. It was taken the Christmas before they died at a supporters' dinner-dance in the boardroom at Anfield. Even now he hasn't turned his back on the game; the office banter is always about football and his secretary brings him his coffee in a Liverpool mug.

'Vicky wanted to be a sports reporter,' he says. 'She'd taught herself to touch-type, and after she died they found a folder full of match reports that she'd written and tickets she'd saved from the games.' She was the more reserved of the two but she could be as determined as her father and the two sometimes clashed. Sarah was more outgoing and untidy, 'a typical boffin type'. She loved maths and sciences but was also interested in the band U2 long before they were famous. 'They had a stereo each in their rooms and I'd often hear them competing to see who could turn up the music the loudest,' Trevor smiles as he recalls.

Sarah left home in September to read chemistry at Liverpool University. 'She was the first to go and Jenny took it hard,' he says. 'The three of them were just like sisters.' Trevor had a flat in the Midlands where he was working at the time and saw his family only at weekends. 'It really matters to me that Vicky and I went to the supermarket together the night before the disaster,' he says.

'There was a lot of traffic on the motorway on my way home and it was a mad rush to make it in time. Vicky was a brilliant organizer and she took charge. She went into Waitrose and I went into Bejam next door to get some ice-creams, then I followed her in. I pushed the trolley while she did the shopping. We had a laugh and a joke and I teased her about missing a couple of things on the list. We had such a good time that I told Jenny that Vicky and I would go shopping together every week. That was the last thing we did together.'

The family left home early the following morning, and listened to the team news on the radio in the car. Trevor forgot to enclose a cheque when he applied for tickets, so they were lucky to get them at all. 'My name was mud when I did that,' he recalls. Vicky said: 'You idiot, if we can't go I'll never speak to you again.' Trevor and the two girls were allocated a standing ticket. They waved good-bye to Jenny who was sitting down and arranged to meet outside a newsagent's after the game.

When Trevor stopped to buy a programme the girls snatched their chance to get away – they didn't want their dad around as they stood on the Leppings Lane terraces. 'They used to like to stand with all the lads and from what I hear there was the odd bit of romance around,' says Trevor. 'I have a vivid memory of Victoria looking over her shoulder and laughing.'

He stood about twenty yards away and lost sight of the girls as the pens started to fill up. Gradually his excitement turned to fear as he realized there were too many people in the ground, and he knew his daughters were at the front. He watched as fans climbed over the fence on to the pitch and collapsed. 'I don't forgive the police for the slowness of their response,' he says. 'It may or may not have helped Vicky or Sarah, they were almost flattened, but I could tell there were problems before anyone started doing anything at all.'

In desperation he battled his way through the crowd towards his daughters. His eyes fill with tears as he remembers catching a glimpse of Victoria as she was passed over a fence. He couldn't mistake her long dark hair. He felt numb as he walked through a gate on to the pitch and found both girls lying side by side.

Dr Colin Flenley, who has since become a friend, was attending to Sarah. Trevor bent down beside him and tried to revive Vicky, watching and hoping for a glimmer of life as he gave her heart massage and the kiss of life. 'The girls were an awful colour,' he recalls. 'There was no response but I had to keep going, sucking vomit out and blowing into Vicky's mouth. We were all shouting for oxygen.' His battle to revive his daughter carried on in the ambulance on the way to the Northern General Hospital in Sheffield. Fifteen minutes after they arrived Trevor was told that Vicky was dead.

He had done all he could for his younger daughter and set off to find Sarah, tears streaming down his face. For half an hour he ran through the chaos, along the hospital corridors, past survivors lying on trolleys, into wards, asking everyone he met if they'd seen his daughter. He'd left her on the pitch but she had to be in hospital by now. He found a policeman and gave him the same descriptions he'd given a dozen times before: both had Swatch watches on, Sarah was wearing Doc Marten boots, Vicky had ankle boots on.

'There's one unidentified female,' another policeman

told him, and came out carrying a Swatch watch. Trevor confirmed it could have been Sarah's. He walked the few hundred yards to the hospital mortuary with a young policeman, a nurse and a minister. In the chapel of rest the trolley was wheeled out, covered in a red table cloth. He stood in silence, filled with dread, believing he was about to see Sarah dead. They pulled back the covers – and it was Vicky again.

Meanwhile his wife Jenny was looking for her family. 'I couldn't believe they could be dead, not all of them,' she says. 'I was getting to the point where I thought I was going crazy.' She'd watched the disaster happening from the north stand. At 2.30 p.m., half an hour before the game started, she turned to the stranger next to her and pointed out how crushed it was in the central pens.

'I can't remember seeing the Liverpool players, I didn't watch the game at all,' she says. 'I was desperately trying to see Trevor and the girls. I ran to the front and the police wouldn't let me on the pitch. I even saw the ambulance but didn't realize Trevor and Vicky were inside.'

She went to the newsagent's where they were supposed to meet and stood as crowds filed past her. 'Maybe she'd missed them?' She was still hoping. It was after 5 p.m. and there were fewer and fewer people coming out when she finally gave up and ran back to the car. 'I knew in my heart they wouldn't go back there without me,' she says. 'Our silver Granada was the only car in the car park so it stood out like a sore thumb. There was no one there and I could see I was running to nothing.

'I had no money and no keys. On the way I passed a Scottish couple and I told them I couldn't find my family. They flagged down a police car and I was taken to a police station.' Eventually a social worker took her to the Northern General but Trevor had already left to search for Sarah in another hospital. Jenny's heart soared when hospital staff told her 'We had a Victoria', because she thought that meant her daughter had been treated and released.

Then a nurse took her into a treatment room and closed the door. A doctor came in carrying a clipboard and asked her to sit down. 'No,' she cried, panic starting to well inside. The doctor didn't lift his eyes from the board. 'Are you the mother of Victoria Hicks?' Jenny screamed, 'You're going to tell me she's dead.' 'I'm sorry, I am,' he replied. Jenny shoved him out of the way, shouting, 'Couldn't you put her on a ventilator?' She felt as if she was out of her body looking down at herself. The accident and emergency department echoed as she walked around repeating the same words over and over again: 'They let you die here, they let my daughter die.'

When Trevor came back Jenny was watching through the hospital's glass door. 'Where's Sarah?' she screamed, as he walked across the car park. The last time Trevor had seen Sarah she was on the pitch looking worse than Vicky.

Trevor and Jenny will never forget the green notice board and the Polaroid photographs of the dead. It was stuck on a corridor wall in a temporary mortuary, set up in the gymnasium at the ground. Jenny had never seen a body before and felt physically sick as her eyes moved from one horrific picture to another. Vicky was number 89, but Jenny couldn't see Sarah. 'I was relieved,' she says. 'Then I looked again, and I saw her. I hadn't recognized her the first time.' The search was over.

The girls were wheeled out on ambulance trolleys, and the black body-bags were unzipped to show their heads. Jenny asked if she could give them a cuddle, her eyes lit up when she put her arms round Sarah because she was still warm. 'Are you sure she's dead?' she asked. 'That was gut wrenching,' says Trevor. 'You feel as if you've been turned inside out.'

It was almost midnight as they walked out of the

ground carrying their daughters' belongings in pathetic,
white plastic bags. Jenny held on to Sarah's leather jacket
and realized she would never have any grandchildren. Like
any parents they had chatted about what it would be like
when the girls left home, how they would have a nice
family house where their daughters could come back with
their own children for Christmas.

It was Sarah's birthday five days before the disaster and
the jacket had been her present. Jenny hugged the jacket
all the way home from Hillsborough, every few minutes
she looked behind her as if she expected the girls to be
sitting in the back seat of the car.

In the early hours of the morning Jenny took out her
scissors and went into the garden to pick the tulips the
girls had planted down the drive in clumps of red and
gold, the Liverpool colours. She switched on every light
in the house and she and Trevor spent all night wandering
in and out of their daughters' rooms, talking and reminisc-
ing. The breakfast things were still there from that morning, the beds weren't made.

'It was as if I was waiting for something to happen,'
says Jenny. 'I couldn't sit down. I lay on the settee but
every time I was about to nod off I jumped. I would like
to have gone to sleep and not woken up.' The next
morning Trevor started to telephone relatives. He hadn't
washed, and was still wearing the same jeans with muddy
patches on the knees from where he had been kneeling on
the pitch. For the next few weeks he felt numb one
minute, blind rage the next. 'Why us, why both of them?'
he asked himself over and over again. If one would have
lived, even if she'd been injured, they'd have been left
with something.

'I didn't realize until then that emotions can cause
physical pain,' he says. 'My chest was tight, I had pains
down my arms and I felt physically ill. I blamed myself

for not standing with them. The fact I would probably have been killed too was irrelevant.' He told himself Hillsborough was a punishment for everything he had done wrong in the past.

Overnight the family became famous. Their detached house was surrounded with the press, and pictures of the girls appeared in newspapers all over the world. As a result thousands of letters and cards arrived including one from a pensioner, with £1 sellotaped inside. A pot of flowers arrived on the porch with a card saying, 'Divided on the pitch but united in grief'. A basket of flowers with two roses came 'with love from fellow Kopites'.

Trevor and Jenny decided the girls would want to be buried in Liverpool. 'It's a nice cemetery,' says Trevor. 'I know that sounds stupid but things like that matter to you.' The weekend before the funeral they brought their bodies home. 'I put on their make-up and made them look nice,' says Jenny. 'I put in their earrings and dressed them in their favourite clothes. Trevor and I sat up all night with them and we put them in their own bedrooms.

'On Saturday evening one of Sarah's friends called, and when she heard that she was upstairs she wanted to see her.' Jenny was concerned that she hadn't seen anyone dead before and told her to ask her parents. The following morning the teenager arrived at 9 a.m. with her dad and they stayed until 10 p.m. Word went round that the girls were home and the house was full until midnight with friends coming to pay their respects. 'I found that very comforting,' says Jenny.

At the funeral, mourners heard that two weeks before the disaster Sarah had had a premonition she was going to die. She told Jenny she had a feeling she would never grow old, she'd had a good life and she wanted her mother to be happy when she died.

In January Jenny and the two girls had watched the

Lockerbie memorial service together. 'We all said how sad it was when we looked at the families,' says Jenny. 'There was so much ahead for all of us, and I thought: "Thank God it isn't me." Three months later I was at a memorial service for the girls.'

Soon after the funeral Trevor spent a full day sitting on a pile of bricks at the back of the garage crying his eyes out. He couldn't be consoled, he wanted to be left alone. Jenny brought him tea. He'd thought he was invincible, 'such a super person', but suddenly everything had been taken away. He was just another guy who could die as easily as anyone else. He needed help like he'd never needed it before and felt as insignificant as a grain of sand on a beach.

'When your children are taken before you, when they're taken in one go everything is topsy-turvy,' he says. 'You're trying to cling on to yourself, not just your sanity. You're adrift with no real purpose in life. It's a frightening experience and I'm not over that yet. I'd spent all my life working up the career path to earn enough money for my family. My main role in life was to be the provider and at times disciplinarian and suddenly there seemed no point in having a job, a pension fund, insurance or money in the bank.' There still isn't.

Trevor went back to work six weeks after the disaster but it was three months before he was able to stay in his flat in the Midlands on his own. 'I remember sitting in the boardroom with the chairman and a couple of directors,' he recalls. 'I was saying to myself: "This is all just trivia. I don't believe how insignificant it is."'

For the first six months he had vivid flashbacks to the pitch at Hillsborough and an imaginary taste of vomit in his mouth. He could only drink water or Marks & Spencer's ginger beer which helped to take the taste away. When he saw a girl with long dark hair walking in front of him, he wanted to spin her round and make sure it wasn't Vicky.

In June he was sitting in his car at a local shopping arcade when he noticed a Father's Day promotion in a newsagent's window. 'I was blubbering my eyes out, everyone was looking and I couldn't have cared less,' he says. He cried too as he drove along the motorway alone, playing at full volume the Simple Minds tape he'd been given by Sarah.

'I don't think I was ever truly suicidal,' he says. In fact he drove more carefully and became obsessed with safety. 'But I remember driving back home one Friday night. There were big strong trees at the side of the motorway and I almost decided to drive into them and make it look like an accident.'

Jenny wanted to die but didn't want to kill herself. 'There were times when I thought I couldn't stand another five minutes,' she says, as she lights another cigarette. She didn't smoke before, now she smokes at least twenty a day. 'I lost a stone in weight in the first six months. I lived on cereal, bananas and chocolate. I felt guilty about picking up a knife and fork because the girls couldn't eat. I couldn't eat anything they would have liked. I couldn't go shopping for clothes because I'd always gone with them.'

Jenny had always been proud of her appearance, but it didn't seem important any more. At 4 p.m., the time when she normally met Vicky off the school bus, she was still in her dressing-gown. There was nothing to dress for after they died. She lay on the settee with her hair not washed or combed. One day she asked her brother to take her to the school bus to see if Vicky got off. 'I remember him talking to me like a toddler, telling me it wouldn't be a good idea,' she says.

At night she hated going to bed so she waited until she was dizzy with tiredness. Her prayer was always the same:

'Please God don't let me wake up tomorrow, I can't go through it again.' Sometimes she crept into Sarah's bed, which still had her smell and the scent of her perfume. She climbed up the little ladder to Vicky's top bunk for the same reason, it felt as if she was having a cuddle. During the day she stood in their wardrobes smelling their clothes.

'I didn't like the fact the sun came up in the morning,' she says. 'I couldn't understand how everything was normal when I walked down the street. When I looked at families in cars I resented the fact that they were still together. For about a year I couldn't sit down. I felt as if I wasn't walking on the ground and I had a horrible hole in my stomach that felt like a physical pain.' She felt guilty that she had been the family's first football fan and has supported the team for over twenty-five years. Pictures flashed into her head of the girls in body-bags and she fought to push them away.

Jenny started going to the spiritualist church every week. She went to the library, read philosophy books about life and death, and spoke to several religious leaders. 'I used to think that good people went to heaven and bad people went to hell and I didn't think too seriously about it,' she says. 'I thought we were pretty average people who hadn't done anything to deserve eternal condemnation and I think Sarah and Vicky were pretty good kids. After they died I needed to know where they were and what they were doing.'

A couple of times she believes she saw Sarah, and that she came back to let her know how she was. The first time was six months after the disaster. 'I'd gone to bed and the next minute I was on the landing with her,' she recalls. I said: "Oh Sarah." I remember going to hug her and I thought it would be like hugging a cloud. I put my arms around her. I said: "Sarah, you're solid."

'Sarah laughed and said: "What do you expect?" I asked

her where Vicky was and she said she was helping in the nursery and that they had jobs to do. It was so positive and comforting. I asked her not to go. She said: "I'm allowed to visit you but I have to go back." I said: "They're not going to miss you when so many millions of people have died." Then I gave her another hug and she went. I woke Trevor up to tell him and he thought I was so lucky.'

Trevor and Jenny decided to go on holiday for a week to Spain. They stayed in the sort of hotel they'd never been able to afford before but within two days they wanted to come home. 'We went to restaurants and there were tables for four,' says Trevor. 'We kept saying: "This isn't right, the girls should be here." There were two empty chairs and the food choked us.'

In the early days after the disaster they considered fostering or adopting but were told they'd have to wait two years. Just eighteen months after the disaster they split up. At first their suffering brought them closer together but then they started to mourn in their own way. When Trevor felt depressed Jenny was cheerful, when he was more cheerful she was feeling down. 'We were two people with no ties, just a lot of memories,' he says. 'We both had nothing to live for in one way and in another we had to do different things. Part of the problem was I was trying to smother Jenny. She was all I had. She also wanted me and I needed space.'

Jenny decided she had to change her life and part of that change was to end her marriage. When the girls died she'd lost her job as a housewife looking after her family. 'I was no longer a mum,' she says. 'I wanted to go out and find out who I was and I needed space to sort myself out. It was my decision initially to split up. Trevor needed me so much and I couldn't handle it. I'd grown quite independent, then suddenly I was all of his life.'

They parted in July 1990 when Jenny moved to Liverpool. She had her long hair cut into a modern bob and decided to go to Liverpool Polytechnic to study psychology and criminal justice – anything to shut out this horrible pain. 'I was convinced that the girls were living on somewhere else and if I was sad they could see it,' she says.

She wanted them to be proud of her and to make up for the fact that Sarah hadn't been able to finish her degree course. 'At the time I thought I was being really positive. People were saying: "She's getting over it, isn't she brave." I just couldn't sit still. I couldn't run the home in a normal way or do what I used to do without the girls. I had to do something different.'

Trevor bought a cottage in a picturesque village in the Yorkshire Dales. He became managing director of England Worthside in Keighley. 'It was a very sad day when we moved out of the house,' he says. 'Jenny and I spent the weekend sorting and packing. We felt as if we were intruding when we went into the girls' rooms.'

The girls' possessions were split between them, he took Sarah's white polar bear with its Liverpool scarf and put it on his dressing table. 'I talked to it as if I was talking to her,' he says.

For the first six months after they separated he drank too much and didn't care if he lived or died. 'I was sorting through some stuff one day and found Sarah's shoe,' he says. 'We only had one of her shoes back. It caught me off guard and I spent the next three hours crying my eyes out. I couldn't throw it away.' He still has Vicky's bunk beds in his spare room.

Jenny brought her daughters' clothes, soft toys and record collections to a mews house in a converted stables in Liverpool. The drawings the girls did when they were toddlers are still in boxes waiting to be unpacked, and her house still looks as if she has recently moved in.

On her living-room floor there's a pinboard with a picture of Trevor. Pinned next to it is a photograph of Sarah blowing out the candles on her last birthday cake, with Vicky making sure she's doing it correctly. On the wall above there's the same photograph of the girls that Trevor has in his office, blown up into a huge painting.

Jenny doesn't regret moving to Liverpool and her daughters' grave is just ten minutes drive from her home. But she believes she made too many other changes too soon. After the first year at college she was so mentally exhausted she had to leave. Two months after the start of the course she was at the inquest in Sheffield when she should have been at lectures. 'Perhaps I made changes for the wrong reasons,' she says. In her cut-off denim jeans and white T-shirt she looks at least ten years younger than her age.

Like Trevor Jenny was forty-two when the disaster happened. 'I couldn't have carried on with my life the way it was, and making changes was a way of surviving. When I look back now perhaps I should have given it another year before I went to college. I think I could tackle the course much better now. Possibly I should have left splitting-up with Trevor for a while. I think separation might have been better than a divorce. It would have given us both thinking time and space.'

Now she's alone and looking for a job. 'The old Jenny died at Hillsborough,' she says. 'I was much more responsible and sensible, like you are when you're a mum; the kids came first. I feel as if I've gone back twenty years, as I no longer have responsibilities, but physically I'm getting older.'

Now instead of cooking dinner she's getting ready to go to a barbecue. She used to be a vegetarian like the girls but now she's eating meat. Trevor was horrified when he saw her drinking pints of lager in the students' union bar.

What happened to his wife who used to have an occasional glass of wine?

'My life was destroyed and I'm trying to rebuild it,' she says. 'I have a heavy sadness inside and I wonder what's the point in anything. People say the pain gets better in time, but I know it gets worse. Now I realize I've lost them for ever.'

On Trevor's birthday Jenny sent him roses with a message pp Sarah and Vicky. He sent her flowers on Mother's Day. They still meet occasionally and the other day he called into their old house in Middlesex and telephoned her. Both are still Liverpool supporters and go to matches, though not together. 'I haven't been this season,' Trevor admits. 'I have great difficulty making the effort. I'll always be a supporter but I suppose I'm putting other things first.'

He is concerned about Jenny. 'She doesn't even have a job to lose herself in,' he says. 'We both like to look after each other and I still have a big soft spot for her. She was an absolutely brilliant mum. I don't think anyone could have done better.' When Jenny dies she will be buried in the same triple-decker grave as the girls. Trevor will go in the one next to it, wherever he lives or with whom.

Trevor is now engaged to Julie. He started seeing her in February 1991 and they live together. They will eventually move into the barn he is busy renovating. 'I assume we'll get married,' he says, 'but I'm reluctant to make the commitment, I don't think I'm ready for it and it's nothing to do with her. I'm not sure if I will expose myself emotionally. There's a little bit of me that doesn't let go just in case I'm hurt again. There's a bit of me that's been killed. I sometimes say I haven't got a heart.

'Julie and I have talked about having children and I have mixed feelings. They make a family, but if I had them would someone come and take them again? The odds must be huge against that happening but I used to think that was the case before. The logical part of me says you've used up your share of bad luck.'

Once a pillar of society, and a Freeman of the City of London, Trevor now has no faith in politicians, the police or the establishment generally. Shortly after the disaster he became chairman of the Hillsborough Families Support Group, set up for mutual support and to seek justice. It became the focal point of his life and he is now a folk hero in Liverpool. 'I was a typical man who didn't show my emotions,' he says, 'but since the disaster I've cried in front of people and not thought twice about it.'

Trevor still has flashbacks, although they are less vivid than they used to be. The pain he feels inside hasn't eased although he is now better at handling it. He doesn't feel he can ever be truly happy again. 'I don't feel the need to role-play,' he says. 'People see me and not the plastic person who used to pretend before. I don't care if people think I'm a bit loopy. Before I would never have dared to say I'd been to see a psychiatrist, now I don't care.'

Every morning he wakes up at 4 a.m., after just four hours sleep. He has put on a stone and a half in weight through eating for comfort. 'Perhaps I'm more honest, more sincere,' he says. 'I think I'm a better person.'

Hillsborough taught him never to put anything off in life. He'd always wanted to go to Disneyland with the girls but thought they could not afford it. He wishes he'd taken them, wishes he'd told them he loved them, and that they had never had a row.

'I have found what seems to be the ideal partner,' he says. 'I live in a nice part of the country and I have a good job. I suppose you could say I have it all. I'd give up everything, even give up my life if I could get Sarah and Vicky back. I feel they were cheated. It was such a waste.'

Dr Colin Flenley will always recall the anguish in Trevor's voice when they met for the first time on the pitch at Hillsborough. The Midlands GP was trying to revive Sarah, Trevor was standing over him shouting: 'Come on Sarah,' willing her to live. Eight months later Colin asked Trevor and Jenny to be godparents for his daughter Libby-Jo.

The baby was born on the first day Liverpool went back to play a game at Hillsborough. 'We felt very close to Trevor and Jenny,' says Colin. 'It seemed to be a way of cementing our relationship. It wasn't in any sense to replace Sarah because Sarah can never be replaced but we felt it was some way of showing Trevor and Jenny how important they are to us.'

The Liverpool-born doctor was standing on the terraces when the crush happened and dashed on to the pitch to help victims. He rushed in among bodies, trying first to revive an elderly man who was already dead. He remembers an ambulance driving over the foot of the body.

Then he went to Sarah and tried cardiac massage and mouth to mouth resuscitation for twenty minutes without success. He remembers how hard he fought to save her life, and how difficult it was to let her go when the ambulance came.

Colin didn't speak to Trevor during the disaster but wrote to him afterwards after he heard his name on television, and recognized Sarah's photograph. 'I didn't want any glory,' he says, 'but I sensed that Trevor needed help emotionally and I wanted to chat about Sarah, to tell him what I'd been doing and to put his mind at rest that nothing more could have been done.' That letter was the start of a firm friendship between the two men, who still meet up regularly.

'When he telephoned to say he'd received my letter I remember chatting to him as though we'd been friends for a long time,' says Colin, a father of three. 'We'd been through such an important experience it had brought us together. We have a deeper relationship than most people will ever have.'

The doctor was thirty-one when the disaster happened, and it changed his attitude to life. He cried the following day as he watched television and saw himself on the pitch. He wandered around not knowing what to do, wanting to go back, to be with others who had been there too.

He told his friends and his wife what had happened but they weren't involved so he felt they didn't really know what it was like. He felt angry that it had happened and wrote letters to the press to let them know. For a couple of months Colin was moody and low, for six months afterwards he felt physically sick.

He believes the disaster took away some of the laughter in his life and that it hasn't returned. Life after Hillsborough became so much more serious. He felt guilty because he hadn't suffered and still feels that maybe he could have done more.

Now Colin has a greater loyalty than ever to the city of Liverpool and takes his eight-year-old son Toby to watch his team play. He copes with the disaster by trying to push it to the back of his mind. When patients ask about it he avoids going into detail. A couple of times a year when he's feeling really low he forces himself to go through it again.

'I have a couple of videos of Hillsborough, taken from television programmes,' he says. 'I sit and watch them and become more depressed, and I read the newspaper reports. Then I can put them to one side and decide I've got to pull myself out of it again and forget it.'

Policeman Peter-John McGuinness also features in Trevor's address book of people whom he met on the day. It was PC McGuinness who told him that Vicky was dead.

The Sheffield policeman cries again when he recalls the disaster. It's as clear to him now as if it had happened yesterday. When he first saw supporters trying to get over the fence he thought there was going to be a pitch invasion. He went and stood in front of the pens, ready to grab the first person who came over. 'I'm glad I didn't put him into a headlock because he was already blue,' he says. 'That's when I realized what was happening. I was surprised by the number of other police officers who didn't realize as quickly as I did. I was shocked and numb. There I was looking at all those poor little faces crushed up against the fence, and there was nothing I could do.'

He remembers how one policeman didn't move throughout the disaster, even when people were being helped on to the pitch and carried off on advertising hoardings. 'I felt like going up and punching him,' he says. 'Afterwards I realized he couldn't move, that same numb feeling had come over me,' he says.

PC McGuinness decided he had to act. He ran round the back of the terraces and pushed his way through the crush down the tunnel. As he was telling the crowd to get back supporters above were spitting down on top of him. Adrenalin was pumping round his body. He thought he was going to be hit or head butted. He pushed his way to the front of the crowd and lifted Vicky over the fence, on to the pitch. He tried in vain to revive her and then went with her and Trevor in the ambulance.

At the hospital Peter held on to the drip while the doctor battled to save Vicky's life. Inside, the young policeman was screaming: 'Please, God, let her live.' He cried when they said she was dead. It was the first time he'd cried since he was a boy. 'I'd always felt before that it wasn't right to cry, that I was letting myself go,' he says.

Peter had faced tough situations before. He'd had bricks thrown at him during the miners' dispute, but he'd been

able to run. It wasn't his first brush with death, either.
Not long before a sixty-year-old farmer had collapsed
with a heart attack in the middle of the road. Peter was on
duty and called to the scene, but there wasn't a lot he
could do. The man was still alive in the ambulance but
died in hospital. It didn't seem wrong for him to die. But
the disaster was different: Vicky was so young, and he
couldn't get over the stupidity of it all.

Afterwards he felt guilty that he hadn't been compassionate enough during the disaster, that he hadn't cared
enough about Vicky. In reality he knew he had, and it's
still painful for him to talk about her today. Peter disagreed
with many of the policemen he worked with, and found
himself defending Trevor who was blaming the police.
'He's lost two daughters, let him do what he likes,' he told
his colleagues, and if any officers spoke about Trevor in a
bitter way he felt upset.

'I felt very close to Trevor and I understood what he
was trying to do,' says Peter. He says that during the
disaster, 'I had no ability to do anything and I wasn't in a
position to. The people who were didn't do very well and
at the time that made me very angry.' Now he doesn't
blame any officers. 'I just have a sense of the tragedy, and
how many lives have been ruined, police officers' lives as
well as everyone else's.'

Peter was in uniform when the disaster happened and
was keen to get out of it as quickly as possible. He didn't
want to be seen as a policeman, he still doesn't, and is now
in CID at the same station.

Recently he came face to face with an officer he'd met
at Hillsborough. As their eyes met he had an instant
flashback to the pitch. He recalled the battling expression
on the other policeman's face as he tried to give mouth to
mouth resuscitation, his heavy tunic covered in sweat. 'I
remember you from Hillsborough,' the officer said. Peter

could say no more than 'Yes'. He felt he wanted to hug him.

Since the disaster Peter has been more aware of death. He doesn't drive as fast, and thinks more about the dangers in his job. He is also more likely to shout or lose his temper. 'I watch my baby daughter Rebecca playing and I think how lovely it is to see her growing up,' he says. 'I also think about Vicky and it makes me realize how I could suddenly lose Rebecca. I pray that nothing similar will happen to her.'

Tony Barnbrock has met Trevor twice since the day they stood on the pitch together. Sarah had been passed over the top of the fence, on to his shoulders and he'd put her down on the floor. He tried to give her the kiss of life but she was dead. He still has nightmares about the moment Trevor came over and found her. 'I never want to see another person like that,' he says. 'Trevor looked as if he was dead himself.'

'That's my daughter,' he said to Tony. 'Sorry mate, I couldn't do anything,' Tony replied. As Trevor held his daughter's head in his hands Tony walked away. 'The first time I met him afterwards I explained who I was and he asked what happened,' says Tony. 'When I told him he said: "OK, thanks." He just seemed to go off into a little world of his own.'

Tony was twenty-four when the disaster happened and had been a Liverpool supporter all his life. He went to the match with his father and fourteen-year-old brother Stephen. He was six yards behind his little brother during the crush, watching him trapped underneath a man who was pushed against the fence. Tony's legs were off the floor and he was in agony. Then the gates at the front opened and he saw Stephen and his father escape.

As Tony went through he broke another boy's arm which was stuck between himself and the gate post. 'The boy collapsed to the ground,' says Tony. 'I pulled him up by the hair and pulled him out with me. I could hear a crush barrier snapping behind me. I heard the bending of metal, then the crash. When you hear people scream like that the hairs on the back of your neck stand up. You know they're dying.'

Tony broke his hand and three of his ribs in the disaster, but his mental anguish has taken longer to heal. At first he couldn't sleep and wandered night after night round the Anfield ground in the early hours of the morning. In desperation he thought about killing himself with an overdose of the insulin he takes for his diabetes. A couple of times he filled the syringe, but thoughts of his children stopped him doing it.

Tony, a father of two, went through six months of depression. He sat in the chair not talking to anyone, staring at the television but not able to say what was on the screen. The same depression comes back every year on the anniversary of the disaster, and if it's ever mentioned on television.

Tony doesn't go out with his friends any more. He developed a stammer after Hillsborough, so bad at first that he could hardly talk. On Saturday when his friends are at the match he washes the car and listens to the game on the radio. He is too frightened of crowds to go himself.

The disaster has also left him in debt despite the £10,000 compensation he received more than three years later. He was off work for nine months and couldn't face going back to his job as an industrial cleaner, where one of his tasks was to clean out a cage. It would have brought back memories of being fenced in at Hillsborough. The family almost lost their two-bedroomed semi but found enough money to save it on the day the bailiffs came. Now even though Tony is working as a fork-lift truck driver he's had to put the house up for sale to pay his debts.

At school they called him the class clown. 'I don't feel I can laugh and joke like I used to,' he says. 'But I do feel better. I can talk about Hillsborough now without getting really upset.'

Survivor Paul Taylor still thinks about the disaster every day. In the back of the van, on the way to his job as a bricklayer, he can close his eyes and see Victoria's face. In the midst of his sadness he imagines what her life was like. When he saw her she was dead. He feels ashamed that he couldn't have done more for her and as a result is too embarrassed to get in touch with Trevor Hicks.

Paul is frightened by his behaviour since the disaster.

'See that door panel there, I punched that a week ago,' he says, looking at the living-room door of his terraced house in Liverpool. 'I normally punch them through.' The top two panels have been replaced at least a dozen times. He's also punched through the bathroom door and the bedroom door a dozen times each.

'I still get depressed over Hillsborough,' he says. 'My wife Julie asks me if I want a cup of coffee, and instead of saying "No, thank you," I refuse to answer. She keeps asking me and the door panel will go. The kids do something silly. I don't touch them but I've got to punch something, and the door is the easiest thing to punch. When it's done it's great, the tension's gone, then I have to spend three hours repairing and repainting it.

'Sometimes it doesn't happen for a month. Then I go through a terrible time when I've just got to do it. I've broken the children's high chair, the little lad was climbing on it and he fell and I was so afraid I punched it and it broke. I'd never have done that before.'

Paul speaks with desperate sincerity. His voice is gentle and barely audible. 'A month after Hillsborough I broke the dining-room table, I thought I was smashing a policeman's face in. Julie was screaming at me to stop. Six weeks ago I smashed up the toy-box, broke one of the chairs in the other room and ran upstairs. I broke two sideboards in the bedroom and threw them at the wall. I was out of control, I could feel my heart pounding. Sometimes I think, what's the next stage?'

All his life Paul has been a Liverpool supporter. As a little boy he dreamt of one day becoming a player. As a teenager he went out with girls during the week but Saturdays were for his mates and Liverpool. He broke off an engagement because his girlfriend thought he was spending too much money on the game.

When he saw that his married friends were not able to go to the match he decided not to settle down until he was in his late twenties. In 1986 he had to miss a season, the first ever, because he was getting married and couldn't afford to go. It was so unbearable he had to join his uncles at the Everton games twenty-five minutes before the end just so that he could watch football.

Hillsborough was the highlight of the season and as he travelled up on the coach his mates were talking about the game, who would be playing and who they thought would score. 'It's in the back of your mind that you might lose,' he says. 'In the seventies Ipswich beat us and on the train on the way back the emergency cord kept being pulled so we had to stop. It took us eight hours to get home; no one was talking, and I was crying.'

There seemed to be a good chance of winning the Semi-Final. Liverpool had beaten Nottingham Forest the year before and they were in good form. It was a nice day and Paul stood talking to an old man and a girl on the terraces. He was thinking of taking his six-week-old son Michael on to the Kop during the next home game and sending a photograph to be published in the programme. In the pen on his right there was so much space two lads were sunbathing.

The crush was in his section. At 2.45 p.m. it was so bad he started to feel uncomfortable. He put his foot on a bar of the fence and used his thigh as a stool to help supporters over into the next pen. At 3 p.m. he could hardly move. 'I was pushed against the side railings and I had trouble breathing,' he says. 'I saw a teenager in front of me die standing up. I couldn't do anything because my hands were pinned to my sides. That's when I panicked.

'I thought I was going to die. Everyone started to fall forwards. I stayed where I was with my arm caught in the railings and people were trying to hold on to me as they went past. They were on top of one another in front of me.' Then when he felt more space around him he started picking supporters up off the floor, heaving them over the fence into the next section. Some were alive, some were limp and lifeless. 'I was on such a high, I just kept going and going,' he says.

He saw Vicky lying backwards, trapped from her waist by a pile of bodies. 'I tend to be protective towards girls,' he says. 'There was a big fat man lying there. I put one foot in the middle of his stomach – he didn't say anything so I knew he was dead. I leaned across and pulled her out by her arms, over the other bodies. Another lad and I carried her to the side. I tried to give her the kiss of life but I thought she was already dead. I knew that she was some mother's little girl and I was so upset. I took her arm out of her cardigan and covered her face with it.'

Then Paul saw a boy lying in the pile of bodies at the front, his eyes moving slightly. He pulled him clear of the crowd, put him next to Vicky and tried to give him the kiss of life. The boy was dead and Paul pulled off the jacket he was wearing to cover his face.

Going back towards the coach Paul was so upset to see people going into shops and eating. 'I was screaming at them, "Don't you know what's happened?" They were staring at me as if I was a zombie.'

Back home in Liverpool Paul struggled to cope with his feelings. He walked around in a trance for weeks, taking sedatives prescribed by his doctor. A fortnight after the disaster he went to a memorial service. When he came home he sat and cried, rocking backwards and forwards, unaware of what he was doing.

'I was scared,' he says. 'I thought I was going to end up in a strait-jacket. The more I tried to force Hillsborough out of my mind, the more it was there.' He was taken by ambulance to hospital and saw a psychiatrist. Paul was worried that the boy he had given the kiss of life to may have died because he put him in the wrong position.

The disaster still affects every area of Paul's life. At work he always had a reputation for being keen. If a job didn't look right it had to be pulled down and built again. Now he's not so enthusiastic. He has never worked on the anniversary of the disaster, and feels he never will again.

Every time his wife goes out he tries to memorize what she's like, as if it is the last time he will ever see her. He has screamed at her for arriving home fifteen minutes late. On his own in the house Paul feels nervous and eats for comfort. He is now nineteen stones, six stones heavier than he was before the disaster. 'If you weren't here now I'd be in the kitchen,' he says. His family are out visiting relatives. Still obsessed with Hillsborough, he watches videos of it over and over again. His flash-backs to the disaster are as clear as watching a video in his head.

Every week Paul visits Victoria's grave and talks to her. She's buried in a plot near to his grandmother's. As he stands on the Kop he always spends five minutes talking to those who have died. 'I tell them I'm back again and ask them what they think about the game,' he says. 'I know it sounds silly, I don't know any of them.'

He's only spoken about Hillsborough once on the terraces. The man he was speaking to was an Evertonian and Paul punched him because he didn't like what he said.

'I've heard people talking about what they went through at Hillsborough,' he says. 'I don't know how they can do that in a pub with people listening. I feel it cheapens it. For me, the disaster will always be remembered with dignity. Can you imagine me standing in the middle of a pub describing Victoria?

'Hillsborough has made me cherish the fact I'm still alive. Life is very precious to me now.'

# CHAPTER TWO

# THE *HERALD* OF FREE ENTERPRISE

## 6 March 1987

Sonia is smiling again. It hardly seemed possible after she saw her husband drown on her fifty-third birthday. She watched helplessly as he disappeared into the bitterly cold waters of the English Channel when the *Herald of Free Enterprise* capsized. Seriously injured and alone, Sonia had to cope with her loss and the trauma of being involved in disaster. A year later she was so lonely she joined a dating agency, not realizing that her future husband lived just across the road.

Sonia and Jim Harwood married in March 1990, three years after the ferry capsized. He is ten years younger than she is, a widower whose wife died of leukaemia a year before Sonia lost her second husband Mick. 'I realize I've been lucky to find someone else,' she says, as Jim hands her a cup of tea. 'We both think the world of each other.'

Sonia had been married to Mick Saunders for eight years when the disaster happened. He was a bricklayer – a large, jolly man, the life and soul of the neighbourhood. Their trip to Belgium was her birthday treat. She had drunk a few brandies by the time they boarded the boat for the return trip and was feeling a bit tipsy.

Mick stood drinking a pint of beer in the bar as she had another double. They were laughing when the 8,000-tonne ferry started to tilt. Then Sonia found herself rising into the air, clinging to a chair as she went higher and higher. The ferry turned on its side and she could see water rushing in at the bottom. Then she watched her husband slide down.

'He seemed to know he was going to die,' she says. 'He just threw himself in there, he seemed to give up and didn't try to get hold of anything. He'd always been scared of water and wouldn't even go swimming.' Sonia watched as chairs, tables and bottles fell on top of him, and the bodies piled up one on top of another.

'There was all this money floating around on top, big rolls of it,' she says incredulously. 'That was what I thought was so funny, no one cared about it.' When the lights went out she was dangling in the dark, forty feet up in the air. 'Everyone was screaming,' she says, 'but I didn't want to waste any breath I might need.' She believes that being a nurse helped her not to panic.

'It was so hard to hang on and I knew I couldn't do it for ever,' she says. 'In the end I let go and fell down, hoping I was going to go into the water and not hit anything. If I'd hit a body I'd have broken my leg.'

Sonia talks about the disaster without emotion. It is Jim who can't listen to her story any longer and has to leave the room. She carries on chattering. 'The water was quite deep – everyone was walking on my head, and they were pushing me down. I had to get to an exit, and I held my breath and tried to swim underneath, pushing myself beneath the bodies.

'I was giving up. It was so cold I couldn't even feel my fingers. I decided to let myself die. It felt better when I went under the water, just like going to sleep. All the anxiety had gone and it was lovely.' A lorry driver saved her life. He pulled her out of the water by the hair, on to a chair and then over on to an upturned toilet block. 'My clothes had been ripped off. I only had half my trousers on and nothing on top,' she says. 'I was freezing and he gave me his soaking wet coat. At least it covered me up.'

Sonia was in so much pain she thought she was having a heart attack. 'I broke all of my ribs, didn't I?' she says, not expecting an answer. Then she continues: 'I broke five of them, that was enough.' She recalls the conversation she had with the lorry driver.

'Don't you dare have a heart attack after what you've put me through,' he said.

'Of course I started laughing,' says Sonia.

'Keep talking,' he said.

'What do you do for a living?' she asked him.

'I'm a lorry driver.'

'I'm cold,' she said.

'I'm cold too and you have my coat.'

'It's wet,' she said.

'No, it's not, it's your imagination.'

They noticed a Toblerone chocolate bar floating in the water, the lorry driver picked it out, took off the paper and broke a piece off. 'Now try to eat this,' he said. 'You're joking, it's been in all that dirty water,' she replied. Then she ate it.

Meanwhile she could see her husband floating face down in the water. 'I knew it was him because he had really white hair,' she says. 'I saw the divers in there turning up the heads to see if people were still alive. I saw them pull his head up and leave it down again. People don't realize what you go through in a situation like that, it's enough to make you go round the bend.'

Sonia was rescued through a window that had been smashed above her head. She tried to climb up a rope-ladder but couldn't move and fell back into the water. Eventually a rope was tied round her and she was pulled up, protesting fruitlessly that she couldn't go unless Mick was taken out too.

In the rescue boat her body was numb with cold and wrapped in sacks. A fisherman's huge smelly socks hung off the ends of her feet, and were red with her blood. Sonia had gashed her legs and was suffering from hypothermia.

She lay unconscious and on a ventilator in St Jans Hospital, in Bruges, for four weeks. When she woke up she was worried about how she was going to pay her hospital bill. 'I knew we didn't have a lot of money in the bank,' she recalls. 'I mentioned it to Margaret Thatcher when she came to the hospital and she said the government paid the bill.'

Sonia was on her own in Belgium, two hundred miles away from home. 'I felt so lonely over there. I didn't really care about myself any more,' she says. A month later she was moved to the Medway Hospital in Gillingham, Kent, where she normally worked. 'I had continuous anxiety attacks,' she says. 'As soon as I shut my eyes it was all happening again.' She could see the heads bobbing up and down in the water, the pitch blackness penetrated occasionally by a glimmer of light as men switched on their cigarette lighters.

Two months later Sonia came home to her house in Rainham where her son Terry lived with her for the next two years. At first she could hardly move and he had to do everything for her, including giving her a bath. 'I cried myself to sleep every night,' she recalls. 'I wondered if I'd be on my own for ever and what I was going to do with my life. I talked to Mick as I lay there and told him I wanted to meet someone else. I asked him questions and I felt he was answering me. There was no one else I could talk to.'

Sonia, already a mother of two and a grandmother, joined a dating agency, but she had just one date before she gave it up. 'He was horrible, not my type at all,' she says. Terry insisted on going to the same pub and watched from a distance with his girlfriend. He told his mother she couldn't go out with the man again. 'I thought I was going to be able to meet a really nice bloke like Mick to settle down with, but they're few and far between,' she says.

Then she decided to go back to work and devote her life to her career as a nurse. Twelve months after the disaster she was back in the operating theatre but stayed for just a year. Every time a serious case came in she had an anxiety attack, and a couple of times ran up and down the hospital corridors oblivious to what she was doing.

One attack happened as she was standing in the theatre sterilizing supply unit packing instruments for a four-hour operation. 'I was in charge of four women and I started flying off the handle at one of them. It sounded like she was really shouting, then all the others seemed to be shouting at me. I started running down to the rest room.'

The anxiety attacks went on for eighteen months after the disaster, and happened anywhere – in the pub, in the car or at home. 'I felt as if I couldn't breathe, as if I was drowning and fighting to get out of the water. I was breathing heavily and pouring with sweat but I felt really cold. The next day all my limbs ached.'

Sonia bought a white rose-bush in memory of Mick and eighteen months after the disaster went in search of a neighbour to help her plant it in her garden. She couldn't bend down or walk very well herself. Jim answered the door. He was going through a bad time. He missed his wife and was getting drunk every night to push the pain away.

Their first night out was at a rock and roll club in London. Sonia and Mick used to go regularly and she discovered that Jim was also a rock and roll fan. They married eighteen months later, and now live in a bungalow in Rainham which they both renovated.

'I had to move, there was too much of Mick in the house I lived in before,' says Sonia. 'Jim and I have had some good laughs working on this one.' In the living-room are a collection of pipes which Sonia and Mick dug up in a Victorian dump. In the conservatory is Jim's collection of golliwogs.

'The night before the wedding I had a little talk to Mick,' says Sonia. 'I told him if the following day was nice I'd know he agreed to me getting married again. It was March but it was a beautifully sunny day.'

Sonia can't stay in the house on her own. If Jim's not there she has to go out, even if it's only for a walk round the block. Inside, her doors are never closed and Sonia can't sit down. She still swims even though just talking about water makes her come out in goose-pimples.

'I took life for granted before the disaster,' she says. Small, plump and full of fun, she loves to keep active. 'I used to go to disco-dancing classes and bowling alleys and I went every Saturday night to rock and roll with Mick,' she says. 'But I've done more since the disaster.'

When she received her £70,000 compensation she decided to spend. 'I lived it up,' she says. 'I was always out shopping and there was never a day when I didn't buy something.' She took her son to America, gave both of her children some money, bought Jim a jeep, and swapped the yellow Cortina she had before the disaster for a white Toyota MR2 sports car. She jumps into it to go off and buy a cabbage in town. When Jim was made redundant from his job as a printer they used what money was left to pay off their mortgage. Now they plan to go and live in Spain and buy a little boat so they can visit the islands.

Last year Sonia went back on a ferry to celebrate her birthday. Before that they'd always gone to the cremato-rium on the anniversary of the disaster with a rose for Mick and one for Jim's first wife. But last year Sonia decided she wanted to go to France. 'Maybe I was trying to reverse what happened,' she says. 'Instead of the trip ending in disaster I was happy as I got off the ferry knowing that my life was going to be with Jim. 'We both know what it's like to lose someone you love and to be able to love again.'

Nicola Simpson was just fourteen when she lost her mother in the Zeebrugge Ferry disaster. Nicola almost died herself. Her heart had stopped beating and she was clinically dead when she was taken to hospital.

Now she's working in a bank in Welwyn Garden City and living in a flat with her boyfriend. They met when she was seventeen and were engaged a year later. 'The disaster made me grow up,' she says. 'I feel I grew up too quickly. When I was a teenager I was paying a mortgage. I come home and do the washing and the cooking but I feel I should be going to nightclubs.'

Nicola was one of thirty children under the age of sixteen years who survived the disaster. She was with her thirty-nine-year-old mother Pat, forty-one-year-old father Tony and fourteen-year-old best friend Cheryl Taylor when the ferry capsized as they were sitting in the café. Nicola and her mother were swept to one end of the boat.

She recalls what happened next: 'We fell against the wall and the water swept us along. I grabbed hold of my mum's arm and she kept saying, "Hold on, hold on." She was telling me to keep moving, keep warm. I was swimming up to my shoulders in water and I took my little pixie boots off because they were pulling me down. When the lights went out I couldn't see anyone.

'The glass partition which was then the roof shattered down on top of me and I could feel it gashing my head even though I only had two little cuts. I could hear someone shouting, "I'm drowning, I love you!" Then someone grabbed hold of me, asked me my name and said, "Hold on to me." I held on to him, and I told him I wanted to hold on to my mum. I don't remember any more.'

Cheryl and Tony, a British Aerospace engineer, were able to swim to a door above their heads and were rescued. Nicola spent over three hours in the water. When divers found her she was blue with the cold and apparently lifeless, but they realized she was actually alive.

They tied a rope round her and tried to pull her up to safety but the rope fell off and she plunged into the water on top of floating bodies. They tried a second and a third time before they managed to pull her up.

Nicola was picked up by helicopter and taken to a nearby naval base before being rushed to St Jans Hospital. She wasn't breathing and her heart had stopped but doctors noticed that her heart muscles were still shivering on the cardiac machine.

Her temperature was 75°F, twenty degrees below normal and too low to restart her heart. A warm saline solution was pumped into her stomach. She was taken to the operating theatre where she was attached to a heart-lung machine and her blood was drained, oxygenated and replaced.

Doctors were worried that they wouldn't be able to stop the deterioration of her lungs and kidneys and feared she would be brain damaged. At 9 a.m. the following day they were delighted when she was able to point to letters on an alphabet card and spell her name.

'I find it hard to believe I didn't die,' says Nicola. A week after the disaster she was told her mother was dead. 'They didn't want me to know but when I was alone with my sister I asked,' she says. 'For a few weeks I had letters and presents and I was really spoilt, so it didn't have a chance to sink in. When it did I can't say in words how I felt.'

Nicola went back to school two months after the disaster, not as shy as she'd been before. 'She was affected by the attention,' her father believes. Nicola giggles. Tony has called round to be at her side as she talks; he still finds it too difficult to talk about the disaster himself. He looks through the press cuttings instead, which Nicola keeps in a cupboard in her living-room. 'When I look at them it makes me feel proud,' she says. Her jeans and denim shirt hide the long scar running down her body. 'It's nice to think that's me.'

In one picture she's meeting the King and Queen of Belgium. 'I look awful there,' she says as she looks at another. Her hair was cut and ragged because of her injuries. 'Skip that one, it's horrid,' she adds, as she looks at a third.

Just after the disaster she was so frightened at night she had to leave the radio on and a light on in the hall. In group therapy with other children who had survived, she talked about how she felt. One little girl had lost four members of her family and the others used to tease her and call her 'orphan'.

Nicola never stopped talking about the disaster to her friend Cheryl but hardly mentioned it to her father. 'My dad didn't like to talk about it, not with me,' she says. 'He didn't want to upset me and I didn't want to upset him. It was as if it had never happened to us. We both liked to avoid talking about mum.'

Like many survivors Nicola felt guilty that she did not die. Now she feels that death could be just round the corner and wants to make a will. 'They say I'm too young; I say I could be dead tomorrow.'

Customers in the bank where she works still remember her from newspaper cuttings at the time of the disaster.

When they recognize her she feels embarrassed. 'It's so long ago,' she says. 'I have to look ahead. If I keep looking back I will ruin the rest of my life.'


Alan Rogers and his family are still suffering as a result of the ferry disaster. The emotional scars they suffered that night haven't healed. In fact the pain is so bad that Alan wishes his children had died in the disaster. 'The people who died that night were the lucky ones,' says Alan, his voice breaking with emotion. 'They haven't had to go through what we're going through now.' His wife Sue is also in tears as she talks about how their once happy family has been torn apart. 'I could quite easily kill myself,' she says. 'A couple of times I've thought about taking a load of tablets.'

Sue and Alan now sleep in different rooms. They have made love just once since the disaster, and stay together because of the children. The children – twins William and Emma, who were three when it happened, and Adrian who was eighteen months old – still wake up screaming.

William went back to playschool a few days after the disaster and covered a piece of paper in black paint. 'It's the naughty ferry,' he told his teacher. Emma drew a picture of a boat with a man beside it, his face covered in blood.

The family had been on a fun day out when the disaster happened. They boarded the ferry for their return trip and had just settled down in the television lounge. Alan still remembers how passengers flew through the air 'as if they were on a trapeze. They plunged through the glass partition next to me and were ripped to shreds. I watched them die,' he says. William fell through a hole in the glass and out into the corridor. Alan was still holding his hand and knew he had to slide through the gap to be with him.

'There was a huge explosion as the ferry hit the sea bed,' he recalls. 'The windows smashed and pitch-black water rushed in.' In the darkness Alan held William to his chest. The freezing water carried them back to the rest of their family. Sue thought Adrian was dead. He was in her arms and wasn't crying or moving. Alan took Emma from Sue and held both of his children in one arm. He held on to Sue with the other and tried to keep them all out of the water as they climbed up on to chairs and tables. 'This is it, love,' he said to his wife. 'We're not going to get out.'

Sue's memory of the disaster is patchy. It has come back gradually but there are still parts her mind refuses to recall. She remembers being up to her chest in water, as Alan passed the children over to a woman who had found a place on a shelf. The family were showered with glass when the window was broken above their heads. Alan climbed up a rope and out on to the side. He went to a lifeboat, found a canvas bag on a rope and lowered it down, then pulled his children out one at a time.

Alan managed to pull his wife three-quarters of the way out but she fell back in. 'I went under the water,' she says. 'The glass partition had become the bottom and I used that to push myself up again. I cut my feet on the broken glass.'

Alan found a ladder next to the lifeboat and lowered it through the broken window. Immediately there was a rush of people clambering up. 'It grew quieter and quieter as people managed to get out,' Sue recalls. Another passenger held her out of the water but he had cut his wrists and was eventually forced to let go. She found out later that he felt guilty because he thought he'd let her die. Sue thought he had died too. It was a year before they discovered through the Herald Families Association newsletter that both had survived.

Sue spent an hour and a half in the water and was one

of the last to be rescued out of the television lounge. Alan went down the ladder to find her but couldn't get her out. She wasn't strong enough to climb up the ladder and he couldn't carry her because he'd injured his arm and his back. The piece of metal embedded in his arm is still there.

'When I climbed out I was chilled to the bone,' he says. He made his way to the children on the tug, convinced he would never see Sue again. He was leaving the boat to have another go at getting her out when he saw that she had been rescued.

Sue lay on the side of the boat so cold she couldn't move. 'Then I heard someone say, "Knock her out, we'll take her up in the helicopter," so I started crawling on my arms,' she recalls.

When the family stepped off the tugboat in the ferry terminal William was suffering from hypothermia. Sue thought it was tiredness that was making him drift off to sleep as she held him in her arms. Then someone from the Red Cross grabbed him from her and rushed him to an ambulance. In the hospital Sue's badly sprained ankle was put in a plaster cast but that didn't stop her hobbling from one cubicle to another to comfort her children.

Alan felt that he'd been a coward. He'd been an ex-Royal Navy reservist and had naval training but he didn't go straight back inside the ferry. He thought that Sue detested him because he'd left her behind. 'I knew he'd done his best,' she says.

Three months after the disaster, the twins were having their fourth birthday party, and Alan was upstairs at their home in Cheltenham taking sleeping tablets and pain-killers. He woke up in hospital. 'I didn't particularly want to come home,' he says. 'I don't know if I was trying to kill myself.' He still recalls the day he grabbed an orna-mental sword and announced he was going to kill the ferry's skipper, Captain David Lewry.

The disaster had destroyed his marriage and his business. Before it happened he was earning £800 a week and had his own building maintenance business. Now he is unemployed, and has lost £100,000 in wages. The family have been given an £11,000 interim payment from P&O Ferries but are still waiting for compensation.

Alan says he can't work now; his back hurts and he can't concentrate so it's impossible to find a job. Three years after the disaster he worked as a lorry driver but gave it up after three months. Shocking flashbacks tormented him as he sat in his lorry in Dover Docks waiting to load up. His trauma was so severe he couldn't concentrate and forgot where he was driving to.

'I feel so angry that no one has been punished for what happened,' he says. 'I wish I'd never got off the ferry.'

The Askey family from Burton upon Trent in Staffordshire were sitting in the same television lounge the night the ferry capsized. Teresa Askey's sixty-seven-year-old mother was killed. 'If I wasn't such a strong person I might never have got over it,' says Teresa. 'I used to ask Trevor if I was hard. We had to be strong for our daughter.'

Trevor bursts into tears as he starts to talk about what happened. He was playing chess when the boat started to tilt. Teresa came flying over his head first and he caught her by the legs; then his mother-in-law was flung across in the same way. He tried to grab her but she was a big woman and he couldn't. Next came his only daughter Rebecca and he caught her and pushed her under a table.

Then he fell too, sliding down the boat to hit the glass partition. 'I hit the handle of a pushchair,' he recalls. 'I remember a woman shouting, "You're on my baby, you're on my baby!" It saved me going through the partition and under the water.' Trevor shouted to his family and when he found out where they were he helped them up on to tables. They all escaped with cuts and bruises.

At first Rebecca had nightmares and wouldn't go to bed in the dark and even now she occasionally leaves a light on. Trevor also had to leave his bedroom light on for months. Every time he slept, he felt as if his body was tilting again.

'I felt very guilty,' he says. 'I still do. I was the one who asked her mum to come and I saved the other two, but not her.' Teresa found it difficult to face the rest of her family at first and was worried they would blame her. 'I didn't go out for four weeks, I felt everyone was looking at me,' she says. She wouldn't have a shower for months and still won't shampoo her hair under the shower or have water on her face. Rebecca doesn't talk about the disaster but has been back on a ferry since.

Both Trevor and Teresa have gone back to their factory jobs. They settled their compensation claim out of court two years after the disaster. 'We've coped so well because we had each other,' says Teresa. 'If one of us is ten minutes late home now we panic. We don't like to be apart for very long.'

Ken Hollingsbee had a wife and two children when the disaster happened. The family lived in a four-bedroomed detached house in Canterbury with its own swimming pool. At thirty-eight Ken had it all.

He even survived the ferry disaster. He never could have anticipated that in the years that followed he would lose everything. Slowly he saw his life fall apart.

Three years after the disaster his wife Susan asked him

to leave. The happy, fun-loving man she had married had become aggressive and had slapped her a couple of times. She was frightened and could take no more. There are times, Ken admits, when he thought he was going crazy.

Ken was one of the crew on the *Herald of Free Enterprise* when the disaster happened. He remembers how the ferry started to tilt as he sat at the till in the duty-free shop. A bottle of brandy hit him on the head. He shielded the woman next to him from the bottles that followed from the shelves. 'I kept thinking how are we going to clear this lot up,' he recalls. 'I thought the ferry would bounce back.'

It took him half an hour to get out after it capsized. Ken climbed up a rope and through a broken window, then he spent six hours on the side of the boat helping passengers to escape.

'There was a woman with a dead baby who wouldn't move,' he recalls. 'A couple of blokes had to coax her out.' Ken tried to resuscitate a teenager and an elderly woman in a brown coat, but without success. He'd never had any training. 'It is an experience I will never forget,' he says.

At one stage he was helping passengers into a tugboat and decided to get in with them. Tired and cold, he'd done enough. A cup of tea was thrust into his freezing hands and he wrapped his fingers around it. Then a woman started crying about how she had trodden on her son and he was dead. Ken stood up and said he had to go back.

'The ship was covered in blood and water and we were sliding all over the place,' he recalls. The draught from the helicopter also made it difficult to stand up. Another crew member, Clive Bush, came out and had lost his glasses. He grabbed hold of Ken's hips and he led him along the side. Ken looked back and there were four others in the line. 'I started to conga,' he recalls. 'It sounds barmy but it relieved the tension of it all.' As he pulled one over-weight woman through the window he told her to go on a diet. The following day she thanked him and said she would.

After four hours on the side Ken heard crying at the back of the ferry. He found a woman clutching a little girl as they sat on the side of the seats on deck. They were strangers clinging together for comfort. He pulled the little girl through the railings and the woman over the top.

Ken's wife had seen him on the ten o'clock news putting someone in a helicopter winch so she knew he was safe. He telephoned her from a Belgian hospital in the early hours of the morning. They already had been through so many traumas together. After they met she was impaled on a railing in a car accident and wasn't expected to live, then one of their twins almost died of meningitis. There was no way they could have guessed that this disaster would have such an effect on their marriage.

Ken went back to his job on the ferries but even though he loved it he couldn't do it any more and left after four months. He went to work as a roofer but gave that up and then set up his own taxi business but lost interest in that. It collapsed in early 1991. He couldn't settle, the sea still had a magnetism and if he was near it he sat looking at it longingly.

'I was angry and taking it out on my wife,' he recalls. 'She didn't know what I'd been through and I wouldn't let her in. She wasn't part of the *Herald* family. I felt she didn't understand but I didn't give her the chance. She wasn't part of that exclusive little club that had gone through it. The crew who were on leave when it happened suffered desperately. When we went back to work they were the outsiders, they weren't part of the crew any more.'

Ken decided he had to confront the assistant bosun Mark Stanley. It had been his job on the day to close the *Herald*'s bow doors. He didn't because he was asleep in his cabin. The ferry headed into the Channel bound for Dover with its bow doors open and capsized. 'I knew him, he was a quiet, reserved chap,' says Ken. The two men bumped into each other at a nightclub. 'We had a drink and a chat and I said, "I've got to tell you what I feel."

'I knew he had a lot to live with and I tried to put it in a way that wouldn't make him feel worse.' Ken told him: 'I don't hate you, but I do blame you.' 'If he had shut the doors it wouldn't have rolled over,' he says. 'I would still have had thirty-eight mates and I wouldn't have had to go to thirty-eight funerals in a month. I just had to tell him. Mark said: "I understand. I think I'd be the same."'

Ken and his wife split up in October 1990 and he went to live with his mother. They are still friends. 'I had absolutely nothing and I owed people money all over the place,' he says. 'I hadn't got the confidence to apply for a job, and I didn't think I could do anything.' Ken was surviving on his credit cards and had spent his compensation.

Then in August 1991, still owing £8,000, he opened his own pub in Canterbury. The pub gave him the chance to make a new start. 'When I found the pub everything I was before came out again,' he says. 'Finding the pub was the best thing that could have happened to me.'


Clive Bush and his wife sold their car and bought a couple of bikes to ride around on. 'We probably get more laughs out of life now than we did before,' says the former barman. There's no trace of the 'living hell' they went through after the *Herald of Free Enterprise* disaster. 'I was frightened of Clive, frightened of what he might do next,' says Pat.

They had been married for fifteen happy years when the disaster happened. Clive loved his life. He had a good time at home in Hythe with his wife and family. He enjoyed his job on the ferry so much that he couldn't imagine doing anything else. Clive was fifty and thought he'd be there until he retired.

When the ferry capsized he was sitting in the crew mess near to a wall which then became the floor. As water rushed in through the door he thought he was going to drown. Luckily it stopped short of the other wall, which had become the ceiling. He clambered up on to tables and, with freezing cold water up to his waist, he waited to be rescued. It was an hour before someone lowered a rope inside and he was able to climb out. Then he stood on the side dragging people through a shattered window.

Clive went back to work on the ferries for three months. During that time his personality changed dramatically. He had always been quiet, never a violent man. 'After the disaster I used to walk down the street and have an overwhelming desire to hit anyone and anything,' he says. 'I had a frightening desire to kill them. I tried to diffuse it by walking for hours into the countryside so I didn't see anyone and could try to calm down. I knew it wasn't me. I didn't hit anyone but my knuckles used to come through my skin with the power I knew I had.'

Five months after the disaster Clive contemplated suicide. 'I felt overwhelming guilt that I was alive and a lot of my pals were dead.' Clive breaks down in tears as he talks about the crew; his wife steps in to help him out. She felt too much love for him to walk away, even when he became unbearable to live with.

'He wasn't physical, he was so nasty with his words,' says Pat. She used to tell their children not to bring over the grandchildren because he was behaving so strangely. 'One day he took me to work and stopped the car about a mile away,' she recalls.

'I just happened to say I didn't realize I was going to have to walk, I had my high heels on. He got out of the car, opened my door, slammed it, used terrible swear words and told me I could walk and he never wanted to see me again. That just wasn't Clive. That evening he said he didn't expect me to come home. The next morning he went to pack his suitcase.'

Pat telephoned a counsellor from the Herald Assistance Unit and she came over and talked to him for hours. Without the unit Pat believes she couldn't have coped. The wives met there once a week and found support in talking to each other. 'It sounds very hard but the ones who had lost their husbands could get on with their lives,' she says. 'We couldn't see any end to it.' Clive was also going to the Herald Assistance Unit, but wasn't talking to Pat about how he felt.

He became impotent and that also put a strain on their marriage. 'I can count on one hand how many times we've made love since it happened,' he says. It didn't worry him, but Pat found that difficult to understand. 'I felt he didn't care for me,' she says. 'I've had to put it to the back of my mind and build on what we have got rather than what we haven't. I used to feel angry with the men who died because I thought that was holding him back.' Clive once said to her about their sex life: 'How can I think of that sort of thing when there are chaps who've died and haven't got a life?'

Even though their sex life hasn't recovered, their relationship has. Clive has lost his aggressiveness. 'I think we're closer than we've been in a long time,' says Pat. 'Clive is unemployed and we seem happier. We have money problems but he's not under pressure at work and he's relaxed a bit more.'

After Clive left the ferries he went on a nine-month course to learn French polishing and upholstery. He started his own business but gave that up after six months. He wasn't good enough, he admits, and his heart wasn't in it. Then he worked in an office, but couldn't bear to be inside, so he stayed only a week. His last job was as an airport security officer but he was made redundant at the end of 1991.

'We still find it difficult to talk to each other sometimes,' says Pat. 'He seems to switch off and doesn't want to bother with everyday problems.' Clive has applied to be a gardener in a zoo. 'The ordinary things in life that used to worry me, don't worry me so much now,' he adds.

He's without a car for the first time since he was twenty. When he walks the seven miles into Folkestone he feels on top of the world. 'Financially I'm worse off than before but I think we get more out of life,' he says. 'I feel physically and mentally better. Recently we both couldn't stop laughing at something and that hadn't happened for a long time.'


Stephen Homewood was Assistant Purser on the *Herald of Free Enterprise*. The night it capsized he spent five hours helping passengers up to safety. The following year, at the age of thirty-four, he received the Queen's Gallantry Medal at an investiture ceremony at Buckingham Palace. Now he is working behind the counter of his own post office.

After the disaster Stephen moved from Folkestone to a picturesque village near Ashford in Kent and now lives in a post office and house dating back to 1700. 'The quality of my life is better than before,' he says. 'I can go out and hear the cuckoo and watch the herons fly. I go down to the canal in my little boat. This year I hope to take it out to sea, but I know that my only responsibility will be myself.'

Stephen has always had a passion for the sea, and always will. He was in the main lounge of the *Herald of Free Enterprise* when the disaster happened and can still picture the blood on the glass before the lights failed. 'The disaster plays on my mind as if it was yesterday,' he says.

Stephen was pulled on to the side of the ferry through a porthole and then put a rope-ladder down to help others escape. Some were so weak they fell down into the water again, on top of the people below. As he pulled others out they were still carrying their duty free goods. 'I was telling them to drop them, not to worry about them. They wanted something to cling on to, like a child who is upset and grabs hold of a cuddly toy.'

Stephen will always remember the three-year-old boy who stood on the side of the ship. His father had rescued him and gone back inside for his pregnant wife. 'As soon as I picked him up I was full of emotion,' he says. 'I had an eighteen-month-old child at the time and I felt like he could have been mine.' The hardy seaman was struck by the innocence of the little boy. As they looked over at the shining lights of Zeebrugge the little boy pointed to them. 'Look at those pretty lights,' he said. 'That gave me the strength to think that perhaps there were more like him below.'

After half an hour on the side Stephen clambered back down into the ferry. His torch gave him enough light to scan the surface of the water. It was held in one hand as he pulled people on to the ladder with the other. Nearby a father was tying his baby to a rope that had been lowered through another porthole.

As the rope was pulled up the baby smacked against the side of the ferry. Stephen was convinced the baby was killed but discovered days later that it had survived. At one stage he slipped off the ladder himself and went into the water for a few minutes. A frantic passenger lunged at him desperate to be pulled out.

Back on dry land Stephen was taken to a naval base twenty-minutes' drive away. When he went to the toilets he forgot that he'd left the ferry. 'They were in a disgusting state, and I decided I had to get them cleaned,' he recalls. He didn't realize then that half of his colleagues had been killed. They'd been one of the happiest crews he'd ever worked with, laid back and easy going. Stephen had to identify two of their bodies in the mortuary.

He felt like a judge as he walked between the corpses, laid out in sections for men, women and children. He was looking at the man of sixty, saying he hadn't had a bad life, staring at the two-year-old child, asking why it had been allowed to happen. 'Shock helped me to cope with it at the time. I felt numb,' he says.

Back home the following day he bought a newspaper to see which of his friends had survived. Stephen went to thirty-two funerals and carried four coffins. He lost about eight close friends. 'To lose so many people in one blow is devastating,' he says. 'I wasn't prepared for it.'

He didn't go out for ten days after the disaster, he didn't want people coming up to him in the street asking questions. Three weeks later he went back to work on an identical ship. Then feelings of bitterness, anger and depression started to come to the surface. 'I wanted someone to blame and there wasn't anyone. There was a proportion of blame everywhere,' he says.

A year after the disaster Stephen went to see a psychologist for six months. 'Several times I thought it would probably have been easier to have died with the others,' he says. 'It's probably a bit of a selfish attitude.

'I still feel I was a bit like God. I had the leave book and I told some people they could have the day off, and others they couldn't. The ones I gave the day off to came up and thanked me.'

There were so many questions to be answered in the aftermath of the disaster. For eighteen months he couldn't forget the limp and lifeless hand that had fallen across his face as the ship rolled over. 'I thought it was a woman, the hand was nice and slim and smooth,' he says. 'I can still feel it now.' He looked at plans of the *Herald* and walked round the identical ship he was working on, trying to work out where the hand had come from. When he did he was able to put it to the back of his mind.

Stephen worked on two other ferries for six months after the disaster but found he didn't enjoy the job any more. The day he left he didn't tell anyone he was going and had no idea what he was going to do next, He went to work as a kitchen porter in a hotel and then bought the post office.

Now he can look back at the good times on the *Herald* as well as the disaster. 'I'm a better person now,' he says. 'I understand more about how people feel. I have no patience with people who think only of themselves. Our society is out to get what it can out of life. I think there's more to it than that.'

Mother-of-two Gail Cook was also praised for her bravery on the night of the ferry disaster. Despite a broken collar bone and three broken toes she calmed hysterical passengers. She comforted mothers and looked after frightened little children.

Gail was in her crew uniform and determined to do her

job. Now if her own teenage daughter wants a cuddle she backs away. 'I can't bear being hugged or any signs of affection,' she says. 'Maybe it's because I don't like to be hemmed in.'

Her husband went through 'three years of hell', she says. 'He'd walk in and I'd say something nasty. I wanted him to be hurt as much as I was.' For almost a year he slept on the settee. 'We didn't talk to each other during the day,' she says. 'We couldn't stand the sight of each other, and we didn't go to bed together at night. How we are still married I don't know. He must have been a saint.'

Gail went back to work nine weeks after the Zeebrugge disaster and worked with a handful of other disaster survivors on the new super ferry the *Pride of Dover*. Once happy-go-lucky, she couldn't understand why she still saw the people who had died walking about. One night she looked up and distinctly saw one of the dead stewards looking down. Then he vanished.

A year after the disaster she went to see a spiritualist and believes she made contact with two of the crew who died. It helped to banish the guilt she felt about not doing enough to help. 'It made me feel a lot better to be told from the crew who had died that I couldn't have done anything else. I now know that when I die they will be there waiting.'

Gail is still emotional as she talks about what happened, several times she is almost in tears. At night she dreams that she's back on the ferry and the same people are still there. When she wakes up it feels as if she has been visiting friends.

Three months after the disaster she had to give up her job and resents losing a way of life she loved. The crew had worked hard and played hard, seeing each other socially when they weren't on duty. Now Gail is working behind a bar in a friend's pub but plans to give it up soon to become an auxiliary nurse.

'I feel I'm more caring than I was before,' she says. 'But

I'm still afraid of getting too close to people or letting them get too close to me. I'm afraid that if I do, something will happen to them. The people I cared about deeply have gone.'

# CHAPTER THREE

# KING'S CROSS

## 18 November 1987

Mariella Santello hunts through a drawer for her photographs. 'I was very photogenic when I was younger,' she laughs as she points to a pretty girl with piercing eyes, tanned skin and hair dyed purple. 'I always wanted to look a bit different, I was so conscious of my image.'

A month after that photograph was taken Mariella lay in a hospital bed. All that remained of her hair was still purple. Her face was blackened, charred and covered in blisters. Her eyes were closed and tubes came out of her mouth and nose.

On the day before her twenty-first birthday Mariella survived the King's Cross fire. Her body was roasted alive. She pulls out another album. This time they're colour photographs, taken during her first twenty-four days in hospital. More than 40 per cent of her body was burnt and she wasn't expected to live. Her mother, who had never been out of Italy before and didn't speak a word of English, didn't recognize her as she walked into the ward.

Mariella was a rebel who had left her little fishing village in Italy when she was eighteen. 'I wanted to be a punk singer and London was the place to be,' she recalls. 'I wanted to be free.' Her eyes light up as she remembers the hopes, the plans she had for the future. San Benedetto del Tronto, halfway down the east coast of Italy, was too small for Mariella. 'I was really famous in my town,' she says, 'probably because of the way I dressed. I always took a very strong approach to things. I was proud to be different.'

Mariella loved London, and was busy learning English at a language school and working part time to make a living as a chambermaid and waitress. She knew she could make it as a singer, her voice was good enough to sing in the church choir at home. When her English was good enough she was planning to have some singing lessons.

Life couldn't have been better for the young Italian girl. A year before she had fallen in love with a boy called Marco from her home town, and he had come over for her birthday. He was studying philosophy at the university in Bologna and had got a lift over on a lorry. Marco didn't know it but she had bought him a ticket so that he could fly home instead of going back on the lorry. Marco never heard about the surprise.

They were travelling together through King's Cross when the disaster happened. As they stepped off the tube they could see smoke but Mariella didn't think there was anything to worry about. No one seemed to be rushing and the policeman directing the people seemed to be calm.

The fire had already started on the Piccadilly Line escalator. The young couple were told to go on to the Victoria Line escalator system. 'I was talking to my boyfriend and kissing him as we went up the escalator,' she recalls. 'He was one step below. When we reached the end I saw the fire. Everything happened so quickly I didn't think of going back down.

'I thought if I could run through the flames I could get out. I shouted: "Run, Marco, let's go", and just set off. I didn't even grab his hand. I saw a gap under the flames, bent down and ran under it. The smoke was so black and so thick on the other side. I hadn't expected that. The flames were so bright that I hadn't been able to see beyond them. I thought I'd get through the flames and see the exit, but it was pitch black.'

Mariella pulled her black plastic jacket off her shoulders. She'd always been so proud of it but as it melted in the heat she couldn't wait to get it off her body. 'I tried to look back or shout Marco's name but the heat was so intense I couldn't really move my head,' she recalls. 'I couldn't open my mouth too much, I couldn't do anything, didn't know what to do. The station was huge and I didn't know where I was. It felt as if I was in there on my own.'

Mariella thought she was going to die, she thought she had no choice but to sit and wait for it to happen. Her only regret was that she hadn't done anything for the world, that her life had not been useful. Then something inside forced her to react, told her she couldn't let herself give up. She tried to walk forwards but banged into a wall, burning herself on the hot tiles.

She had to choose whether to go left or right and luckily chose left because the other way would have led her back to the fire. Then she bumped into some stairs and dropped to the floor. Mariella went on: 'I stood up again and grabbed a handrail but it was burning me, it was so hot. I went up the stairs and the smoke was becoming less thick. That's when I found the exit.

'I came out into the open air and someone came towards me. I was shouting, "This is not true", and screaming like crazy. I said, "My boyfriend is in there – you've got to get him out."' Inside the station Mariella had felt no pain but as soon as she stepped out into the street she felt as if she was dying in agony.

A man led her to a bench but she was in too much pain to sit down. It seemed like ages as she waited to be taken to hospital. When the ambulance arrived she was lowered on to a stretcher and put inside. Her clothes were cut off and the water thrown on her to cool her down rose as steam from her burning body. Gasping for air she was put on a ventilator.

Mariella was taken to University College Hospital with burns to her face, right arm, legs and buttocks. It was twenty-four days before she regained consciousness. Her boyfriend died in the fire and when she woke up he had already been buried. Two weeks later her mental torture started. 'I felt guilty because I didn't go back for Marco,' she says. 'He had come to England for me. I felt he should have survived, not me; he was such a good person.'

She smiles shyly as she recalls how close she came to 'insanity'. She became clinically depressed and had to take anti-depressants. Mariella realized her recovery was going to take time and that she was going to be disfigured. 'What sort of life am I going to have?' she wondered.

'I lost the willingness to fight,' she recalls. 'I would have preferred it if I'd died. I didn't have an appetite or a willingness to eat and I lost weight. My dreams and my aspirations had been put in a bag and thrown out of the window. Every five minutes I just cried and cried and cried.'

Her days were spent wondering if she was going to be able to eat, sleep, or see any improvement. She couldn't move for the first two months after she woke up. The pain was so bad the nurses used to burst into tears and leave the room. Mariella was on four-hourly medication and the effects wore off in two. The caring hospital staff couldn't do anything for her. She cried in desperation but her lungs were so badly damaged her voice could not be heard.

Mariella came out of hospital three months after the disaster but her ordeal was far from over. In April she went to Italy for a holiday and fifteen people drove for four hours to the airport to meet her. They had all heard different stories about the extent of her burns. She considered going back home to live, but decided it was easier to be in London on her own. 'In a small town it's all gossip, whereas in this city no one knows me,' she says.

When Mariella came out of hospital she had to wear a specially made pair of tights, gloves and elastic sleeves to help the skin on her body to heal. She also had to wear a face mask for a year. 'I tried to wear the mask when I went out a couple of times but it was far too difficult,' she says.

When she walked down to the road two workmen pointed at her. 'It's the new phantom of the opera,' they jeered. 'They were laughing, I was crying,' she recalls, 'but my face was squashed into the mask so I couldn't cry properly. I could have exploded into tears. I walked over to them and said: "King's Cross did this to me", and kept on walking. I decided then that I wouldn't go out.'

For a year she only went to the hospital for treatment or to the supermarket. At home she couldn't concentrate long enough to read and spent hours in front of the television.

It wasn't easy to venture out into the world again when the mask came off to reveal her scars. 'I felt people didn't want to know me,' she says. 'I ran away from them. I wasn't cheerful company. In the beginning I couldn't help talking about the accident. I didn't have anything else to say. If I mentioned I'd been in the King's Cross fire it made people shut up.

'I was putting on a brave face so that people wouldn't

be pushed away by my feelings of self-consciousness but at home I'd feel that I didn't like myself and people didn't like me.'

Mariella decided to join an art class, and on the first day had to introduce herself to the group. 'As I stood up and said my name I tried not to look at them to see if they were looking at me,' she says. One of the pictures she painted was a coloured panel representing burnt broken skin. There were black and white photocopies of her burns around it.

In the autumn of 1990, almost two years after the disaster, Mariella turned to food for comfort. The weight piled on to her normally slim body. She put on almost a stone and a half in the year she was binge eating and went up to ten stones. 'I'd go off and buy three different kinds of cakes or four packets of biscuits and eat them all,' she recalls. 'Then I'd feel unhappy because I'd done something wrong. I'd start crash dieting for a few days then go off and make a pig of myself again. I didn't like my body so I thought I might as well. My eating was out of hand, I'd lost control. I got to the stage where I didn't want to look in the mirror because of my weight and the scars on my face. My overeating was compensating for the affection I wasn't getting.'

On top of her fridge there's a tiny framed photograph of Marco, and next to it a picture of Mariella's father who died when she was a child. 'It was very difficult in the beginning to get over Marco's death,' she says. 'I got to the point where I decided I had to leave it behind. When I look at the photograph I remember him.'

Mariella hasn't had a boyfriend since the disaster. At times she didn't have the confidence, at others she believed that men were put off by her scars. 'At different points I felt it would be really nice to have someone to love me and take care of me,' she says. 'I don't feel that now. I don't want to get married, I don't want children. To me that isn't what gives life a purpose.'

Mariella believes she has now recovered from the disaster. 'I am happy,' she says. 'It's as if one veil after another was lifted from my eyes. Obviously I'm aware of my scars, and I'm aware of the excess stone that's still there, but my eyes have grown accustomed to it. I look in the mirror and see myself as pretty.'

Her confidence is back again, and she doesn't feel the need to hide away. When a butcher asked her recently what happened to her face she wasn't offended or hurt. Instead she was indignant at his cheek. 'If I was worried about my image I would have gone home and committed suicide,' she laughs.

Mariella's punk outfits have been replaced by jeans and a striped grey T-shirt. She's not so concerned about how she looks any more. Instead she's thinking about how she should invest her compensation and hopes one day to be a full-time artist. 'I can't pretend I'm an ordinary person,' she says, 'I'd rather have an ordinary life.'

Ron Lipsius has had twenty-four operations on his hands since the King's Cross disaster. In the space of a few minutes he lost his living as a guitarist, and hasn't played since. His hands were so badly burned that charred flesh was falling off the bones.

'I used to play the guitar for two or three hours a day,' he says, as he holds his scarred fingers out to the physiotherapist. She's on one of her regular visits to his London home. 'I had a musical brain and playing the guitar kept it ticking over. After fifteen years it had become pretty routine and a part of my fulfilment.

'Suddenly all that was gone for ever, as most of the doctors would have liked me to believe. When I left hospital my guitars were still in the house. I tried to pick them up again but I couldn't do anything and it just hurt. I had to put them away really quickly.'

Ron has had operation after painful operation in a bid to play again. 'I haven't grieved for the loss of guitar playing,' he says. 'I have this big plan that I will eventually do it again.' Ron has to admit that his hopes are beginning to fade. The physiotherapist bends his fingers backwards and forwards on the kitchen table. He winces occasionally, but after years of treatment he's used to it and barely seems to notice. He carries on talking and she helps him to recall what happened.

Ron wants to talk about the night of the disaster but finds it difficult. He starts: 'So many things about it were beyond my earthly experience. It was such a disgusting place to be; it was like an incinerator. The heat was so severe it felt as if I had put my face in the oven and left it there. I wanted to pull it out but I couldn't. It had to be the most disgusting smell I'd ever smelt, like a hundred years of filth, skin cells and chemicals. The sound of the fire was creepy and the atmosphere didn't have a drop of water. It was dry, crackly, echoing, like a whispering gallery, and I could hear everybody's little prayer to Jesus.

'Visually it was totally bizarre, like science fiction. I saw the biggest cloud of billowing flame in front of me – it put the fear of God into me. I felt so insignificant. I felt as if this thing could eat me up and do anything it wanted to.' He remembers hitting the ground, his jacket and hair on fire, and yet he still picked up his hold-all, he wasn't going to leave it behind in hell.

Ron was on his way from a session at the studios to play basketball when it happened. The mother of a close friend, who was with him, failed to get through the fire and died. When Ron made it out of the inferno he wandered round the pavement in a daze.

He tried to cross a normally busy road, to make it to the firemen on the other side and tell them he needed an ambulance. The road had been closed off and was empty of traffic. 'My legs started going and I had to turn round and go back,' he says. 'My whole body started trembling and shivering in shock. I felt uncontrollably cold and I could hardly breathe.

'An old woman, who I think was a beggar, was standing on the central reservation. I was mumbling and I'm sure she didn't know what I was talking about. She looked at my face in a strange way and I had no idea why, then she looked down at my hands and pointed to them. That's when I first noticed that my hands were burnt.' They were so badly burnt that the nerves had been killed and he didn't feel the pain. He was in agony with the less severe burns under his neck and on his back.

Ron spent three months in University College Hospital in London. He was twenty-seven, and at first he couldn't come to terms with the fact that his life had been shattered and he would have to make a new start. It was enough to cope with the appalling images of the disaster that came into his mind every time he dozed off, waking him up, and making him jump up in bed every five minutes.

Ron was separated from his wife Sally at the time of the disaster, but 'she was superb,' he says. 'She was there all the time and was almost like a nurse. She used to sleep at the bottom of my bed. The disaster completely changed our marriage.' They are now back together again and have two children.

In those early days in hospital Ron cried in agony and had to be given heroin for the pain. He pulls out a series of photographs showing his burns at different stages. 'That's really good horror movie stuff,' he says as he turns the pages of the album.

One photograph shows where the surgeon had cut flaps into his skin near his groin and put his hands inside. They were stitched in to try to get skin from his body to grow on. Afterwards his hands had huge chunks of flesh on and the flesh had to be cut down to make them a normal size again.

Ron felt ashamed of his hands when he left hospital. 'Before the fire I used to look at people who had hideous things wrong with them and think, "You poor man, I wouldn't want to be you for all the world." Suddenly it *was* me. I didn't want pity. If I wanted a good little cry I could start feeling sorry for myself, but it's not good to feel sad so I avoid it.'

He doesn't enjoy socializing as much as he used to and is conscious of the scars on his face. 'I used to have really nice skin. Now if the sun shines it goes bright red and blotchy. It's not nice to age ten years overnight. I don't feel as good about myself.'

Nine months after the disaster Ron and Sally went out for the evening to visit friends. 'As soon as I came home I went into an incredible depression,' he recalls. 'I couldn't stop crying into the pillow and I couldn't tell Sally what was wrong. I had never cried like it before, it was really deep sorrow and anguish.'

Ron fears that the disaster was a punishment. His mind goes back to the vagrant who once approached him at King's Cross station asking him for money. 'I was in a hurry and told him he was obstructing me,' he recalls. 'He turned round as I was walking away and gave me a volley of abuse, like something out of a movie. He was condemning me, telling me that I'd come to a sticky end. I remember walking away feeling uneasy.'

Ron still feels that life is unreal. There's an incredible bitterness inside. 'I want to assemble a little courtroom and get all those people together who were responsible for the disaster. I want to hold them by the hair and say: "See what happens when you do that." I want them all to say: "I'm really sorry, it's dreadful." '

At the same time the fight has gone out of his life and he has lost his drive and ambition. The disaster has made him realize that he's not as lucky as he thought he was. 'That's a really big cutting–down to size,' he says. 'I could say that life is great and it was a little hiccup. I really want to see it that way but I can't.

'Everyone has goals but I think I'm not going to pursue anything with any vigour at all. When I was in hospital people used to come in and visit me, taking lunch–breaks off from their manic little lives. It seemed so foolish. I wished they could step back for a second.

'I don't enjoy going back to the way of life I used to have. What most people see as a successful way of life doesn't impress me. It could be that I'm rebelling against doing anything.'

Ron has started composing music again and is trying to convince himself that any way of making music will do. He has excavated the basement of his terraced house and plans to use it as a studio. He wants to create music using computer technology. 'If I had that I might have some fun again in life,' he continues.

'I do like composing music and my guitar isn't my exclusive interest as an instrument to compose for.' The guitar used to be his composing partner, now he has started playing the piano. 'I do still get a buzz from music,' he says, 'but if I thought about how much fun I had with the guitar I would be really desolate.'

★

Rosalind Leech plays with the cross on the chain round her neck as she speaks. Her long slender fingers are still scarred from her burns. Well worn and dry, they look like the fingers of a fisherman. Her slightly scarred cheek is almost hidden beneath her mid-brown hair. She wears small pearl earrings and a flowered dress.

Rosalind has changed since the King's Cross disaster and she's pleased about it. Before she didn't feel too much emotion at all, never too much joy, or too much sadness. 'Now because I have experienced a greater degree of depression and pain I can also experience greater joy,' she says.

In her twenty-eight years Rosalind had never found it easy to be close to people. She was close to God and she was beginning to feel close to her friend Liz when Liz was killed in the disaster. Rosalind had never been able to show anger in her life. But after the disaster she had to cope with her new-found feelings of fury and her rage against the God she'd trusted.

'Why have you let Liz die?' she asked him. 'I felt that Liz was perhaps the person who was getting to know me best,' she says. 'It wasn't fair. I felt that God had abandoned me, that my prayers weren't even reaching the ceiling. For a very long time I couldn't feel his presence close to me at all and that was frightening.'

Rosalind was working as a secretary for the Church of England's hospital chaplaincy's council when the disaster happened. Liz had been a friend for five years, and had attended the same church as Rosalind. Liz played the saxophone and clarinet, Rosalind played the clarinet and they were both in the worship band at church. They met once a week to pray for each other and regularly went out for dinner together

The day of the disaster had been much like any other.

Rosalind had opened the post, had eaten lunch in the canteen, organized a council meeting, and then met Liz after work. They went for tea together and caught the underground train to King's Cross station on their way home.

When they got off the train they noticed smoke on the platform as they made their way towards the exit to the main line station. They decided to use the Thames Link exit but the gates were locked. Liz shook them and Rosalind tried to find a key mounted on the wall but there was none. The smoke had followed them along the northbound platform so they joined other passengers on the southbound platform which was still clear.

As a voice said, 'Everybody out', the two women began to pray, following the other passengers along a smoky corridor. Rosalind recalls how Liz had started to panic. 'I tried to avoid panicking the others by walking slowly up the stairs,' she says. 'Jesus help, Jesus help,' the two women repeated over and over again, holding on to each other as the smoke became thicker and the atmosphere hotter. Ron Lipsius remembers hearing their desperate words. When they reached the top of the stairs the lights went out.

'Liz and I parted, I don't know how,' Rosalind recalls. 'I suddenly realized I'd lost her hand. I went straight on, running and running, knocking into things as I went. I occasionally tripped. It's a miracle I didn't fall over. Half of me thought I'd wake up any second, but this was for real. I was petrified. My glasses melted off my nose, I lost a shoe.

'I remember losing my bag and thinking that maybe I should go back for it, then I thought, "Don't be so ridiculous."' She repeats the words again as if she's a schoolmistress scolding herself. 'I felt like I was getting weaker, as if I was running for ever with my mouth and eyes closed, trying to breathe as shallowly as possible.'

Rosalind collapsed at the bottom of a flight of stairs, and pleaded with God, telling him she didn't want to die, promising to set up a centre for young people if he allowed her to live. 'I believe he gave me the energy to go up those stairs,' she says.

'You're OK, you're out.' Rosalind couldn't believe the words she was hearing. She thought she'd been running up the stairs but the man who found her told her later that she was crawling. 'He could tell I was trying to say something important but he couldn't understand what. I was trying to tell him my friend was still in there.'

Rosalind was critically ill for forty-eight hours. She spent six weeks in University College Hospital in London and had four operations. Two days after the disaster the hospital chaplain told her that Liz was dead. 'I was sad but the intense grief came much later,' she says. 'In those early days it was as though the feeling part of me had completely shut down. I wanted to concentrate on getting my hands better and that took all my energy.'

Doctors didn't know if Rosalind would ever be able to dress herself, play her clarinet or drive again. For a year she had to wear pressure garments: gloves on her hands, and a mask covering her cheeks and neck. The mask was hot and itchy and had to be worn twenty-four hours a day. 'Some people stared and turned away,' she says. 'I wanted to tell them what had happened and to ask them why they were staring. But there was another part of me that didn't want to say anything at all. When I told some of the people I worked with what had happened I had to cope with their shock. My injuries were proof that we're all vulnerable. It could have happened to anyone.'

Rosalind went back to work after nine months. In April 1989 she started a new job as an administrator for the health authority that had treated her. 'It took me many months to admit to myself that I was depressed,' she says, 'even though I was waking early and feeling incredibly hot as if I'd left the electric blanket on.'

It was in July 1989, eighteen months after the disaster, when she felt the full impact. Rosalind went on holiday with her sister and a Christian group to Austria. 'Perhaps it was a train journey through the Alps that triggered my feelings,' she says. 'I felt claustrophobic and ill and couldn't wait for the journey to end. During that holiday I had nightmares about trying to escape from something, and I grieved for Liz. I felt distanced from everyone and couldn't make the effort to get to know them. The beauty of the countryside made me want to cry and on the train on the way home I couldn't stop crying.'

Rosalind had two weeks off sick and decided she would try to help out at a church holiday club for children. A few years before she had organized a week of evening activities. This time if anyone had asked her to look after a class for five minutes she'd have panicked. 'I enjoyed doing the washing-up because it was something familiar and it meant I didn't have to talk to anyone,' she remembers.

Her acute depression lasted for four months and during that time she saw a psychiatrist. 'I went back to work after two weeks but the slightest thing upset me,' she says. 'I used to exist between my weekly counselling sessions. They were hard work – it's painful to bring up emotions you'd rather not deal with. Sometimes I came away feeling worse than I'd done before.'

As she sat in her flat, she had to deal with new emotions. 'It was so exhausting experiencing them, I was constantly tired,' she recalls. 'I was angry with the people, whoever they were, who had allowed the King's Cross fire to happen. I felt afraid of my anger, afraid of being out of control. I questioned God's wisdom at not taking me with Liz. I was furious with him for taking her away and furious because I felt so absolutely desperate.

'Life was pointless and meaningless. I believed God was there but it was difficult to see evidence of it. It took me ages to do things. I couldn't make decisions. I wanted people to ring me, but I hadn't the energy to initiate anything myself. I'd become hyper-vigilant and avoided ordinary risks which had never bothered me before. I was dangerously slow crossing roads and neurotic about checking that I had turned off the cooker and pulled out plugs. At work I was anxious about not making mistakes and afraid that I would forget something important.'

Rosalind now believes her trauma has gone. 'I feel really well. It's wonderful,' she says. Physically she has also recovered, even though extremes of heat and cold make her hands feel uncomfortable and she can't use her right hand as well as she could before. She's playing the clarinet and driving again.

'Counselling has taught me about myself, made me more confident, more prepared to take risks in relationships and be open with people.' She's not as scared of feeling out of control as she was before the disaster. She dares to be late whereas before she had to be punctual. Rosalind is now a part-time secretary to the Bishop of Hertford. She also kept the promise to God she made on the night of the disaster and helps to run a caravan in Hatfield where young people can drop in for a chat.

'I find it difficult now to blame God for King's Cross,' she says. 'I was in the wrong place at the wrong time. I believe that whatever happens in the future God will be there with me and bring ultimate good out of it. I don't know why Liz was taken and I wasn't, but I know she's secure and with Jesus. I reckon she'll be playing her saxophone too. I know she has gone to a better place but I still miss her.'

# CHAPTER FOUR

# PIPER ALPHA

## 6 July 1988

'Holy queen, mother of mercy,' he prayed, as he crouched in a foetal position. A dozen other men around heard him mutter an act of contrition. Andy Mochan was hiding from a raging inferno. Outside he could hear a succession of explosions blowing the Alpha Piper rig apart. Inside the hut he was thinking of his mother.

Andy pleaded with her to save him, just like she'd always done before. 'I'd been a bit of a lad in my early years and she was the one who always bailed me out,' he says. She'd died two years before but surely there was something she could do. The rig was his second home, the men like a family. He watched as both went up in flames.

Andy was forty-seven and a superintendent in charge of the maintenance contractors. When the first explosion rocked the platform he was in his office. 'There was a tremendous bang, then there were ceiling tiles and filing cabinets everywhere,' he says.

The muster point was on the top level of the accommodation module and more than half the crew went there to wait to be evacuated by helicopter. Fire and smoke prevented the helicopters arriving. Andy believes some of the men had given in to the fact that they were going to die. 'I kept kicking people to get up and they didn't,' he says. 'Looking back I torture myself with what I could have done.'

Most of those who survived leapt or clambered down the external superstructure into a sea covered with burning oil. Andy spent an hour trying to find a way out of the accommodation block. He was stumbling along passages, stopping off occasionally in a cabin to wet a towel he'd put over his head. When he stepped out on to the pipe deck he says: 'it was like going out of a frying pan into a fire.' The platform was disintegrating in front of him.

Andy sheltered in the hut known as the white house for twenty minutes. Inside the hut drilling equipment and blocks of steel were being thrown about like matchsticks. As Andy huddled up he hoped he wouldn't be hit by the flying missiles.

'There was another tremendous explosion and a body landed on top of me,' he says. 'I had to get out of my boots to push him off.' Only twelve of the twenty people who sheltered with him in the hut survived.

They clambered outside and crouched on the deck which by now was at a 45-degree angle. One man was sitting on a crane which had toppled over and he waved at them to come up. Andy climbed up on to it but it was so hot he burnt both hands, his elbows and buttocks. 'I felt the pain but my mind was on more important things,' he says.

From the crane he could see over into the water and jumped down a hundred and fifty feet. 'I just stepped off,' he says. 'It seemed like for ever as I was going down. All the breath was knocked out of me. I don't know whether I blacked out. Then when I hit the sea it seemed to take for ever to come up. I swallowed so much water, and I felt angry. I'd come through so much that I'd have felt cheated if I'd drowned.'

As Andy surfaced in his life-jacket he looked at the rig. 'There wasn't an inch of it that wasn't ablaze,' he continues. A couple of men were in the water beside him, one who didn't have a life-jacket put his hands on Andy's chest to stay afloat. Together they held on to a piece of wood which kept them chest high out of the water. That's when the burns started to hurt.

Andy was in the water for half an hour before he was rescued and was suffering from hypothermia. As he got to the edge of the rescue boat he remembers putting out his burnt hands to reach for the scramble net. 'I held on to it but I couldn't get any further,' he says. 'I was totally spent.'

Andy was in hospital for seven days. 'I heard the doctors say they'd given me enough morphine to knock out a donkey, but I didn't go to sleep. I was frightened that if I closed my eyes I wouldn't wake up again.'

He spent three months receiving treatment for his burns. Now his hands are still scarred and painful and he uses an inhaler to help him breathe. 'I used to be quite a fit person for my age,' he says. 'I don't work for a living now.'

Instead he spends his days at home in Glasgow, in the house he bought with his compensation. He also bought his father's house for him and his mother-in-law's house for her. 'My relationship with my wife is different,' he says. He admits that stress had left him almost completely impotent. 'Sex makes a big difference, and more to women than men,' he says. 'It's a woman's way of showing love.'

As he speaks he is surrounded by the photographs of his three grown-up daughters who came so close to losing their dad. Even though he's safe his struggle isn't over. Andy is still battling to cope with depression.

'It's a feeling of total hopelessness,' he says. His mind brings him back regularly to that awful night. 'I can see people running up and down the corridors. I saw them that night and I never saw them after it.

'I used to love going to football matches but I can't go to big games now because I feel claustrophobic.' Andy cannot even get on a bus if there are too many passengers on board. Just after the disaster he was on a bus that broke down. It was a wet morning and the driver kept the door closed as he called for help on his radio. There were people standing in the aisles and Andy almost knocked them over in his frantic bid for freedom.

One woman who lost her husband in the tragedy has ignored him ever since. 'I got this lad a job and he was killed two months later,' says Andy. 'He'd been on the rig for a couple of months. I felt terrible. I sent her Christmas cards saying I was sorry. Her husband was out of work at the time and I thought I was doing him a favour.'

Andy wasn't the only Piper Alpha survivor to take the blame. Drilling supervisor John Gutteridge received a series of abusive telephone calls from the wife of a colleague who died.

'She phoned about once a month for six or seven months,' he says. 'She was very nasty and rude. I knew that she was also going through hell. She wished I was dead, not her husband, and wanted to blame someone. She knew I was the boss out there at the time. I got off and her husband didn't. It was affecting me but I tried to be positive about it. When I was sensible I realized she was really upset and had to let her anger out. Then a week later if I was feeling down I'd wonder if she was right.'

John, a father of two, was divorced and living at his mother's house. The calls stopped when he bought a house in Kent and kept his new telephone number ex-directory.

Six weeks after the disaster he faced more abuse at a memorial service for those in his firm who had died. Just ten of his thirty-six colleagues survived and only six of those could be at the service; the others were still in hospital with burns. After the service there was a reception in a hotel.

'We suffered there,' he says. 'As soon as one family stopped talking to me another family wanted information. After ten hours I was feeling the strain. There was a lot of anger coming out. They were asking, "Why are you alive when my brother isn't?" and saying, "My husband should be alive, not you." I wanted to run, but where to? I felt I was helping them.'

Many times John wished he hadn't survived. He felt jealous and angry that those who died didn't have to go through what he was going through. 'They're all heroes and we are suffering all of this,' he thought.

John never believed he wasn't going to get off the burning rig, and even took his passport out of his bag so that he could go on the holiday he'd planned the following month. He spent half an hour trying to fight his way out of the accommodation module.

In the thick hot smoke he felt his way along the walls until he got to the doors. He ran through a wall of fire to get out. John survived by climbing down the derrick, then sliding down a hose into the water.

The weekend after it happened he decided to escape again. Without telling anyone where he was going, he disappeared to a cottage in Wales for three days. 'I realized I was famous,' he says. 'I was part of something that had hit the headlines and no longer just a working man in the street. I was getting the same sort of treatment as most stars and I didn't like it. I felt guilty and I still feel a bit of guilt now, although I try to brush it aside. Many young men who worked with me didn't survive and I was kind of responsible for them. I left them behind really. I know I couldn't have helped them, I've accepted that. If I had I'd have probably lost my own life, yet I sometimes feel that if I'd done this or that one or two more might have got off.'

Soon after the disaster he went to see the wife of his friend Jeff who was killed. 'I went through hell the night before,' he says. 'Facing the bereaved contributed more to my stress than what happened.' The men he'd worked with had chatted about their wives and though John had never met them he felt as if he had.

When he went to see Sue he knew all about her shoes – Jeff had said she had more shoes than a shoe shop. They were able to share their memories of Jeff. Sue knew the man he was at home, the well-known rugby player who had played for Cardiff. John knew the man at work, one of the toughest men on the rig.

John had to cope with six months of depression, and post-traumatic stress that went on for two years. 'I used to spend hours lying in bed during the day,' he says. 'I wasn't a very nice person. I argued with friends and relatives and I shouted a lot. I thought about all the guys on the rig, things that irritated or amused me about them, and I thought about how much I missed them.'

He'd known some of the men for twenty years. They'd worked around the world together in harsh and uncompromising conditions. After their deaths he imagined he saw their faces in the High Street. 'I'd walk up to within a couple of paces of them and their faces would change,' he recalls. 'When I discovered it wasn't them I'd panic and have a flashback to the disaster. I'd feel shaky as if I'd just walked out of a car crash.'

A year after the disaster John lost his licence for speeding. It was the early hours of the morning, a Remembrance Sunday, and a beautiful sunny day. He was on his way up to Aberdeen to spend the day with friends and was driving at 100 m.p.h. He had a feeling that he couldn't die. He had faced death once and escaped so it wouldn't happen to him. Now years later he feels more vulnerable than ever.

'I'm emotionally weak and it takes me a while to recover from an argument,' he says. 'I spend more time listening than I used to and I'm more compassionate.' John doesn't have the confidence to look for a job any more. Most of his £550,000 compensation was awarded for loss of earnings. He used to earn £44,000 a year and had been doing the same job for twenty-two years.

Two months after the disaster he went back off shore but stayed for just two weeks. 'I was still in a senior position but I had trouble motivating myself without jumping out of my skin every time something banged on deck,' he says. His job was highly skilled but wasn't useful in any other industry.

Afterwards he trained to be a goldsmith. He completed a foundation year but didn't have the confidence to go on to the full-time course. 'I don't know what I'm going to do now,' he says. 'My whole career has gone.'

Like many others John found support talking to his friends who had also survived. He regularly speaks on the telephone to Fred Busby who worked with him as a driller on Piper Alpha. John lives in the south of England, Fred in the north of Scotland, but despite the distance they are closer than most friends because of what they've been through together.

Fred had worked off shore for fifteen years when the disaster happened. It had been his life ever since he was eighteen, and his complexion was rugged from years of exposure to wind and rain. Since the disaster he has swapped the harsh conditions on an oil rig for a completely different occupation.

Fred now sells clothes in the fashion shop he bought with his compensation and he loves his new way of life.

'I'm not interested in going back off shore,' he says. 'I miss the friendship and the laughs we used to have, but it's not a good job. It's dirty and noisy and I feel lucky to have got away. I value my family more now and life as a whole.'

Fred, his wife and four young children live in a picturesque stone cottage in Huntley near Aberdeen. 'It's hard for me to talk about personal things,' he admits, as he gets up from the table to walk round the kitchen. Fred still shakes if his wife burns the toast. The smell of smoke takes him back to the worst night of his life.

The picture of the rig is still in front of his eyes, he could see it from the water as he waited to be rescued. He can still see the men he left behind desperately trying to escape. 'It looked like a frying-pan sitting on a gas ring,' he says, pointing over to the cooker in his cosy kitchen.

Fred was with John Gutteridge when the first explosion happened. 'I don't remember hearing anything,' he says. 'I was sitting on my chair in the drilling office when suddenly I was lying on my back. I ran outside and I could see a big tunnel of black smoke sweeping across the pipe deck. I got down on to my knees and crawled beneath it.'

Fred spent forty-five minutes trying to get off the burning rig. The noise of the fire was deafening as he squeezed through hatches, climbed up windbreaks and crawled along walkways, his nose scraping the metal.

Like John he survived by sliding down a four-inch-wide hose that stopped twenty feet above the sea and dropping off the end. He was in the water for five minutes before he was rescued. A multinational flotilla of ships helped to pull survivors from the sea.

Fred and John were taken to the Tharos, a semi-submersible rig which was alongside the Piper Alpha at the time of the blast. It had full medical equipment and trained medical staff. The two men watched the inferno they had left behind through the porthole windows. Even in the most desperate of situations they were trying to make light of things.

The following night Fred was safely back home and his house in Aberdeen was full of friends who'd come to visit. At 3 a.m., long after they'd gone, he walked alone, in pitch blackness, through the peaceful lanes nearby. 'I felt as if a big weight was lifting off me,' he recalls.

In the months that followed that euphoria disappeared. Fred became short tempered, drank too much and even thought about suicide. 'I'd blow my top for no reason. I'd shout and storm out of the house into the car and I'd come back eight hours later. I'd snap at the children for no apparent reason,' he recalls. At night he slept for just a couple of hours, during the day he sat around feeling lethargic.

Five months after the disaster Fred went to a reunion of survivors in a local hotel. He got drunk and started running round looking for doors, behaving as if he was trying to get off the rig again. 'I was crying but I can't remember what was going through my head.' he says. 'It was a sort of grief. I went on a binge for two days after that and I didn't come home.

'The reunion was on Friday and I drank all through Saturday and didn't phone my wife. I booked into another hotel in Aberdeen and drank all the next day. After that my wife didn't talk to me.' His relationship with his wife Alison is now closer than ever. 'I love her,' he says. 'She supported me through the bad times and helped me through it.'

Fred wasn't used to revealing his feelings but for seven months he talked about them openly to a psychiatrist. There isn't a day when the disaster doesn't go through his mind. Every time he has a flashback he tells himself to relax, he breathes deeply and counts. 'My feelings are the same as they were at the start,' he continues. 'I've just got used to them and I'm coping better. It's not such a big shock now.'

Billy Barren went to twenty-three funerals in the weeks after the Piper Alpha disaster. He dressed day after day in his black suit. Like Fred he sought comfort in alcohol, and spent three months drinking his way to oblivion. 'I was drinking a bottle and a half of whisky a day,' says Billy who was fifty-three when the disaster happened. 'I must have been turning into an alcoholic.

'I went to places where I knew other oil guys would be before they went off shore. I intended to speak to them, to get back to what it used to be like. But when I knew there were oil men at the bar I couldn't bring myself to start talking to them. When it came to the crunch I couldn't say I'd worked off shore.'

Billy spent all day in the pub, all night watching television. He was too frightened of his dreams to sleep. Then one day he decided that drinking wasn't the answer. 'I saw someone worse off than myself falling about the place,' he recalls. 'I thought that could be me. I came home, got a spade out of the shed and dug the garden, six feet deep. The neighbours asked me if I was trying to dig to Australia. Thank God it wasn't a big garden – I'd still be there now.'

Billy used to drive his car at speeds of over 120 m.p.h. 'I think I had a death wish,' he says. Even now he thinks he's living on borrowed time. 'My father died a month ago and I didn't show any emotion. I've probably blocked off feeling,' he says.

Billy admits that if he hadn't received his £290,000 compensation he'd have probably gone off shore again. Instead he's working as a part-time gamekeeper, a dramatic change from his job as foreman in charge of the painters on Piper Alpha.

When the disaster happened Billy was in the cinema on the rig, watching a comedy film. 'I heard a loud bang. It brought us out of our seats and I remember the screen falling down,' he says. 'I knew it was a big one, but I always thought if an explosion happened they'd get us off. I'd make my way to the muster station and the supervisor would see to it.' The canteen was so full he could hardly squeeze through the door.

Billy tried to make his way outside but was turned back by the flames and smoke. The men inside had started to cough and splutter. He tried to get out again and was relieved to discover that the flames he'd seen at the end of the passageway came from nothing more than a burning skip. Out on the pipe deck he made his way down to the 84-foot level by scaling a siren used to warn ships.

Another major explosion shook the rig and there were flames everywhere. Gripped with terror, he knew he couldn't stay on the burning platform, but he couldn't swim and it was just as frightening to jump into the sea. 'All I could think about was getting into the water but I didn't know what I was going to do when I got there,' he says.

Billy had no choice. He climbed down a rope and dangled on the end five feet above the water. Burning pieces of metal cascaded from above on top of his head. His arms were aching but he clung on, going up and down with the swell of the water. It was seven minutes before he was rescued.

From the Tharos Billy watched the remains of the rig disappear. 'The worst part was seeing the accommodation section fall into the sea,' he says. 'I knew a lot of people in there would have still been alive.'

It took a year for him to decide he needed to see a psychiatrist, before that he was determined not to have anything to do with the 'head shrinks'. One of his best therapies was to model for the Piper Alpha memorial.

Billy spent almost a year posing for the huge bronze figures featured on top. Standing still for up to four hours at a time in different offshore uniforms, he thought about the rig and the men he'd known. The memorial was unveiled in the North Sea Rose Garden in July 1991 by Her Majesty Queen Elizabeth, the Queen Mother.

Billy, who has a wife and grown-up daughter, started feeling better at about the same time. There are weeks now when he feels as if the disaster never happened. Then he reads a story about it in a newspaper and it comes flooding back again.

His family say his character has changed. 'I'm a bit short tempered,' he says. 'If I'm doing a job and I don't remember where I put something I go mad. Last week I smashed up the dog kennel and rebuilt it. I felt I had to do something destructive that day and it was the one thing that needed repairing.'

Survivor John Wood decided to reshape his whole life after the Piper Alpha disaster. The father of three changed jobs and moved house with his family. They gradually fell out with most of their neighbours. 'We lived in a close-knit community and before the disaster we'd regularly go round for a drink or maybe go out with them,' he says. Afterwards John craved isolation and started to show that he didn't want to be part of the community.

'The lifestyle we had and the way we were had gone. We were like new people to them,' he says. 'They couldn't understand and started dictating what we should be doing and what was best for us. They were making comments like: "You should be all right now. Don't you think it's about time you did this or that?"

'The garden was looking a mess because I wasn't interested in it and they said: "Isn't it about time you cut your grass?" When we moved I wanted to make a fresh start. A lot of people thought we were running away; instead we were doing what we wanted to do.'

The family moved from Gosport in Hampshire to Somerset in 1991. John, once a respected diving technician, is now a science technician in a senior school, 'a fetch and carry merchant for the teachers', he calls himself.

He has told no one except the school secretary that he survived Piper Alpha. 'People can be so cruel,' he says. 'You wonder if they really understand or if they think you are feeling sorry for yourself. No one knows anything about me now. It's pointless telling them.'

It isn't John's first job since the disaster. He also worked as an engine fitter but the job reminded him too much of the rig. He could see the faces of those who died and imagined they were working there. Three weeks after the disaster he tried to go off shore but stayed for just a month. 'I went on to a diving ship but I was useless,' he says. 'We were working alongside a platform and I could imagine it blowing up.

'I couldn't wait to get off but I was frightened of the future and where money was going to come from. I felt that I'd let myself and my family down by not carrying on as normal. I'd always been a good provider. I felt that if I couldn't do that any more I wasn't such a man.'

John still misses his life off shore. He'd been on Piper Alpha for five years and had a responsible job. When the first explosion happened he was working on the dive complex, sixty-eight feet above sea level.

He remembers the huge bang. 'Everything fell on to

the floor and I couldn't understand how the heavy duty emergency exit doors had blown open. There was a strange silence. Things had stopped working. There was a noise in the background I wasn't used to, a high-powered furnace noise which was obviously the fire burning.'

John found himself trapped with about thirty other men in a corner of the platform, gasping for breath as his lungs filled with smoke. 'We couldn't go up because the fire above our heads was worse than where we were at,' he recalls. 'We couldn't go forward because that was where the smoke was coming from.'

He found a rope and lowered himself into the water. On the rescue boat he shouted and waved, desperate to help those who were still on the rig. From a distance he could see the escape routes but it was hopeless trying to communicate. He felt so helpless. He didn't realize that seconds later he was about to face death again himself as a fireball rolled across the top of the rescue boat. 'I saw and felt it,' he says. 'The heat was incredible. I thought I was going to be roasted. I dived to the bottom of the boat and hoped for the best.'

When he first came home John didn't want to believe his friends were dead. He tried to convince people that he was still the same person but in conversations he was so preoccupied with the disaster he forgot to listen to what others were saying. 'I'd stay on the settee in the lounge all day with a blanket thrown over me to shut myself off. I wanted to be left alone.'

He constantly lost his temper with his three children then aged five, seven and nine. Occasionally the eldest would ask him what was wrong. But how could he explain? 'I had a lot of anger but nowhere to direct it,' he says. 'I was bitter towards everyone. It was satisfying to have some sort of argument; it would give me a direction for my anger.'

Over and over again his mind went through what had happened to him, frame by frame, like a film. In recurring nightmares he twisted the events. In one dream he escaped from the rig but was burnt. He always felt that people would be more understanding if he was physically injured. In another he didn't make it off and woke up at the point his life was about to be taken. In a third he was in the water and one of the men who died was dragging him down with him. Night after night he woke up screaming.

His nightmares were also a melting pot of events that had happened over the eleven years he'd worked off shore. There was the odd fire or explosion and memories of the men who had been hurt or killed on the platforms.

In November 1988 John went on a month-long trauma therapy course, along with survivors of the *Herald of Free Enterprise* ferry disaster, Falklands veterans, nurses, policemen, firemen and someone who had been mugged. He was listening to other people who felt the same. 'I said to a lot of the chaps at the time that I was being a wimp and why did they want to bother listening to me,' he says. 'In a peculiar way you think you're on your own, that you're a complete nutter.'

Now he feels that he's over the worst of his trauma and his family are happy again. 'The last few years have been absolutely awful but we've really worked at it,' he says. 'It's a completely different lifestyle to what we had but we're all together and that's the main thing.

'The disaster has given me a different outlook on life. Before, the grass had to be cut every Sunday with stripes across it. Now I don't worry about petty things like that. I realize that life is very short and sweet.'

*

Survivor Mike Jennings thought his life was over on the night of the disaster. He shook hands with his friends when he thought he was about to die. 'It was nice knowing you,' he said, his voice barely audible above the groaning of the metal as it melted and broke up around him. The fire raged and another huge explosion rocked the level below. There seemed to be no escape as they said their goodbyes.

The rig started to collapse, tilting twenty feet. Mike was standing on the drill deck and as that broke away a gap opened up beside him. He clung on to cable wiring to stop himself falling through the hole. Mike couldn't believe his eyes when the smoke cleared. He saw the Tharos in the distance – the first time he'd seen anything but black smoke for three-quarters of an hour. Then he saw someone else jump off the rig and realized there was a way to escape. Sitting on the pipes he worked his way along to the edge of the platform.

'I looked down and thought I've got to go,' he recalls. 'You're supposed to put your arm across your life-jacket to stop it riding up and breaking your neck as you hit the sea. Someone came up behind me and shoved me before I had time to do it. The man had lost his shoes and said his feet were burning. He wanted to get off fast.'

Mike plunged towards the sea spinning over and over. 'I'd escaped from the rig but I thought I was going to break my neck. I don't remember hitting the water, I just remember coming to the surface and lying on my back with my life-jacket on.' The water was warm and he felt relieved. He pulled himself on to a partition from the accommodation module and sat in silence, not saying a word to the man who'd scrambled up beside him. 'I found some training shoes floating in the water and I used them to paddle away,' he continues.

'I could feel the heat from the platform and I thought we were going to go under it.' He stood up and waved at the stand-by boats. Twenty minutes later a boat threw him a line and he pulled himself up to it from his piece of wood. He scrambled up the netting and as soon as he knew he was safe his legs wouldn't hold him up any longer. He reached the deck and collapsed, coughing and spluttering from the effects of smoke and water. His body was black from oil and smoke as they wrapped him in a survival blanket.

Mike spent three days in hospital suffering from burns to his left hand and smoke inhalation. The men he'd shaken hands with also survived. 'I knew that people in the beds around me had horrific burns and I couldn't believe how lucky I was,' he says. Two weeks later Mike and his wife Doreen were on their way to the memorial service, sharing a bus ride with the wives and families of those who had died. When Doreen put her hand in his he pushed it to one side. Those who had lost their partners had been denied the chance to do the same and he didn't want to hurt them.

Three weeks later Mike went back off shore and has worked on the Claymore, a sister platform, ever since. He's still doing the same job, dealing with flight information and logistics. 'I felt I had to go off shore again,' he says. 'I feel I belong there.

'At first I thought: "What am I doing here?" When I went on to the platform I wanted to be shown all the escape routes.' Now he doesn't worry about working on the rig. His real fear is that the helicopter will crash on its way to the platform. He can imagine the horror of hitting the water again, of having to fight his way up through the darkness as he did on the night of the disaster.

Mike works off shore for two weeks at a time. He comes home to a beautiful bungalow near Aberdeen and never forgets that Piper Alpha gave them the chance to live there. They bought it with the compensation and there's a drawing of the rig in the hall to remind them.

Mike went to meetings with other survivors for a year, but decided he didn't have enough in common with them. 'I think they were disappointed in me because I'd gone off shore and they thought I was stupid and letting the side down,' he says. He thought they were focusing on being a survivor too much. 'I have become very intolerant of people and I was becoming more intolerant of them than anyone else.'

The sea laps the bottom of his garden, and stretches into the distance. He looks through the window and his mind seems far away as Doreen explains how he's changed. 'He used to have all the patience in the world, now he's very short tempered,' she says. 'He was always very quiet and would never speak up; now he gets very angry. He used to do everything around the house, now he starts so many different things and never finishes anything. For three and a half years it felt as if we were living a nightmare. It has been better since then, we're learning to live with it.'

Doreen would be happier if Mike didn't work off shore. 'We fall out quite often and we never used to before,' says Mike. 'I worry more than I used to. I don't like doing things at the drop of a hat and I have to plan.'

At times Mike feels he needs to be alone. When he's at home he enjoys gardening and spends his days in the garden of the cottage they used to rent. 'I enjoy being out in fresh air more than I used to. I really throw myself into nature,' he says. A log fire crackles comfortably in the grate. 'I'm just glad to be alive. It's all extra, it's a bonus.'

★

Another fire crackles in the grate in Bob Ballantyne's house in Aberdeen. It barely breaches the silence in the study where he sits with his head bent over a book. He is middle-aged and bearded, with a rugged appearance that makes him look strangely out of place indoors. The door opens and he lifts his head, then turns to greet his wife and baby daughter.

As Naomi toddles over there's a warmth and a pride in his eyes. Bob cried at Naomi's birth. 'I cried because I had witnessed a miracle,' he says. 'I also cried because my mates who died on the platform would never have the same privilege.'

His wife Pat had to become like a mother to him after the Piper Alpha disaster changed their lives. She wrote a list of things for him to do every day. Whenever he had a tantrum she took a pair of his shorts out of the drawer to remind him that he was behaving like a schoolboy.

Bob was forty-five and working as an offshore electrician when the disaster happened. As the first explosion shook the rig he was in the accommodation block. He went to the canteen where about a hundred men had gathered, listening in the darkness to the deafening sound of continuous explosions outside.

As their names were taken few realized how serious the situation was. Bob even took a book to read as he set off with two dozen others to make his way out on to the pipe deck. The doors were so hot they couldn't touch them, they could feel the heat of the fire raging on the other side.

Eventually the group found a way out through the offices, and Bob will never forget the scene as he stepped outside. 'It was like a surrealist painting, a nightmare,' he recalls. 'Some of the lads went back inside, they couldn't take it. We could see the platform disintegrating in front of us. Twenty-four-inch pipes were being thrown about like matchsticks. A fireball shot past me and I jumped out of the way.'

Another engulfed the helideck and he knew some of his mates were up there. Bob decided he was going to see Pat again. He was shouting and screaming above the explosions: 'You're not going to take me. I'm going to survive.' The noise was so deafening he couldn't hear his own voice.

Bob followed the others to the drill deck but was last in line. Fire blocked his path as he watched the rest go through. He didn't realize they were going to their deaths. He turned and made his way to the south side of the platform with pieces of pipe and flaming wood falling on to his head. 'I felt as if I was looking down on myself,' he says. 'Every move I made I thought might be the last.'

He couldn't believe his luck when he found a rope on the side of the platform and lowered himself down twenty feet, then he slid down another cable to a level just twenty feet from the sea. 'I was on my own and it was terribly frightening,' he recalls. A ladder led down to the water and as he climbed down it he watched his mates at the same level on the other side of the platform.

As he watched they were engulfed in a huge fireball. 'It wiped them right out,' he says. 'I was totally devastated.' Only two of the original twenty-four who left with him survived.

Bob climbed into the sea and hung on to the platform, dipping his head under the water to cool down. It felt as warm as a baby's bath water. As he swam away there was a gas explosion in the sea in front.

It set up a fireball which came towards him. 'My face was covered in oil and debris and I was burning up,' he recalls. He turned away from the fireball, just as a child would turn away from anything it didn't like. If he couldn't see the danger, it couldn't see him, he thought. He swam the other way, only to be caught up in an oil slick.

Bob was eventually picked up after forty minutes in the water. At that stage he was so weak he couldn't pull himself up into the rescue boat and was banging against its huge tyres. A rescuer helped him up and a packet of frozen peas was put on his burning face. It was the only first aid left in the boat. It was then Bob realized how lucky he was. They told him he was the forty-second survivor and he knew there were over two hundred men on the rig.

'The further away I go in time the more I realize how fortunate I was,' says Bob. 'I used to get terribly upset at first when people told me how lucky I was. I told them I was there, that wasn't lucky. I didn't realize they were glad to see me alive.'

He vowed when he was in the water that he would never go off shore again, he knew it wouldn't be fair to Pat. The police knocked on her door early the following morning to tell her what had happened. When she saw Bob in Aberdeen Royal Infirmary she says: 'He was totally shell-shocked. I still didn't realize the significance of what he'd been through. He was trying to explain what had happened and how all his friends were dead. I was saying: "Maybe they're not."'

All Bob wanted to do when she took him home was contact the wives of his closest friends who had died on the rig. He felt so guilty he wanted to apologize for having lived.

Bob went on to become obsessed with the disaster. 'The research he did was unbelievable,' says Pat. 'He was working at three times his normal speed and this continued for months. It ruined my career.

'I had been teaching and I really loved it. He came to

collect me from school and could be anything up to an hour late. I had to switch off instantly from school, in spite of any preparation I had to do, and switch over to him. I had to listen to and be interested in anything that had happened, anything that had been found out.'

Before the disaster Bob had always put his wife first. He was fifteen years older than she was, and it was his second marriage. He'd always been the perfect partner, and a true romantic. 'Afterwards I must have felt I was being pushed out of his life,' she says, 'but I remember thinking that what had happened to him was more important than anything. I learned pretty quickly that I had to forget about me. We'd seen a lot of survivors' relationships break down and I was determined that wasn't going to happen to us.'

Bob set out to campaign for improved safety off shore. He lobbied MPs and appeared on Scottish Television. He watched every news bulletin and read all the newspapers every day searching for information about Piper Alpha. The survivors held regular meetings arranged through social services and then set up their own Piper Alpha support group.

'I became terribly angry about the passiveness of survivors meetings,' he says. 'I found that because of the power of the oil companies survivors felt they couldn't do anything. I was trying to get them to get mad, fight back.' He wanted survivors to use the support groups to campaign. 'It didn't take me long to realize that other people were there just to talk about their experience,' he says. 'It's quite a daunting task to campaign if you've never done it before but I'd been an active trade union member.'

At home Bob relied heavily on his wife. 'I ran his life for him,' she recalls. 'He'd wash the dishes and ask me what to do next. I wrote a list of things for him to do that included cleaning, shopping and remembering to pick me up in the evening. I'd send him to my sister's house and he'd take her little boy out. If he didn't have her son with him he'd disappear for hours or meet people and talk. He's become very compassionate since the disaster and is prepared to spend hours with someone even when he should be doing something else.'

Bob's anger came out in abstract drawings. 'I had to do them really fast,' he recalls. 'I used colours like reds and blacks, mixing the colours to get the ambers in. I had to ask Pat to tear the edges of the paper so they would be ragged.'

Pat also discovered that Bob had no patience with her, and in the first couple of years after the disaster they frequently argued. 'I had to be perfect and we still suffer from that,' says Pat. 'I'm not allowed to make ordinary mistakes.

'I've always been an accident prone person and if I blunder into something he gets mad and says: "I would have noticed that. It's because I noticed things I survived."' Bob always checks for exits in shopping centres and never gets caught up in a crowd going through doors.

If he hears a car horn he feels like stopping his own car and curling up in a ball. 'I have always jumped when a car horn blows,' says Pat, and she tells her husband he is going to have to put up with it.

Pat admits there were times when she considered leaving Bob but their relationship survived because they were both prepared to fight for it. They married sixteen months after the disaster and their daughter was born in July 1991. 'There are times he's terrific or I wouldn't have married him,' she says.

Bob's whole way of life has now changed. Both he and Pat are students at Aberdeen University. 'Now our lifestyle is much more rewarding and fulfilling,' says Pat. 'I sometimes resent the compassion Bob has for everyone else, but he is still very considerate to me.'

Bob's obsession with the disaster has also diminished. 'I realize that people much more capable than myself have now taken up the fight through the union,' he says. A new union, called the Offshore Industry Liaison Committee, was set up in 1991 as a result of the Piper Alpha disaster.

Pat is proud of her husband. 'He is a hero,' she says. 'I'm angry and bitter about what he's had to suffer. He really is wonderful, and that's why I'm able to cope.'


Iain Leetham is awake bright and early every morning. Life is short enough, he complains, and he's determined not to miss any of the day. Before Piper Alpha he lived life for the moment. 'People used to ask me when I was going to act my age,' he remembers. 'Life was a game I enjoyed playing, now it's a game I have to conquer.'

He was twenty-seven when the disaster happened and he believes it made him grow up. He has responsibilities now: a daughter born just after it happened, and a house in Montrose.

Iain was a crew member on a stand-by vessel, the Sandhaven. In his three years on the ship, he'd joked about what it would be like if Piper Alpha blew up. Never in his worst nightmare did he really imagine it happening.

When the 'man overboard' alarm sounded Iain and two of his colleagues jumped into a fast rescue craft. In the fading light of dusk they could see smoke billowing from the platform. As they came closer they saw flames underneath. 'Oh my God, this is what we're getting paid for,' they thought. Iain can't remember feeling afraid.

It seemed like an eternity as they watched another boat, tucked in against the legs of the platform, picking up survivors. As they waited for it to move they rescued one man out of the water. Then it was their turn to go in. Three men came down and were helped into the boat. 'It was so hot it felt as if we were underneath a grill,' says Iain.

As the boat was pulling away two men landed in the water behind them and they turned around to pick them up. The boat became tangled up in ropes and the debris from the rig. They were trapped to the legs of the rig like flies to fly paper.

With hearts thumping in terror, Iain and his friend Malcolm tried slashing off the ropes with knives. Then they heard a huge explosion above. A fireball blew out from the sides and blasted straight over the top of the boat. Iain was lucky, he was blown over the side and into the water, but his two colleagues and the six rescued men were killed.

The water was alight and as Iain lay on his back flames burnt his hands and his face. His natural instinct was to get below the fire but the equipment he was wearing kept him on the surface. He thought he was going to die.

Iain was about to give up when he looked around and the fire in the water had disappeared. He lay still, trying to decide which way to swim. Back underneath the leg of the rig he went and out at the far side. Hanging on to another leg he could see a fire-fighting ship about forty feet away. 'If only I could get to that,' he thought. Above him explosions were destroying the rig, and with every bang the leg shook ferociously. He was so hot his ears were burning and he occasionally dipped his head into the water to cool off.

There was no choice but to let go of the leg. 'Rage and fury kept me going,' he says. He'd been furious ever since the fireball hit the boat and that had helped him to survive. Iain swam out to the ship. Just as he was about to climb the ladder the ship rolled and he was sucked under the surface. 'I thought I was going to be minced,' he recalls. Then a crew member threw him a rope and pulled him along to the ladder. Anger and determination helped him to climb up.

Iain didn't go home to Inverness for two days. 'I couldn't face anyone,' he says. 'I felt guilty that my friends had died. Malcolm had a wife and two children and I had no one at the time.' He went to see Malcolm's wife a few days later. Iain had worked with Malcolm for eight years and knew Susan because she used to meet him off the ship.

'She wanted to know all the things that people wouldn't tell her, like how he died,' he says. 'I was the only person who could answer so many questions for her. When she said the children wanted to speak to me I wanted the ground to open up. They were nine and thirteen at the time. They just asked me how I was and they didn't mention their dad.' Iain would rather go through another disaster than have to face Susan in that situation again.

After he went to Malcolm's funeral he pledged never to go to another funeral in his life. 'If Malcolm had died in normal circumstances I would have been a bystander,' he says. 'It was different because I was with him at the time. We were both fighting for the same ends. One day you are standing together saying "Christ almighty", the next he's not there.'

All of Iain's anger about Piper Alpha has been directed against religion. Iain admits he's probably more bitter and cynical than he was before. He has never believed in God and never been to church but now he says: "I go out of my way to be nasty to ministers. If they say "God has obviously shone on you," I say, "He should have shone brighter to save the other people." A few of the ministers say, "I know what you're going through." How do they know?'

Iain has had to see four psychiatrists as part of his compensation claim. One said he was like a time bomb waiting to go off. 'They scare me more than anyone else in the world,' he says. 'They know what triggers a response from you, they're waiting for you to explode. I refuse to go near them. They know what I'm thinking, they get too familiar and I don't entertain that.

'Everyone expects people to talk about their problems, a problem shared is a problem halved. That's rubbish. I see it as my problem and I'll deal with it. My way of doing it is to stick it to the back of my mind and forget it, it doesn't exist any more. It might be dangerous, I don't know. But I've said this isn't going to ruin me.'

Iain went back to the same ship eight weeks after the disaster, but he had already planned to change jobs. 'Going back was a nightmare,' he says. 'I used to spend a lot of time on deck on my own thinking about it.' He is now a senior instructor for a company responsible for training crew members for the stand-by industry. He teaches men about first aid and how to drive fast rescue craft in emergencies.

As part of his job he has to show a video of Piper Alpha. Time and time again, he's watched it, but it has no effect. In fact he believes it's the best thing he could have done. His heart does start racing if he's on a ship late at night and the 'man overboard' alarm sounds. He knows it's only an exercise but it still produces the same response.

Iain believes some people in the industry were bitter about the fact that he received compensation. They also resented the fact that he was given awards. 'I didn't ask for the awards, but I'm not going to turn them down,' he says. 'That has distanced me from some of the people in the industry. I won't have anything to do with them.'

His awards included the George Medal, a gold medal from the Transport and General Workers Union for bravery and the Silk Cut nautical award for outstanding bravery. His mother looks after them, he refuses to keep them in the house. 'They remind me of the disaster,' he says. 'I have to deal with Piper Alpha at work and I won't have anything to do with it at home. When I come home I don't want to think about it.'

# CHAPTER FIVE

# THE CLAPHAM RAIL DISASTER

## 12 December 1988

Helen screamed at the man she used to love. 'I sometimes wish you'd been killed in the crash. It would have been better for all of us.' She didn't recognize the character she was talking to. The father of her children had become so dark and angry. 'I was really frightened that at some point he might just explode and hit me,' she recalls.

She had known Bob for five years when the Clapham rail disaster tore their happy family apart. 'It used to be one of those relationships that was absolutely right,' she says. He was thirty-seven, Helen ten years younger. They had married the year before and had a three-year-old son and a three-month-old daughter.

Bob Mintram, like hundreds of others, commuted to work in London every day. It was a three-hour trip from his home in Southampton but he was used to it. He'd been doing the same journey for eight months and knew many of the people on the busy Bournemouth to Waterloo express. Office staff and business executives, they swapped stories about what was happening in their lives.

Bob's routine was always the same. The alarm went off at 4 a.m. and he caught the 7.10 a.m. train from Southampton station. Then he travelled through London to Edgware where he worked as a computer consultant.

It was 8.13 a.m. when the disaster happened and he was

sitting in the buffet car drinking coffee and reading his book. The train started to shake and he heard a loud explosion. When he regained consciousness other passengers were helping him out of the rubble. The crowded passenger train had ploughed at speed into the back of another, and the buffet carriage had been ripped in half.

As Bob brushed off the debris he looked around to see what had happened to the other commuters he travelled with. One woman had been telling him how she was looking forward to visiting her grandchildren. He turned round and saw her lying dead on the floor. For a second he couldn't help hoping she was still alive. She looked cold so he took off his jacket and gave it to the fireman who was with her. The fireman looked up. 'I don't think she needs it,' he said.

A girl opposite was screaming. A man, buried up to his shoulders in debris, died as firemen reached him. 'I can't imagine that kind of carnage,' says Helen. 'When my son fell off his bike and cut his head open I felt sick.'

Bob had thirty stitches in a cut above his right eye. Another passenger used a tie to bandage his head. The bridge of his glasses had broken his nose and he had two broken ribs. For over a year after the disaster he had a constant headache and tingling in his scalp.

The first Helen knew about the disaster was when Bob phoned from a pub at 9.20 a.m. 'Can you telephone the office and tell them I won't be in. There's been a minor bump with the trains.' he said. 'They're taking me to hospital, I've just got a cut on my head.' Helen put on the one o'clock news and discovered the truth. 'I couldn't believe what I was seeing,' she recalls. 'I was really upset. I wondered what state Bob would be in.'

Bob arrived home in a taxi at 4.30 p.m. 'He was covered in blood and tar from head to toe,' she recalls, 'and he was obviously in an awful lot of pain. He went to have a bath and I picked up his clothes to put them in a bin bag. His underpants had blood all over them and it couldn't have been his. He must have sat or landed in a pool of blood. I realized then that it must have been one hell of a mess.'

That night they talked about what had happened, they called into the pub on the way home from the doctor's. 'He sounded so cheerful, it was almost like bravado,' she recalls. 'His attitude seemed to be: "I've been in this and I've survived, I'm lucky."' Bob's cheerfulness lasted for a week.

The disaster happened on a Monday. On Wednesday he discovered that his friend Jill who was sitting on the next table had been killed. He went back to work on Thursday and on Friday it was his firm's Christmas dinner. Helen and Bob went to London and stayed in a five-star hotel. They got off the train at Clapham on the way to collect his belongings. 'Bob was still in shock,' Helen recalls. 'He seemed to be quiet and going through the motions. There was no sign of depression; in fact we both felt a bit guilty that we were having such a good time.'

The following Monday the panic attacks started. Bob had cut short his normal journey to London and got off the train at Basingstoke station. As he walked across the platform to catch a train back to Southampton he saw another commuter who was going to Jill's funeral in Bournemouth so Bob went with him. He didn't go back to work until after Christmas. Three days after that his problems started.

'He came in so wound up I could feel that he was about to explode,' says Helen. 'I felt as if he was trembling inside. He was bright red and he said: "If I do that journey again I'll have a coronary." He said he was absolutely terrified.'

Bob was released from his contract and found a job three miles away from where they lived, but couldn't stay. 'He used to sit and look at his computer terminal, get up and come home,' says Helen. 'He couldn't even comprehend what he was supposed to be doing. He looked at the screen and it was almost as if he had never seen one before.' He terminated the contract after six months and accepted another contract in Havant and then one in Stevenage.

At home his trauma started to have an effect. 'It seemed that the nice side of him had vanished,' says Helen. 'He wasn't talking and he withdrew from us all. The only way he communicated with me was in anger. He'd argue with me and call me everything under the sun, tell me how dreadful I was and that I needed locking up because I was totally crazy and a danger to the kids. He told friends that I'd threatened to kill the children.

'I thought: "Who is this man?" He was behaving totally out of character. He was distant with the two children, and didn't want to play with them. Our little boy saw his father go from being a wonderful person to someone who was always shouting at him and rebuffed him if he wanted a cuddle. It confused him.'

Sometimes Bob would stare straight ahead as if there was another picture in his mind. He was tortured by flashbacks to the disaster. Over and over again he saw the window of the train coming at him. The striped duvet cover on their bed had to be thrown away because he looked at it and saw railway lines.

It didn't help that Helen had her own problems at the time. Doctors had discovered her thyroid gland had failed and she was weak and so ill she spent most of the time asleep. If she'd been well she feels she could have handled the situation better.

In October 1989 Helen told her husband he was being

'an absolute pig', and went to see her solicitor to talk about divorce. In her heart she knew she couldn't leave him when he needed her most, but she wanted to shock him into going for help.

At the beginning of 1990 Bob accepted a three-month contract in Nottingham. He stayed there during the week and came home at weekends. 'I wrote him a long letter saying we were letting circumstances destroy everything we had,' she recalls. 'I thought I'd lost him because he wasn't the same any more. When he came home at weekends some of the anger had gone. He used to say he couldn't cope with his job and he wasn't interested in life any more.' Then one Monday morning when the alarm went off he couldn't move. 'He had completely frozen,' Helen recalls. 'He couldn't move his arms or legs.'

That night Bob went for the first time to a support group run by Clapham survivors. It was the first time he admitted he needed help. Before that he'd always said there was nothing wrong. For the next six months he withdrew from everything. 'He hardly ever spoke to us, he hardly ever slept and he hardly ate, but he did get very drunk. He drank all day,' Helen recalls. 'He had about three hours sleep a night and if he wasn't in the pub he was wandering around the garden transferring books between our two sheds.'

Towards the end of the six months Bob started to talk. In September 1990 he took a part-time job teaching mathematics in a local school. Shut in a classroom he felt claustrophobic and depressed. Then in November 1990 he found a job working as part of the technical support team at GEC, seven miles away from his home.

Helen and Bob's problems were still not over. In January 1991 Helen was diagnosed as suffering from myalgic encephalomyelitis (ME). Bob was still having flashbacks. Five months after he started at GEC he had a particularly bad one. It was at a time when there was tension in the office and talk of redundancies. One morning as he sat at his desk he could see a three-dimensional train coming at him out of the wall. He got up, came home and had three days off work.

Two years later Bob is still working at GEC and has learnt how to cope with the after-effects of the crash. He still has headaches if he thinks about it. He doesn't drive far and doesn't like getting on the train. He takes the bus to work.

In 1992 he was paid £50,000 compensation which didn't pay off their debts but meant the family could finish refurbishing the kitchen. They had started work on the extension in October 1988 and finished construction two weeks after the crash. The building had been completed, and the plaster put on the walls, but because of the effect of the crash they didn't have enough money to decorate. 'Every day for years, when I looked at the wreck in the kitchen, I thought what a wreck had been made of our lives,' says Helen.

When Bob was contracting in London his firm was charging him out at £1075 per week. Now his salary is £780 a month. She says: 'I had to beg British Gas not to cut us off because we couldn't pay the bill. It was winter and we had two little children. Bob is stuck in a dead-end job which he may not have in a few months' time. He has already survived two rounds of redundancy. There's no way he could now travel round the country contracting.

'Every day for the last few years I have woken up with the disaster in my mind, wondering if it's ever going to get back to normal, and knowing that it won't because we're both different.'

Helen never used to be cynical. 'By God I am now,' she says with determination in her eyes. 'I was never a person who believed in retribution but I do now, I want people to be made accountable for what happened.'

Helen doesn't blame Bob for his behaviour, although she did at first. 'Even though I can find reasons for what we went through it doesn't mean I can forgive him,' she says. 'There was a lot of bitterness and anger and it's hard to overcome. Once things have been said you can't wipe them out.'

Helen says it is much harder to make Bob laugh now. 'There's no real physical contact between us at all. He doesn't put his arms round me or touch me very often.' They haven't made love since the crash. The years of bad feeling have destroyed the mutual trust they had.

Helen admits she wouldn't have married the person he is now. 'When you make your marriage vows no one knows what's round the corner,' she says.


Marilyn Robinson made love with a friend on the day she survived the Clapham rail crash, even though she had been married for twenty-three years. The forty-three-year-old mum walked through the doors of a plush London office that evening.

'Thank God you're alive,' said the businessman as he stepped from behind his desk.

'I think I am but I feel so numb,' she replied. 'You must make love to me so that I will really know.'

'But you can't,' came the businessman's astonished reply.

'I can,' she said.

'Do you really want to?'

'Yes, that's what I really want,' she told him.

'But you're married.'

'Who cares,' she replied.

They made love in his office, long after everyone else had gone home. She laughs as she recalls. 'I didn't feel very much, and it wasn't as if it was exciting. It just seemed like the normal thing to do. I'd known him for a very long time. It could have been anyone I knew. I have seen him since but we don't mention it,' Marilyn hasn't told anyone except for her psychologist.

After her 'encounter' she got into her car and drove home. She was determined to be there in time to watch the ten o'clock news and to make sure that the crash had really happened.

Ten days before the disaster Marilyn's husband had announced he was leaving. Two days after it happened he went. The morning he left he walked round the room packing his case – folding his shirts immaculately, she recalls. That day Marilyn, a mother of two sons, decided she had to start again.

It was a frightening prospect. She had never run a house on her own and didn't know the first thing about the mortgage. She was also alone to cope with the trauma of the crash. 'When I look at photographs of me at Christmas a few days later I look like a china person,' she says. 'I'm all dressed up but I have a glazed look.'

Within a couple of weeks Marilyn was so desperate she sat on the floor beating the carpet with a stick. 'I'd do it for a short time, then I'd think, "What's the point?" I'd get up and carry on,' she says. Marilyn was in agony from injuries to her neck and the base of her spine, but she struggled through.

The crash happened on her normal Monday morning train journey to Kingston Business School where she was on a course for a diploma in management studies. For the rest of the week she worked as a lecturer in computer studies at Basingstoke College. Marilyn boarded the train at Basingstoke station just before 8 a.m. and was reading a newspaper when it happened.

She was sitting near the back of the twelve-car Basingstoke to Waterloo train when the Bournemouth train following ploughed into it. 'There was an enormous triple bang,' she says. 'The shock was like an explosion and I could feel it go all the way down my body. I remember thinking this is a crash and I suppose this is what it feels like.'

As one man tried to run out in terror she grabbed the back of his leg and told him she was a nurse to stop him panicking. The carriage was in total chaos; she laughs at how the passengers started tidying it up. Some mopped up their blood as others put their belongings back into overhead racks.

The man sitting next to her picked up a newspaper and started reading it, even though he was looking at it upside down. The man diagonally opposite looked over. 'I think that's my newspaper,' he said as he tapped him on the shoulder. 'Oh, is it? Sorry.' The other man handed it back. They sat in silence, as if the train would continue its journey any minute.

Marilyn watched through the window as a train went past on another line. It was packed and the passengers were looking out of the window with frightened expressions on their faces. To her it looked like a scene from a horror film and the people seemed to be on their way to be executed. She didn't realize that they were horrified because they were looking at the crash.

When Marilyn got out of the train she saw the carnage around her. She saw people lying among the tangled metal, obviously injured or dead. It wasn't until she went for therapy years later that she remembered seeing them. She had conveniently remembered only her own carriage and the people in it.

In therapy as she closed her eyes her face screwed up in pain and tears rolled down her cheeks. She remembered the people lying half in and half out of the train as they were rescued. 'I remember someone in a royal blue coat,' she recalls. 'They are only images. I was so shocked I couldn't believe they were human.'

Covered in mud Marilyn walked up the line to the crowded Clapham station. She couldn't see anyone taking names and addresses so she decided to continue her journey, and someone put her on the right platform for the Kingston train. 'A woman gave me some sugar lumps,' she recalls. 'Other people obviously thought I looked shocked and dishevelled and I had some blood on me, which wasn't mine.' Concerned commuters came up to her and asked her: "Are you OK?"

'Not really, because I think I've been in a train accident,' she replied. 'But don't worry.' She didn't want to upset them.

Marilyn got off the train at a station. She wasn't sure if it was Kingston. She remembers the flower-seller outside. 'I got on a bus and to my amazement someone said "Hallo",' she recalls. 'It was a student from the course I was on and I walked with her to the business school.

'I went to the canteen and told a policeman on the course I wanted a coffee with at least eight sugars in. I told him I thought I'd been in a train accident. "Oh my God, not the one where people died," he said. I was really annoyed that he knew,' says Marilyn. 'I thought it was our accident.' He said it was on the news and she collapsed.

She was half supported, half dragged out of the canteen shouting: 'I've got to tell someone I'm alive, I'm supposed to be meeting him.' Marilyn picked up the telephone to her friend, the man she later made love with.

'Hallo, it's me,' she said.

'How are you?' the voice said, not realizing she had been involved in a crash.

'Well, I'm alive,' said Marilyn, without explaining what had happened.

'Well, that's good,' said the voice.

'Yes, isn't it?' she replied, and put the telephone down.

Her whole body felt numb. She went to the last lecture of the day, and the husband of one of the other students drove her back to her car, parked in the railway station at Basingstoke. Her husband would be angry if she left it there, she thought. She drove home and there was nobody in. That's when she decided to go to her friend's office.

'The following morning I went to the doctor's,' she recalls. 'I was sitting in the waiting-room and had a terrible panic attack just because I was in a chair with someone each side of me. It seemed like a train carriage. I was just hysterical. I thought, "You silly woman, shut up," but I couldn't. I was crying and screeching and saying, "I've got to go in now."'

Marilyn went back to work two days after the disaster but left within two months. She had a responsible job at the college and was on various committees. It was her career and she was ambitious. When she went back she found that her vocation had gone. Every time a student shouted it sounded like the shouting she heard after the disaster. Since then she has had three different jobs in computer sales and is now selling computer systems to the gift-wear trade.

Marilyn hid her trauma behind closed doors. 'I had screaming fits in the house but no one knew,' she says. In the early hours of the morning she phoned the Samaritans but no one realized she wasn't coping. Her husband had gone and she didn't want to tell her children how bad she was. One of her sons was at boarding school and the other in the Navy and at sea.

'In order to keep up my career and the house and the façade I had to act in a certain sort of way,' she says with mock primness. 'You very soon realize that any strange behaviour is totally unacceptable. You're a mental case if you behave strangely so if you do you don't tell.'

*Above:* Hillsborough, 15 April 1989
(courtesy Rex Features)

*Left:* Vicky and Sarah Hicks, 1988

*Top:* The Hicks family: Vicky, Trevor, Sarah and Jenny

*Right:* Jenny and friend, 1992

*Above Left:* Trevor Hicks, 1988

the M1 air crash, 8 January 1989 (courtesy Camera Press)

*Right:* Tony Brown before the M1 air crash

*Top Left:* Tony Brown after the M1 air crash.

*Bottom Left:* Stephen McCoy, in London on his first trip away from home, January 1989

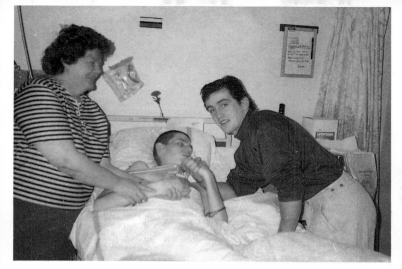

*Top:* Stephen McCoy in Queen's Medical, Nottingham. Barry McGuigan paid the aspiring boxer a visit.

*Left:* Jackie James, 'the white witch of Brixton'

*Right:* Madeline Anderton

**Mariella Santello before and just after the fire at King's Cross**

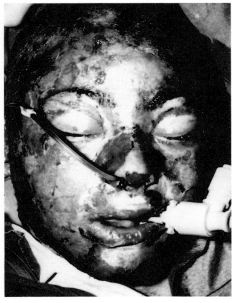

*Above:* Adam Spearritt, who died at Hillsborough. His father was seriously injured.

*Right:* Tony Bland: his case made legal history

*Above:* Sonia Harwood with Mick, who died on the *Herald of Free Enterprise*

*Right:* Sonia and Jim

In the car, if anyone drove too close behind her, she screamed. She was fined for speeding after having a clean licence for twenty-eight years. 'I wasn't speeding, I was trying to get away from the cars behind,' she says. In her nightmares the train carriages had become writhing snakes and were hanging on the wall with their insides gouged out.

Marilyn was angry that she had been left to look after herself and couldn't understand why no one noticed she needed help. There were times she felt that she had gone mad.

'I was totally out of control. I screamed and shouted and battered the furniture. I don't think I'd have done it if there was anyone here. I'd stop and think how pathetic my behaviour was and carry on with the day as if nothing had happened.'

After one particularly bad patch when Marilyn cried for three days, she saw an advertisement for a job selling computer training. She sat down, wrote out her application, put on her make-up and best dress. She delivered it, and was given the job.

At work she was successful and earning a good salary. No one knew how she felt inside. 'Out on site I had panic attacks while I was trying to sell computer training,' she recalls. 'I felt total hysteria but I couldn't let the customer know.'

In February 1991 Marilyn had to cope with another devastating blow. Her twenty-eight-year-old daughter-in-law suffered serious head injuries in a car accident and now has brain damage. Night after night she sat up with her son as he wondered if his wife would live or die. It was a year later when Marilyn finally admitted how much she was suffering. She was referred to a psychologist for a report as part of her compension claim but continued to see him in the months that followed.

Now she says her trauma has lessened but in its place
has come an extreme sensitivity. 'Before I was behaving
how people thought I should behave and I hadn't noticed
I'd developed quite a hard brittle shell. That shell has
disappeared but it has left me feeling much more vulnerable,' she says.

Marilyn still cries at times with the pain in her head,
neck and spine. She is still alone. Her only company is her
Persian cat Bluebell who wanders around the garden on a
lead.

She believes it would be difficult for her to have another
relationship. 'Unless people have had a similar experience
they don't live their lives on the same plane,' she says. 'If I
met someone who had been a victim and recovered then
at least they would understand. I don't expect ever to live
with anyone again.'


Barrie Knight relied heavily on his wife after the Clapham
disaster. 'I became so terribly demanding I wanted her
around all the time. I was worried in case anything
happened to her, worried about the sheer uncertainty of
life.'

Barrie had already survived one brush with death before
he was involved in the disaster. In 1985, after leading what
seemed like a charmed life, he discovered he had bowel
cancer. It was a 'deeply traumatic' time, but he believes
the experience helped him to cope with the disaster he
faced three years later.

Barrie became a patient at the Bristol Cancer Help
Centre which helps cancer sufferers in an holistic way. He
learnt all about positive thinking and, after the Clapham
crash, decided to count his blessings rather than worry
about his injuries. 'I saw a medical report which said that I

was a positive person and that had helped me in my recovery,' he says.

Barrie used the trains often and was a regular commuter to London, catching the train four days a week from Branksome station near Bournemouth. A freelance marketing consultant in publishing, he was on his way to see a client when the disaster happened.

'I was spun round almost like a top,' he says. 'I remember putting my hand across my chest for protection, everything disintegrated and I was dumped on the floor. On my left I could see someone's arm hanging down but I couldn't see the body. A hole had been ripped in the carriage roof.'

Barrie had broken his back in the crash and couldn't move. When he looked down he noticed that his chest bone was fractured and visibly sticking out. He spent four weeks in St George's Hospital, Tooting, and had two metal rods inserted either side of his spine. Doctors said he was lucky the fracture hadn't affected his spinal cord. 'Positive thinking was with me from the beginning,' he says. 'I thought: "I'm still alive. I have to thank God I haven't been paralysed."'

Initially he felt euphoric. Margaret Thatcher shook his hand, the Duchess of York came to see him. It all seemed so unreal. 'People were doting on me, hand and foot,' says Barrie, the father of two grown-up children. 'That gave way to a sense of anger that it had been allowed to happen and that anger is still with me on and off.'

His wife Ann refused to let him mope. 'If I got a bit morose she'd say: "you have just come back from intensive care and you have to be thankful." It was a verbal clip round the ear.' Barrie believes that Ann suffered more than he did.

She had to travel up and down to London to see him in

hospital. 'I took it for granted but it put a tremendous strain on her,' he admits. After he came home he became so dependent on her he wouldn't let her out of his sight.

'Ann found herself getting desperately depressed and not able to cope with simple things,' he says. 'She went through a worse time than me.' Ann recovered with the help of a psychologist and as a result of her experiences is now a bereavement counsellor. She and Barrie are closer than ever, and have both realized how much they depend on each other.

Barrie didn't receive any counselling although he regularly attended a support group meeting for two years. He found that he wanted to read newspapers about the crash over and over again and had a plan of the carriage that he was sitting in. If he heard about a certain person he could take out his plan to see where they were sitting at the time.

He was interviewed on local radio and played the recording of the interview over and over again to reassure himself he was still alive. Two men whom Barrie used to meet at the station died. When he went back to work six months later he still expected them to come down the steps.

Now Barrie works fewer hours than he did before. If he walks for more than a mile he has a pain in his back and has had to give up playing tennis. The metal rods in his back are there for life. Emotionally he says: 'I like to think the disaster made me stronger; at times of crisis you find inner strengths you never knew you possessed.'

Those inner strengths helped him in July 1991 when Barrie discovered he had cancer of the bowel again. 'The first time round I was absolutely shattered emotionally,' he says, 'even though I managed to recover fairly quickly through people talking to me sensibly and positively. The second time round, I had complications and was in and out of hospital three times, but I coped with it better mentally. I didn't think it was the end of the world; I thought it was another thing I had to cope with.'

Barrie was fifty-seven when he first discovered he had cancer. He was fit, had never been in hospital in his life and had always thought that bad things happened to other people. Then he had three shocking experiences one after the other.

'I think I've become a bit more humble and a bit more appreciative of life,' he says. 'I realize there's a miraculously thin line between life and death. It makes me realize I have to live every day as it comes. I never plan too far ahead now. I enjoy life much more.'

# CHAPTER SIX

# LOCKERBIE

## 21 December 1988

There are strangers in Lockerbie these days. The townsfolk can no longer be sure they know everyone as they walk down the street. It's not unusual to hear an American accent in the newsagent's, find a carload of tourists asking the way to Rosebank, or see a photographer taking a picture in Sherwood Crescent. The once quiet Scottish market town is on the map, whether the residents like it or not.

There's no getting back to normal for the 3,500 inhabitants of Lockerbie. Their cosy obscurity was snatched away one cold December evening when a bomb exploded in the cargo hold of a Pan Am Boeing 747, 31,000 feet above the town.

The main part of the fuselage fell and exploded in Sherwood Crescent, sending burning metal and flaming fuel showering over the houses. Another large part of the fuselage landed across town in the Rosebank Crescent/Park Place area.

The terrorist bomb killed the 259 passengers and crew of flight 103 and another eleven residents in Lockerbie. The community survived and came together to cope with their trauma.

Among those worst affected was Ella Ramsden whose home at Rosebank was wrecked by falling debris. The body of a passenger was embedded in her roof and she found another outside her garden gate.

Ella has lived in Lockerbie all her life, as did her mother

and grandmother before her. Her reaction is typical of many in the town. 'I think I'm the same,' she says as she curls her hair ready to go out and play bowls. 'I'm no more nervous than I was before. I just plod on.'

Ella was opening Christmas cards in her council house in Park Place on the Rosebank Estate when disaster struck. The fifty-nine-year-old widow was feeling lost and alone. Her son Ian, his wife and two young sons had been staying with her, but had left to go home to Germany earlier that day. Ella had only her Jack Russell terrier Cara and the television for company as she sat on her knees in front of the fire. *This is Your Life* had just started. It's an evening Ella will never forget.

'Cara came to me and her fur was standing on end,' she recalls. 'I was saying to her, "What's wrong?" Then suddenly I heard this noise, I still can't describe it.' Ella rushed over to the window of her living-room and looked outside. 'The whole place was lit up with an orange glow,' she says. 'I'd never seen anything in the sky like it. I wondered what was going on. I'd heard people before talking about the end of the world, and I knew there was something very wrong.'

Ella saw the explosion in Sherwood Crescent and the clouds of black smoke. 'I wonder what I should do?' she said to Cara, with desperation in her voice as she tried to decide whether to go out or stay in the house. Ella only knew that she didn't want to be alone, so she picked Cara up and ran to the back door in the kitchen. Just as she reached it the lights went out.

The door wouldn't open. 'I bent down to see if it had been jammed by the mat,' she says. 'That was when a piece of the plane landed on my house and it really started to shudder.' Ella felt herself being sucked into the house. The dirt and dust that flew past her bruised her legs, and plaster fell down around her.

The weight of Cara in one arm stopped her being carried along as she clung on to the handle of the door. Then suddenly it was quiet. 'I didn't know if I'd died or not for a wee while,' she says with a giggle. 'I've been able to laugh about things since but not at the time.'

Ella was too frightened to move. As she looked up she noticed that the ceiling had moved and she could see the stars above her. Carefully she reached inside her pan cupboard for a stew pot. Then, still holding Cara in her arms, she turned round and flung the pan backwards 'with such a heave'. It smashed through the glass in the back door.

Outside there was an eerie silence. It was so quiet Ella felt she couldn't scream or yell. Instead, in the politest voice imaginable she said: 'If there's anyone there will they please come and get my wee dog?'

One of Ella's neighbours had gone to the front of the house and when he saw that the gable end had gone he presumed she must be dead. Then he heard her voice and ran to the back. Ella climbed on to a chair and stuck her head through the door so that she could be pulled out.

She made sure she handed Cara over first. 'I'm a silly old woman,' says Ella, looking back. 'I probably could have managed to get out of the house on my own, but I was frightened to put Cara down in case she took off.'

Ella stood at the top of her garden looking back at what was left of her house. 'I'm not going to mourn for a house,' she told her neighbour and thanked God that the rest of her family had left that day. For hours Ella was left wondering what had happened. When she climbed over her fence and saw a body in the road she never imagined they had been on a plane; she thought it was someone local.

Watching television at her brother's house later that

evening she found out the extent of the disaster. Afterwards when she looked at the house on television and in newspapers it didn't seem real, didn't look like her home.

Ella decided she was never going back to Park Place. Night after night she tossed and turned in her bed unable to sleep. During the day setting up a new home helped to keep her busy. There were so many things to buy and replace, it was like starting all over again.

A few items survived with her, including a picture that is still dented from the explosion. Her three goldfish were miraculously unharmed and her budgie was found on a hedge the day after the disaster.

Ella also kept herself busy helping to serve thousands of meals to those involved in the search and recovery operations. 'I've never seen so many people working together,' she says. 'It helped to remove a lot of my frustration and stress. I was washing the pots and pans in the sink and it did me a lot of good. I was side by side with the minister's wife. A lot of good things came out of the disaster.' The search went on for four weeks and at its peak 2,300 people were involved including police officers, RAF and Army personnel and voluntary organizations.

Ella was surprised at how many people wanted to meet her. They wanted to see her because the body of someone in their family had been found in her garden. 'I couldn't believe how sympathetic they were that I had lost my home,' she says. She became involved in a friendship group set up by people in Lockerbie to meet relatives of victims and if necessary take them to the places where their loved ones' bodies had been found.

The bereaved wanted to visit Lockerbie to express their grief and find out as much as they could about what had happened. Ella had so many invitations to go over to America and still keeps in touch with an American and a

British family. At its peak there were ninety people in the friendship group but now there's so little demand for help it rarely meets.

There's not a day goes by when Ella doesn't think about the people who died. She recalls the moment when she had thought she was dying: 'I could see my three kids as plainly as if they were in front of my eyes. I remember telling them I loved them very much. We're dour Scottish people and we take a lot of things for granted. That's something that has changed since. Now when I telephone the kids I always finish by telling them I love them.'

Ella admits that she felt some stress, but she says: 'I didn't let it take over, I didn't want it. I told myself that all my family had escaped and I had to go on. Life is sweet and I'm awfully glad to be alive.'

Ella's neighbour Bunty Galloway doesn't remember feeling any stress, even though part of the plane's fuselage came down in front of her house. Like Ella she was watching *This is Your Life* when she heard the awful noise that seemed to come closer until she was running to get away.

She ran to the back door but couldn't open it the first time she tried. The second time she escaped but when she tried to get into the coal-house outside she fell over the cat who was trying to get out with her.

Bunty, who was sixty-five when the disaster happened, ran to the front of her house. 'There were spoons, underwear, headsquares, everything on the ground,' she recalls. 'A boy was lying at the bottom of the steps on to the road, a young laddie with brown socks and blue trousers on.' Later that evening her son-in-law asked for a blanket to cover him.

'I didn't know he was dead,' says Bunty. 'I gave him a lamb's wool travelling rug thinking I'd keep him warm.' Two more girls were lying dead across the road, one of them bent over garden railings. 'It was just as though they were sleeping,' she says.

The boy lay at the bottom of her steps for days. Every time Bunty came back to the house for clothes he was still there. 'My boy's still there,' she used to say to the waiting policeman. Eventually on Saturday she could take no more. 'You've got to get my boy lifted,' she told the policeman who stood over her. That night he was moved.

Bunty stayed with her daughter for two weeks and was frightened when she first moved back into the house on her own. The rain had blown through the windows and the clothes on her bed were so damp they were sticking to her. She wondered if a disaster would happen again.

Bunty never found out the name of the boy at the bottom of her steps and often wondered who he was. In 1992, more than three years after the disaster, someone laid a bouquet of flowers not far from where he was found. Until then she had always imagined he was unknown.

As time has passed the effect of the disaster has faded. Bunty says she doesn't think about it much these days.


Lockerbie residents don't chat about the disaster over the garden fence any more, but it's still a topic of conversation for those who make a special visit to the town. As long as they come Ruth Jameson will never be able to put the disaster behind her.

She was in the Townfoot petrol station the night the bomb exploded, showering her in debris. Despite her trauma she's still working there now, and acting as a reluctant guide for sightseers. The petrol station is on the main road through Lockerbie and visitors call in on their way to Sherwood Crescent. 'I wish they'd leave me alone,' she says. 'They drive me up the wall.'

'I had a carload of Americans the other day and I get

quite angry with them. Some of them could be relatives so you feel you have to be nice just in case. They said: "We want to see where this plane is and the big hole."'

The crater where houses had stood in Sherwood Crescent became well known. It was about a hundred feet long and thirty feet deep. Ruth told them it had been filled in and they replied: 'So soon?' They still expected it to be there years later. The other day the pilot's best friend stopped off at the petrol station. 'He was quite upset,' she says.

Ruth, a thirty-four-year-old mother of two, was on the forecourt when the disaster happened. A low rumble like thunder came first, then the whole sky lit up. The noise was deafening. 'I was absolutely petrified,' she says.

'Everything started falling down – lumps of plane, bits of seat belts, packets of sugar, bits of bodies. There were burning bits all over the forecourt. It seemed to shower for ages, but it was only for about five minutes. We had just had a delivery of petrol that morning and I thought the whole forecourt was going to go up.'

It was next morning before Ruth realized what had fallen from the sky. The two fingers on her roof stayed there for a fortnight.

Ruth ran inside and hid under a shelf. She tried to ring the police but the lines had gone. When the horror stopped she ran across the road with two of her customers. Ruth got 'absolutely legless' that night in a pub.

For six months she was depressed and on tranquillizers. It was impossible to take in what had happened, impossible to believe she might have died. 'I had palpitations at any time and I just started crying for nothing,' she recalls. 'It was terrible.' Every Wednesday someone had to stay with her in the garage after dark. The disaster had happened on a Wednesday.

A couple of months afterwards she considered giving

up her job because of the constant questions from visitors, but enjoyed it too much to leave. 'We try to discourage them from going to Sherwood Crescent,' says Ruth. 'It's good for business to have visitors in the town but she would hate to live in Sherwood. 'I've never been there since,' she says. 'I couldn't face it.'

Mary Ward moved back into Sherwood Crescent in November 1990, but it didn't feel as if she was coming home. Her three-bedroomed bungalow had been razed to the ground in the disaster almost two years before. Besides hers, seventeen other homes were destroyed and eleven neighbours died.

The new bungalow was exactly the same and built on the same spot. It had new carpets, new furniture, and a new picture on the wall. There were no photographs and none of those special little treasured possessions that used to make her feel at home. Even the clothes in her wardrobe had never been worn before.

Mary was living alone at number 6 Sherwood Crescent when the disaster happened, shortly after the first anniversary of her husband's death. 'I used to ask my husband what was the point of paying all that house insurance every year,' she says. 'I thought there wouldn't be a fire if everyone was careful. I never thought something was going to come down from the sky and set the whole place ablaze.'

It was four days before Christmas when it happened and Mary was sitting in front of her fire wrapping a box of biscuits and a box of shortbread for one of her elderly neighbours Jean Murray. Ten minutes later she would have been in Miss Murray's home and died with her.

The noise came first, it sounded like a low-flying aeroplane. Then Mary was thrown from her chair and across the room. Her home was ablaze and as she crouched in terror burning pieces from the walls and ceiling fell on the carpet and furniture.

Outside, the footpath and the road were a mass of flames and flames were going up the curtains of the house across the road. Mary thought she could see her husband's face in front of her, she believed she was about to die and be with him.

'Then I pulled myself together and I prayed hard, as I've never prayed before,' she says. She prayed for life so that she could see her daughter and grandchildren again. Picking the pieces of debris off her arm and leg she staggered out of the front door. If it had been locked she would have been overcome with smoke. Mary escaped and went to live in a flat with her cat Misty, who was found ten days later.

While she was away her bungalow was rebuilt exactly the same as it had been, by a local builder. 'I couldn't have cared less at the time what it was like,' she says. 'Unless they've come through it people don't really understand what it's like to lose everything – everything they had when they were first married.'

All that Mary took were the clothes she was wearing. Items that can never be replaced were lost, including her mother's gold watch and a silver charm bracelet given to her by her late husband. A gold chain was replaced with money sent in an anonymous letter signed 'from American friends'. 'I thought that was nice of them,' she says. 'They must have seen me on television.'

Mary still reads the letters and cards she received from all over the world. 'To begin with, I used to think the disaster would happen again,' she says. 'Now I've tried to put that out of my mind.'

It hasn't been easy to settle back into her bungalow. Misty died a month after she moved in and she now has two new cats. The photographs in the living-room have been given to her by friends. Sometimes she thinks she's back in her old bungalow and walks into a room expecting it to have the same memories.

Despite the problems she's had, Mary is pleased to be back in Sherwood Crescent. 'I have to live somewhere so I might as well make a go of it here,' she says. 'I feel bitter that so many innocent people lost their lives because of an act of violence. At least I'm here and I'm reasonably happy.'

Robert Hunter feels unsettled in Lockerbie and would be happy to move. He lives with his wife and two children just round the corner from Mary in Sherwood Park. 'Lockerbie is known as a very violent place now, and it wasn't before,' he says.

After the disaster Robert occasionally became involved in a fight. 'I drank a lot for two years afterwards,' he says. 'I'd go out about once a week and get absolutely legless.'

Robert was in a hotel in the middle of town when it happened. He still feels guilty that he wasn't at home with his wife and children. The house, just over a hundred yards away from the crater, was slightly damaged but the family escaped. They didn't escape the effect of the disaster.

'Lockerbie was like a different town for a while,' says Robert, a machine operator in a local dairy. 'You'd see glum faces walking along the street. They looked as if they would have felt guilty if they'd smiled.' For the first year there were so many sightseers in the area he sometimes found it difficult to get into his drive.

'The ones who were here for a reason would stop and ask you questions,' he says. 'The ones who were here to be nosy were too embarrassed.' In amazement he watched from his window as a photographic club parked their minibus at the corner and started taking photographs. Some visitors took cuttings from hedges, and flowers from the gardens.

Well over a thousand media representatives descended on the small town and they met with hostility from some of the residents, including Robert. 'At the time I was very bitter towards the media, and most people would have nothing to do with them,' he says.

'On Christmas day the kids had new bikes. There was rubble everywhere around here so we took them up to the main road. Half way up we were approached by the press. If I met someone from the media on the street I would swear at them even if they didn't ask me a question.' Robert went on to be a member of the media awareness group who volunteered to talk to reporters in an effort to protect others in the town.

He also became chairman of the Sherwood Park Residents Association. The Associations were set up in the Sherwood and Rosebank areas to discuss rehousing and rebuilding and went on to become involved in wider aspects of future town planning. At the end of November 1989 contractors started building eleven houses in Sherwood.

'About the time the building work was going on there were a lot of unhappy people,' he says. 'There was a lot of mess. It upset some people that their house was being repaired when someone along the road was getting a brand-new house.'

Initially everyone in the area pulled together, he believes. At the first few meetings of the Association they wanted information on what to do. 'Once people started building they seemed to look after their own interests,' he adds. The Residents Association folded.

Robert doesn't believe there is a good community spirit

now in the town. 'At the end of the day I would say it's down to money,' he says. 'There is a lot of bad feeling about, a lot of hearsay about money.'

On one side of Lockerbie there is local authority housing and on the other, the Sherwood side, the houses are privately owned. 'This was known as the snob's end and it has been said that the money went to the wrong people, to the people who've got, not the people who haven't,' he says. Robert believes that Lockerbie will never be the same again.

Local authority personnel manager Alec McElroy was given the task of helping Lockerbie return to normal. The Dumfries and Galloway regional council was determined that the community itself should be involved in its own survival and development. Volunteers came forward in their hundreds to help clear up the town.

Alec's task was to make the population of Lockerbie aware of the support available and put them in touch with it if necessary. He was based in the town for a year in an office in the High Street. 'The disaster brought the community together,' he says.

Lockerbie resident Max Kerr believes that being Scottish helped them to get over the disaster. 'We're quite tough,' says Max, the chairman of the Rosebank Community Liaison Committee. In the days that followed the disaster, the Committee visited every house in the area requesting help. Residents were asked if they wanted to bake scones, knit socks – anything to keep them busy and stop them dwelling on what had happened.

Max remembers the reaction of one old man in the neighbourhood. 'It's sad but I've seen a lot worse and I'm lucky to be alive,' he told Max. As he spoke there were twenty bodies in his garden. They were lying around his back door and sitting in his hedge. 'It's past now, people don't talk about the disaster any more,' says Max.

# CHAPTER SEVEN

# THE M1 AIR CRASH

## 8 January 1989

The once-proud sergeant-major wakes every day with a shock. In sleep he has forgotten he is paralysed. In the morning he opens his eyes and it hits him again. 'Oh Christ, it has happened.' He can hardly believe it. The years have done nothing to dull the horror that dawns with every new day. 'I look at my body and it sickens me,' he says.

Tony Brown used to be one of the fittest men in the army. 'I wasn't a vicious bloke, but I was known as a bloke you didn't muck about with. My reputation went before me,' he says. 'When I punished one of the soldiers it wasn't with a menial job, it was with a physical test. When they were parading the streets at 11 p.m. or working out in the gym after twelve hours of duty they knew they were getting something out of it.'

Now he lies in bed every morning waiting for a nurse to wash and dress him. 'I've been helped every day for years but I still find it a really humiliating experience,' he continues. 'My legs are twisted and scarred, my stomach hangs out. I feel disgusting.'

Tony's self-esteem was snatched away in the Kegworth air disaster. His arms and legs were paralysed and he lost the life he loved. 'I left home at fifteen and joined the army,' he recalls, as he sits slumped in a wheelchair in the kitchen. 'I thought the world was my oyster, that I was going to have a great time and I did.'

He was already fit, a 'hard bean pole', who had played truant from school when he was thirteen to work on the land. 'When they said do fifty press-ups, I could have done them all day,' he recalls. 'When they gave me huge boots and told me to run for miles it was nothing to me – I'd been used to working in ploughed fields. It was a life of such brutality, but there was such comradeship and fun. I loved playing sport, loved travelling about, loved the hardship. My life was a dream, and I did everything I wanted to.'

Tony, the father of three young children, was thirty-six when the disaster happened. He was on his way back to Northern Ireland after spending Christmas at home in Dereham, near Norwich. It was never easy to say goodbye to his family, but this time something didn't feel right.

The feeling stayed with him as he made his way to Heathrow Airport, a trip he made at least once a month. 'Normally I enjoyed the train journey, but not this time,' he remembers. 'I felt uneasy on the tube, and when I got to Heathrow I almost ran to the telephone to speak to my family. I never do that, normally I ring them when I arrive or the following day.'

There were twenty-six members of the armed forces on board the Boeing 737–400 to Belfast. Tony arranged to meet his friend David at the airport and sat next to him on the flight. As the British Midland plane lifted off at 7.52 p.m. he was reading the last chapter of a book he has never finished.

The plane was flying at 29,000 feet when the young woman next to him noticed flames coming out of the left-hand engine. She started to cry and Tony tried to joke about it, even though he knew they were in trouble. The crew shut down one of the engines to correct the problem, but the passengers didn't know they had chosen the wrong one.

As the plane diverted to East Midlands airport, the right-hand engine had been shut down. The left-hand engine appeared to be working normally. Then at 900 feet the left-hand engine failed completely. The whole aircraft started to resonate. The vibrations were so great Tony couldn't hear himself speak.

As the pilot told passengers to prepare for crash landing Tony had his arm around the girl next to him. 'I was telling her everything was going to be all right,' says Tony. 'Meanwhile I was really angry, more angry than I'd ever been before. I knew my life would never be the same again. It was the end or the beginning of something else.'

The plane crashed at 8.26 p.m., just short of East Midlands airport. It struck a field adjacent to the eastern embankment of the M1 and then suffered a second severe impact on the sloping western embankment of the motorway. It crumpled into three sections and overhead fixtures and fittings rained down on the passengers.

Tony was trapped in a wreckage of crushed airline seats and tangled metal. 'A luggage holder was on top of me and I believe that's what broke my neck,' he says. 'I was really angry because I knew I was in deep trouble. I felt very cold and in a lot of pain. Then the pain went and I felt nice and warm and cuddly and wanted to drift off. I had a second burst of anger and that's what kept me going.'

Tony was able to move slightly until the paralysis took over. The woman beside him was calling out, 'My leg, my leg.' His friend on the other side was talking normally asking Tony how he was. Then he was silent. 'I just knew he'd died,' says Tony. 'I knew he wasn't going to say any more.'

Tony stayed calm until he was rescued in the early hours of the morning. 'A bloke behind me was going out of his head,' he recalls. 'He was in pain, wanted to be rescued, wanted to be dragged out. He was shouting and swearing, I couldn't see the point in doing that. There were people dead and dying all around me.

He remembers feeling annoyed when the rescuers rushed to get into the cockpit. 'Someone in authority said: "For God's sake get into that damned cockpit and see what's going on in there,"' he recalls. 'They climbed over everything to get into the cockpit. I felt they were leaving us to deal with them. It felt like the old army thing of officers first and riff-raff second.'

In the ambulance Tony tried to hit an ambulance man who was standing over him but he was so weak the blow flicked past his chin. 'I had to do it, I don't know why,' he says. 'It could have been that I wanted to be left alone.' Tony doesn't remember any more for weeks.

The ambulance took him to Derby Royal Infirmary where he spent six weeks in intensive care. He suffered a broken neck, head injuries, broken shoulder blade, badly broken ankle, broken pelvis and injuries to his chest, kidneys and bladder. His right leg was so badly damaged it almost had to be amputated. His family were told he was going to die. When he didn't local newspapers dubbed him 'the miracle man'.

During the weeks of floating in and out of consciousness he had vivid dreams and hallucinations. During the night the large light used to examine his wounds would appear to come closer. A black head suddenly seemed to dash out of it and snarl at him. He imagined that his wife Carolyn was leaving him and taking the children, and he didn't want to let her out of his sight. He dreamt that he was in an aeroplane crash but disappeared from it, and the army posted him as a deserter. He imagined that when they found him he was dying of cancer and the Queen gave him a royal pardon. His daughter put him in a coffin. As she put the lid down on the coffin he heard that a third world war had broken out.

In reality Carolyn kept telling her husband he was paralysed, but it didn't sink in. When he was transferred to Stoke Mandeville Hospital he still thought he was going to walk again. Gradually he realized that he wasn't. 'One night in the sick bay I started sobbing and I sobbed all night,' he recalls. 'They moved me into another room where I sobbed and sobbed and sobbed.'

Tony spent a year in the same ward as the plane's flight captain, Kevin Hunt, who suffered spinal and leg injuries in the crash. Tony didn't blame Captain Hunt; he knew he'd made mistakes himself in the past. A young man had broken his arm when Tony was in charge of a physical training lesson. Tony had to take responsibility and admit it was his fault.

It did upset him when Captain Hunt had a visit from a steward who had been on the flight. It reminded him suddenly and without warning of the disaster. Tony can still recall the shocking moment when the steward arrived at Stoke Mandeville Hospital, as he was waiting in reception for a visitor. 'All of a sudden I looked up and he was standing there. It just blew me away, dismantled me, I was howling, sobbing, hysterical for the first time in my life.'

Tony and Captain Hunt never talked deliberately about the accident, but it was obviously mentioned. One day a patient answered the telephone. 'It's for you, it's British Midland,' the man said. Quick as a flash Tony replied: 'Tell them I'm not paying for the bloody ticket.' He looked round and Captain Hunt was sitting behind him. 'He didn't laugh,' says Tony. 'I felt uncomfortable and guilty because of what I'd said.'

Another day Tony and some of the lads were on their

way to the lift in their wheelchairs, laughing and joking. Being in a disaster had given Tony a certain notoriety among the patients and he got on well with them all. 'Kevin Hunt arrived at the lift first,' he recalls. 'As the boys got closer one turned round and said: "If you're pressing the buttons there's no way I'm getting in that lift." I thought, "Oh no," but the others were howling with laughter.'

Tony spent two years in hospital, and still hasn't come to terms with his paralysis. 'The world goes on but I'm like a ghost looking in through the front-room window,' he says, as his wheelchair rolls from the table, slowly back towards the wall. He feels vulnerable, pathetic and tearful.

Before the disaster Tony went for a run at 6.30 a.m. every day. Every lunchtime he played indoor football, trained in the gym or played squash. He had medals in every sport. 'It seems silly to get so much out of a lunch-time five-a-side game, but I did,' he says. 'When I scored in hockey and heard the ball hit the back of the board it was the greatest buzz in the world. Finishing a half marathon and standing having a can of beer afterwards was a buzz. Life had to be a buzz. I was bored so easily.'

Now he spends his days breeding canaries in his garage or going with his wife to the garden centre. He isn't strong or agile enough to get in and out of the car on his own and so he doesn't bother driving. 'There isn't one thing I love doing now apart from spending time with the kids,' he says.

'Carolyn and the kids would have been better off if I'd died. She would have married again, she's an attractive woman. I had to sit there and tell her what to do while she taught my son to ride a bike. I can't teach him how to play cricket or fish and if I took him to a football match he'd be in the disabled area when I'd want him to be with the howling mob.'

Every day Tony watches other people running round his old jogging route, the one he used to love. He knows he could run better, if only he could move. At times he feels as if the joggers have come into the house and punched him in the face. 'I was a hugger and a kisser, and a ranter and a raver,' he says. 'If things went wrong the dustbin was kicked over. I was a physical person and I'm not any more.'

He flashes back to the lack of control he felt as the plane plunged to the ground. 'That lack of control has stayed with me. I have no control over my life. Sometimes I try to work out a way out of it but there isn't one.'

Tony remembers the day he sat in his wheelchair and cried because he couldn't reach the telephone directory. He was alone, and desperate to talk to the Samaritans. He defied his paralysis somehow to slip the directory from the table on to his knees. Then he watched it slowly slip off. The telephone number was out of reach and there was nothing he could do.

'I needed someone at that moment more than I'd ever needed them in my life,' he says. 'They were there, two feet away from me, and I couldn't reach them. I just screamed and howled, despair crushed over me.'

Tony is scared of the future, worried about his health, has a fear that stress could give him cancer, and is in need of constant reassurance from his wife. He was never afraid of anything before. He survived shooting incidents in Northern Ireland, a helicopter crash, parachute jumps that went wrong and a truck accident.

'When my old friends come to visit I look forward to it so much,' he says. 'It's great while they're here. When we're sitting talking and having a can of beer I'm not paralysed. When they leave it's awful, they're going back to the life I loved.'

Tony believes he is still grieving. 'When you're paralysed you have to grieve as if you've lost a loved one, and I don't think I've finished going through that,' he says. 'My paralysis is so restricting and dominating, it has always beaten me. My life has been ruined. Everything I got a buzz out of is gone.'

Margaret Dawson also lost the life she loved in the M1 disaster. She was climbing mountains in Spain just before the crash. Slim, fit and elegant, she was the envy of many other women of her age. At fifty-two she had made it. She had a wonderful social life and had travelled all over the world as national sales manager for a computer company. Now she is paralysed from the chest down, trapped inside the body she calls a 'physical prison'.

She says: 'I find the constant pain, the spasms, the inability to sit up without holding on all the time very tough. So much of my time is taken up with personal hygiene, having a meal or wheeling my chair from one point to another.' As she talks she grips the sides of her wheelchair. Her body occasionally shudders. 'The Margaret Dawson that was no longer lives,' she adds.

The new one is just as determined. Margaret smiles through tears that cloud her eyes. Doctors believe she will never walk again, but she says: 'I still have hope in my heart. I don't think I will be in a wheelchair for ever. I believe the Lord will let me walk again.'

Margaret, a divorcée, was on her way back home to County Down in Northern Ireland when the disaster happened. 'I have no real memory of the crash apart from the sensation of blacking out into oblivion,' she says. 'I remember spiralling out and the sound receding. It must have been on impact when I fractured my skull.'

She was unconscious for eight days and on a life support machine. Her fifteen-year-old daughter Alexandra was told she wouldn't survive. Margaret had a broken shoulder and pelvis, and her ankle was almost severed. Her shoulder and arm had to be built down to her elbow on the left side. It was five months after the disaster when doctors discovered she also had spinal cord damage.

'I thought I would be out and physically fit within a short time,' she recalls. 'I was supposed to be learning to walk again but there was obviously something wrong. I could stand and transfer from the chair to the bed but I couldn't walk and balance very well without holding on to someone. They thought it was because I'd been in bed for so long.' Then she started having spasms in both her legs.

Margaret had a seven-hour operation on her spine and was told that she would walk again. Afterwards there was no improvement. The operation hadn't been a success and Margaret had to go back into the operating theatre for another operation.

In September, more than eight months after the disaster, she left hospital able to walk a short distance with crutches. She was able to walk around the house, make a cup of tea, and look after herself slowly and painfully. She wasn't able to go far but she was able to drive her car. Then she started feeling numbness in her left side, left arm and into her head. It was obvious there was something wrong again.

By the time she had another operation in November 1990 she was paralysed and couldn't walk. Four feet of plastic tubing was inserted to drain the cysts which had appeared on the spinal cord. When she left hospital six days later she was walking again, but disappointment was just round the corner.

A month later her condition deteriorated and in 1991 Margaret gradually lost her ability to move. It was a tragic blow. 'It was as if I had been hit with the whole crash all over again,' she says.

Now she is paralysed from the chest down. Her only real feeling is in her right arm. She can move her left arm but has limited use of her shoulder so she can't put it above her head, across her body or straight out to the side.

'I have no balance,' she says. 'If I reach forward for a cup my elbows have to rest on the chair, if I butter bread my elbows still have to be resting. It's agony on my neck and shoulders. Sometimes I forget. Someone wheeled me over to a table in hospital. I lifted my arms and fell right over the dinner plate, mouth, nose, everything.'

In the kitchen of her home a voluntary care worker is making her a bowl of cauliflower cheese for lunch. Margaret would have been on holiday in Australia this year if it hadn't been for the accident. Instead she's preparing to move into a purpose-built flat. Her unmarried daughter and baby granddaughter Ashleigh have been living with her. They moved out of the bungalow yesterday and she's moving out tomorrow to live alone.

Margaret calls to her care worker: 'Winnie, can you move the iron please. Someone has put it on the polished table in the dining-room and the water has run out of it.' She continues with another request: 'Can you put some hot water in a flask? I'll ring a neighbour and see if she will come up and put me on the bed. I wouldn't want to ask her to make tea.'

Margaret knows her limitations but she doesn't like to be too demanding. She goes to bed at 4.30 p.m. and lies flat on her back for twelve hours at night; she can't move or turn. 'The loss of privacy and dignity, and the fact that I'm back to a lot of baby stages is very difficult,' she says. 'It probably depresses me more than anything else. I cannot programme my paralysed body to suit nurses and visitors.'

Despite her severe pain and the struggle she faces, Margaret still has an air of elegance. It can't be easy for her to admit: 'If I want to go to the toilet during the night, it's too bad. I stay with it until morning. I can take care of my catheter but I can't take care of my bowel.'

Margaret sits in her track suit, a crochet blanket over her knees. A telephone rings and stops before she can get to it. 'I've had to cope with the fact that I'm ageing rapidly,' she says. 'Before the accident I looked ten years younger than I was. I hadn't a grey hair in my head. Now I'm going grey, and my hair is in a simple style so I can brush it. I can't wear the same clothes and I've had to give up my nice heeled shoes and dresses.'

A nurse comes in to dress her in the morning. A home help comes in to make lunch every day except Sunday when Winnie takes over. Margaret sits in her chair from 9.30 a.m. to 4.30 p.m.

'The realization of what someone who is paralysed lives with has been daunting,' she says. 'When I looked at someone in a wheelchair I always thought they merely couldn't walk. That is so far from the truth. There is nothing to hold me in the right place and I'm forever struggling to sit in the right position or hope I'm straight. It's as if my bones, my vertebrae and my ribs are in a stocking with no support or control. If anyone moves me or twists me I stay like that.'

Sometimes she feels as if she can't take any more pain. She lies flat to take as much pressure off her spine as she can, and prays for peace. 'I often wish I could magic other people into my body,' she continues. 'I find it amazing when they complain about a sore leg. If they were in my body for two minutes they'd say: "This is dreadful, murder, get me up to casualty."'

If she didn't believe in God Margaret says she would have had the option of committing suicide, or taking the slow option of killing herself with drink or drugs. They are not options open to her. 'Sometimes I have a desire to withdraw and see no one,' she says. 'I think perhaps it would be much better. It would be helpful if I could choose whom I see.' The disaster has taken away that freedom.

She goes on: 'I don't think I've come to terms with it, but I look at things I can do, not the things I can't. Fortunately I have an interest in painting and studying theology and psychology. My mind is sharp from programming computers but I can concentrate for a shorter time now because of the intrusion of pain.'

In many ways her mind is more focused. There were so many demands on her time before, so many places to go. 'I have more time now to look out of the window at the different colours of the trees and shrubs and to see the different varieties of birds and insects.'

'I've also been able to spend more time with Ashleigh, my granddaughter, than I did with Alexandra because I was so busy then. I have the normal happiness that any grandmother would have when she puts her little arms up and kisses me.' Margaret's voice breaks with emotion as she continues: 'That happiness is tinged with sadness because I can't lift her up and I can only hold her when someone holds her on me. If I'm in bed and she sits on top of me it makes me go into spasm. Now that Ashleigh's getting older, though, she comes and puts her little hand in mine.'

Margaret goes to a day centre once a week to study art. It's her only outing. She used to collect water-colours and antiques but now she doesn't value her material possessions. She would be happy with just her wheelchair, a table and another chair for someone to sit in.

'I only look at today,' she says. 'Recently I went through a fairly deep depression and that's when I realized

I was dwelling far too much on the past.' Margaret was thinking too much about what she could have done to avoid the disaster, wishing she hadn't gone over to England that weekend. 'There comes a time when you have to call a complete halt,' she says. 'You have to say that nothing from the past will intrude.'

Sometimes she allows herself to look back at the good times. 'I use them as a picture book of happiness,' she says. 'If it's a nasty dull day and I'm in a lot of pain I'll take myself off to a beach in the West Indies or to some of the nice times I've had.' She doesn't dwell on the memory and is careful not to allow any remorse.

To start looking to the future is equally stupid, she believes. Margaret has never asked, 'Why did it happen to me?' 'It's a pointless question,' she says. 'I didn't say, "Why me?", when I was having a wonderful life, living in Australia or travelling around Scandinavia. So if I get on an aircraft and I happen to be there when the disaster happens it's my bad luck.

'To say it was a total disaster for me wouldn't be true. I have learnt tremendous things about myself and other people and it has made me more caring. I'm here for a reason, I have to believe that.'


Stephen McCoy walks his fingers in the air and points outside. The council estate is alive with the sound of children laughing. A couple of teenagers idly kick a football up and down the street. 'You want to walk, Stephen,' his sister translates as he sits in a wheelchair in the corner. 'You can see the children outside walking and you can't, and you can't box either.' Yvonne talks slowly, listening to the sounds her younger brother makes and the movement of his hand as he pretends to box the air.

Stephen was sixteen years old when the M1 air disaster

ended his promising future as a boxer. It left him a prisoner inside his body, unable to speak and paralysed down his left side.

His hair was once bleached blond, now it's black again and the spikes have been replaced by a more conservative style. 'He still likes to keep himself as good looking as possible,' Yvonne whispers. But these days Tony's punk fashion is left hanging in the wardrobe. Instead he insists on wearing high-necked shirts to cover the hole left by a tube inserted into his neck. 'He's so vain he's scared of people seeing him in a wheelchair,' she adds. 'When we take him out he wants to come home again.'

Stephen was on his way back home to Toombridge in Northern Ireland when the crash happened. It was the end of a week's holiday spent with his cousin in England and he was looking forward to telling his eight brothers and sisters all about it. He had telephoned his mother Rose during the week to tell her what he'd bought and spoke to her again just before he boarded the plane.

Rose remembers that the sky was 'an awful gloomy colour', as she and her husband Idris made their way to Belfast International Airport to meet him. Rose was relieved she wasn't travelling by air that night. When they reached the airport she decided to wait in the car, then changed her mind. 'I wanted to see his smiling face, as he came through with all his shopping,' she says. Stephen smiles over at her now as she talks.

The announcement came as they were waiting in the arrivals hall. Anyone waiting for flight BD92 was asked to go to the VIP lounge. There had been a crash, they were told, but no one knew at that stage how many fatalities or casualties there were. Meanwhile Stephen's brothers and sisters were crowded round the television at home when the news flash came on – there had been a disaster.

Rose and Idris waited all night for news of Stephen.

Around them relatives wept uncontrollably, others numbed by the horror sat and stared in disbelief. Every time another passenger was accounted for, and another name on the computerized list ticked off, they hoped it was Stephen. 'I knew he had to be badly hurt,' says Rose. 'If not he would have been able to give his name. We came home at eight in the morning still not knowing if Stephen was alive or dead.'

The knock on the door came at midday. 'Stephen has substantial head injuries,' the policeman said. 'He is critically ill.' Rose's son was in intensive care as a result of travelling on an aeroplane. The following day she had to travel on one for the first time in her life. She didn't expect he would still be alive when she reached the Queen's Medical Centre in Nottingham.

The other children cried as their parents left home, pleading with them not to switch off Stephen's life support machine and to give their brother every chance to live. 'When I first saw Stephen I wouldn't have known him,' says Rose. 'He had a bandage on his head, his face was swollen and he was covered in tubes. I recognized him because of his teeth and his long eyelashes.'

A week after the accident the family were told that Stephen had an hour to live. Stephen had always been his 'daddy's blue-eyed boy', and they'd often gone fishing together. Idris had shared his thoughts with his kind, hard-working, son. It seemed unbelievable, a nightmare come true, as Idris stood at his son's bedside. He didn't reply when the doctor asked him if he would donate his son's organs.

Rose had already decided what clothes she would dress Stephen in if he died. The tartan trousers and red checked shirt were his favourites. Stephen had never let his father see him dressed as a punk, but Rose had been in on his secret. She'd let him in when he knocked on the window after a night out and he'd rush upstairs to change into his jeans and comb his hair back down.

Stephen survived but spent six months in a coma after the crash. 'When I first saw him I hoped he'd tell me to go home,' says Yvonne. 'Stephen and I didn't get on before the accident. I'm three years older, and we were jealous of each other.' Their past bickering was forgotten as Yvonne tried desperately to wake her brother up again.

She took stones into hospital, put them on fishing lines and clicked them together. 'I'm winning,' she told her one-time rival. 'If you don't wake up all the eels will have gone.' She took worms into hospital and let them crawl on his stomach. She got into bed with him and tried to coax him to push her out. 'You wouldn't want me in bed with you,' she teased.

Gradually Stephen came out of his twilight world. 'I used to hold his hand and put it on to his eyes, nose and mouth, but there was no response,' says Yvonne. 'Then three weeks later he was able to show me where they were himself. It seemed like a miracle, as rewarding as if I'd been given a million pounds. I was crying as I ran to the telephone to tell everyone. I almost knocked a nurse down I was running so fast.' Another breakthrough came the day Stephen took a spoonful of water. Before that he'd been fed through a tube.

Stephen's plight made world news. The boxer Barry McGuigan went to see him in hospital. Stephen laughs and punches the air excitedly as Yvonne mentions his hero's name. Stephen's favourite punk band GBH booked into a studio to record personal messages to him and make a tape of their best-known songs.

Stephen was in London for most of the two years he spent in hospital. Rose and Idris rented a flat there and travelled backwards and forwards to be with their son. They became accustomed to the silence of living together without their children and when they came home they found it difficult to adjust to the squabbles and fights of a large family.

The children used to dread their parents' return. 'They were like two bears,' says Yvonne. Eventually she decided to ease the pressure. She gave up her job as a care assistant in a home for the elderly and spent seven months with Stephen in London.

The family had a party for Stephen to welcome him home in September 1991. Idris asked Yvonne if she would continue to look after him. She agreed, and the two now live in a council house next door to the rest of the family. The wall between the two kitchens has been demolished. Stephen's bed is on the ground floor and has cot sides to stop him falling out. Yvonne sleeps upstairs and gets up four times a night to turn him and put cream on him. 'I didn't mind taking on the job, but I do miss going out to work and meeting other people,' says Yvonne. 'I get depressed.'

Her day starts at 8 a.m. when she helps Stephen out of bed, washes and dresses him. Doctors have said that Stephen will never be able to speak but Yvonne spends hours trying to teach him to repeat words. His only means of communication is through a portable keyboard and screen. It's a slow and laborious process.

Yvonne tells her brother everything. The night that her boyfriend proposed she came home and asked Stephen whether she should accept; he indicated that she should say 'yes' and she did.

The strain has had an effect on the family. Rose says: 'I have no patience now. I'm like an animal sometimes and I can't help it. I used to be easygoing but I'm not any more.'

Yvonne agrees: 'She's not the same mammy.' Rose hides her head in her hands. 'I wouldn't wish this on my worst enemy,' she weeps. 'It has wrecked our lives.'

Stephen looks over at her. One of her daughters can't listen any more and runs out of the room in tears.

The family will soon be forced to move out of the house where Rose and Idris have lived since they married thirty years ago, and into a bungalow which has been especially adapted for Stephen. 'We will never get over what has happened,' Rose continues. 'I can never explain how much it hurts. It breaks his daddy's heart. Idris says: "If only Stephen could do this or do that."'

Yvonne searches for a video of Stephen winning an amateur boxing match just before the disaster. His loyal group of supporters cheer him as he celebrates his victory. The one-time champion cheers again as he watches it. Eventually his mother has to switch it off as the memory becomes too painful.

Stephen now makes chopping boards and bird boxes at a day centre. He blames Yvonne and his parents for the crash. 'One day he had us all crying he was so frustrated,' says Rose. 'If he had a gun he was going to shoot us all.' Stephen knows what he wants to say but often isn't able to make his family understand. 'He gets very bad tempered,' says Yvonne. 'Some mornings he's a real treat to get up to, other mornings when I get up he pulls my hair. He calls me his monkey. Stephen doesn't realize how seriously ill he was. If he did he'd be delighted to be sitting here today, but he doesn't look at it that way.'

Michael Gilbert stepped on to flight BD92 not knowing it was going to change his life also. He was trapped in the wreckage of the Boeing 737 for four and a half hours. The anguish is still in his voice as he recalls what happened. He was twenty-eight at the time, and had spent Christmas in America with his girlfriend Susie, who is now his wife. His first flight from Washington was delayed so he was late arriving at Heathrow. He missed the earlier flight he should have been on to Belfast. As flight BD92 took off Michael was tired, he was missing his girlfriend and wishing he was home. The events that followed read like a horror story.

'I was at the back of the plane as we came down,' he says. 'I asked the guy to my left what the crash-landing position was. He told me to get down, but I was getting down and looking up. I wanted to see what was going on. I said my goodbyes to everyone. I didn't think about being injured, I thought I was going to die.'

Michael was in the tail section of the plane near to where it broke off from the rest of the fuselage. 'There were so many bumps and bangs before we came to a complete standstill,' he says. 'I was thinking: "Is this the way a crash is supposed to be?"'

He put his hand down to what should have been the floor of the plane and was able to pick up soil and debris. Michael was trapped. He recalls the chilling details: 'I was lying like a little baby tucked up in a pram with everything curled up apart from my leg which was straight through another seat.'

He couldn't see any of the other passengers, or the hand that came through the seat in front and grabbed his. They held on to each other palm to palm. Michael knew it was a woman; the hand felt soft against his skin, rough from years of farming. 'It was strange but rewarding,' he recalls. The hand was warm. Then the hand went cold. The woman had died.

'I was afraid to touch it again,' he says. 'It was worse than having nothing.' Michael tried to use what little energy he had left to get away from the hand, in desperation he tried to push the seats and lockers away but couldn't move. The air felt hot around him, it was hard to breathe, and he was gasping.

He was so afraid that something would happen. If he struggled he could see part of the embankment through the little window next to him. He knew that they had crashed on the ground, but he was still worried that water was going to come in from somewhere, that he was going to drown.

Michael drifted in and out of consciousness. 'It felt as if I was down in the dungeons,' he says. Around him other passengers had started to make contact with each other, no conversation, just short sentences. 'I'm so and so. Who are you? How are you doing? Can you see anything? Is anyone coming? I'm being rescued now.'

'People started to become aggravated,' he says. 'When the rescue services came they were saying, "I'm worse than she is, and he's worse than I am." How could they know? I didn't scream for a long time but other people were being rescued because they screamed and swore and cursed so I did the same to get attention.'

Michael was in agony and knew he had a terrible injury. His energy was draining away and he felt that time must be running out. Then he became aware that the rescuers were close by even though they hadn't reached him.

He begged them for a glass of water. The rescuers managed to push through a can of soft drink but Michael couldn't move enough to drink it. He spilled it on to the palm of his hand and splashed it up to his mouth.

They told him they were coming and tried to keep his spirits up as they sliced away at the wreckage. Three-quarters of an hour later Michael was taken out, attached to a drip. 'I begged them to take my leg off or leave me with it in the plane,' he recalls. 'It was practically off anyway. The rescuers had found me, I wanted them to hold me and be there. I was safe in their hands, but I didn't want them to move me. The pain was so severe.'

Michael was taken to Leicester Royal Infirmary suffering

from fractures to his knee, a dislocated shoulder, broken ribs and a spinal injury. 'For the first week I wanted to shut off and quietly die,' he says. 'I listened to music on my headphones continuously. I had plenty of visitors but I had to be wheeled out of the ward several times. I had to be totally on my own, in a separate room, to cry. I didn't want to hear anybody or see anyone.'

Michael knew he'd been in a plane crash so he didn't feel he should still be alive. When he looked out of the hospital window everything seemed unreal. 'I looked at the rows of houses, at the cars and the people and everything seemed so small. It was as if we'd crashed on a different planet.'

Michael spent three months in hospital and it was ten months before he walked again without crutches. One of his legs is now one and a half inches shorter than the other, and he suffers constant pain in his leg and his back. Michael was always active before the crash. He used to walk, run marathons, go skiing and roller-skating. Now he walks with a limp.

He still works on his father's farm but now he cannot tackle many of the major jobs which require lifting and pushing. Instead he helps to milk the cows and works with the poultry flock. 'I feel claustrophobic in a small room, or at the farm if I'm under something or looking inside something,' he says.

There isn't a day when he doesn't think about the crash. Sometimes he forces himself to relive it. 'I don't know why,' he says. He closes his eyes – he has to be in the dark – and goes back through the whole disaster, through everything that happened. He feels that perhaps he is trying to remember something that he hasn't recalled.

Michael is not as complacent about life any more. Susie wakes up in the middle of the night to find him sitting up in bed crying. 'On bad days I want to be alone,' he says.

'I want to go away far, not physically, but in my mind. I'm reluctant to do anything or share anything. In the plane I was on my own.'

On the second anniversary of the disaster he was in America. 'I was so lonely, and I wanted to be lonely,' he says. 'Susie was there but she couldn't do anything. I remember her saying: "What can I do?" She was scared. We went to someone's house and I had to get out of the house, out of four walls to a place where there were no people.

'We left the house and got into the car. I drove to the woods and stopped in the car park. Susie held my hand, I think that made it worse. I told her I had to be on my own and she left me in the car. There seemed to be no escape, just confusion. I wanted peacefulness, no thoughts, but how was I going to find that?

'Sitting in the car on my own I rubbed my temples and ended up just coming through it all. I heard a bird chirp outside the window and woke up to reality again.'

That nightmare was over, but there were days of trauma still to come. Now he says he has learnt to cope with the after-effects of the disaster. 'I live with it,' he says. 'I enjoy life as it is.'


Noel Crymble didn't just lose his job as a result of the air crash, he lost his whole way of life. Almost every waking minute used to be taken up with his business. He was a dealer in light engineering equipment, a successful man who was always on the go. At home the telephone started ringing at 7.30 a.m., and people called during dinner. Now the house is quiet and his feeling of achievement has gone.

In the years since the M1 air disaster Noel has watched his business collapse. Even as it was winding up he didn't want to admit it was happening. 'I thought I would be able to carry on with work the same as before,' he says. 'I thought I would be able to put the crash behind me. I appeared not to be seriously injured and had always been a quiet, calm, cool person. I assumed I would have no long-lasting problems. Unfortunately that has not been the case.'

Noel was on his way home to County Antrim in Northern Ireland when the disaster happened. He had spent the day at an engineering exhibition in London. The girl beside him on the plane was working and borrowed his pen. When the problems started she told him she'd had a premonition that something was going to happen. Noel told her not to be concerned. 'I feel guilty about saying that,' he says. The girl was killed in the disaster.

'Just after the crash there seemed to be an immense silence, then people started to scream and yell. Those screams have never left me.' Noel opened a hatch beside him. A fireman who came to the door handed over a torch and told him to shout to the people inside that help was at hand. He thought he was going to be able to shout loud but his voice didn't work. He had to shout a few times before he could complete the sentence. Noel had damaged his pelvis and couldn't move his legs.

He tried to talk to the girl next to him whom he thought had been knocked unconscious. Then he pushed himself out on the wing, which was slippery with foam, held on to a rope and bumped down the wing to the embankment.

When he came home two weeks later he was determined that life was going to get back to normal and tried to act as if nothing had happened. 'I was stunned and numb for a year,' he says. 'It's harder now to talk about the disaster than it was then.'

His business continued at first. Goods arrived at his

door that he'd bought at the exhibition and Noel had to do something about them. He couldn't concentrate to do anything. It was hard enough to make a cup of tea. There were times when he'd think he'd put on the electric kettle and wait for it to boil when he hadn't switched it on.

'The ability to remember, decide and do anything seemed to elude me,' he says. Customers knocked on his door to tell him they owed him money, and he'd forgotten. 'I was always trying to convince myself that I could get back to normal, always tomorrow,' he recalls.

It didn't help that he was also in pain. The impact has had an effect on his pelvis, back, legs and knees. 'It is reasonable now, after this length of time, to expect no big improvement and this means that I have to consider a new way of life,' he says. In his heart he hopes to revive his business.

'I enjoyed doing it and I felt I was able to help a lot of people,' he says. His life is empty without it. 'Sometimes I feel that I just want to withdraw and sit and read books,' he says. 'Many times I feel I'd be quite happy to have a smallholding completely away from everyone.'

He lives only a few miles away from the airport in Belfast and most of the planes fly over his house. 'The noise of an aeroplane never meant anything to me before. Now the drone brings the disaster right back,' he says. 'There can be an aeroplane every fifteen minutes and I'm always aware of the one that flies over at 1.45 a.m. Even if I've fallen asleep I wake up again in time to hear it.'

Noel has turned his study into a library of information for the Air Safety Action Group, formed as a result of the disaster. Because of his problems concentrating, tasks that should take half an hour can take a day, and he finds it difficult to absorb what he's reading. He could never have imagined feeling depressed before. When depression first came after the disaster he didn't recognize it. 'I no longer

looked forward to life,' he says. 'I had no hopes or plans
and life seemed to be very immediate.'

He still doesn't look to the future. 'It worries me that I
don't have a new direction,' he continues. 'I have considered many other jobs and other self-employed occupations and educational courses but never feel able to make a
decision one way or the other. The last few years seem to
have disappeared. At times I've said I might as well have
been in gaol with no real quality of life. When you come
out of gaol it's over, but this is like a life sentence.'

Debbie Griffith loved her job as an air stewardess. She was
twenty-four, vibrant, and keen to see as much of life as
she could. Life in the air had a certain glamour and she
couldn't imagine doing anything else.

The M1 air disaster changed that. Now her days are
spent looking after the sick as a trainee nurse at St James's
Hospital in Leeds. 'I feel that I'm living in the real world
now,' she says. 'I can't tell you why I'm a nurse. I just
knew it was the right thing to do.'

Debbie had been an air stewardess for two and a half
years when the disaster happened. She remembers how
the aeroplane landed with 'an almighty thud' that threw
her around like a rag doll. The jump seat that she'd been
sitting in collapsed and chairs and overhead lockers came
hurtling towards her. The passengers were blocked off by
the debris.

'I could hear people crying out for help and I couldn't
do anything about it,' she recalls. Maybe that's why she's
a nurse now. 'I could only hear about half a dozen voices
and that worried me. There was a woman with a baby and
she was screaming: "Get the baby out, for God's sake get
the baby out!" I was shouting back: "It's going to be all
right!"'

Debbie was trapped for an hour before she was rescued, then she spent another hour lying on a stretcher on the motorway. She had injured her hip, foot and leg. 'They put a young boy in his twenties down in front of me,' she remembers. 'I can still see his face now. I thought he was sleeping or unconscious. He seemed to be at peace among all the mayhem, the sirens, and the people running around. An ambulance man came and put a blanket over his head and I remember thinking, "What's he doing that for?"'

It was a week later the horror and tragedy of it all sank in. Debbie was lying in a hospital bed, listening to a girl in her ward crying. Every morning as soon as she woke up the girl had cried for her fiancé who had died. That morning Debbie started crying too. 'I wasn't crying for myself, I was crying for what happened to other people,' she says. Another morning, half awake, she watched a patient get up at 6 a.m. The nurses dressed her in a black suit and she went off to her sisters' funeral.

During the month that Debbie spent in hospital she decided to change her life. 'I didn't want to go back to flying. I knew immediately it had lost its sparkle for me,' she says. 'I decided to become a nurse. It was as if something was pushing me into it, nagging and nagging until I said yes. I kept dismissing it, thinking it wasn't me. I hadn't thought of doing it before.' Nursing certainly didn't seem glamorous. Debbie imagined days spent giving injections and changing bedpans. Friends who were nurses told her not to do it.

Debbie went back to flying ten months later, thinking she had to give it another go. After three months she left and worked as a secretary until she could start her training to be a nurse in October 1991.

The disaster has left her feeling insecure about talking to other people and about her abilities. That didn't make it easy to start a new career. 'I could have gone for an easier life than this,' she admits. 'I've chosen to climb this huge mountain and I think when I reach the top I'll see a most wonderful view.'

The crash has left her with an occasional limp and a twelve-inch scar on her leg. If she can avoid it she doesn't tell her colleagues she's been involved in a disaster. 'I don't think people know how to handle it,' she says. When they ask her what she did before she tells them she was a secretary. 'It's as if my whole life has been thrown into the air like a jigsaw. Some bits go behind the settee and are never found again. Something deep inside you has to change.' She's no longer happy-go-lucky. 'I'm prepared to give a bit more,' she says.

Chris Thompson woke up in hospital after the M1 air disaster. He looked up and saw a nurse bent over him, her face almost hidden in a mask. His eyes were so swollen he could barely see her.

'You're all right now,' she whispered soothingly. 'You're in hospital, you were in a plane crash.'

Chris was so confused he didn't know what a plane was. 'I was horribly cold,' he says. He stared at the ceiling.

Her face moved into view again. 'We're cutting off your left shoe. Can you feel it?'

Chris was so dazed he didn't know what his left shoe was. He didn't feel a thing. His clothes were soaked in blood and urine.

A few hours before the thirty-two-year-old business-man had been sitting on flight BD92, talking about his plans for the future. The father of two runs a sports shop in Belfast and had gone over to visit the Boat Show in London. It had been a good day and on the way home he was talking to his partner Nick Stevenson about the new ideas they'd picked up.

Twenty minutes into the flight they heard a loud bang and the plane shuddered. 'Suddenly I was aware that we were very high up in the air and I started to feel vulnerable,' he says. 'My palms were a bit sweaty and my mouth was dry. I just wanted to get to our destination. I thought I'd tell my friends about it in the pub the following day and we could have a bit of a laugh.'

The plane started a gradual descent. Then there was another bang. 'I could feel my skin crawling,' he recalls. 'The plane shook violently and it was obvious there was something wrong. We must have been about 1500 feet up, but I didn't know it. I was sitting in the front row with the window beside me and I could see a row of lights which turned out to be the motorway. I didn't envisage the plane would crash, I had no concept of what that meant. The remaining engine started choking and dying like a car running out of petrol.

'There was total and utter silence. I could hear people hold their breath. It was like going over the top of a roller-coaster. I remember thinking how unfair it was that my wife was going to be left on her own, there was no one to cut the grass for her. Everyone was waiting, there was nowhere to run to. There was a look of disbelief on their faces.'

As Chris put his head down into the brace position he could see the church spire in the village of Kegworth; it seemed to be only ten feet from the window. 'Then I felt this huge impact, and an unbelievable crushing. I remember being crushed and crushed and crushed. It didn't stop, I couldn't move, I was just held there.'

Chris fractured his skull and lay unconscious in the wreckage for two and a half hours. His legs were shattered, his left foot crushed and broken, and his back injured. His body was bruised from the chest down and covered in tiny cuts. He spent five months in hospital.

He was taken first to the Queen's Medical Centre in Nottingham where doctors told him he might not walk again. Within a week they told him he probably would walk but would have to use a stick or crutches. 'At that point I didn't care,' he says. 'I felt so lucky I could have hugged the bed. I was on the ground again and the euphoria was absolutely unbelievable. It was total joy and happiness at being there. All the colours and smells were so vivid.'

In his diary he wrote: 'If only people would realize how easy it is to die without making it happen with bombs and bullets they might wake up to see how short life is.'

Two weeks after the disaster Chris was transferred to the Royal Victoria Hospital in Belfast by air ambulance. That's when his depression started. In England, everyone knew he had survived a disaster, he was made to feel special. In Ireland he felt like just another patient. 'I was in so much pain that if the drugs trolley was five minutes late with the painkillers I was at the point of killing someone,' he says.

He wrote in his diary: 'During the night I had a cyclomorphine shot for pain. I woke up screaming in agony convinced my legs had tangled and had to be shown them to convince me they weren't.' The diary went on: 'Another survivor died suddenly today and it makes me worry about my operation on Friday and sudden death while unconscious.'

Another entry reads: 'I always feel as if I'm waiting to come to the end of some test or something, then I can cry, scream and unwind. I am a drowning man who keeps swimming towards a far-off shore – don't think, forget the distance, just one stroke after another.'

One night Chris had taken a tranquillizer and was just about to go to sleep when a vibrating noise came up through the radiator. Instantly he was back in the disaster.

The noise in the radiator reminded him of the cutting machines the rescuers used to free him from the tangled mess. 'The hospital staff brought up the engineer to reassure me and explain that he'd been cutting a pipe,' says Chris. 'I was terrified. I could see I was in a room but I wasn't, I was there in the wreckage. I could see it, smell the fuel.'

Chris spent three weeks in the Royal Victoria Hospital before he was transferred to a private clinic. By March he was becoming institutionalized and settled in his own little room. He had plants, a bookcase and a drinks cabinet beside his bed. It was his own little world and if anything was moved out of its place he was upset.

'It got to the point where I felt I hadn't got a second to see a visitor,' he says. 'I got up in the morning, had a wash before breakfast, ate my breakfast, watched television to see if there was anything on about the crash, then shaved, wrote my diary; morning tea arrived, then I had to fill out the lunch menu.' Before the crash he would have been busy running his business.

In his diary he wrote: 'I still think sometimes that if I blink and shake my head, when I open my eyes I will be back to normal.'

As the weeks passed Chris began to be affected more by outside events and disasters. One night he heard on the news about a plane crash in South America and was devastated. His diary reads: 'If you could catch all the fear and terror of those 200 passengers and put it together and expose one person to it it would be the most horrific weapon in the world.' For three months after the disaster he cried himself to sleep every night. On the surface he was friendly and jovial but underneath he felt depressed.

Chris believes that when he was in hospital he was looked after by an invisible person whom only he could see. The shadowy outline appeared two weeks after the disaster and stayed until he was ready to go home. 'It never left my room unless someone came to visit me,' he says. He talks seriously about his friend. His belief seems strangely out of place as we sit in the stockroom of his Belfast city centre shop, surrounded by training shoes and sweatshirts. One of the assistants comes in to look for a pair of size nines.

'Maybe it was my guardian angel,' Chris says seriously, talking about the shadow. 'It had no features, not male nor female. Occasionally it would get up and look out of the window. If someone came to visit me it would walk around the room. If it looked as if they were staying for a while it would step round them and disappear out into the corner.

'When they left it came in again. It used to sit in the chair and would move away if someone else tried to sit there. Occasionally I woke up in the middle of the night to find it straightening my bedclothes. It didn't frighten me, it was very reassuring.'

When Chris left hospital for the first time he could smell every blade of grass and the hospital car park seemed miles wide. He told his wife to slow down as she drove him home at 20 m.p.h. It felt like they were driving at five times that speed. 'The buildings seemed so tall and everything seemed larger than life,' he recalls. 'We drove through town and the shops seemed so bright and so pretty I couldn't believe it. My house felt enormous.'

Chris was determined that he would sleep upstairs and crawled up at night on his arms. 'At home I felt depressed that I'd been in the crash and it was so unfair,' he says. 'I hadn't felt that before. The last time I'd left the house it was the morning of the crash. I was back home but things were not the way they should have been.'

After the disaster he felt immune, as if no one could hurt him. 'They could have wheeled me around terrorists and I felt I could have stopped them and changed them,' he says. 'I felt that if I met a group of murderers they'd listen to me. I don't feel that now. Now I feel more fragile and I don't take chances any more.'

Eight months after the disaster he was still in plaster and on crutches when he went on his first flight, this time to Jersey. He took some sedatives and told British Midland he wanted to sit in the same seat. On the way back his seat had been given to another man with the same surname. 'I felt destroyed,' he says. 'I had to get it back, it was my seat. They called the guy back to the desk on the intercom.'

Chris has flown since but admits: 'With every flight I feel worse and I don't fly now unless I have to. I used to love flying, my wife bought me flying lessons for Christmas just weeks before the disaster but I was given a refund a year later.'

Chris had to learn to walk again two years after the crash. He now walks unaided but he still can't run or go skiing. If he sits in the chair too long he walks with a limp, and his back is painful every morning.

In his wardrobe Chris still has the blood-stained training shoes he was wearing on the night of the disaster. 'I know they've been through a lot with me,' he says.

'I think I'm happier than I would have been before. If it rains it's lovely to feel it splashing on my face, it's great to be alive. I still feel like a very special person.'

Chris's partner Nick Stevenson thought his life was over in the M1 disaster, but it was a feeling he'd known before. The hardened rock climber had already stared death in the face in the mountains of South America and survived. Danger was no stranger and he believes that helped him to cope with the trauma of the crash.

'As a climber you're frightened all the time, but you control it,' he says. 'There's nothing like it when you are on a route just within your capabilities and your body and the rock are in harmony. It's a major kick, it's fantastic.'

After the disaster Nick sat confidently in the psychiatrist's chair and told him: 'I don't think there's anything wrong with me.' The psychiatrist agreed. It was two years after the disaster when he felt depressed but believes that may not have been related to the crash. 'I don't know what brought it on, but it worried me,' he says. 'I felt frustrated with life, and that I couldn't be bothered with anyone. I wanted to be left alone.'

Nick, the father of two, was thirty when the disaster happened. When the plane started to vibrate, he says, 'It was so loud you couldn't hear yourself scream. I remember thinking that if it continued the aircraft was going to disintegrate and I could see myself flying through space in my seat.'

He didn't panic. 'There was nowhere to go. If when you're climbing you're faced with a particularly difficult move and it's impossible to reverse you can only go forwards,' he says. 'You dare not think that you can't go back down. You tend to exclude the bad possibilities.'

This time the feeling was different because Nick wasn't in control. 'That's what made it worse,' he recalls. 'There was no piece of rock to hold on to. I had to rely on the aircraft and the people flying it.' He couldn't believe the plane was about to crash. 'No one survives a plane crash,' his mind was telling him. 'I wonder will I?'

Nick doesn't remember the impact. When he regained consciousness he was amazed that he was still alive. 'I thought there was going to be a fire and I had to get out. I looked to my left and there was a huge hole in the fuselage. I could see the motorway embankment and the overhead lights for the junction. The stewardess was strapped into her jump seat – she was unconscious or dead, I wasn't sure which.

'I stood up and my seat came with me. I undid my seat belt and walked over to where the aisle would have been. After three or four steps I had a sudden pain in my left leg. When I looked it was sitting at a peculiar angle so I realized my femur was broken.' Nick decided to walk on. 'I put my hands on to my trousers and lifted my leg with my hand. I was determined to get out and nothing was going to stop me.

'It felt as if the aircraft was on a slope. I had to step over floor panels and I was standing on suitcases, as I went. A man was lying under one of the panels with his head and upper torso covered by it. He was groaning, that was the only noise I heard. I had to put my bad leg down beside him, and I can remember thinking, "Don't grab my ankle."'

Nick struggled to the side of the aircraft and clung on to a branch of a tree hanging inside. He was standing on a suitcase desperately trying to keep his balance. There was no way he was going to make it out. He couldn't lift his leg out with one hand, and he couldn't let go of the tree with the other. 'I was getting ready to dive out on to the ground, thinking that a compound fracture was better than being torched,' he says. 'Then I heard a noise in the trees and two men were coming up the embankment. I shouted: "Help me!" They lifted me out and took me down to the roadside.'

Nick spent three weeks in hospital. 'At first I thought it was brilliant,' he recalls. 'I had survived a plane crash. Then I started to be greedy. I thought: "This is not so good, I've got a broken femur, I may not be able to go running or climbing. I could have got away unscathed." After that I started to feel guilty that I'd survived.'

Initially the disaster changed his outlook on life. 'I had this feeling that I was like God and I could suddenly see the meaning of it all. I remember thinking how trivial the terrorist campaign in Northern Ireland was, what a total and utter waste of time and effort. For a moment I understood the meaning of life, what it was all about. Then it disappeared.'

Nick decided that life was going to carry on as normal after the crash, and he is now able to run and do everything he could do before. Before it happened he had already decided to give up climbing. In fairness to his family, he didn't feel he should be taking risks any more. The crash reinforced that decision.

As a child it had been his dream to climb all over the world, and he never believed anything would happen to him. It almost did when he was twenty-one and climbing in the Andes in South America.

'The glaciers in the Andes move rapidly so there are lots of big ice cliffs,' he says. 'They're falling over all the time. We were right in the middle of the most badly creviced bit and my friend was about thirty metres ahead of me. Suddenly there was a crashing noise. We looked at each other and thought it was an earthquake.' Nick and his friend thought they were about to die. Then they realized: 'It was a big ice cliff further down collapsing and the vibration was coming through the glacier.'

Nick hasn't climbed since the crash but he is planning to go on an expedition to the Himalayas as base camp manager organizing food and equipment. 'The crash made me realize I'm mortal and one day I will die,' he says.


Alistair McCorry ambles round the grounds of Castle Ward, his face battered by years of wind and rain. The impressive eighteenth-century mansion is his territory, and as head gardener of the National Trust estate he knows almost every blade of grass.

He's a man who likes doing things his way, stubborn, some would say, including Alistair himself. 'Right from the crash I was determined to get back to where I was before,' he says. 'I don't suffer from an awful lot of stress.'

In typical style Alistair proposed to his girlfriend on the night of the M1 air disaster, then was shocked when everyone including the press was so excited. Alistair had been with Pat for ten years at the time, although they had never lived in the same country. Pat had looked after his aunt and they met when Alistair went over to Cornwall after she died to sort out her affairs. After that they continued to see each other several times a year.

Alistair had spent Christmas in Cornwall and was on his way home to Downpatrick in Northern Ireland when the disaster happened. As the plane took off, 'I was tired and in bad form,' he says. 'It had been a long journey up from Cornwall and I wasn't happy about leaving Pat.'

On his knee was the questionnaire British Midland had given him, asking what he thought about the service. He hated filling in forms and was more interested in the fact that dinner was being served.

Alistair was sitting in a window seat and as he glanced sideways he noticed flames coming out of the engine. It was dark outside and they were burning brightly against the sky.

'I knew I couldn't do anything so I had to sit and make the best of it,' he says. 'I carried on eating. I also decided it would be the last time I would fly because of the sense of helplessness. Some passengers panicked but I was too relaxed.'

Alistair tightened his seat belt another four inches. He believes that helped to save him from serious injury along with his heavy sheepskin coat thrown over his knees and legs. 'I thought the world of that coat and I never let it out of my sight,' he says. 'If the stewards had tried to move it they would have had a row.'

'Prepare for crash landing,' he heard the captain say, and the man at the end of his row suggested, 'Maybe we'd better put our heads down.' Alistair put his head down on his coat. 'Then it started happening,' he recalls.

'I was lucky that I was conscious all the time and I can remember how I got my injuries. On impact all the lights went off. It was almost like a hurricane, a fantastic sensation of speed as we hit. The first bang was bad enough, the second was far worse.

'I tried to keep my head down on my coat but I hadn't the strength to do it. My spectacles shot off my face at about eighty miles an hour. My legs went up and my arms flung everywhere. I tried to put my left hand in front of me to save myself.

'My head came down very hard and hit the seat in front. I was fighting not to do that as I felt a bit of a fool flying around. I was trying to control myself. I straightened up again and hit the seat in front with my legs. To me the accident seemed to go on for quite a while. The plane was breaking up around us.'

When the mayhem finally stopped Alistair tried to get out but realized he couldn't use his right leg or left arm. His side of the plane had been ripped out and long strips of it were lying over his shoulder. There was a jagged opening behind him where the plane had broken up, and the roof had been flattened above him by the broken tail section.

A few times Alistair tried to climb over his crumpled seat but couldn't do it. 'I knew that it had been a bad landing but I didn't realize it was as bad as it was,' he says. 'I sat down and tried to rest.'

After a few minutes rescuers stepped into the plane

behind him. 'They were obviously shocked at what they saw,' he says. 'They asked what size of plane it was to see if anyone was still alive. I turned round and said it had twenty-seven rows and six seats across, and I told them about my injuries.'

Alistair was rescued four minutes after the crash and put down on the edge of the motorway. 'I'm used to being outside all the time and I was glad to get out into the fresh air,' he says. 'It was a very mild night. I was asked if I was cold but I wasn't.'

There seemed to be no one else about as he lay in darkness, suffering from the severe pain of his injuries. One of his eyes was swollen and sore, so it was easier to keep them closed. 'All I could do was sit and relax,' he says. 'I wasn't sure what to expect.'

He didn't expect to be covered in foam as emergency services battled to stop a massive blaze developing. 'I began to think I might drown in the stuff,' he recalls. 'I wasn't sure whether to shout or try to drag myself away. I decided to stay where I was and I put my head down and my good arm over my mouth.'

Gradually other passengers were rescued and laid on the motorway around him. One girl he described as 'a little bit of a thing, no size at all', was walking around. 'I was very cross with myself that she could walk and I couldn't. I have funny joints anyway, gardeners tend to have them, it's a funny kind of rheumatism which I've had since I was very young. I knew if I could move it would be much better for me.'

The girl kept on asking the date and the time, over and over again, but as soon as he told her she forgot. 'It helped because it diverted me,' he recalls. 'I was in a fair bit of pain.'

Alistair was taken to Leicester Royal Infirmary with a dislocated hip, dislocated shoulder, a cut on his nose and bruising from head to toe. 'I always felt I wasn't too bad,' he says. 'I'd never been in hospital before so I didn't know much about it.'

In the early hours of the morning Alistair telephoned his girlfriend to tell her he was alive. She'd already learnt this from an off-duty nurse who was passing the scene of the crash and had written Pat's telephone number on her blouse and later phoned her. Pat couldn't believe he was alive when she saw pictures of the plane on television.

'She couldn't believe she was speaking to me,' says Alistair. 'I told her roughly what my injuries were. Then in the middle of the conversation I said to her: "It's time we got married and the sooner the better." We'd always felt we'd get together and a disaster tends to concentrate the mind.'

The policeman standing at the end of the ward was the first person to congratulate him. 'He nearly died of shock,' says Alistair. 'He overheard the conversation and came over as soon as I was off the phone. There were two nurses there as well. I thought that was it – I wasn't expecting the whole world to know.

'Then the press picked it up and went totally mad. They brought Pat up from Cornwall and we were not allowed to be alone, they were always there.' Princess Anne heard about the proposal when she visited the hospital. It received so much attention Alistair didn't have time to dwell on the crash.

After a couple of days he was concerned because he hadn't suffered any traumatic reaction, and mentioned it to the hospital staff. The following day he was watching coverage on television, and shed a few tears for a few seconds. That was the only reaction he noticed.

Alistair spent two months in hospital and then another six months in Cornwall with Pat before going back to work. He hasn't had a day off since.

When is he going to get married? He laughs. 'As soon as I can find a job in England. Pat comes over on holiday but she's not happy here. I see her about every three months. It works out very well at the moment and it wouldn't make any difference if we were married.'

Alistair feels he was probably slightly more carefree before the disaster, but it hasn't had a great effect. 'I tend to be very much an individualist and that went against me at school. I liked doing my own thing and the school I was at was terribly regimented. The fact that everyone probably thought some of the things I was saying or doing at school were totally mad didn't concern me.'

Alistair did his best to be in control after the disaster. 'Right from the beginning I realized how well things were going for me and because of that I coped.'

When Sharon Freestone survived the M1 air disaster she decided it wasn't going to change her life. She's now working again as a stewardess on the same type of aircraft that plunged to the ground with her on board. Sharon was twenty-two when the disaster happened and had been flying with British Midland for just two weeks.

Her love affair with the air started when she was at school and her dream was to travel around the world as cheaply as possible. Although she'd never been in an aeroplane Sharon had already decided on her career.

After she left school she joined the Royal Air Force and became a stewardess on their VC10s. It was a job that took her all over the world. One week was spent in Canada, on a trip with then Prime Minister Margaret Thatcher; on another trip she went to Australia and the Far East.

Two years was the longest she was allowed to spend flying with the RAF. When she was about to be grounded

Sharon left to continue her career in the air with British Midland. Even then she had a premonition that something was going to happen. 'I just kept pushing it to the back of my mind,' she says. That premonition came back to her on the night of the disaster, and as soon as the problems started she was worried she wasn't going to survive.

As she rushed about collecting meal trays her heart was racing. 'Do what you've got to do,' she kept telling herself. It helped that she was able to keep busy. Then the passengers were told to prepare for crash landing and Sharon sat in the brace position in her seat praying as she had never done before.

The plane crashed, her seat collapsed, and the bulkhead in front of her came forward. 'Initially I wasn't able to breathe, and I thought this is it,' she says. 'Then I told myself to calm down, I had a severe chest pain as though someone had hit me hard.'

Sharon tried unsuccessfully to open the door, not realizing that her arm was broken. 'I went to the flight deck door, but it was so badly mangled I couldn't get inside,' she continues.

'The captain was slumped back in his chair with his head back and blood dripping down his face. I kept shouting to him, "Are you OK?" He said: "I think I've broken my back." I asked the first officer if he was OK and he said, "Yes, just my legs." I said: "I can't get in to help you." I looked back into the cabin and thought: "Oh God, it doesn't matter if I open the door or not, these people aren't going to go anywhere."'

Sharon couldn't believe the plane had crashed; it all seemed so unreal. 'I thought any minute everyone would stand up and brush the dust off themselves. Then someone would say, "Cut, we'll take that shot again."'

She started shouting to an elderly man who had been sitting in the front row with his wife. All she could see was his head rocking backwards and forwards. His wife had vanished. 'I couldn't go any further because if I'd stepped forward I'd have fallen through into the hold,' she recalls.

Outside she could hear the sirens so knew the emergency services were not far way. 'Can you hear me, can you hear me?' she shouted to the elderly gentleman. 'The firemen are here and they will have you out in no time.' Another woman was saying: 'I can't move my leg.' 'I can't get to you, please stay where you are,' Sharon called back through the dust and darkness. 'I was asking people to stop moving,' she says. 'As one person was trying to fight their way out they were knocking something on to someone else who was then screaming.'

Half an hour later Sharon was being carried down the embankment, complaining to firemen that her skirt was up so far people could see her knickers. 'I knew we'd been through a crisis but I still wanted to look fairly respectable,' she says.

On the ground Sharon was able to use her RAF training to look after other passengers. Despite the trauma of what she'd been through, she bravely decided to help those who had been injured.

'There's a chap over there in absolute agony and he wants a painkiller,' she told the doctor, pointing to a man who had injured his leg. Sharon expected the doctor to give her a tablet and a glass of water, instead he gave her a syringe.

'There's morphine in there, do you know what to do?' he said as he handed it over. 'Push it into his thigh,' Sharon replied. She'd been taught how to do it in the Air Force. 'Make sure you pinch the skin when you're doing it,' said the doctor. Sharon went off clutching the syringe; she ripped the man's trousers and gave him an injection.

Another passenger was brought down the embankment

with blood spurting from his head and Sharon went into action again. She held his head while the emergency services bandaged it up, then she put him in the recovery position.

Time went by so fast Sharon didn't realize she'd been on the ground for an hour. Someone asked her who she was: 'Actually I've just come out of that aircraft,' she told them, and couldn't believe the words she was saying. It wasn't until she was in the ambulance and allowed herself to relax that she felt the pain in her back.

Three months later doctors discovered she had several fractures. Although she can cope now with the occasional back pain doctors have told her that one day she may have to wear a spinal brace.

Sharon was determined to get back into the air immediately after the disaster. 'I just wanted to go back, there was nothing else I ever wanted to do,' she says. Four weeks after the crash she tried to fly again but wasn't fit enough, and had to work in an office at Heathrow Airport instead. It was fifteen months before she was able to go back to the job she loved. Sharon now works for British Airways and travels all over Europe.

'I decided from day one that I wasn't going to let the disaster affect my life,' she says at her home in Wiltshire. 'The most important thing was that I wanted to get back to normal.'

Just after the crash Sharon saw a psychiatrist but she says: 'I had nothing to say to her. I felt as though I had to try to make things up or say I was stressed about something because that was what she wanted to hear. I've never had a nightmare or been upset about it, or anything. If I had I couldn't have gone back to flying. Maybe if I'd been a passenger it would have been different.'

Sharon believes it was her Air Force training that helped her to cope. 'Freestone!' She can hear the bellowing in her ears as she struggled through her initial six-week training. She was just eighteen, and it was her first time ever away from home. Her task was to camp out for three days during a freezing cold winter. Of the eight girls who shared her tent, two were sent to hospital with hypothermia.

Knee-deep in snow Sharon battled on, a tiny figure in combat gear, crying, and desperate for a warm fire. 'We were up at the crack of dawn, marching, marching, marching, so absolutely shattered we didn't want to go any more, but they told us to keep going,' she recalls. 'They wanted us to crack, to say, "I've had enough of this, I'm going home." If we'd done that we'd have failed ourselves so it made us more determined.'

There were times when she questioned: 'Why am I doing this?' The answer was because she wanted to be an air stewardess. 'I was pushed so far I felt I couldn't be pushed any more,' she says. 'I thought: "If I don't break now I never will."'

Sharon never has. She has survived.

# CHAPTER EIGHT

# HILLSBOROUGH

## 15 April 1989

Allan Bland sat on the side of the bed gently stroking his son's white face, his eyes brimming over with affection. Tony's eyes, lifeless and staring straight ahead, didn't see the clutter of the red and white mementoes around him, or the photographs of his heroes Bruce Grobbelaar and Kenny Dalglish on the walls. He didn't see the Liverpool shirt signed by his team, the flowers sent by a girl he had never met, or the picture of the baby nephew he had never been able to cuddle.

Just seven months after I saw Tony he was finally allowed to die. On 3 March 1993 he was released from the twilight world in which he'd lived for almost four years, ever since he was involved in the Hillsborough disaster.

His father, described by High Court Judge Sir Stephen Brown as a 'splendid straightforward Yorkshireman', recalls the day that changed their lives. It was a normal Saturday afternoon and he was watching television before taking the washing to the laundry. His eighteen-year-old son Tony was off enjoying the FA Cup semi-final between Liverpool and Nottingham Forest, or so he thought. Tony had waved through the window that morning as he set off in his Liverpool colours.

The first Allan knew of trouble was a news flash that came on television – reports of a pitch invasion, nothing to be worried about. By the time Allan came back from drying the washing the story was that three were dead.

As the numbers rose Allan tried to get through on the Hillsborough hotline. Then a friend rang to say that Tony had not come back to the car as arranged. His body was one of the last to be pulled out of the crush. His brain had been starved of oxygen and that had sent him into a coma. Allan drove to Sheffield and scanned photographs of the dead for his son. In the early hours of the morning he found him lying motionless in a hospital ward.

When Tony was released from intensive care his devoted parents brought him home to the Airedale Hospital in Keighley where they live. The brain damage Tony suffered was total. He couldn't talk, see or hear. Every day for the rest of his life Tony's parents visited his bedside, but Tony never knew they were there. The vibrant fresh-faced teenager they had known was gone, and his body had been left in limbo.

Allan, a warehouseman at a shoe factory, took six months off work and spent the time at the gym with Tony trying to move his limbs. Gradually they watched as Tony's muscles atrophied so much that his arms were bent up against his chest. His fists were tightly clenched and his legs twisted.

At first his parents didn't give up hope. Barbara chatted to him continually, asking him if he wanted beefburgers for his tea, watching for every movement. Gradually that hope disappeared. Towards the end Barbara read or did a crossword during her visits. The best she could do for her son was his washing. 'To me Tony has been dead for years,' she said. 'It's like sitting next to his shell.'

Occasionally a tear fell from Tony's empty brown eyes, but Barbara believed it was nothing more than his eyes cleaning themselves.

Allan rubbed his son's shoulder and his hand touched a tiny 'Liverpool' tattoo; in the same place on his other arm the tattoo said 'Keighley'. They were done the night before the Hillsborough disaster, and Tony hadn't wanted his mother to know. Allan smiled: 'He didn't have a hair on his chest when he came in here but look at him now,' he said, as he stroked his son's hairy chest.

'Tony wasn't a clever boy, but he had more more money than I had,' said Allan. 'He worked with his mother as a machine-minder at the local factory, making paper tubes.'

It seems incredible that any father could have wanted his son to die, particularly a father who obviously loved him so much. 'It's what's best for him,' said Allan. 'He has no quality of life, in fact it's undignified. It would be so much more humane if he was allowed to die and we'd know he was at peace.'

As we talked Allan asked a nurse to put a painkiller into the feeding tube. He was worried there was something bothering Tony because he was grinding his teeth. Even though he had been told his son couldn't feel pain he still couldn't bear the thought of him being hurt.

'It hurts me when I see his mates courting and getting married,' said Allan. Tony was the younger of his two children and his only son. Not long before the disaster Allan had started taking him to the men-only club in Keighley. It's a long-standing tradition that men take their sons along when they come of age. Afterwards he had to watch as other young men came through the door, knowing that his lad would never be at his side again.

All he could do was keep Tony up to date with what was happening in the local pub and tell him how his team were doing. He knew there would be no reply, no chatter between father and son.

The three-year campaign to end Tony's life took its toll on Allan and Barbara. Three years after Hillsborough Allan had to take ten weeks off work because of stress. He fell asleep one afternoon in the warehouse as he was writing his despatch notes. When he woke up his writing had trailed across the labels. Barbara also suffered from depression.

The strain affected their marriage as they struggled to cope in different ways. Allan wanted to talk to the media about Tony. Barbara didn't, yet she found she was continually answering the telephone to journalists. Now their telephone number is ex-directory and their relationship has improved.

'From the beginning I was determined Tony wouldn't be forgotten,' says Allan. 'It would have been kinder if he hadn't survived.' He was convinced that his son would want to die. 'If he knew the facts, that he wasn't going to recover, I'm sure he'd want what we want,' he said. 'I'd like it to be as comfortable an ending as possible because he has suffered enough.'

Tony would want to die with dignity. And Allan was determined that he should. In November 1992 a High Court judge said it was lawful to stop feeding him and allow him to die. The decision by Sir Stephen Brown, president of the Family Division, meant Tony's doctor James Howe could disconnect his feeding tube without being accused of murder. Sir Stephen was satisfied that there was 'no reasonable possibility' of Tony emerging from his coma.

He paid tribute to Allan Bland who gave evidence during the two-day hearing. 'He has faced the terrible tragedy which has befallen his family with remarkable realism and dignity,' he said. 'He has not allowed emotion to influence his judgement.'

He added: 'To his parents and family, Tony is dead. It is a desperately tragic situation both for what remains of Anthony Bland and for the devoted members of his family.' He hoped Tony could 'die with the greatest dignity and least distress'. 'His spirit has left him and all that remains is the shell of his body. May his soul rest in peace.'

It was a decision the Blands had been waiting for but their anguish wasn't over. The Official Solicitor representing Tony's interests in court contested the ruling at an Appeal Court hearing on 30 November. Master of the Rolls Sir Thomas Bingham agreed that doctors should be allowed to let Tony die with dignity. The case then went to the House of Lords.

On 4 February 1993 five Law Lords ruled that the feeding was medical care and that it was not in his interests to continue it.

The Law Lords gave only a glimmer of hope to the families of hundreds of other people lying in a 'persistent vegetative state'. They said that the line dividing life and death should be decided by Parliament and urged laws to close the gap between 'old law' and new medicine.

The decision was a great relief for the Bland family, but met with opposition from anti-euthanasia campaigners.

Tony's physician, Dr Jim Howe, ceased all hydration, nutrition and drug therapy on Monday, 22 February 1993.

'The tube was removed when we were present,' says Allan.

'We didn't have to touch anything. We had seen him with a tube up his nose for four years. When it has removed he looked so much better – like his old self again. His death was very peaceful. He just slipped away.'

Tony died nine days after the tube was removed. He lived longer than he was expected to. 'The nurses were brilliant,' says Allan. 'They handled him as if he was their own son. You could almost touch their love.

'The day he died a nurse told us there would be two more breaths. Barbara sat at the bottom of the bed and I sat next to Tony with my hand on his chest. I held his hands and that was it. He was gone. I felt relieved for him, that he was at peace. Our aim was to do the best for Tony and this was the only way.

'Tony wouldn't have wanted to be left as he was. He loved life too much for that. He lived for the day. There was a time when we said we'd like him back, that we'd give everything we had and I'd sweep the roads. But we knew that couldn't happen. You have to get on with your lives the best that you can.'

Allan and Barbara have felt no remorse. They were doing what they thought was best for Tony. More than one thousand people who wrote to them after Tony's death thought the same.

'It was an emotional time and there were a lot of tears,' says Allan. He and Barbara grieved again for the son they have missed for the last four years. They had already cried so much they thought they couldn't cry any more. When he died they cried again.

Allan suffered so much stress after Tony's death he had to have time off work. The last few years have had a profound effect on their lives. 'I feel I understand life better than most,' says Allan. 'If I see a tragedy on television I feel so much for the people involved. We have met so many nice people but in the wrong circumstances. It has given me a different outlook on life.'

Eddie Spearritt lost his fourteen-year-old son Adam at Hillsborough. Three years after the disaster, in April 1991, he and his wife had another baby, Daniel Adam, who now toddles around the garden of their home in a village near Runcorn.

Little Daniel kicks a football past a basket of flowers recently removed from Adam's grave and runs over to the goal as fast as his little legs will allow. His father walks protectively behind.

The nearest Daniel will come to seeing his big brother is a tiny photograph of him on top of the television. It's tucked inside an eighteenth-birthday card from his mum and dad. They still sent Adam a card even though he won't be able to celebrate his birthday. On top of the cupboard are Adam's football trophies and another picture taken with the school team.

'Adam and I were mates,' says Eddie. 'We did a lot together and we got on really well. I think about the times we had because I know they won't happen again, and I think about the times we should have had. I'd always said I'd buy him a car on his eighteenth birthday and we'd have a big party.' That never happened.

Eddie, a former taxi driver, had to give up his job as a result of the Hillsborough disaster. 'I was in charge of my son at Hillsborough and I failed miserably,' he says, fighting back the tears. 'How can I take responsibility for anyone else's life when I'm driving? I still feel guilty.'

Eddie and Adam were at the front of the pens, next to the fence, when the crush started. 'It felt just like a vice getting slowly tighter and tighter,' he says. 'Adam fainted. I was trying to lift him up. I turned him around to face me, but I couldn't lift him over the fence.

'I was screaming and bellowing at this policeman, at this so-called fellow human being, and he was doing nothing.' Eddie started punching the fence, trying to break it down with his bare hands. He doesn't remember doing it, but the evidence was there afterwards when he looked at the holes in his battered hands. He doesn't remember the moment he lost consciousness.

Eddie's son died nearly two hours later, in the intensive care unit at the Northern General Hospital in Sheffield. His father was in the same intensive care unit, and was on a ventilator for twenty-four hours. Eddie had been trampled on and crushed. His lungs were damaged and his feet were crushed where they'd been stood on. Jan, his wife, was told he might not make it through the first night, and if he did he could have brain damage.

As Eddie regained consciousness on Sunday he was asking about his son. The hospital staff wanted to wait until Jan was there so that she could break the news that Adam was dead. Eddie was determined to find out and started pulling out tubes to force them to tell him. When they did, 'everything seemed black,' he recalls, even though it was spring and the sun was shining outside.

On Monday he went to the mortuary with Jan to see Adam's body. Eddie was in his pyjamas, with a blanket wrapped round his shoulders as he travelled across Sheffield in a taxi. When they arrived there were so many journalists he couldn't go through the front doors in his wheelchair. Instead he had to go through a back door and walk across derelict land in his bare feet. Jan carried his drip as he stepped over bricks and broken glass. Inside he stared at his son's body through a glass partition, the first time he'd seen him since they stood on the terraces together dreaming about Liverpool winning at Wembley.

The following day as he left hospital he saw other children on their way home from school and it sank in for the first time that Adam was dead. On the day of the funeral the cars drove past the school. It was a freezing cold morning. 'There were 300 kiddies standing there on the road and I nearly cracked up,' he says.

Eddie went back to work but left again after three months. Instead of concentrating on the road he was thinking about Adam and Hillsborough. On one trip he was stopped for speeding even though he'd been warned there was a speed trap on the road. When he arrived in town he almost crashed into a van full of police. He started having doubts about whether he should carry on taxi driving.

Now he spends his days reading transcripts of the Hillsborough inquiry and the inquest, determined to know as much as possible. The information is stored in huge boxes in Adam's room, which hasn't been touched since the disaster. His school books still litter the floor and near to them are his football boots, lovingly cleaned by Eddie.

Adam's younger brother Paul, who was nine at the time of the disaster, uses his brother's golf clubs. 'Paul has grown up far too early,' says Eddie. 'Adam was a bubbly person who had loads of mates and there was always loads of girls knocking on the door. Paul is a bit withdrawn and doesn't seem to have any friends.'

Eddie goes to football matches with Paul occasionally. 'Once on the way out I found myself throwing Paul above my head,' he recalls. 'I thought there was going to be another crush. It seemed to go on a long time but in reality it lasted for seconds. People were staring at me.'

Hillsborough has taken over Eddie's life. He doesn't like to be out of the country in case it comes up in the news and he can't say or do anything about it. Recently he took his family to Cyprus but he didn't enjoy it and vowed never to go abroad again.

'I'm bitter and I have every right to be,' he says. 'What I want is justice. That anger will always be there.' He says if he wanted revenge he wouldn't target the police officers in charge on the day of the disaster, he'd target their children. 'Then they would know exactly how I feel. If I was single and didn't have a wife or children I would probably be in gaol. I don't know what I would have done but I would have done something. I'd only have myself to think about, and I don't think much about myself anyway.'

The disaster has brought him closer than ever to his wife, who was forty-two when Daniel was born. 'After Adam's death I used to think about having another baby and that maybe it would help to occupy our minds,' he says. 'Then I thought that if he looked like Adam and had Adam's ways it would be more painful.'

One day Jan announced she was pregnant. 'My first reaction was that I'll be sixty when he's sixteen. We hadn't planned Daniel, but it's lovely to have him. He makes me laugh and people have said he looks like Adam.' Eddie reacted angrily when a neighbour said there would never be another Adam. 'I don't need you to tell me that,' he snapped back at her. 'Dan is not here to replace him.'

Now he hopes that Daniel and Paul will go to university, but has no ambitions for himself. 'I have terrible nightmares,' he says. 'I dream I'm in a pen, everywhere's black and all I can see are faces, faces I don't know. I try to take it further but unfortunately I can't. I don't remember any more.'


Billy Pemberton's son was twenty-six when he was killed at Hillsborough. 'I haven't accepted he's dead yet,' he says. 'I'm running away from it. I feel he's in Australia and I haven't seen him for a long time. I'm still looking for him, as if there's a faint chance that he's still alive somewhere. It's stupid but it keeps me going. If that goes I might as well throw myself off a bridge.'

Billy spoke to me about the disaster at Jenny Hicks' house. His wife Sheila prefers not to talk about it, even though there's a picture of their son Roy on the wall of their Liverpool home. Their marriage has suffered under the strain of the disaster. Like Eddie, Billy feels he lost a friend when his son died. 'I haven't got someone I can talk to, I haven't got a pal now,' he says.

Billy offered to travel to the match with his son because all Roy's friends were away and he hadn't got anyone to go with. 'I decided to wait in the coach outside and be company for him on the way home.' Billy had fallen asleep when there was a knock on the window of the coach. He woke up and saw three teenagers crying outside.

They told him there had been a terrible accident. 'I put on the television and after a few minutes the cameras went to the ground,' he says. The memory is so painful he has to pause, and apologizes for being emotional.

Billy set off to find his son, 'I was actually hoping he'd been injured,' he says, his voice barely a whisper. He walked through the streets carrying a plastic box containing food, a syringe and insulin for Roy who was a diabetic and had to be injected twice a day. Every time he met a policeman he asked for information.

Billy was determined to do the right thing, and still is. 'I realized I had to be a responsible person and I mustn't let the name of Liverpool and Liverpool supporters be tarnished,' he says.

It was later that night when Billy scanned the pictures of the dead looking for Roy. He could barely recognize him, Roy could have been number 35 or 65, he didn't know which. Then he went in to see his son's body. 'I had a look at him and knelt down beside him,' Billy recalls. 'You've been battered,' I said. His voice still has as much compassion as it must have had then.

Billy set up a family support group for the bereaved and organized the first meeting. He is now vice-chairman. 'I thought other people must feel the same. I needed their suffering to help my suffering and I wanted my suffering to help them,' he says.

'Sheila and I were devastated. My son was on a computer sciences degree course at Leicester Polytechnic. He was our only son, the only Pemberton to carry the name forward. We'd struggled to bring our three children up to be good honest citizens and we were proud of them. I felt betrayed – it was only a football game he went to.'

Billy, now in his sixties, has hardly worked since the disaster. He's a draughtsman by trade but it now takes him longer to do a drawing than before. Like Eddie Spearritt, Billy has had problems coping with the fact that he took his son to a football match but didn't bring him home.

'We were in the Cup Final recently and I was fortunate enough to have a ticket,' he says. 'Two young lads who had both lost brothers in the disaster were not able to go because their father couldn't make it. I offered to take them. I was asking them to trust me to bring them back, and I made it plain I wouldn't be offended if they couldn't go with me. They said they could, we had a bloody good game, and we enjoyed ourselves. I was so pleased.'

Brian Anderton came home from Hillsborough without his father Jack and, like Billy, has not accepted that someone he loved is dead. The family had always gone to the match together ever since he was a child. His father, a former factory worker, and his mother Eileen both stood in the same place on the Kop, even when Brian grew up and started going with his friends. Eileen didn't go to the semi-final, there would have been too much excitement. 'She wouldn't have wanted to be there if they were beaten,' says Brian, who works as a mechanic. 'The semi-final is more for men, there's so much pressure.'

He was thirty-three when the disaster happened. He remembers running into the ground laughing when the gate opened. As the crowds came behind them they were pushed forward. 'My arm was pushed against the crush barrier, and the rest of me was on someone's back,' says Brian. 'I knew Dad had come up beside me and that he'd also be against the barrier. I couldn't turn round to see him but I could hear him saying he was being crushed.

'In a couple of minutes the pressure increased. I could hear my dad crying that he was dying. I shouted to him, "Dad!" The lad in front of me had died, his stomach was over the barrier. I was crying, fighting for breath. I was right up against the back of the heads of two lads on the other side of the barrier. I remember saying to them, "Help me, I'm dying," but they said they couldn't. It was just as bad on the other side.'

Brian lost consciousness. When he woke up again the crush had eased, the boy who died had disappeared and he couldn't see his father. Hoisted up on to the stands, he sat for a couple of minutes trying to focus before deciding to find sixty-two-year-old Jack. He walked through the stands, down the steps and outside the ground. There were bodies everywhere. 'I had a little look and spotted my dad,' he says. 'His shirt was off and over his face, but I knew him straight away. I took the shirt off, and his face was marked, I don't know if he'd been stood on. I couldn't even cry, I felt so hopeless, I didn't know what to do. I sat there for ages holding his hand. The police came and put a coat around me.

'After I'd been there for a while I thought I should check if he was dead but I didn't know how to go about it. I felt frightened to touch his face. I went near him and checked if he was breathing but I didn't know what I was doing.'

The nerves in Brian's arm had been crushed and his back was badly bruised. 'I started feeling a pain in my arm so I lay down beside my dad, but then I thought, "They'll think I'm dead," so I sat up on the concrete again,' he recalls.

'I stayed there for about an hour. There was a girl sitting next to her boyfriend on the ground not far from me. She was screaming and I thought: "Why am I not doing the same?" I don't know if I had the strength to scream.'

Brian cried that night in the mortuary when he saw his father's body for the second time. He cried again the following morning when he woke with a start at 6 a.m. in his parents' home where he'd stayed the night. Over the next few days visitors flocked to the house.

'People were coming in crying all the time. I thought I was supposed to cry with them and I couldn't cry to order,' he says. 'I didn't feel I could properly show any emotion, I was numb. I kept trying to say stupid things to Mum like, "Dad lived for Liverpool and if he had a choice he would have died the way he did." I tried to believe it then, but I don't now. I didn't know what to say.'

Brian still feels that he's trying to shut out his father's death. 'Sometimes I hurt a bit – well, a lot,' he admits. He tries not to think about the disaster and finds it difficult to look at photographs of his dad or read about Hillsborough. 'Mum has photographs around the house and I have to look past them. No one knows I do that.' There are no pictures of his father up in his Liverpool home. 'I blame myself. If I look at the photographs, I feel that I'm looking at him and I want to cry.'

Brian started going to church again to find answers to his questions. 'It's funny how you start believing in heaven,' he says. He went every Sunday for twelve months. Like many bereaved he feels in some way responsible: it was his idea to go into the tunnel, his idea to go to the pub, his idea that his father should have a third pint when he said he couldn't drink any more. 'I almost feel that I should have died but I know that would have killed my mum,' he says.

Now he is short tempered with his own children, and can't stand their screaming and shouting. Brian has lost some of his confidence and most of his friends. He is frightened to talk to people. 'I've stopped going out,' he says. 'After a few drinks I'd always end up on the same subject with me feeling sorry for myself. People got fed up with it.'

Brian tried to protect his mother by not talking about the disaster. 'Every day I went to Mum's because I felt so guilty, and everything revolved around her. I wasn't giving time to my family,' he admits. He still takes her to bingo twice a week and they go to football matches together.

Brian went back to a match, three weeks after the disaster, and stood in his father's spot on the terraces. 'I used to stand thirty yards away where I could swear a bit. If Liverpool scored we'd always acknowledge it to each other from a distance,' he says.

'Dad had stood in the same place for years and I'd stood there too when I was younger. Many people I'd grown up with still stood there and Dad knew them almost like sons. They laid flowers for him on the steps of the Kop and I had to go back to the same spot to thank them.'

Brian's mother had said she wouldn't go to another football match, but she changed her mind. She now sits in the stands and still enjoys the game. Jack was cremated and his ashes scattered in the Liverpool goal. 'Whenever I go I always have a little look and say a prayer,' says Brian. 'As far as I'm concerned that's the cemetery.'

The disaster has now started to feel like a dream to him. 'I remember the whole day very clearly but it has a vague feeling almost as if it didn't happen to me. It seems such a long time ago. '

Ian Price survived the Hillsborough disaster but it left him with an overwhelming fear of death. Ian was so frightened of dying after the disaster that he clung to his family for protection. In the months that followed the twenty-year-old bank clerk retreated in terror from the outside world. 'I thought I was going to die in my sleep, going out in the car, walking across the road, anywhere,' he recalls. 'I felt frightened all the time.' At his home in Liverpool he only felt safe if his family were with him. When they were out there was no one to rescue him if anything happened.

He didn't go out for six weeks. Unwashed and unshaven, he sat in his chair too frightened to move, to go to bed, or get up again in the morning. At 10 p.m. he regularly went out on to the doorstep of his terraced home to wait for his older brother to come home. The front door and living-room door were open so that he could still see his family. When his brother came back at 11.30 p.m. he closed the door and came inside. 'I had to make sure my family were safe,' he says. 'I was scared of them suffering.'

When Ian went to bed the curtains and the bedroom door had to be left open. During the night his parents played children's board games with him when he was too terrified to go to sleep. One night they woke up to hear him shouting downstairs. He couldn't open the sliding door from the living-room into the kitchen. In panic he'd fainted and taken the door with him.

Every morning it took him up to an hour to have breakfast. 'I was so slow,' he recalls. 'I was petrified of food poisoning and checked my food to see if there was anything in it. I looked for bits in the milk around the cereal. I had no control over that milk so it had to be checked. Then I sat in the chair for half an hour before I went into the kitchen to make toast. I was scared to move. I was worried that maybe I'd burn myself on the cooker. I lived in constant fear.'

Ian was so frightened of scissors he wouldn't have his

hair cut and it grew down to his shoulders. 'I was frightened of cutting myself when I was shaving and drowning in the bath water,' he says. 'Sometimes I didn't wash or shave for a week. When I did it had to be with the bathroom door open just in case something happened.'

It was his mother Irene who decided the family needed help. 'We were really down,' she recalls. Ian had lost about two stones in weight and had stopped eating. He was asking her why he was still alive when other people had died. 'That particular morning we had a terrible row over a piece of fish,' she says. 'He wanted the fish, I bought it and he wouldn't eat it.'

She telephoned the Hillsborough Centre, which offers support to those affected by the disaster, and arranged for them to go over. Irene asked her son which way he wanted to travel, by bus or taxi. He asked her which was the safest. 'I couldn't tell him,' she recalls. Months before she'd been able to hold discussions with an adult. Now she was answering the questions of a child.

'The first taxi didn't know where the Centre was.' She remembers her frustration. 'I dragged Ian out of that taxi and hailed another one. I felt it must be degrading for him as a man to be dragged along, but he was like a three-year-old. I was desperate for help. I couldn't do any more for him and I thought I was going to lose him.'

Ian ventured out of the house again with the help of a counsellor who set him goals. The first was to walk round the block every night for five minutes. 'That was the worst thing I'd ever done in my life,' he says. 'I knew everyone round the block but I was so petrified I had to run. I used to wait until 4 p.m. every day. Then I'd go to the window, make sure no one was out, run round and come back again. The worst part was going into the next street. I was frightened because I was going out of my street and away from my family.'

As he ran he wore a coat with the hood up, and flip-flops because his toenails had been crushed in the disaster. 'I was frightened that people would talk to me and hold me up,' he recalls. 'I was frightened of being out too long in case something happened. It was a relief to come back in.'

With the help of the counsellor he gradually went further away from home. His next goal was to go to the Centre in a taxi on his own, the one after that to go to town with his counsellor and come home on the bus on his own. 'I was terrified,' he says. 'I didn't want anyone to sit next to me.'

Ian's mother tried to persuade him to go out even when he didn't feel like it. Together they walked up to the shops, and she walked cn the outside to protect him from the traffic. He walked slowly, continually looking behind.

Ian was pleased that he had to wear the open-toed shoes for a year. It meant there was something visibly wrong so maybe people would realize he had been in the disaster. At the same time he was embarrassed at not looking the same as everyone else. The Christmas after Hillsborough he wore his flip-flops to town in the snow. The other shoppers were wearing duffel coats and wellingtons. 'I met a friend and was so pleased to be able to talk to him so that people could see I wasn't by myself. They would think I had to be normal because the other lad was,' he recalls.

Ian was off work for four months, then went back, part-time at first, gradually returning to his full-time job fifteen months after the disaster. His anxiety attacks continued. If a customer in the bank was annoyed it could bring one on. 'I'd feel tense, there would be a burning in my ears, a tightness in my heart and a feeling that my body had lost control.' They were so severe he was taken to hospital six times.

Over the years they became less frequent. The last serious attack was in October 1991, and happened as he was working in the bank. He felt his arm tensing up, tried to grab his pen and couldn't. Two months before, the pain in his head had been so severe he had had to lie down in an ambulance on the way to hospital. Ian went on a course to relieve his anxiety, and also went to yoga. 'I'll try anything to get better,' he says. 'I don't want to sit back and let it happen.'

It took two years for his phobias to go and the fear of death has still not gone completely. He still doesn't feel relaxed unless his family are at home. Two years after the disaster Ian's brother married. He could walk to his new house but still felt upset that someone in the family had left home.

'Maybe I held on too much to my family,' he says. 'They were there all the time and they knew what I was going through.' They were always there when he needed help. A year after Hillsborough Ian wanted to go to a friend's twenty-first birthday party. His mother had to go to the function room half an hour before to check where the escape routes were, where the telephone was and whether it was working so that Ian could ring home if he needed to. His father went back to a football match with him at Anfield but Ian had to leave after twenty minutes.

Ian believes his values have changed since the disaster. He now sponsors a child in Peru, and helps to run a youth club and a boys' brigade. 'I want to help people and give all the time rather than receive,' he says. 'I used to want to go up and up the career ladder, now I realize money isn't everything, my health and my life are. At my age I should be moving away from home, but I have no intention of doing that.'

He sits in a chair opposite his mother, in a neat suit with neatly cropped hair. 'Next week I'm going away with my friends on holiday for the first time since it happened and I'm frightened,' he says. 'I'm only going to Wales, and it's not far, but I know my family won't be there.'

Keith Martin lost his voice as a result of the Hillsborough disaster. For over a year a tiny squeak was the only sound he made. Now hoarse and barely audible he explains how his vocal cords stopped working as a result of stress. It meant he had to give up his job as a careers officer at the largest secondary school in Coventry. In his early forties, he has had to start all over again and is now studying for a degree in biological sciences at Birmingham University.

Keith doesn't find it easy to recall what happened on the day of the disaster. 'There are one or two instances I've never been able to talk about at all,' he says. As he speaks he is full of emotion, once or twice he breaks down in tears. 'The journey to Sheffield has come to be my worst nightmare,' he starts.

Keith boarded the train at Coventry station. He can remember every detail, even down to the bacon, lettuce and tomato sandwich he had when he changed trains in Birmingham. A little girl with blonde, shoulder-length hair sat opposite him when he boarded the second train to finish his journey. She was two, he smiles as he recalls. She brought over her book and asked him to read her a story. It was a book about ducks and geese and rabbits at a birthday party.

'I live in absolute dread of ever seeing that book again,' he says, trembling. 'It would be the worst thing I could ever see. I worked in a junior school afterwards and had to make sure it wasn't there.' In his nightmares he dreams about the journey but never gets as far as seeing the little girl. 'I'd hate it all to come together,' he says. As she got off the train with her mother at Chesterfield, he called after them, 'Liverpool for the Cup'. It was going to be such a good day.

Keith describes the rest of the journey to the Hillsborough ground in detail. It's only when it comes to the crush that he has problems talking about what happened. He moves on swiftly to explain what happened afterwards, how he helped those who had been injured and carried outside. 'There was an absolute sea of death out there,' he says in a whisper.

A boy sitting on the bottom of the steps had broken his ribs and Keith picked him up and put him into an ambulance. 'I was in the ambulance on my own with Robert,' he says. 'There was a clatter and a clash on the bottom steps and a stretcher was thrust into it. I picked up the stretcher and it amazed me how light it was.'

In shock Keith's body felt rigid, and it was a struggle to move. The terror also gave him an incredible strength. 'I picked someone far bigger than I was up in my arms and they weighed nothing,' he recalls.

Keith spent hours helping the injured. It was spring, and a hot day. On the banks of the river the trees were coming into bud. He thought about pulling off some branches to splint a boy's leg. 'He was sitting up and his legs were absolutely smashed,' says Keith.

'I knelt down beside him, but it was so hard, it felt as if there were steel rods in my arms and legs. I asked him, "Are you all right?" What a stupid question that was. He looked at me, he must have had bad internal injuries. What was I able to do for him? Watch him die?' All that is left of Keith's voice sounds disgusted. 'I stood up again and I was so angry.'

Keith tried to find an ambulance man to take the young supporter to hospital but when he looked back he was convinced the boy was dead. He still lives with the fear that he helped him to die because he moved him. 'I always fear that someone isn't here now because I made a mistake,' he says. 'That's hard to live with.'

'I've never wanted to help people so much in my life but I felt so helpless.' Keith feels he was tested in a difficult situation and failed. 'Perhaps the death toll would have been one less if I'd done the right thing instead of the wrong thing?' he says.

He remembers bending down to talk to one lad. There was something over his face and Keith thought it was there to protect his eyes from the bright sunlight. He asked him where it hurt but there was no reply. 'I was trying to talk to him and he was dead,' he says, as if he can hardly believe what he's saying.

Keith went back and looked at the twisted metal on the terraces. 'I stopped for a few seconds, I couldn't believe what was going on. My mind switched off and gradually fed back all the horrors. I was still getting those fifteen months later.'

Two weeks after the disaster Keith's voice disappeared. He thought he had a cold and the doctor gave him a fortnight off work. He was off work for six months. There was no way Keith could give careers advice with a voice that was just a squeak. It was difficult enough to be understood over the telephone. 'It's dreadful when you rely on communicating,' he says. 'It's so frustrating when you squeak at someone and they say, "Pardon?" If I was close enough they could understand me.'

Keith still didn't have a voice when he went back to his job at Coundon school in Coventry. 'I remember when my first client talked to me and I couldn't hear a word she was saying. I was thinking: "Why aren't you dead, why aren't you dead?" as I looked at her.'

Keith couldn't cope with the school environment. 'There wasn't much space in my office, just enough to

have two people in,' he says. 'If the clerk came in to get
out the records or anyone else came in I started to panic.'
It became even worse when a temporary member of staff
was put into his office. Keith had to go out and sit in the
unheated conservatory. It was easier to stay out there and
shiver.

He stood outside the school in the mornings, sometimes
for up to twenty minutes, telling himself he couldn't go
in. 'My confidence in dealing with situations and in
making new relationships disintegrated,' he says. 'It
stopped me making friends and asking girls out.'

Keith often walked the streets all night, too afraid of
his nightmares to go to bed. He also became more
aggressive, smashed bottles and threw objects at walls.
Some of the doors in his house have holes where he has
punched them.

Just before the first anniversary of the disaster Keith
tried to commit suicide. It started when he put his fist
through the glass in the front door. Covered in blood he
stormed out of the house and found himself near a railway
line. The signal light was on green and Keith sat on the
track, waiting in the darkness for a train to come and put
an end to his misery. Then the light turned to red and two
cars stopped nearby. 'I think someone had seen me so I
got out of the way before I was found,' he says. 'I didn't
want anyone to see me in that state.'

'When it hadn't worked I felt really confused.' Keith
went for help to a local priest whom he hadn't met before.
He burst into tears and told him he'd been at Hillsborough.
'He blessed me,' says Keith. 'That's what you really need,
isn't it? I went back to the railway line to do it again.' This
time there were more people around so Keith decided he
wouldn't even try and went to hospital.

They put plasters on his cut hand and asked him if he
wanted to see anyone to talk about his problem. Keith

refused, he went home and after a sleepless night went to school the following day. He told no one.

Keith went back to work for ten months before deciding he had to give up his job. He then spent six months at Warwick University studying for a Bachelor of Arts degree with qualified teacher status but had to give that up too. It was too claustrophobic in the crowded lecture rooms and he found it difficult to manage financially without a grant.

He went on to work as a voluntary helper at Courthouse Green Junior School in Coventry, and stayed there for eighteen months. With a door open he found he could cope. He gathered the children around him when he talked so that he wouldn't need to have a loud voice.

Now he goes for regular speech therapy, his voice is stronger, and he is convinced it will return. He believes it disappeared because he hasn't talked about the worst aspects of the disaster. 'I still have nightmares, some aggression and lack of confidence,' he says.

He has no definite plans for the future. 'I love children but it's difficult to say if I want to be a teacher,' he says. 'When I was giving careers advice I used reference points like people's achievements and the type of person they were. I feel those reference points don't exist for me any more. I'm not the same person.'


Bernard Mayne's life was never the same again after Hillsborough. He used to be a bus driver – a big man, with plenty of cheek and confidence. He didn't seem the sort of person to be frightened by anything. After Hillsborough Bernard was so frightened he couldn't go back to work.

Terrified to sit in the cab of his bus, he had to give up the job he'd been doing for twenty-five years. Now he's back in the classroom, a brave move for a man who admits he was an idiot at school and left without any qualifications. Barny, (as he's known to his mates) is on an access course and hopes to go on to further education.

Hillsborough couldn't have happened at a worse time for him. He was forty-one and struggling to rebuild his life after a recent and messy divorce. Back living with his mum, and without his wife and two children, he was single again. He was drinking fourteen pints a night, going to nightclubs at the weekend and travelling abroad twice a year with the lads. Then the disaster happened and changed his life again.

Barny went to the match with his brother Owen and seventeen-year-old nephew Jonathan. He'd been a fanatical supporter ever since he was fourteen and had followed the club all over Europe. They were like part of his family. 'We're going to die!' Barny can still remember Jonathan's screams as they fought for life in the crush. 'This man's dead,' Jonathan shouted again, looking in horror at the man standing trapped and motionless beside him.

Barny told him to shut up and save his breath. Then he watched as Jonathan disappeared down among the legs in the crowd. In a second he grabbed his hair and dragged him up again. A teenager walked across Barny's balding head, and when the boy slipped he thought his ear had been taken off.

The crush eased and Barny was able to pull his nephew to the back of the terraces, leaving him propped up against a wall. He went back for his brother, pushing his way through the crowd. Owen had nine-month-old twin girls and they couldn't be left without a dad. Afterwards Barny felt guilty that in his desperation to reach Owen he could have given someone a final push.

When he reached Owen he had to pull him free of the crowd. 'I could see he was standing on other people, on their arms and legs,' he says. 'I couldn't believe it. I was so sick.' Barny dragged Owen to the back and as he was going into the crowd to help again he collapsed. 'I felt myself going down,' he recalls. 'I had a feeling that I was going to die and I was terrified. Then I remember thinking there was no point fighting it and I relaxed.'

He woke up outside the ground to find a policeman giving him the kiss of life. Barny suffered fractured ribs and lost the use of one of his kidneys. He was in hospital for eight days and went in regularly for treatment over the next fourteen months.

For the first few days he was afraid to close his eyes. They are times he will never forget. 'I was in the first bed in the ward. At the end of the ward there was a fella in his late forties, and he was moaning and in a bad way. The curtains were drawn around him most of the time.

'Then his wife came in and she must have been to identify his son's body. She came and told him. They drew the curtains back. My dad used to wear one of those docker's macs and she had one over her arm. The man got out of bed and pulled the tubes out of his hand and his arm, the woman was crying. She put the mac round him and he walked up the ward towards me.

'I was in a hell of a lot of pain. I dragged myself to the end of the bed, and stood up and put my arms round him. He said, "I've lost my lad." I just felt as if I didn't want to look.'

It was all too much for Barny. When he came home eight days after the disaster he felt numb. 'I was walking around the streets and I didn't know what I was doing,' he says. 'A couple of people asked me if I was all right and I asked them why. They told me I was crying – I didn't even realize it. I'd lost all control.'

His seventy-three-year-old mum Lily found him sitting with a box of tablets on the bed a month after the disaster.

After that she sat with him night after night to try to help
him over his despair. 'I told my mother I was going round
the twist. I couldn't stop crying,' he says. 'I felt as if I'd
been stitched up the sides and the stitches were coming
out. I was trying to hold myself together.'

Like so many other survivors, Barny had lost his
confidence. When he went down to the bus garage it was
great to see his mates but there was no way he could get
back into a cab. Even travelling on a bus was difficult. 'I
stood back and let buses go if there were too many people
on,' he says. 'The drivers let me stand on the platform and
left the doors open.'

Barny spent half his compensation on buying a car so
that he could travel on his own. The other £4,000 he gave
to his mother.

Everything changed after the disaster, including his
love of football. Nothing would have made him miss a
game before. He was delighted afterwards when the team
gathered round his hospital bed and gave him a signed
shirt.

When he left hospital he went to pay his own tribute to
the dead at Liverpool's Anfield stadium. Standing at the
gates he held on to his bunch of flowers but wasn't brave
enough to go in. 'Can you put these on the Kop for me,'
he asked a steward. Liverpool manager Kenny Dalglish
was walking past at the time. 'He grabbed hold of me and
said, "Come on." I felt like one of the royal family going
through the main door. He took me up on to the Kop, I
put my scarf on it and sat there sobbing.' The stadium was
a sea of floral tributes.

Barny would never have believed he could lose interest
in the game but soon started to question whether it was
worth going through what he did for football. He also lost
interest in drinking alcohol and gave up smoking his sixty
cigarettes a day. Some of the changing may have been for

the better. 'Maybe it was a good thing I had to stop working on the buses,' he says. 'At the time it looked as if everything was going down the tubes. At the moment I live from day to day.'

Sean Luckett has changed. He doesn't even look the same as he did before the Hillsborough disaster. Now his hair is long and his face unshaven. 'Around here that's quite strange and people are wary of me,' he says.

Sean was working as a chef at Warwick Hospital when the disaster happened. As a survivor he was given the chance to be different.

Sean gave up his job and is now playing in a band called 'Porridge'. 'I had the opportunity to say to my dad that I want to be a writer, I want to be an actor, I feel I have something to offer. It gave me the opportunity or the excuse to do what I wanted with life. I'm a lot better because of it. I've learnt a lot more.

'I'm in a position now where I honestly believe I know about everything I want to understand about. Nothing is shocking now. My mum left and I just went, "Well, so what?" I know the world is totally messed up. I have become more cynical about life; I think nothing is going to hurt me again.'

Hillsborough made him look at life in a different way. 'I realized I didn't have to go to work to please Dad,' he continued. 'Whatever you want to do you should do it, because you only have a limited amount of time.'

Sean lives in Hope Cottage in the pretty Warwickshire village of Claverdon. He doesn't remember the journey to Sheffield on the day of the disaster and has no memory of the disaster either. He doesn't remember being woken from his two-day coma by Kenny Dalglish. His first memory is of the day after he opened his eyes. He recalls seeing the Nottingham Forest team standing around his bed at the Royal Hallamshire Hospital.

When he came home he watched videos of the news coverage every day for six months and cried every time. 'I hated everything and niceness annoyed me,' he says. 'Friends of my mother came round and I hardly knew them. I thought, "It's nothing to do with you, just leave me alone."'

When he got out of bed weeks later he thought he had recovered. With so much energy he couldn't wait to go out again and went back to work. Sean stayed just three days. 'I hated it anyway, but I never had an excuse before not to work there,' he says. He started work at a private hospital in Warwickshire but couldn't cope with the stress and had to leave.

'I don't think there was a night when I was sober for a year,' he recalls. 'For two years I was a very strange person. I'm quite strange anyway. Part of my appeal to people is that they think I'm a bit oddball. It's almost as if I try to be wild deliberately to ruin my body.'

At parties if he drank too much he burst into tears and questioned why others had died and he hadn't. 'For those two years I felt as if my brain was made of mercury and if it got too hot it would explode out of the top of my head,' he says. 'I used to attack trees and cars and rip them to shreds until I had no energy and collapsed in a heap. That was frightening to other people who knew me.

'I'm relieved I didn't take it out on people. I felt a lot of anger against society. I was angry with people who worked for big companies and the government who thought they stood for something which was good and proper and it's not.'

When he couldn't install the car stereo he beat it with a stick and felt better. When he tried to play guitar and couldn't concentrate he smashed it to pieces outside his house. His father John came out to find the fret-board in his hands.

Sean's father, also a keen Liverpool fan, was sitting in the stand during the disaster. They have never talked to each other about it. Sean has discovered he was helped over the fence by a sixteen-year-old boy. The boy wrote to him saying he was pleased he had recovered. Sean tried to ring him but he wouldn't come to the telephone. 'I was quite relieved,' says Sean. 'We'd have had nothing else in common except football and the fact that he saved my life.'

Sean hasn't been able to concentrate on anything since the disaster. He used to ride horses and enjoyed football and hockey, but has given them all up. When it comes to a job he has the same problem. Three months is the longest he has worked anywhere, and that was in a wine bar. He went to Newcastle Polytechnic to study psychology but only stayed for six months.

If it hadn't been for the disaster, he says, 'I'd have been sucked more and more into the machine and I'd probably have a mortgage now.' Instead he sings and writes lyrics for the band. 'I always wanted to be a bit different,' he says. 'Hopefully one day I'll make a living from it.'

Steve Whittall could have used Hillsborough as a chance to be different too. He was just nineteen and a first-year student at Leeds University when it happened. He had all his belongings in the car ready to start his final term.

Steve survived the disaster but then faced a desperate battle to hold his life together. Two days after he stood in the crush on the terraces Steve was back in lectures. The 9 a.m. lecture on Monday was on data analysis. 'I was in a different world,' he recalls. 'I wasn't taking anything in. I was still trying to take in what had happened to me. I went to a lecture in organization studies after that and it was just the same.'

Steve decided it would be easier to go home to Wiltshire to revise. 'I was trying to minimize the effect and deny it was happening,' he says. 'It didn't make any difference, I couldn't work at home. All my books were laid out on the table but my mind was elsewhere. It was like a constant picture on a television screen and I couldn't turn it off.' Steve could see the bodies on the terraces, he could feel the crushing, hear the shouting, and the sirens of the ambulances.

It was a relief when he was told he didn't have to take his exams in May, but he wasn't happy about it and felt he'd failed. The summer was spent trying to revise so that he could take the exams in September. 'I felt my head was in a cloud of confusion,' he recalls. 'There were times when I felt, "What's the point in trying?" I was becoming more and more frustrated. I became very depressed and broke down a few times by myself. I didn't show my emotions in front of people.'

Steve passed three of the six papers. 'I felt gutted,' he says. All that time had been spent revising, working through the night to cram it in; all his hopes had been on doing well and he'd failed. He found a job as a contract manager for a roofing company in Manchester. 'I took several sick days because everything was getting on top of me,' he recalls. 'I was just lying on my bed pondering my future and asking myself if it was what I really wanted to do. My direction had gone and I wasn't sure I had the ability to take the exams again.'

Steve's area manager was worried about his performance. His concentration wasn't there and his heart wasn't in the job, but he needed to work to survive financially. When he decided to leave in January the firm offered him more money and a company car to stay. It wasn't enough.

A delighted Steve was given £5,000 out of the disaster fund and that wiped out his debts and meant he was able to go back to studying. He took his exams again and passed them, even though the marks weren't great. 'I felt very ill and mentally and physically tired when I was revising,' he says. 'I wasn't just fighting the trauma; I was fighting the fact that I'd failed before.'

Steve continued with the course but it took him two years to build up his confidence again. In 1992 he was awarded a BA (Hons) degree in management studies and decided to travel for fifteen months. After that he plans to do a master's degree, looking at how people cope with change.

'This year I wanted to go to Liverpool on the anniversary but I hadn't got time because of my finals. I decided not to. That showed me I had more control,' he says. 'Sometimes I feel guilty for feeling better. I know it hasn't been easy, but I know I've suffered so perhaps that takes away some of the guilt.'

Survivor Ron Holmes couldn't forgive himself after the Hillsborough disaster. A boy had been crushed to death in front of him – and he hadn't been able to do anything about it. Ron had always been in control before. His wife Thelma had never seen him cry, not in all their twenty years of marriage. She'd always thought he was a bit on the hard side. He was an assertive type, who lived life to the full and had bags of confidence. The day after the Hillsborough disaster Ron was heartbroken, a changed man. In the eighteen months that followed he thought he was coping with the disaster, but his family knew he wasn't.

Ron, who works in the Ford factory on Merseyside, was forty-two when the disaster happened, Thelma was five years younger. He was standing a couple of steps from the wire fence directly behind the goal. 'I felt the crush was getting tighter and tighter,' he recalls.

'I became aware of a lad struggling, he was shouting for help. I couldn't see his face or his body, all I could see was an arm and a leg sticking up. I put his foot on my chest and got hold of his arm, and I was trying to lever him up. Then a crush barrier collapsed and we fell on top of him. I was pressing him against the concrete, I could feel my knees across the top half of his body. I could hear him screaming, "Get me up! Help! Help!" Then I felt him shuddering, and he stopped shouting.'

Ron managed to push his own head up above the crush. 'This sounds stupid,' he says, as he recalls what he did next. 'I tried to get a message to my wife through telepathy. I thought I was going to die and I wanted to say I was sorry that I was leaving her on her own. I was thinking of my two teenage sons and hoping I'd given them a good life.'

Ron's shoes had been ripped off and his feet were off the ground. 'I was looking at the sky and it was a lovely sunny day,' he recalls. 'I was thinking it was such a nice day to die.' He could hear the screams, see people trying to pull down the fence in front of him, but he was in another world.

Then he tripped over, the crush eased and someone started pulling him up. 'We've got to help this lad,' Ron was crying out in desperation. He didn't have a clue where the boy had gone to. The man spoke to Ron: 'Leave it lad, there's nothing you can do for them now,' he said. Ron looked around and saw so many bodies he couldn't tell who the lad was. He never found out.

He walked back through the tunnel in a daze and went with his mates to get drunk. On Tuesday he was back at work and at the end of the first week decided he had to

put the disaster to the back of his mind. Thelma knew her
husband had changed. "When he went to bed he couldn't
settle unless I had my arm across him or he was holding
my hand. It was just so out of character. If he was going
to the shop or the bank he wanted me to go with him. I
couldn't understand it but I didn't think it was because of
the disaster.'

To Ron life didn't seem real any more. 'I finished work
every Friday and went straight on the ale,' he says. 'At
weekends I drank myself silly and I was rarely sober. My
memory suffered terribly, my confidence had gone and I
was just a million miles away all the time. I didn't bother
with my wife and children. My two lads couldn't understand why I didn't spend any time with them, why I never
talked to them and was snappy with them.'

Thelma was worried. 'We'd always been pretty close
and we'd had a good relationship but we just seemed to
lose it. I told him we didn't seem to be friends any more.
He began to look really haunted; I'd never seen him look
so ill.'

Ron felt more in common with the people who were
involved in the disaster than he did with his own family
and friends. 'The people who were at Hillsborough could
understand and they were my family,' he says. 'I felt the
only thing that was real was that day and that day was my
whole life.'

Ron started going to watch Liverpool FC more than
ever, following them to away as well as home matches.
Yet he had to give up running the local football team he'd
been manager of for thirteen years. 'I wasn't enjoying it
any more,' he says. 'I had to upset some of the players by
leaving them out and telling them they weren't good
enough and I didn't want to do it any more.'

He knew there was something wrong the day he had to
go on to the pitch to sponge down an injured player. An

argument started with someone from the other team. 'They punched me in the face and I couldn't feel the pain,' he recalls. 'I didn't feel any anger, any emotion at all.'

Eighteen months after the disaster Ron first admitted that he wasn't coping, and went to the Hillsborough Centre. 'One day I just couldn't take it any more. I came out of work and told my wife I thought I needed help. I felt everything was closing in on me.'

Ron had been working at the factory for twenty years and for ten of those years had been a supervisor on the shop floor. After the disaster he felt he wasn't doing his job properly. 'As a supervisor I had to go in and discipline people and sort trouble out. It just didn't seem important when I'd been in the middle of all those people being crushed to death. I started to question why I wanted to argue.'

Ron had two months off work. One morning he put on his shirt and tie and set off to go back. It was 7.30 a.m. as he approached the factory. He looked at his watch again and it was 10.30 a.m., and he was walking along the promenade in Southport. He doesn't remember anything in between.

Ron admitted to himself that his behaviour was different because of Hillsborough. 'I went to the Centre and jpoured all my feelings out,' he says. 'It was the first time I had spoken in depth about the disaster. I'm glad I was talking to a woman. If I'd started crying in front of a man I think I'd have felt a bit stupid.'

Thelma admits she was jealous of the counsellor. 'She was a really nice person but I was jealous because I knew she was giving him something I couldn't,' she says. At the Centre Ron and Thelma watched a video of the disaster, and both cried.

As Ron saw himself walking through the turnstiles he realized it hadn't been a nightmare: it had really happened to him. Thelma could also see what he'd been through. 'I couldn't believe it,' she recalls. 'I'd imagined it was like a busy Saturday morning in Liverpool, but it was totally different. It made it easier for me to talk to him about it.'

They're even closer now than they were before the disaster and Thelma is relieved to see the mischievous sparkle back in her husband's eyes. Both are happy that Ron was eventually downgraded because of the strain he felt at work.

'Now I've gone into the office and there is no stress involved,' he says. 'I don't have to tell people what to do and my confidence is coming back. I don't try to force my opinions on people as I used to. The disaster has made me realize that everyone has the right to live on this planet, and everyone has the right to their opinion. I don't criticize people as much as I used to, I just want to get on with everyone.'

Ron doesn't feel guilty about the death of the teenager any more. He says, 'I just wish I'd known who he was so that I could have gone to his funeral and said sorry to his family for not being able to save him. I remember him shouting for his mum and I'd like to have told her that. I felt he was a friend even though I'd never spoken to him.'

# CHAPTER NINE

# THE *MARCHIONESS*

## 20 August 1989

A year after the *Marchioness* disaster Madeline Anderton was arrested. She had survived the river boat disaster but then found herself in a prison cell next to Moors murderer Myra Hindley. Her life had fallen apart. 'Life in prison was hell,' says the once flamboyant party goer. 'I'm too much of a lady to be there. I've always lived in a clean house, and had clean clothes, and I've never eaten crap food. If I had to go back I'd kill myself.'

Maddy was jailed for fifteen months at Croydon court in January 1992 after pleading guilty to having five ounces of cocaine with intent to supply. The cocaine was worth £11,000. She insists that the cocaine had been left in her fridge for half an hour by someone she knew.

Maddy served six months in prison. Now she is out but has no bank account, no business and no credibility. 'I never hated anybody before, but now I hate everybody,' she says. 'I'm completely different to the woman I was before the disaster.'

Maddy was in the upstairs bar of the Thames pleasure cruiser when it happened. Her good friend Antonio de Vasconcellos was celebrating his twenty-sixth birthday. He was so much younger than Maddy who, at forty-five, was older than most of the guests on the boat. Yet she had always fascinated him. 'Darling, you're going,' he'd said when she'd tried to tell him she wouldn't be at his party.

They had known each other for eighteen months and she watched him with affection as he unwrapped his presents. He was admiring an art deco tortoise, a gift from a fashion model friend. Downstairs the other guests were dancing, she could hear the music, 'Ladies Night', a song by Kool and the Gang. Those in the restaurant were sampling a selection of hors d'oeuvre.

Maddy's present to Antonio was a tarot-card reading. What else could she give the man who had everything? She'd brought along her friend, the white witch, Jackie James, to look into his future. Jackie wasn't happy. She couldn't swim, she told Maddy, as the two went to the bar together. Maddy was busy reassuring her when the collision happened.

At 1.46 a.m. as the revellers danced the night away there was a collision near Southwark Bridge between the dredger *Bowbelle* and the *Marchioness*. Antonio and fifty others died.

'The glass window caved in and the boat tilted so fast,' Maddy recalls. 'The people slid and crumpled on top of each other. I was trying to keep my feet, grabbing a stainless steel bar on the window with one hand, and holding on to Jackie with the other.'

As the water washed her out through the window she stretched out her arms in front in a dive position. Terrified, she thought she was going to be cut to pieces on the jagged glass. No sooner was that terror over than another took its place.

Maddy found herself inside a pipe on the riverbed. 'I started moving my feet, and I was shocked I still had them after coming through the window,' she says. 'Then I felt the skin on my arms and legs coming off and realized I was in a pipe. I thought that no one would find me and that I was going to drown.' Then suddenly she popped out like a champagne cork.

Maddy was treated in hospital and came home to her London flat the following morning. Straight away she drank a bottle of brandy but still felt sober. Her black silk trouser suit, with its pink and yellow orchids, was in shreds. Covered in grease and dirt, Maddy was put to bed by her neighbours; there was no way she was going to get into a shower.

In the months that followed Maddy turned to alcohol for comfort. After the disaster she says: 'I hit the bottle and was boozing quite badly for a year. I was drinking about four bottles of wine a day. I'd wake up in the morning and have another drink.'

The once fun-loving Maddy wished she had died in the disaster. It made her angry, brought out an aggressiveness she hadn't felt since she was a child coping with the frustrations of dyslexia. Growing up she found a way to control that aggressiveness but suddenly the control had gone. In prison she rebelled all the way.

'I had a row with a girl who gave me plenty of grief,' she says. 'I was sick and in bed for a week with a bad throat infection. The girls said there was salad that night so I thought I'd have some. I queued for twenty minutes and this girl who was doing eight years for cocaine refused to serve me. I slung some tea over her. If I'd got my hands on her I'd have killed her. The screws got me up against the wall with my arm up my back.'

Maddy was moved to the hospital wing at Cookham Wood prison, physically and mentally exhausted. During the night she had a panic attack in her cell. 'I was locked up on my own with just a stainless steel sink. I started shaking and couldn't breathe, I thought I was having a heart attack. I hit the button but the screws wouldn't come into my cell. They said: "Try to relax." The doctor came and gave me an injection.'

Maddy woke up at 6.30 a.m., an hour before the doors

were unlocked. 'I could hear them saying, "Myra, Myra, are you up yet?" I thought: "What am I doing here with Myra Hindley in the next cell?"'

The inmates in East Sutton Park open prison, where she spent most of her time, formed their own complaints committee, and Maddy was on it. They needed more irons, so she had a meeting with senior officers to get them. Her jobs included looking after the chickens and in winter working in the gardens wearing huge, heavy boots. Before the disaster Maddy had been a products demonstrator and had worked in Canada, America and Holland. She also had her own secondhand stall in Brixton market.

Now she has nothing. She still suffers from severe depression and has seen a series of psychoanalysts since the disaster. 'It comes over me like a blanket,' she says. 'It's the same sort of feeling you have when someone close to you dies.' Maddy says she isn't strong enough to open her market stall again. How could she stand in the market again after being in prison, she asks. 'It's not nice, people always think you're guilty,' she says. 'I have come home to nothing, I've never been skint in my life.' Despite her problems Maddy refuses to give up. She has plans to start again, and set up her own business importing antiques into Israel.

Before the disaster, she says, 'I was the sort of lady you'd want at your party. I was fun, I loved to dance, to see people enjoying themselves, I loved to entertain and cook lovely food.' A single woman, she did what she wanted to do and had a wonderful life.

'Now I'm boring and I don't want to go anywhere,' she says, she didn't even want to go to the party her friends organized to welcome her home. 'It's sad, isn't it?' she says.

*

Jackie James, the friend who accompanied Maddy on the night of the disaster, has also become something of a recluse. She is called the white witch of Brixton and everyone there knows her. They call to her in the market, shout hallo as she walks down the street.

Jackie doesn't allow her friends into her second-floor flat. It's been out of bounds to visitors since February 1991, and hasn't been cleaned since. 'It's dusty and a mess,' she says. 'There's a kind of knitting pattern growing over everything. I drink a bit too much since the disaster and the cans and bottles are piled up. I've piled clothes on the chairs so people can't sit down. I plan to clean the place up but then my knee hurts. I start to do a few things but I have to have a rest. I can't understand how people can't find anything to watch on television.'

We meet in a friend's house. Jackie lowers herself into the chair, and takes a vodka bottle out of her bag. Her friend goes off in search of the orange juice. 'I live on my own and I've become a complete hermit,' she says. 'I feel there has to be somewhere where I can get the shakes, where I can scream and cry and someone isn't going to catch me out. If they knock on the door I don't answer. I sometimes feel that I want to smash the place up. I live my life either laughing or crying; it's a tightrope between bliss and hell.'

Jackie is in her early sixties, a mother of three grown-up children and a reader of tarot cards. She has walked with a stick since her leg was shattered in the disaster. The fact that Jackie survived when so many people died has only added to her reputation as a witch. 'Some people are sceptical and ask why I put myself in a dangerous position,' she says. 'I say it's because I didn't listen to the signs. I didn't want to go but I was determined not to let Maddy down.'

The water looked so black and evil that night and she felt frightened. She was in the second deck saloon bar when the collision happened, reading cards for one of the guests.

The cards predicted a dangerous river crossing but the boy said he was modelling abroad in the near future. 'There were a lot of Hooray Henry types picking up the cards and making jokes,' she recalls. 'It made me cross. My cards are holy and I didn't want people picking them up, saying: "What does this mean?" and tossing them down again.

'Suddenly someone was kneeling on a seat beside me, shouting out of the window and saying, "They haven't seen us." Everyone was looking out of the windows. The next second the *Bowbelle* ploughed into the side. It made a horrible grating noise.' The anchor on the front of the boat came through the window beside her. She can still remember its rusty smell.

As the water rushed in it swept Jackie underneath the table where she had been sitting. She was completely submerged in water and unable to swim. She held her breath and thought she was about to die. Her scarlet dress with its full sleeves and long skirt was billowing around her. The table had fallen on top of it and trapped her. She could feel the other guests grabbing at the material, desperate to stay alive. The noise as it ripped sounded so much louder under water.

Eventually the dress was torn off and Jackie was free. The water swept her again, this time pushing her underneath something else. She felt the cushion and realized it was a seat. As she tried to escape she was struck by swimming feet and thought she was going to be kicked to death.

'Out of the darkness someone grabbed my arm,' she remembers. 'I could feel the bubbles coming out of their mouth and I knew it was a person. The bubbles stopped, the hand fell off, and I was relieved they died before they killed me.

'The next thing I knew I was free. I don't know how, but I remember having to tear my hair to escape. I was flapping my arms like flippers going up through the water. I got to the top and I thought I was safe.'

The fast-moving current tipped her upside down. 'Help! I can't swim!' she shouted as she struggled to stay on the surface. She was naked apart from her boots and could feel what she thinks was crustaceans biting her. Then another girl called over: 'I can't swim either, but I'm going to try to get to you.' A black shape came surging out of the water, two strangers facing death together.

The girl grabbed a piece of wreckage and pushed it under the older woman's chin. Jackie called out, 'Hold my hand,' and the two linked their fingers together. 'She saved my life,' says Jackie. 'I started to get hypothermia. I was so tired and so cold I couldn't shiver any more. I could hear the girl's voice in the distance, but I couldn't be bothered answering.

'As I was drifting off to sleep I heard her say there was a boat coming, then she screamed; "They haven't seen us!"' Jackie was hit by the rescue launch, and two of her teeth were knocked out. As she rolled underneath it the propeller caught her and spun her around. Climbing on board, she begged the man who was helping her not to drop her back into the water again.

Jackie was in St Thomas's Hospital in London for nine weeks. One night she thought she saw a party going on, and watched for hours as young revellers enjoyed themselves on the window ledge of a block opposite. 'I realized they were in a life-threatening situation,' she says. 'They were twenty-two storeys up with nothing to protect them and they were drinking. I told a nurse but she told me there was no one there.

'They were looking at me, shrugging, as if to say, "She can't see us." They seemed to be floating on the window ledge. They were looking down at me saying; "We're having a ball, we all went together."' Jackie believes it was the people who died. They were trying to tell her not to feel so guilty about the fact that she had survived.

Jackie carried enormous guilt because of the way she felt when the person hanging on to her died. It was her own life or that of the other person – who was a perfect stranger – but she didn't like the fact that she'd felt relieved. 'I've met some of the bereaved parents since the disaster and they know the story,' she says. 'They all look at me wondering if it was their son or daughter.'

'At first when they read that a woman of fifty-seven had survived when their children had died I know they all hated me. When I went in a wheelchair to the first group meeting I felt such hostility from the bereaved. Then a mother came up to me and said: "I'm glad to meet you, we were all hating you, but now we know you." I've grown very close to a lot of the mothers.'

Jackie knows her leg will not get any better. 'I still feel I'm going to wake up and it's just a dream,' she says. 'I can't be a cripple for the rest of my life, not able to go dancing ever again or walk long distances. It has destroyed me. A friend of mine for eighteen years has had to terminate the friendship, as every time she sees me she gets a migraine.'

When Jackie was thirty she modelled stockings and photographs of her legs were up in the underground. 'Everything I've done in my life has been centred on my appearance,' she continues. Her waist–length hair has been cut to her shoulders since the disaster.

'My mother deteriorated into a bent shaky person over thirty years but it has happened to me overnight,' she says. 'I feel resentful, robbed and cheated. I look in the window and think: "Who is that old granny?" I can't go on demonstrations now. I raised my children on marches. "Save the whales." "Ban the bomb." I was anti–this and anti–that, but I can't do it any more.'

The disaster has left Jackie so frightened of water that she can't drink it and has to have bubbles in her bath. 'I think if anything bad is going to happen it will happen to me,' she says. 'The other night I thought lightning was going to strike the flat. I think it will crumble and fall down and that aeroplanes are going to crash through the window.' Jackie flashes back to the disaster if she hears the growing rumble of a child on roller-skates. Sometimes she is so upset she can't eat, at other times she eats for comfort.

She has been to see three psychologists, her 'Aries lady', her 'Sagittarius lady' and her 'Leo lady'. 'I saw the Leo lady last week and she said I'd gone backwards,' says Jackie. 'I laugh and joke and make out I'm getting better for my friends. I don't like miserable people.'


Erika Spotswood is fed up with crying. She was twenty-five when she survived the *Marchioness* disaster along with her boyfriend Roger. 'The saddest thing is that our relationship is coloured by it,' she says.

The couple share a flat in London's fashionable Chiswick. She sings in a band called Ruby Blue and he plays guitar. 'We both handled it in different ways,' she says. 'I involved myself with fund-raising and putting on concerts. Roger was the opposite, he didn't really want to think or talk about it too much.'

'I'd spend ages on the telephone trying to organize a concert, he wanted to shut it out of his life and I dragged it in front of his face.'

If only one of them had been involved in the disaster the other would have been more understanding, she believes. 'We are both demanding of each other and we can't give to each other because we're trying to handle it ourselves,' she says. They associate the disaster with each other. 'I associate that horrific time with him and he does with me. There's no way you can ever escape that,' she continues. 'We had just bought this flat and we stayed here the night it happened. We decorated it and moved in our stuff while the funerals were going on. The disaster is also associated with this place.'

Erika knew about twenty people at the party and went to funerals and memorials for a month. 'The disaster aged me and took a lot of joy away,' she says. She couldn't read, she couldn't disappear into another world in a book when her own had so much confusion.

When the £8,000 disaster payment came the cheque felt dirty. 'At the time I really needed the money. I felt really guilty for having wanted it. It was like pay-off time. I felt I had no right to my emotions after that.'

Erika believes she lost her excitement about life as a result of the disaster, but a strength is coming in its place, a determination to be in control. She feels a need for certainty and security in her life.

'People keep asking me when I'm going to write some happy songs,' she says. 'I was never so inward-looking before, never so searching.'

★

Clare Smith, another passenger on the *Marchioness*, believes the disaster robbed her of her youth. It happened days before her twenty-sixth birthday and Clare, who lives in London, has hardly socialized since. It also robbed her of her livelihood.

'I was self-employed as an illustrator, but my little business went completely down the drain,' she says. 'I thought I was OK but unknown to me I was neglecting the business and not doing any work. I was putting tax returns somewhere and finding them a couple of months later.

'I neglected my personal appearance and became very scruffy. I went through a phase where I kept forgetting to clean my teeth. It was an immense strain to hold my life together and it's still very difficult.'

For three years Clare had a telephone phobia and if she was alone in the house and it rang she wouldn't answer it. If there was someone else there they answered unless she was expecting an important call.

'I put so much trouble, time and money into being an illustrator,' she says. 'I associate it now with failure and disaster.' Clare has now found a part-time job, teaching English to foreign students; eight hours a week is all she can manage. 'I'm generally more nervous and anxious,' she says. 'I'm gradually trying to regain my confidence.'

Frederick Lupson is terrified that he is going to die. 'For the past year I've been convinced I've got a terminal illness,' he says. 'I think maybe I've got Parkinson's disease, maybe I've got breast cancer – I'm sure men can have that too.'

His nineteen-year-old cousin Lee was killed in the *Marchioness* disaster. Frederick had taken him to the party, and like many bereaved survivors blames himself. The two men were like brothers. When he was a child Lee spent the summer staying with his seven cousins in the Kent countryside. Frederick, who was three years older, taught him to ride and swim. They went on holiday together, they were planning to go to Ibiza two weeks after the disaster.

Frederick was on the deck of the *Marchioness* talking to friends when it happened. He saw the *Bowbelle* seconds before the collision. 'I slid down into the water, the boat turned over on top of me and pushed me down. When I tried to get up I banged my head, I remember thinking I needed to swim down and away, and that's what I did.' Frederick took off his training shoes – as a follower of fashion he had laced them loosely for effect – and when he kicked they slipped off. 'I was crying under water,' he recalls. 'I thought I was going to die.'

Then he started swimming up through the water. 'I felt people beneath me and they were clawing at me as I was trying to get out. It was almost like hell. When I surfaced it was like waking up to a nightmare. There was relief that I could breathe but it was the end and the beginning. Around me there was terror, people were screaming and crying.' A life-belt surfaced near him and he held on to it. Then he saw a large raft with people on floating past about two hundred yards away. He took his jeans off and swam for it, and they were later picked up by the police boat. 'I sat and screamed as if I knew my cousin had died,' he says.

Frederick couldn't accept his cousin's death. 'For two years I tried to put it to the back of my mind. It made me neurotic, nervous and violent. I became disillusioned with my parents and my brothers and sisters. I didn't want any contact with them. I became obsessed with death, convinced I was going to die any time, as if every evening was the last supper. I slept all day and when I woke up I wanted to bite someone's head off.'

Frederick found it difficult to trust people. 'I didn't trust anyone,' he says. 'I thought I was being used. I didn't think they liked me for myself and I thought family and friends were planning behind my back.'

Frederick's behaviour also changed. 'If anything was to hand I'd smash it. I smashed cups, glasses, plates and a telephone answering machine. I don't smash anything now because I can't afford to replace it.'

For two years he was dependent on drink to help him escape. 'Many days I'd wake up and it was as if all the wrong parts of my brain were functioning and I was going over the edge. If I hadn't got my family around me then I would have signed myself into a psychiatric hospital.'

His parents helped him financially but cut back the allowance when they found out what he was spending money on. Despite their help he ran up a bank overdraft of £3,000, and borrowed from friends telling them he'd pay them back when he was working.

In some ways his relationship with his family has improved, because they all realize how fragile life is. Sometimes Frederick convinces himself he doesn't need or like them. 'Every now and then I pick an argument with my father. We don't talk and I think that's just how I want it,' he says. 'I don't need any closeness with my family because I'm afraid of being hurt again.'

He hasn't been able to talk to his aunt about the death of her son although they'd always had a good relationship before and she'd been like a second mother to him. She'd been so understanding when he told his family he was homosexual. 'There are some things now that we can't talk about whereas we talked about everything before,' he says. 'I'd like to be able to clear the air so that we can cry together. I know that she doesn't blame me. But her son's death is slowly killing her; she was so devastated, so crippled by it.'

Frederick still blames himself for not looking after Lee enough and as a result has become overprotective of his friends. He started seeing a counsellor in March 1992.

He says: 'Before, I was a young kid trying to make good in life, enjoying every minute of it. Now I'm cynical and desperate.' He hasn't worked since the disaster. He was studying for A levels when it happened, but never went back to college. His plans to go on to university and become a journalist were abandoned.

'I have no ambition whatsoever,' he says. 'I really don't care. I'd be quite happy to lose myself in oblivion. Now I try to fill my life as much as possible with mundane things. I have a little dog and that helps.' Before he used to walk around his London flat in a trance.

'I feel I am no longer in control of my job, my financial situation or my future. I hope I will work one day. I'd like to think one day I could get on with my life.'

*Marchioness* survivor Annette Russell has been able to get on with her life, and she believes that work has helped her to cope. 'I think many of those who attempt to get better prior to working are taking the wrong option,' she believes. 'Occupying your mind and forcing yourself to do something productive is good therapy. You're giving yourself another pressure to take the pain away.'

The former model and beauty queen was less than two months away from opening her own model agency when the disaster happened. Antonio de Vasconcellos, who was killed, was going to be the financier and her partner and just days before they had been to the solicitors to register the company. She had invited four models to the party and two died. Two of the agency's proposed staff, whom she'd invited, also perished.

Annette had invited about twelve people in all but many of her other close friends were on board. Like Frederick she felt guilty that they'd died. She now finds it difficult to invite friends to anything.

Annette was twenty-six when the disaster happened. She was on the deck and dived off the side at the moment of impact. The tide took her underneath the boat and out the other side.

'I didn't think I was ever going to come up,' she says. She swam to the shore and along with three other people climbed up a rickety steel ladder set against a huge brick wall. They climbed over the wall, into the street, and stopped a passing car to take them to hospital. He charged them £10 for the trip.

Annette went to nine of the funerals. 'It was awful looking at the mothers,' she says. 'You know they're looking at you thinking: "Why did she live and why did my child die?"' Annette plucked up courage to visit the mother of one of the models and went alone. Her heart was racing as she knocked on the door. 'I walked in and she sat me down on the sofa,' Annette recalls. 'She was holding her little baby who had been born a couple of nights before the disaster. Her son hadn't seen it. She took my hand and said, "Do you want to cry now? You must be feeling terrible pressure because no one is going to notice that you're hurting." She was strong for me.'

For the first year Annette admits she was 'a complete mess'. 'I was running around like a mad woman, trying to escape. It was horrible. Crossing the road was a nightmare, walking along the street on my own was a nightmare and trying to communicate with anyone other than a survivor was virtually impossible. I thought no one else would understand and I didn't do anything unless there was another survivor around. We clung to each other.'

Despite her suffering she went ahead and set up her business. 'I wasn't going to come back into the business but the models I represent forced me to,' she says. 'We had to be self-financing because I couldn't find another financier. I started with a phone, and an old desk and chair. My parents gave me some money which created financial pressure for them.'

Before the disaster Annette worked for another agency, booking models. 'I was earning quite a lot of money and was quite a valuable asset,' she says. 'I chose to go into business with a partner. Now I'm in business alone, earning a quarter of what I was then.'

She is too afraid to book travel for any of her models in case something happens to them, so someone else in the agency has to do it. 'I don't think I have ever given my company anywhere near as much as I gave to the other agencies before because I've never been capable of it,' she says. 'When I'm on form I'm good,' she laughs. 'It's just that I'm not on form all the time.'

Annette sleeps between two and six hours a night and that means she is sometimes tired and stressed. Her mood swings are still severe, but she has now come to terms with them. At least now she's feeling high or low whereas before it was low or very low.

Now she will cry in public whereas before the disaster she wouldn't have dared. 'When I'm at the very bottom it hurts,' she says. 'But I don't know quite what it is that hurts. There's still a lot of guilt. I've done a lot of sitting around in desperation behind closed doors. I've stayed in my bed for long periods of time, not asleep but hidden, ignoring the telephone.'

In some ways she feels more joy than she did before, just because she's grateful to be alive. But also, like

Frederick, she feels that death is round every corner. 'I worry that I might do something stupid like walking out in front of a car because my mind is so full of things or I'm crying too much or I'm in a daze of escapism. I feel like I've been dealt a very difficult sentence. I don't know what for, obviously I did something wrong. I believe we all get our come-uppance and perhaps that was what happened to me.'

Photographer Iain Philpott was on the brink of bankruptcy as a result of the *Marchioness* disaster. He was twenty-six when it happened and at the party with his twenty-four-year-old girlfriend Tamsin Cole. Tamsin drowned and Iain didn't realize that he would have to fight for his own survival in the years that followed.

'I was the classic case of Thatcher's children,' he says. 'I suppose all of us were to some extent. When Mrs Thatcher came to power I was sixteen. At eighteen I left art college and went straight into fashion photography. I had a wonderful girlfriend, I was earning a fair amount, I owned a flat and I had no money worries. It was probably as close as one could get to having a Utopian life. I now believe that nothing good lasts for ever and nothing bad lasts for ever either.'

He had known Tamsin, a model's agent, since she was sixteen. When she was twenty-one they started having a relationship and had talked about getting married. He recalls how he shouted and screamed for her as he was in the water. Iain spent most of the following month going to the funerals of his friends. Soon his business started to suffer.

Clients disappeared. With fashion shoots costing up to £30,000 a day, they were not going to trust a photographer who'd been through such a traumatic experience. 'This business is so competitive,' he says, as we talk in his new London studio

In October, two months after the disaster, two of Iain's fashion shoots didn't go well, one had to be done again. 'I blame myself because I wasn't in the right frame of mind to do them,' he says, 'but gossip like that spreads fast.' For eighteen months after the disaster his pictures were dropped or regularly re-shot. That had never happened to him in his five years as a photographer. 'Word was out across town that Iain Philpott couldn't do a shoot.'

At Iain's worst point, in July 1991, he was three months behind with his mortgage, £32,000 overdrawn at the bank, had creditors' debts of £15,000 and owed about £5,000 for his car. 'It was extremely worrying. I was going to lose my house and every single thing I'd worked for,' he says.

Incredibly he has managed to fight back. At a time when the industry was heading deeper into recession his business was booming again. 'I think we did an amazing job persuading clients that I can still take pictures,' he says. 'It's been a battle.' It was January 1992 before he was taking pictures anything like the standard he was shooting before. 'I lost three years out of my life as a result of the *Marchioness*, and I can't replace them,' he believes.

Iain lost £60,000 in earnings alone. When it comes to compensation he says: 'I won't settle for a cent less than I think I should, even if it takes another ten years.' He helped to set up the *Marchioness* Action Group to represent survivors and relatives. He has spent hours finding out about marine safety and why disasters happen. 'I'm fairly cynical now,' he says. 'I'm certainly nowhere near as happy-go-lucky as I was and I find it difficult to trust people. I find that I won't let anyone get close. I don't know if I ever will.'

Now he has a new relationship with a girl he knew before the disaster. He was working with her after it happened and she'd just lost a good friend in a car crash. They found comfort talking to each other. 'It's been difficult,' he says. 'She's had to put up with a hell of a lot.'

He still has to cope with flashbacks to the disaster. They can be triggered by an advertisement on television showing a swimming pool. He can't go near a school playground because the screams remind him of the noise he heard in the water. He doesn't enjoy sailing now, he hates the nightclubs he used to love and doesn't go out very much. The first thing he does when he checks into a hotel is find out where the fire exits are. He can't travel on the underground and his fear of flying is increasing. 'I don't trust people to take care of me,' he says. 'I don't want to depend on anything or anyone. At the end of the day I can only depend on myself.

'I hated the thought of death with a passion before; now I think it's inevitable. God knows why I felt I had to be immortal, with hindsight it was completely stupid. I find I analyse things more – "Why am I doing this? Why do I feel like this?" – rather than just accepting it as I did before.

'I take life more seriously in some ways but the materialistic side of life holds nothing for me now. Before, money was a major draw. Now, so long as I can pay my bills I have no great desire for all the trappings of success. I'm probably far more caring. If all I had was taken away tomorrow I wouldn't give a damn whereas before it would have been a major trauma in my life. I don't care about the future. I'm living and I think I enjoy it.'

Odette Penwarden loves her life and likes the woman she's become since the *Marchioness* disaster. 'I went through hell but in many ways it was a learning process.' she says.

Before it happened she was a successful marketing executive aiming for the top of the tree in the tourism industry. She travelled throughout Europe, dined in all the best restaurants. She was popular, vivacious, wanted everyone to know her. 'There goes Odette,' she wanted them to say. Now as she strolls through London she still stands out from the crowd in her bright yellow jumper, red hair and red-rimmed spectacles. But her aims have changed.

The new Odette is on a two-year college course in counselling, enjoys charity work, and wants to become a bereavement counsellor. 'I want to spend my time helping people,' she says as she sips a slimline tonic. 'I have a much simpler life now than I had before the disaster. I really wouldn't want to be the person I was then. I'm much more caring now, a lot more patient with people who have problems. I was always searching for more exciting things to happen. Now I've settled into me, and it's all thanks to therapy.'

Odette was forty-one when the disaster happened, and was marketing boats on the Thames. The party had been her idea and she had booked the boat. It was Odette who insisted that her closest friend Peter should come along too. When he was killed she wished that she was dead too. Her guilt was enormous. Peter had been tired that night but she had dragged him along. 'We were very close, everything but lovers really,' she says.

Odette felt like Peter's widow. 'The day of his funeral we all went for a bite to eat afterwards at the wine bar that Peter and I used to go to all the time,' she recalls. Odette was left sitting on her own and decided to walk out and down to the river. 'I nearly threw myself in,' she says. 'I remember thinking: "That's where Peter is and I want to be with him." Something made me walk away.'

Odette didn't know what to do with her life any more and left her job after a few weeks. She went home and stayed in bed for a fortnight. In three months she put on two stones in weight. 'It was disgusting,' she says as she recalls the nights when she crept underneath the cover with bags of cashew nuts, crisps and pieces of cheese. In the shocking aftermath of the disaster taste was the only sensation she could feel, so she ate all the time for comfort.

'I remember being invited to a party because I was a survivor of the *Marchioness*,' she says. 'It was at a neighbour's house and she'd told everybody before I got there.' Odette spoke to a couple of people before she realized. 'Then I picked up my coat and said I was leaving. I said: "I'm not being treated as the cabaret." I was livid.'

A risk-taker all her life, Odette couldn't understand how the disaster had happened to her. 'Nothing bad had ever happened to me and it never occurred to me that it could,' she says. She'd enjoyed the thrill of flying in light aircraft and loved the excitement of water sports. Then on a lovely summer night she almost died.

She became obsessed with the disaster, wanted everyone to know she'd been on the *Marchioness*, and grabbed any excuse to talk about it. On the bus she smiled at the person sitting next to her, they smiled back. Then she said: 'Well, I'm lucky to be alive.' 'Crazy, absolutely crazy,' she says looking back.

'Part of me could operate, I could go and do the shopping, but the other part was screaming, terrified all the time.' When her psychologist told her it was Post Traumatic Stress she says: 'It was such a relief. I thought: "There's a name for this; I'm not on my own."'

When Odette first went to see the psychologist she sat and sobbed. 'That went on for weeks and then I started to tell him about my feelings,' she says. 'I'd already talked about the accident to the press and to the police and to loads of people. After a while you talk on a very superficial level, but I talked to him in depth about it. I told him how privileged I'd felt that night to be among that crowd of people.'

That night at the party, before disaster struck, she'd felt: 'This is it, this is what life is all about.' 'I couldn't believe that Antonio liked me,' she says. 'He was so much younger than me and so much cleverer.' The year before she was with him and some of his friends in Madrid. 'Why me, Antonio?' she asked, not able to understand why he wanted her there. 'Because, darling, you have a talent to amuse,' he replied.

A *Marchioness* Action Group was set up after the disaster and Odette joined but stopped going to meetings in November 1990. She found that most of the survivors and bereaved had nothing in common with her other than the disaster. That wasn't enough for her to want to spend time with them. 'My main aim was for it to be a support group but it turned out to be a fighting and lobbying group,' she says. 'I had worked through my anger. I still wish them well but I need all my energy to recover myself.'

Odette wants to give hope to others who have gone through trauma. 'I want to say that you can get better. You have to work hard, but you can actually do it. I just saw misery for the rest of my life, but I'm happy now.'

# CHAPTER TEN

# THE CAMPAIGNING SURVIVOR

Years after the disasters, many survivors continue to campaign for improved safety. Most knew nothing about the subject before their lives were changed overnight. Now they have become experts on safety at work, on public transport and in football grounds. They fear that if society does not become more safety conscious more disasters will happen in the future.

Survivor Trevor Hicks fights tirelessly for increased safety in all football grounds. He is an eloquent spokesman for the cause of improved spectator safety. Anyone who meets him cannot fail to admire his strength of purpose. Since the Hillsborough tragedy, where his two daughters were killed in the terrible crush, he has devoted a large amount of his time to the cause.

He often interrupts his busy work schedule as a company director to speak out for greater safety. Whether in the television studio or radio station, or on his car phone giving interviews to newspapers, he is determined to help the campaign. He has spent days at public inquests and inquiries and been involved in long court cases.

Trevor has become extremely knowledgeable about safety at football grounds, a subject he knew very little about before the Hillsborough disaster. He is a well-known and highly regarded figure in the city of Liverpool.

'I would like to turn the clock back,' he says, with obvious frustration. 'I did not want to get involved in this. I am a celebrity, and I don't want to be. It is the last thing I want.'

Trevor had been a senior manager for years before the disaster, and was the natural choice for chairman of the Hillsborough Families Support Group. 'I operate on two levels,' he says. 'As chairman of the Group I try to operate as professionally as I can. Underneath that level I am a grieving father who basically had his life destroyed.' Trevor's psychologist has recommended that he should give up the chairmanship of the Group for his own good. He has been told that he is suffering from Post Traumatic Stress Disorder.

Since the Hillsborough tragedy on 15 April 1989 Trevor has spoken out in favour of all-seated football grounds. He says: 'Hillsborough was like a tidal wave of people pushing into the barrier. Those who died were smashed from behind by a sea of people. That can't happen if supporters are sitting down.' Trevor believes that supporters should not be segregated and caged together in large groups.

He has visited grounds all over the country without witnessing any serious crowd trouble from Liverpool supporters. On the day of the disaster they came from all over to watch the FA Cup Semi-Final between Liverpool and Nottingham Forest. Supporters of both teams arrived in cars and coaches and parked in the same car parks. It was only when they entered the Sheffield Wednesday ground that they were separated into opposing sides.

At 2.40 p.m., twenty minutes before kick-off, queues of supporters started to build up outside the main entrance gates. Inside, the Liverpool supporters were milling around, making their way to the stands and terraces.

Many walked through the gates, down the tunnel, that was then directly in front of them, to the Leppings Lane Terraces, situated behind the goal.

By this time pens three and four at the end of this tunnel were already full to capacity. There was nothing to stop even more supporters walking down the tunnel, into the dangerously overcrowded pens, as kick-off approached.

Due to the build-up of very large numbers of supporters outside the main entrance gates, gate C was opened by the police at approximately 2.50 p.m. This allowed a wave of 2,000 supporters to move down the tunnel to the Leppings Lane Terraces.

Extreme overcrowding caused the fatal crush which killed ninety-five supporters standing in pens three and four. Although the match had started it was abandoned after six minutes when it became clear that there was a catastrophe.

Trevor Hicks feels that the crush could have been avoided. The supporters were caged in. They had no means of escape. There was no one directing them away from pens three and four. He is angry that supporters were allowed to continue pouring in.

'The whole disaster could have been avoided by putting two police officers at the end of the tunnel,' he says. 'People were allowed to walk along the downward slope of the tunnel. There was a tidal-wave effect which washed down at 45 degrees.'

The numbers on the terraces rose to horrific levels. The control over numbers and the avoidance of overcrowding depended on visual monitoring of the crowd. The gruesome pictures of supporters crushed against barrier fences are testimony to the inadequacy of this system of crowd density control.

'Police were pushing people back,' says Trevor. He has watched hours of video recordings of the disaster taken on the day by television companies, police and amateurs. 'The police were trying to prevent people getting on to the pitch. There was a policeman on video with his hand on a man's head, who was obviously in distress, pushing him back.'

Trevor cannot understand why senior police officers were not held accountable for what happened. Many of the junior officers appeared to be obeying orders to prevent a pitch invasion even though it was clear that too many Liverpool fans had entered the terraces behind the goal. 'You don't wait for orders – you dive in,' he says.

After years of campaigning, which has taken Trevor Hicks all over the country and through every level of the legal system, he remains dissatisfied. 'We have achieved a little, but we have not achieved justice. We have not received recognition for what really happened,' he says. 'The Families Group has been sickened. I am the figure-head of a Hillsborough battleship that has been torpedoed and cut up for scrap.'

Trevor Hicks believes passionately that the Hillsborough disaster could have been avoided if greater care had been taken to ensure the safety of the supporters. He doesn't feel sympathy for the senior police officers who were responsible for crowd control on the day. But he says: 'I also know that they are men and they made a mistake. If they had stood up publicly and said, "We made a mistake, we're sorry," then I'd have been in a difficult position. I would have realized, they are guys like me, they got it wrong on the day.

'The fact that they went underground and tried to bury it cemented us into action. More people would have walked away if they had stood up and said, "Sorry."'

Trevor feels that the system is grinding the Families Group down. 'It is even working on me and I have probably had the strongest spirit,' he says. 'It is like an army situation. You've got to out-think the opposition. It is no good charging in like the Light Brigade every time. Sometimes you have to outflank the opposition.'

The survivors and bereaved were disappointed with the coroner's verdict of accidental death on the victims of the Hillsborough disaster. Trevor Hicks says that he sometimes feels he is in a 'no win situation'.

The final blow came when the House of Lords dismissed a test case on pre-death pain and suffering in March 1992. Trevor and his wife Jenny brought the case against the police on behalf of their daughters' estates. The case hinged on whether the two girls suffered in the minutes before they died in the terrible crush. Lord Bridge, sitting with four other Law Lords, upheld the decisions of the High Court and the Court of Appeal, that the girls died of traumatic asphyxia causing 'swift and sudden' death and had not therefore suffered any compensatable physical injury. Trevor describes this decision as 'the final insult'.

Trevor Hicks says that he used to put his faith in the system but now feels frustrated enough to do something physical. 'I have thought of burning Hillsborough Stadium down,' he says. 'I have got a struggle within myself. The reasonable side of me says, "No, you've got to play the game, you've got to beat them at their own game." That is the side that has won through so far, but what has it got me? Nothing. I am sinking at the moment. I am losing my way and I wonder, How will I ever get back? I may leave the Group and get on with my grieving. You can't escape it, you have to grieve.'

Survivor Andrew Parker has become an expert in safety on roll-on roll-off passenger ferries. He used to use the ferries, like most of the travelling public, oblivious to the risks. All that changed when he was a passenger on the *Herald of Free Enterprise*. Andrew became famous overnight when he formed a human bridge to allow other passengers to escape. Since that day he has fought hard to press for increased safety in ferry transport.

Andrew has appeared on several television programmes about ferry safety, contributed to newspaper articles and written to Government ministers. Like many survivors, he is not satisfied with the care that some companies take to avoid major accidents.

He feels that all ferries should be able to stay upright and afloat long enough for passengers to abandon the ship safely even in an emergency. The ships that can't do that should not be in service, he believes.

He also calls for more safety information to be given to the passengers when they buy their ticket. 'All we want is for ferries to be made so that they cannot capsize in a matter of seconds,' he urges.

Andrew's life changed on 15 July 1987. The *Herald* accelerated out of Zeebrugge at 6.05 p.m., to a speed of approximately eighteen knots. The assistant bosun, Mark Stanley, whose job it was to close the inner and outer bow doors, was asleep in his cabin. No one checked to see if he had carried out his duties before leaving port.

Water was pouring into the car deck as the ship moved away from the harbour. The large open deck space was awash with sea water. The ferry became totally unstable. It capsized at approximately 6.30 p.m., coming to rest on one side in shallow waters.

Andrew Parker is concerned that ferry companies now have until the year 2004 to comply with stringent international regulations covering ferry stability. The regulations were agreed in 1990 by the shipping companies' governing body, the International Maritime Organisation.

Andrew feels that ferry companies have an immediate duty to ensure the safety of their ferries. He believes that the older ferries should not be carrying passengers unless they are made more stable. 'It is not practical for the travelling public to refuse to travel on them, given that we are an island,' he says anxiously.

*Marchioness* survivor Iain Philpott shares Andrew Parker's concern about maritime safety. He is an active committee member of the *Marchioness* Action Group, set up in March 1990 following the collision of the pleasure boat the *Marchioness* with the aggregate dredger the *Bowbelle*. Initially a support group, it soon also became a campaigning body demanding greater safety on rivers and waterways.

'I think we have achieved quite a lot,' says Iain. 'I don't believe that the *Bowbelle* would have been banned from the River Thames were it not for the action our Group took. I think the Group as a whole has an awful lot to be congratulated upon in endeavouring to ensure greater public safety on the waterways in the United Kingdom.'

It was a fine moonlit night when the small cruiser, filled with party goers, was struck from behind by the much larger dredger. The faster moving *Bowbelle* was not aware of the other craft until it was too late. The huge impact virtually pushed the *Marchioness* under the water. The upper saloon was completely torn away. She sank in under a minute.

Due to the design of both vessels the visibility from their respective wheelhouses was very poor. The *Bowbelle* skipper had to rely on lookouts placed at the front of the long craft to warn him of any danger. The discothèque lights on the *Marchioness* were indistinguishable from the lights on shore.

Iain believes that there should have been a full public inquiry into the cause of the tragedy. He says the public have a right to know why the *Bowbelle* was still using the Thames despite being previously involved in collisions.

The survivors and relatives fear that without a thorough

and open investigation of the incident lessons will not be learned from their tragedy.

Following the disaster many of the Action Group bought shares in Ready Mixed Concrete, the company that owned the *Bowbelle*. This gave them the opportunity to attend the company's annual general meeting to voice their concerns about safety and compensation.

Noel Crymble, a survivor of the Kegworth air disaster, is a member of the Air Safety Action Group. It was set up in 1991, two years after the tragedy, by the survivors and bereaved. The group has fifty members and meets once a month to discuss strategy in their fight for improved safety on the airlines. Like survivors of other disasters they are in regular contact with Government and industry, urging them to give safety matters the utmost priority.

Noel uses his engineering background to campaign, and often works all day and half the night grappling with the complexities of the aviation industry. 'Different parts of planes are made all over the world,' he says.

He fears that due to the complexity of the industry, basic questions of safety and air worthiness could be glossed over. 'The aviation industry has done a good job at making flying look very professional,' he says. 'When you get on a plane you don't think that anything is going to happen to you.'

He feels that there should be tighter international safety regulations to ensure that all planes satisfy rigorous safety standards. 'You have to build an aircraft so that it does not crash,' says Noel.

The shelves in his study are packed full of the information he has collected since the disaster. Carefully read reports spill over into boxes on the floor.

The doomed Boeing 737-400 aircraft was a new plane that had previously completed only seven flights. It left

Heathrow Airport for Belfast at 7.52 p.m. As it was climbing to its cruising altitude of 28,000 feet, the captain and his co-pilot smelt smoke on the flight deck and felt the plane juddering violently. One of the engines was on fire, but which one?

Throttling back the right-hand engine seemed to cure the problem so they shut it down. Unfortunately, they switched off the wrong engine. Decreasing the speed of the right engine had lessened the strain on the left one, which meant that it now appeared to be working normally.

The only instrument that could have alerted them to their mistake was a small vibration level dial, the size of a thumb nail. It was situated in a non-priority position and gave a high reading for the left engine. There were no external cameras giving the pilots a view of the fire in the left engine which many passengers saw.

The plane was diverted to East Midlands Airport. It was able to fly on one engine, so no further trouble was expected. However, approximately two miles from the airport the damaged left engine began to vibrate once more.

A broken fan blade had been sucked in. It caught fire and failed on the approach to runway 27. The captain told passengers to prepare for crash landing. The plane crashed into the sloping western bank of the M1, near the village of Kegworth in Leicestershire.

A large number of the Kegworth survivors sustained serious injuries on impact. The Air Safety Action Group is therefore encouraging the airline companies to improve impact survivability of passengers. Noel says: 'The aviation industry is approximately twenty years behind the motor-car industry in impact survivability.'

Most of the overhead luggage bins became detached during the crash. These fast-moving, dangerous projectiles

struck some survivors from behind causing serious neck
and head injuries. Others received injuries when they
struck sharp edges on the seat in front. These injuries
could have been lessened by softening the rear of seats.

It was found that many passengers who received injuries
to their limbs did not adopt a brace position before impact.
Research has shown that injuries to head, arms and legs
can be reduced if passengers hold their head down in a
crouched position, with elbows in towards the knees and
feet pulled back. Safety experts recommend that cabin
crew give a brace position demonstration prior to each
flight.

Noel and the Air Safety Action Group will continue to
press the airline companies to raise safety standards.

Piper Alpha survivor Bob Ballantyne escaped from the
burning rig by refusing to follow the company evacuation
plan. He has no faith in oil companies. As the men
gathered in the canteen just below the helideck Bob was
urging them not to wait to be rescued by helicopter and to
head for the sea with him.

Gas explosions and dense black smoke meant that the
rig could not be approached from the air. The men who
remained, desperately waiting to be rescued, did not
survive.

'I never thought I was going to be rescued by helicopter,' he says. 'It would take at least an hour and a half for
one to arrive from the airport. It was a totally impractical
evacuation plan.'

He was also shocked to find that oil and gas continued
to flow into Piper Alpha through pipelines from other rigs
for up to an hour after the initial explosion. The rig was
being heated from below by what amounted to a giant
blowlamp.

Bob Ballantyne would like to see those who work on
the rigs taking a more active role over safety in their own

workplace. He believes that, 'Until the workforce has a greater say in how real safety issues are decided, then the North Sea is still going to be a very dangerous place to work in.'

After the disaster, the survivors group began a media campaign calling for greater safety on the oil rigs. They saw this as the only way to confront a large and influential industry.

Bob Ballantyne believes that companies should always put the safety of the workforce before commercial gain. He was one of the first members of a new trade union, the Offshore Industry Liaison Committee, founded in 1989 following the Piper Alpha disaster. With safety of the workers on the rigs its main concern Bob Ballantine sees that 'This Union stands out like a shining beacon as the only hope in the North Sea.'

The campaign for safety is an ongoing process. Long after their involvement in a disaster the survivors continue to press for higher standards of care.

The organization 'Disaster Action' was launched in October 1991. It was set up by survivors and bereaved relatives of recent UK disasters as a charity and pressure group. The members aim to prevent others suffering in the way they have done. Although their own personal tragedies may be very different, the common aim of mutual support and concern for public safety has fused them into an action group. They are anxious that lessons are learned from the terrible events.

Many survivors had to attend post-disaster inquests and inquiries. This was in itself a harrowing experience. Often, after travelling long distances, they were questioned in a courtroom situation. The lawyers asked in precise detail about their recollection of the disaster.

The survivors have also had to face a complex legal process in their fight for compensation. They were usually required to undergo several psychiatric examinations. Compensation for 'psychiatric damage' is now a well-established claim in the courts following disasters. It includes compensation for Post Traumatic Stress Disorder.

As the understanding of the psychological effects of trauma has increased so too has the courts' willingness to award substantial damages in such cases. If the defendant admits liability and a psychologist's report says that the plaintiff has suffered psychiatric damage, then the only issue to be decided is how much compensation is due.

No one can seriously doubt the significant physical and psychological harm that has been caused to many disaster survivors. Lives were wrecked, careers have been ruined. All the survivors have a different account of the effect of the trauma on their lives. Their compensation claims can therefore differ greatly.

Following the *Herald of Free Enterprise* disaster many claims still remained unsettled years later. In May 1989 ten of the claims were put before a panel of three senior personal injury lawyers. Each of the cases was assessed individually. Expert psychiatric evidence was heard and read. The compensation figures arrived at have since been used to determine many other claims made by survivors in that and other disasters.

The compensation awarded for psychiatric injury ranged from £1,750 to £30,000 depending on the severity of the psychological reaction to the trauma. Additional sums were awarded to compensate for loss of earnings, physical injuries and the cost of medical care.

While legal battles and settlement negotiations dragged on many survivors found themselves in a desperate financial situation. Inability to work through trauma plunged many survivors and their families into debt. *Marchioness* survivor Iain Philpott found himself on the brink of bankruptcy while waiting for compensation.

Psychologists believe that the longer the compensation claim remains outstanding the worse the suffering is likely to be. Clapham survivor Bob Mintram found himself unable to commute to work in London due to increased anxiety. The huge reduction in family income left them struggling to pay their bills. Meanwhile they waited for compensation.

Even though the vast majority received relatively small amounts of compensation, some survivors have been awarded larger sums. In theory, the amount reflects the seriousness of the loss. The more damage caused to the survivor the greater the necessary compensation to alleviate the loss and suffering. The larger figures arise only where, for example, there has been serious damage to their ability to earn a living or the need for expensive medical care.

But compensaton, too, brought its own problems. Some survivors found that even close friends believed that they had somehow benefited from the disaster because of the financial settlement. But compensation, no matter what the amount, cannot alone bring the peace of mind that all survivors crave.

In order to deal with the survivor claims as quickly and efficiently as possible the solicitors' governing body, the Law Society, operates a disaster coordination service. The solicitors representing individual claimants register their claims with the service and a steering group of solicitors is elected. All information relating to the progress of the claims is circulated to the solicitors.

Michael Napier, a solicitor of Pannone Napier Solicitors, has represented many survivors of recent disasters in their claims for compensation. He found that the best settlement results were obtained when a steering group of solicitors coordinated the negotiations with the defendant companies. In this way a united front was maintained in the battle for proper compensation for those affected by a disaster.

Many survivors and bereaved also feel that the criminal law has proved ineffective in prosecuting those responsible for recent major disasters. They point out that the lack of successful corporate manslaughter prosecutions illustrates the injustice of the present situation.

Disaster Action would like to see a body similar to the Serious Fraud Office set up. This could investigate possible cases against companies or individuals in the wake of a major disaster. They believe that companies will pay far more attention to the safety of the public if irresponsible ones are held properly accountable for their lack of care.

The inquiries into many of the recent disasters have shown gross neglect to have been the overriding cause of the accidents. The common theme has been lack of concern for public safety. The survivors hope their efforts to encourage safety will help to prevent future disasters. Prevention is always better than cure.

# CHAPTER ELEVEN

# THRUST INTO THE LIMELIGHT

'I'm a priest,' said Marcus Saville-Deane as he stood at the doors of the Roman Catholic Cathedral. Around him, 5,000 people were waiting to pay their final respects to those who had died at Hillsborough. Inside, the cathedral was packed with 3,000 more. 'I knew the only way I was going to get inside was to say I was a priest,' he says.

An enthusiastic nun led Marcus down to the basement and pointing to a set of robes, asked him to put them on. It was too late for Marcus to confess that he was an Anglican curate. Before he knew what was happening he was marching up on to the altar with a group of Catholic priests, standing two away from the Archbishop of Liverpool, the Most Reverend Derek Worlock.

'I'm probably the only Protestant to concelebrate in the Roman Catholic Cathedral in Liverpool,' he says. 'I like breaking all the rules. I'd just seen ninety-five people die and the Reformation seemed to be a long way away.' The television cameras were on him, and at home his curate friends were bewildered. 'What's Marcus doing there?' they wondered as they watched him. Marcus wondered too.

'When I was dishing out the bread and wine to the Catholic laity I thought, "This is really odd." I had to go through with it because we were on television. I couldn't suddenly say, "I shouldn't be here." I put my hands in the right place at the right time, there was a little card on the altar telling us what to do. No one would have known I wasn't a true blue.'

Marcus had already found fame in the newspapers. He was well known for his part in helping a family who lost a son in the disaster. The family never knew that Marcus' own life was in crisis at the time, that he was depressed and receiving psychotherapy. 'I was going off my head,' he says. The disaster gave him back his self esteem, if only for a few weeks. 'I loved being famous,' he admits. 'I loved being valued and a saviour figure. It made me feel I was worthwhile and that I had something to give in life.'

Marcus was thirty when the disaster happened and at St Mary's Church, in Osterley, Middlesex. He was given a ticket for the Semi-Final by a member of his congregation who was a scout for Liverpool. 'For me it wasn't only a football match, it was a great sociological experience,' he says with sincerity. 'I find the whole thing fascinating, the atmosphere and all the working-class people turning up.'

He was cautious in such a massive crowd and felt that he wasn't really part of it all. 'My background was public school, university, theological college and Christianity,' he says. 'I went into the ministry because I wanted to convert the world. I've always been a religious chap.'

Marcus watched the crush from his seat in the stands. When he saw supporters climbing over the fence he thought they were 'football hooligans'. 'I've come all the way from London to see a good match and these blokes are going to invade the pitch,' he thought. Then he realized he was wrong. 'One was sitting in one's comfortable seat and could see all the people down there in real agony,' he says. 'I felt there was nothing I could do. It was like being a spectator at a bullfight.'

Marcus was walking out of the ground when he decided to go to the gymnasium that had been turned into a temporary mortuary. 'I went up to two Liverpool lads, Kevin and Joe, who were crying,' he recalls. 'Their dead brother Patrick, who was thirty-six years old, and thirteen and a half stone, was lying dead at their feet.' Marcus told them he was a priest. 'The first thing we have to do is ring your parents,' he said, and went off with Joe to find a telephone.

It was a battle to fight back his tears as Marcus lifted the receiver. He told the boys' father that Joe wanted to talk to him, then handed over the telephone. 'I've got something to say: "Patrick is dead,"' said Joe. They were the only words he could manage before he broke down in tears.

Marcus then had to persuade Kevin to let go of the body. Patrick was their eldest brother, 'the big man of the family'. Kevin was determined to stay the night with him. Marcus took the boys home to Liverpool. When they arrived just before midnight the house was full of relatives.

Kevin and Joe introduced him as a friend and the priest who had helped them. Their parents, both in their late sixties, assumed he was Roman Catholic and called him Father. 'I let them believe it,' says Marcus. 'I was aware of the Protestant–Catholic tensions in Liverpool and I wasn't going to say, "I'm a Protestant." That would have been an awful thing and something else for them to deal with. They were thrilled that I'd performed the last rites; I didn't know what the last rites were. I didn't tell them I hadn't.'

He also told them his name was Marcus Deane. 'I didn't want to use my double-barrelled surname – they would have thought I was some sort of upper-class twit with a posh accent.' That night Marcus stayed with a relative of the family.

The following morning he went in a taxi to Anfield. 'I have to be honest, I'm not sure if I was self-seeking,' he says. 'I was on a bit of a high. Maybe I was suddenly

being useful right out there in the market-place with a load
of Catholics. Maybe there was a part of me that felt, "I'm
somebody important in this whole thing."'

At the ground Marcus said that he was a priest and that
he had been at the match. He was taken into the boardroom where he talked to Kenny Dalglish and Liverpool
goalkeeper Bruce Grobbelaar. Footballer John Barnes gave
him a lift home. He went back later in the day with Joe
and his father. Still assuming he was a Catholic priest the
family told him about the service at the cathedral and they
all went together.

When he went back to London Marcus rang all his rich
friends to raise money for Patrick's widow, who had five
children. He took a bundle of cheques back to Liverpool,
when he went up to read a lesson at the funeral. It was on
that second visit that Marcus confessed he wasn't a
Catholic.

It didn't make any difference, he recalls. 'The father
who was very fond of me took me under his wing and
said: "Marcus is a family friend and it doesn't matter
whether he is Church of England or Catholic. The important thing is that he brought my boys home."'

Patrick's body was lying in the living-room of their
council house, dressed in a black suit. At his feet was a
shirt signed by the Liverpool players and rosary beads
were wrapped round his little fingers. Marcus sat next to
the coffin for two days and two nights and stayed with the
local Catholic priest.

'I quite enjoyed meeting all these people. I didn't think
about God really,' he confesses. 'The world is a nightmare
in some ways. If there is a God of Love what's he doing
about it? All I can think is that God has identified with all
the awfulness through the cross of Christ.'

Marcus used Hillsborough to preach the gospel in
schools and at his church in London. 'If you trust in

Christ you'll never walk alone,' he told those who listened. They didn't realize that he had already considered leaving the ministry. He says. 'I was ordained at St Paul's Cathedral in 1987 and was doing superbly well in my parish life, bringing people to Christ, getting people converted and housing refugees. I was feeling alive and thrilled. I had a girlfriend and that was going really well.'

His problems started when he met the girl's brother, who was a petroleum engineer for BP. 'Instead of saying, "I'm Marcus, I'm a curate and looking forward to being a vicar and then going on to be a bishop," I looked at him and thought, "You have everything and I have nothing." I came back and said to my girlfriend: "I also went to Imperial College and I could have done what he's doing." I never thought about working for BP until I met him and then I would have sold my soul to work for them.

'I said to the vicar: "I don't want to do this job any more." I went downhill from then on. My life has been destroyed by envy.' His engagement to his girlfriend broke up. 'She thinks I'm a complete nutter,' he says.

Since then he has been through the worst time in his life. 'Hillsborough was a bit of a lift, a bright spot in all this,' he says. 'If I died tomorrow at least I could feel I've done something important in my life. I look back at Hillsborough as one of the best things I've done. It gave me confidence.' That feeling of confidence lasted about a month, before the euphoria disappeared. Marcus eventually left the ministry in 1991.

He went to York determined to find a good job and start a new life, but it didn't work. Instead he found himself living rough for three days, among the sort of tramps he had once helped. As he slept on park benches he thought of how he had once slept in a cardboard box for the weekend, to raise money for the homeless. He never imagined he would one day be homeless himself. As he walked the streets he found himself questioning whether God really did exist. It always used to be so obvious.

Now he has reached a conclusion. 'I think I'm going to believe that God does exist,' he says. Some would say it's only because he wants a job and somewhere to live. Marcus is aware of that but denies it's the reason. 'I'm going to believe he exists because of my own personal experience,' he says. 'I know I've been much happier in my life when I've been actively serving Christ although I have a lot of problems with it.

'Leaving the ministry was a very silly thing to do. It hasn't got me anywhere; it has taken me further downhill. It's not as if I'm now a smart person wearing striped shirts with a good job. I need to get back to it otherwise my life's going to be wasted. I'm a religious person, I can't help it. I feel I've got to go back to the church and carry on preaching the gospel.'

Marcus is now living in Oxford and working as a gardener for five hours a day. He is still taking anti-depressants although he has started to feel more positive and is taking steps to go back into the church. 'I've made some colossal mistakes,' he admits. 'I've crucified myself, I'm my own worst enemy. Life has been very painful. I feel at times it's all over for me. Looking back at Hillsborough I feel I'd like to come alive again. I feel I've got more resources than I think I have. It's criminal to be wasting my gifts.'


The eyes of the world were on talented soccer star John Aldridge long before the Hillsborough disaster. Afterwards he admitted publicly that he had been affected by the experience. Years later the Liverpool-born striker has noticed another change. 'I think I'm a different person, and I'm not a better person for it,' he says. 'I go off my head easier, I lose control of myself when I shouldn't and I go like a lunatic. If there's an argument on the pitch something clicks and I go like a nutter.'

It happens to him off the pitch too. At home he loses control and does things he wouldn't have done before. 'You pick up a pot and throw it against a wall, that type of thing,' he says with an embarrassed laugh. 'There's nothing I can do about it. I used to have arguments with my wife and we'd have a go at each other but the last couple of years I've found that when I do I go like a nutter. My head goes. I was a bit hotheaded before but not as bad as I am now.'

It was John's wife Joan who persuaded him to play football again after the disaster. He lost interest in the game and didn't train or play for two weeks. 'I'd always felt close to the fans and I know they did to me,' he says. John's love of Liverpool Football Club began in the 1960s. From the age of six he rarely missed a match and stood watching from the Kop. 'When I got the chance to play for them I couldn't take it in for a while, I couldn't believe it.'

He speaks softly as he talks of the disaster. The game started at a hectic pace, he recalls. 'I remember Peter Beardsley hitting the bar and there was a massive big roar. The next minute there was a spillage behind the goal and they told us to get off the pitch immediately.'

It was an hour later when John realized that fans had died. That night he sat with his wife watching the coverage on television. 'I was crying all night, every time it came on the news,' he recalls. 'I thought I'd wake up the following day to find it had all been a dream.'

The reality hit him hard. 'I've never been hit by anything like it in my life,' he says. Two days after the disaster he went to Sheffield Royal Infirmary. 'There was a young lad of about thirteen, his face was similar to my lad. His family were all around him and they were in a mess. They asked me to say something to him. I was whispering in his ear. Then I went to the doctor and asked him when the young lad was going to come round. He told me he was going to die within hours. The thump hit me straight away. I looked at his family and I thought: "He went to watch his heroes play football and lost his life." I was his hero.'

John went to eleven funerals. At the sixth, the funeral of two brothers, he almost fainted. Sweat poured out of his body and he had to sit down to recover.

John admitted publicly that he couldn't face playing again. He pulled out of the Republic of Ireland squad for the World Cup match against Spain in Dublin. He telephoned Jack Charlton to say it would be better if he didn't play because his heart wasn't in the game. 'I just sat there watching television, I couldn't motivate myself to get up in the mornings. I withdrew into myself and I didn't want to have conversations. I lost weight and I felt as if it wouldn't bother me if I never played football again.'

Sackloads of letters poured in from fans urging John to go back to the game, telling him that those who died wouldn't want to see him moping. They would want to see him out there playing well for the team he loved. It was John's wife who eventually persuaded him. She told him he had to go back and earn money to secure the future of their two young children. John realized she was right.

The Semi-Final replay at Old Trafford gave him the confidence he needed. It was the most important game of his life. Liverpool won 3–1 and he scored two of the goals. He was delighted. 'That was for the people,' he says.

'They were the two most important goals I've scored in my career.'

John was sold to Spanish club Real Sociedad five months after the disaster. 'I was pushed out for money,' he says. The Spanish club offered over £1 million for him. Liverpool accepted the bid. 'I never wanted to leave Liverpool but I could see I wasn't wanted so I had to be strong,' he says. 'The supporters and the players didn't want me to go. It would have been nice to have ended my career with Liverpool but it wasn't to be so I accepted it.'

John came back to England to play for Tranmere in the summer of 1991. He has carried his memory of the disaster with him wherever he has gone. In bed at night he still thinks about it. He prays for his family and with them he prays for those who died.


Andrew Parker would rather have achieved fame for scoring the winning goal at Wembley. Instead he became, overnight, one of Britain's best-known heroes as a result of the Zeebrugge ferry disaster. The media called him The Human Bridge. He was awarded the George Medal for his bravery and is still recognized in the street.

He can't deny he enjoyed the fame – having a photograph on the front page of a newspaper would be exciting to almost anyone. But his kind of fame carried a heavy price. Along with it came the traumatic aftermath of disaster: depression, aggression, and a strain on his relationship with his wife.

'We were famous for all the wrong reasons,' he says. 'I was pushed into the limelight and I didn't have a great deal of choice. We started living a lifestyle we didn't really want. We were appearing in the newspapers every five minutes, appearing on television and documentaries and being invited to big dinner parties and lunches.

'The newspapers were talking about £90,000 being paid in compensation which was all rubbish. Certain of our so-called friends believed we had moved into a different financial bracket and they became jealous. They considered we had moved up in the world and no longer had time for them. I lost all the friends I had at the time. It's no loss but it is upsetting. There was a time when I didn't have any friends at all. Some people didn't know what to do and walked away because they couldn't handle it.'

Andrew's part in the disaster is well known. The 6ft 3ins city bank official hurled himself across two metal barriers. His back formed a human bridge across the water-filled chasm. Andrew hung on while his wife Eleanor and twelve-year-old daughter Janice scrambled across, followed by twenty other women and children.

He helped to set up a fireman's chair with a knotted rope that had been lowered to passengers through a door above. The women and children were rescued first. When Andrew tried to get up the rope he was too heavy and was left hanging in the air for five minutes until someone got a ladder. He was able to hold on to it and free himself from the rope which had started slipping up towards his shoulders.

Andrew was named Man of the Year by the Royal Association for Disability and Rehabilitation (RADAR) in 1987. 'As far as I'm concerned I'm not a hero,' he says modestly.

'All I did was save myself and my family and a few other people who joined in as well. Other people suggested I was unselfish or brave. As far as I can remember it, and I remember it moment by moment, I don't consider I did anything special. It's a bit like a map. You come to a series of junctions and make a choice. I don't consider I put myself in any danger. I can remember times when I've

witnessed an accident in the street and I've not known
what to do. I've been as frightened as anyone else.'

Andrew felt guilty that he had survived, and still feels
guilty that he didn't help one woman who was shouting
and screaming for help. 'I think possibly I could have done
something but my mind was on other things,' he says. 'It
would have been a big struggle to get to where she was. I
have no idea if she survived or not.'

It was 7.30 a.m. the following day when Eleanor
discovered that Janice was safe and 2 p.m. when she found
her thirty-four-year-old husband. She ran across the hospital corridor and jumped on him in relief. Now years
later they have been unable to regain the easy closeness
they had before the disaster, and that has made life difficult
at home.

Eleanor still suffers from agoraphobia. 'The worst thing
is I'm incapable of helping her,' says Andrew. Janice, who
is still at school, avoids talking about the disaster. 'If I try
to prompt it I might as well be talking to a brick wall. I
suppose she's still suffering the same way the rest of us
are,' he says.

Andrew's worst period of suffering came a year after
the disaster and lasted for eighteen months. The euphoria
had died down and he had to deal with the depression that
came in its place. His life had changed and his feelings
were different, he had to learn to cope with them. For two
years he took anti-depressants. He became so angry that
he put his fists through doors at home.

In November 1989 he went on a month-long residential
course. It was on post-traumatic stress and run by a
psychologist. 'I could have done with more help earlier,'
he says. 'It would have helped me to understand what was
going on. I felt there was no one to talk to. No one can
understand the concept of a ship sinking. We've all seen

films, but all that is fantasy. People can't understand it happening for real.

'I've done some things that other people wouldn't understand. We had the opportunity to visit the *Herald* when she was in the dock in Holland. I picked up handfuls of broken glass and some oily rope.' His wife did the same. It was something to remind him of the reality at times when it all seemed like a dream.

'I sometimes think if you have lost someone in a disaster it's easier to come to terms with it,' he says. 'There's something tangible in what happened, an emptiness. Your husband used to sleep next to you but now he's dead and buried. In our case no one died, everyone is still here, there's nothing tangible to hold on to.'

Andrew looks at photographs, reads about himself in press cuttings and struggles to believe it's true. He has always been willing to talk to the media and has been an avid campaigner for ferry safety. People all over the world wrote him letters of support. One letter came from a Battle of Britain pilot, now living in Canada, who was keen to swap stories with him. He met someone who fought in Burma during the Second World War, still suffering the effects of trauma. Not all the letters were friendly. 'I had some angry anonymous letters telling us to stop drawing attention to ourselves and protect the survivors and people suffering,' he says. 'Those people don't know what they're talking about.'

Fame has given Andrew a new confidence, and he's not as shy as he was before the disaster. Before he had opinions but never dared to voice them; if there was a confrontation he backed away. Now that's not the case. 'If I have an opinion I mean it to be heard. It doesn't bother me if it's not accepted. I don't feel a moment of my life should be wasted. Every minute of every day I've got to be doing something positive. God must have had a reason for me surviving; probably one day I'll know what it is.'


A model of a Jumbo Jet sits on top of Jamie Carter's television. He travels in them all over the world: one week Nairobi, the next Tokyo. No two weeks are ever the same and that's the way he loves it. Jamie was an air steward, on his first operational flight, when it crashed on the M1. For most people that would have been enough to put them off the job for ever, but not Jamie.

Jamie was twenty-three when the disaster happened. He shouldn't have been on doomed flight BD92 but stepped in at the last minute when a stewardess cried off with flu. He was feeling nervous as this was a new job. He'd only joined British Midland the previous month and was keen to make a good impression with the flight services manager on board. Jamie was busy handing out meals to passengers. There was a couple he'd missed first time round and he was rushing back to them. Then he heard a loud bang.

'The floor seemed to start shaking violently,' he recalls. 'The Lockerbie disaster had been eighteen days before and I thought that maybe it was a bomb in the hold. Wispy smoke started to appear at the back of the aircraft. Suddenly everyone started screaming on the left-hand side and I heard comments like, "The wing's on fire!" I ran to the galley at the back, my heart in my mouth. Barbara, the supervisor, looked out of the window and screamed, "No!" It seemed to go through the whole cabin.'

Jamie and two of the cabin crew rushed quickly up the cabin towards the flight deck. Then a woman in her mid-twenties jumped out of her seat next to the aisle. 'She was literally on top of me beating me up,' Jamie recalls. 'She had rugby tackled me to the ground, people were pulling her off me. She was saying, "What's happening, what's happening?" She was punching with her fist on top of my back and shoulders. I was trying to push her off saying, "Let me find out." I was elbowing her and people were pulling her off me. She'd been so quiet and studious, reading a book; suddenly the shock hit her.'

The smell of burning and smoke in the cabin disappeared, but some passengers were still anxious. A woman at the back started screaming, and triggered screaming from the back to the front of the cabin. 'If people had their emergency cards out we were telling them to read them,' says Jamie. 'Some said: "Stop trying to frighten us."'

The flight services manager went on to the flight deck. 'He came out and said everything was flashing in there and he didn't like what was happening,' Jamie recalls. 'He told us to remove every piece of hand luggage lying around passengers' feet or on spare seats. I remember going all goose-pimply. That was the point when Dan started to tell us what was going to happen.'

It was Jamie's job in the junior position to look after small children and mothers on the flight. Dan was a little boy aged about ten. He started saying: 'I'm never going to see my daddy again.' Jamie gave him a boiled sweet and tied him as tightly as he could in his seat-belt. 'I couldn't get it very tight because he was so small,' Jamie recalls. 'My eyes were full of water.' He fights back the tears again as he remembers.

Jamie was with Dan when the pilot told passengers to prepare for crash landing. He didn't know whether to jump into the empty seat beside him, but decided instead to go to his seat at the back so that he could open the doors in an emergency. 'On impact everything seemed to fall on top of me,' he says, 'the oven, the trolleys, the whole galley. I felt myself being thrown up into the cabin.'

A piece of the aeroplane had fallen on top of him and protected him from serious injury.

Jamie and fellow flight attendants Barbara Jones and Jonathan Collins were in the tail section. 'Suddenly I heard a woman screaming, "We're on fire!"' he recalls. 'I could see that we couldn't get out of the door. Barbara and I just looked at each other and started crying. Jonathan kept saying: "Breathe in." He thought we would die of toxic fumes instead of burn. Then someone shouted: "The firemen are here!"'

Jonathan and Barbara were both injured and trapped by their seat harnesses. Jamie tried to get them out: 'I managed to find a knife and I was cutting through but the knife fell down into the cabin somewhere. I found a vodka bottle and smashed that. Using a little piece of glass I managed to cut through both their harnesses.' Jonathan was able to pull himself out from beneath the trolleys. Both ankles were broken but he was walking on them. He and Jamie pulled debris away from the door and were rescued by firemen. Barbara came out ten minutes later, suffering from a broken pelvis.

Jamie walked up and down the motorway looking for sticks to make a splint for Jonathan's foot. 'There was a bridge beside where it happened,' he recalls. 'There were people in dressing-gowns who had come to watch. They had brought the kids. Jonathan started getting very angry shouting at them to go away.' Jamie didn't realize at first why they were there.

He went in an ambulance with Barbara to the Queen's Medical Centre in Nottingham. A soldier in the ambulance with them was so shocked he thought the plane had crashed in Belfast. 'He was worried that something was going to happen to him,' says Jamie. The three held hands on the way. When they arrived Jamie refused to get into bed.

'I was on cloud nine – I had every emotion you could think of,' he says. 'I was laughing one moment, and crying the next.' He was running between the beds trying to find news of loved ones for those who had been injured, carrying messages between them. 'Tell her I love her and think of the kids,' one man asked him to tell his wife. Some of the passengers told him 'in a stupor' that the wrong engine had been turned off. 'We didn't realize that but some of the passengers did,' he says. 'I kept saying to the doctor: "They're telling me he turned the wrong engine off." I wanted someone to confirm it. No one could.'

British Midland officials arrived at the hospital and whisked Jamie away to a hotel. 'They told me to order anything on room service I wanted to,' he says. 'I locked myself in the hotel room. I rang my mum to tell her I was all right.' His white, short-sleeved shirt was covered in blood, most of it Barbara's. He had cuts on his hands and arms and discovered later that he had also injured his back. 'I washed my shirt in the bathroom and put it on the radiator to dry,' he recalls. 'I thought I had to get it dry for morning because I didn't know what was going to happen to me.'

Jamie was watching news of the disaster on late-night television when there was a knock at the door. He checked through the peep hole and a blonde-haired woman on the other side said: 'Can you tell me if you were on the aircraft that crashed on the M1?' She said she was a journalist. 'I've been told I can't say anything to anyone,' Jamie replied.

'Did it crash or was there an explosion on board?' she asked.

'It crashed.'

'Is there anything else you'd like to say?' she went on.

'I said: "Passengers keep telling me they turned the

wrong engine off." It still wasn't sinking in; I was saying it almost in disbelief.'

The journalist went away but knocked on the door again five minutes later. 'Take my advice, get yourself to a hospital. I don't think you should be here,' she told him. Jamie rang British Midland and told them. In his now damp shirt he went in a taxi to British Midland's head office in Castle Donington. A receptionist gave him her cardigan because he was so cold. In the operations room he learned the awful truth that Dan, the little boy he had looked after, was dead.

Jamie flew home later that day, but wasn't happy about getting back on an aeroplane. The first time he tried he had to turn back. A woman with a bunch of flowers was going through security at the same time and Jamie started crying. It brought back memories of the woman on the flight who didn't want to part with her flowers when he was putting belongings into the overhead lockers.

Jamie came home to instant publicity and that helped, he says. Newspapers called him the 'brave steward', and the kitchen of his flat was taken over by ITN. Jamie thought he was a celebrity. Two days after the crash he went back to work and was flying again within two months. Jamie's world was back to normal; at least that was how it seemed.

Jamie didn't realize that his battle was far from over. The disaster left him feeling so depressed he didn't want to go out. When he came home from work he sat watching television, eating two family-sized bars of chocolate at a time. His relationship with the boyfriend he'd been with for four years broke up.

Three weeks after the disaster the police asked Jamie to identify where passengers had been sitting when they died and whether they had moved before the impact. They asked him to look through some photographs. Jamie thought he was going to be shown holiday snaps or passport pictures. The policeman pulled out a small photograph album. Jamie opened it up and jumped back in horror.

They were mortuary photographs, and the first was of the little boy Dan. Dan's brother and mother were numbers two and three. On the pages that followed he saw the woman who had jumped on top of him, and the man at the front who had offered to help collect the meal trays when the emergency started. Jamie recognized half of the pictures. 'It was like seeing some of your family dead,' he recalls. 'It really upset me and I kept having nightmares. I had never seen a dead body before.'

Jamie didn't find it easy to go back in the air again. He had to leave British Midland because he couldn't bear to fly in the same type of aircraft. Before he left he had a particularly bad flight. As he started serving passengers his eyes filled up with tears. He was back on the doomed BD92 again and all the passengers had the same faces. 'I was thinking if we crash you're going to die in that seat and you're going to survive.'

Jamie went to work as a member of the ground staff for British Airways. After six months he started to miss flying and British Airways gave him a job as a flight attendant. He is now a health and safety representative with the union, Cabin Crew '89. 'I feel I'm a different person,' he says.

'I'm much more confident and competent at almost everything I do. I'm not afraid of people as much as I used to be because I've had the opportunity to question MPs and those involved in air safety. I decided to change everything about me I didn't like. I changed my job, changed friends and moved house. The friends I have now are much closer, before I was a bit more superficial.'

Even though he is now confident Jamie dreads criticism

and anything that will make him feel insecure. In the autumn of 1991 he was on a flight to Miami. 'An awful American woman wanted immediate service,' he recalls.

'She was asking for a soft drink. I was carrying two tea pots and said: "I've only got one pair of hands, I'll be with you in a second." That wasn't good enough for her and she reported it to my supervisor. The supervisor said, "What are you playing at?" I took that as criticism and went into the toilet. I was crying for a minute or two until I pulled myself together.'

Jamie was crying not about what had happened but about the crash, going through it again in his mind, thinking about the impact and the passengers on board.

A year after the disaster he went to the Air Accident Investigation Branch headquarters at Farnborough, Hampshire, to see the crashed aircraft. The Boeing 737 was in a hangar next to the aeroplane involved in the Lockerbie disaster. The seats had been reassembled, the aircraft seemed so much smaller than Jamie remembered.

He sat in his own seat first and then went to seat 8D where Dan had been sitting. Inside the seat pocket was the green boiled sweet that Jamie had given him. He picked it out and put it in his pocket. The seat next to where Dan was sitting was buckled up; if Jamie had sat there he would have been killed. 'I felt anger when I saw that sweet,' he says. He expected to feel angry at the aircraft, but didn't. The aircraft felt like a person and his anger was towards the captain.

Now he says he feels more emotional than he used to. 'I find myself in tears for no reason. Sometimes when I go to a pub or a nightclub I feel I just want to blend into the background. If a weepy song comes on I start thinking about the disaster. I want to be in the club but I just don't want to talk to anyone.'

Every anniversary he still thinks about the crash. In

1992 he was in Australia at the time. He sat on his bed in the hotel room counting the minutes in UK time to when it happened. He says: 'I was trying to put myself on BD92, sitting there as though I was waiting for a crash landing. I felt very sad.'

Jamie's memories haven't stopped him flying all over the world. 'I just love my job, everything about it,' he says. 'The chances of a disaster happening to me again must be slight. Lightning doesn't strike twice.' For twelve months after the crash there was a photograph in his hall of the crashed plane. Now it's in the garage gathering dust.


Gareth Jones will always be remembered as the man who faced the television cameras the day after the air crash. It was a brave move for a man who had been injured the night before in an horrific disaster. Thousands watched as thirty-eight-year-old Gareth sat in his wheelchair, at the Queen's Medical Centre in Nottingham, talking about what had happened. There was a cut on his head where he had hit the seat in front, and he also suffered bruises, torn ligaments and broken ribs. 'In some respects I was glad to have been able to help the hospital,' he says, 'but it didn't help my feelings of guilt.'

That evening he shuffled down to the day room to watch the press conference on television. Watching it with him were two people who had lost their son. 'They were asking me questions about what it was like. They could see I had been there because I was on the box. I felt really low that I'd bothered to watch it,' he says.

Gareth felt dirty and guilty for having survived and for having found fame through a crash that had killed so many people. The hospital had asked him to take part in the conference because he worked for the health service. A month before the disaster he'd started work as a buyer in Northern Ireland. He was returning to Ireland after one of his weekend trips home to see his wife and two children when the crash happened.

Gareth went home to Berkshire two days later and found the press waiting for him outside. That night the television cameras were in his home. When he went to bed he says: 'I just wanted to curl up in a ball and for everyone to leave me alone. I wanted people to be there, I just didn't want them touching me. I thought I didn't deserve all the attention.' Gareth was still talking to reporters two weeks after the disaster but didn't find it easy to talk to his family about what had happened.

They found out by listening to him tell his story. 'I found it easier to talk to people who weren't close to me because I knew I wasn't burdening them and hurting them,' he recalls. 'My father would never talk about his experiences in the war, probably because he didn't want to pass on horrible bits, and I felt the same.'

Gareth still feels guilty but the feeling isn't so severe. He was given the Royal Humane Society Medal for helping to rescue another passenger. 'In one way it was tremendous and I was very proud to get it, but in another it reinforced the guilt.'

Dr John Ashton is regarded in Liverpool as the man who spoke out about what really happened at Hillsborough. The Head of the University's Department of Public Health was there on the day and wanted to tell the world. He said that the emergency services weren't doing their job and that more lives could have been saved if staff and equipment had arrived earlier.

In the aftermath of the disaster he spoke out against the stigmatization of Liverpool and its people by the press. He was stopped in the street by people who wanted to thank him. Dozens of supportive letters arrived. But Dr Ashton has come in for criticism as a result of his views from some of his own profession. He still finds he has to defend his actions.

In the *British Medical Journal* he wrote: 'Sadly, among the letters have been a handful that one can only describe as sick, including one from a medical practitioner who in essence accused me of acting unprofessionally.'

Dr Ashton gave evidence at Lord Justice Taylor's inquiry into the disaster at Sheffield. He didn't prepare himself for walking into the lion's den of the country's best barristers, he recalls. 'I assumed because I'd always enjoyed a lot of credibility in the public arena I would be able to go in and give my testimony. I didn't expect to be taken to bits and to have my credentials challenged. They were trying to say I didn't know what I was talking about because I wasn't a proper doctor.'

John set up a working party of thirteen doctors, nurses and a medical student who had all been involved with the emergency response at Hillsborough. Some were there as football supporters and were either standing on the terraces or in the stands when the disaster happened. Others were among those who responded to media requests for assistance at the ground and turned out to help.

They submitted a report to the second stage of the inquiry. The group looked at on-site emergency services and the capability of coping with normal medical emergencies at sporting events. It took the view that even the normal eventualities were not adequately catered for and concluded that the medical facilities at football grounds in the United Kingdom were amateurish.

Dr Ashton had gone to the match with his two sons and a nephew. After the crush he went to the injured behind the stand. 'Quite a few people had been brought out and I realized that people were being put indiscriminately into ambulances. It was necessary for someone to take charge,' he says. He divided people into three groups, depending on whether they were dead or should have priority to go to hospital.

Dr Ashton had been a Liverpool supporter for thirty-five years and, in his then role as senior lecturer in community health, regularly spoke to the press. He contacted them when he came home from Hillsborough and was interviewed by media from all over the world. 'I realized it was important to come home to represent a view of what happened, and that's what I did,' he says.

He paid a price for airing his views. For a year after the disaster Dr Ashton suffered from the skin problem psoriasis. 'I reached a point where I felt I had to stop taking an interest because it was something that wasn't doing a great deal of good,' he says. 'I felt sullied and as though my professional good name was besmirched. I had a hard time at the inquiry. After the disaster I felt angry, stressed and exhausted. But after the inquiry I felt traumatized.'

His experience has made him more cautious of speaking out and becoming involved in public situations. 'I felt I had done what I had to do and behaved in a responsible professional way and then the establishment turned on me. I think I do my job as well as I did before but I've become more reluctant to be in the public domain.'


Clapham survivor Allison Killerby found it difficult to live with the pressure of fame. She was seen by millions of television viewers telling Mrs Thatcher she hoped her facial injuries would heal in time for her wedding six months later. She managed to joke with the then Prime

Minister even though her left eye was swollen shut and she had deep scars cutting across her nose and forehead.

The press followed Allison and were at her wedding in June. When she arrived at the Bradford church in a horse-drawn carriage she says: 'There must have been 500 camera lenses peering at me over the wall. My first reaction was to feel great that I had so much attention.' She soon changed her mind.

'They followed me as I tried to get to the door of the church, sticking their lenses up my nose and it was really intrusive. When I came out of the church my photographer couldn't get near me to take pictures because of all the press. It was absolutely chaotic and they were all fighting over who could get into the wedding reception.'

Allison, now Mrs Sherry, had no preparation for fame. She was a twenty-six-year-old recruitment officer with a City firm of accountants when the disaster happened. 'I was standing on the train with my elbows resting on seats either side of me,' she says. 'I was reading a really romantic part of my book and thinking about flowers for my wedding. I was trying to decide what colour I should have and whether I should get orchids from Singapore.'

Then she remembers a huge bang like a hammer hitting a tin. 'I felt myself falling, felt myself being squashed and my clothes being ripped. I struggled to open my eyes, there was so much dirt in them. There was a metal bar across my leg and I struggled to get out. I didn't know I was bleeding heavily from my nose. I could feel it stinging so I knew I'd cut myself. When I looked up I could see either steam or a dust cloud.'

The air smelt of greasy oil and dirty bits of metal. Allison could see blue sky above her – it was a clear winter's morning. She climbed up towards it and was pulled clear of the wreckage.

She was taken to St George's Hospital in Tooting and has had plastic surgery on her injuries. Two days after the disaster she saw her face for the first time, not in a mirror, but covering the front page of a tabloid newspaper. 'My brother brought it in to me and he was distressed that I was in that condition. I was more upset for him than me,' she says.

Back home again Allison found she couldn't go shopping without being recognized. 'Everyone in the country knows who I am,' she thought, even the bus driver asked her how she was. She decided to make a fresh start, and moved from Basingstoke to her home county of Yorkshire.

In August 1990 her daughter Ailsa was born. The media still followed Allison, even though she was living in another part of the country. Two weeks after she came home with her new baby they knocked on her door. 'It makes me wonder how the prime minister copes,' she says.

# CHAPTER TWELVE

# HELPING SURVIVORS

Coping with the effects of the disaster aftermath meant that many survivors had to overcome intense feelings of fear and anxiety. 'In order to survive you have to believe that if you look after yourself you are going to live, and what the disaster survivors learn is that they were looking but still something catastrophic happened,' says psychologist Peter Hodgkinson, who is a director of the Centre for Crisis Psychology in Yorkshire. 'Their sense of invulnerability in the world goes so they are instantly vulnerable, along with those they love and those around them.

'Suddenly the world is no longer predictable in situations in which they previously thought they were safe. People tend to believe that good things happen to good people and bad things happen to bad people. Therefore, as something bad has happened to them some survivors believe that they must be bad.'

Psychologists found that it was necessary to help the survivors manage their thoughts of the disaster, in order that they could properly process the event in their minds. The memories then lost their frightening power and could fade like any other.

The onset of psychological problems following trauma is usually quite soon after the event but there may be a delay. Some survivors who thought they were not affected by the trauma began to notice that their ability to cope with their lives was not what it used to be.

The unsettling flashbacks and feelings of anxiety were

triggered by anything that reminded them of the disaster. Psychologists therefore tried to teach the survivors to manage this anxiety by exposing them to the feared stimulus in manageable chunks. The gradual process of desensitizing the survivors to thoughts of the disaster was achieved by progressively exposing them to the frightening stimulus.

Dr James Thompson, based at the stress clinic, Middlesex Hospital, London, went over and over the events with the survivors in the clinic. Then he spent up to seven hours at a time with the survivors visiting the scene of the disaster. King's Cross survivors were escorted back into the underground. *Marchioness* survivors were taken back to the Thames.

If the thoughts of the disaster are not properly dealt with they are unlikely to fade with time. Time alone does not heal. The untamed beast could rear its ugly head when it is least expected.

Psychiatrist Morgan O'Connell the Surgeon Commander who runs four-week courses for trauma victims at the Hasla Naval Hospital, Portsmouth, says: 'On our programme we say to them that we are going to travel with them part of the way on the road to recovery. What we don't want them to do is to become dependent on us.

'The first thing we say to people is that we don't think we can cure them. We try to teach them to cope with their emotional responses. We teach them how to manage their anxiety whilst emphasizing to them that their response is understandable in the light of the trauma they have been exposed to. The first stage is getting them to recognize that they have a problem. The second stage is getting them to explore the detail of the traumatic experience. We get them to talk about it, write it down, share it with others, however upset they get.'

Given the known benefits of early intervention, psychologists believe that a properly coordinated system for offering support to survivors should be available in the wake of major disasters. In these situations, regular avenues of medical help are not enough. Peter Hodgkinson says: 'Due to the very nature of the trauma reaction many survivors are reluctant to seek help.' The doctor's referral system is therefore inappropriate when dealing with a large group of people from a particular disaster. Very few survivors would be helped if this were the only method open to them. Early contact with the survivors is essential.

In the major disasters it was not always possible to identify those who were involved. There was no register of names of supporters entering the Hillsborough ground or passengers using the King's Cross underground station on the day of the disaster.

Psychologists and social workers used a pro-active approach in offering help to survivors. Given that many had witnessed terrifying events it was safe to assume that they would benefit from caring professional assistance to cope with the aftermath. Telephone helplines and emergency numbers manned by social workers and psychologists were advertised in the media. Helpful leaflets entitled 'Coping with a Major Personal Crisis' were distributed. Survivors were advised that what they were feeling was a normal reaction to an abnormal event; they were not going mad.

David Tumelty, a social worker who worked with the survivors of the Piper Alpha disaster, recalls that initially the survivors wanted information. They were trying to piece it all together. They wanted to know what had happened, why it had happened, what was happening to them now and what was likely to happen to them in the future. Survivors were encouraged to seek help if they needed it. In this way a larger proportion of the survivor population was reached.

The sooner survivors are given an opportunity to discuss in detail what has happened to them the better. Peter Hodgkinson says: 'This generally helps them begin to put their mental house in order. They can then start to process their thoughts about it.' The problems do not become ingrained and are easier to deal with. In order to process the thoughts of the disaster properly it is necessary for the survivors to talk about what has happened to them in depth and with full and genuine feeling.

The Hillsborough Centre was set up by Liverpool Social Services following the football stadium tragedy. Part of its role was to give the survivors a place where they could go and talk freely about the terrifying images that filled their minds. Many were reluctant to burden their families with the harrowing memories.

Although a caring supportive family is one of the best antidotes to stress, psychologists have found that there is a tendency among those exposed to trauma to isolate themselves. They feel that the best way of dealing with the painful thoughts is to block them out, to try to avoid thinking about them. But total denial is not possible in the long term. Some turned to drink or drugs in an attempt to block things out, coping strategies which often proved very damaging to their health. The survivor's family and friends were exposed to secondary trauma as a result of living with the traumatized survivors. They too needed help and support to cope with the disaster aftermath.

The staff at the Centre have an open door policy, encouraging survivors and bereaved to stroll in without the need for an appointment or a doctor's referral. They sat and watched video recordings of the horrific crushing that occurred on the terraces. The survivors found that the images became less frightening after a while.

Jan Crawley, a social worker at the Centre, recalls how

many of the young football fans thought they were going mad. Young men who were not used to showing their emotions found themselves unable to cope with their feelings of fear, anxiety and depression.

The Hillsborough Centre remains open for the disaster survivors and now also accepts referrals of people suffering from the effects of any serious trauma, including victims of physical and sexual assault and serious road traffic accidents.

If the identity of those involved in a major accident is known, psychologists and social workers feel that if possible help should be offered to them all in person. Following the *Herald* disaster, the Herald Assistance Unit wrote a letter of sympathy to the survivors and bereaved with a home visit from a member of the Unit. Most welcomed the visit. The survivors were able to find out more about what was happening to them and receive more help if they wanted it.

The most important reference group for people who are traumatized is other traumatized people. Newsletters run by the survivors themselves kept them all abreast of developments. They shared advice and information.

Dr David Alexander believes that survivors should be told at an early stage of the possible psychological reactions they might have to trauma. 'To be forewarned is to be forearmed,' he says. 'They would not then be further shocked by their own emotional reactions. I take the view that whatever happens is normal.'

There are still no nationally coordinated disaster trauma aftercare plans. Each region is left to respond to a disaster situation in whatever way it feels is appropriate. Most regions do not have a rehearsed plan for dealing with the trauma aftermath and psychological aftercare. In the wake of many of the recent major disasters the lack of coordinated plans meant that some survivors received as many as eleven visits from social workers, clergy, voluntary agencies and the police, while others received none.

A working party was set up in 1988 by the Department of Health and Cruse Bereavement Counselling. They gathered information, spoke to professionals and disaster survivors. Their intention was to draw from the experiences and knowledge gained from the recent disasters. A set of guidelines of best practice was published in 1991 ('Disasters: Planning for a Caring Response'). The guidelines contain a framework for coordinating the short-and long-term regional response to caring for the survivors of a major disaster. They were sent to all regional Directors of Social Services. They are not, however, obliged to implement the recommendations and many areas remain without such a plan.

Marion Gibson, a social worker and member of the Government working party, is disappointed with the lack of Government funding made available to implement the guidelines at local and regional level. Such plans would have to be funded by the local authorities whose budgets are already overstretched. Without any obligations upon them many local authorities have failed to implement the guidelines.

The British Psychological Society regrettably failed to obtain Government backing for a Private Member's Bill in February 1992, in which they called for a legal obligation on Local Authorities to take all appropriate steps to supply the necessary support to disaster survivors.

Some psychologists would like to see a panel of trauma experts set up. They could help to train and advise local areas in the event of a disaster. The pockets of expertise dotted around the country could also be brought together if and when required.

Peter Hodgkinson believes that the avenue for seeking

professional help in a disaster plan should be open to disaster survivors for at least two years. They should be able to tap the support if and when they need it. This makes financial sense as, if help is not supplied it is likely that a proportion of survivors will develop serious problems which would be far more difficult and expensive to overcome in the long term.

The first International Traumatic Stress Conference was held in Amsterdam in June 1992. Leading psychologists from all over the world shared their knowledge and experience.

Professor Charles Figley of Florida State University, USA, and a founder member of the International Society for Traumatic Stress, says: 'We are at a much higher level of sophistication with regard to assessment, prevention, treatment and theory development. Trauma is now a field of study.'

Professor Figley believes that psychologists the world over now have a broadly similar approach to trauma victims. 'There is such a wide variation in how individuals respond and recover from highly stressful events that you should not use a cookie cutter intervention approach for everyone,' he says. 'You should tailor your assistance based on the individual and context.'

The vast majority of disaster survivors come to terms with their experiences in time. Psychologists believe, however, that they are unlikely to get down to the general anxiety level they had before the disaster.

Dr David Alexander says: 'I don't think they can erase the emotional scars from their minds. They must come to terms with what has happened to them and find a place for it in their minds. Many wives of Piper Alpha disaster survivors have said to me, "He's not the same man," and they are right. Very few are unchanged. Sometimes they take a long time to come to terms with their new selves.

They may be more emotional. They must develop this new person and push this one forward.'

Dr James Thomson says: 'Many survivors ask me, "Will I be like I was?" I say to them, "The person you will be is probably a close relative to the person you might have been anyway." The key to good psychological adjustment is knowing when to kiss something goodbye, knowing when an issue is not worth thrashing about. Having thought about an event, and got rid of it, kiss it goodbye and put it behind you.'

# Post Traumatic Stress Disorder – A Clinical Description

At the present time the criteria for a diagnosis of PTSD are contained in the Revised 1987 3rd edition of the *Diagnostic and Statistical Manual of Diseases* (DSM III R):

A.   The person must have experienced an event that was outside the range of usual human experience that would be markedly distressing to almost anyone, e.g. serious threat to one's life or physical integrity; serious threat or harm to one's children, spouse or other close relatives and friends; sudden destruction of one's home or community; or seeing another person who has recently been or is being seriously injured or killed as the result of an accident or physical violence.

B.   The traumatic event is persistently re-experienced in at least one of the following ways:

(1)   recurrent and intrusive distressing recollections of the event (in young children, repetitive play in which themes or aspects of the trauma are expressed);

(2)   recurrent distressing dreams of the event;

(3)   sudden acting or feeling as if the traumatic event

were recurring (includes a sense of reliving the experience, illusions, hallucinations and dissociative (flashback) episodes, even those that occur upon waking or when intoxicated);

(4)  intense psychological distress at exposure to events that symbolize or resemble an aspect of the event, including anniversaries of the trauma.

C.  The person persistently avoids stimuli associated with the trauma or shows a numbing of general responsiveness (not present before the trauma), as indicated by at least three of the following:

(1)  efforts to avoid thoughts or feelings associated with the trauma;

(2)  efforts to avoid activities or situations that arouse recollections of the trauma;

(3)  inability to recall an important aspect of the trauma (psychogenic amnesia);

(4)  markedly diminished interest in significant activities (in young children, loss of recently acquired developmental skills such as toilet training or language skills);

(5)  feelings of detachment or estrangement from others;

(6)  restricted range of affect, e.g. unable to have loving feelings;

(7)  sense of a foreshortened future, e.g. does not expect to have a career, marriage or children, or a long life.

D.  Persistent symptoms of increased arousal (not present before the trauma), as indicated by at least two of the following;

(1)   difficulty falling or staying asleep;

(2)   irritability or outbursts of anger;

(3)   difficulty concentrating;

(4)   hypervigilance;

(5)   exaggerated startle response;

(6)   physiological reactivity upon exposure to events that symbolize or resemble an aspect of the traumatic event (e.g. a woman who was raped in a lift breaks out in a sweat when entering any lift).

E.   Duration of the disturbance (symptoms in B, C and D) of at least one month.

# APPENDIX TWO

# Disaster Action Network Committee Guide to Organizations

## Disaster Action
11 Lamb Street, London E1 6EA
Tel: 071 377 6691. Fax: 071 377 8434.

## Alder Centre
Royal Liverpool Children's Hospital, Alder Hey,
Eaton Road, Liverpool L12 2AP. Tel: 051 228 4811.
The Alder Centre is for all those affected by the death of a child. Now there is a helpline staffed by bereaved parents and trained volunteers. Tel: 051 228 9759 (7 to 10 p.m.).
Alder Centre leaflet in Disaster Action library.

## Bereaved Parents Helpline
6 Canons Gate, Harlow, Essex CM20 1QE.
Tel: 0279 412745.
Support to bereaved parents by telephone counselling and visits.

# Campaign Against Drinking and Driving — C.A.D.D.

83 Jesmond Road, Newcastle upon Tyne,
Tyne & Wear NE3 1NH. Tel: 091 281 1581.
Practical advice and information to support the families of
victims killed and injured.

# Centre for Educational Response to Disaster

Roselyn House, 93 Old Newton Road, Newbury,
Berks. R914 7DE. Tel: 0635 30644.
Director: Elizabeth Capewell

# The Compassionate Friends

6 Denmark Street, Bristol BS1 5DA. Tel: 0272 292778.
An international organization of bereaved parents offering
friendship and understanding to other bereaved parents.
They also have a library on child bereavement and you can
apply for the list – contact the Librarian.
Compassionate Friends leaflet in Disaster Action library.

# Construction Relatives Support Group

Contact: Anne Elvin. 8 Chalfont House,
Keaton's Road, London SE16. Tel:071 252 1621.
Dealing with individual workplace deaths.

# Cruse-Bereavement Care

5 Bute Gardens, London W6 7DR. Tel: 081 748 7275.
Christine Mead. A service of counselling, advice and
opportunities for social contact to all bereaved people
through branches around UK. Newletter and publications.
Local contacts via national office. Cruse held a symposium
on Disasters in June 1990 and there is a copy of the
discussion papers/list of lecturers etc. in Disaster Action

library. Cruse/Disasters Working Party contact: Alec San-
dison (Director – Cruse).

## Disaster Staff Network

Director: Elizabeth Capewell, Roselyn House,
93 Old Newton Road, Newbury, Berks. R914 7DE.
Tel: 0635 30644.

A forum for people who become involved in disaster work
in the course of the normal work role.

## Foreign and Commonwealth Office

Mr Ron Dodoo, Consular Department,
Room 626, Clive House, Petty France,
London SW1H 9HD.

This department deals with UK nationals who have died
overseas. Contact was made after the Lauda air disaster in
Thailand.

## Inquest

Alexander National House, 330 Seven Sisters Road,
London N4 2PJ. Tel:081 802 7450/7430.

Currently struggling to maintain funding to support their
office. June Tweedie, and her assistant Deborah, deal with
any queries regarding inquests and have been involved
with Hillsborough. They are fighting to make changes in
the legal system, but with a question mark over funding,
they may not have the resources to be effective in this area.

## London Association of Bereavement Services

See National Association of Bereavement Services.

Umbrella organization for over fifty bereavement projects
and practitioners in London and the Home Counties,
borough-based and specialist, offering counselling and
visiting services. Referrals by telephone or letter.

# Maudsley Hospital

99 Denmark Hill, London SE5 8AS. Tel: 071 703 6333.
The Psychological Treatment Unit at the Maudsley has
treated many victims of disasters and other traumatic
events and is further researching and developing treat-
ments for PTSD (Post Traumatic Stress Disorder).
Professor Yule, Katrina Lovell, David Richards.

# National Association of Bereavement Services

20 Norton Folgate, London E1 6DB.
Tel:071 247 0617/247 1080.
List of specialist bereavement services, from Bereaved
Parents' Helpline to Age Concern.
Leaflet and listing in Disaster Action library.

# National Association of Widows

54–57 Allison St, Digbeth, Birmingham B5 5TH.
Tel: 021 643 8348.
Branches throughout UK offering practical advice and
supportive counselling to widows.

# Northern Ireland Widows' Association

137 University St, Belfast BT7 1HP. Tel: 0232 228263.
Has a local network offering information, advice and
support.

# RoadPeace

Brigitte Chaudhry, RoadPeace, PO Box 2579,
London NW10 3PW. Tel: 081 964 1021.
Formed by families and friends of victims of road death.
Committed to: (1) offer support and information to road
traffic victim families; (2) endeavour to ensure all practic-
able efforts are made to reduce danger on roads by those

responsible for road safety; (3) network; (4) carry out research and publish information.

## Samaritans — National Office

17 Uxbridge Road, Slough, Berks. SL1 1SN.
Tel: 0753 32713/4

Will refer to local branches (which are listed in telephone directories) who offer a 24-hour service for all in despair. Di Stubbs, Outreach Officer.

## UCL Stress Clinic

University College and Middlesex School of Medicine
Stress Clinic: Wolfson Building, Middlesex Hospital,
Ridinghouse Street, London W1N 8AA.
Tel: 071 380 9662.

The Stress Clinic aims to provide assessment and therapy for those who may have been affected by traumatic events. Location map available in Disaster Action library.

## Victim Support

Cranmer House, 39 Brixton Road, London SW9 6DZ.
Tel: 071 735 9166.

Practical help and advice and basic emotional support to victims and their families following crime. Local branches listed in telephone directories.

Victim Support – Families of Murder Victim Project, final report, April 1990. This booklet in Disaster Action library.

# FOR PRACTICAL INFORMATION CONCERNING WILLS OR FUNERALS:

## British Humanist Association

13 Prince of Wales Terrace, London W8 5PG.
Tel: 071 937 2341.

A network of local Humanist groups. Produces a guide to non-religious funerals.

## Local Citizens' Advice Bureaux

See telephone directories.

## National Association of Funeral Directors (NAFD)

618 Warwick Road, Solihull, West Midlands B91 1AA.
Tel: 021 711 1343.